Federal Legislative Branch
Updated through November 2008.

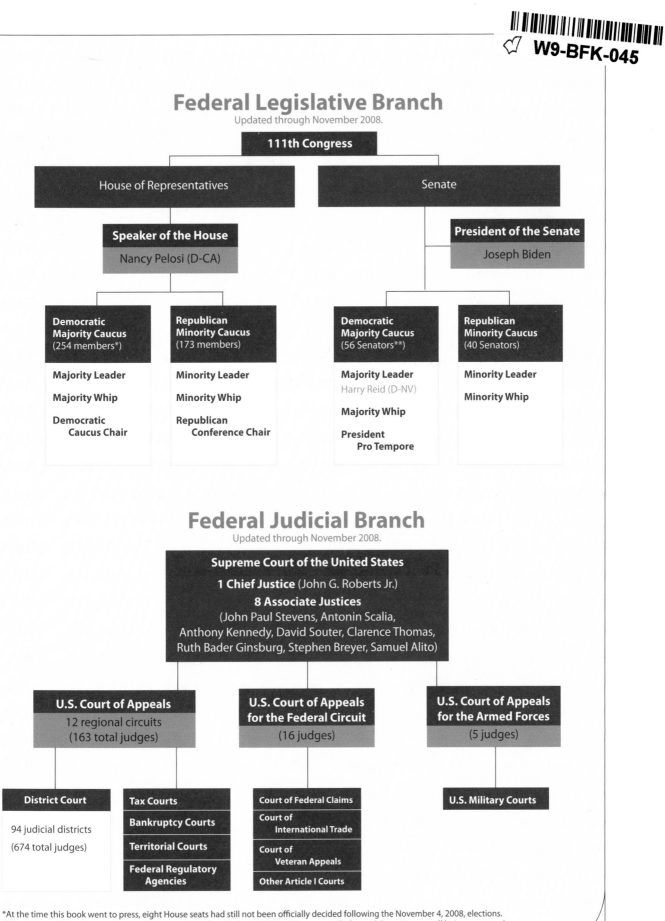

111th Congress

House of Representatives

Senate

Speaker of the House

Nancy Pelosi (D-CA)

President of the Senate

Joseph Biden

Democratic Majority Caucus (254 members*)

Majority Leader

Majority Whip

Democratic Caucus Chair

Republican Minority Caucus (173 members)

Minority Leader

Minority Whip

Republican Conference Chair

Democratic Majority Caucus (56 Senators**)

Majority Leader
Harry Reid (D-NV)

Majority Whip

President Pro Tempore

Republican Minority Caucus (40 Senators)

Minority Leader

Minority Whip

Federal Judicial Branch
Updated through November 2008.

Supreme Court of the United States

1 Chief Justice (John G. Roberts Jr.)
8 Associate Justices
(John Paul Stevens, Antonin Scalia,
Anthony Kennedy, David Souter, Clarence Thomas,
Ruth Bader Ginsburg, Stephen Breyer, Samuel Alito)

U.S. Court of Appeals
12 regional circuits
(163 total judges)

U.S. Court of Appeals for the Federal Circuit
(16 judges)

U.S. Court of Appeals for the Armed Forces
(5 judges)

District Court

94 judicial districts
(674 total judges)

Tax Courts

Bankruptcy Courts

Territorial Courts

Federal Regulatory Agencies

Court of Federal Claims

Court of International Trade

Court of Veteran Appeals

Other Article I Courts

U.S. Military Courts

*At the time this book went to press, eight House seats had still not been officially decided following the November 4, 2008, elections.
**At the time this book went to press, Senate seats up for election in 2008 in Minnesota, Alaska, and Georgia were still being contested.

AMERICAN GOVERNMENT

AMERICAN GOVERNMENT

HISTORICAL, POPULAR, AND GLOBAL PERSPECTIVES

ELECTION UPDATE

Kenneth Dautrich
Associate Professor of Public Policy
University of Connecticut

David A. Yalof
Associate Professor of Political Science
University of Connecticut

WADSWORTH
CENGAGE Learning™

Australia • Brazil • Japan • Korea • Mexico • Singapore • Spain • United Kingdom • United States

WADSWORTH
CENGAGE Learning™

American Government: Historical, Popular, and Global Perspectives, Election Update Edition

Kenneth Dautrich
David A. Yalof

Publisher: Suzanne Jeans

Executive Editor: Carolyn Merrill

Development Editor: Betty Slack

Assistant Editor: Katherine Hayes

Editorial Assistant: Nathan Gamache

Associate Development Editor: Caitlin Holroyd

Marketing Manager: Amy Whitaker

Marketing Communications Manager: Heather Baxley

Senior Content Project Manager: Josh Allen

Art Director: Linda Helcher

Print Buyer: Linda Hsu

Permissions Editor: Tim Sisler

Production Service: Lachina Publishing Services

Image Acquisitions Manager: John Hill

Cover Designer: Didona Design

Cover Image: ©Rudy Sulgan/Corbis; Digital Vision/©Media Bakery

For product information and technology assistance, contact us at
Cengage Learning Academic Resource Center, 1-800-423-0563
For permission to use material from this text or product,
submit all requests online at **www.cengage.com/permissions.**
Further permissions questions can be e-mailed to
permissionrequest@cengage.com.

Library of Congress Control Number: 2008939569

Student Edition:

ISBN-13: 978-0-495-56808-7

ISBN-10: 0-495-56808-2

Alternate Edition:

ISBN-13: 978-0-495-56978-7

ISBN-10: 0-495-56978-X

Wadsworth
25 Thomson Place
Boston, MA 02210-1202
USA

Cengage Learning products are represented in Canada by Nelson Education, Ltd.

For your course and learning solutions, visit **www.cengage.com**

Purchase any of our products at your local college store or at our preferred online store **www.ichapters.com**

Printed in Canada
1 2 3 4 5 6 7 12 11 10 09

This book is dedicated to the next generation of responsible citizens who will inherit the American government; in particular, our students and our own children:

Allison, Benjamin, Jane, Kenny, and Rachel

Brief Contents

American Government: Historical, Popular, and Global Perspectives

Contents

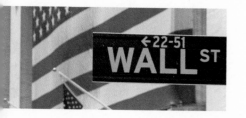

ANNOTATED CONSTITUTION OF THE UNITED STATES OF AMERICA   C-1

American Government: Historical, Popular, and Global Perspectives

PART II

Institutions

Chapter 7 The Presidency

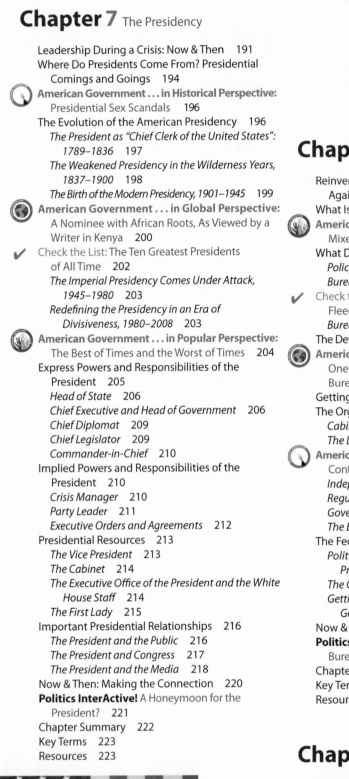
Chapter 8 The Federal Bureaucracy

Chapter 9 The Judiciary

PART III

Political Behavior

Chapter 10 Public Opinion

Chapter 11 Interest Groups

Chapter 12 The Media and Politics

Chapter 13 Political Parties

Chapter 15 Campaigns and Elections

PART IV

Public Policy

Chapter 16 American Economic Policy

Chapter 18 American Foreign Policy

Chapter 17 American Social Policy

Appendix

Glossary   G-1

Credits   CR-1

Index   I-1

Special Features

American Government . . . in Historical Perspective

American Government . . . in Popular Perspective

American Government . . . in Global Perspective

✔ Check the List

Politics InterActive!

Preface

This is a textbook about the American government, the success of which depends upon a responsible citizenry willing to ask tough questions of its leaders and demand reasonable answers in return. We live in an increasingly interconnected world; more than at any time in American history, the policies and actions of the U.S. government have an impact on the citizens of other nations, just as their governments' policies in turn have an impact on American citizens. Despite all the changes that have occurred over the course of the nation's history, the past is replete with examples from which we can learn. The challenge facing instructors of American government today is how to take adequate account of all these changes while never losing sight of the issues and events from the nation's past and their significance today.

We offer in this textbook all the nuts and bolts of the U.S. government and how it works, but we do not settle for mere surface descriptions and analysis of American government and politics. We also seek to educate students about American politics in ways that go beyond the essentials of government by placing current political issues and debates in perspective. By examining the current state of American politics from different angles, we hope to encourage students to think critically about the significance of certain persons, places, and events in American politics and consider all the different ways in which they might be viewed and interpreted.

As educators, we never want to let students accept at face value essential aspects of American politics—we thus offer alternative perspectives to help students think more critically about American government and politics. For example, we don't want students to assume that all victories in the American political system are equally important; rather, we want them to realize that prevailing political circumstances exert a powerful influence on how different entities may define "victory." For example, although the story may be apocryphal, it is still instructive: When Lyndon Johnson, at the height of his party's political power in early 1965, was informed by an aide that the White House had just won passage of a desired piece of legislation by a wide margin, Johnson purportedly remarked: "How much more could we have gotten had we been willing to win by just one vote?" In similar fashion, some defeats may still advance the given cause, such as when losses generate attention or publicity for a previously unrecognized issue. For instance, the newly formed Republican Party's defeat in the 1856 presidential election set the stage for Abraham Lincoln's election as the first Republican president in 1860, and the eloquent dissents written by Supreme Court Justice Oliver Wendell Holmes in the 1920s pointed the way to the more liberal free speech doctrines embraced by a majority of Supreme Court justices in the 1960s.

Throughout the chapters of this textbook, we offer students of American government and politics the means by which to think critically about those topics. Blinded by what is in front of us now, we often ignore lessons from the past. American government and politics have changed dramatically in the more than 200 years of the nation's existence, yet certain issues persist. In this textbook we investigate America's political institutions and processes from a number of different viewpoints in an effort to take the full measure of American politics.

Three Perspectives on American Politics

We offer in these pages no polemic or theoretical argument about what American politics should look like or stand for, either now or in the years ahead. To the degree it is possible, we attempt to avoid normative judgments about American political institutions or individuals based on a particular ideological point of view—whether conservative or liberal, radical or moderate. Instead, we aim to provide a more measured view of government institutions and processes. We complement the text presentation of the essentials of American government with a focus on three perspectives, allowing students to view American government from a variety of different angles.

The Historical Perspective

The historical perspective places issues and problems of contemporary American politics within the context of past events and circumstances. Looking back provides important lessons applicable today. In examining the past we find that some of our new and "unprecedented" political controversies are neither new nor unprecedented. The faces may have changed and the policies may have been transformed, but the challenges the nation faces today are often newer versions of past dilemmas and problems.

Viewing American politics through the prism of history allows students to gain a greater appreciation for American government, both its flaws and its successes. Furthermore, placing American government in historical perspective facilitates an understanding of how the modern political system works. For example, the smoke-filled rooms of the nineteenth century in which political party bosses often selected political candidates threatened democracy and undermined accountability to the majority. Those smoke-filled rooms no longer exist today, as progressive reforms introduced in the early part of the twentieth century forced major political parties to use slightly more democratic means to choose candidates. Still, party bosses continue to exert considerable influence by determining where the party will allocate its resources. A thorough examination of past problems, issues, and conflicts does not negate the uniqueness of the current American condition, but it does offer a better understanding of contemporary issues. In some cases, studying the past assures us that the political process does work in a positive way; in other cases, it reminds us that we are not the first to face certain difficulties, and it suggests that we may want to seek more direction from the past about what works and what does not.

The Popular Perspective

The popular perspective offers yet another useful framework for examining political issues. At its core, American government is built upon the bedrock of popular consent. The U.S. Constitution itself and the institutions of government underscore the importance of the role of the people in American government. The biennial election of every member of the House of Representatives and the frequent elections of many state and local officials remind us that securing the popular will has been essential to our system from the beginning. The number and frequency of public opinion polls are further testament to the importance of the popular will.

Of course, public opinion polls can be manipulated and abused—after all, respondents can only answer the questions that are posed to them at the time they are asked, based on the information (often quite limited) that is provided to them. That said, public opinion polls do offer a valuable perspective on where hot and not-so-hot political issues stand in the court of public opinion. As popular opinion on the war in Iraq shifted, Bush administration officials responsible for foreign policy were forced to make decisions and advise the president in a more complex (and increasingly hostile) political environment. Students need to take account of these shifting political winds to understand why certain events transpired as they did. A popular perspective on American government promotes a deeper appreciation for the nuances of the American political system.

The Global Perspective

The global perspective offers viewpoints and opinions *about* U.S. government institutions and processes from the media, political elites, and the public in other parts of the world. (This global perspective should not be confused with a *comparative* analysis of political institutions and processes in different countries.) Over the years the nations of the world have become increasingly interconnected through communications advances (such as TV, satellite, and the Internet), the improved mobility of people (such as by more routine air travel), economic interdependencies (such as the North American Free Trade Agreement), and political changes (such as the creation of the United Nations after World War II). Now more than ever, American government affects and is affected by events, circumstances, and conflicts all over the world.

Though few would argue that the American government should develop policies based primarily on the views of others, awareness of how "outsiders" view the American government lends a valuable perspective to our understanding of the subject. Franklin Delano Roosevelt's controversial lend-lease agreement with Britain in 1940 (by which he "traded" war materials to Britain with little hope of repayment) angered many Democrats from his own party who wanted the United States to stay absolutely neutral in the conflict in Europe. FDR knew, however, that Western European hopes for victory in the war against the Nazis were fading, and he wanted to assure both the leaders and the citizens of Britain in particular that they were not alone. Almost 60 years later, many were surprised when in 2003 some of the long-time Western European allies of the United States refused to support American military operations in Iraq. American officials' awareness of how their actions are viewed in other parts of the world can only benefit decision-makers as they guide the United States through the increasingly interconnected world of global politics.

These three different perspectives offer students a broader view with which to enhance their understanding of American government and politics. Even more importantly, these perspectives provide the means for students to engage in critical thinking about American political issues—in effect, they allow students to challenge more effectively what they read and hear in the media and elsewhere. Does that television news anchor understand that the political rivalry he or she is discussing has roots in the early nineteenth century? Does knowing the history affect the significance of an event or change the way political officials should treat the issue? To what extent does that state legislature's controversial policy confront popular approval in its own state and region? Did officials know how the newly occupied nation would react, and did they craft their policies accordingly? These perspectives are not just helpful—they may be critical to helping students see beyond the here and now.

Organization of the Textbook
Part I Foundations

Part I ("Foundations," Chapters 1 through 5) of the textbook begins with a discussion of how three different perspectives on American politics can add to and help shape our understanding of American politics and the creation and evolution of its institutions and processes. In Chapter 1, after reviewing the forms and functions of government in general and highlighting fundamental aspects of American political culture, we pose a hypothetical question: Is American democracy on the decline? We then consider evidence that has been offered in recent years to support and contradict that controversial proposition, using an examination of historical perspectives in order to place contentions such as these in their proper contexts. Chapters 2 through 5 begin the textbook's consideration of the American political system with a discussion of the origins of the American government and the Constitution (Chapter 2), the federal system and the rights and liberties that derive from the Constitution (Chapter 3), and the Bill of Rights and subsequent amendments that guarantee equality (Chapters 4 and 5).

Part II Institutions

Part II ("Institutions," Chapters 6 through 9) considers the major institutions of government formed under the Constitution. Congress (Chapter 6), the executive branch (Chapter 7), and the judiciary (Chapter 9) were all established by the first three articles of the Constitution, though their appearance and functions today might surprise many of Founders who designed them. The bureaucracy (Chapter 8) is not specifically mentioned in the Constitution but it is an inevitable product of a government expected to tackle the problems of a nation that is home to a diverse population of over 300 million people.

Part III Political Behavior

In Part III ("Political Behavior," Chapters 10 through 15), we consider political behavior and its evolution. Interest groups (Chapter 11) and political parties (Chapter 13) are not modern phenomena; they were outgrowths of the American political system from the beginning. Public opinion (Chapter 10), the media (Chapter 12), voting (Chapter 14), and campaigns and elections (Chapter 15) receive extended attention in this part of the textbook.

Part IV Public Policy

In Part IV ("Public Policy," Chapters 16 through 18), we discuss public policy at national, state, and local levels. Following a discussion of the nature of public policy in general, we consider aspects of the nation's economic (Chapter 16), social (Chapter 17), and foreign policies (Chapter 18).

Special Instructional Features

We offer a number of recurring special instructional features designed to engage students' interest and provide pedagogical support to help them master chapter material. Several of the recurring features highlight the three perspectives that underlie the book's presentation.

Now & Then

Each chapter (except Chapter 1) begins with an opening vignette entitled **"Now & Then,"** in which some situation relevant to the chapter topic is presented. Many students with at least some exposure to American politics will be able to identify the more recent issue or event (i.e., "Now") to which the situation appears to refer. At the same time, however, the situation also refers to some event or issue in the past (i.e., "Then") that may not be as familiar to students. Those who correctly identified the more recent event may be surprised to learn that the situation presented also describes another event from the nation's past. The "Now & Then" opening vignette thus demonstrates that although people and circumstances may change dramatically, certain issues and problems persist. At the end of the chapter, the section entitled **"Now & Then: Making the Connection"** revisits the two examples from the beginning of the chapter, ties them together, and then connects them to major themes of the chapter as a whole.

Perspectives Features

Each chapter also includes three features that focus on the three perspectives (historical, popular, or global). **"American Government . . . in Historical Perspective"** compares different moments in American history in which the same event or circumstance recurred, albeit with different actors and in somewhat different forms. **"American Government . . . in Popular Perspective"** offers evidence (usually from public opinion data) about where the American public stands on some issue relevant to the chapter. **"American Government . . . in Global Perspective"** presents material from other countries—perhaps a newspaper editorial, a quote from a foreign politician, or evidence from foreign public opinion polls—that offers outsiders' perspectives on some aspect of American politics.

✔ Check the List

Late night television host David Letterman is not the only one to offer "Top Ten" lists—such lists have become part of American culture, whether they feature the top ten movies of the year, the top ten political cartoons of the month, or the top forty songs of week. In each chapter of the textbook the **"Check the List"** feature presents a list (sometimes, but not always, a ranked list) of people, places, events, issues, and so on that addresses some aspect of American politics.

Study Aids and Resources

Aids to facilitate study of the material include a **chapter summary** of key points at the end of each chapter. Additionally, within each chapter **key terms** are highlighted in boldface type and defined in the margins of the pages. These key terms are also listed at the end of the chapter, and the terms and definitions are repeated in a glossary at the end of the book. Also at the end of each chapter is a list of **resources,** both print and electronic, that students can explore on their own.

Politics InterActive!

The **Politics InterActive!** feature at the end of each chapter presents some contemporary political event or conflict related to the chapter content and instructs students to visit the Wadsworth website (http://academic.cengage.com/dautrich) accompanying this textbook to explore further Internet resources that offer historical, popular, and global perspectives on that same topic. These Internet resources encourage students' critical thinking and help them realize just how much their views of American politics may be shaped—or reshaped—by their exposure to alternate perspectives. The interactive exercise component of the Politics InterActive! feature then poses a similar issue and asks students to explore Internet resources that offer varying perspectives on that topic.

Many other textbooks subtly (and, in some cases, not so subtly) offer the authors' own "take" on American politics. Although some instructors may appreciate that more polemical approach, we aim to provide something different. Recognizing that students come to the introductory American government course from a variety of different backgrounds and with varying levels of understanding about American politics, we present all the nuts and bolts they need to understand the system in as straightforward and clear a manner as possible. But then we go a step further: To complement that foundation of basic information, we offer materials that present different perspectives on each topic. These different perspectives are intended to encourage students to engage in critical thinking about the political process as a whole.

The historical, popular, and global perspectives presented in Chapters 2 through 18 do not interfere with the description of essential foundations. If anything, they should spark students' interest in revisiting what they learned in high school, from the media, and elsewhere about American politics with a more discerning and critical eye. Perhaps many students will take this critical approach beyond the course itself and become actual participants in the process. If they do so with a more critical and skeptical eye, our democratic system can only benefit.

Supplements for Instructors
Media
Power Lecture with JoinIn contains:

Interactive PowerPoint Lectures This one-stop lecture and class preparation tool makes it easy for you to assemble, edit, publish, and present custom lectures for your course, using Microsoft PowerPoint. The interactive Power Point lectures bring together text-specific outlines, audio and video clips from historic to current day events, animated learning modules illustrating key concepts, and tables, statistical charts and graphs, and photos from the book, as well as outside sources. In addition, you can add your own materials—culminating in a powerful, personalized, media-enhanced presentation.

Test Bank in Microsoft Word and ExamView computerized testing with a large array of well crafted multiple-choice and essay questions, along with their answers, page references, and difficulty level.

Instructor's Manual with learning objectives, chapter outlines, discussion questions, suggestions for stimulating class activities and projects, tips on integrating media into your class, including step-by-step instructions on how to create your own podcasts, suggested readings and Web resources, and a section specially designed to help teaching assistants and adjunct instructors.

Resource Integration Guide outlines the rich collection of resources available to instructors and students within the chapter-by-chapter framework of the book, suggesting how and when each supplement can be used to optimize learning.

JoinIn on TurningPoint for American Government Wadsworth is now pleased to offer you book-specific **JoinIn** content for Response Systems tailored to the Dautrich/Yalof text, allowing you to transform your classroom, assess your students' progress, and examine concepts in political science with instant in-class quizzes and polls. To support this book, we also provide **JoinIn** questions in three formats:

★ Visual Literacy Questions that promote critical thinking and analysis in interpreting visual data.

★ Political Polling consisting of pre-built public opinion polling questions meant to stimulate interest and discussion in the course/lecture.

★ Book Specific Quizzing Content that provides content knowledge and assessment from material covered in the text itself.

All of these question types display students' answers seamlessly within the Microsoft PowerPoint slides of your own lecture, in conjunction with the "clicker" hardware of your choice. Enhance how your students interact with you, your lectures, and one another. For college and university adopters only. Contact your Wadsworth representative for more information about **JoinIn on Turning Point** and our exclusive infrared or radio frequency hardware solutions.

Political Theatre 2.0 DVD

Political Theatre 2.0 offers the most comprehensive, rich collection of audio and video clips available. Covering seventy-five years of key political events—from Roosevelt's first Fireside Chat in 1933 to the U.S. Presidential Debates in 2008—this collection gives you instant access to the very best of presidential speeches, campaign ads, debates, news reports, national convention coverage, demonstrations, speeches by civil rights leaders, and more. This free instructor ancillary can be shown in class as a lecture launcher, to prompt class discussion, or to provide a platform for homework assignments and research. Your local Wadsworth sales representative can provide you a sample DVD and will send you the full set upon the adoption of a Wadsworth textbook.

JoinIn on TurningPoint for Political Theatre

Transform your classroom by combining the power of Political Theatre with the innovative teaching tool of a classroom response system through **JoinIn.** Instantly poll your students with questions we've created for you! We've done the work by providing over 100 Political Theatre-related questions from which to choose. Additionally, you can choose to create your own custom questions.

2010 ABC News DVD

This collection of short video clips on relevant political issues has been updated to include coverage of the Democratic and Republican National Conventions, the selection of Sarah Palin as John McCain's running mate, and the economic bailout plan. They serve as great lecture or discussion launchers.

Video Case Studies for American Government

Free to adopters, this award-winning video contains twelve case studies on the debate on recent policy issues, such as affirmative action. Each case ends with questions designed to spark classroom discussion.

Online Resources

Resource Centers—Just What You Need to Know and Do Now! Resource Centers, updated and enhanced for 2009, direct students to the appropriate premium resources, including an integrated online e-book, new interactive Simulations focusing on the 2008 presidential elections, Animated Learning Modules illustrating key concepts, case studies, updated Internet activities, updated videos for each chapter, maps, podcasts, flashcards, Associated Press content, InfoTrac, and Timelines. Adopting instructors will be given password-protected access to course management tools so that they can assign and supervise their students' use of Resource Centers if they wish to do so.

The **Election 2008 Website,** available via Resource Centers, will provide information on the 2008 elections, updated throughout the year with current polling data and analysis of the key races, with a particular focus on the race for the White House.

The Instructor's companion website contains an author-written newsletter that will be updated as needed with teaching tips and information about current events.

Rich with content for your American government course, this **WebTutor** is a Web-based teaching and learning tool that includes course management, study/mastery, and communication tools. Use WebTutor to provide virtual office hours, post your syllabus, and track student progress with WebTutor's quizzing material. For students, WebTutor offers real-time access to interactive online tutorials and simulations, practice quizzes, and Web links—all correlated to *American Government: Historical, Popular, and Global Perspectives.* Available in WebCT and Blackboard.

Other Teaching Support

Turnitin This proven online plagiarism-prevention software promotes fairness in the classroom by helping students learn to correctly cite sources and allowing instructors to check for originality before reading and grading papers. Turnitin quickly checks student papers against billions of pages of Internet content, millions of published works, and millions of student papers and within seconds generates a comprehensive originality report. A booklet, *How to Avoid Plagiarism Using Turnitin,* is also available; ask your Wadsworth representative for details.

Building Democracy: Readings in American Government This extraordinary collection provides access to over 500 historical documents and scholarly readings to create the ideal supplement for any American Government course. Cengage Custom Solutions' intuitive **TextChoice** website at **www.textchoice.com/democracy/** allows you to quickly browse the collection, preview selections, arrange your table of contents, and create a custom cover that will include your own course information. Or if you prefer, your local Wadsworth representative will be happy to guide you through the process.

The Handbook of Selected Court Cases Includes more than thirty Supreme Court cases.

The Handbook of Selected Legislation and Other Documents Features excerpts from laws passed by the U.S. Congress that have had a significant impact on American politics.

American Government: Using MicroCase ExplorIt, **Ninth Edition** By Barbara Norrander. Windows-compatible package that includes access to MicroCase datasets and workbook. Students make their own decisions about the issues as they analyze and interpret current NES and GSS data.

For students, available packaged with the book

Resource Centers Updated and enhanced for 2009, Resource Centers direct students to the appropriate premium resources, including an integrated online e-book, new interactive Simulations focusing on the 2008 presidential elections, Animated Learning Modules illustrating key concepts, case studies, updated Internet activities, updated videos for each chapter, maps, podcasts, flashcards, Associated Press content, InfoTrac, and Timelines.

Visit **academic.cengage.com/now** today for more information and a sample chapter!

Study Guide includes a chapter summary, key terms, and a practice exam for every chapter of the book.

Also for Students

Companion Website for *American Government: Historical, Popular, and Global Perspectives*—students will find free and open access to Learning Objectives, Quizzes, Chapter Glossaries, Flash Cards, Crossword Puzzles, and Internet activities. This site also features **Politics InterActive!**, a feature created by the authors that allows students to examine the three perspectives on government— historical, popular, and global—through online research and exercises.

About the Authors

Kenneth J. Dautrich (Ph.D., Rutgers 1995) is an associate professor of public policy at the University of Connecticut in Storrs. He is also the founder and former director of the Center for Survey Research & Analysis at the University of Connecticut. Previously, Dr. Dautrich was a Research Fellow at the Media Studies Center in New York, and has served as a senior faculty fellow at the Heldrich Center at Rutgers. His first book, *How the News Media Fail American Voters* (Columbia University Press, 1997), received scholarly praise in numerous political science circles. He also co-authored *The First Amendment and the Media in the Court of Public Opinion* (Cambridge University Press, 2002) and *The Future of the First Amendment* (Rowman & Littlefield, 2008). Dr. Dautrich's research and teaching focus on public opinion and American elections. For the past four years he has directed a set of national surveys on civic literacy in the American public and the role of higher education in advancing knowledge about American government. He is currently writing a book on findings from this project.

David A. Yalof (Ph.D., Johns Hopkins University 1997; J.D., University of Virginia 1991) is an associate professor of political science at the University of Connecticut. His first book, *Pursuit of Justices: Presidential Politics and the Selection of Supreme Court Nominees* (University of Chicago Press, 1999), was awarded the American Political Science Association's Richard E. Neustadt Award as the best book published on presidential studies in 1999. He is also the co-author of *The First Amendment and the Media in the Court of Public Opinion* (Cambridge University Press, 2002), *The Future of the First Amendment* (Rowman & Littlefield, 2008), and another textbook, *Constitutional Law: Civil Liberty and Individual Rights* (Foundation Press, 2007). Dr. Yalof has written extensively on issues in constitutional law and Supreme Court appointment politics—his work has been published in *Political Research Quarterly, Judicature, Constitutional Commentary,* and various other journals. He is currently nearing completion of a book-length manuscript about executive branch wrongdoing and the due process of law.

Acknowledgments

I n preparing this Election Update Edition of *American Government: Historical, Popular, and Global Perspectives,* we have been exceedingly lucky to be in the company of high-quality publishers and editors at Cengage. Certainly Sean Wakely's faith in this project from high above has never wavered, and we only now continue to learn about the important role he's played in this project from behind the scenes. Yet the primary credit for everything positive that emerged belongs to Carolyn Merrill. Her intellect, professionalism, and ability to stay cool under pressure continue to turn the impossible into a reality. This edition would not have been possible without her, and that's putting it mildly.

Of course one of Carolyn's greatest contributions to the enterprise was her decision to once again bring back development editor Betty Slack. Betty's editing skills know no equal, and we're thankful that Carolyn and Cengage know a good thing when they see one. As always, we must also pay homage to the formidable contributions and support of P. J. Boardman and Clark Baxter.

Needless to say, this Election Update Edition is a product of many cooks. On the production and editing end, Annie Beck helped us turn around a blizzard of chapters in a very short time; Joshua Allen continued in his role as project manager overseeing numerous details; Nina Smith had picture options ready for us in a hurry. Thanks also to Mark Klippinger for his help with the newsletters.

On the marketing end, we will no doubt look back on the arrival of Amy Whitaker as one of the most critical events in the success of this book. Anyone who spends an hour or two with her is left dazed at all the fresh ideas and marketing ingenuity that pours forth. Thanks also to the countless sales reps out there (Davene, Houston, Nick, Sally, and everyone else—you know who you are!!) who got the good word out on this book before it had even been produced.

Naturally, a textbook such as this also requires the endless patience of colleagues back home at the two author's respective departments at UCONN. In the Department of Public Policy, Mark Robbins, Amy Donahue, Bill Simonsen, Eric Brunner, Deneen Hatmaker, and Thomas Craemer offered their support and encouragement, and numerous staff and graduate students lent a hand in the search for website materials. In the Department of Political Science, Howard Reiter, Garry Clifford, Betty Hanson, Carol Lewis, Rich Hiskes, Mark Boyer, and all the public law folks (Virginia Hettinger, Kristin Kelly, Jeff Dudas, and Rob Venator) were especially supportive. Nor should we forget all the support we received from home, led (of course) by our wives, Andrea and Mary Beth (our *much* better halves, to be sure), and the five children to whom this book is first dedicated. Also, a special note of thanks to Stephen Pelletier and Kenny Dautrich for their help in identifying some of the pictures found in the book.

Finally there are the many members of our profession who put in countless hours and personal energy commenting on (and greatly improving) this manuscript from the beginning. Some participated in focus groups; others marked up chapters. Our debt to these many people knows no bounds. A list of these fine contributors to the cause is provided below. But please know this: Any errors that remain are entirely our own.

We thank the reviewers who commented on drafts of the manuscript:

Reviewers

David Gray Adler
Idaho State University
Scott Ainsworth
University of Georgia
Noe Aguado
University of North Alabama
Dr. Lydia Andrade
University of the Incarnate Word
Yan Bai
Grand Rapids Community College
Christine M. Bailey
Ferris State University
Ross K. Baker
Rutgers University
Bethany Barratt
Roosevelt University
Timothy Barnett
Jacksonville State University
Brian Bearry
University of Texas–Dallas
William T. Bianco
Indiana University
David E. Birch
Tomball College
Scott E. Buchanan
Columbus State University
Jeffrey Bumgarner
Texas Christian University
Alexander M. Burton
South Texas College
Tom Caiazzo
East Georgia College
Douglas Camp Chaffey
Chatham College
Mark A. Cichock
University of Texas–Arlington
Stanley Clark
*California State University–
    Bakersfield*
Dewey M. Clayton
University of Louisville
Carolyn Cocca
SUNY–Old Westbury
Christopher A. Cooper
Western Carolina University
Kimberly Cowell-Meyers
American University

Brian Cravens
Montgomery College
Lane Crothers
Blinn College
Nicolas Damask
Scottsdale Community College
Andrew James Dowdle
University of Arkansas
LaVonne Downey
Roosevelt University
Dennis Driggers
California State University–Fresno
Anthony J. Eksterowicz
James Madison University
Charles Epp
University of Kansas
Matthew Eshbaugh-Soha
University of North Texas
Teri Fair
Suffolk University
Jeff Fox
Fort Lewis College
Brian Frederick
Northern Illinois University
Raymond Frey
Centenary College
Anthony Gabrielli
High Point University
G. David Gerson
North Carolina State
Joe Gershtenson
Eastern Kentucky University
Randy Glean
Midwestern State University
Timothy Gordinier
SUNY–Potsdam
Paul Goren
University of Minnesota–Twin Cities
Nathan Griffith
Belmont University
Joel Grossman
Johns Hopkins University
Willie Hamilton
Mount San Jacinto College
Thomas Haymes
*Houston Community College,
    Northwest*

Peter Heller
Manhattan College
John R. Hermann
Trinity University
Marjorie Hershey
Indiana University
Richard Himmelfarb
Hofstra University
Samuel Hoff
Delaware State University
Jennifer E. Horan
University of North Carolina–
  Wilmington
Timothy Hoye
Texas Women's University
Lisa Huffstetler
University of Memphis
Charles F. Jacobs
St. Norbert College
W. Martin James
Henderson State University
Mark S. Jendrysik
University of North Dakota
Irina S. Khmelko
Georgia Southern University
Quentin Kidd
Christopher Newport University
Richard Kiefer
Waubonsee Community College
Kimi King
University of North Texas
Marvin P. King Jr.
University of Mississippi
Anders Michael Kinney
Calhoun Community College
Dina Krois
Lansing Community College
Paul Labedz
Valencia Community College
J. Celeste Lay
Tulane University
Nancy Lind
Illinois State University
Thomas H. Little
University of North Carolina–
  Greensboro
Eduardo Magalhaes III
Simpson College
Gary Lee Malecha
University of Portland

Steven Marin
Victor Valley College
Wendy Martinek
SUNY–Binghamton
Tina Mavrikos-Adamou
Hofstra University
Scott D. McClurg
Southern Illinois University–
  Carbondale
Eddie L. Meaders
University of North Texas
Scott Meinke
Bucknell University
Philip Meyer
University of North Carolina–
  Chapel Hill
Mark C. Miller
Clark University
Richard Millsap
Texas Christian University,
  University of Texas–Arlington
Craig Mulling
Prairie State College
Jason C. Newman
Consumnes River College
Patrick Novotny
Georgia Southern University
Anthony J. Nownes
University of Tennessee
Laura Olson
Clemson University
Richard Pacelle
Georgia Southern University
David Penna
Gallaudet University
Ronald Pettus
St. Charles Community College
John Queen
Glendale Community College
Donald R. Ranish
Antelope Valley College
Russell Renka
Southeast Missouri State
  University
Heather Roberson
St. Petersburg College
J. Philip Rogers
San Antonio College
Donald Roy
Ferris State University

Martin Saiz
California State University–Northridge
Kay Scott
University of Central Florida, retired
T. M. Sell
Highline Community College
Ronald Seyb
Skidmore College
Youngtae Shin
University of Central Oklahoma
Rebecca L. Sims
South Georgia College
Fred Slocum
Minnesota State University–Mankato
John Speer
Houston Community College, Southwest
Mary Stegmeier
University of Virginia
Marcia B. Steinhauer
Rider University, retired
John P. Tuman
University of Nevada–Las Vegas
Brian Vargus
Indiana University at Purdue University, Indianapolis
John Vento
Antelope Valley College
Kevin Wagner
Florida Atlantic University
Adam L. Warber
Clemson University
Carl Anthony Wege
Coastal Georgia Community College
Paul Weizer
Fitchburg State College
Matt Wetstein
San Joaquin Delta College
Sharon G. Whitney
Tennessee Technological University
Kenneth C. Williams
Michigan State University

From the Advanced Placement community:

Karen Coston
Blacksburg High School (Blacksburg, VA)
Rebecca Small
Herndon High School (Herndon, VA)

Many thanks to those who attended focus groups:

Sharon Alter
Harper College
Lynn Brink
North Lake College
Randy Burnside
Southern Illinois University–Carbondale
Peggy Connally
North Central Texas College
Erwin Cornelius
McHenry County College
Renee Ann Cramer
Drake University
Rebecca Deen
University of Texas–Arlington
Louis DeSipio
University of California–Irvine
Victoria Farrar-Myers
University of Texas–Arlington
Susan Gluck Mezey
Loyola University–Chicago
Donna Guerin
Moraine Valley Community College
Ellen Lazarus
University of Texas–Arlington
Larry Martinez
California State University–Long Beach
Debra Moore
Southern Illinois University–Carbondale
Patrick Schmidt
Macalester College

Valerie Simms
Northeastern Illinois University, retired
Rorie Solberg
Oregon State University
Abigaile Van Horn
Purdue University
Richard Vollmer
Oklahoma City Community College
Molly Waite
Harper College

Charles Weston
Western Illinois University
David Wigg
St. Louis Community College
Laura M. Wood
Tarrant County College
Robert Wood
University of North Dakota
Mark Wrighton
Millikin University

AMERICAN GOVERNMENT

Perspectives on American Government

1

★ Introduction to Perspectives on

    American Government

★ Forms and Functions of Government

★ American Government and Politics

★ American Political Culture

★ Is American Democracy on the Decline?

    Assessing Both Sides of the Debate

★ Historical, Popular, and Global Perspectives

EMMANUEL DUNAND/AFP/GETTY IMAGES

Democrat Barack Obama, winner of the 2008 presidential election, greets supporters

Introduction to Perspectives on American Government

The collapse of the U.S. stock market in September 2008 and the subsequent $700 billion government rescue plan of Wall Street did not occur in a vacuum; these were seismic events in what were already shaping up to be historically bad economic times. During the previous year Americans had resolutely faced up to the reality of record high gas prices, plunging real estate values, and a substantial credit crisis that had already claimed several well established financial institutions as victims. President George W. Bush, a Republican, was a lame duck chief executive at the end of his second term in office. Thus in the 2008 presidential race, voters looked to the candidates of the two major parties for answers. The Republican nominee, John McCain, and the Democratic nominee, Barack Obama, both sought to distance themselves from what they agreed were the failed economic policies of the past. Both promised to bring change to Washington. Yet try as he might to avoid that fate, McCain found himself invariably linked to the current holder of the White House, both by party association and by their shared economic philosophy. On Election Day 2008, voters turned out in record numbers to defeat the "in party" candidate and send the young and energetic Barack Obama to the White House to clean up the financial mess.

President-elect Barack Obama and Vice President-elect Joe Biden

The Five Largest Daily Losses and Percentage Drops in Stock Market History

The Largest Daily *Point Losses* in the Dow Jones Industrial Average:

✔ 1. September 29, 2008: A **778-point drop** (7.0%) following the U.S. House of Representatives' failure to pass the Bush Administration's $700 billion bailout plan.

✔ 2. September 17, 2001: A **684-point drop** (7.1%) on the first day of trading following the September 11 terrorist attacks.

✔ 3. April 14, 2000: A **618-point drop** (5.7%) was the result of a massive sell-off of technology stocks.

✔ 4. October 27, 1997: A **544-point drop** (7.2%) came amid troubles in the Hong Kong Hang Seng Index, which fell 6% in trading. (The Dow was actually forced to close 30 minutes early that day.)

✔ 5. September 31, 1998: A **513-point drop** (6.4%) after reports of a drop in new home sales and business deterioration among domestic manufacturers led to a bearish correction.

The Largest Daily *Percentage Losses* in the Dow Jones Industrial Average:

✔ 1. October 19, 1987: A **22.6% drop** (508 points) on what later came to be known as "Black Monday," when most of the world's stock markets crashed.

✔ 2. October 28, 1929: A **12.8% drop** (38 points) on the original "Black Monday." This was actually the second day of an extended crash that lasted over three separate days (including October 24, 1929, and October 29, 1929 (see #3, below), setting off a widespread panic with long-lasting consequences for the American economy, including the onset of the Great Depression.

✔ 3. October 29, 1929: An **11.7% drop** (31 points) on "Black Tuesday."

✔ 4. November 6, 1929: A **9.9% drop** (26 points).

✔ 5. December 18, 1899: An **8.7% drop** (6 points).

Historical Perspective

The history of presidential elections helps put the 2008 election results into perspective. Economic crises have had profound and predictable effects on presidential election politics; in most instances, a bad economy has driven the party in control of the White House out of power. This occurred in the wake of the various panics that jarred the American economy during the nineteenth century: The Panic of 1837, which halted business growth for three years, spelled certain trouble for President Martin Van Buren and the Democrats in the 1840 election; a decade after the Civil War, the panic of 1873 kicked off a severe six-year economic depression that made the previously downtrodden Democratic Party suddenly competitive at the national level (the 1876 Democratic nominee, Samuel Tilden, actually defeated Republican Rutherford Hayes in the popular vote); and the Panic of 1893 set off a series of bank failures that made it near impossible for the Democrats to win an 1896 election dominated by economic issues. More recently, several twentieth-century presidents watched as the poor economy all but doomed their prospects for reelection, whether it was Herbert Hoover in 1932, Jimmy Carter in 1980, or George H. W. Bush in 1992. In each of those cases the out-party candidate promised change during uncertain times; in 2008 Barack Obama benefitted from the same type of economic forces to forge his own electoral success. Placing events of the past in historical perspective certainly helps explain the results of the 2008 election.

Popular Perspective

Understanding the opinions of American voters provides yet another perspective from which to examine and seek greater understanding of the 2008 presidential election outcome. Each of the two presidential campaigns obsessed over and catered to the vagaries of public opinion in their strategizing. The public mood during the 2008 general election campaign was certainly palpable: by early October nearly nine in ten Americans indicated that they thought things in the country had gotten "seriously off track," and 62 percent placed the economy atop their list of concerns. Naturally, both Senators McCain and Obama were eager to respond to public opinion that demanded a quick fix to the Wall Street crisis right way. Political scientists have long documented the nature of public opinion during elections, including the strong inclination of voters to hold the party in power accountable for a problematic economy. Under the theory of "retrospective voting," voters assess their own economic standing and accordingly either blame or reward the party in power. In 2008, most voters held a dim view of their economic prospects and thus were more likely to vote to "throw out the rascals"—in this case that meant jettisoning Republicans from the White House. Senator Barack Obama clearly benefitted from this wave of public opinion to secure a resounding Electoral College victory.

Global Perspective

It is perhaps a truism that America's economy in the twenty-first century is inextricably intertwined with the world's economy; accordingly, understanding how the rest of world views the 2008 presidential election and its implications has become increasingly important. When the U.S. stock market plunged from mid-September through October 2008, officials in markets around the world watched nervously. They were right to do so: Asian markets soon plummeted as well, and Europe's various financial authorities prepared for the economies of their nations to follow suit. Once England and France began to coordinate their nations' bailout efforts, the U.S. government was forced to take joint global action as well so it would not be viewed as working in isolation on this critical matter. Thus on October 14, 2008, President Bush announced measures to implement a plan of action that had been agreed to by the Group of Seven major advanced countries and to strengthen the banking industry. Barack Obama's election would naturally affect the course taken by the U.S. government in the crisis, and world opinion would prove crucial in achieving a consensus for how to proceed. Few would contend that world opinion should ever guide U.S. foreign policy; still, most agree that at a minimum the global perspective helps shape what government does, including how the Bush administration and the Obama administration addressed the Wall Street collapse of 2008.

In this book we examine the major topics and concepts in American government and politics. We attempt to answer sweeping questions about how American government works: How does public policy get made? Who are the major players and institutions that make laws? How do these major players achieve their position? How do disputes get settled? What is the role of the American people in governing? In this discussion of American government, we draw on three perspectives to provide a deeper understanding of and appreciation for American government and how it works. From a historical perspective, we view contemporary American government as a product of American history. From a popular perspective, we recognize the significant role that the American people play in influencing what government does. And from a global perspective, we examine how the rest of the world views American government and consider how those views might help shape policy.

Forms and Functions of Government

★ **Government**

The collection of public institutions in a nation that establish and enforce the rules by which the members of that nation must live.

★ **Anarchy**

A situation in a society where there is no government and which is characterized by lawlessness and discord in the political system.

★ **Social contract**

From the philosophy of Jean-Jacques Rousseau, an agreement people make with one another to form a government and abide by its rules and laws, and in return, the government promises to protect the people's rights and welfare and promote their best interests.

★ **Authority**

The ability of public institutions and the officials within them to make laws, independent of the power to execute them.

★ **Democracy**

Form of government in which the people, either directly or through elected representatives, hold power and authority. The word *democracy* is derived from the Greek *demos kratos,* meaning "rule by the people."

★ **Oligarchy**

A form of government in which a small exclusive class, which may or may not attempt to rule on behalf of the people as a whole, holds supreme power.

★ **Theocracy**

A form of government in which a particular religion or faith plays a dominant role in the government.

Government is the collection of public institutions in a nation that establish and enforce the rules by which the members of that nation must live. Even the most primitive of societies have found government to be necessary. Without government, society would be in a state of **anarchy,** a situation characterized by lawlessness and discord in the political system. Thomas Hobbes, a seventeenth-century British political philosopher, wrote that without government life would be "solitary, poor, nasty, brutish and short."[1] Government is necessary to make the rules by which citizens must abide, promoting order, stability, and protection for the society. It exists in part to resolve conflicts that naturally arise when people live in communities. Elaborating on the role of government, Jean-Jacques Rousseau, an eighteenth-century French philosopher, posited that in fact a "social contract" exists.[2] A **social contract** is an agreement people make with one another to form a government and abide by its rules and laws. In return, the government promises to protect the people's rights and welfare and to promote their best interests.

A government's **authority** over its citizens refers to the ability of public institutions and the officials within them to make laws, independent of the power to execute them. People obey authority out of respect, whereas they obey power out of fear. There are a number of different forms of government with governing authority that can be found around the nations of the world. One such form—the form that will receive extended attention throughout this book—is **democracy,** defined as a government in which the people, either directly or through elected representatives, hold power and authority. The word democracy is derived from the Greek *demos kratos,* meaning "rule by the people."

By contrast, an **oligarchy** is a form of government in which a small exclusive class, which may or may not attempt to rule on behalf of the people as a whole, holds supreme power. In a **theocracy,** a particular religion or faith plays a dominant role in the government; Iran is just one example of a theocratic nation in the world today. A **monarchy** is a form of government in which one person, usually a member of a royal family or a royal designate, exercises supreme authority. The monarch may be a king, such as King Abdullah of Saudi Arabia, or a queen, like Queen Elizabeth II of Great Britain. In the past monarchies were quite common; today they are rarely practiced in the absolute sense. Although the United Kingdom continues to pay homage to its royalty, true political power rests in the Parliament whose members are elected by the people.

Many of the nations in the world today have an **authoritarian** form of government in which one political party, group, or person maintains such complete control over the nation that it may refuse to recognize, and may even choose to suppress, all other political parties and interests. The nation of Iraq, before the American military intervention in 2003, was considered by most to be an authoritarian government under the dictatorial rule of Saddam Hussein. North Korea under Kim Jong-Il is an authoritarian government that still exists today.

An important characteristic of any government, whether democratic or not, is its power to exercise authority over people. **Power** is the capacity to get individuals to do something that they may not otherwise do, such as requiring them to pay taxes, stop for red lights, or submit to a search before boarding an airplane. Without power, it would be very difficult for a government to enforce rules. The sustained power of any government largely rests on its legitimacy. **Legitimacy** is the extent to which the people (or the "governed") afford the government the authority and right to exercise power. The more that people subscribe to the goals of a government, and the greater the degree to which that government guarantees the people's welfare (for example, by supporting a strong economy or providing protection from foreign enemies), the higher will be the government's level of legitimacy. When the governed grant a high level of legitimacy to their government, the government wields its power to make and enforce rules more successfully.

[1] See Thomas Hobbes, *Leviathan* (London: A. Crooke, 1651).

[2] For a collection of Rousseau's work, see Jean-Jacques Rousseau, *The Social Contract and Discourses,* translation and commentary by G. D. H. Cole (London: Guernsey Press, 1983).

American Government and Politics

Politics is defined as the way in which the institutions of government are organized to make laws, rules, and policies, and how those institutions are influenced. More than seventy years ago, political scientist Harold Lasswell proposed a brief but very useful definition of politics as "who gets what, when and how."[3] In American politics, the "who" includes actors within and outside the formal government such as citizens, elected officials, interest groups, and state and local governments. The "what" are the decisions the government makes and take the form of what government funds, the way it raises revenue, and the policies it produces and enforces. The "when" relates to setting priorities about what government does. The concerns and issues that government addresses differ in importance, and issues of greater importance tend to be addressed more quickly. Finally the "how" refers to the way in which the government goes about its work, based on the political institutions that exist and the formal and informal procedures and rules that define the governing process. In describing American politics, this book provides answers to Lasswell's "who gets what, when and how?"

Government in the United States is especially complex. It is organized into multiple layers (national, state, and local), it encompasses a number of political institutions that share power—the executive (the president), the legislature (Congress), and the judiciary (the courts)—and it provides countless methods for individuals and groups to influence the decisions made by those institutions. In this book, we will examine this complex organization of American government, describe the political institutions that exercise power, and explore

©BETTMANN/CORBIS

Painting of George Washington and the Constitution's drafters at the Constitutional Convention in 1787.

the varied ways that people and groups exert influence. As we sort through this complexity of American government, we will seek to explain how and why the American

★ Monarchy

A form of government in which one person, usually a member of a royal family or a royal designate, exercises supreme authority.

★ Authoritarianism

A form of government in which one political party, group, or person maintains such complete control over the nation that it may refuse to recognize and, if it chooses to, suppress all other political parties and interests.

★ Power

The ability to get individuals to do something that they may not otherwise do, such as pay taxes, stop for red lights, or submit to a search before boarding an airplane.

★ Legitimacy

The extent to which the people afford the government the authority and right to exercise power.

Table 1.1 **Governments in the United States**

Government	Number
Federal	1
State	50
County	3,034
Municipal	19,429
School District	13,506
Township/Town	16,504
Special Districts	35,052
Total	87,576

The government of the United States might be more correctly described as a system of governments. In addition to the federal government, there are fifty state governments and thousands of local governments. The 2002 edition of the *Statistical Abstract of the United States* listed these totals for the number of governments operating throughout the nation.

[3]Harold Laswell, *Politics: Who Gets What, When and How* (New York: McGraw-Hill, 1936).

Chapter 1: Perspectives on American Government

7

American Government . . . in Global Perspective:

World Views on American Democracy

Even within the United States itself some people express hostility toward the nation's democratic system, as nearly a quarter of all Americans say they dislike American ideas about democracy. As surveys taken in 2002 and 2005 reveal, the United States' friends and enemies can be found in some of the most unlikely places; survey results reveal no obvious geographic lines and divisions among the nations that like the U.S. political system and those that oppose it.

Which of these comes closest to your view? "I like American ideas about democracy"
OR "I dislike American ideas about democracy" (2002 survey)

	Like	Dislike	DK/Ref.*
North America			
United States	70%	23%	7%
Canada	50	40	10%
Western Europe			
Germany	45	45	7
Italy	45	37	18
Great Britain	43	42	15
France	42	53	5
Eastern Europe			
Czech Republic	64	30	6
Slovak Republic	54	38	8
Bulgaria	50	23	27
Russia	28	46	26
Latin America			
Venezuela	67	10	3
Peru	47	36	17
Bolivia	27	60	13
Asia			
Philippines	69	25	6
Vietnam	68	24	8
India	36	27	37
Africa			
Kenya	87	6	7
Uganda	67	17	16
Tanzania	43	31	25

*Indicates the percentage of respondents who either said that they "don't know" or otherwise refused to answer.

(*continued*)

★ Politics

The way in which the institutions of government are organized to make laws, rules, and policies, and how those institutions are influenced.

political system has been able to endure the conflicts, both internal and external, that it has faced and currently faces. We will attempt to show how the American government is uniquely designed to stand up to its many challenges.

The strength and stability of the U.S. government is grounded in the high level of legitimacy it maintains with the American public. Americans may disagree vehemently with public officials, but rarely do they question their claim to authority.

"Do you have a favorable opinion of the United States?"

	2000	2002	2003	2004	2005
Canada	71	72	63	—	59
Britain	83	75	70	58	55
Netherlands	—	—	—	—	45
France	62	63	43	37	43
Germany	78	61	45	38	41
Spain	50	—	38	—	41
Poland	—	79	—	—	62
Russia	37	61	36	47	52
Indonesia	75	61	15	—	38
Turkey	52	30	15	30	23
Pakistan	23	10	13	21	23
Lebanon	—	35	27	—	42
Jordan	—	25	1	5	21
Morocco	77	—	27	27	—
India	—	54	—	—	71
China	—	—	—	—	42

Source: Pew Global Attitudes Project, 2002, 2005.

The Framers of the U.S. Constitution were keenly aware of the importance of the legitimacy of the system. They knew that if the government was to withstand the test of time, it must serve the people well. These ideas about legitimacy drew largely on the theories of the seventeenth-century British political philosopher John Locke (1632–1704).[4] Locke proposed that people are born with certain *natural rights,* which derive from **natural law,** the rules of conduct inherent in the relationship among human beings and thus more fundamental than any law that a governing authority might make. Government cannot violate these natural rights, which include life, liberty, and property. Therefore, government, or human law, must be based on the "consent of the governed." That is, citizens are responsible for choosing their government and its leaders. This theory loomed large in the mind of Thomas Jefferson as he drafted the Declaration of Independence to justify the American colonies' split with the British government: "All men . . . are endowed by their creator with certain unalienable rights . . . [and] whenever any form of government becomes destructive of these ends, it is the right of the people to alter or abolish it." A government maintains legitimacy as long as the governed are served well and as long as government respects the natural rights of individuals.

Drawing on this philosophy, the Framers drafted a Constitution that created a political system able to manage the inevitable conflicts that occur in any society. Mindful of Thomas Hobbes's notion that the essence of government is to manage naturally occurring conflicts, the Framers designed a government that encourages conflict and competition rather than attempts to repress it. As we shall see in the chapters that follow, the U.S. Constitution includes a number of mechanisms that allow naturally occurring conflict to play out in as productive a manner as possible.

★ Natural law

According to John Locke, the most fundamental type of law, which supersedes any law that is made by government. Citizens are born with certain natural rights (including life, liberty, and property) that derive from this law and that government cannot take away.

[4]John Locke, *Two Treatises of Government,* ed. Peter Laslett (Cambridge: Cambridge University Press, 1960).

Mechanisms are also in place to resolve conflicts and arrive at consensus on issues. Those who disagree and come up on the short side of political battles are guaranteed rights and liberties nonetheless. Further, the rules by which conflicts are settled are predicated on fairness and proper procedures.

The significance of what the Framers of the Constitution accomplished cannot be overstated. They not only addressed the short-term problems challenging the new nation; they also drafted a blueprint for how government should go about dealing with problems and conflicts into the future. The U.S. Constitution has served as the cornerstone of an American political system that routinely attempts to tackle some of the thorniest problems imaginable. In Chapter 2 of this book, we examine the enduring principles and processes outlined in the Constitution.

The Constitution provides a way for the American government to navigate through the many problems and conflicts that have faced the nation, including severe economic depressions, two world wars, nuclear confrontations with the former Soviet Union, and persisting questions of equality. Through all these difficulties, the American government has endured. The foresight of the Framers to create a Constitution that possesses the flexibility to adapt to changing times has served as a basis for the United States' enduring democracy.

The preamble to the U.S. Constitution perhaps best summarizes the broad goals of American government:

We the People of the United States, in Order to form a more perfect Union, establish Justice, insure domestic Tranquility, provide for the common defense,

★ **Popular sovereignty**

The idea that the ultimate source of power in the nation is held by the people.

★ **Representative democracy**

A form of government designed by the U.S. Constitution whereby free, open, and regular elections are held to allow voters to choose those who govern on their behalf; it is also referred to as *indirect democracy* or a *republican* form of government.

American Government . . . in Historical Perspective:
Constitutional Amendments that Have Extended Voting Rights in the United States

In several states, approval of the new U.S. Constitution drafted in 1789 hinged on adding a bill of rights. Supporters of the Constitution agreed, and the first ten amendments, which comprise the formal Bill of Rights, were added to the Constitution in 1791. Since then, the Constitution has been amended seventeen times. Six of these seventeen amendments extend Americans' voting rights, and no amendment has ever in any way restricted voting rights. Over the years, changes to the original Constitution have led to greater empowerment of the American people in determining the direction that government takes. The six amendments that have extended voting rights are:

In 1870, the Fifteenth Amendment: provides that the right to vote may not be denied on the basis of race.

In 1913, the Seventeenth Amendment: changes the method of selection of U.S. senators from having state legislatures choose senators to having senators directly elected by the voters of a state.

In 1920, the Nineteenth Amendment: provides voting rights to women by not allowing states to deny women the right to vote.

In 1961, the Twenty-third Amendment: provides residents of the District Columbia with electoral votes in presidential elections.

In 1962, the Twenty-fourth Amendment: prevents states from levying a tax on people in order for them to vote in federal elections. Some states used a poll tax to discourage poor people and African Americans from voting.

In 1971, the Twenty-sixth Amendment: provides voting rights to those who are eighteen years of age by not allowing states to deny the franchise to those who have obtained this age.

promote the general Welfare, and secure the Blessings of Liberty to ourselves and our Posterity, do ordain and establish this Constitution for the United States of America.

It is no accident that the first three words of the Constitution are "We the People." With this phrase the Framers acknowledged that the ultimate source of power rests with the people, a concept known as **popular sovereignty.** This "popular perspective" frames our understanding of how the American government works.

The U.S. Constitution provided for a form of **representative democracy,** under which regular elections are held to allow voters to choose those who govern on their behalf. In this sense, individual citizens do not directly make policies, rules, and other governing decisions (a system of government known as a **direct democracy**). Rather, representative democracy, also referred to as *indirect democracy* or a *republican* form of government, rests on the notion that consent of the governed is achieved through free, open, and regular elections of those who are given the responsibility of governing. An important source of the legitimacy of the U.S. government is the nation's commitment to representative democracy, which features the notion of majority rule. Majorities (more than 50 percent of the voters) and pluralities (the leading vote getters, whether or not they constitute absolute majorities) choose the winners of election contests, and so officeholders take their positions on the basis of who most voters prefer. If officeholders fall from public favor, they may be removed in subsequent elections.

Legitimacy is also enhanced by broad public support for the specific purposes of government stated in the preamble to the Constitution: to "insure domestic tranquility" (produce laws that maintain a peaceful and organized approach to living in the nation), to "provide for the common defense" (establish and maintain a military force to protect the nation from outside threats), to "promote the general welfare" (develop domestic policy programs to promote the welfare of the people), and to "secure the blessings of liberty" (guarantee basic freedoms, such as the rights of free expression and the ownership of property, even to those in the minority). Though people may have different opinions on how to achieve these broad goals, few in the United States would disagree with the ideals as stated in the abstract, or with the broad outlines of our republican form of government. Problems arise when public officials stray so far from these goals that their actions are deemed illegitimate by a near, if not absolute majority. Yet the political system as a whole has been able to maintain its legitimacy, even under such trying circumstances, because it has been flexible enough to eventually rid itself of those ineffective actors, whether through elections, impeachment, or some other means. The relatively high degree of legitimacy that is maintained in the United States has helped the American government persist under the U.S. Constitution through good times and bad since 1789.

American Political Culture

Political culture refers to the core values about the role of government and its operations and institutions that are widely held among citizens in a society. Political

©ARPL/HIP/THE IMAGE WORKS

"I agree to this Constitution, with all of its faults, if they are such: because I think a general government necessary for us, and there is no form of government but what may be a blessing to the people if well administered. I doubt too whether any convention we can obtain may be able to make a better constitution. For when you assemble a number of men to have the advantage of their joint wisdom, you inevitably assemble with those men all their prejudices, their passions, their errors of opinion, their local interests, and their selfish views. From such an assembly can a perfect production be expected? It therefore astonishes me . . . to find this system approaching so near to perfection."

—Benjamin Franklin (1788)

★ Direct democracy

A system of government in which all citizens participate in making policy, rules, and governing decisions.

★ Political culture

The values and beliefs about government, its purpose, and its operations and institutions that are widely held among citizens in a society; it defines the essence of how a society thinks politically and is transmitted from one generation to the next.

culture defines the essence of how a society thinks politically. It is transmitted from one generation to the next, and thus has an enduring influence on the politics of a nation. Every nation has a political culture, and the United States is no exception.

Whereas common ancestry characterizes the core of many other nation's political cultures, the United States has no common ancestry. Most other nations around the world, such as France, Britain, China, Japan, are bound by a common birth lineage that serves to define the cultural uniqueness of the nation. For example, the Russian people share common political values and beliefs as part of their ancestors' historical experiences with czars, and then later with the communist regime. Britain, despite being a democracy, retains a monarchy as a symbolic gesture toward its historical antecedents. In many nations rich with such common ethnic traditions, these routines often serve to underscore the political culture of the nation.

The United States has no such common ancestry to help define its political culture. Its land was occupied by many different Native American tribes, and then settled by people from many different parts of the world. Most of the immigrants who settled the colonies were seeking a better life from the political or religious persecution they experienced in their native countries, or they were seeking better-improved economic opportunities for themselves or their families. As America continued to grow through the centuries, it attracted immigrants from around the world, anxious to find a better life. These circumstances had a profound influence on the core values that have become engrained in the American political culture. The ideas generated by democratic political philosophers such as Thomas Hobbes and John Locke also significantly contributed to American political culture. These ideas were used by the founders to justify the Declaration of Independence and the U.S. Constitution, and they continue to underlie American political culture today.

The circumstances surrounding America's first and current immigrants, as well as the great ideas generated by enlightenment philosophers, form the core set of values that define the American political culture. One of these core values is **majority rule.** From its earliest times, the American nation has been committed to the notion that the "will of the people" ought to guide public policy, thus underscoring the importance of popular sovereignty in the thinking of the founders. Majority rule is the way in which popular sovereignty is actually exercised. Rarely will all of the people agree all of the time; and so it is what the majority of people prefer that generally guides decision-making. Early local governments, such as town governments in some of the New England colonies, relied on town meetings, where all citizens were invited to attend, discuss, and vote, to make governmental decisions. Elections for most local and state offices, and elections for the U.S. Congress, are all based on the idea that those who make and enforce laws are duly elected by majorities. A more recent aspect of U.S. commitment to majority rule is its heavy reliance on public opinion polling as a gauge to assessing the performance of elected leaders, and to ensure that leaders respect public preferences for certain policy positions.

While the preferences of the majority rule the day, another core value in the American political culture is minority rights. Those in the minority enjoy certain rights and liberties that cannot be taken away by government. The idea of the natural law (e.g., that people are "endowed by their creator with certain unalienable rights" which government cannot deny) is an important corollary to majority rule. The right to speak freely, to choose a religion, or to decide not to practice religion at all, are among the many liberties that are protected by the U.S. Bill of Rights, and are widely endorsed by the American public.

These rights are intended to inspire debate on issues, to guarantee religious freedoms, to afford due process rights to those accused of crimes. The American political culture places a high value on individual liberty. The fact that many immigrants came to this country for the promise of greater freedom adds further credence to this proposition. Certainly there are some terrible black marks in American history which belie this claim. Among them are the perpetuation of slavery in the country up until the Civil War, the internment of Japanese Americans during World War II, and the treatment of early 1960s civil rights protesters in the South. Still, many Americans today view their nation as the

★ Majority rule

The notion that the will of the majority should guide decisions made by American government.

Table 1.2 Daniel Elazar's Typology of American Political Culture

Many observers of American politics have used different approaches and typologies to describe American political culture. The late political scientist Daniel Elazar described three competing political subcultures, which he believed differentiated American political culture from that found in any other country in the world.* The subcultures that Elazar identified are:

An individualistic subculture, which is skeptical of authority, and keeps government's role limited and celebrates the United States' general reliance on the marketplace

A moralistic subculture, which has faith in the American government's capacity to advance the public interest and encourages citizens to participate in the noble cause of politics

A traditionalistic subculture, which maintains a more ambivalent attitude toward both government and the marketplace, believing that politicians must come from society's elite, whereas ordinary citizens are free to stand on the sidelines

According to Elazar, different subcultures can be found in different geographic areas, and sometimes within a single area itself. For example, he described the political subculture in Texas as part traditionalistic (as manifested in the long history of one-party dominance in state politics) and part individualistic (as seen in the state government's commitment to support for private business and its opposition to big government).

*See Daniel J. Elazar, *American Federalism: A View from the States* (New York: Thomas Y. Crowell, 1966).

world's "garden" of freedom and liberty, even if it has come to this status only slowly and sometimes with reluctance during its more than two centuries of existence.

Another core value in American political culture is the idea of **limited government.** Americans have generally supported the idea expressed by Thomas Jefferson that "the government that governs least governs best." From the days of the American Revolution, the colonists believed that the corruptive power of King George III and the British Parliament led to unfair treatment of the colonies. Suspicion of the government and those with power is firmly rooted in the psyche of American political culture. The "watchdog" function of the press, the separation of powers and the system of checks and balances among political institutions, and the rather negative connotation of the word "politics" all reflect an appreciation for limits and checks on those with authority. Corresponding to the value of limited government is the notion that communities and the private sector should take a role in helping fellow citizens. Problems that may be solved without government should be solved that way. The French journalist Alexis de Tocqueville observed this tradition when he visited the United States in the early 1800s and credited the success of the American political system in part to citizens' strong interest in community and helping one another apart from government.[5]

★ Limited government

The value that promotes the idea that government power should be as restricted as possible.

Since the United States has no common ancestral or cultural bloodline, American political culture recognizes the value and strength derived from the diversity of its population—another important core value. At the base of the Statue of Liberty in New York harbor is inscribed the poem by Emma Lazarus beginning with the phrase: "Bring me your huddled masses, yearning to be free." Until the U.S. government adopted a restrictive immigration policy in the early 1920s, those huddled masses arrived in waves from different parts of the world, as the United States became the chosen destination for those seeking a better life. Joining freed African American slaves who were originally brought here against their will were legions of Italians, Irish, Germans, and other immigrants from Europe and elsewhere. The United States today is one of the most racially and ethnically diverse nations in the world. Integrating these many peoples into a united nation has not come easy; in fact, resistance to the notion of a "melting pot" has been common. The nation has been wracked at times with racial and ethnic strife to a degree that more homogeneous countries can more easily avoid.

[5]Alexis de Tocqueville, *Democracy in America, 1835* (edited by Richard Hefner, Penguin Books, 1956).

Government officials occasionally exacerbate these tensions by promoting policies that discriminate against various groups, including Native Americans, African Americans, Asian Americans, and Hispanic Americans, among others. No stranger to ethnic and racial tensions himself, the German dictator Adolph Hitler calculated that the diversity of the United States would eventually hamper the nation in resisting his own country's totalitarian aggression; in fact, American soldiers of different backgrounds, ethnicities, and religions fought in World War II. Much to Hitler's chagrin, U.S. diversity proved a source of strength, rather than weakness. Indeed, many Americans today believe that the heterogeneity of our society enhances the quality of our culture and helps guarantee the fairness of the government.

Americans also generally subscribe to the notion that individuals are primarily responsible for their lot in life—a value referred to as **individualism.** The seeds of this value were sown hundreds of years ago with the Puritans and their commitment to a strong work ethic that stressed that "what one sows determines what one reaps." In other words, hard work and intelligence should be rewarded. While the U.S. government has assumed some responsibility to provide a safety net for citizens who suffer economically, the American political culture, through its primary reliance on a capitalist economic system, free markets, and individual effort, is one that promotes individual initiative and responsibility. The value of individualism promotes another

★ **Individualism**

The value that individuals are primarily responsible for their own lot in life and that promotes and rewards individual initiative and responsibility. This value underlies America's reliance on a capitalist economy and free-market system.

RICK BOWNER/AP PHOTO

Barack Obama's bid for the presidency in 2008 represented a new chapter in the history of diversity as a value in American political culture.

core value—equality of opportunity, or the idea that the role of government is to set the stage for individuals to achieve on their own, and that everyone should be given the same opportunity to achieve success. Indeed, America has been an attractive place for highly motivated individuals from around to world to immigrate to so that they might have a fair chance of achieving personal success. Many immigrants today, particularly from Asia and Latin America, are attracted to the United States for the opportunities to achieve individual success.

The United States has long set itself apart from those nations whose histories include traditions of a rigid class system of privileged aristocracies and oligarchies and peasants with few or no rights or freedoms. In the United States there is no formal recognition of a class system; nor is there a tradition of royalty, nobility, or monarchy. Indeed, Article I of the Constitution specifically prohibits both the federal government and the state governments from granting any title of nobility upon its citizens. Instead, American political culture values the so-called Horatio Alger myth. Alger was a popular writer in the late 1800s whose characters came from impoverished backgrounds but through pluck, determination, and hard work achieved huge success.

Although this idealistic rags-to-riches notion often ignores the many harsh economic disparities that exist in the United States, it remains central to the American political culture. The stories of Benjamin Franklin and Abraham Lincoln exemplified this road to success, as do the more recent examples of Presidents Bill Clinton and Ronald Reagan, both of whom came from less-than-privileged circumstances to win the nation's highest political office and become leaders of the free world. Perhaps it is because of these success stories that so many Americans believe that they have boundless opportunities to better their lot on the basis of diligence and hard work.

These core values provide a window into American political culture. To be sure, there is plenty of room for disagreement as to how these values might be applied to specific situations, which we address in Chapter 10. In addition, these values are often in conflict. At the heart of the debate over affirmative action, for example, lies the value conflict pitting individualism against equality of opportunity. Those who oppose affirmative action in hiring claim that individuals should be evaluated exclusively based on who they are and what they can do rather than on their gender, race, or other demographic characteristic. Those supporting affirmative action claim that historical discrimination has led to a current job market that provides unequal opportunities for certain groups, such as racial minorities and women. While these values do not always solve problems and policy debates, they do lay the groundwork for how American politics goes about settling problems and debating issues.

Is American Democracy on the Decline? Assessing Both Sides of the Debate

The old saying that "those who ignore the problems of the past are destined to repeat them" holds as true in American politics as it does in any other context. Certainly new issues and problems may arise, requiring innovative new thinking to address them. But many other difficulties the United States faces can be effectively addressed by casting an eye on the distant or not-so-distant past. A historical view can help place modern dilemmas in proper perspective.

The Case for Decline

Some recent observers of American politics have suggested that the American political system is in decline. Are we currently witnessing a deterioration of democracy in the United States? Is the American political system in jeopardy? Are the problems that the American system of government faces today beyond repair? To try to answer these questions, let's first look at the factors some cite as contemporary indicators of the decline of American democracy:

★ **The decline in voter turnout:** Democratic theorists regard an active, participatory citizenry as a sign of a healthy, vibrant democracy. Thus many point to the half-century trend toward lower voter turnout as a sign of decline.

In the 1960s, for example, the percentage of eligible voters who cast a ballot in presidential elections ranged from 62 percent to 65 percent, whereas the range since 1996 has been lower, from 51 percent to a little more than 60 percent. Ratification of the Twenty-sixth Amendment to the U.S. Constitution in 1971, which guaranteed eighteen-, nineteen-, and twenty-year-olds the constitutional right to vote, expanded the pool of eligible voters, but many of those younger voters have stayed away from the polls in disproportionate numbers, explaining at least in part this downturn in voter turnout. With a smaller percentage of people choosing to participate in elections, many have interpreted the decline as a sign of an ailing democracy.

★ **The 2000 presidential election crisis:** For nearly one month after the 2000 presidential election, it remained unclear whether the next president would be Republican George W. Bush or Democrat Al Gore. The closeness of the race in the key state of Florida, along with controversies over how or whether to count certain ballots, left open the question of which candidate actually won the Electoral College vote. In the end, the U.S. Supreme Court indicated that there was insufficient time for a manual recount of Florida's paper ballots, thus effectively awarding Florida's twenty-five electoral votes to Bush, and with them, giving Bush the Electoral College victory. Confounding this outcome was the stark reality that Gore had received approximately half a million more popular votes in total than did Bush. Many regarded this situation as a true constitutional crisis, and called for the abolition of the Electoral College as a means of selecting the president on the basis that a president who takes office without having won the highest number of popular votes lacks the required legitimacy to govern. Four years later a similar electoral crisis was only narrowly averted. A swing of just sixty thousand votes in Ohio would have given the Electoral College victory to Democrat John Kerry, even though he garnered several million fewer popular votes nationwide than did the Republican candidate, incumbent President George W. Bush.

★ **The suspension of civil liberties to protect national security:** The terrorist attacks of September 11, 2001, exposed a variety of security vulnerabilities in the United States. In response to these attacks, Congress passed and President Bush signed into law the USA Patriot Act, which gave the federal government increased authority to exercise wiretapping and other surveillance over citizens and to detain individuals deemed "suspicious." Rights advocates viewed this increased authority as a violation of the rights and liberties guaranteed to individuals by the Constitution, and indicative of how American society has become increasingly intolerant of the rights and freedoms of minorities. The willingness of the president and Congress to support laws that allow the government to jail individuals for an indefinite period of time, whether or not those individuals have been charged with a crime, suggests to critics of the USA Patriot Act that some of the core values upon which the American nation is built may now be under siege.

★ **The disproportionate influence of money and wealth on politics:** In American politics today, most successful election campaigns require large amounts of money. Those who have the financial resources—corporations and wealthy individuals—provide the bulk of the financing. During the 2008 presidential primaries alone, candidates from both major political parties raised more than $1 billion. The winning congressional candidates in the 2006 elections for the House of Representatives and the Senate collectively raised nearly $750 million. Do these huge sums of money, most of which come from corporations and wealthy individuals, influence the behavior of those who win elections? If so, what does that indicate about the state of American democracy?

★ **Politics that are more negative and conflictual:** Negative political advertising, partisan conflicts that degenerate into personal attacks, and exploitation of personal affairs into public spectacles seem to characterize a good deal of modern-day American politics. The inclination of political figures to "go negative," combined with the news media's taste for negative stories has created a political atmosphere fraught with attacks, counterattacks and much partisan wrangling. From the Republican-driven impeachment of President Bill Clinton in 1998, to claims during the 2004 election that President George W. Bush had avoided serving in the Vietnam War, to the constant barrage of negative political ads throughout the 2006 midterm elections (such as the claim that Tennessee Senate candidate Harold Ford Jr. was a play-boy), to the Republican attacks on Barack Obama

CHARLES KNOBLOCK/AP PHOTO

One of the negative ads of the 2008 presidential campaign attacked Democratic candidate Barack Obama for his association with William Ayers, a co-founder of the Weather Underground, a radical 1960s anti-Vietnam War group that carried out bombings at the Capitol and the Pentagon. The Web video ad questioned Obama's judgment for his association with Ayers, seen here in a 1980 photo entering the Criminal Courts Building in Chicago. Ayers, labeled as a ter-rorist in the ad, is now a college professor, and he and Obama served together on the board of a school reform organization in the mid-1990s.

comparing his celebrity status to that of Britney Spears and Paris Hilton, the measured and orderly democratic process envisioned by the Founders seems to have become much less deliberative and civil and much more strident and negative.

★ **The "red" state/"blue" state divide:** The Electoral College maps that the media used to follow the 2008 presidential election returns showed states that Democratic candidate Barack Obama won in blue, and states that Republican candidate John McCain won in red. Whereas the blue states were for the most part clustered in the northeastern United States, the northern Midwest, and the West Coast, the large land block between coasts and throughout the South was predominant red, with few exceptions. The results of the 2000 and 2004 elections revealed an even sharper divide, with a sea of red extending from Nevada, Arizona, and Idaho in the West, all the way to the Southeast Coast and Florida. (In the 2000 election, New Mexico offered a lone island of blue, while New Hampshire stood by itself as a red state in the Northeast.). It is perhaps no wonder that commentators, referring to this "blue versus red" division of the American public, argue that it represents an electorate widely divided not only along partisan lines, but also along cultural lines. These observers emphasize the divide between the socially moderate-to-liberal values of the Northeast and West Coast and the more conservative values embraced by the Great Plains states and the South.

These dilemmas in contemporary American politics have led some observers to conclude that American democracy is in sharp and deep decline. Yet even with the evidence provided, this may be a rather superficial examination of contemporary American government. If we examine these characteristics of American politics with the benefit of some historical perspective, it is possible to draw quite different conclusions, which in turn suggest that our system of government is designed to allow conflict and controversy to be managed in a productive way. The system promotes clashes of ideas, sometimes characterized by personal animosity. The system also allows for multiple points of input from a large number of citizens and organized interests.

The Case against Decline

If we re-examine some of the criticisms of contemporary American politics with the benefit of historical perspective, we may reach far different conclusions about whether American democracy is now in a state of decline:

★ **Decline in voter turnout:** As shown in the figure on page 19, there has indeed been a general decline in voter turnout since the 1950s. In the presidential elections of 1952, 1956, 1960, 1964, and 1968, the percentage of eligible voters who cast a vote in the presidential election exceeded 60 percent. Yet in eight of the last ten presidential elections, the percentage voting has been in the 50 percent to 56 percent range. Voter turnout exceeded 60 percent in the 2004 and 2008 presidential elections, but it remains to be seen whether this jump in turnout will sustain itself in the future. A historical perspective reveals, however, that it has not been uncommon for only half—or even less than half—of voters to cast a ballot in a presidential election. In the elections of 1924 and 1928, turnout dropped below 50 percent. Even in the historically important election of 1932—the election that put Franklin Roosevelt's New Deal coalition into office—voter turnout was less than 60 percent. In the 1948 contest in which Democratic candidate Harry Truman came from far behind to defeat the Republican Thomas Dewey, turnout was a mere 53 percent. Thus by early-to mid-twentieth-century standards, a turnout rate of around 50 percent is not all that unusual. In fact, low voter turnout may even indicate the public's general contentment with the state of the union.

★ **The 2000 presidential election crisis:** The confusion surrounding the outcome of the 2000 presidential contest was not unique to that presidential election. In fact, there have been other presidential election contests that either produced no clear winner in the Electoral College or produced an Electoral College winner different from the popular vote winner. The Framers of the Constitution may have even contemplated these possibilities, because they created a compromise that sought to give less populated states disproportionate influence over the outcome. In 1888, for example, Grover Cleveland won the popular vote, but lost the Electoral College vote (and thus the presidency) to Benjamin Harrison. In 1876, Samuel Tilden won 51 percent of the popular vote but failed to capture a majority of electoral votes, and Rutherford B. Hayes became president as part of a brokered deal among political party elites. In the 1824 election, Andrew Jackson defeated John Quincy Adams by more than 10 percentage points of the popular votes cast; however, neither candidate won a majority of electoral votes, and the House of Representatives chose Adams as the new president. Even in one of the earliest presidential contests in 1800, the lack of an Electoral College majority was resolved by the House of Representatives awarding the presidency to Thomas Jefferson (it took more than thirty ballots for the House to arrive at this conclusion). What in 2000

American Government ... in Popular Perspective:
Voter Turnout in U.S. Presidential Elections

The popular perspective of the American people finds multiple ways to influence the outcome of policy debates, including reporting poll results, working on campaigns, and donating time and/or money to political candidates and interest groups. But the most basic way in which the people affect policy is through voting. Prior to 1828, only a limited number of states held popular elections to help determine how a state's electoral votes would be allocated in a presidential election. Since then, most states have held popular elections for electors who in turn select the president. This figure shows the percentage of the eligible electorate that cast a vote in presidential elections since 1900.

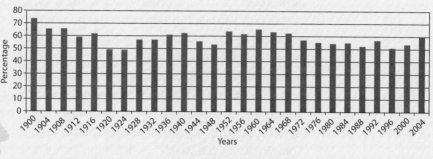

Source: From Harold W. Stanley and Richard G. Niemi *Vital Statistics on American Politics,* (CQ Press, 2006). Copyright ©2006 CQ Press, a division of Sage Publications.

seemed like a unique controversy in American politics was only the latest among many in the history of presidential elections.

★ **The suspension of civil liberties to protect national security:** Under the terms of the USA Patriot Act, many individuals suspected of having connections with terrorist organizations have been detained by the U.S. government without being formally accused of having committed some specific crime. Some civil liberties organizations, including the American Civil Liberties Union (ACLU), claim the Patriot Act thus allows gross and unprecedented violation of individuals' due process rights. But there have been other instances in the nation's history when the government has curtailed individuals' rights. During the Civil War, President Abraham Lincoln closed down several newspapers and suspended the writ of habeas corpus, by which a prisoner can demand a trial or hearing before a judge so that the judge can determine whether the prisoner is being legally detained. Immediately after the Japanese attack on Pearl Harbor in 1941, the federal government ordered

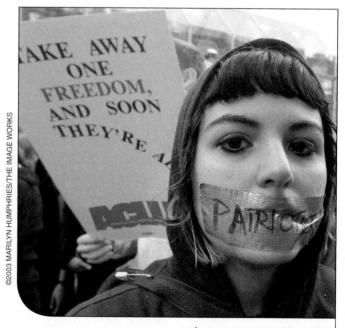

©2003 MARILYN HUMPHRIES/THE IMAGE WORKS

A young woman participates in a protest of the controversial USA Patriot Act at Boston's historic Faneuil Hall in September 2003.

that more than one hundred thousand individuals be placed in internment camps; most of those interned were American citizens of Japanese ancestry. Thus although such actions may run counter to the American political culture, which places great value on individual liberties, allegations that the government has violated some of those liberties are nothing new in American politics, particularly when national security is severely threatened.

★ **The disproportionate influence of money and wealth on politics:** There is no doubt that the bulk of money for political campaigns comes from corporations and wealthy Americans, and few would question the degree to which money influences political decisions. In addition, some of the most successful interest groups in the United States are funded by the wealthy. But this is by no means a new phenomenon in American politics either. Most of the Founders, all of whom were white males, were wealthy landowners. It has been reported that George Washington himself bought one and a half quarts of liquor for each vote he received in his first run for public office in 1758.[6] Just as today's large corporate contributors (such as Microsoft and IBM) and powerful interest groups (such as the American Medical Association and the American Trial Lawyers Association) enjoy disproportionately large influence over politics, so too did the so-called robber barons of the late nineteenth century, such as the financier J. Pierpont Morgan, the industrialist Andrew Carnegie, or the railroad magnate Cornelius Vanderbilt, wield considerable influence over the nation's politics.

★ **Politics that are more negative and conflictual:** The negativity, combativeness, and personal conflict that characterize modern American politics—distasteful though these may be—are nothing new. Negativity and conflict are the product of the vigorous and spirited debate that occurs in a free and open democracy. One of the most negative political campaigns ever waged was the 1800 presidential battle between Thomas Jefferson and John Adams. During that campaign, Jefferson used partisan newspapers to launch a very negative campaign against Adams. The personal attacks that pervaded the impeachment hearings of President Bill Clinton in 1998 were no match for the character assassinations featured during the impeachment of President Andrew Johnson in 1868. And in neither of those cases could the personal attacks match the fatal wounding in 1804 of Alexander Hamilton by Aaron Burr in a duel over political differences that became personal. Nor is the general tone of negativity of the modern-day news media anything new. The intense partisanship of some of the nation's early newspapers, such as Ben Franklin's *Pennsylvania Gazette,* and the sensationalist "yellow journalism" of the late nineteenth century provide a good match for today's focus on negative news.

★ **The "red" state/"blue" state divide:** The Electoral College vote totals of the 2000, 2004, and 2008 presidential elections may appear to depict an unprecedented new geographical divide among the nation's states. Yet nearly half of those states—twenty-three of the fifty—including a handful of states located in every region of in the country, failed to give either presidential candidate as much as 55 percent of the popular vote, a signal that these were in fact not the die-hard "red" or "blue" states that the media often portray them as. In the 2006 congressional elections, Democratic Senate victories in

[6]Robert Goidel, Donald A. Gross, and Todd G. Shields, *Money Matters* (Lanham, MD: Rowman & Littlefield, 1999), p. 17.

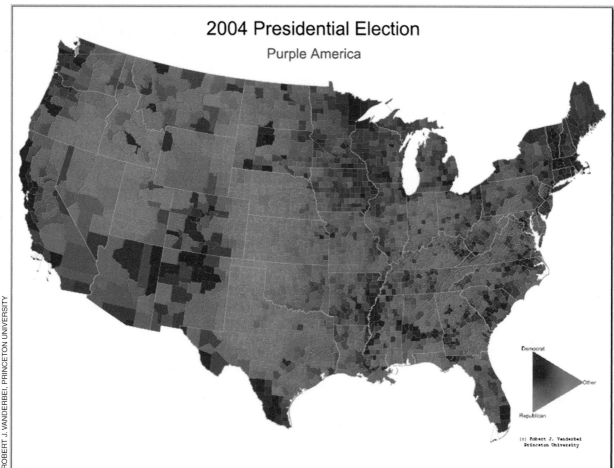

2004 Presidential Election

Purple America

"red" Republican states such as Virginia and Montana helped put Democrats back in the majority not only in the House of Representatives but also in the Senate. In fact, within some states, such as Ohio, Florida, and Pennsylvania, divisions may be sharper than ever. As political scientist Morris Fiorina argued in his 2005 book, *Culture War? The Myth of a Polarized America*,[7] the percentage of American citizens who went to the polls at the beginning of the twenty-first century with a fairly set idea of how they would cast their votes was actually no greater than it had been a quarter century earlier, or even a full century earlier. Fiorina also discovered that geographic regions differ far less on such issues as abortion, gun control, or the role that religion should play in politics than the stereotypes of red state versus blue state would suggest. Reports of a sharp red–blue divide may be nothing more than a convenient story created by pundits and journalists to generate interest in news stories.

Discussion of the "blue vs. red" political divisions in America ignores the possibility that there may actually be a "purple America," as shown in this map from Time magazine. (Closely contested districts in 2004 are shown in purple; one-sided Republican districts are shown in red, and one-sided Democratic districts are shown in blue.)

Historical, Popular, and Global Perspectives

History does not literally repeat itself. The specific people, circumstances, and events certainly change. But history can help us identify patterns, recurring problems, and trends in how the American political system functions and resolves conflicts. The preceding discussion of some of the contemporary arguments for why American democracy may be in a state of decline helps us

---

[7]Morris Fiorina, *Culture War? The Myth of a Polarizing America* (New York: Pearson Longman, 2005).

frame current conditions. In doing so, we may gain a greater understanding of the challenges facing the nation today. Certainly, many contemporary challenges are no less daunting than problems the nation has encountered over the past two centuries. Throughout this book, a historical perspective on contemporary problems offers a sense of how the past might help us understand politics today.

As past events provide perspective on contemporary American politics, they also make quite clear the significant role that people play in influencing political outcomes and public policy. The "will of the people" is not just a rhetorical phrase used by politicians. Rather, it has guided American politics and government since the country's founding. Throughout this book, we employ a popular perspective to understand better how our system of government works. Citizens who actively participate in politics through voting, working on campaigns, contributing time and effort to interest group activities, participating in demonstrations, writing to elected officials and the op-ed pages, and running for office have an impact on public policy. In this book, consideration of the popular perspective allows us to see how the will of the people has an impact on American politics.

Finally, a look at American government would not be complete without some perspective on how the rest of the world views the United States. Through advanced technologies such as the Internet, satellites, and air travel, life in the modern world increasingly interconnects people from different nations. The governments of the globe, for better or for worse, are affected by this interconnectedness of the world's peoples. Throughout this book, a global perspective offers insights into how people around the world perceive American government.

"Isn't it sad that politics have become so negative these days?" Such is a common complaint about contemporary American politics in general, and political campaigns in particular. Just in the most recent 2008 campaign, candidates were accused of being celebrities, liars, plagiarists, adulterers, and terrorist supporters. Poll after poll depicts how much Americans deplore negativity in campaigns, though that doesn't seem to deter its prevalence.

www.factcheck.org, a web page developed and maintained by the Annenberg School at the University of Pennsylvania, is an antidote to some of the negativity and misrepresentation of candidates, records. This web page examines many of the negative claims that candidates launch against each other in political advertising, and seeks to verify the claim or vilify the false accusation.

At http://academic.cengage.com/dautrich, find the politics interactive link for details and examples of negative campaigning in American politics. Consult as well the various links that relate to negativity in American politics in historical, popular, and global perspectives.

The duel between Aaron Burr and Alexander Hamilton, which killed Hamilton, is perhaps one of the most famous and extreme instances of negativity in American politics.

http://academic.cengage.com/dautrich

Chapter Summary

★ The development of the American political system is grounded in the philosophy of John Locke and Jean-Jacques Rousseau, who argued that government is necessary and that it exists for the purpose of protecting the people that it serves. The "social contract" theory states that natural law gives people certain unalienable rights that government cannot take away, and that the people give government authority to rule, but the people can withdraw that authority if government does not serve the people's interests.

★ Democracy includes at its core the idea of popular sovereignty. The United States practices a form of democracy known as "representative democracy," where the people indirectly rule by electing leaders who are responsible for making and carrying out policies and laws.

★ The political culture in America is reflected in the Constitution and the way in which the political system deals with and decides political debates. Among the core values guiding the American political culture are majority rule, liberty, individualism, equality of economic opportunity, diversity, and limited government.

★ Although the current American government has been in place for more than two hundred years, there have been questions raised about whether this political system is in a state of decline. Lower voter turnout, negativity in politics, the influence of money in policy outcomes, and confusing election outcomes have been offered as evidence of a decline. However, a review of historical patterns in American politics suggests that these seemingly contemporary problems are chronic, and the American political system has effectively dealt with these and many other problems.

★ Viewing American government from a historical perspective may enrich our understanding of how the political system works. History can help us identify patterns, recurring problems, and trends in how the American political system functions and resolves conflicts. Many contemporary challenges are no more significant than problems the nation has encountered over the past two centuries.

★ Viewing American government from a popular perspective also informs our appreciation of the important role that citizens play in the political system. People play a large role in influencing political outcomes and public policy. The "will of the people" is not just a rhetorical phrase—it has guided American politics and government since the country's founding. Citizens who actively participate in politics through voting, working on campaigns, contributing time and effort to interest group activities, participating in demonstrations, writing to elected officials, authoring letters in op-ed pages, and running for office, all have an impact on public policy.

★ Viewing American government from a global perspective has become increasingly important in a world that has become interconnected. Through advanced technologies such as the Internet, satellites, and air travel, life in the modern world increasingly interconnects people from different nations. The governments of the globe, for better or for worse, are affected by this interconnectedness of so many different peoples. A global perspective offers insights into how people around the world perceive American government.

Key Terms

Anarchy (p. 6)

Authoritarianism (p. 7)

Authority (p. 6)

Democracy (p. 6)

Direct democracy (p. 11)

Government (p. 6)

Individualism (p. 14)

Legitimacy (p. 7)

Limited government (p. 13)

Majority rule (p. 12)

Monarchy (p. 7)

Natural law (p. 9)

Oligarchy (p. 6)

Political culture (p. 11)

Politics (p. 8)

Popular sovereignty (p. 10)

Power (p. 7)

Representative democracy (p. 10)

Social contract (p. 6)

Theocracy (p. 6)

Resources

Important Books

Anderson, Terry H. *The Pursuit of Fairness: The History of Affirmative Action.* New York: Oxford University Press, 2004.

Fiorina, Morris. *Culture War? The Myth of a Polarizing America.* New York: Pearson Longman, 2005.

Gilliam, Howard. *Votes That Counted: How the Court Decided the 2000 Presidential Election.* Chicago: University of Chicago Press, 2001.

Greenberg, Stanley B. *The Two Americas: Our Current Political Deadlock and How to Break It.* New York: Thomas Dunne Books, 2004.

Putnam, Robert. *Bowling Alone.* New York: Simon and Schuster, 2000.

Internet Sources

www.nara.gov (this is the site for the National Archives and contains a wealth of information on documents relating to American culture)

www.whitehouse.gov (the official home page of the White House)

www.fjc.gov (the site of the Federal Justice Center, which provides detailed information on the federal judiciary)

www.house.gov (the site for the U.S. House of Representatives)

www.senate.gov (the site for the U.S. Senate)

The Founding and the Constitution

2

President Bill Clinton

WIN MCNAMEE/REUTERS/LANDOV

Impeachment by the "Book": Now & Then

The president of the United States had been under political siege for months—all that now stood between him and the end of his political career were the safeguards inherent within the constitutional mechanism of impeachment. The designers of the U.S. Constitution had made the process of removing an elected official from office extremely difficult—thus although his impeachment was now a matter of record, it would take a two-thirds vote of the Senate to oust him from the White House. The president hoped that it would be difficult, if not impossible, to collect such a large number of votes against him. On that score the president was right—although the highly partisan House of Representatives had impeached him by a wide margin, he was ultimately acquitted in the Senate, with several members of the opposition casting nay votes to keep the embattled president in office. The removal of a sitting president had proven to be an extremely difficult endeavor, just as the Framers of the Constitution hoped it would be.

President Andrew Johnson

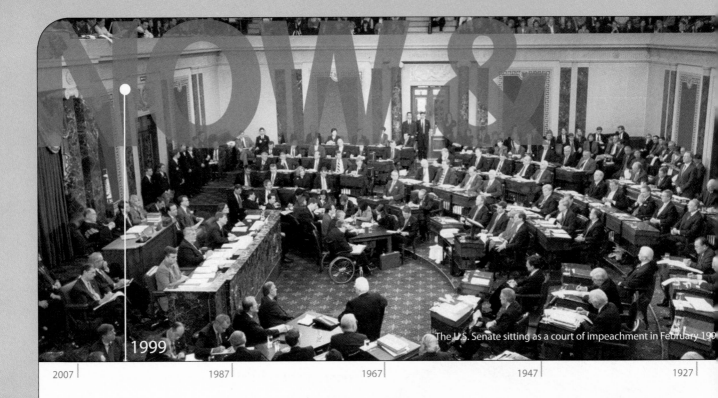

NOW &

1999

The U.S. Senate sitting as a court of impeachment in February 1999

2007   1987   1967   1947   1927

Now . . . For a six-month period during President Bill Clinton's second term in office—from August 1998 through February 1999—this young and energetic chief executive from Arkansas saw his presidency threatened by an emboldened House Republican opposition, which only a few years earlier had captured control of that institution for the first time in decades. On the morning of August 17, 1998, President Clinton testified before a grand jury that he had engaged in an "inappropriate" physical relationship with onetime White House intern Monica Lewinsky in late 1995, and that he had ended that relationship in 1997. That same evening, Clinton addressed the nation on the matter, admitting that he had engaged in an "inappropriate relationship" with Lewinsky, but repeated his denials of any wrongdoing. Reacting to these events, the House of Representatives approved two articles of impeachment against the president on December 19, 1998. The first count, that of perjury, charged that the president had lied to a grand jury investigating Clinton's conduct in a sexual harassment lawsuit brought by a former employee, Paula Jones; at that time Clinton denied having "sexual relations" with Lewinsky. The second impeachment count charged Clinton with obstruction of justice on the basis of allegations that he had pressured aides to lie to investigators about his involvement with Lewinsky. On February 12, 1999, after a five-week trial in the Senate, the president was acquitted on both counts. Once the constitutional mechanism of impeachment was officially invoked, critics complained about its suitability to the task at hand—Clinton's actions were embarrassing and perhaps unethical—but was the time and effort that went into Congress's investigation of such charges truly justified? Clinton's supporters and opponents no doubt disagree on that issue. To date, no changes to the two-century-old constitutional provisions for impeachment have made much headway, and none are expected any time soon.

The U.S. Senate trying the impeachment of President Johnson in 1868.

THEN

1868

1907 1887 1867 1847

Then . . . Clinton's predicament may have seemed unprecedented to contemporary observers, but in many ways it was a near replay of events that had occurred 130 years earlier involving another southern president of the United States, Andrew Johnson. In 1864 Johnson, a pro-Union Democrat from Tennessee, had been elected vice president of the United States as the running mate of Republican President Abraham Lincoln. Lincoln's assassination in April 1865 thrust Johnson into the presidency, where his attempt to carry out Lincoln's conciliatory policies toward rebel Southern states brought him into conflict with radical Republicans in Congress, who had won significant majorities in the 1866 elections. In February 1868, Johnson fired his Secretary of War in apparent violation of the 1867 Tenure of Office Act, which required congressional assent prior to any such dismissals. Radical Republicans in the House of Representatives, who were determined to get rid of Johnson, used the occasion to bring articles of impeachment against the president. The trial in the Senate began in March and continued through April and into May. When the Senate vote repeatedly fell short of the two-thirds majority required for conviction, the Senate adjourned as a court of impeachment in May 1868 and Johnson served out the rest of his term as president.

Andrew Johnson and Bill Clinton are the only two presidents in history to have been impeached by the House of Representatives according to the provisions in Article II, Section 4 of the Constitution. At the Constitutional Convention of 1787, James Madison had argued that without provisions for presidential impeachment, the chief executive might "pervert his administration into a scheme of peculation and oppression. He might betray his trust to foreign powers."[1] In an attempt to extend the check beyond the crime of treason, the convention delegates agreed to allow impeachment also for "bribery and other high crimes and misdemeanors." At the same time, the drafters applied the supermajority vote requirement (two-thirds) to the Senate vote for conviction, to ensure that this new deliberative body would be "most careful" when considering an issue of such critical importance.

Bill Clinton's Senate impeachment trial played out just as the Founders might have predicted, and just as Andrew Johnson's trial played out in the same Senate chamber 130 years earlier. Indeed, the United States had already survived the impeachments of one president, one Supreme Court Justice, eleven lower court judges, one Cabinet Member, and one U.S. Senator in the 210 years before Clinton's trial took place. In the cases of both Johnson and Clinton, the Founders' carefully designed mechanism for combating certain types of crimes was invoked at a time when the presidents' enemies might well have preferred a quicker and more decisive way of forcing the chief executive out of office.

The Beginnings of a New Nation

Throughout the seventeenth and early eighteenth centuries, thousands of people, many of them British subjects, migrated to North America. Many came in search of greater economic opportunities; others fled to escape religious persecution and sought freedom to worship as they pleased. Slowly, a culture dedicated to the protection of social and civil rights began to take shape in the colonies.

The political structures that governed the colonies up through the early 1760s roughly paralleled those of England during the same period: (1) royal governors served as substitutes for the king in each individual colony; (2) a governor's council in each colony served as a mini House of Lords, with the most influential men in the colony serving effectively as a high court; and (3) the general assembly in each colony was elected directly by the qualified voters in each colony and served essentially as a House of Commons, passing ordinances and regulations that would govern the colony. Up until the middle of the eighteenth century, the colonies' diverse histories and economies had provided little incentive for them to join together to meet shared goals. In fact, Great Britain feared other European powers attempting to encroach on their American holdings far more than they feared any form of uprising on the part of the colonists.

The French and Indian War that was waged in the colonies from 1754 through 1763 was a significant turning point in British-colonial relations.[2] For nearly a decade the French, from their base in Canada, fought the British in the colonies for control of the North American empire. Both nations were interested in rights to the territory that extended west of the colonial settlements along the Atlantic seaboard and over the Appalachian Mountains into the Ohio Valley. Britain defeated France, and under the terms of the Treaty of Paris (1763), which settled the war, all territory from the Arctic Ocean to the Gulf of Mexico between the Atlantic Ocean and the Mississippi River (except for New Orleans, which was ceded to Spain, an ally of Britain during the war) was awarded to Britain. But along with the acquisition of all this new territory came a staggering debt of approximately 130 million pounds. Administering its huge new North American empire would be a costly undertaking.

[1] For a full account of the convention, see Max Farrand, *The Records of the Federal Convention of 1787* (New Haven, CT: Yale University Press, 1967).
[2] Fred Anderson, *The War That Made America: A Short History of the French-Indian War* (New York: Viking, 2005).

British Actions

Following the war, Britain imposed upon its colonies a series of regulatory measures intended to make the colonists help pay the war debts and share the costs of governing the empire. To prevent colonists from ruining the prosperous British fur trade, the Proclamation of 1763 restricted them to the eastern side of the Appalachian chain, angering those interested in settling, cultivating, and trading in this new region. The Sugar Act (1764) was the first law passed by Parliament for the specific purpose of raising money in the colonies for the crown. (Other regulatory acts passed earlier had been enacted for the purpose of controlling trade.) The Sugar Act (1) increased the duties on sugar, (2) placed new import duties on textiles, coffee, indigo wines, and other goods, and (3) doubled the duties on foreign goods shipped from England to the colonies. The Stamp Act (1765) required the payment of a tax on the purchase of all newspapers, pamphlets, almanacs, and commercial and legal documents in the colonies. Both acts drew outrage from colonists, who argued that Parliament could not tax those who were not formally represented in its chambers. Throughout late 1765 and early 1766, angry colonists protested the Stamp Act by attacking stamp agents who attempted to collect the tax, destroying the stamps, and boycotting British goods. When English merchants complained bitterly about the loss of revenue they were suffering as a result of these colonial protests, Parliament repealed the Stamp Act in March 1766.[3]

Patrick Henry, a leading revolutionary who coined the phrase "Give me liberty or give me death," speaking before the Virginia House of Burgesses in 1775.

---

[3] Robert Middlekauff, *The Glorious Cause* (New York: Oxford University Press, 1982).

Colonial Responses

As a result of the Stamp Act fiasco, positions on the state of British rule were articulated both in the colonies and in Parliament. Following the lead of the Virginia assembly, which sponsored the Virginia Resolves that had declared the principle of "no taxation without representation," an intercolonial Stamp Act Congress met in New York City in 1765. This first congressional body in America issued a Declaration of Rights and Grievances that acknowledged allegiance to the Crown, but reiterated the right to not be taxed without consent. Meanwhile, the British Parliament—on the same day that it repealed the Stamp Act—passed into law the Declaratory Act, asserting that the king and Parliament had "full power and authority" to enact laws binding on the colonies "in all cases whatsoever."

Despite the colonists' protests, Parliament continued to pass legislation designed to raise revenue from the colonies. The Townshend Acts, passed in 1767, imposed duties on various items, including tea, imported into the colonies and created a Board of Customs Commissioners to enforce the acts and collect the duties. When the colonists protested by boycotting British goods, Parliament repealed all the duties except that on tea in 1770. The Tea Act, enacted in 1773, was passed to help the financially troubled British East India Company by relaxing export duties and allowing the company to sell its tea directly in the colonies. These advantages allowed the company to undersell colonial merchants. Angry colonists saw the act as a trick to lure Americans into buying the cheaper tea and thus ruining American tea sellers. On December 16, 1773, colonists disguised as Mohawk Indians boarded ships in Boston Harbor, and threw overboard their cargoes of tea. Outraged by this defiant Boston Tea Party, Parliament in 1774 passed the Intolerable Acts (known in the colonies as the Coercive Acts), designed to punish the rebellious colonists. The acts closed the port of Boston, revised the Massachusetts colonial government, and required the colonists to provide food and housing for British troops stationed in the colonies.

The colonists had had enough. In September 1774, fifty-six leaders from twelve colonies (there were no delegates from Georgia) met in Philadelphia to plan a united response to Parliament's actions. This First Continental Congress denounced British policy and organized a boycott of British goods. Although the Congress did not advocate outright independence from England, it did encourage the colonial militias to arm themselves and began to collect and store weapons in an arsenal in Concord, Massachusetts. The British governor general of Massachusetts ordered British troops to seize and destroy the weapons. On their way to Concord, the troops met a small force of colonial militiamen at Lexington. Shots were exchanged, but the militiamen were soon routed and the British troops marched on to Concord. There they encountered a much larger group of colonial militia. Shots again were fired, and this time the British retreated. The American Revolution had begun.

After the skirmishes at Lexington and Concord in early 1775, a Second Continental Congress met in May of that year, this time with all thirteen colonies represented. This Congress established a continental army and appointed George Washington as its commander in chief, initiating the process that resulted in independence for the colonies and the formation of a new nation, the United States of America.[4]

BOYCOTT

NO TAXATION WITHOUT REPRESENTATION

[4] Events of these years are nicely recounted in Pauline Maier, *From Resistance to Revolution: Colonial Radicals and the Development of American Opposition to Britain, 1765–1776* (New York: W. W. Norton, 1992).

Top Ten Most Important Founders?

Jim Allison, an independent researcher from Virginia Beach, Virginia, recently tried to identify those Founders who most influenced the early republic. Rejecting traditional forms of subjective or impressionistic analysis, Allison invented his own ranking system, which allotted to each Founder a specific number of points for participation in selected activities. For example, he awarded two points for signing the Declaration of Independence, two points for attending the Constitutional Convention, one point for authoring documents that had an impact on state government, and so on. The ranking system can be found at http://members.tripod.com/~candst/tnppage/quote1.htm. Allison's system has its flaws; most notably, it awards to each person the same number of points for participating in an activity, even though some obviously had more influence on the outcome of these activities than others. Thus the appearance of James Madison at the top of the list seems reasonable, whereas Thomas Jefferson's low ranking (19th) may be explained in part by his absence from America (he was in France) during both the Constitutional Convention and subsequent congressional debates over the Bill of Rights. Perhaps what is most surprising about Allison's list is the absence of such well-known figures as George Washington, Benjamin Franklin, and John Adams.

Who would you list as the ten most important founding fathers? The list of Allison's top ten is as follows:

Founder	Points	State
✔ **James Madison,** key drafter of Constitution, author of some Federalist Papers, Congressional sponsor of Bill of Rights, fourth President of the United States	364	VA
✔ **Roger Sherman,** author of the Great Compromise that saved the Constitutional Convention	295	CT
✔ **James Wilson,** played a leading role at the Constitutional Convention, one of the first Supreme Court justices	276	PA
✔ **Rufus King,** delegate to Constitutional Convention, early 18th-century candidate for president, vice president	272	MA
✔ **Elbridge Gerry,** delegate to Constitutional Convention, American commissioner to Paris, vice president	214	MA
✔ **Edmund Randolph,** proposed Virginia Plan at the Constitutional Convention, first U.S. Attorney General, Second Secretary of State	154	VA
✔ **George Mason,** key revolutionary statesman, opposed the Great Compromise, fought for federal Bill of Rights	131	VA
✔ **Alexander Hamilton,** author of Federalist Papers, Secretary of Treasury, inspired creation of national bank	125	NY
✔ **Gouverneur Morris,** led floor debates at Constitutional Convention, prepared final draft of Constitution	119	PA
✔ **John Rutledge,** member of Continental Congress, delegate to the Constitutional Convention, associate justice of the Supreme Court, nominee for Chief Justice	112	SC

The Decision for Independence

Despite the events of the early 1770s, many leading colonists continued to hold out hope that some settlement could be reached between the colonies and Britain. The tide turned irrevocably in early 1776, when one of the most influential publications of this period, *Common Sense,* first appeared. In it, Thomas Paine attacked King George III as responsible for the provocations against the colonies, and converted many wavering Americans to the cause of independence.[5]

The Declaration of Independence.

On June 7, 1776, Richard Henry Lee, a delegate to the Second Continental Congress from Virginia, proposed a resolution stating that "these United Colonies are, and of right ought to be, free and independent States." Of course the Congress needed a formal document both to state their list of grievances and to articulate their new intention to seek independence. The Congress thus appointed a committee to draft a document that would meet those objectives.

The committee, consisting of Thomas Jefferson, John Adams, Roger Sherman, Robert Livingston, and Benjamin Franklin, appointed Jefferson to compose the document. At first, Jefferson may have seemed an unlikely choice to produce such a declaration. The thirty-three-year-old lawyer and delegate to the Continental Congresses of 1775 and 1776 had played a relatively minor role in those bodies' deliberations. But according to historian David McCullough, Adams initially believed that the document was really just a symbolic "side show," and quickly justified the choice of Jefferson over himself as follows: "Reason first: you are a Virginian and a Virginian ought to appear at the head of this business. Reason second: I am obnoxious, suspected and unpopular. You are very much otherwise. Reason third: You can write ten times better than I can." Later, Adams fumed for decades over the larger-than-life reputation Jefferson gained on the basis of authoring the nation's first great political document.[6]

The committee submitted its draft to Congress on July 2, 1776; after making some changes, Congress formally adopted the document on July 4. The **Declaration of Independence** restated John Locke's theory of natural rights and the social contract between government and the governed.[7] Locke had argued that although citizens sacrifice certain rights when they consent to be governed as part of a social contract, they retain other inalienable rights. In the Declaration, Jefferson reiterated this argument with the riveting sentence: "We hold these truths to be self-evident, that all men are created equal, that they are endowed by their Creator with certain inalienable rights, that among these are life, liberty and the pursuit of happiness." Jefferson went on to state that whenever government fails in its duty to secure such rights, the people have the right to "alter" or "abolish" it and institute a new one. Through the centuries, America's political leaders have consistently invoked the Declaration of Independence as perhaps the truest written embodiment of the American Revolution. Before independence could become a reality, however, the colonists had to fight and win a war with Great Britain.

★ Declaration of Independence

Formal document listing colonists' grievances and articulating the colonists' intention to seek independence; formally adopted by the Second Continental Congress on July 4, 1776.

[5] *The Political Writings of Thomas Paine, Vol. 1* (Boston: J. P. Mendum Investigator Office, 1870).
[6] David McCullouch, *John Adams* (New York: Simon & Schuster, 2001), p. 119; Joseph Ellis, *Founding Brothers* (New York: Alfred A. Knopf, 2000), pp. 212–213.
[7] Pauline Maier, *American Scripture: Making the Declaration of Independence* (New York: Vintage, 1998).

American Government: Historical, Popular, and Global Perspectives

TAXI/GETTY IMAGES

The First National Government:
The Articles of Confederation

The colonies also needed some sort of plan of government to direct the war effort. The Second Continental Congress drew up the **Articles of Confederation,** a written statement of rules and principles to guide the first continent-wide government in the colonies during the war and beyond. Although the document was initially adopted by Congress in 1777, it was not formally ratified by all thirteen states until 1781. The Articles of Confederation created a "league of friendship" among the states, but the states remained sovereign and independent with the power and authority to rule the colonists' daily lives. The sole body of the new national government was the Congress, in which each state had one vote. The Congress enjoyed only limited authority to govern the colonies: it could wage war and make peace, coin money, make treaties and alliances with other nations, operate a postal service, and manage relations with the Native Americans.[8] But Congress had no

★ Articles of Confederation

The document creating a "league of friendship" governing the thirteen states during and immediately after the war for independence; hampered by the limited power they vested in the legislature to collect revenue or regulate commerce, the Articles eventually proved unworkable for the new nation.

Table 2.1 The Articles of Confederation and the U.S. Constitution: Key Features

Articles of Confederation Provisions	Problems Generated	1787 Federal Constitution
1. Unicameral (one-house) Congress with each state having one vote, regardless of population	Gave smaller, less populated states disproportionate power in lawmaking	Bicameral (two-house) legislature with one house apportioned by population (House of Representatives) and second house (Senate) apportioned equally among states (two senators from each state)
2. Approval by nine of thirteen states required for most legislative matters	Restricted lawmaking by simple majorities, halting the legislative process in most cases	Approval of simple majority (one-half plus one) of both houses required for most legislation
3. No separate executive or judiciary	Legislative abuses went unchecked	Three separate branches of government: legislative, executive, and judicial
4. Congress did not have the power to regulate foreign or interstate commerce	States negotiated separately among themselves and with foreign powers on commercial matters, to the detriment of the overall economy	Congress given power to regulate interstate and foreign commerce
5. Congress did not have the power to levy or collect taxes	Suffering from the economic depression and saddled with their own war debts, states furnished only a small portion of the money sought by Congress	Congress given power to levy and collect taxes
6. Congress did not have power to raise an army	Once the war with Britain had ended, states were reluctant to provide any support for an army	Congress given power to raise and support armies
7. Amendments to articles required unanimous approval of state legislatures	Articles were practically immune from modification, and thus inflexible to meet changing demands of a new nation	Amendments to Constitution require two-thirds vote of both houses of Congress, ratification by three-fourths of states

[8] Merrill Jensen, *The Articles of Confederation: An Interpretation of the Social-Constitutional History of the American Revolution, 1774–1781* (Madison: University of Wisconsin Press, 1959).

power to raise troops, regulate commerce, or levy taxes, which left it dependent on state legislatures to raise and support armies or provide other services. Congress's inability to raise funds significantly hampered the efforts of George Washington and the Continental Army during the war against Britain. Although Congress employed a "requisition system" in the 1780s, which essentially asked that states voluntarily meet contribution quotas to the federal government, the system proved ineffective. New Jersey, for example, consistently refused to pay such requisitions. Reflecting the colonists' distrust of a strong centralized government, the Articles made no provision for a chief executive who could enforce Congress's laws.

The limited powers of the central government posed many problems, but changing the Articles of Confederation to meet the needs of the new nation was no easy task. The Articles could be amended only by the assent of all thirteen state legislatures, a provision that made change of any kind nearly impossible. Wealthy property owners and colonial merchants were frustrated with the Articles for various reasons. Because Congress lacked the power to regulate interstate and foreign commerce, it was exceedingly difficult to obtain commercial concessions from other nations. Quarrels among states disrupted interstate commerce and travel. Finally, a few state governments (most notably, Pennsylvania) had come to be dominated by radical movements that further threatened the property rights of many wealthy, landowning colonists.

These difficulties did not disappear when the war ended with the Americans' victory in 1783. Instead, an economic depression, partially caused by the loss of trade with Great Britain and the West Indies, aggravated the problems facing the new nation. In January 1785, an alarmed Congress appointed a committee to consider amendments to the Articles. Although the committee called for expanded congressional powers to enter commercial treaties with other nations, no action was taken. Further proposals to revise the Articles by creating federal courts and strengthening the system of soliciting contributions from states were never even submitted to the states for approval; congressional leaders apparently despaired of ever winning the unanimous approval of the state legislatures needed to create such changes.

Then in September 1786, nine states accepted invitations to attend a convention in Annapolis, Maryland, to discuss interstate commerce. Yet when the Annapolis Convention opened on September 11, delegates from only five states (New York, New Jersey, Delaware, Pennsylvania, and Virginia) attended. A committee led by Alexander Hamilton, a leading force at the Annapolis meeting, issued a report calling upon all thirteen states to attend a convention in Philadelphia the following May to discuss all matters necessary "to render the constitution of the federal government adequate to the exigencies of the Union." At the time, few knew whether this proposal would attract more interest than had previous calls for a new government.

Daniel Shays leads a rebellion of farmers to a Massachusetts courthouse in 1786 to protest the state legislature's inaction.

Events in Massachusetts in 1786–1787 proved a turning point in the creation of momentum for a new form of government. A Revolutionary war veteran, Daniel Shays, was also one of many debt-ridden farmers in Massachusetts, where creditors controlled the state government. Shays and his men rebelled against the state courts' foreclosing on the farmers' mortgages for failure to pay debts and state taxes.[9] When the state legislature failed to resolve the farmers' grievances, Shays's rebels stormed two courthouses and a federal arsenal.[10] Eventually the state militia put down the insurrection, known as **Shays's Rebellion,** but the message was clear: a weak and unresponsive government carried with it the danger of disorder and violence. In February 1787, Congress endorsed the call for a convention to serve the purpose of drafting amendments to the Articles of Confederation, and by May eleven states had acted to name delegates to the convention to be held in Philadelphia.

TIME LIFE PICTURES/GETTY IMAGES

Portrait of George Washington, circa 1775.

The Constitutional Convention

The **Constitutional Convention** convened on May 25, 1787, with twenty-nine delegates from nine states in attendance. Over the next four months more than fifty-five delegates from twelve states would participate. Fiercely resistant to any centralized power, Rhode Island sent no delegates. Some heroes of the American Revolution like Patrick Henry refused appointments due to their opposition to the feelings of nationalism that had spurred the convention to be held in the first place. Meanwhile, lending authority to the proceedings were such well-known American figures as George Washington, Alexander Hamilton, and Benjamin Franklin. (The thirty-six-year-old James Madison of Virginia was only beginning to establish a reputation for himself when he arrived in Philadelphia; meanwhile John Adams and Thomas Jefferson were both on diplomatic assignment in Europe.)

The delegates, who unanimously selected Washington to preside over the convention, were united by at least four common concerns: (1) the United States was being treated with contempt by other nations, and foreign trade had suffered as a consequence; (2) the economic radicalism of Shays's Rebellion might spread in the absence of a stronger central government; (3) the Native Americans had responded to encroachment on their lands by threatening frontiersmen and land speculators, and the national government had been ill-equipped to provide citizens with protection; and (4) the postwar economic depression had worsened, and the national government was powerless to take any action to address it.[11] Of course, on many other matters the delegates differed. Those from bigger, more heavily populated states such as Virginia and Pennsylvania wanted a central government that reflected their larger population bases, whereas those from smaller states like Georgia and Delaware hoped to maintain the one-state, one-vote principle of the Articles.

Plans and Compromises

It quickly became evident that a convention originally called to discuss amendments to the Articles of Confederation would be undertaking a more drastic overhaul of the American system of government. Members of the Virginia delegation got the ball rolling when they introduced the **Virginia Plan,** also known as the "large states plan," which proposed a national government consisting of three branches—a legislature, an executive, and a judiciary. The legislature would consist of two houses, with membership in each house proportional to each state's population. The people would elect members of one house, and the members of that house would then choose members of the second house.

★ Shays's Rebellion

Armed uprising by debt-ridden Massachusetts farmers frustrated with the state government.

★ Constitutional Convention

Meeting of delegates from twelve states in Philadelphia during the summer of 1787, at which was drafted an entirely new system of government to govern the United States.

★ Virginia Plan

A proposal known also as the "large states plan" that empowered three separate branches of government, including a legislature with membership proportional to population.

[9] For an account of Massachusetts public policy during this period, see Van Beck Hall, *Politics Without Parties: Massachusetts 1780–1791* (Pittsburgh: University of Pittsburgh Press, 1972).

[10] Robert Gross, ed., *In Debt to Shays* (Charlottesville: University of Virginia Press, 1993).

[11] Christopher Collier, *Decision in Philadelphia: The Constitutional Convention of 1787* (New York: Ballantine Books, 2007).

Chapter 2: The Founding and the Constitution

The legislature would have the power to choose a chief executive and members of the judiciary and authority to legislate in "all cases to which the states are incompetent" or when the "harmony of the United States" demands it. Finally, the legislature would have power to veto any state law. Under the plan, the only real check on the legislature would be a Council of Revision, consisting of the executive and several members of the judiciary, which could veto the legislature's acts.

To counter the Virginia Plan, delegates from less populous states proposed the **New Jersey Plan,** which called for a one-house legislature in which each state, regardless of size, would have equal representation. The New Jersey Plan also provided for a national judiciary and an executive committee chosen by the legislature; expanded the powers of Congress to include the power to levy taxes and regulate foreign and interstate commerce; and asserted that the Constitution and national laws would become the "supreme law of the United States." Both the Virginia and New Jersey plans rejected a model of government in which the executive would be given extensive authority.

By July 2, 1787, disagreements over the design of the legislature and the issue of representation had brought the convention to a near dead end. The delegates then agreed to submit the matter to a smaller committee in the hope that it might craft some form of compromise.

The product of that committee's deliberations was a set of compromises, termed the **Great Compromise** by historians. (Formally proposed by delegate Roger Sherman of Connecticut, the agreement is also known as the Connecticut Compromise.) Its critical features included: (1) a bicameral (two-house)

★ New Jersey Plan

A proposal known also as the "small states plan" that would have retained the Articles of Confederation principle of a legislature where states enjoyed equal representation.

★ Great Compromise

A proposal also known as the "Connecticut Compromise" that provided for a bicameral legislature featuring an upper house based on equal representation among the states and a lower house whose membership was based on each state's population; approved by a 5–4 vote of the state delegations.

Table 2.2 The Virginia Plan, the New Jersey Plan, and the Great Compromise

	The Virginia Plan	The New Jersey Plan	The Great Compromise
	Introduced on May 29, 1787, by Edmund Randolph of Virginia; favored initially by delegates from Virginia, Pennsylvania, Massachusetts	Introduced on June 15, 1787, by William Paterson of New Jersey; favored initially by delegates from New Jersey, New York, Connecticut, Maryland, Delaware	Introduced by Roger Sherman of Connecticut; approved at the convention by a narrow 5–4 vote on July 16, 1787
Branches	1. Bicameral legislature with one house elected by the people and second house chosen by the first	1. Unicameral legislature elected by the people	1. Bicameral legislature with one house elected by the people and second house chosen by state legislatures
Legislature	2. All representatives and senators apportioned by population	2. Equal representation among states	2. Members of one house (representatives) apportioned by population (five slaves counted as three free men); members of second house (senators) apportioned equally among states
Other Powers	3. Singular executive chosen by the legislature	3. Plural executive chosen by the legislature	3. Singular executive (method of election to be determined)
	4. Congress can legislate wherever "states are incompetent" or to preserve "harmony of the United States"	4. Congress has power to tax and regulate commerce	4. Congress has power to tax only in proportion to representation in the lower House; all appropriation bills must originate in lower house

legislature with an upper house or "Senate" in which the states would have equal power with two representatives from each state, and a lower House of Representatives in which membership would be apportioned on the basis of population; and (2) the guarantee that all revenue bills would originate in the lower house. The convention delegates settled as well on granting Congress the authority to regulate interstate and foreign commerce by a simple majority vote, but requiring that treaties be approved by a two-thirds vote of the upper house. The Great Compromise was eventually approved by a narrow 5–4 margin of the state delegations. Connecticut, New Jersey, Delaware, Maryland, and North Carolina approved; Pennsylvania, Virginia, South Carolina, and Georgia opposed; New York and New Hampshire were absent, and the Massachusetts delegation was deadlocked. Thus a vote margin of just one state paved the way for the creation of a new federal government.

Compromise also resolved disagreement over the nature of the executive. Although rejecting the New Jersey Plan's call for a plural executive, the delegates split on whether the executive should be elected by members of Congress or directly by the people. The agreement reached called for the president (and vice president) to be elected by an electoral college. Because the number of electors equaled that of the number of representatives and senators from each state, this system gave disproportionately greater influence to smaller states. As chief executive, the president would have the power to veto acts of Congress, make treaties and appointments with the consent of the Senate, and serve as commander-in-chief of the nation's armed forces.

The Slavery Issue

The issue of representation collided with another thorny issue looming over the convention proceedings—the issue of slavery. Four Southern states—Maryland, Virginia, North Carolina, and South Carolina—had slave populations of more than a hundred thousand each. Meanwhile, two New England states, Maine and Massachusetts, had already banned slavery and another four Northern states—Vermont, New Hampshire, Rhode Island, and Connecticut—had a combined total of just four thousand slaves within their borders. The steady march of abolition in the North was matched by a Southern slave population that had been doubling every two decades. The convention delegates who advocated a new form of government were wary of the role slavery would play in this new nation, but they were even more wary of offending Southern sentiments to the point that consensus at the convention would be endangered.

Some delegates from the Northern states that had already voted in favor of banning slavery sought a similar emancipation of slaves in all the colonies by constitutional edict. Southerners hoping to protect their plantation economy, which depended on slave labor, wanted to prevent future Congresses from interfering with the institution of slavery and the importation of slaves. Moreover, even among Northerners there was disagreement on how emancipation should proceed: some favored outright freedom, whereas others argued for some form of colonization of the slaves, which would in effect ship them back to Africa. Many delegates feared that any extended discussion of slavery at the convention would become so divisive that it might bring the entire gathering to a standstill.

★ Three-Fifths
    Compromise

A compromise proposal in
which five slaves would be
counted as the equivalent of
three free people for purposes
of taxes and representation.

Southern delegates also wanted slaves to be counted equally with free people in determining the apportionment of representatives; Northerners opposed such a scheme for representation because it would give the Southern states more power, but did want slaves counted equally for purposes of apportioning taxes among the states. In an effort to forestall the convention's collapse, the delegates crafted a series of compromises that amounted to misdirection, and in some instances out- right silence on the issue of slavery.[12] By the agreement known as the **Three-Fifths Compromise,** five slaves would be counted as the equivalent of three "free per- sons" for purposes of taxes *and* representation. Delegates from Southern states also feared that a Congress dominated by representatives from more populous Northern states might take action against the slave trade. Most Northerners continued to favor gradual emancipation. Once again, neither side got exactly what it wanted. The Constitution said nothing about either preserving or outlawing slavery. Indeed, the only specific provision about slavery was a time limit on legislation ban- ning slave importation: Congress was forbidden from doing so for at least twenty years. In 1807, however, with the slave population steadily outgrowing demand, many Southerners allied with opponents of the slave trade to ban the importation of slaves. Not until the Civil War decades later would the conflict over slavery be finally resolved.

Figure 2.1 Concentration of Slavery (by County) circa 1790

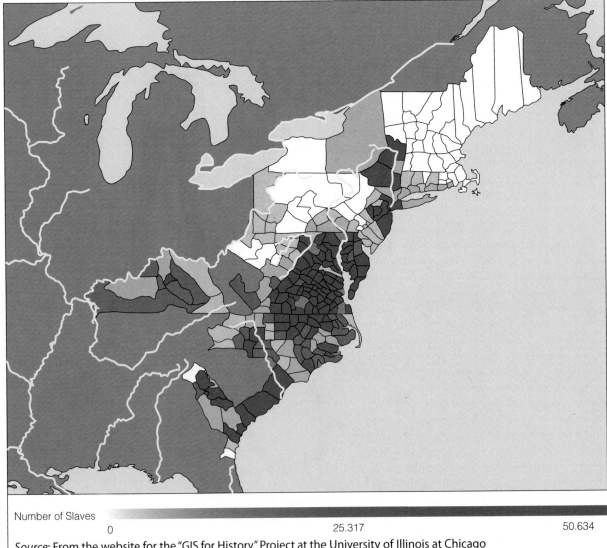

Number of Slaves

0   25.317   50.634

Source: From the website for the "GIS for History" Project at the University of Illinois at Chicago http://www.gisforhistory.org.

[12] For a discussion of the Founders' silence on slavery, see Joseph Ellis, *Founding Brothers* (New York: Knopf, 2000), pp. 81–119.

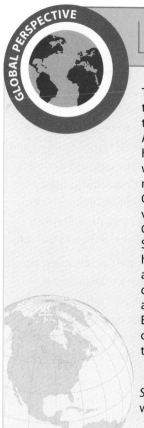

On September 17, 1787, after four months of compromises and negotiations, the twelve state delegations present approved the final draft of the Constitution. By the terms of Article VII of the document, the Constitution was to become operative once ratified by nine of the thirteen states.

The New Constitution

As a consequence of the many compromises in the draft Constitution, few of the delegates were pleased with every aspect of the new document. Even James Madison, later heralded as the "Father of the Constitution" for his many contributions as a spokesman at the convention, had furiously opposed the Great Compromise; he hinted at one point that a majority of the states might be willing to form a union outside the convention if the compromise were ever approved, and he convinced the Virginia delegation to vote "no" when it came up for a formal vote.

Nonetheless, the central desire of most of the delegates to craft a new government framework did lead them to consensus on a set of guiding principles that are evident throughout the document. The principles below continue to guide politicians, lawyers, and scholars today as they study the many ambiguous provisions of the Constitution:

★ Recognizing that calls for fairer representation of colonists' interests lay at the heart of the Declaration of Independence, popular sovereignty was a guiding principle behind the new Constitution. The document's preamble beginning with "We the People" signified the coming together of people, not states, for the purposes of creating a new government. Under the Constitution, no law could be passed without the approval of the House of Representatives, a "people's house" comprised of members apportioned by population and subject to re-election every two years. Of even greater significance, the delegates agreed that all revenue measures must originate in the House, an explicit affirmation of the principle that there would be "no taxation without representation."

★ The delegates recognized the need for a **separation of powers.** The Founders drew upon the ideas of the French political philosopher Baron de Montesquieu, who had argued that when legislative, executive, and judicial power are not exercised by the same institution, power cannot be so easily abused. Mindful of the British model in which Parliament combined legislative and executive authority, the drafters of the Constitution assigned specific responsibilities and powers to each branch of the government—Congress (the legislative power), the president (the executive power), and the Supreme Court (the judicial power). In the new government, individuals were generally prohibited from serving in more than one branch of government at the same time. The vice president's role as president of the Senate was a notable exception to this rule.

★ While establishing separate institutions, the drafters of the Constitution also created a system of **checks and balances** to require that the branches of government would have to work together to formulate policy. This system of "separate institutions sharing power" helped ensure that no one interest or faction could easily dominate the government. Through the exercise of presidential vetoes, Senate advice and consent, and judicial interpretations and

★ Separation of powers

The principle that each branch of government enjoys separate and independent powers and areas of responsibility.

★ Checks and balances

A system of limits imposed by the Constitution that gives each branch of government the limited right to change or cancel the acts of other branches.

Figure 2.2
Checks and Balances in the U.S. Constitution

CHECKS BY JUDICIARY

Checks on Congress
✓Federal judicial power extends to all cases arising under the laws of the United States (Art. III, § 2, Cl. 1) **(subsequently interpreted to include power to invalidate unconstitutional laws passed by Congress)**

Checks on Executive
✓Federal judicial power extends to all cases or controversies to which the U.S. government is a party (Art. III, § 2, Cl. 1) **(subsequently interpreted to include power to invalidate unconstitutional acts by president)**

✓Chief justice shall preside over Senate impeachment trials of the president (Art. I, § 3, Cl. 6)

CHECKS BY EXECUTIVE

Checks on Congress
✓Presidential power to sign or veto bills (Art I, § 7, Cl. 2)

✓In alternate role as president of Senate, vice president of United States can cast votes to break ties in a divided Senate (Art. I, § 3, Cl. 4)

✓President can bypass Senate temporarily by filling vacancies during Senate recess that expire at end of next Senate session (Art. II, § 2, Cl. 3)

✓President may "on extraordinary occasions" convene or adjourn either or both houses of Congress (Art. II, § 3)

✓President must "take care" that congressional laws are faithfully executed (Art. II, § 3)

Checks on Judiciary
✓President nominates and (with Senate advice and consent) appoints Supreme Court justices (Art. II, § 2, Cl. 2)

CHECKS BY CONGRESS

Checks on Executive
✓Impeachment by House (Art. I, § 2, Cl. 5) and removal by Senate (Art. I, § 3, Cl. 6) of president, vice president, and all civil officers of the United States (Art. II, § 4)

✓Congressional override of presidential vetoes by two-thirds vote of both houses (Art. I, § 7, Cl. 2)

✓Senate must approve all treaties by two-thirds vote (Art. II, § 2, Cl. 2)

✓House selection of president and Senate selection of vice president in event there is no Electoral College majority (Art. II, § 1, Cl. 3, Twelfth Amendment)

✓Senate advice and consent required for appointment of "Officers of the United States" (Art. II, § 2, Cl. 2)

Checks on Judiciary
✓Senate advice and consent required for appointment of Supreme Court Justices (Art. II, § 2, Cl. 2)

✓Impeachment by House (Art. I, § 2, Cl. 5) and removal by Senate (Art. I, § 3, Cl. 6) of Supreme Court justices

✓Congress can make exceptions to appellate jurisdiction of the Supreme Court (Art. III, § 2, Cl. 2)

other tools, each institution would have an opportunity to contend for influence.

★ A system, later termed federalism, featuring two sovereign powers for both the states and the federal government is also a defining characteristic of the government, established by the Constitution. Rather than entrusting all powers to a centralized government and essentially reducing the states to mere geographical subdivisions of the nation, the convention delegates divided powers between two levels of government: the states and the federal government. The distinction drawn between local concerns—controlled by state governments—and national concerns—controlled by the federal government—was as confusing then as it is today. But the delegates determined that such a division was necessary if they hoped to achieve any consensus. It would be politically impossible to convince the states to become mere geographic subdivisions of a larger political whole.

★ Although united by the belief that the national government needed to be strengthened, the framers of the Constitution were products of a revolutionary generation that had seen governmental power abused. Thus, they were committed to a government of **limited** or **enumerated powers.** The Constitution spelled out the powers of the new federal government in detail, and it was assumed that the government's authority did not extend beyond those powers. By rejecting a government of unlimited discretionary power, James Madison argued that individual rights, including those "inalienable rights" cited in the Declaration of Independence, would be protected from the arbitrary exercise of authority.

★ Finally, some delegates believed that the new Constitution should be a "living" document; that is, it should have some measure of flexibility in order to meet the changing demands placed on it over time. Perhaps the most frustrating aspect of the Articles of Confederation was the near impossibility of any sort of modification: because any change to the Articles required the unanimous consent of the states, even the most popular reform proposals stood little chance of being implemented. Thus, the Framers decided that the new Constitution would go into effect when it had been ratified by nine of thirteen states. Furthermore, once ratified, the Constitution could be amended by a two-thirds vote of each house of Congress (subject to subsequent ratification by three-fourths of the state legislatures).

The Ratification Battle

Federalists versus Anti-Federalists

Once Congress submitted the Constitution to the states for approval, battle lines were formed between the **Federalists,** who supported ratification of the new document, and the **Anti-Federalists,** who opposed it. From the outset, the Federalists enjoyed a number of structural and tactical advantages in this conflict:

★ **Nonunanimous consent.** The rules of ratification for the new Constitution, requiring approval of just nine of the thirteen states, were meant to ease the process of adopting the new document. The delegates understood that once

DIGITAL VISION

Benjamin Franklin at the time of the Constitutional Convention—statue, Franklin Institute, Philadelphia.

★ **Enumerated powers**

Express powers explicitly granted by the Constitution such as the taxing power specifically granted to Congress.

★ **Federalists**

Those who supported ratification of the proposed Constitution of the United States between 1787 and 1789.

★ **Anti-Federalists**

Those who opposed ratification of the proposed Constitution of the United States.

the Constitution had been approved, it would be difficult for even the most stubborn of state holdouts to exist as an independent nation surrounded by this formidable new national entity, the United States of America.

★ **Special "ratifying conventions."** The delegates realized that whatever form the new constitution might take, state legislatures would have the most to lose from an abandonment of the Articles. Thus they decided that the Constitution would be sent for ratification not to state legislatures, but instead to special state ratifying conventions that would be more likely to approve it.

★ **The rule of secrecy.** The Constitutional Convention's agreed-upon rule of secrecy, which forbade publication or discussion of the day-to-day proceedings of the convention, followed the precedent established in colonial assemblies and the First Continental Congress, where it was thought that members might speak more freely and openly if their remarks were not subject to daily scrutiny by the public at large. In the fall of 1787, the rule of secrecy also gave the Federalists on the inside a distinct advantage over outside opponents, who had little knowledge of the new document's provisions until publicized. Because the number of convention delegates who supported the new Constitution far exceeded the number of delegates opposed, the rule of secrecy gave the Federalists a distinct advantage. As it turned out, five state ratifying conventions approved the Constitution within four months of the convention's formal conclusion, just as Anti-Federalist forces were collecting their strength for the battle ahead.

★ **Conventions held in the winter limited rural participation.** Winter was approaching just as the fight over the new Constitution was being launched. This timing gave the Federalists another advantage, especially in the critical ratification battle-grounds of Massachusetts, New Hampshire, and New York. It would be difficult for rural dwellers—mostly poor farmers resistant to a strong central government and thus opposed to the new Constitution—to attend the ratification conventions if they were held in the dead of winter. Supporters of the Constitution successfully pressed for the ratifying conventions to be held as soon as possible. And of the six states that held such conventions over the winter, all voted to ratify by substantial margins.

Portrait of James Madison, the "Father of the Constitution."

The Federalist Papers

Between the fall of 1787 and the summer of 1788, the Federalists launched an aggressive media campaign through newspapers that was unusually well organized for its time. James Madison, Alexander Hamilton, and John Jay wrote seventy-seven essays explaining and defending the new Constitution and urging its ratification. Signed under the name "Publius," the essays were printed in New York newspapers and magazines. These essays—along with eight others by the same men—were then collected, printed, and published in book form under the title *The Federalist*.[13] The essays allayed fears and extolled the benefits of the new Constitution by emphasizing the inadequacy of the Articles of Confederation and the need for a strong government. Today these essays are considered classic works of political philosophy. Among the most frequently cited Federalist Papers are:

[13] Jacob E. Cooke, ed., *The Federalist* (Middletown, CT: Wesleyan University Press, 1961).

★ **Federalist No. 10.** In Madison's first offering in the **Federalist Papers,** he analyzes the nature, causes, and effects of *factions,* by which he meant groups of people motivated by a common economic and/or political interest. Noting that such factions are both the product and price of liberty, Madison argued that by extending the sphere in which they can act, "you make it less probable that a majority of the whole will have a common motive to invade the rights of other citizens." Political theorists often cite Federalist No. 10 as justification for pluralist theory—the idea that competition among groups for power produces the best approximation of overall public good.

★ **Federalist No. 15.** Alexander Hamilton launched his attack on the Articles of Confederation in this essay. Specifically, he pointed to the practical impossibility of engaging in concerted action when each of the thirteen states retained virtual power to govern.

★ **Federalist No. 46.** In this essay, Madison defended the system of federalism set up by the new Constitution. He contended that the system allowed the states sufficient capacity to resist the "ambitious encroachments of the federal government."

★ **Federalist No. 51.** In perhaps the most influential of the essays, Madison described how the new Constitution would prevent the government from abusing its citizens. His argument is that the "multiplicity of interests" that influence so many different parts of the government would guarantee the security of individual rights. Because the federal system of government divides the government into so many parts (federal versus state; legislative versus executive versus judicial branches, and so on), "the rights of the individual, or of the minority, will be in little danger from interested combinations of the majority."

★ **Federalist No. 69.** Hamilton in this essay defined the "real character of the executive," which, unlike the King of Great Britain, is accountable to the other branches of government and to the people.

★ **Federalist No. 70.** In this essay, Hamilton presented his views on executive power, which had tempered considerably since the convention when he advocated an executive for life. Still, Hamilton argued for a unitary, one-person executive to play a critical role as a check on the legislative process (that is, by exercising vetoes), as well as in the process of negotiating treaties and conducting war. According to Hamilton, "energy in the executive is a leading character in the definition of good government"; by contrast, "the species of security" sought for by those who advocate a plural executive is "unattainable."

★ Federalist Papers

A series of articles authored by Alexander Hamilton, James Madison, and John Jay, which argued in favor of ratifying the proposed Constitution of the United States; the Federalist Papers outlined the philosophy and motivation of the document.

In late 1787 and early 1788, Anti-Federalists countered the Federalist Papers with a media campaign of their own.[14] In letters written under the pseudonyms "Brutus" and "The Federal Farmer" and published by newspapers throughout the colonies, the Anti-Federalists claimed that they were invoking a cause more consistent with that of the revolution—the cause of freedom from government tyranny. For them, the new national government's power to impose internal taxes on the states amounted to a revival of the British system of internal taxation. Perhaps the Anti-Federalists' most effective criticism was that the Constitution lacked a bill of rights that explicitly protected citizens' individual rights. They rejected Madison's contention in Federalist No. 51 that limitations on the central government provided those protections.

---

[14] Saul Cornell, *The Other Founders: Anti-Federalism and the Dissenting Tradition in America 1788–1828* (Chapel Hill: University of North Carolina Press, 1999).

American Government . . . in Historical Perspective:
The Continuing Call to the Federalist Papers

The Federalist Papers had a significant impact on the birth of the new nation. The essays argued persuasively that the Articles of Confederation were inadequate. Many scholars today attribute the narrow margin in favor of ratification of the Constitution at New York's ratification convention to the sophisticated media campaign waged by the Federalists, especially through the Federalist Papers.

In 1905, the Supreme Court's controversial decision in *Lochner v. New York,* which invalidated a New York State health regulation restricting the hours that bakers could be exposed to flour dust, set off a furious political debate about the role government should play in a newly industrialized society. Advocates on both sides of the debate repeatedly cited the Federalist Papers to bolster their arguments. Those who supported government regulation argued that it was not the job of courts to disagree with the decisions of legislatures on such public interest issues; even if factions and interest groups had produced such legislation, they cited Federalist No. 10 to justify the proposition that the corrupting spirit of "factions" distinguished democracy from true republics. Opponents of government regulations countered that Madison's preference for more factions was simply his way of reaching toward an ideal politics in which all these factions would cancel themselves out— by contrast, they argued that factions remained heavily influential in state legislatures. In support of the Court's

ruling, they cited Federalist No. 78 in which Hamilton argued that "the independence of the judges may be an essential safeguard against the effects of occasional ill humors in the society." Only a sudden switch by the Supreme Court to stop interfering with industrial regulations in 1937 saved the nation from a constitutional crisis fueled in part by dramatically contrasting readings of the Federalist Papers.

In 1996, President Bill Clinton (a Democrat) signed a welfare reform bill that slashed federal welfare spending, reduced welfare benefits, and shifted major responsibilities for welfare programs from the federal government to state governments. To defend the president's actions against incensed Democratic Party leaders like Senator Patrick Moynihan (D-NY), who feared the bill unfairly turned the government's back on the poor, the White House dug into the Federalist Papers for its defense. In Federalist No. 51, James Madison defended the Constitution against charges that it unduly transferred excessive powers to the new government: "A double security arises to the rights of people . . . the different governments will control each other, at the same time that each will be controlled by itself." The White House argued that shifting major welfare responsibilities to the states represented a sharing of the duties and responsibilities of government that was consistent with the intentions of the Founders.

President Bill Clinton listens to former welfare mother Rhonda Costa in 1998. Two years earlier, Clinton signed a major welfare bill that shifted primary responsibilities for overseeing welfare to the 50 state governments.

AFP/GETTY IMAGES

Table 2.3 Ratifying the Constitution

State	Vote	Date of Ratification
Delaware	30-0	December 7, 1787
Pennsylvania	43-23	December 12, 1787
New Jersey	38-0	December 18, 1787
Georgia	25-0	January 2, 1788
Connecticut	128-40	January 9, 1788
Massachusetts	187-168	February 16, 1788
Maryland	63-11	April 26, 1788
South Carolina	149-73	May 23, 1788
New Hampshire	57-46	June 21, 1788
Virginia	89-79	June 25, 1788
New York	30-27	June 26, 1788
North Carolina[1]	194-77	November 21, 1789
Rhode Island	34-32	May 29, 1790

[1] Despite strong Federalist sentiment at the convention, North Carolina withheld its vote in 1788 until a Bill of Rights was formally introduced. The submission by Congress of twelve proposed amendments to the states on September 25, 1789, led North Carolina to hold a second ratifying convention the following November.

Ratification ultimately succeeded, but by a somewhat narrow margin. Of the first five states to ratify, four (Delaware, New Jersey, Georgia, and Connecticut) did so with little or no opposition, whereas Pennsylvania did so only after a bitter conflict at its ratifying convention. Massachusetts became the sixth state to ratify when proponents of the Constitution swung the convention narrowly in their favor only by promising to push for a bill of rights after ratification. By June, three more states (Maryland, South Carolina, and New Hampshire) had voted to ratify, providing the critical threshold of nine states required under the Constitution. Still, the Federalists worried that without ratification by the major states of New York and Virginia, the new union would not succeed.

Opposition in Virginia was formidable, with Patrick Henry leading the Anti-Federalist forces against James Madison and the Federalists.[15] Eventually Madison gained the upper hand with an assist from George Washington, whose eminent stature helped capture numerous votes for the Federalists. Madison also promised to support adding a bill of rights to the new Constitution. Then, Alexander Hamilton and John Jay capitalized on the positive news from Virginia to secure victory at the New York ratifying convention. With more than the required nine states—including the crucial states of New York and Virginia—the Congress did not wait for the votes from North Carolina or Rhode Island; on July 2, 1788, it appointed a committee to prepare for the new government.

A Bill of Rights

Seven of the state constitutions created during the Revolutionary War featured a statement of individual rights in some form. The Virginia Declaration of Rights

[15] Henry Mayer, *A Son of Thunder: Patrick Henry and the American Republic* (Charlottesville: University of Virginia Press, 1992).

of 1776, for example, had borrowed (from John Locke) its grounding of individual rights in a conception of natural law and social contract: "All men are by nature equally free and independent, and have certain inherent rights, of which, when they enter into a state of society, they cannot, by any compact, deprive or divest their posterity." Later, during the battle over ratification, five state ratifying conventions had stressed the need for amendments to the Constitution in the form of a bill of rights, which would expressly protect fundamental rights against encroachment by the national government.[16]

Still, not all the Federalists saw the need for a federal bill of rights. Madison, for one, believed a bill of rights was unnecessary because the central government held only those powers enumerated in the Constitution. He explained: "The rights in question are reserved by the manner in which the federal powers are granted . . . the limited powers of the federal government and the jealousy of the subordinate governments afford a security which has not existed in the case of the state governments, and exists in no other." Madison was also concerned about the dangers of trying to enumerate all important rights: "There is great reason to fear that a positive declaration of some of the most essential rights could not be obtained," leaving some essential rights omitted for the future. Hamilton underscored this sentiment in Federalist No. 84, arguing that such a list of rights might invite governmental attempts to exercise power over those rights not included in the list.

Among the most ardent supporters of adding a bill of rights to the Constitution was Thomas Jefferson, who warned about the dangers of abuses of power.[17] From his distant vantage point in France, where he continued to serve as an American minister, Jefferson was in the dark about the new constitution until November 1787. Then, in a December 20, 1787, letter to his friend and political protégé from Virginia, James Madison, Jefferson wrote: "A bill of rights is what the people are entitled to against every government on earth, general or particular, and what no just government should refuse, or rest on inference." Although recognizing Madison's fears of omissions as legitimate, Jefferson continued to argue the point. In a subsequent letter dated March 15, 1789, Jefferson argued that "half a loaf is better than no bread. If we cannot secure all our rights, let us secure what we can."

In the end Jefferson's arguments prevailed, and Madison (by this time a congressman from Virginia) became a principal sponsor of a bill of rights in the first Congress. Introducing the bill in the House of Representatives, he declared: "They will be an impenetrable bulwark against every assumption of power in the legislative or executive." On September 9, 1789, the House of Representatives voted to submit a list of twelve **amendments** to the states; ten of these were ratified by the required nine states by December 15, 1791, and comprise today's **Bill of Rights,** which are the first eight amendments to the Constitution.

Among the rights protected by the Bill of Rights are the rights of free religious exercise, free speech, free press, and assembly (First Amendment); rights against search and seizure without a warrant stating "probable cause" (Fourth Amendment); and rights of due process and no self-incrimination (Fifth Amendment). The two amendments not ratified in 1791 did not relate to individual rights at all. They were: (1) a prohibition on salary increases for legislators taking effect prior to the next congressional election (in 1992—more than two hundred years later—this became the Twenty-seventh Amendment); and (2) a provision defining the rules for determining the number of members of the House of Representatives.

Changing the Constitution

The Formal Amendment Process

Though political circumstances dictated that the Bill of Rights be passed in a relatively speedy fashion, future proposed amendments would not have it so easy. In crafting the rules for amending the new constitution, the Framers sought to balance

---

★ Amendments

Modifications or additions to the U.S. Constitution passed in accordance with the amendment procedures laid out in Article V.

★ Bill of Rights

The first eight amendments to the U.S. Constitution, which protect various rights of the people against the new federal government.

---

[16] Paul Murphy, *The Historic Background of the Bill of Rights* (New York: Taylor & Francis, 1990).
[17] See Jefferson–Madison correspondence republished in Philip Kurland, ed., *The Founders' Constitution* (Indianapolis: Liberty Fund, 2000).

two competing interests: (1) the need to protect the Constitution from short-lived or temporary passions by making amendments exceedingly difficult to pass; and (2) sufficient flexibility to allow for amendments to be added when the needs of the nation demanded change. Their determination to strike such a balance was shaped by their experience in dealing with the Articles of Confederation, whose "unanimous consent of states" rule had left them immune from even the most necessary of reforms.

Article V of the Constitution specifies two ways in which amendments can be proposed and two methods of ratification. Congress may propose an amendment by a two-thirds vote of both houses; alternatively, two-thirds of the state legislatures may apply to Congress to call a special national convention for proposing amendments. Amendments take effect when ratified either by a vote of three-fourths of the state legislatures or by special ratifying conventions held in three-fourths of the states. To date, all twenty-seven amendments (including the Bill of Rights) have been proposed by Congress, and all but one (the Twenty-first) have been ratified by the state legislatures.

Figure 2.3 How an Amendment Gets Proposed and Ratified

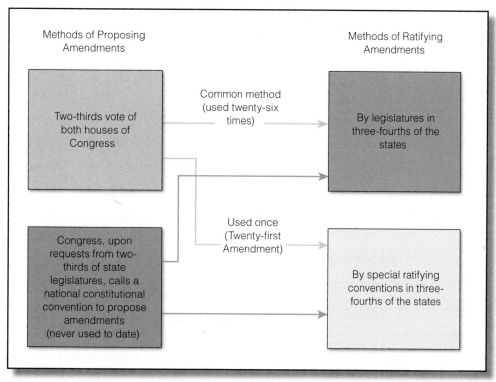

No national convention has ever been called for the purpose of proposing amendments. Indeed, the closest the states have ever come to applying to Congress for such an event occurred in 1967, when thirty-three states (just one short of the required number) petitioned Congress to call a convention that would propose an amendment reversing the 1964 Supreme Court ruling requiring that both houses of each state legislature be apportioned according to population. Given the ambiguity of Article V, numerous questions have been raised about the form such a convention would take. How would delegates be chosen? When Congress proposed the Twenty-first Amendment, it left it to each state to determine the manner in which delegates to the ratifying conventions would be chosen. How would the convention be run? Could a convention go beyond the limitations placed on it by Congress? What would happen if a convention went far afield and proposed an entirely new constitution, just as the convention in 1787 did? Congress has to date refused to pass laws dictating the terms of future conventions, in part because it has not wanted to encourage such an event.[18]

Critics of the amendment process charge that it is undemocratic, as today just thirteen of the fifty states can block amendments desired by a large majority. Additionally,

---

[18] Indeed, there may be numerous legal problems implicated by the holding of such a convention, as noted in Russell Caplan, *Constitutional Brinksmanship: Amending the Constitution by National Convention* (New York: Oxford University Press, 1988).

Table 2.4 Amendments, Date of Ratification, Length of Ratification Process

Amendment	Subject of Amendment	Date Proposed	Date Ratified	Length
Bill of Rights				
First	Free speech, press, religion, assembly	Sept. 25, 1789	Dec. 15, 1791	2+ years
Second	Right to bear arms			
Third	No quartering of troops in homes			
Fourth	No unreasonable searches/seizures			
Fifth	Right to due process, grand jury, no double jeopardy, self-incrimination			
Sixth	Right to speedy & public trial, counsel			
Seventh	Right to trial by jury in civil cases			
Eighth	No excessive bail, fines, cruel/unusual punishment			
Ninth	Rights not enumerated retained by people			
Tenth	Powers not delegated to Congress or prohibited to states belong to states or people			
Subsequent Amendments				
Eleventh	No federal cases between state, citizen of other state	March 5, 1794	Jan. 8, 1798	3+ years
Twelfth	Modified electoral college rules	Dec. 12, 1803	July 16, 1787	9+ months
Thirteenth	Ban on slavery	Feb. 1, 1865	Dec. 18, 1865	10+ months
Fourteenth	States can't deprive right to due process, equal protection, privileges & immunities	June 16, 1866	July 28, 1868	2+ years
Fifteenth	Right to vote can't be denied by race	Feb. 27, 1869	March 30, 1870	1+ years
Sixteenth	Congress can levy individual income taxes	July 12, 1909	Feb. 25, 1913	3+ years
Seventeenth	Direct election of senators	May 16, 1912	May 31, 1913	1+ years
Eighteenth	Prohibition of liquors	Dec. 18, 1917	Jan. 29, 1919	1+ years
Nineteenth	Right to vote for women	June 4, 1919	Aug. 26, 1920	1+ years
Twentieth	Dates for inauguration, Congress's session	March 2, 1932	Feb. 6, 1933	11+ months
Twenty-first	Repeal of prohibition	Feb. 20, 1933	Dec. 5, 1933	9+ months
Twenty-second	Presidential term limits	March 24, 1947	Feb. 26, 1951	3+ years
Twenty-third	D.C. residents' vote for president	June 16, 1960	March 29, 1961	9+ months
Twenty-fourth	Ban on poll taxes	Aug. 27, 1962	Jan. 23, 1964	1+ years
Twenty-fifth	Appt. of new vice president, presidential incompetence	July 6, 1965	Feb. 10, 1967	1+ years
Twenty-sixth	Right to vote for eighteen-year olds	March 23, 1971	July 1, 1971	3+ months
Twenty-seventh	Congressional pay raises effective only after election	Sept. 25, 1789	May 7, 1992	202+ years

amendments, especially those ratified by special conventions, may be adopted even if they lack widespread popular support.

Although twenty-seven amendments have been ratified since 1789, only seventeen of those were ratified after 1791. More than five thousand amendments have been introduced in Congress since that time, but only thirty-three have been formally proposed by Congress. Among the proposed amendments not ratified have been:

★ an amendment that would withdraw citizenship from any person who has accepted a title of nobility or who has received (without the consent of Congress) an office or salary from a foreign power (proposed in 1810)

★ an amendment proposed on the eve of the Civil War in 1861 that would have prohibited further interference by the federal government with slavery in any state

★ an amendment that would have prohibited labor by young children (proposed in 1924)

The Equal Rights Amendment (ERA) proposed by Congress in 1972 also came up short during the ratification process, although only after years of effort to secure its passage failed. Although the courts have consistently held that ratification of an amendment must take place within a "reasonable time," it has been left up to Congress to determine what constitutes a reasonable time. When drafting the proposed Eighteenth Amendment in 1917, Congress placed into the text of the amendment a seven-year limit on ratification and continued to do so with sub-

MICHAEL KLEINFELD/UPI/LANDOV

Demonstrators (including Rep. Carolyn Maloney (D-NY), pictured at the podium) urging reintroduction of the ERA as an amendment to the Constitution.

sequent amendments it proposed up until 1960. That year, when Congress proposed the Twenty-third Amendment giving residents of the District of Columbia the right to vote in presidential elections, it began the practice of setting time limits in the resolution accompanying submission of the amendment to Congress, rather than in the formal part of the amendment. As a consequence, when it appeared that the ERA would not be ratified, proponents of the amendment managed to get the ratification period extended to June 30, 1982 (an additional three years and three months beyond the original deadline) by a majority vote of both houses. Despite the extension, however, the proposed amendment died when it failed to win the approval of more than thirty-five state legislatures, three short of the thirty-eight necessary for passage.

The "reasonable time" requirement for ratification of an amendment reached an extreme with the Twenty-seventh Amendment (forbidding congressional pay raises from taking effect until an intervening election in the House of Representatives has occurred). Originally proposed in 1789 as part of the Bill of Rights, it was finally ratified in 1992, fully 203 years later, thanks largely to the efforts of Gregory Watson, whose campaign to ratify the amendment began in 1982 when Watson—then a sophomore at the University of Texas—discovered the amendment while doing research for a paper on American government. Watson's final paper—in which he argued that the

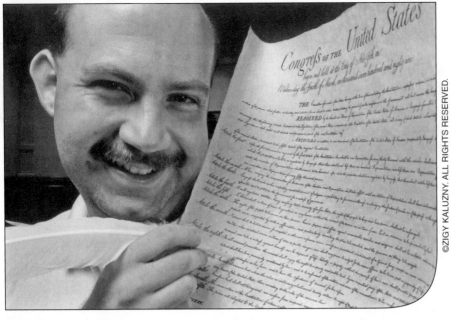

amendment was still viable for ratification—garnered a mere "C" from his professor. But Watson continued his quest to secure ratification of the amendment. Tapping into the resentment of citizens over various instances in which Congress had quietly passed pay raises for itself without calling attention to its actions, he joined forces with several state lawmakers to get the required number of states to ratify the provision. Their efforts succeeded, and the Twenty-seventh Amendment was ratified in May 1992. Although Watson's grade from a decade earlier remained unchanged, he at least had the satisfaction of knowing that he had made history . . . literally.

Greg Watson, whose efforts helped to ratify the Twenty-Seventh Amendment in 1992.

Informal Processes of Change

After the Constitution and Bill of Rights were ratified, there remained the difficult task of interpreting those documents for use by the different branches of government. Among the framers, Alexander Hamilton was perhaps most attuned to the danger that Anti-Federalists and other opponents of the new Constitution might attempt to overturn the convention's carefully crafted compromises so many years later by judicial fiat. Certainly most of the Constitution's provisions were vague enough that they allowed discretion for maneuvering by the generation that interprets them—but how much discretion was justified in the process of constitutional interpretation?

As it turned out, the Supreme Court under Chief Justice John Marshall was the first to put its own lasting imprint on the Constitution. Marshall, who hailed from Virginia, served as the Chief Justice of the United States[19] from 1801 until his death in 1835. Marshall believed in a **loose construction** (or interpretation) of the Constitution, meaning that under his leadership, many of the Constitution's provisions enjoyed broad and quite open-ended meanings. Thus, for example, Article I, Section 8, Clause 18 empowered Congress "to make all laws which shall be necessary and proper for carrying into execution" any of the powers specifically listed in the Constitution. Marshall's loose construction of that provision gave the federal government considerable implied powers (those not explicitly stated) to regulate the economy. For example, in the 1819 case of *McCulloch v. Maryland,*[20] Marshall's court ruled that Congress had the power to create a national bank, even though the Constitution said nothing explicitly about such a power. The Court determined that a national bank was "necessary and proper" to assist in regulating commerce or raising armies. This philosophy of loose constitutional interpretation underlies the concept of a "living Constitution," one that is adaptable to changing times and conditions.

Thomas Jefferson, James Madison, and many others viewed the powers of the central government more narrowly. They favored a **strict construction,** arguing that the government possessed only those powers explicitly stated in the Constitution. Thus although Article I, Section 8, Clause 3 gave Congress the power to regulate interstate commerce, it could not do so by creating a national bank or utilizing any

★ Loose construction

Constitutional interpretation that gives constitutional provisions broad and open-ended meanings.

★ Strict construction

Constitutional interpretation that limits the government to only those powers explicitly stated in the Constitution.

American Government: Historical, Popular, and Global Perspectives

[19] One of the better recent works on Marshall's tenure at the Court is R. Kent Newmyer, *John Marshall and the Heroic Age of the Supreme Court* (Baton Rouge: Louisiana State University Press, 2002).

[20] 17 U.S. 316 (1819).

American Government . . . in Popular Perspective:
Constitutional Interpretation

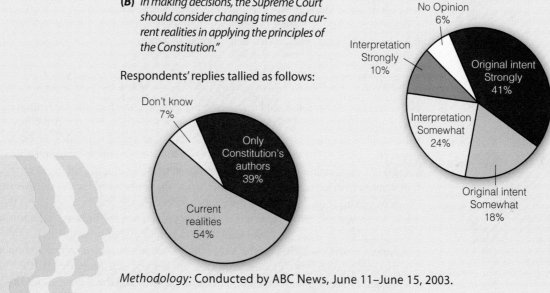

Consider this strange contradiction. In the abstract, the public tends to prefer a flexible view of the Constitution over a fixed view. But in the context of being asked about potential Supreme Court nominees, respondents' replies indicated that the Founder's ideas on restrictions on judges carried considerably greater appeal. Consider this question from a spring 2003 poll:

"Which comes closer to your point of view?"

(A) *In making decisions, the Supreme Court should only consider the original intentions of the authors of the Constitution.*

(B) *In making decisions, the Supreme Court should consider changing times and current realities in applying the principles of the Constitution."*

Respondents' replies tallied as follows:

Don't know
7%

Only Constitution's authors
39%

Current realities
54%

Now compare that to when the public is asked about potential nominees:

"Do you think the next person nominated to join the U.S. (United States) Supreme Court should be someone who tries to follow the original intent of the U.S. Constitution as it was written, or someone who tries to follow an interpretation of what the Constitution means in current times?" (If Original intent/Interpretation, ask: *"Do you feel that way strongly, or somewhat?"*)

The tally of responses to this question showed:

No Opinion
6%

Interpretation Strongly
10%

Original intent Strongly
41%

Interpretation Somewhat
24%

Original intent Somewhat
18%

Methodology: Conducted by ABC News, June 11–June 15, 2003.

other means not specifically mentioned in the Constitution. They supported a "fixed" constitution, one that could be changed only by the formal amendment process, not by congressional action or judicial ruling.

The tension between advocates of strict and loose constructions of the Constitution continues to this day. Robert Bork, a former Yale law professor and failed Supreme Court nominee, argues that overly loose interpretations of the Constitution are outside the court's proper task. In particular, Bork says, the Supreme Court has "simply abandoned" the Constitution by refusing to enforce limits on the subjects that come within congressional reach.[21] In accordance with this philosophy, the more conservative Supreme Court of the late 1990s struck down federal statutes regulating guns in the schools and domestic violence, on the theory that such regulations were not grounded in any specifically enumerated power of Congress, such as the power to regulate interstate commerce.

This strict-construction approach contrasts markedly with the approach advocated by Professors Lawrence Tribe[22] and John Hart Ely,[23] as well as former Supreme

---

[21] See Robert Bork, *The Tempting of America* (New York: Simon & Schuster, 1990).

[22] Lawrence Tribe, *Constitutional Choices* (Cambridge, MA: Harvard University Press, 2004).

[23] John Hart Ely, *Democracy and Distrust* (Cambridge, MA: Harvard University Press, 1980).

Court Justice William Brennan, who argued for a loose or more flexible interpretation of the Constitution. Advocates of a loose construction view the document as evolving with the times. In the 1960s and 1970s, the Supreme Court utilized a loose-construction approach to interpret congressional power more broadly to include the power to create civil rights legislation and federal criminal laws.

With so few amendments proposed and ratified during the nation's history, students of American politics may wonder how a Constitution written in 1787 has developed to meet the needs of a changing nation. In truth, an informal constitutional convention occurs on a frequent basis in the American political system. Congress, the president, and the courts engage in constitutional interpretation every day through their respective activities, both official and unofficial. Thus the Constitution has not been a straitjacket at all—rather, its elegant vagueness has opened it up to a variety of interpretations.

Much of the rise in presidential power during the twentieth century occurred in the absence of any formal amendments conferring new powers on the chief executive; the president of the United States reacted to circumstances facing the executive office by assuming greater authority over foreign and domestic policy making, and the other branches of government have allowed the president considerable latitude to do so. With its ruling in *Marbury v. Madison* (1803),[24] the Supreme Court asserted its right of judicial review, that is, its authority to review acts of Congress for their constitutionality and void those that the Court determines are contrary to the Constitution. As part of its decision in *McCulloch v. Maryland* (1819), the Court ruled that when state and federal powers collide, federal powers take precedence. With some notable exceptions, the other branches of the federal government and state courts have more or less acquiesced to such exercise of power.

Now & Then: Making the Connection

For several weeks in 1868, and then again in 1999, the president of the United States was at the mercy of the U.S. Senate. First Andrew Johnson, and later Bill Clinton, sat on trial before the full Senate body; each fought to keep his job despite being impeached by the House of Representatives. It may seem surprising to some that Congress's application of its powers of impeachment—including the rules of procedures, internal organization, and trial practices—have occurred largely outside the scope of constitutional review by the courts. Indeed, in the one case (in 1990) when the U.S. Supreme Court reviewed the Senate's procedures for impeaching a lower court judge, the justices bent over backward to point out that their role in the impeachment process—including the review of procedures—was in fact quite limited. The House has on its own created procedures to help it determine whether the "high crimes and misdemeanors" standard has been reached, and the Senate alone has determined what rules of evidence govern at Senate trials, such as whether a committee could be named to hear evidence. The impeachment provisions in place in 1789 (like most other provisions of the Constitution) have never been altered, and so the Congress that impeached and tried Bill Clinton followed the same pattern as that of the Congress that impeached and tried President Andrew Johnson in 1868.

Although it has become fashionable in recent years to proclaim a "constitutional crisis" whenever the system doesn't run quite the way many believe it should, the Clinton impeachment episode demonstrates just how misleading that label really is. Clinton's impeachment may well have diverted the country from more pressing matters, such as the atrocities being committed in Kosovo or Iraq's noncompliance with nuclear inspection teams, but it was never a constitutional crisis. The rules of the Constitution were followed, a president was impeached though not convicted, and afterward all the players in the episode returned to their everyday jobs to conduct business as usual. Within weeks of his acquittal, Andrew Johnson was combing over a list of candidates for the attorney general post that had recently been vacated; less than a week after his own acquittal, Bill Clinton was out storming the country to drum up support for his new Social Security proposal.

---

[24] 5 U.S. 137 (1803).

Although Americans like to celebrate the notion that anyone can grow up to be president, a quick scan of Article II of the Constitution squarely rejects that claim: A president must be thirty-five years old, a resident within the United States for fourteen years, and a "natural born citizen." That final provision eliminates those born in foreign countries from ever qualifying to serve as president. Yet what about persons born in U.S. territories or in other lands controlled by the United States, but not technically within the fifty states themselves? For a time, this question worried supporters of 2008 Republican presidential candidate John McCain, who was born in 1936 in the Panama Canal Zone, where his father was stationed as a military officer. Even though both of McCain's parents were U.S. citizens, the question arose whether an individual not born in one of the fifty U.S. states could be considered a "natural born citizen" under Article II.

One legal scholar, Gabriel Chin of the University of Arizona Law School, has argued that Congress's attempt to fix the problem in 1937 by conferring full citizenship on all children of American parents born in the Canal Zone came a year too late for McCain, as the law was not passed until a year after his birth. Chin's analysis makes some sense, but political reality points in a different direction. Specifically, a bipartisan legal review (led by lawyers working for McCain and his Democratic opponent, Barack Obama) and a unanimous Senate resolution both indicated that McCain is a natural-born citizen, notwithstanding the legal controversy. The bottom line? Because courts are unlikely to ever get near the issue, questions over McCain's eligibility for the presidency promise to become little more than a footnote to history. Just try telling the offspring of a U.S. soldier that the White House lies outside his reach.

On http://academic.cengage.com/dautrich, find the politics interactive link for details on the controversy over McCain's birthplace and the question of citizenship, including the research done on the subject by legal experts and the full text of the 1937 law passed by Congress to try to remedy the problem. Consult as well the various links that relate to qualifications for president and other related issues. Historical, popular, and global perspectives on the issue are also presented.

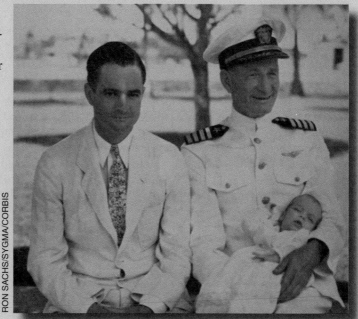

RON SACHS/SYGMA/CORBIS

Three generations of McCains: Future presidential candidate John McCain, as an infant, in the arms of his grandfather, John S. McCain. McCain's father, John S. McCain Jr., is at left.

http://academic.cengage.com/dautrich

Chapter Summary

★ British attempts to collect revenue from the American colonies to help pay debts incurred during the French and Indian War (1754–1763) spurred angry colonists to protest. By the 1770s, colonists' outrage against duties imposed by the British Parliament on tea and other goods led to acts of outright defiance, including the Boston Tea Party in 1774.

★ After a series of military skirmishes at Lexington and Concord, the Second Continental Congress in 1776 authorized the drafting of a Declaration of Independence listing the colonists' grievances and justifying its call for independence based on John Locke's theory of natural rights and the social contract.

★ The Articles of Confederation created a "league of friendship" among the thirteen states by vesting them with equal authority in the central government during and immediately after America's successful war for independence. Under the Articles, the central government also possessed only limited powers to raise revenue and regulate commerce, hampering the U.S. government's war effort and its economic relations with foreign nations.

★ A Constitutional Convention consisting of delegates from twelve of the thirteen states convened in May of 1787 in an attempt to revise the Articles; however, the delegates immediately began to consider the "Virginia Plan," which proposed to overhaul the Articles by empowering a new government with three separate branches and the power to raise revenue.

★ The Virginia Plan favored large and more populous states by allotting membership in its proposed legislature based on each state's population; delegates from less populous states countered with the "New Jersey Plan," based on the principle of equal representation of the states. The Constitutional Convention eventually resolved the conflict by accepting the so-called Great Compromise, which proposed a bicameral legislature with a House of Representatives apportioned by population, and a Senate that allots equal power to each of the states.

★ With the issue of slavery dividing Northern and Southern states, the convention sidestepped the issue by settling on the "three-fifths compromise" (counting five slaves as three people for purposes of taxes and representation) and by deferring a ban on slave importation for at least twenty years into the future.

★ The new Constitution combined features of popular sovereignty, separation of powers, and checks and balances with a commitment to a system of "federalism," which divides sovereignty between state and federal governments.

★ The battle over ratification was waged between Federalists (who supported the new Constitution) and Anti-Federalists (who opposed it). The Federalists' carefully crafted media campaign, which included publication of the Federalist Papers justifying various provisions of the new Constitution, helped to ensure its ratification. Several state ratifying conventions insisted that the new government add a bill of rights to the Constitution; overcoming his initial reluctance to propose such a bill for fear that it might omit important rights, the "father of the Constitution," James Madison, eventually sponsored a new Bill of Rights in the first Congress.

★ Article V of the Constitution makes it exceedingly difficult to amend the Constitution. Since the Bill of Rights was ratified in 1791, only seventeen additional amendments have been ratified.

★ The Supreme Court under Chief Justice John Marshall favored a loose construction of several constitutional provisions, giving the federal government considerable implied powers; Thomas Jefferson and Jeffersonian Republicans favored a stricter construction of the Constitution's provisions.

Key Terms

Amendments (p. 48)

Anti-Federalists (p. 43)

Articles of Confederation (p. 35)

Bill of Rights (p. 48)

Checks and balances (p. 42)

Constitutional Convention (p. 37)

Declaration of Independence (p. 34)

Enumerated powers (p. 43)

Federalist Papers (p. 45)

Federalists (p. 43)

Great Compromise (p. 38)

Loose construction (p. 52)

New Jersey Plan (p. 38)

Separation of powers (p. 42)

Shays's Rebellion (p. 37)

Strict construction (p. 52)

Three-Fifths Compromise (p. 40)

Virginia Plan (p. 37)

Resources

Important Books

Amar, Akhil Reed. *America's Constitution: A Biography*. New York: Random House, 2006

Bailyn, Bernard. *The Ideological Origins of the American Revolution*. Cambridge, MA: Harvard University Press, 1967.

Beard, Charles S. *An Economic Interpretation of the Constitution*. New York: Macmillan, 1941.

Federalist Papers, various editions, including paperback version edited by Isaac Kramnick. New York: Penguin Press, 1987.

Kammen, Michael. *A Machine That Would Go of Itself: The Constitution in American Culture*. New York: Alfred A. Knopf, 1986.

McDonald, Forrest. *Novus Ordo Seclorum*. Lawrence: University Press of Kansas, 1985.

Maier, Pauline. *American Scripture: Making the Declaration of Independence*. New York: Alfred A. Knopf, 1997.

Monk, Linda R. *The Words We Live By: Your Annotated Guide to the Constitution*. New York: Hyperion, 2003.

Rakove, Jack N. *Original Meanings: Politics and Ideas in the Making of the Constitution*. New York: Alfred A. Knopf, 1996.

Wood, Gordon S. *The Creation of the American Republic*. Chapel Hill: University of North Carolina Press, 1998.

Wood, Gordon S. *The Radicalism of the American Revolution*. New York: Alfred A. Knopf, 1991.

Internet Sources

http://lcweb2.loc.gov/ammen/bdsds/bdsdhome.html (Library of Congress exhibit on documents from the Continental Congress and the Constitutional Convention)

http://www.constitution.org/ (web page of the Constitution Society, founded in response to growing concern about noncompliance with the U.S. Constitution)

http://www.usconstitution.net/constfaq.html (a site with frequently asked questions about the Constitution)

http://www.constitution.org/dfc/dfc-0000.htm (the debates of the Constitutional Convention of 1787)

http://www.archives.gov/exhibits/ (exhibit hall of the National Archives and Records Administration on the charters of freedom: Declaration of Independence, U.S. Constitution, Bill of Rights, and so on)

ANNOTATED CONSTITUTION OF THE UNITED STATES OF AMERICA

THE CONSTITUTION OF THE UNITED STATES OF AMERICA

We the people of the United States, in order to form a more perfect union, establish justice, insure domestic tranquility, provide for the common defense, promote the general welfare, and secure the blessings of liberty to ourselves and our posterity, do ordain and establish this Constitution for the United States of America.

As a statement containing the essential reasons for drafting the Constitution and the purposes of the new central government, the Preamble theoretically does not confer any actual power on government. Nevertheless, on numerous occasions the Supreme Court has cited the preamble to illustrate the origin, scope, and purposes of the Constitution, as well as to help discern the meaning of certain constitutional provisions that follow it. Most notably in McCulloch v. Maryland (1819), Chief Justice John Marshall quoted from the Preamble at length to confirm that the Constitution comes directly from the people, and not from the states.

Article I

Section 1. All legislative powers herein granted shall be vested in a Congress of the United States, which shall consist of a Senate and House of Representatives.

The placement of provisions for congressional power in Article I confirms what the Founders undoubtedly assumed to be true: that Congress would be the preeminent branch of the new central government. Section 1 established two important principles. First, by specifying "powers herein granted" it declared that the national government is one of enumerated powers. Despite the broadening of powers implied by the necessary and proper clause of Section 8, this statement of Section 1 still means that Congress theoretically cannot do whatever it wants to do. Rather, it must ground its exercise of power (whether explicitly stated or implied) in a specific provision of Article I. Second, Section 1 established the principle of bicameralism—the presence of two separate, but equally powerful legislative bodies as a further safeguard against government tyranny.

Section 2. The House of Representatives shall be composed of members chosen every second year by the people of the several states, and the electors in each state shall have the qualifications requisite for electors of the most numerous branch of the state legislature.

No person shall be a Representative who shall not have attained to the age of twenty five years, and been seven years a citizen of the United States, and who shall not, when elected, be an inhabitant of that state in which he shall be chosen.

Representatives and direct taxes shall be apportioned among the several states which may be included within this union, according to their respective numbers, which shall be determined by adding to the whole number of free persons, including those bound to service for a term of years, and excluding Indians not taxed, three fifths of all other Persons. The actual Enumeration shall be made within three years after the first meeting of the Congress of the United States, and within every subsequent term of ten years, in such manner as they shall by law direct. The number of Representatives shall not exceed one for every thirty thousand, but each state shall have at least one Representative; and until such enumeration shall be made, the state of New Hampshire shall be entitled to chuse three, Massachusetts eight, Rhode Island and Providence Plantations one, Connecticut five, New York six, New Jersey four, Pennsylvania eight, Delaware one, Maryland six, Virginia ten, North Carolina five, South Carolina five, and Georgia three.

When vacancies happen in the Representation from any state, the executive authority thereof shall issue writs of election to fill such vacancies.

The House of Representatives shall choose their speaker and other officers; and shall have the sole power of impeachment.

Section 2 of Article I establishes a House of Representatives as the lower House of the Congress. The membership of the U.S. House of Representatives is apportioned according to each state's population; the so-called three-fifth compromise (only three-fifths of the population of slaves would be counted for enumeration purposes) helped to resolve an impasse at the Convention between Southern states (who wanted slaves to count as more) and Northern states (who wanted them to count as less). Although the number of House members has grown with the population, since 1911 it has been fixed by statute at 435. As constituted, the House is as powerful as the U.S. Senate, and in one respect is even more powerful: the House has the sole power to originate revenue bills. Section 2 also lays out the two-year term rule and qualifications for each House member, as well as providing procedures for apportionment and filling vacancies. Finally, it authorizes the House to choose top officials, including the Speaker.

Section 3. The Senate of the United States shall be composed of two Senators from each state, chosen by the legislature thereof, for six years; and each Senator shall have one vote.

Immediately after they shall be assembled in consequence of the first election, they shall be divided as equally as may be into three classes. The seats of the Senators of the first class shall be vacated at the expiration of the second year, of the second class at the expiration of the fourth year, and the third class at the expiration of the sixth year, so that one third may be chosen every second year; and if vacancies happen by resignation, or otherwise, during the recess of the legislature of any state, the executive thereof may make temporary appointments until the next meeting of the legislature, which shall then fill such vacancies.

No person shall be a Senator who shall not have attained to the age of thirty years, and been nine years a citizen of the United States and who shall not, when elected, be an inhabitant of that state for which he shall be chosen.

The Vice President of the United States shall be President of the Senate, but shall have no vote, unless they be equally divided.

The Senate shall choose their other officers, and also a President pro tempore, in the absence of the Vice President, or when he shall exercise the office of President of the United States.

The Senate shall have the sole power to try all impeachments. When sitting for that purpose, they shall be on oath or affirmation. When the President of the United States is tried, the Chief Justice shall preside: And no person shall be convicted without the concurrence of two thirds of the members present. Judgment in cases of impeachment shall not extend further than to removal from office, and disqualification to hold and enjoy any office of honor, trust or profit under the United States: but the party convicted shall nevertheless be liable and subject to indictment, trial, judgment and punishment, according to law.

Just as Section 2 does for the House of Representative, Section 3 establishes various powers and procedures for the U.S. Senate. Individual senators may be more powerful than their counterparts in the House because of the longer length of their terms (six years) and because there are far fewer members in the body; however, there is no constitutional basis for the claim that the Senate is a superior chamber. Although the vice president theoretically presides over the Senate as its president, and the president pro tempore serves in the vice president's absence, in actual practice the president pro tempore usually deputizes a more junior senator to preside over most Senate business. The provisions of clause 1 and clause 2 that state legislatures choose senators have been overturned by the Seventeenth Amendment, which now provides that senators are chosen by popular election.

Section 4. The times, places and manner of holding elections for Senators and Representatives, shall be prescribed in each state by the legislature thereof; but the Congress may at any time by law make or alter such regulations, except as to the places of choosing Senators.

The Congress shall assemble at least once in every year, and such meeting shall be on the first Monday in December, unless they shall by law appoint a different day.

According to Article I, Section 4, states can regulate the time, place and manner of all federal elections, but Congress can still establish a single uniform date for elections (and it has done so on "the first Tuesday following the first Monday in November").

Section 5. Each House shall be the judge of the elections, returns and qualifications of its own members, and a majority of each shall constitute a quorum to do business; but a smaller number may adjourn from day to day, and may be authorized to compel the attendance of absent members, in such manner, and under such penalties as each House may provide.

Each House may determine the rules of its proceedings, punish its members for disorderly behavior, and, with the concurrence of two thirds, expel a member.

Each House shall keep a journal of its proceedings, and from time to time publish the same, excepting such parts as may in their judgment require secrecy; and the yeas and nays of the members of either House on any question shall, at the desire of one fifth of those present, be entered on the journal.

Neither House, during the session of Congress, shall, without the consent of the other, adjourn for more than three days, nor to any other place than that in which the two Houses shall be sitting.

Section 6. The Senators and Representatives shall receive a compensation for their services, to be ascertained by law, and paid out of the treasury of the

United States. They shall in all cases, except treason, felony and breach of the peace, be privileged from arrest during their attendance at the session of their respective Houses, and in going to and returning from the same; and for any speech or debate in either House, they shall not be questioned in any other place.

No Senator or Representative shall, during the time for which he was elected, be appointed to any civil office under the authority of the United States, which shall have been created, or the emoluments whereof shall have been increased during such time: and no person holding any office under the United States, shall be a member of either House during his continuance in office.

Article I, Section 6 extends to members of Congress various immunities. The speech and debate clause of Section 6 prevents House members or Senators from being sued for slander during congressional debates, committee hearings, or most other official congressional business. In deference to the principle of separation of powers, Clause 2 ensures that members of Congress cannot hold another civil office while retaining their legislative seats.

Section 7. All bills for raising revenue shall originate in the House of Representatives; but the Senate may propose or concur with amendments as on other Bills.

Every bill which shall have passed the House of Representatives and the Senate, shall, before it become a law, be presented to the President of the United States; if he approve he shall sign it, but if not he shall return it, with his objections to that House in which it shall have originated, who shall enter the objections at large on their journal, and proceed to reconsider it. If after such reconsideration two thirds of that House shall agree to pass the bill, it shall be sent, together with the objections, to the other House, by which it shall likewise be reconsidered, and if approved by two thirds of that House, it shall become a law. But in all such cases the votes of both Houses shall be determined by yeas and nays, and the names of the persons voting for and against the bill shall be entered on the journal of each House respectively. If any bill shall not be returned by the President within ten days (Sundays excepted) after it shall have been presented to him, the same shall be a law, in like manner as if he had signed it, unless the Congress by their adjournment prevent its return, in which case it shall not be a law.

Every order, resolution, or vote to which the concurrence of the Senate and House of Representatives may be necessary (except on a question of adjournment) shall be presented to the President of the United States; and before the same shall take effect, shall be approved by him, or being disapproved by him, shall be repassed by two thirds of the Senate and House of Representatives, according to the rules and limitations prescribed in the case of a bill.

Article I, Section 7 is often referred to as the presentment clause. It establishes the procedures by which Congress presents bills to the president for approval; it also lays out the process by which the president may veto legislation, either by refusing to sign it and sending it back, or by keeping the bill for a period of 10 days without signing it while Congress has adjourned in the interim (referred to as a "pocket veto"). In 1996, Congress passed the Line Item Veto Act, which allowed the president to veto specific expenditures at the time of signing; the Supreme Court declared the Line Item Veto Act unconstitutional in Clinton v. City of New York (1998) because it gave the president the power to repeal parts of duly enacted statutes in a manner different from the "finely wrought and exhaustively considered procedure" described in this section.

Section 8. The Congress shall have power to lay and collect taxes, duties, imposts and excises, to pay the debts and provide for the common defense and general welfare of the United States; but all duties, imposts and excises shall be uniform throughout the United States;

To borrow money on the credit of the United States;

To regulate commerce with foreign nations, and among the several states, and with the Indian tribes;

To establish a uniform rule of naturalization, and uniform laws on the subject of bankruptcies throughout the United States;

To coin money, regulate the value thereof, and of foreign coin, and fix the standard of weights and measures;

To provide for the punishment of counterfeiting the securities and current coin of the United States;

To establish post offices and post roads;

To promote the progress of science and useful arts, by securing for limited times to authors and inventors the exclusive right to their respective writings and discoveries;

To constitute tribunals inferior to the Supreme Court;

To define and punish piracies and felonies committed on the high seas, and offenses against the law of nations;

To declare war, grant letters of marque and reprisal, and make rules concerning captures on land and water;

To raise and support armies, but no appropriation of money to that use shall be for a longer term than two years;

To provide and maintain a navy;

To make rules for the government and regulation of the land and naval forces;

To provide for calling forth the militia to execute the laws of the union, suppress insurrections and repel invasions;

To provide for organizing, arming, and disciplining, the militia, and for governing such part of them as may be employed in the service of the United States, reserving to the states respectively, the appointment of the officers, and the authority of training the militia according to the discipline prescribed by Congress;

To exercise exclusive legislation in all cases whatsoever, over such District (not exceeding ten miles square) as may, by cession of particular states, and the acceptance of Congress, become the seat of the government of the United States, and to exercise like authority over all places purchased by the consent of the legislature of the state in which the same shall be, for the erection of forts, magazines, arsenals, dockyards, and other needful buildings;—And

To make all laws which shall be necessary and proper for carrying into execution the foregoing powers, and all other powers vested by this Constitution in the government of the United States, or in any department or officer thereof.

Article I, Section 8 may be the most heavily cited clause in the original Constitution, as it lays out all the enumerated powers of Congress. The 18th clause listed, the necessary and proper clause, was the source of significant controversy in the early republic. In McCulloch v. Maryland (1819), Chief Justice John Marshall interpreted the clause as essentially aiding Congress in carrying out its expressed powers. Combining the powers granted by the 18th clause with other powers allows Congress to exercise implied powers not explicitly listed in the Constitution, so long as those powers offer a theoretical means of achieving the enumerated powers. Thus Congress successfully incorporated a bank of the United States because it was deemed necessary and proper to achieve the power to coin money and regulate its value (clause 5), as well as other powers. Similarly, Congress chartered a railroad company as a necessary means of promoting commerce (clause 3) and waging war (clauses 11–14). No wonder the necessary and proper clause has also been called the elastic clause: It gives Congress the power to enact laws on almost any subject it desires. The power to regulate interstate commerce under clause 3 has been especially useful in this regard. Citing the commerce clause, Congress since 1937 has regulated minimum wages of state employees, outlawed loan sharking, and passed numerous civil rights laws, among other legislation. The only current limits to that practice were outlined by the Supreme Court in United States v. Lopez (1995) and United States v. Morrison (2000)—the law in question must regulate activities that are at least directly economic in nature.

Section 9. The migration or importation of such persons as any of the states now existing shall think proper to admit, shall not be prohibited by the Congress prior to the year one thousand eight hundred and eight, but a tax or duty may be imposed on such importation, not exceeding ten dollars for each person.

The privilege of the writ of habeas corpus shall not be suspended, unless when in cases of rebellion or invasion the public safety may require it.

No bill of attainder or ex post facto Law shall be passed.

No capitation, or other direct, tax shall be laid, unless in proportion to the census or enumeration herein before directed to be taken.

No tax or duty shall be laid on articles exported from any state.

No preference shall be given by any regulation of commerce or revenue to the ports of one state over those of another: nor shall vessels bound to, or from, one state, be obliged to enter, clear or pay duties in another.

No money shall be drawn from the treasury, but in consequence of appropriations made by law; and a regular statement and account of receipts and expenditures of all public money shall be published from time to time.

No title of nobility shall be granted by the United States: and no person holding any office of profit or trust under them, shall, without the consent of the Congress, accept of any present, emolument, office, or title, of any kind whatever, from any king, prince, or foreign state.

Section 9 places some explicit limits on congressional power, including restrictions on the power to ban the import of slaves (at least through 1808), the power to bestow titles of nobility, and the power to lay direct taxes not apportioned to the states' populations. (This last restriction was effectively removed by ratification of the Sixteenth Amendment in 1913. It also prohibits Congress from issuing bills of attainder [legislative acts that inflict punishment without a judicial trial] or from passing ex post facto laws [criminal laws that apply retroactively to acts committed in the past].)

Section 10. No state shall enter into any treaty, alliance, or confederation; grant letters of marque and reprisal; coin money; emit bills of credit; make anything but gold and silver coin a tender in payment of debts; pass any bill of attainder, ex post facto law, or law impairing the obligation of contracts, or grant any title of nobility.

No state shall, without the consent of the Congress, lay any imposts or duties on imports or exports, except what may be absolutely necessary for executing its inspection laws: and the net produce of all duties and imposts, laid by any state on imports or exports, shall be for the use of the treasury of the United States; and all such laws shall be subject to the revision and control of the Congress.

No state shall, without the consent of Congress, lay any duty of tonnage, keep troops, or ships of war in time of peace, enter into any agreement or compact with another state, or with a foreign power, or engage in war, unless actually invaded, or in such imminent danger as will not admit of delay.

The final section of Article I limits states from exercising powers reserved exclusively to the federal government. Most controversial of these clauses was the contract clause, which prohibits states from impairing the obligation of contracts. Added to the Constitution largely to prevent state laws that undermined the collection of valid debts, it was later used to protect certain franchises or special privileges that corporations had received from state legislatures. Thus the Supreme Court held in Trustees of Dartmouth College v. Woodward (1819) that the charter given to Dartmouth by a colonial legislature in 1769 could not be changed without Dartmouth's consent. State legislatures complained that the contract clause unduly restricted their ability to legislate; thus, the Supreme Court over the course of two centuries has narrowed the meaning of the clause to allow states greater freedom to operate, relying on the theory that such contracts are by implication the laws of the state and thus may be modified by the state. The Court has also upheld state bankruptcy laws when the laws are applied to debts incurred after passage of the law.

Article II

Section 1. The executive power shall be vested in a President of the United States of America. He shall hold his office during the term of four years, and, together with the Vice President, chosen for the same term, be elected, as follows:

Each state shall appoint, in such manner as the Legislature thereof may direct, a number of electors, equal to the whole number of Senators and Representatives to which the State may be entitled in the Congress: but no Senator or Representative, or person holding an office of trust or profit under the United States, shall be appointed an elector.

The electors shall meet in their respective states, and vote by ballot for two persons, of whom one at least shall not be an inhabitant of the same state with themselves. And they shall make a list of all the persons voted for, and of the number of votes for each; which list they shall sign and certify, and transmit sealed to the seat of the government of the United States, directed to the President of the Senate. The President of the Senate shall, in the presence of the Senate and House of Representatives, open all the certificates, and the votes shall then be counted. The person having the greatest number of votes shall be the President, if such number be a majority of the whole number of electors appointed; and if there be more than one who have such majority, and have an equal number of votes, then the House of Representatives shall immediately choose by ballot one of them for President; and if no person have a majority, then from the five highest on the list the said House shall in like manner choose the President. But in choosing the President, the votes shall be taken by States, the representation from each state having one vote; A quorum for this purpose shall consist of a member or members from two thirds of the states, and a majority of all the states shall be necessary to a choice. In every case, after the choice of the President, the person having the greatest number of votes of the electors shall be the Vice President. But if there should remain two or more who have equal votes, the Senate shall choose from them by ballot the Vice President.

The Congress may determine the time of choosing the electors, and the day on which they shall give their votes; which day shall be the same throughout the United States.

No person except a natural born citizen, or a citizen of the United States, at the time of the adoption of this Constitution, shall be eligible to the office of President; neither shall any person be eligible to that office who shall not have attained to the age of thirty five years, and been fourteen Years a resident within the United States.

In case of the removal of the President from office, or of his death, resignation, or inability to discharge the powers and duties of the said office, the same shall devolve on the Vice President, and the Congress may by law provide for the case of removal, death, resignation or inability, both of the President and Vice President, declaring what officer shall then act as President, and such officer shall act accordingly, until the disability be removed, or a President shall be elected.

The President shall, at stated times, receive for his services, a compensation, which shall neither be increased nor diminished during the period for which he shall have been elected, and he shall not receive within that period any other emolument from the United States, or any of them.

Before he enter on the execution of his office, he shall take the following oath or affirmation:—'I do solemnly swear (or affirm) that I will faithfully execute the office of President of the United States, and will to the best of my ability, preserve, protect and defend the Constitution of the United States.'

Article II, Section 1 lays out the manner by which the president and vice president are selected, the qualifications for those two offices, and the means for removal and succession. (Clause 2 on presidential elections has been replaced by the Twelfth Amendment.) Section 1 begins with the vague declaration that the "executive power shall be vested in a president of the United States of America ..." Does this clause serve as a source of independent power for the chief executive? Beginning in the 20th century, the Supreme Court has held that the president possesses broad "inherent powers" to exercise certain powers not specifically enumerated in the Constitution. These vast executive powers included, for example, Franklin Roosevelt's various executive agreements extending the scope of the federal government during the 1930s. On the other hand, the Supreme Court ruled in Youngstown Sheet and Tune Co. v. Sawyer (1951) that a president's inherent powers did not include President Truman's attempt to seize the steel mills to avert a strike without congressional approval; similarly, in U.S. v. Nixon (1974) the Court held that the chief executive's inherent powers did not encompass President Richard Nixon's refusal to turn over important documents in a criminal matter.

Section 2. The President shall be commander in chief of the Army and Navy of the United States, and of the militia of the several states, when called into the actual service of the United States; he may require the opinion, in writing, of the principal officer in each of the executive departments, upon any subject relating to the duties of their respective offices, and he shall have power to grant reprieves and pardons for offenses against the United States, except in cases of impeachment.

He shall have power, by and with the advice and consent of the Senate, to make treaties, provided two thirds of the Senators present concur; and he shall nominate, and by and with the advice and consent of the Senate, shall appoint ambassadors, other public ministers and consuls, judges of the Supreme Court, and all other officers of the United States, whose appointments are not herein otherwise provided for, and which shall be established by law: but the Congress may by law vest the appointment of such inferior officers, as they think proper, in the President alone, in the courts of law, or in the heads of departments.

The President shall have power to fill up all vacancies that may happen during the recess of the Senate, by granting commissions which shall expire at the end of their next session.

Article II, Section 2 is striking for how few express powers are granted to the president, as compared to the long list of powers granted to Congress in Article I, Section 8. In the 20th century the powers granted to the president expanded to create a far more powerful presidency than the founders envisioned. Thus, invoking their power as commander-in-chief, modern presidents have deployed troops around the world in military battles even without a formal declaration of war by Congress. Recent presidents have occasionally terminated treaties without the consent of the Senate. Presidents have also asserted the power to terminate officers of the United States without cause. The combined Supreme Court precedents of Myers v. United States (1926) and Humphrey's Executor v. United States (1935) authorize them to do so in the case of purely executive officers, but not in the case of independent agency heads.

Section 3. He shall from time to time give to the Congress information of the state of the union, and recommend to their consideration such measures as he shall judge necessary and expedient; he may, on extraordinary occasions, convene both Houses, or either of them, and in case of disagreement between them, with respect to the time of adjournment, he may adjourn them to such time as he shall think proper; he shall receive ambassadors and other public ministers; he shall take care that the laws be faithfully executed, and shall commission all the officers of the United States.

Article II, Section 3 lists numerous presidential responsibilities, including the obligation to give a report on the "state of the union" to Congress (today this occurs in the form of a yearly address), and the duty to "take care that laws be faithfully executed." Citing this latter phrase, presidents have asserted the power to impound money appropriated by Congress, and to suspend the writ of habeas corpus. Whenever called upon, the Supreme Court has held such actions to be unconstitutional—usually the Court does so long after the fact. Additionally, the Supreme Court has upheld efforts by the president to call upon the military to assist in faithfully executing the law. President Eisenhower exercised this power when he used federal troops to enforce desegregation decrees in Arkansas and Mississippi in the late 1950s.

Section 4. The President, Vice President and all civil officers of the United States, shall be removed from office on impeachment for, and conviction of, treason, bribery, or other high crimes and misdemeanors.

Article II, Section 4 lays out the process of impeachment and conviction of civil officers, but the phrase "high crimes and misdemeanors" is vague and subject to conflicting interpretations. Regardless, the House of Representatives has asserted its authority to decide on its own how to define the term. Only two chief executives have ever been formally impeached under this section: Andrew Johnson in 1868, and Bill Clinton in 1998. However, in both cases, the U.S. Senate failed to provide the required two-thirds vote necessary for conviction.

Article III

Section 1. The judicial power of the United States, shall be vested in one Supreme Court, and in such inferior courts as the Congress may from time to time ordain and establish. The judges, both of the supreme and inferior courts, shall hold their offices during good behaviour, and shall, at stated times, receive for their services, a compensation, which shall not be diminished during their continuance in office.

Section 2. The judicial power shall extend to all cases, in law and equity, arising under this Constitution, the laws of the United States, and treaties made, or which shall be made, under their authority;—to all cases affecting ambassadors, other public ministers and consuls;—to all cases of admiralty and maritime jurisdiction;—to controversies to which the United States shall be a party;—to controversies between two or more states;—between a state and citizens of another state;— between citizens of different states;—between citizens of the same state claiming lands under grants of different states, and between a state, or the citizens thereof, and foreign states, citizens or subjects.

In all cases affecting ambassadors, other public ministers and consuls, and those in which a state shall be party, the Supreme Court shall have original jurisdiction. In all the other cases before mentioned, the Supreme Court shall have appellate jurisdiction, both as to law and fact, with such exceptions, and under such regulations as the Congress shall make.

The trial of all crimes, except in cases of impeachment, shall be by jury; and such trial shall be held in the state where the said crimes shall have been committed; but when not committed within any state, the trial shall be at such place or places as the Congress may by law have directed.

Section 3. Treason against the United States, shall consist only in levying war against them, or in adhering to their enemies, giving them aid and comfort. No person shall be convicted of treason unless on the testimony of two witnesses to the same overt act, or on confession in open court.

The Congress shall have power to declare the punishment of treason, but no attainder of treason shall work corruption of blood, or forfeiture except during the life of the person attainted.

Article III establishes a U.S. Supreme Court, spells out the terms of office of its members, and lists the various cases to which its judicial power extends. Just as important, it provides the basis for a more elaborate judicial system featuring numerous levels of courts, which Congress may establish at its discretion. Note how vague and general this Article is compared to Articles I and II: Only one court (the Supreme Court) is specifically mentioned, and there are no provisions that specify the size or composition of the court. Congress subsequently established that federal judges on the courts of appeals and the district courts, like justices of the Supreme Court, are appointed by the president and confirmed by the Senate. They too serve for indefinite terms on good behavior, which provides the equivalent of life tenure to federal judges on those three levels of courts. Article III does not specifically grant the Supreme Court the power of judicial review, that is, the power to review the actions of other branches for their constitutionality. The Supreme Court seized that power for itself in Marbury v. Madison (1803), and it remains a fundamental precept of the federal judicial system today.

Article IV

Section 1. Full faith and credit shall be given in each state to the public acts, records, and judicial proceedings of every other state. And the Congress may by general laws prescribe the manner in which such acts, records, and proceedings shall be proved, and the effect thereof.

Section 2. The citizens of each state shall be entitled to all privileges and immunities of citizens in the several states.

A person charged in any state with treason, felony, or other crime, who shall flee from justice, and be found in another state, shall on demand of the executive authority of the state from which he fled, be delivered up, to be removed to the state having jurisdiction of the crime.

No person held to service or labor in one state, under the laws thereof, escaping into another, shall, in consequence of any law or regulation therein, be discharged from such service or labor, but shall be delivered up on claim of the party to whom such service or labor may be due.

Section 3. New states may be admitted by the Congress into this union; but no new states shall be formed or erected within the jurisdiction of any other state; nor any state be formed by the junction of two or more states, or parts of states, without the consent of the legislatures of the states concerned as well as of the Congress.

The Congress shall have power to dispose of and make all needful rules and regulations respecting the territory or other property belonging to the United States; and nothing in this Constitution shall be so construed as to prejudice any claims of the United States, or of any particular state.

Section 4. The United States shall guarantee to every state in this union a republican form of government, and shall protect each of them against invasion; and on application of the legislature, or of the executive (when the legislature cannot be convened) against domestic violence.

Article IV describes the responsibilities states have to each other under the Constitution, and the obligations of the federal government to the states. It also provides the procedures for admitting new states to the union (no state has been admitted since Alaska and Hawaii's entry in 1959). In recent years, the most controversial aspect of Article IV has been the full faith and credit clause of Section 1, which theoretically binds states to respect the public acts and proceedings of other states, including the granting of drivers' licenses, child custody rulings, etc. Does the full faith and credit clause apply as well to the institution of same-sex marriage? The federal government and the states have sought to evade the recognition of gay marriages sanctioned elsewhere (only Massachusetts, Connecticut, and California allowed such marriages at the time of this writing, although voters in California sent their state's law into flux in November 2008 when they approved a constitutional amendment to ban the right) through legislation, including the Defense of Marriage Act of 1996. The ambiguous privileges and immunities clause of Article IV, Section 2 requires that states not discriminate against citizens of other states in favor of its own citizens, although the Supreme Court has allowed states to establish more favorable terms for in-state residents when distributing certain recreational rights such as amateur fishing licenses or permits to use state parks; taxes on commuters, by contrast, may be unconstitutional if they penalize out-of-state residents who work or do business in the state. The requirement in Section 4 that the United States guarantee to every state a republican form of government was invoked in the 1840s when President John Tyler threatened the use of federal troops after a rebellion occurred in Rhode Island. Today that provision is obscure and little-used.

Article V

The Congress, whenever two thirds of both houses shall deem it necessary, shall propose amendments to this Constitution, or, on the application of the legislatures of two thirds of the several states, shall call a convention for proposing amendments, which, in either case, shall be valid to all intents and purposes, as part of this Constitution, when ratified by the legislatures of three fourths of the several states, or by conventions in three fourths thereof, as the one or the other mode of ratification may be proposed by the Congress; provided that no amendment which may be made prior to the year one thousand eight hundred and eight shall in any manner affect the first and fourth clauses in the ninth section of the first article; and that no state, without its consent, shall be deprived of its equal suffrage in the Senate.

Article V spells out the process for amending the Constitution. By far the most common form of constitutional amendment has been by congressional proposal, with state legislatures ratifying the proposal. Twenty-six of the twenty-seven amendments have been adopted in this way. The sole exception was the Twenty-first Amendment, which was ratified by specially chosen state ratifying conventions to assure that farmer-dominated state legislatures would not undermine the effort to repeal Prohibition. Meanwhile, the procedure by which the requisite number of state legislatures (two thirds) apply to Congress to call a convention for proposing amendments has never been used. Article V does not provide a deadline for considering proposed amendments, although Congress has the power to set such deadlines in the language of the proposed amendment. Congress did not do so in the case of the Twenty-seventh Amendment, which received the approval of the required three-fourths of states necessary for ratification in 1992—fully 203 years after the amendment was first proposed.

Article VI

All debts contracted and engagements entered into, before the adoption of this Constitution, shall be as valid against the United States under this Constitution, as under the Confederation.

This Constitution, and the laws of the United States which shall be made in pursuance thereof; and all treaties made, or which shall be made, under the authority of the United States, shall be the supreme law of the land; and the judges in every state shall be bound thereby, anything in the Constitution or laws of any State to the contrary notwithstanding.

The Senators and Representatives before mentioned, and the members of the several state legislatures, and all executive and judicial officers, both of the United States and of the several states, shall be bound by oath or affirmation, to support this Constitution; but no religious test shall ever be required as a qualification to any office or public trust under the United States.

Article VI establishes that the Constitution, laws, and treaties are to be the supreme law of the land. In interpreting this supremacy clause, the U.S. Supreme Court has countenanced little resistance. Thus the Supreme Court has consistently struck down attempts by states to control federal institutions, and it has reminded state governments that even state constitutions are subordinate to federal statutes. Even more important, in Cooper v. Aaron (1957) the U.S. Supreme Court stated in no uncertain terms that its own rulings are to be treated as if they are the words of the Constitution itself, heading off attempts by some state governments to resist Supreme Court rulings on desegregation by offering their own interpretations of the federal Constitution as authority.

Article VII

The ratification of the conventions of nine states, shall be sufficient for the establishment of this Constitution between the states so ratifying the same. Done in convention by the unanimous consent of the states present the seventeenth day of September in the year of our Lord one thousand seven hundred and eighty seven and of the independence of the United States of America the twelfth. In witness whereof We have hereunto subscribed our Names,
G. Washington—Presidt. and deputy from Virginia

New Hampshire
John Langdon
Nicholas Gilman
Massachusetts
Nathaniel Gorham
Rufus King

Connecticut
Wm. Saml. Johnson
Roger Sherman

New York
Alexander Hamilton

New Jersey
Wil. Livingston
David Brearly

Wm. Paterson
Jona. Dayton

Pennsylvania
B. Franklin
Thomas Mifflin
Robt. Morris
Geo. Clymer
Thos. FitzSimons
Jared Ingersoll
James Wilson
Gouv Morris

Delaware
Geo. Read
Gunning Bedford jun
John Dickinson

Richard Bassett
Jaco. Broom
Maryland
James McHenry
Dan of St Thos.
Jenifer
Danl Carroll

Virginia
John Blair—
James Madison Jr.

North Carolina
Wm. Blount
Richd. Dobbs
Spaight
Hu Williamson

South Carolina
J. Rutledge
Charles Cotesworth
Pinckney
Charles Pinckney
Pierce Butler

Georgia
William Few
Abr Baldwin

Amendments to the Constitution of the United States

The Bill of Rights, ratified in 1791, consists of the first ten amendments to the Constitution. Since that time, seventeen additional amendments have been ratified by the states. Originally the Bill of Rights applied only to the federal government and not to the state governments; however, through a process known as incorporation, the Supreme Court has ruled that the Fourteenth Amendment (adopted in 1868) made most of the provisions found in the Bill of Rights applicable to the states as well. Subsequent amendments have extended the franchise, established (and repealed) Prohibition, and clarified important procedures that the federal government must follow.

Amendment I (1791)

Congress shall make no law respecting an establishment of religion, or prohibiting the free exercise thereof; or abridging the freedom of speech, or of the press; or the right of the people peaceably to assemble, and to petition the government for a redress of grievances.

Although many provisions of the original Bill of Rights are based on aspects of English law, the extensive guarantees found in the First Amendment have no true English equivalent. The First Amendment offered one of the first written guarantees of religious freedom, and it formed the basis for extensive free speech and free press protection as well. Yet its unqualified language notwithstanding, the First Amendment has never conveyed absolute freedom to Americans. Whether it was the Alien and Sedition acts of 1798, the aggressive application of the Espionage Act during World War I, or the "red scare" of the late 1940s, government has often found ways to evade the First Amendment, especially during times of crisis. The Supreme Court has also specifically exempted obscenity, libel, fighting words, and incitement from free speech protections. Nor has the separate and independent provision for the freedom of the press been interpreted to give members of the press any more protection than is afforded to ordinary citizens. Finally, as noted above, although the first word of the amendment implies that its protections apply only against actions of the federal government, today the First Amendment offers protection against the state governments as well.

Amendment II (1791)

A well regulated militia, being necessary to the security of a free state, the right of the people to keep and bear arms, shall not be infringed.

The Second Amendment originated as a compromise in the debate between those who feared mob rule by the people, and those committed to give the people everything they need to fight governmental tyranny. In 2008, the U.S. Supreme Court ruled for the first time that certain gun control laws may violate an individual's Second Amendment right to "bear arms," but it remains unclear whether that holding applies to state governments. See District of Columbia v. Heller, 554 U.S. ____ (2008).

Amendment III (1791)

No soldier shall, in time of peace be quartered in any house, without the consent of the owner, nor in time of war, but in a manner to be prescribed by law.

The Third Amendment has been all but lost to history. The Quartering Act, which required the American colonists to provide shelter and supplies for British troops, was one of the grievances that provoked the Declaration of Independence and ultimately the Revolution. Many colonists resented having to house British soldiers in private homes. The Third Amendment aimed to protect private citizens from such intrusions.

Amendment IV (1791)

The right of the people to be secure in their persons, houses, papers, and effects, against unreasonable searches and seizures, shall not be violated, and no warrants shall issue, but upon probable cause, supported by oath or affirmation, and particularly describing the place to be searched, and the persons or things to be seized.

Like the First Amendment, the Fourth Amendment is a uniquely American right. It arose out of colonists' anger over the warrantless searches and so-called General Warrants, by which British authorities would conduct raids of colonists' homes virtually at their own discretion. The Fourth Amendment guarantees that with certain carefully specified exceptions (consent of the owner, urgent circumstances, etc.), government authorities can conduct searches only when they possess a reasonably specific warrant demonstrating probable cause. Enforcement of the Fourth Amendment occurs primarily through application of the controversial exclusionary rule, which excludes from trial all evidence seized in violation of a defendant's constitutional rights.

Amendment V (1791)

No person shall be held to answer for a capital, or otherwise infamous crime, unless on a presentment or indictment of a grand jury, except in cases arising in the land or naval forces, or in the militia, when in actual service in time of war or public danger; nor shall any person be subject for the same offense to be twice put in jeopardy of life or limb; nor shall be compelled in any criminal case to be a witness against himself, nor be deprived of life, liberty, or property, without due process of law; nor shall private property be taken for public use, without just compensation.

The Fifth Amendment is a collection of various rights, most of which are important primarily to those accused of a crime. Those who "take the Fifth" under oath are normally invoking the privilege against self-incrimination; under current precedents they can invoke that privilege in other contexts as well, such as whenever they are being questioned by police or other authorities. The grand jury requirement has never been incorporated to apply against state governments. The requirement against double jeopardy prevents defendants who have been acquitted from being retried for the same offense by the same government. The due process clause of the Fifth Amendment was later duplicated in the Fourteenth Amendment and applied to states as well. Finally, the takings clause limits the traditional power of eminent domain by requiring that the government must pay compensation whenever it takes private property for public use.

Amendment VI (1791)

In all criminal prosecutions, the accused shall enjoy the right to a speedy and public trial, by an impartial jury of the state and district wherein the crime shall have been committed, which district shall have been previously ascertained by law, and to be informed of the nature and cause of the accusation; to be confronted with the witnesses against him; to have compulsory process for obtaining witnesses in his favor, and to have the assistance of counsel for his defense.

The Sixth Amendment offers the accused numerous constitutional protections. The need for a speedy and public trial dates back to concerns raised by imprisoned enemies of the British crown who were detained indefinitely and without notice. The right to a jury trial—considered a sacred aspect of the American political culture—is not all-encompassing either: It applies only to non-petty offenses (punishable by more than six months of prison).

Amendment VII (1791)

In suits at common law, where the value in controversy shall exceed twenty dollars, the right of trial by jury shall be preserved, and no fact tried by a jury, shall be otherwise reexamined in any court of the United States, than according to the rules of the common law.

The Seventh Amendment is the only amendment in the Bill of Rights that focuses on elements of civil trials exclusively. It preserves the distinction the English system draws between courts of common law (in which juries grant monetary relief) and courts of equity (in which a judge grants non-monetary relief, such as an injunction).

Amendment VIII (1791)

Excessive bail shall not be required, nor excessive fines imposed, nor cruel and unusual punishments inflicted.

The Eighth Amendment offers protections that come directly from the English Bill of Rights. The prohibition against excessive bail was established to prevent judges from keeping the accused indefinitely imprisoned while waiting for trials on minor offenses; it has subsequently been interpreted to allow judges to deny bail in instances where the charges are sufficiently serious, or where preventative detention is warranted for the safety of the community. The prohibition against cruel and unusual punishment forbids some punishments entirely (drawing and quartering, burning alive, and other forms of torture), while forbidding other punishments only when they are excessive compared to the crime. Aside from the four-year period from 1972 through 1976, the Supreme Court has consistently held that with proper safeguards, capital punishment is not cruel and unusual punishment. However, consistent with this clause it may not be imposed for rape or crimes lesser than murder, and it may not be imposed against the mentally retarded or against juvenile offenders.

Amendment IX (1791)

The enumeration in the Constitution, of certain rights, shall not be construed to deny or disparage others retained by the people.

The Ninth Amendment has been nicknamed the Madison Amendment in deference to James Madison's general concerns about the Bill of Rights. During debates over ratification of the Constitution, Anti-Federalists called for a bill of rights to protect the people against a potentially abusive new central government. In correspondence with Thomas Jefferson, Madison expressed the fear that by listing exceptions to congressional powers, such a bill of rights would effectively deny the existence of rights that did not happen to appear on the list. Eventually, as a member of the House of Representatives in the First Congress, Madison sponsored passage of the Bill of Rights, but he included this amendment as a way to ensure that the listing of certain rights did not mean that other rights were denied. As interpreted, the Ninth Amendment has not had much impact on the Constitutional landscape. Likened by some to an "inkblot," it has been most commonly viewed not as a source of rights, but rather as a loose guideline on how to interpret the Constitution.

Amendment X (1791)

The powers not delegated to the United States by the Constitution, nor prohibited by it to the states, are reserved to the states respectively, or to the people.

The Tenth Amendment lays out in explicit terms that the federal government is limited only to the powers granted to it in the Constitution. For most of the 20th century, the Supreme Court regarded the amendment largely as a redundant truism, adding little to the Constitution as it was originally ratified. Yet since the early 1990s the Supreme Court has began to put teeth into the amendment, interpreting it as a prohibition on attempts by Congress to force states to participate in federal programs.

Amendment XI (1798)

The judicial power of the United States shall not be construed to extend to any suit in law or equity, commenced or prosecuted against one of the United States by citizens of another state, or by citizens or subjects of any foreign state.

The Eleventh Amendment was ratified to modify the Supreme Court's controversial decision in Chisholm v. Georgia (1793), which upheld the authority of federal courts to hear lawsuits brought by citizens of one state against another state. The Supreme Court has ruled that the Eleventh Amendment provide states with some form of sovereign immunity, which means that it generally protects states from civil or criminal prosecution. The Supreme Court has also determined that under the Eleventh Amendment, a state cannot be sued by one of its own citizens, either.

Amendment XII (1804)

The electors shall meet in their respective states and vote by ballot for President and Vice-President, one of whom, at least, shall not be an inhabitant of the same state with themselves; they shall name in their ballots the person voted for as President, and in distinct ballots the person voted for as Vice-President, and they shall make distinct lists of all persons voted for as President, and of all persons voted for as Vice-President, and of the number of votes for each, which lists they shall sign and certify, and transmit sealed to the seat of the government of the United States, directed to the President of the Senate;—The President of the Senate shall, in the presence of the Senate and House of Representatives, open all the certificates and the votes shall then be counted;—the person having the greatest number of votes for President, shall be the President, if such number be a majority of the whole number of electors appointed; and if no person have such majority, then from the persons having the highest numbers not exceeding three on the list of those voted for as President, the House of Representatives shall choose immediately, by ballot, the President. But in choosing the President, the votes shall be taken by states, the representation from each state having one vote; a quorum for this purpose shall consist of a member or members from two-thirds of the states, and a majority of all the states shall be necessary to a choice. And if the House of Representatives shall not choose a President whenever the right of choice shall devolve upon them, before the fourth day of March next following, then the Vice-President shall act as President, as in the case of the death or other constitutional disability of the President. The person having the greatest number of votes as Vice-President, shall be the Vice-President, if such number be a majority of the whole number of electors appointed, and if no person have a majority, then from the two highest numbers on the list, the Senate shall choose the Vice-President; a quorum for the purpose shall consist of two-thirds of the whole number of Senators, and a majority of the whole number shall be necessary to a choice. But no person constitutionally ineligible to the office of President shall be eligible to that of Vice-President of the United States.

The Twelfth Amendment altered the Constitution's original procedures for holding presidential elections. Under Article II, the winner of a majority of Electoral College votes would become president, and the runner-up would become vice president. The election of 1800 exposed the peculiarity that if every member of the Electoral College voted for both members of a party ticket, each member of the most popular ticket would receive the same amount of votes, resulting in a deadlock. The Twelfth Amendment cured that flaw by requiring electors to cast separate votes for president and vice president, and by ensuring that if a deadlock occurred anyway and the House of Representatives failed to choose a president, then the candidate who received the highest number of votes on the vice presidential ballot would act as president (thus all vice presidents must be constitutionally eligible to serve as president).

Amendment XIII (1865)

Section 1. Neither slavery nor involuntary servitude, except as a punishment for crime whereof the party shall have been duly convicted, shall exist within the United States, or any place subject to their jurisdiction.

Section 2. Congress shall have power to enforce this article by appropriate legislation.

*The Thirteenth Amendment was the first of the three Civil War Amendments. It officially pro-
hibited slavery in all states, and with certain exceptions (such as in the case of convicts) involuntary servitude. Immediately prior to its ratification in December 1865, slavery remained
legal in only two states: Kentucky and Delaware. (Slavery in the former confederate states
had been outlawed by the Emancipation Proclamation of 1863.)*

Amendment XIV (1868)

Section 1. All persons born or naturalized in the United States, and subject
to the jurisdiction thereof, are citizens of the United States and of the state
wherein they reside. No state shall make or enforce any law which shall
abridge the privileges or immunities of citizens of the United States; nor shall
any state deprive any person of life, liberty, or property, without due process
of law; nor deny to any person within its jurisdiction the equal protection of
the laws.

Section 2. Representatives shall be apportioned among the several states according to their respective numbers, counting the whole number of persons in
each state, excluding Indians not taxed. But when the right to vote at any election
for the choice of electors for President and Vice President of the United States,
Representatives in Congress, the executive and judicial officers of a state, or the
members of the legislature thereof, is denied to any of the male inhabitants of
such state, being twenty-one years of age, and citizens of the United States, or in
any way abridged, except for participation in rebellion, or other crime, the basis
of representation therein shall be reduced in the proportion which the number of
such male citizens shall bear to the whole number of male citizens twenty-one
years of age in such state.

Section 3. No person shall be a Senator or Representative in Congress, or elector of President and Vice President, or hold any office, civil or military, under
the United States, or under any state, who, having previously taken an oath, as a
member of Congress, or as an officer of the United States, or as a member of any
state legislature, or as an executive or judicial officer of any state, to support the
Constitution of the United States, shall have engaged in insurrection or rebellion
against the same, or given aid or comfort to the enemies thereof. But Congress
may by a vote of two-thirds of each House, remove such disability.

Section 4. The validity of the public debt of the United States, authorized by
law, including debts incurred for payment of pensions and bounties for services
in suppressing insurrection or rebellion, shall not be questioned. But neither the
United States nor any state shall assume or pay any debt or obligation incurred in
aid of insurrection or rebellion against the United States, or any claim for the loss
or emancipation of any slave; but all such debts, obligations and claims shall be
held illegal and void.

Section 5. The Congress shall have power to enforce, by appropriate legislation, the provisions of this article.

The Fourteenth Amendment was ratified in an attempt to secure rights for freed slaves by broadening the definition of national citizenship and offering all persons equal protection of the law as well as due process of law from state governments. In the Slaughterhouse Cases (1873), the Supreme Court held that the privileges and immunities of national citizenship are actually quite limited: They include visiting the seat of government, petitioning Congress, using the nation's navigable waters, and other narrow privileges. By contrast, the equal protection clause provided the basis during the 20th century for dismantling legally enforced segregation in Brown v. Board of Education (1954) and other cases. It also has been used to extend equal protection to groups other than African Americans, including women and other ethnic minorities. Of equal significance, the Supreme Court has also interpreted the equal protection clause to require states to apportion their congressional districts and state legislative seats on a "one-person, one-vote" basis.

The due process clause has been interpreted to provide procedural safeguards before the government deprives a person of life, liberty, or property. More controversially, in the early part of the 20th century the Supreme Court in Lochner v. New York (1905) interpreted the clause as providing substantive protection to private contracts and other economic agreements. In later rulings the clause sparked considerable controversy when the Court used it as the basis for protecting substantive privacy rights not explicitly spelled out in the Constitution, such as that of a woman's right to an abortion (in the Court's 1973 Roe v. Wade decision), and of homosexual sodomy (in its 2003 ruling in Lawrence v. Texas).

Amendment XV (1870)

Section 1. The right of citizens of the United States to vote shall not be denied or abridged by the United States or by any state on account of race, color, or previous condition of servitude.

Section 2. The Congress shall have power to enforce this article by appropriate legislation.

The Fifteenth Amendment was ratified in order to enfranchise all the former male slaves. (As was the case with all women, former female slaves would have to wait for passage of the Nineteenth Amendment to gain the franchise as well.) Unfortunately, the promise of the franchise was subsequently undermined in many states by the proliferation of rigorous voter qualification laws, including literacy tests and poll taxes. Not until passage of the Voting Rights Act of 1965 and the elimination of poll taxes did the franchise become a reality for African American voters in many parts of the South.

Amendment XVI (1913)

The Congress shall have power to lay and collect taxes on incomes, from whatever source derived, without apportionment among the several states, and without regard to any census of enumeration.

The Sixteenth Amendment was ratified in response to the Supreme Court's controversial decision in Pollack v. Farmer's Loan & Trust Co. (1895), which held that a tax on incomes derived from property was a "direct tax." Prior to the Pollack case, income taxes had been considered "indirect" taxes, and thus well within the powers given to Congress by the Constitution. "Direct taxes," by contrast, could only be imposed if they were apportioned among the states according to each state's population (Article I, Section 9). The effect of the Pollack decision was to make an income tax all but impractical; the Sixteenth Amendment remedied the situation by placing income taxes back in the category of "indirect taxes."

Amendment XVII (1913)

The Senate of the United States shall be composed of two Senators from each state, elected by the people thereof, for six years; and each Senator shall have one vote. The electors in each state shall have the qualifications requisite for electors of the most numerous branch of the state legislatures.

When vacancies happen in the representation of any state in the Senate, the executive authority of such state shall issue writs of election to fill such vacancies: Provided, that the legislature of any state may empower the executive thereof to make temporary appointments until the people fill the vacancies by election as the legislature may direct.

This amendment shall not be so construed as to affect the election or term of any Senator chosen before it becomes valid as part of the Constitution.

The Seventeenth Amendment changed the method by which U.S. Senators were elected, overturning the provisions in Article I, Section 3. The amendment was the culmination of an extended effort of Progressive Era reformers at the beginning of the 20th century, who frequently targeted institutions marked by economic privilege and corrupt politics. Eventually they demanded that U.S. senators should be more responsive to the public will—the best way to accomplish that goal was to require that senators should be chosen by popular election, rather than by state legislatures. Prior to the amendment's ratification, many states had already amended their primary laws to allow a popular vote for party nominees, and a handful of states had bound their respective legislatures to select the candidate who received the highest number of popular votes in the general election. The Seventeenth Amendment soon followed, receiving the approval of the required number of states (three-fourths) less than a year after it was first introduced.

Amendment XVIII (1919)

Section 1. After one year from the ratification of this article the manufacture, sale, or transportation of intoxicating liquors within, the importation thereof into, or the exportation thereof from the United States and all territory subject to the jurisdiction thereof for beverage purposes is hereby prohibited.

Section 2. The Congress and the several states shall have concurrent power to enforce this article by appropriate legislation.

Section 3. This article shall be inoperative unless it shall have been ratified as an amendment to the Constitution by the legislatures of the several states, as provided in the Constitution, within seven years from the date of the submission hereof to the states by the Congress.

The Eighteenth Amendment slipped into the Constitution on the strength of efforts by the Anti-Saloon League and other groups who believed that intoxicating liquors were harmful and sinful. The amendment was proposed immediately after the end of World War I, and the Prohibition era began a year after its formal ratification on January 16, 1919.

Amendment XIX (1920)

The right of citizens of the United States to vote shall not be denied or abridged by the United States or by any state on account of sex.

Congress shall have power to enforce this article by appropriate legislation.

The Nineteenth Amendment was a reform spurred by the Progressive movement. Although women had been fighting for their right to vote since before the Civil War, the drive for woman suffrage started achieving success only with the entry of Western states such as Wyoming, which extended the right to vote to women upon its admission to the Union in 1890. (Five other Western states followed suit in subsequent decades.) By concentrating their efforts on a federal constitutional amendment guaranteeing women the right to vote, woman suffrage activists brought immediate pressure to bear on Congress and the president to support the movement. With momentum clearly on its side, the Nineteenth Amendment was ratified less than fifteen months after it was first proposed.

Amendment XX (1933)

Section 1. The terms of the President and Vice President shall end at noon on the 20th day of January, and the terms of Senators and Representatives at noon on the 3d day of January, of the years in which such terms would have ended if this article had not been ratified; and the terms of their successors shall then begin.

Section 2. The Congress shall assemble at least once in every year, and such meeting shall begin at noon on the 3d day of January, unless they shall by law appoint a different day.

Section 3. If, at the time fixed for the beginning of the term of the President, the President elect shall have died, the Vice President elect shall become President. If a President shall not have been chosen before the time fixed for the beginning of his term, or if the President elect shall have failed to qualify, then the Vice President elect shall act as President until a President shall have qualified; and the Congress may by law provide for the case wherein neither a President elect nor a Vice President elect shall have qualified, declaring who shall then act as President, or the manner in which one who is to act shall be selected, and such person shall act accordingly until a President or Vice President shall have qualified.

Section 4. The Congress may by law provide for the case of the death of any of the persons from whom the House of Representatives may choose a President whenever the right of choice shall have devolved upon them, and for the case of the death of any of the persons from whom the Senate may choose a Vice President whenever the right of choice shall have devolved upon them.

Section 5. Sections 1 and 2 shall take effect on the 15th day of October following the ratification of this article.

Section 6. This article shall be inoperative unless it shall have been ratified as an amendment to the Constitution by the legislatures of three-fourths of the several states within seven years from the date of its submission.

The Twentieth Amendment brought an end to the excessively long period of time between the November election and the March inauguration of a new president. Given advances in transportation and communications systems over the previous century, such a delay in the president taking office—with the outgoing president reluctant to act even during times of crisis—could no longer be justified. The amendment also limited Congress's lame duck sessions that followed the November elections: Newly elected members of Congress could now begin their service to constituents in early January, rather than waiting thirteen months until the following December. Finally, the amendment authorized Congress to provide for a line of succession in the event that neither a president-elect nor a vice-president-elect qualified to serve by the January 20th date.

Amendment XXI (1933)

Section 1. The eighteenth article of amendment to the Constitution of the United States is hereby repealed.

Section 2. The transportation or importation into any state, territory, or possession of the United States for delivery or use therein of intoxicating liquors, in violation of the laws thereof, is hereby prohibited.

Section 3. This article shall be inoperative unless it shall have been ratified as an amendment to the Constitution by conventions in the several states, as provided in the Constitution, within seven years from the date of the submission hereof to the states by the Congress.

The Twenty-first Amendment repealed Prohibition. The enforcement of the Eighteenth Amendment had proven too difficult and expensive, as thousands of illegal sources arose to meet the continuing public demand for alcohol. Crime gangs involved in the illegal liquor trade spread violence and bloodshed throughout the nation, pressuring politicians to end Prohibition. Finally, when both parties came out in favor of repeal during the 1932 election, Prohibition's days were clearly numbered. After the Twenty-first Amendment was ratified on December 5, 1933, states would thereafter have the exclusive power to prevent the import and use of liquor in their respective jurisdictions.

Amendment XXII (1951)

Section 1. No person shall be elected to the office of the President more than twice, and no person who has held the office of President, or acted as President, for more than two years of a term to which some other person was elected President shall be elected to the office of the President more than once. But this article shall not apply to any person holding the office of President when this article was proposed by the Congress, and shall not prevent any person who may be holding the office of President, or acting as President, during the term within which this article becomes operative from holding the office of President or acting as President during the remainder of such term.

Section 2. This article shall be inoperative unless it shall have been ratified as an amendment to the Constitution by the legislatures of three-fourths of the several states within seven years from the date of its submission to the states by the Congress.

Franklin Roosevelt's election to a record fourth term as president in 1944 sent politicians clamoring for a means of restoring the unwritten two-term tradition originally established by George Washington. Within two years of FDR's death, Congress proposed the Twenty-second Amendment, and it was adopted soon thereafter. In addition to setting a limit on the number of terms (two) to which a president may be elected, the amendment also sets a maximum of ten years less one day for a president to serve in the event he or she also succeeds to a part of another president's term. The amendment was worded so as not to apply to the then-sitting president, Harry S Truman, but it has applied to Dwight Eisenhower and all other presidents since.

Amendment XXIII (1961)

Section 1. The District constituting the seat of government of the United States shall appoint in such manner as the Congress may direct:

A number of electors of President and Vice President equal to the whole number of Senators and Representatives in Congress to which the District would be entitled if it were a state, but in no event more than the least populous state; they shall be in addition to those appointed by the states, but they shall be considered, for the purposes of the election of President and Vice President, to be electors appointed by a state; and they shall meet in the District and perform such duties as provided by the twelfth article of amendment.

Section 2. The Congress shall have power to enforce this article by appropriate legislation.

The Twenty-third Amendment cured the anomaly of U.S. citizens being denied the right to vote for federal officials (including president of the United States) so long as they remained permanent residents of the District of Columbia. Since ratification of the amendment in 1961, DC residents have been entitled to vote for presidential and vice-presidential candidates, but the amendment did not authorize residents of DC to elect members to either branch of Congress. Nor did it provide DC residents with home rule or the power to run their own local government. Since 1973 Congress has authorized the DC government to be run primarily by locally elected officials, subject to the oversight and supervision of Congress.

Amendment XXIV (1964)

Section 1. The right of citizens of the United States to vote in any primary or other election for President or Vice President, for electors for President or Vice President, or for Senator or Representative in Congress, shall not be denied or abridged by the United States or any state by reason of failure to pay any poll tax or other tax.

Section 2. The Congress shall have power to enforce this article by appropriate legislation.

The Twenty-fourth Amendment eliminated yet another vestige of legally enforced racism in the South and elsewhere. Many states had already eliminated the requirement that voters pay a tax before voting, a restriction that created an undue hardship on lower economic classes, including disproportionate numbers of racial minorities. Still, as late as 1964, five states (Alabama, Arkansas, Mississippi, Texas, and Virginia) continued to tie a poll tax to the voting privilege. In 1966 the Supreme Court ruled in Harper v. Board of Education that poll taxes also violated the equal protection clause of the Fourteenth Amendment.

Amendment XXV (1967)

Section 1. In case of the removal of the President from office or of his death or resignation, the Vice President shall become President.

Section 2. Whenever there is a vacancy in the office of the Vice President, the President shall nominate a Vice President who shall take office upon confirmation by a majority vote of both Houses of Congress.

Section 3. Whenever the President transmits to the President pro tempore of the Senate and the Speaker of the House of Representatives his written declaration that he is unable to discharge the powers and duties of his office, and until he transmits to them a written declaration to the contrary, such powers and duties shall be discharged by the Vice President as Acting President.

Section 4. Whenever the Vice President and a majority of either the principal officers of the executive departments or of such other body as Congress may by law provide, transmit to the President pro tempore of the Senate and the Speaker of the House of Representatives their written declaration that the President is unable to discharge the powers and duties of his office, the Vice President shall immediately assume the powers and duties of the office as Acting President.

Thereafter, when the President transmits to the President pro tempore of the Senate and the Speaker of the House of Representatives his written declaration that no inability exists, he shall resume the powers and duties of his office unless the Vice President and a majority of either the principal officers of the executive department or of such other body as Congress may by law provide, transmit within four days to the President pro tempore of the Senate and the Speaker of the House of Representatives their written declaration that the President is unable to discharge the powers and duties of his office. Thereupon Congress shall decide the issue, assembling within forty-eight hours for that purpose if not in session. If the Congress, within twenty-one days after receipt of the latter written declaration, or, if Congress is not in session, within twenty-one days after Congress is required to assemble, determines by two-thirds vote of both Houses that the President is unable to discharge the powers and duties of his office, the Vice President shall continue to discharge the same as Acting President; otherwise, the President shall resume the powers and duties of his office.

The Twenty-fifth Amendment clarified several ambiguous aspects of presidential succession. At the outset, it formalized an unwritten precedent first established by John Tyler, who succeeded to the presidency upon the death of William Henry Harrison in 1841: If the office of president becomes vacant because of the president's death or resignation, the vice president becomes president and assumes all powers and duties of the office. If the vice presidency is vacant, the amendment establishes new procedures for filling the position between elections:

the president nominates a successor, to be confirmed by a majority vote of both houses of Congress. Since its adoption in 1967, two vice presidents have been selected in this manner: Gerald Ford in 1973, and Nelson Rockefeller in 1974. When he succeeded to the presidency upon the resignation of Richard Nixon in 1974, Gerald Ford became the first—and to date, the only—president in American history to hold that office without being formally elected to either the presidency or the vice presidency.

The amendment also addresses the vexing problem of presidential disabilities. In the early 20th century, Woodrow Wilson was an invalid for more than a year of his presidency; in the 1950s, Dwight Eisenhower suffered a stroke once during each of his two terms in office. The Twenty-fifth Amendment addresses the problem of presidential disability by providing procedures for the president to temporarily discharge the duties and powers of the office to the officer next in line (normally the vice president), who then becomes "acting president." This has happened only twice: in 1985, when Vice President George H. W. Bush received a transmission of power temporarily while President Ronald Reagan underwent a minor medical procedure; and in 2002, when President George W. Bush temporarily transferred his powers to Vice President Dick Cheney while he underwent a colonoscopy. The amendment further authorizes the vice president and certain members of the executive branch to declare the president disabled or incapacitated, subject (within twenty-seven days) to Congress upholding the finding of incapacity. This final provision has never been invoked.

Amendment XXVI (1971)

Section 1. The right of citizens of the United States, who are 18 years of age or older, to vote, shall not be denied or abridged by the United States or any state on account of age.

Section 2. The Congress shall have the power to enforce this article by appropriate legislation.

The Twenty-sixth Amendment extended suffrage to those age eighteen and older. At the time of its passage, soldiers under the age of twenty-one were fighting in Vietnam, creating intense pressure on Congress and state legislatures to extend the vote to all those who were old enough to fight. The amendment does not apply to the denial of rights other than voting to those who are between eighteen and twenty-one years of age. Thus the National Minimum Drinking Age Act of 1984 obliges states to establish a twenty-one-year-old drinking age or risk the loss of federal highway funds. Additionally, Utah and Alaska have established nineteen as the minimum age for tobacco use.

Amendment XXVII (1992)

No law, varying the compensation for the services of the Senators and Representatives, shall take effect, until an election of Representatives shall have intervened.

The Twenty-seventh Amendment was intended to serve as a restraint on the power of Congress to raise its own pay—it may only do so if the raise takes effect after a subsequent general election. Although the Supreme Court has never ruled on the issue, lower courts have held this amendment does not prevent Congress from receiving cost of living adjustments immediately.

Federalism

3

PHOTO: MARK WILSON/GETTY IMAGES

Dueling Sovereign Powers in the United States: Now & Then

At the time of the nation's founding, worries about an excessively powerful central government threatening the states' sovereignty nearly brought a halt to the American experiment before it had even begun. Now it seemed like some of the Founders' worst fears were being realized, as Congress was attempting to interfere with a matter that until then had been under the strict control of state authorities. State authorities were divided on the issue in question; some were shocked at the federal intrusion, whereas others welcomed federal assistance in dealing with this difficult matter. Yet for those who favored federal influence, there was no basis in tradition or in the words of the Constitution, to support such unprecedented infringement in what appeared to be a strictly state matter. Ultimately, the courts stepped in to reassert state control over the matter, and the central government saw its hopes for influence frustrated, at least for the time being. Still, local officials had been put on notice that when Congress disagrees with a state action, that body will not stand by silently and defer without a struggle.

2005

2007   1987   1967   1947   1927

Now . . . It was a matter of family law, a subject traditionally controlled by state authorities. On March 31, 2005, forty-one-year-old Terri Schiavo died in a Florida hospice thirteen days after her feeding tube was removed by court order. Schiavo first went into respiratory and cardiac arrest in 1990; temporarily denied oxygen to her brain, she fell into a short-lived coma. Although she emerged from the coma after two and a half months, Terri Schiavo would live for the next fifteen years in a persistent vegetative state, exhibiting no awareness of her environment. In 1998, Schiavo's husband and legal guardian, Michael Schiavo, petitioned to remove his wife's feeding tube on the grounds that there was no longer any hope for his wife's recovery. His petition thrust him into a protracted legal dispute with his wife's parents. Michael claimed that his wife would never have wanted to be kept alive if she were in a vegetative state; Terri's parents disagreed, and they sought a series of stays against removal of any apparatus necessary to keep their daughter alive.

On September 17, 2003, after five years of hearings, trials, and back-and-forth court orders, a Florida state judge ordered the removal of the feeding tube; less than a month later, the order was executed. Just days after the tube was removed, Governor Jeb Bush ordered the tube to be reinserted in accordance with a new Florida law recently passed to give him that authority. Consistent with their earlier orders, the Florida courts struck down the law as unconstitutional and ordered the tube to be removed; the court's removal order was eventually reinstated on March 18, 2005. Yet at this point the unthinkable happened: federal authorities chose to insert themselves into the state proceedings. On March 21, 2005, President George W. Bush signed newly enacted legislation from Congress that transferred the case over to federal courts for what he hoped would be a different resolution. Unfortunately for Terri Schiavo's parents, this extra layer of federal court review proved no more fruitful once the U.S. Court of Appeals for the 11th Circuit refused to overturn the state court decision. Thus on March 31, 2005, Terri Schiavo died. In the final analysis, the decision over who had the power to determine the medical fate of a patient remained with the state judiciary, Congress's efforts notwithstanding.

1916

1907   1887   1867   1847   1827

Then . . .

The Terri Schiavo case was not the first instance in which the U.S. Congress intervened in a state matter when there was no legal precedent to do so. At the beginning of the twentieth century, many reformers were growing increasingly concerned about child labor. By some accounts as many as two million children, often as young as five or six years old, were working long hours in brutal conditions for barely any compensation. In response, state legislatures around the country began passing laws limiting or banning the use of child labor. The result was a patchwork quilt of state regulations, varying in their effectiveness. Reformers in Congress became frustrated with the slow pace of reform at the state level; they wanted uniform standards imposed immediately to prohibit child labor across the nation. But a string of judicial precedents dating back one hundred years cautioned that states alone had the constitutional power to regulate the manufacturing process. Congress tried a back-door approach to the problem by deploying its power to regulate interstate commerce under the Constitution: in 1916 it passed the Keating-Owen Child Labor Act, which banned the interstate transport of all goods made by children under age fourteen. Some state legislatures were stunned at this aggressive exercise of federal authority. But with its ruling in the case of *Hammer v. Dagenhart* (1918), the U.S. Supreme Court struck down the federal child labor law as unconstitutional. Consistent with its precedents, the Court held that Congress could not ban certain goods from entering interstate commerce if its intention in doing so was to regulate manufacturing.

Nineteen years later the Supreme Court—spurred in part by the harshness of the Great Depression and by the appointment of justices more disposed to defer to Congress—gave its approval to federal laws that regulated manufacturing, including new child labor laws. In the end Congress did have its say over the issue. Unfortunately for those who demanded a national solution to the problem of child labor law, conflict between federal and state sovereigns—interpreted by the Supreme Court to prohibit federal intervention in 1918—hamstrung the federal government for the better part of two decades.

Only once in the nation's history have state–federal tensions ignited an all-out military conflict among the parties: the U.S. Civil War of 1861–1865. There have been countless other incidents, however, when the tensions inherent in a system of dual sovereigns have given rise to conflicts between the federal government and state authority. In addition to the Terri Schiavo case in early 2005 and the battle over child labor laws in the early part of twentieth century, other examples of such conflicts include the protests by many Arizona state officials against a national movement to honor Martin Luther King Jr. with a federal holiday, the movement by Georgians to hoist a state flag with the controversial confederate symbol, and the efforts by Florida state officials to hinder federal attempts to return a young emigrant named Elian Gonzalez to his father's custody in Cuba. In all such instances, tempers eventually cooled and the crisis passed. Passed, but not soon forgotten.

What Is Federalism?

The term *federal* comes from the Latin *foedus,* which means a covenant, or an agreement linking different entities. A federal (or federated) system of government is one in which power is divided between a central authority and constituent political subunits. Both types of government are linked in order to provide for the pursuit of common ends; at the same time, each government maintains its own integrity. **Federalism** is the doctrine underlying such a system. It generally requires the existence of a central government tier and at least one major subnational tier of governments (usually referred to as "states" or "provinces"). Each tier is then assigned its own significant government powers. For a system of federalism to maintain itself, it must sustain this division of powers by whatever means possible, including—but not limited to—a resort to the courts to define the proper bounds of authority.

Perhaps the greatest challenge facing any federalist system is the task of determining **sovereignty,** defined as the supreme political power of a government to regulate its affairs without outside interference. In a system based on federalism, sovereignty resides not just in the central government, but also within each of the subunits or federated states, which in the case of the United States are the individual fifty states. Yet how can there be two separate sovereign governments sharing power over the exact same territory? The distribution of national and local responsibilities to more than one sovereign power depends on how the terms *national* and *local* are defined. These definitions are important, for a government based on federalism must both achieve national unity for certain overarching purposes and also preserve local governments' autonomy so they can respond to diverse subsets of citizens.

Related to these issues are complex questions concerning the nature of national citizenship. American federalism rests on the principle that two separate sovereigns—the state government and the federal government—both exert authority over the individual. But can an individual citizen really be subject to two separate sovereign governments at the same time? U.S. citizens have official status as citizens both of the state where they reside and of the nation as a whole. Many take pride in *both* associations. What remains unclear are the obligations and duties that dual citizenship requires. Is national citizenship every citizen's primary form of identification? To which sovereign government is the citizen obligated when the nation and individual states are in conflict? Although these conceptual difficulties tend to be unique to a federal system, there are other forms of government that involve multiple governments or tiers of government, and these alternative forms have significant problems of their own.

Comparing Federalism to Other Systems of Government

A federal system of government can be thought of as existing on a continuum of forms of government. At one end of the continuum is a **confederation** (or "confederacy"), defined as a league of two or more independent states that unite to achieve certain specified common aims. Those aims may be quite limited, as is often the case with offensive or defensive military alliances. For example, the Articles of Confederation, which prescribed the rules of government for the newly independent colonies until 1788, featured thirteen states entering into "a firm league of friendship with each other, for their common defense, the security of their liberties, and their mutual and general welfare. . . ." Recently the European Community, a collection of European nations united in a commercial alliance, has acquired its own status as a type of confederation.[1] Similarly, the United Nations is a league of countries from around the world that work together to enforce various provisions of international law. Although a confederation may be a useful arrangement to achieve some aims, it can result in political chaos, as when separate member countries bound only by limited rules strike out on their own at critical times, often to the detriment of the larger confederation.

---

[1] Stanley R. Sloan, *NATO, The European Union and the Atlantic Community: The Transatlantic Bargain Reconsidered* (New York: Rowman & Littlefield, 2002).

★ **Federalism**

The doctrine underlying a system of government in which power is divided between a central government and constituent political subunits.

★ **Sovereignty**

The supreme political power of a government to regulate its affairs without outside interference.

★ **Confederation**

A system of government (or "league") in which two or more independent states unite to achieve certain specified common aims.

Figure 3.1 Comparing Systems of Government

The three figures below illustrate the most common configurations for (1) federal systems of government, (2) unitary systems of government, and (3) confederate systems of government. The directions of the arrows indicate the relationship that exists between the different forms of government. Note the two-way arrows found in the federal system.

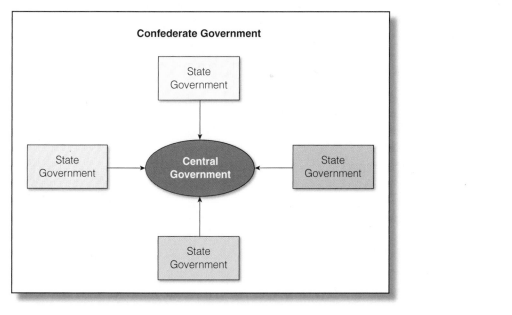

At the other end of the continuum is a **unitary system of government,** which subordinates the independent aims of constituent states (if any even exist) to the goals of the central whole. Although individual states within such a government may enjoy some form of representation in the central legislature (such as through the election of state senators) and may even assert their own systems of municipal law, sovereignty rests in the central government alone, with states exerting authority over citizens only through the larger government entity. Of the Western industrialized nations, Great Britain and France come closest to this unitary government ideal, with their provinces and subunits having little or no power independent of the national government. Problems with a unitary system of government often arise from the tendency toward *hypercentralism,* that is, the more or less complete reliance on the central government and the extinguishing of individual state differences. Such a system often hampers local officials from responding to the particular needs of their varying constituencies.

As Figure 3.1 on the previous page illustrates, a federal system of government sits in the middle of this continuum, granting its member states significant power but still subordinating them to the national government in critical instances. James Madison believed this federal system was the preferred "middle ground" of government types. At least twenty countries today, including Canada, Germany, Australia, and Switzerland, may be characterized as federal systems. It is the United States' brand of federalism, however—first established with the ratification of the Constitution in 1788—that represents the most significant breakthrough in the evolution of this government type among modern nation-states.

Table 3.1 The Powers of the Federal and State Governments under the Constitution

Federal Government Powers (Enumerated Powers)	State Government Powers (Reserved Powers)	Concurrent Powers (Shared Powers)
Borrow money on U.S. credit	Regulate intrastate commerce	Spend money for general welfare
Regulate foreign commerce	Regulate state militias	Regulate interstate commerce
Regulate commerce with Indian nations	Conduct elections/qualify voters	Establish bankruptcy laws
Conduct foreign affairs	Regulate safety/health/morals	Lay and collect taxes
Coin money/punish counterfeiting	Ratify amendments	Charter/regulate banks
Establish courts inferior to Supreme Court		Establish courts
Establish post offices		Establish highways
Establish patent/copyright laws		Take private property for public purposes (with compensation)
Define/punish high-seas offenses		
Declare war		
Raise and support armies, navy		
Call forth militias		
Govern District of Columbia matters		
Admit new states to union		
Establish rules of naturalization		

Government Powers in a Federal System

Under the U.S. Constitution, the national government of the United States was formed to serve a community of thirteen states, and each state delegated to the new central government significant powers while retaining full powers within its own constitutionally designated sphere of authority. The Framers of this new government relied on no overarching philosophy or political theory in designing this federalist form of government; federalism was simply a political compromise calculated to build consensus among them. The powers delegated to Congress under Article I of the Constitution are called enumerated powers. The powers retained by the states are **reserved powers.** And the powers shared by the federal and state governments are generally referred to as **concurrent powers** (see Table 3.1).

Article I, Section 8 enumerates the specific powers held by the national legislature. Among these are economic powers such as the authority to levy and collect taxes, borrow money, coin money, and regulate interstate commerce and bankruptcies; military powers such as the authority to provide for the common defense, declare war, raise and support armies and navies, and regulate the militia; and legislative powers such as the authority to establish regulations governing immigration and naturalization. Congress also enjoys the prerogative to make laws that are "necessary and proper" to carry out these foregoing powers.[2]

On its face, the Constitution appears to draw clear and explicit lines between the powers afforded the state and national governments. In brief, the national government is to assume responsibility for great matters of national importance, including the protection of national economic interests, relations with other countries, and the military security of the United States. All local and/or internal matters—including the health, safety, and welfare of citizens—were to be to the province of state governments. Indeed, in a delayed victory for states' rights advocates who had opposed the new Constitution, the Tenth Amendment restates this fundamental division of powers: that any specific power not assigned to the federal government by the Constitution may be exercised by the states, unless the Constitution prohibits the states from exercising that power.

The Framers of the Constitution believed that Congress should legislate only within its enumerated powers under Article I; in their view the **necessary and proper clause** (later referred to as the elastic clause) was *not* to be used as an instrument to expand federal legislative authority unnecessarily. Yet within a few years, competing views of the necessary and proper clause would arise, giving the national government far more discretion in determining how to carry out its enumerated powers.

★ Reserved powers

Those powers expressly retained by the state governments under the Constitution.

★ Concurrent powers

Those powers shared by the federal and state governments under the Constitution.

★ Necessary and proper clause

The clause in Article I, Section 8 of the Constitution that affords Congress the power to make laws that serve as a means to achieving its expressly delegated powers.

---

[2] See *McCulloch v. Maryland,* 17 U.S. 316 (1819).

The Supremacy Clause

★ Supremacy clause

The provision in Article VI, Paragraph 2 of the Constitution that
provides that the Constitution
and federal laws override any
conflicting provisions in state
constitutions or state laws.

Overlaying this explicit system of enumerated powers for Congress and reserved powers for the states is the **supremacy clause** of Article VI, which provides that the Constitution and the laws passed by Congress shall be "the supreme law of the land," overriding any conflicting provisions in state constitutions or state laws. The supremacy clause gives special weight to the federal Constitution by ensuring that it cannot be interpreted differently from state to state. In the landmark case of ***Martin v. Hunter's Lessee* (1819),**[3] the U.S. Supreme Court rejected the Virginia Supreme Court's attempt to interpret the federal Constitution in a way that conflicted with the U.S. Supreme Court's own rulings. Accordingly, each state legislature and state judiciary not only

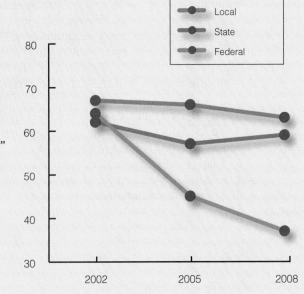

American Government . . . in Popular Perspective:
Comparing Views of Federal, State, and Local Government

Surveys conducted by the Pew Research Center for the People and the Press monitor Americans' views of the performance of federal, state, and local governments. As the figure below demonstrates, Americans hold their local and state governments in fairly high esteem. However, positive views of the federal government in 2008 were at their lowest point in at least a decade. Only 37 percent of people said they held a favorable view of the federal government, while 58 percent expressed an unfavorable opinion. By contrast, 59 percent held favorable views of their state governments and 63 percent held favorable views of their local governments.

Favorability ratings of the federal government in Washington tumbled during 2008. As recently as January 2007, as many Americans offered a favorable (45 percent) as unfavorable (46 percent) opinion. In December 2002, favorable opinions of the federal government outnumbered unfavorable opinions by more than two-to-one (64 percent vs. 27 percent).

"Now, I'd like your opinion of some organizations and institutions. . . . is your overall opinion of (the federal government/your state government/your local government) very favorable, mostly favorable, mostly unfavorable, or very unfavorable?"

[3] 14 U.S. 304 (1816).

must abide by the terms of the federal Constitution; it must also abide by the interpretation of those terms laid out by the U.S. Supreme Court.

The language of the supremacy clause also gives rise to the doctrine of preemption. When Congress exercises power granted to it under Article I, the federal law it creates may supersede state laws, in effect "preempting" state authority. In practice, when a federal law clearly bars state action, the doctrine of **preemption** is relatively uncontroversial. For example, when the federal government acted to regulate the commercial advertising of tobacco products, it essentially "occupied the field," and all state rules governing tobacco advertising immediately gave way to the new federal standard. But when Congress enacts a law that does not clearly articulate its intentions with regard to state laws, a court may have to decide whether the doctrine of preemption applies, subject to later court review. In addition, Congress's lack of action within its enumerated powers opens the door to limited state regulations. For example, a state government can enact transportation regulations affecting truck drivers in the state so long as Congress has not passed any similar laws, and the state law does not burden interstate commerce.

Relations Between the States

A federalist system must not only manage relations between the state governments and the federal government; it must also arbitrate disagreements among member states. A feature of American federalism in this regard is the requirement that individual states must respect the civil laws of all other states, as guaranteed by the **full faith and credit clause** of Article IV, Section 1 of the Constitution. This clause provides that each state abide by the decisions of other state and local governments, including their judicial proceedings. This clause acts to assure stability in commercial and personal relations that extend beyond one state's borders. For example, contracts duly entered into in California under the laws of that state cannot simply be ignored or invalidated by the courts in Arizona or any other state. Similarly, when an unhappy married couple meets the legal requirements of divorce in one state and ends their marriage, they are not required to meet new divorce requirements in other states, as the divorce decree of one state must be recognized as valid by every other state.

In recent years, the proliferation of more controversial family law provisions, such as gay marriage or "civil union" laws in seven separate states and the District of Columbia,[4] has placed considerable strain on the full faith and credit clause of Article IV. On July 1, 2000, Vermont became the first state in the nation to provide for same-sex "civil unions." In the first year after the law was passed, more than eighteen hundred couples obtained civil union certificates, with two-thirds of those couples traveling to Vermont from out of state. Since then six other states and the District of Columbia have passed similar civil union laws, which attempt to extend to same-sex couples in the state nearly the same rights and privileges as those enjoyed by married heterosexual couples, especially with regard to inheritance laws, applications for insurance, the distribution of state pensions, and medical care decision making.

Though controversial, civil union laws have provoked far less outrage from political majorities than full-fledged gay marriage laws, which allow same-sex couples to gain formal state recognition on an equal plane with everyone else under the traditionally accepted institution of "marriage." Opponents of same-sex marriage contend that equating same-sex and opposite-sex marriage in this way changes the meaning of marriage and its

Gay marriage ceremony in Massachusetts.

★ *Martin v. Hunter's Lessee* (1819)

The Supreme Court case that established that state governments and state courts must abide by the U.S. Supreme Court's interpretation of the federal Constitution.

★ Preemption

The constitutional doctrine that holds that when Congress acts affirmatively in the exercise of its own granted power, federal laws supersede all state laws on the matter.

★ Full faith and credit clause

The provision in Article IV, Section 1 of the Constitution that forces states to abide by the official acts and proceedings of all other states.

---

[4] David Moats, *Civil Wars: The Battle for Gay Marriage* (New York: Harvest Books, 2005).

traditions. Massachusetts, Connecticut, and California are the only three states to have formally recognized same-sex marriage. (At the time this book went to press, California's law was in flux, as voters in the state narrowly passed a constitutional amendment overturning the right in 2008.)

Even though the full faith and credit clause has traditionally required states to respect the public proceedings of every other state, many state legislatures have attempted to prevent homosexual couples from asserting their newfound status as married couples. At least thirty states have passed laws denying recognition to same-sex marriages. Legislatures in most other states, including some of those that have sanctioned civil unions, considered but ultimately failed to pass laws of their own that would have denied legal recognition to such out-of-state, same-sex marriages. In denying this recognition, these states enjoy the support of Congress, which in 1996 passed the Defense of Marriage Act, which authorizes any state to deny a "marriage-like" relationship between persons of the same sex, even when such unions are recognized by another state. As a further sign of the heated feelings over this issue, in the 2004 election, voters in eleven states approved referenda preventing gay marriages in their own states, putting them squarely at odds with Massachusetts. Ultimately, the U.S. Supreme Court may have to determine whether the Defense of Marriage Act and similar laws at the state level evade the full faith and credit clause of the Constitution.

Another clause that provides for the equal treatment of out-of state citizens is the privileges and immunities clause of Article IV. Through this clause, which guarantees that the citizens of each state are "entitled to all Privileges and Immunities of Citizens in the several States," the Constitution protects the rights of every citizen to travel through other states, to reside in any state, and to participate in trade, agriculture, and professional pursuits in any state.[5] Some states have tried to limit bar memberships to in-state residents, or to impose hefty commuter taxes on out-of-staters who cross state lines each day for work. Such legislative efforts potentially conflict with the privileges and immunities clause. Article IV also provides that the criminal laws of individual states must be respected across state lines. When a criminal in one state escapes to another state, he or she is normally "extradited" or handed over to the original state either to stand trial or to complete a previously imposed sentence.

Ellis Island.

Article III, Section 2 of the Constitution gives the U.S. Supreme Court the authority to decide disputes between states. Although such jurisdiction is rarely exercised, the Court has taken its responsibility to arbitrate state conflicts seriously on those occasions when it has been asked to do so. So when officials in New York and New Jersey were battling in the late 1990s over which of those two states could claim sovereign authority over Ellis Island, the site where millions of immigrants to the United States were initially processed, the Supreme Court authorized a fact-finding investigation on the issue. Presented with the evidence of that investigation, the Court ruled that Ellis Island lay within the state boundaries of New Jersey—news no doubt to the millions of immigrants who thought they had disembarked in New York.[6] The Framers of the Constitution believed it was critically important that the highest federal court enjoy the power to arbitrate disputes between state governments, a key component of American federalism.

The History of American Federalism

In the more than two centuries that have passed since the ratification of the Constitution, different conceptions of federalism have prevailed during different eras. Some of these shifting patterns in state–federal relations were inevitable given the changing state of the nation and the increasingly important role it would play in world politics. The dominance of a global economy in the late twentieth and early twenty-first centuries, changing patterns in population growth, and techno-

[5] For example, in *Supreme Court of New Hampshire v. Piper,* 470 U.S. 274 (1985), the Supreme Court interpreted the privileges and immunities clause of Article IV to forbid states from excluding nonresidents from admission to the practice of law.
[6] See *New Jersey v. New York,* 523 U.S. 767 (1998).

State Legislatures Staffed with Professionals

America's federalist system relies on state and local governments to perform many functions on behalf of citizens. State legislatures are a key engine in the process, passing laws and overseeing state agencies charged with implementing those laws. Unfortunately, state legislatures are not all equally equipped to meet the many challenges of modern governance; in fact, their memberships vary widely in their professional-ism and time spent on the job. Some large states like California employ legislators and staffs all year long, whereas smaller state legislatures are often in session just three months or less per year. Below is a list of the only ten states that have full-time, well-staffed, well-paid legislatures in session for almost ten months per year or longer. (Note that Texas, one of the more populated states in the union, does not appear on this list.)

✔	California	✔	New Jersey
✔	Florida	✔	New York
✔	Illinois	✔	Ohio
✔	Massachusetts	✔	Pennsylvania
✔	Michigan	✔	Wisconsin

logical developments in communication and transportation all spurred wholesale re-examination of the nature of federal and state governmental functions. Various government figures—presidents, Supreme Court justices, and members of Congress—have also played a role in shaping the nature of federalism. The flexibility of the federalist system has allowed it to adapt to changing circumstances.

Although a clear delineation of periods may oversimplify history, scholars have identified at least five eras of American federalism: (1) state-centered federalism, 1789–1819; (2) national supremacy period, 1819–1837; (3) dual federalism, 1837–1937; (4) cooperative federalism, 1937–1990; and (5) the "new federalism," 1990–present. Each of these periods is defined by some shift in the power relationship between the national and state governments.

State-Centered Federalism, 1789–1819

The Framers' vision of federalism was relatively clear at the time the Constitution was ratified: other than in those policy areas clearly identified as subject to the national government's control (the military, foreign affairs, creation of currency, and so on), state governments would have full sovereignty over all other matters. Indeed, it is tough to imagine the Constitution being ratified by the requisite number of states had it called for any further subordination of traditional state authority. And with some notable exceptions, the national government's reach was exceedingly limited during the first thirty years of the Constitution's history.[7] At the urging of Treasury Secretary Alexander Hamilton, the Washington administration cautiously undertook some first steps in nationwide economic planning when it chartered the first National Bank of the United States and the federal government assumed all the debts of the state governments. Nevertheless, during this earliest period of federalism states remained the principal authority for American citizens. For the most part, each state managed its own affairs, often with little interference from the federal government.

---

[7] Stanley Elkins and Eric McKitrick, *The Age of Federalism: The Early American Republic 1788–1800* (New York: Oxford University Press, 1995).

President Thomas Jefferson took office in 1801 on the strength of a campaign in which his party, the Democratic-Republicans, offered to curtail the national government's occasional excesses, such as its passage of the Alien and Sedition Acts of 1798, which (among other things) punished individuals who criticized the national government. Jefferson articulated his own "principled distaste" for centralized authority. Notwithstanding his administration's authorization of funds to purchase the Louisiana Territory from France for $15 million, thereby doubling the size of the United States and speeding westward development, federal government functions during Jefferson's administration were usually linked to enumerated national powers. State governments exercised a nearly exclusive role in the administration of education, family and criminal law, civil and property rights, elections, and labor relations during this same period.

National Supremacy Period, 1819–1837

Just before leaving office in 1801, President John Adams installed as chief justice of the United States a fellow nationalist, John Marshall of Virginia. That appointment may have been the most significant act of Adams's presidency; although the Federalists would never again occupy the White House or control Congress, the national government–oriented party would influence American politics through Chief Justice Marshall for the next three decades.

Marshall's **national supremacy doctrine** of federalism is most evident in the Supreme Court decision in **McCulloch v. Maryland (1819),** 17 U.S. 316 (1819), which concerned the National Bank of the United States. As secretary of the treasury during the Washington administration, Alexander Hamilton successfully pushed for Congress to charter the first bank of the United States in 1792, arguing that such an institution would help provide for a sound national currency and a national system of credit. Thomas Jefferson, then secretary of state, and James Madison opposed the bank, believing that the Constitution gave Congress no authority to charter such a bank. Consequently when the bank's twenty-year charter expired, the Jeffersonian Republican-controlled Congress declined to recharter it. Recognizing that the lack of a national bank had hindered American efforts to obtain needed financial resources throughout the War of 1812, many in the Democratic-Republican Party, including Madison, who was now president, swallowed their pride and supported the chartering of a second national bank in 1816.

The bank still remained unpopular in many states where state-chartered banks were forced to compete (often unsuccessfully) with local branches of the National Bank for business and influence. The Maryland legislature passed a law that levied taxes on the notes of all banks—including the Baltimore branch of the National Bank—that were not chartered by the state. When James W. McCulloch, the cashier for the National Bank's Baltimore branch, refused to pay the tax, Maryland sued and won in its own state courts, setting up a monumental showdown on the future of the bank in the U.S. Supreme Court.

Writing for a unanimous 7–0 Supreme Court on March 6, 1819, Chief Justice John Marshall upheld the constitutionality of the bank. According to Marshall, the necessary and proper clause of the Constitution gave Congress the power to do nearly anything it wanted, so long as it was a means to exercising their expressly delegated powers, which included the power to borrow money and regulate interstate commerce. The Maryland tax amounted to an unconstitutional interference with national supremacy. "The power to tax involves the power to destroy," the Court declared. Marshall used the occasion of the Court's ruling to articulate a broad vision of the national government's power, asserting that the national government could exercise its powers flexibly to meet the unexpected problems of changing national times. "This . . . is . . . a constitution we are expounding," Marshall noted, "intended to endure for ages to come, and consequently, to be adapted to the various crises of human affairs." According to Marshall, the Constitution altered the position of the states; no longer were they sovereign entities on a par with the federal government. Within the sphere of its own powers, Congress was supreme.

★ National supremacy doctrine

Chief Justice John Marshall's interpretation of federalism as holding that states have extremely limited sovereign authority, whereas Congress is supreme within its own sphere of constitutional authority.

★ *McCulloch v. Maryland* (1819)

The Supreme Court case that established that Congress enjoys broad and extensive authority to make all laws that are "necessary and proper" to carry out its constitutionally delegated powers.

Marshall's Court also refuted the power of state courts to interpret and apply the Constitution in ways that conflicted with the Supreme Court's own interpretations. Thus the Constitution assumed its status as the uniform governing law of all the states. To Marshall, the Court's duty was not to preserve state sovereignty, but rather "to protect national power against state encroachments." Consistent with this view, the Marshall Court routinely interpreted Congress's legislative authority quite broadly. In **Gibbons v. Ogden (1824),**[8] for example, the Court invalidated a monopoly granted by the New York legislature covering the operation of steamboats in New York waters, because the New York monopoly was in conflict with a federal license.

The national supremacy doctrine articulated by Marshall was not without its critics. State politicians accused the Court of ignoring the sovereign power of the states. Some national politicians were no less sympathetic. As president, Andrew Jackson opposed the National Bank and all internal improvements (such as the building of roads or canals) ordered by Congress as unconstitutional. He even vetoed a rechartering of the bank in 1832. Yet, at the same time, he also applied Marshall's national supremacy doctrine in defending the Tariff of 1828. After Congress passed a highly protectionist tariff over the objections of Southern free-trade adherents, the South Carolina legislature adopted a series of resolutions negating the tariff on the theory that state sovereignty allowed each state to nullify any law passed by Congress that the state deemed unconstitutional. (New Englanders had used that same argument during the War of 1812 when a convention of the region's states met in Hartford, Connecticut in early 1815 and endorsed the right of states to interpose themselves against "dangerous infractions" of the Constitution by the federal government.) In response to the action by South Carolina, President Jackson declared that such a nullification was an "impractical absurdity" and rejected the right of individual states to refuse to obey federal laws. A call by South Carolina Senator John Calhoun and others for a "general convention of the states" to reconsider state–federal relations, including possible secession from the Union, elicited enthusiasm from numerous Southern states, but eventually the nullification crisis passed when Congress approved a compromise tariff that progressively lowered rates until they reached the same level they had been at in 1816.[9]

Portrait of John Calhoun, circa 1830.

★ *Gibbons v. Ogden* (1824)

The Supreme Court case that held that a federal license to operate steamboats overrides a state-granted monopoly of New York water rights under the Constitution.

Dual Federalism, 1837–1937

Marshall's successor as chief justice, Roger B. Taney of Maryland (1836–1864), dedicated much of his twenty-eight-year tenure on the Court to rearticulating a vision of federalism more consistent with that of the Framers. Significantly, Taney did not overturn decisions of the Marshall Court asserting the authority of the Supreme Court over state judiciaries to interpret the Constitution, nor did he deny the broad power to regulate interstate commerce that Marshall had announced in *Gibbons v. Ogden*. The Taney Court was not a radical champion of state sovereignty. But Taney did abandon the more sweeping aspects of the national supremacy doctrine, which had heralded the federal government as "superior" to state governments. Instead, he maintained that the Constitution was a "compact of sovereign states," with the powers reserved to the states by the Tenth Amendment serving as a limit on congressional power. In a series of cases in the 1840s and 1850s, the Taney Court raised the status of state involvement in contract and corporate affairs. For example, in *Cooley v. Board of Wardens of the Port of Philadelphia* (1852),[10] the Court upheld a Pennsylvania statute imposing a fee on vessels that passed through the port of Philadelphia because the fee went into a fund for the relief of

---

[8] 22 U.S. 1 (1824).
[9] H. W. Brands, *Andrew Jackson: His Life and Times* (New York: Doubleday, 2005).
[10] 53 U.S. 299 (1852).

pilots and pilots' widows, and was thus deemed a "local subject." Even though the fee affected interstate and international commerce to a degree, the nature of the subject matter counseled against a rigid interpretation that favored national supremacy.

Although slavery was a crucial component of the fight between the Union and the Confederacy, the Civil War was at its core a struggle about the relationship between the states and the federal government. The Union's victory undermined dual federalism's "compact of states" premise by rejecting the authority of states to leave the compact. Then, in a series of cases handed down after the Civil War, a newly constituted Supreme Court acknowledged national power and congressional authority to set the terms for readmitting former Confederate states into the Union. This power was considered an outgrowth of Congress's exclusive and unquestioned authority not only to regulate the territories of the United States, but also to oversee the admission of new states to the Union. With twenty-four of the fifty states joining the Union between 1836 and 1912 (see Figure 3.2), admission to statehood was an important function of the federal government during this period.

Figure 3.2 Admission of States to the Union

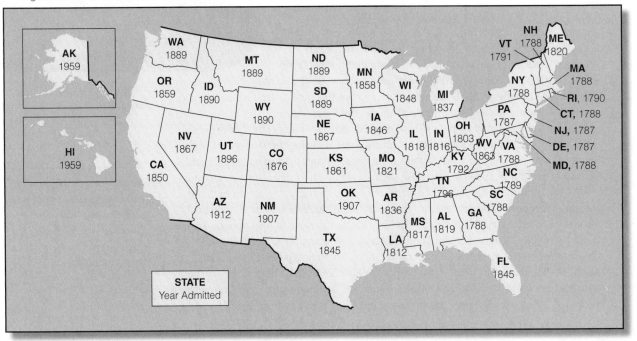

★ Dual federalism

The doctrine of federalism that holds that state authority acts as a limit on congressional power under the Constitution.

Under **dual federalism,** however, the states did retain considerable authority to regulate economic affairs that were not directly within the "stream of commerce" between two or more states, including matters concerning the manufacturing of products and the health and safety of factory workers. Ignoring *McCulloch v. Maryland*, the Supreme Court refused to give Congress the discretionary authority it enjoyed during the era of the national supremacy doctrine. Regulatory legislation passed by Congress, such as the child labor laws referenced in the opening section of this chapter, was set aside as unconstitutional. Once again the Court had greatly diminished the scope of the necessary and proper clause. Despite the onset of the Industrial Revolution, Congress was eventually rendered helpless to regulate the abuses of some businesses. Later, in the 1930s, the Court struck down a series of New Deal laws implementing pension and retirement systems for workers and regulating industrial relations.[11] In this way, dual federalism prevented Congress from addressing the hardships brought on by the Great Depression.

[11] *Railroad Retirement Board v. Alton Railroad Co.,* 295 U.S. 330 (1935); *Carter v. Carter Coal Co.,* 298 U.S. 238 (1936).

Cooperative Federalism, 1937–1990

Faced with judicial opposition to New Deal policies regulating the workplace, retirement policies, and other subjects traditionally ceded to the states, President Franklin D. Roosevelt (FDR) and his supporters grew increasingly frustrated. To them, the economic hardships of the Great Depression demanded an activist federal government, and a conservative Supreme Court now stood in the way. FDR and his allies in Congress proposed expanding the size of the Supreme Court from nine to fifteen, which would allow Roosevelt to "pack" the Supreme Court with advocates of a broader vision of federal legislative power.[12] The proposed "court-packing plan" became unnecessary, however. As public frustration with the Court was mounting, one or two members of the Court in 1937 suddenly did an about-face, abandoning dual federalist principles in favor of a more expansive view of congressional authority. A shift in just one vote had a significant impact; a shift in two votes on the Supreme Court meant that nearly all federal legislation would now survive high-court scrutiny. Once Roosevelt was able to add his own judicial appointees to the mix, the Court as a whole was ready to support unprecedented exercises of congressional power.

Social scientists speak of the post–New Deal period as marking a shift from **layer cake federalism** in which the authority of state and federal governments is distinct and more easily delineated, to a system of **marble cake federalism** in which state and federal authority are intertwined in an inseparable mixture. This new era, later labeled as the period of **cooperative federalism,** in some ways harkened back to the national supremacy doctrine articulated by John Marshall. Congress once again became the judge of its own powers, including those powers implied under the necessary and proper clause. Congress could, for example, restrict the activities of labor unions, criminalize loan sharking, or enact any policy under the theory that it may be "necessary and proper" to exercise enumerated powers such as the power to regulate interstate commerce. The limits on congressional power under so-called cooperative federalism were thus quite small: so long as some link to commerce could be offered, for example, no matter how tenuous such a link might be, Congress remained free to exert its authority over the states. When Congress passed civil rights laws in 1964 under the premise that racial discrimination in restaurants and hotels "burdened" interstate commerce, the Supreme Court barely batted an eye at what was in fact an extremely broad reading of congressional authority.[13]

Cooperative federalism, however, can be distinguished from Marshall's doctrine of national superiority. Whenever concurrent legislative power is exercised, Congress can act in one of three ways. It can:

1. preempt the states altogether and assert exclusive control over the subject matter

2. leave the states to act on their own

3. provide that the operation of its own law depends on or is qualified by existing state laws

This last category provides an opening in state–federal relationships that even Marshall could not have anticipated: the possibility that the federal government might actually enlist state officials and other state actors to implement federal policies.

The positive aspects of cooperative federalism are obvious. The expansion of the central government beginning in the 1930s into the $2.5 trillion per year behemoth that it is today means that federal officials now have huge sums of money at their disposal. Individual states can benefit from this pool of funds whenever the federal government passes on some of its revenues directly to the states to initiate and administer programs. **Grants-in-aid** from the federal government to the states

★ Layer cake federalism

Description of federalism as maintaining that the authority of state and federal governments exists in distinct and separate spheres.

★ Marble cake federalism

Description of federalism as intertwining state and federal authority in an inseparable mixture.

★ Cooperative federalism

The doctrine of federalism that affords Congress nearly unlimited authority to exercise its powers through means that often coerce states into administering and/or enforcing federal policies.

★ Grants-in-aid

Grants from the federal government to states that allow state governments to pursue specific federal policies such as highway construction.

---

[12] William E. Leuchtenburg, *The Supreme Court Reborn: The Constitutional Revolution in the Age of Roosevelt.* (New York: Oxford University Press, 1995), pp. 132–162.
[13] *Heart of Atlanta Motel v. United States*, 379 U.S. 241 (1964); *Katzenbach v. McClung*, 379 U.S. 294 (1964).

have been used to fund state educational initiatives, build roads, and provide unemployment relief, among other programs that fulfill purposes expressly approved by Congress and/or its federal regulatory agencies. Federal grants also help balance the economic inequities that arise because states have vastly different tax bases. Occasionally the federal government has transformed grants-in-aid, which are allocated

Figure 3.3 Comparing Federal Expenditures to State Expenditures The system of federalism dictates that the federal government, not the states, must provide national defense. By contrast, state expenditures focus on educational expenses, criminal justice, and social services in particular. Although different systems of categorization make budget comparisons among governments difficult, a glimpse of the budgets of the federal government and two state governments provides some interesting insights as to where your tax dollars are going . . . or not going.

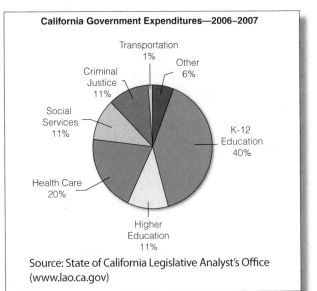

California Government Expenditures—2006–2007

- Transportation 1%
- Other 6%
- Criminal Justice 11%
- Social Services 11%
- Health Care 20%
- Higher Education 11%
- K-12 Education 40%

Source: State of California Legislative Analyst's Office (www.lao.ca.gov)

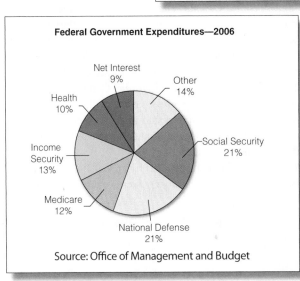

Federal Government Expenditures—2006

- Net Interest 9%
- Other 14%
- Health 10%
- Social Security 21%
- Income Security 13%
- Medicare 12%
- National Defense 21%

Source: Office of Management and Budget

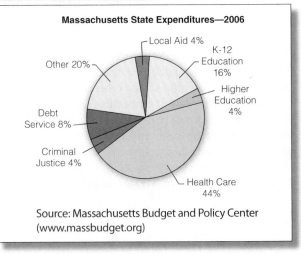

Massachusetts State Expenditures—2006

- Local Aid 4%
- K-12 Education 16%
- Other 20%
- Higher Education 4%
- Debt Service 8%
- Criminal Justice 4%
- Health Care 44%

Source: Massachusetts Budget and Policy Center (www.massbudget.org)

only for specific programs or policies, into **block grants,** which a state or local government may use at its discretion for more generalized programs.

The collaboration between state governments and the federal government in the era of cooperative federalism also carried some negative implications for state sovereignty. Federal government officials increasingly insisted that federal appropriations to the states be accompanied by various conditions. Often these consisted of "protective conditions," designed to ensure that the state would administer its program consistent with the objectives of Congress. For example, Congress required that states receiving educational assistance meet federal requirements for educating handicapped children, including the creation of individualized education programs for special needs students. On occasion, however, Congress has imposed coercive burdens on states that increasingly rely on such federal assistance. In 1984, for example, Congress passed the National Minimum Drinking Age Amendment, which withheld 5 percent of federal highway funds from any state "in which the purchase or public possession of any alcoholic beverage by a person who is less than 21 years of age" is lawful. The purpose of the law was to decrease the number of serious automobile accidents among those aged eighteen to twenty—statistics showed that this group was responsible for a high percentage of accidents on the nation's highways.

All the states but one rushed to comply with the directive. South Dakota permitted individuals aged nineteen or older to purchase beer containing 3.2 percent alcohol, and the state legislature did not want to modify that law. The state then sued to keep its highway funds, asserting that the law was "coercive" and exceeded Congress's constitutional powers of taxation and spending. By a 7–2 decision, the Supreme Court rejected South Dakota's claim. "The spending power is of course not unlimited," Justice Sandra Day O'Connor wrote for the majority, as "in some circumstances the financial inducement offered by Congress might be so coercive as to pass the point at which 'pressure turns into compulsion.'" But the Court determined that such was not the case in that instance. "All South Dakota would lose if she adheres to her chosen course as to a suitable minimum drinking age is 5% of the funds . . . the argument as to coercion is shown to be more rhetoric than fact." With its highway funds threatened, the South Dakota legislature voted to raise the drinking age in the state.

Although the conditions imposed by the National Minimum Drinking Age Amendment essentially coerced state governments to pass laws at the behest of the federal government, the Supreme Court generally approved of such tactics. Yet when Ronald Reagan was elected president in 1980, he openly trumpeted federal initiatives to return policy-making authority to the states. In his first State of the Union Address in early 1981, Reagan proposed to terminate the federal role in welfare and return to the states forty-three other major federal grant programs.

The voluntary transfer of power by the central government to state or local governments is known as "devolution."[14] If Reagan's proposals had been fully implemented, such a large-scale devolution of federal programs would have returned federal–state relations to the version of federalism that existed before the New Deal. As it turned out, however, strong resistance from the Democratic-controlled House led to the defeat of many of Reagan's devolution initiatives. Nonetheless, Reagan administration rhetoric emphasizing federal deregulation and increased state responsibilities set the stage for more sweeping reforms to be implemented in the years ahead.

"Sorry, but all my power's been turned back to the states."

1981 *New Yorker* cartoon depicting President Ronald Reagan's plans to return some federal programs to the states.

---

[14] For an application of the term to welfare policy, see Pamela Winston, *Welfare Policymaking in the States: The Devil in Devolution* (Washington, DC: Georgetown University Press, 2002).

The "New Federalism," 1990–Present

Scholars assessing the state of federalism since 1990 have failed to reach a consensus on the proper label for characterizing what appears to be a counterthrust favoring states' rights. This new era of federal–state relations has been marked by a resuscitation of state authority, helped by a Supreme Court which, since the early 1990s, has been far more attentive to protecting states' rights. The changed composition of the Court accounts for this shift. Between 1991 and 2005, four Reagan appointees to the Court (Chief Justice Rehnquist and Associate Justices Antonin Scalia, Sandra Day O'Connor, and Anthony Kennedy) and one of George H. W. Bush's appointees (Associate Justice Clarence Thomas) generally favored states' rights in federalism disputes.[15] (President George W. Bush's recent appointments of Chief Justice John Roberts and Associate Justice Samuel Alito to the Supreme Court did little to reverse this trend.) The modern Court's decisions on federalism fit into a number of different categories.

First, although the Supreme Court has continued to allow Congress to place conditions on federal appropriations to the states, it put a stop to coercive conditions that leave the states with no discretion to form their own policies. Faced with the difficult challenge of encouraging states to build radioactive-waste dumps within their own borders, Congress

A radioactive waste isolation plant in New Mexico.

JOE RAEDLE/GETTY IMAGES

American Government . . . in Historical Perspective:
Maintaining the Delicate Balance of Federalism

HISTORICAL PERSPECTIVE

When nationwide crises arise, Congress has usually been able to offer innovative solutions. Yet quite often those solutions trample over state notions of sovereignty. And when that is the case, the U.S. Supreme Court usually offers the first line of defense in helping to maintain the delicate balance of federalism.

In the 1880s, when big businesses were greatly expanding their power, numerous corporate mergers and secret agreements among these large companies placed heavy restraints on trade, often burdening small businesses and consumers. Reacting to the anticompetitive fever of the times, Congress in 1890 passed the Sherman Anti-Trust Act, which banned combinations or conspiracies that restrained interstate commerce and prohibited individual companies from monopolizing entire markets. The federal government believed that the law gave it the authority to prosecute the E. C. Knight Company, whose control over 95 percent of the sugar production in the United States had led to artificially high sugar prices. Not so, said the Supreme Court, which in 1895 held that the company did not violate antitrust laws, because the sugar production process itself never crossed state lines and thus did not really

constitute a restraint of "interstate commerce." This narrow view of congressional power would continue to stymie antitrust prosecutions for the next four decades.

In 2000, Congress suffered a setback in its effort to pass groundbreaking social legislation. For more than two centuries, state legislatures alone had been responsible for regulating domestic violence, sexual assault, and other crimes normally committed by men against women. The result was a patchwork of laws and rules governing those crimes. With sexual assaults inside and outside the home mounting into a nationwide epidemic by the end of the twentieth century, Congress responded by passing the Violence against Women Act, which provided a civil remedy in federal court for any person in the United States victimized by a "crime of violence motivated by gender." But in the spring of 2000, the Supreme Court held in the case of *United States v. Morrison* that the federal government had acted unconstitutionally in passing the act— Congress could not regulate noneconomic, violent criminal conduct based solely on the conduct's aggregate effect on interstate commerce. Despite the Court's decision, victims of domestic violence could still sue perpetrators in state courts.

[15] David Savage, *Turning Right: The Making of the Rehnquist Supreme Court* (New York: Wiley, 1993).

in the mid-to-late 1980s passed a series of laws that created monetary and other forms of incentives for states to assume that responsibility. Even more extreme, Congress warned that states that shirked their responsibility on the matter might be forced to assume legal ownership of the waste from private companies, and thereafter incur all the legal liability that would arise from its hazards. In *New York v. United States* (1992), the Supreme Court ruled that this final provision crossed the line, and was unconstitutionally coercive.[16] Recent Supreme Court decisions have also prevented Congress from requiring state officials to implement or carry out federal policies; when the Brady Bill required that local sheriffs conduct background checks of gun purchasers, the Supreme Court in *Printz v. United States* (1997) struck down that provision as unconstitutional.[17]

Second, since the mid-1990s, Congress's virtually unlimited authority to regulate interstate commerce has been scaled back somewhat. In *United States v. Lopez* (1995), the Supreme Court declared that Congress could not ban guns in school zones.[18] Whereas during the cooperative federalism era Congress regulated all manner of criminal and social activities, the present-day Supreme Court has more strenuously insisted that Congress show a clear connection with commerce when exercising its power to regulate interstate commerce, for example. Then, in 1997, Congress ran into more obstacles when it enacted a law entitling sexual assault victims to sue their perpetrators in federal court. Once again, the Supreme Court stood firm for state sovereignty, ruling in *United States v. Morrison* (2000) that the law was unconstitutional, on the theory that domestic abuse had only a slight connection to commerce.[19]

Third, a series of recent Supreme Court decisions has scaled back the doctrine of preemption, at least as applied to Congress's regulation of state governmental workers and employees. In *Alden v. Maine* (1999), the Supreme Court refused Congress the authority to allow private citizens to sue state governments for damages when they fail to pay minimum wages required under federal law.[20] A year later, the Supreme Court issued a similar ruling, disallowing private lawsuits against state governments that violated federal age discrimination laws.

Meanwhile a Supreme Court increasingly intent on protecting states' rights has given new teeth to the Eleventh Amendment, which bars citizens of one state from bringing suit against another state in federal court. As a result of Court decisions, many plaintiffs are now restricted from bringing lawsuits in federal court against public employers; instead, plaintiffs must bring suit in state courts.[21]

AP PHOTO/JOHN DURICKA, FILE

Then-House Minority Whip Newt Gingrich addressing Republican Congressional candidates during the 1994 election campaign. The "Contract with America" was credited in part with helping the Republicans take back the Congress in November 1994 and with making Gingrich the first Republican Speaker of the House in forty years.

Of course Supreme Court decisions are not solely responsible for the resurrection of state sovereignty that has occurred over the past decade and a half. Political developments have also altered the character of American federalism in important ways. Many of President Reagan's federalism initiatives met with limited success in a Democratic-controlled House of Representatives. For example, his own Republican Party's platforms in the 1980s called for the abolition of the Department of Education; yet that controversial proposal proved a nonstarter in the Congress. Still, his administration managed to push through deregulation initiatives in a number of partially preempted programs, and it relaxed federal oversight of state performance to a considerable degree. In addition, six years after Reagan left office, Republicans took control of both the House and the Senate for the first time since the early 1950s. In 1994, Newt Gingrich (R-GA), then House Minority Whip, and 366 other Republican candidates for Congress rallied around the "Contract with America," a series of initiatives they promised to introduce in the first one hundred days of the 104th Congress. (Republicans would maintain control of at least one, but normally both houses of Congress for more than a decade, up until the Democratic sweep of both houses in 2006.)

---

[16] 505 U.S. 144 (1992).
[17] 521 U.S. 898 (1997).
[18] 514 U.S. 549 (1995).
[19] 529 U.S. 598 (2000).
[20] 527 U.S. 706 (1999).
[21] John T. Noonan Jr., *Narrowing the Nation's Power: The Supreme Court Sides with the States* (Berkeley: University of California Press, 2003).

Republican leaders hoped to institute major changes in the nature of the relationship that existed between the federal government and state and local governments. With the Republican takeover of Congress complete after the 1994 midterm elections, newly elected Speaker of the House Gingrich and other House leaders introduced legislation

GLOBAL PERSPECTIVE

American Government . . . in Global Perspective:

Old Rivals Georgia and Florida Duke It Out in a Brand New Venue

Free trade between the United States and Latin American countries is theoretically the province of the federal government. Reality tends to be a bit more complicated. In 2003, talks began among thirty-four countries in the Americas to propose an extension of the North American Free Trade Agreement (NAFTA) to countries in Central America and South America as well. The location of this proposed Free Trade Area of America (FTAA) headquarters caused a bit of controversy beginning in 2005. The city of Miami, Florida, believed it would be a shoo-in for the headquarters, and the Florida state government—with so much to gain from the FTAA—tried mightily to secure Miami as the headquarters. The U.S. government, concerned about the massive anti-corporatization and anti-globalization protests that had taken place at the FTAA negotiations held in Miami and elsewhere, generally steered clear of these lobbying efforts. The federal government was apparently concerned not just about the possibility of violence; it also wanted to stay neutral in a contest among Florida, Georgia, and other states and cities, all vying to be the FTAA headquarters.

Where does this leave Latin American countries concerned that the U.S government's "neutrality" about the headquarters site creates a vacuum that may slow down, if not outright derail the process? A recent issue of the *Latin American Post,* a journal that represents the issues and concerns in common to people from Latin American nations, followed the competition between the states of Georgia and Florida in particular with some amusement:

If it seems like Mr. [Jorge] Arrizurieta [a Florida-born Cuban-born working on behalf of his home state] is maintaining a busy traveling schedule, his counterpart in Atlanta, José Ignacio González, is just as frenzied . . . Mr. González and Mr. Arrizurieta crossed paths as they met with the president of Uruguay, Jorge Batlle, and other government representatives on the same day in late August in Montevideo, the Uruguayan capital. Though they did not see each other, they heard of each other's movements from the officials they were meeting with, both men said. . . . Mr. Batlle later endorsed Miami's bid, becoming the first government leader in the region to publicly side with any city, even though it is ultimately the Uruguayan trade minister who will put forward his position in a consensus process involving negotiators from throughout the region . . .

Mr. González, the [Georgia] envoy, has taken a different approach from Mr. Arrizurieta's by declining to discuss the negative attributes of his competitors in favor of promoting Atlanta's advantages. "Initially," he said in an interview, "Atlanta might not seem like the most obvious choice but we bring the most to the table economically, culturally and historically" . . . Atlanta, buoyed by support from local and state political leaders, appears to be doing fairly well in increasing visibility for its bid. Earlier this month, for example, ministers from five Andean countries—Bolivia, Ecuador, Colombia, Peru and Venezuela—met in Atlanta to discuss preparations for next month's talks in Miami. While in Georgia, they dined with former President Jimmy Carter and met with executives from large Atlanta companies . . .

"We're the indisputable gateway to the Americas," Mr. Arrizurieta said, adding that he bristled upon seeing that exact phrase, "Gateway to the Americas," as part of an extensive advertising insert purchased by Atlanta recently in the magazine *Latin Trade* to win support for its bid. "That really got to me," Mr. Arrizurieta said.

Source: http://www.latinamericanpost.com/index.php?mod=seccion&secc=82&conn=2589

in early 1995 that would have required states to reduce the level of benefits paid to welfare recipients specified as "undeserving." The targets included mothers who gave birth to more children while they were already on welfare, and mothers who had refused to determine paternity. The 104th Congress also proposed budget resolutions in May 1995 that would have created a new series of block grants to states; consolidated or eliminated hundreds of federal programs, agencies, and commissions; and abolished three federal departments—the Departments of Energy, Education, and Commerce.

In the end, that Congress passed few revolutionary new laws. A standoff between President Bill Clinton, who refused to sign the budget resolutions, and Congress, which threatened to close down the government unless the president gave way, led to government shutdowns in November 1995 and January 1996; eventually on April 26, 1996, Clinton signed a budget bill that cut federal domestic discretionary spending for the first time in three decades. Yet the bill did not achieve anything close to the revolution that the leaders of the 104th Congress had hoped for. Devolution of programs to the states has instead evolved far more gradually, through legislation like the Personal Responsibility and Work Opportunity Reconciliation Act of 1996, which capped federal block grants to states for welfare aid. States have been encouraged by the law to create their own, cost-efficient welfare benefits programs. But the states' rights movement stopped significantly short of the vaunted "devolution revolution" promised by Republican House leaders when they first took control in 1995.

Why Federalism?
Advantages and Disadvantages

Advantages of Federalism

Supporters of federalism point to several advantages offered by this form of government. Specifically, they note that a federalist system is more likely to accommodate the needs of a diverse citizenry, to strengthen liberty by dividing powers between levels of government, to encourage experimentation, and to respond to change.

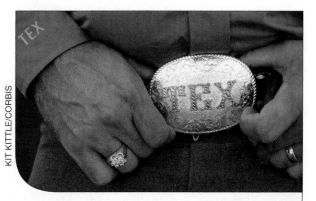

Like this Texan, many citizens take pride in their home states.

★ **Accommodation of Diversity.** If a unitary system of government threatens to treat citizens of different states as interchangeable parts for purposes of quick and easy administration, federalism acts as an important counter-balance to this trend. A citizen of the United States can also take pride in being a citizen of Texas or some other state with a clearly defined culture or character. State and local politicians can perhaps better respond than a central government to the specific demands or needs of its citizens. The culture of a state may be reflected in that state's handgun control laws, its rules on the distribution of alcohol, or its laws concerning abortion, prostitution, the use of land, and many other issues that tend to receive differing levels of support across America.

★ **Strengthening of Liberty Through the Division of Powers.** In Federalist No. 51, James Madison argued that "in the compound republic of America" the power surrendered by the people is divided between two distinct governments. This division provides security against a concentration of power in a single, unitary government. Madison also considered the division of such power "essential to the preservation of liberty," because it becomes harder for a corrupt agreement between these two separate governments to last for long. The existence of two distinct levels of government, combined with the separation of executive, legislative, and judicial powers within each of those governments, offers individuals considerable protection. Accordingly, Madison argued that "a double security arises to the rights of the people."

★ **Throughout American history,** Madison's prophecy has often proven true, as state governments have rallied against federal government abuses of the rights of the people, and vice-versa. For example, the Kentucky and Virginia resolutions drafted by legislatures of those states in the late 1790s negated the power of the federal government to pass federal laws restricting seditious speech and the free movement of aliens.[22] The respective roles of these governments in protecting liberty were reversed 160 years later, when the federal government sent federal troops to Arkansas to protect the rights of African American citizens to attend public schools in the segregated South. "Liberty through government" thus became a principle of the civil rights movement, aided by the rivalry between two sovereign governments.

★ **Encouragement of Laboratories of Democracy.** In 1932, Supreme Court Justice Louis Brandeis made famous a metaphor for creative federalism when he wrote that "a single courageous state may, if its citizens choose, serve as a laboratory, and try social and economic experiments without risk to the rest of the country."[23] This notion of states serving as "laboratories of democracy" is encouraged by a federalist system that gives the states authority to craft policies at the outset, while at the same time affording the central government authority to implement polices that prove successful throughout the nation. During the 1930s, FDR borrowed from the experience of various states in crafting many New Deal policies. In 1993, the Brady Bill drafted by Congress drew heavily on successful state gun control provisions that established waiting periods for handgun purchases. School voucher programs in states such as Wisconsin have been studied carefully by the administration of President George W. Bush, which may seek to duplicate such programs nationwide. The flip side of such successes is also significant: state policies that proved to be failures discourage broad-based applications by the federal government. For example, given that California's deregulation of utilities helped bring about an energy crisis in that state in early 2001, it seems unlikely that other states or the federal government will seek similar forms of deregulation anytime soon.

★ **Adaptability to Changing Circumstances.** Some areas of policy making clearly lie within the purview of the central government: foreign affairs, the development of a strong military, and the resolution of conflicts between states lead the list. By way of comparison, state and local governments maintain relatively strong control over public education in the state and local communities. Similarly, over the past decade responsibility for social welfare policies has rested primarily with state governments. In these and other policy areas, state and local control affords considerably more flexibility to officials wrestling with various ways of addressing policy problems. Changing circumstances, such as a sudden influx of students in a state's K–12 educational programs or a migration of welfare recipients to a state, may require a quick and flexible response from government. Federal control over such issues may ensure the benefits of uniformity, but the cost is some loss of flexibility. State control provides the opportunity for legislative reform over a bureaucracy that may be far more manageable in its size.

An interstate highway beset with construction. Many states must rely heavily on federal construction funds to help them maintain roads and highways.

[22] William Watkins, *Reclaiming the American Revolution: The Kentucky and Virginia Resolutions and Their Legacy* (New York: Palgrave MacMillan, 2004).
[23] *New State Ice Co. v. Liebmann,* 285 U.S. 262, 311 (1932).

Disadvantages of Federalism

Opponents of federalism present arguments of their own concerning the disadvantages of this form of government. Chief among their objections to a federalist system are the unfairness caused by economic disparities among the states, questions about government accountability for many public programs that are inherent with competing sovereigns, and its heavy reliance on the courts to define the nature of federalism.

★ **Fiscal Disparities among the States.** States differ markedly in the wealth of their citizens, and thus in the taxable resources available to them for programs. According to the U.S. Department of Commerce's Bureau of Economic Analysis, Connecticut's citizens in 2006 boasted a per capita personal income of $49,852, almost twice that of citizens in West Virginia ($27,897) or Mississippi ($26,535).[24] Because of these fiscal differences, the amount that states have to spend on governmental programs varies widely. Furthermore, when the central government defers to state entities in the governing process, such as when it requires states to fund their own welfare programs, wide fiscal inequalities among states (and localities) may mean disparate—and inequitable—programs for citizens in different states. Advocates of social equity and justice routinely complain about this consequence of federalism. Although federal financing of state developmental projects or other state programs relieves some of these inequities, the current trend toward reducing state dependency on the federal government promises more, not less, equity in the distribution of government benefits across states.

★ **Lack of Accountability.** Numerous government programs fall under the exclusive authority of neither the state nor the federal governments; both may act, either may act, or, in some cases, neither may act. At least in the abstract, federalism creates the prospect of multiple levels of government vying for the opportunity to address economic or social problems. In practice, however, the federal and state governments often play a game of "chicken," each hoping the other will act first and assume greater economic responsibility, and perhaps accountability for failures. In an era when public frustration with rising taxes discourages government spending, this "blame game" may go on for years, with both sides accusing the other of shirking its responsibilities to the public. During the 1990s, for example, many state governments eliminated benefits for the needy and imposed stricter requirements on those seeking welfare. State legislatures facing growing budget deficits hoped to "push" the poverty problem onto other states by passing laws that encouraged poor people to move to states with more liberal benefits programs. During this same period Congress passed welfare legislation in 1996 that transferred welfare responsibilities back to states. Critics charge that this arrangement of shared accountability quickly transforms into a lack of accountability, with neither government accepting responsibility for dealing with problems.

AP PHOTO/SUSAN WALSH

President George W. Bush, meeting with Louisiana governor Kathleen Blanco and FEMA workers in the aftermath of Hurricane Katrina.

---

[24] See BEA News Release No. 07-11, "State Personal Income Tax 2006" (Released March 27, 2007).

★ **Undue Reliance on Courts to Define the Rules of Federalism.** Because of the ambiguities inherent within a federalist system, courts play a far greater role in defining this form of government than in defining other forms. Because the federalist system is grounded in a political compromise, the rules are unclear; the limits of governmental power fit into no neat or simple formula. Judicial decision making is a mainstay of most federalist systems because it is necessary; without judicial rulings, it may be difficult if not impossible to balance the competing goals of national and subnational governments. This continued reliance on courts to make these weighty decisions exacts a price, however. Unlike legislators or high-level executives who must court public support to be elected, most judges are appointed and thus never need to directly curry the public's favor. When the courts fail to acknowledge public opinion, as the Supreme Court did when it struck down extremely popular measures to fight the Great Depression in the 1930s, a democratic system such as ours may find the delicate balance of powers tipping too far in favor of the unelected branches of government.

Those who favor expanding states' rights and responsibilities can cite a number of advantages that accrue with a healthy brand of federalism, while those who doubt the capacity of state governments to address complex modern problems are just as passionate when citing its various disadvantages. Debates over the merits of federalism are likely to continue well into the future, as political actors at every level of government stake a claim in difficult public policy problems that have few clear solutions.

Current Problems in American Federalism

Beginning in the 1980s, the national Republican Party identified itself closely with the states' rights movement. In seeking to decrease the size of government programs at the national level, President Ronald Reagan and congressional Republicans invited state governments to assume greater responsibilities for their own citizens. Unfortunately, it was never made clear where the money to support such state programs would come from. As state governments continue to shoulder greater responsibilities for some programs, the issue of funding has moved front and center in the debate over federalism.

A public school in Camden, New Jersey, which first opened in 1887.

Unfunded Mandates

Unfunded mandates are directives from the federal government to the states requiring them to perform regulatory tasks at their own expense. By placing conditions on federal grants to states, and then threatening to withdraw those funds if the states don't meet the conditions, the federal government can impose a whole range of such mandates on states seeking their share of federal funds. Even in the 1980s, when the trend was toward deregulation and devolution, Congress continued to place coercive requirements on states that received grants-in-aid. Laws were passed mandating national standards on a host of subjects such as transportation, school and work safety, and environmental hazards. According to social scientist Timothy Conlan, the number of major new intergovernmental regulatory provisions enacted during the 1980s surpassed that of any previous period.[25] States complained that many of these regulations posed considerable economic hardships on their budgets, without any compensatory economic support from the federal government. For example, compliance with federal environmental requirements imposed since 1970 cost all state and local governments combined more than $19 billion per year by the end of the 1980s.

One of the legislative successes claimed by Republicans under the Contract with America was the Unfunded Mandates Reform Act, which President Clinton signed into law in the spring of 1995. On its face, the law made it harder for Congress to impose mandates on the states without accompanying funds for implementation—the law allowed individual members of Congress to block consideration of such mandates unless the requirement for funding was waived by Congress as a whole. Federal agencies were also prevented from carrying out mandates that were unfunded (or underfunded) without the direct consent of Congress. Such mandates have continued in the years since the act was passed, as Congress has continued to enact legislation providing directives to states. As it turned out, the Unfunded Mandates Act could do little to counter the federal legislative zeal for ordering states to carry out initiatives at their own cost.

The Growing Crisis in Big Cities

The inequities arising in a federal system that relies heavily on each state to fund many of its own social programs have created a crisis in many large cities in the United States. Big-city government programs can be expensive, and the needs of poor urban populations (for social and economic services, for example) often outstrip the city's tax base. Education is a particular concern: big-city education has always been more expensive to deliver than education in the suburbs and rural towns

★ Unfunded mandate

A directive from the federal government to the states requiring that they perform certain functions, with no accompanying funds to support those functions.

AP PHOTO/LUKE PALMISANO

A modern public high school in the wealthy suburb of Hudson, Ohio.

[25] Timothy Conlan, *New Federalism: Intergovernmental Reform from Nixon to Reagan* (Washington, DC: Brookings Institution Press, 1988).

Chapter 3: Federalism

because of high land prices, the higher salaries needed to retain teachers in big-city schools, and the high costs of school safety and other problems that are most commonly associated with inner-city education.

The structure of the American federalist system does not benefit urban cities to the degree that their high populations would seem to require. Congress—which includes members from all states and congressional districts—is reluctant to pass laws that exclude nonurban areas. Moreover, states with small populations enjoy disproportionately greater influence in the Senate, where they can stymie legislation aimed at assisting big cities. State aid to big cities increased during the cooperative federalism era, with grants to cities quadrupling between the late 1950s and the late 1970s. However, as the national government scaled back its financial support to states, cities, which benefited disproportionately during the 1960s and 1970s, have started to suffer.

Now & Then: Making the Connection

The pride citizens take in their home state connections is inevitable in a republic that celebrates state identities through its formal institutions and structures. The Constitution of the United States guarantees that each state (from California, the most heavily populated, to the least populated states of Delaware, Wyoming, and Alaska) is represented by exactly two members of the U.S. Senate, through which all federal legislation must pass. The presidential election in 2000 came down to the vote count of one state (Florida), whose state-specific and county-specific rules, regulations, and practices figured prominently in the final outcome. Citizens continue to face a dizzying variety of rules and regulations when they move from one state to another. Sometimes the different rules governing citizens in two different states are more akin to the rules that govern different countries. Indeed, citizens of western New York State crossing by car into Canada often suffer far less culture shock than when they deplane in Texas, Louisiana, or another southern state.

State politicians often push the envelope on the legitimate bounds of state authority, both to win popularity among the state's citizens and to protect what they consider the state's best political interests. In recent years some states—New York and Pennsylvania, for example—have sought to impose "commuter taxes" on people who live in other states but work in their respective states. In an extreme case of state government action, Massachusetts, to protest human rights violations in the country of Burma (Myanmar) and to encourage reform in the nation's domestic policies, attempted to apply indirect economic pressure against Burma by prohibiting the state and its agents from purchasing goods or services from anyone doing business with the Union of Myanmar.

Are these modern federalism disputes any different from disputes over the reach of federal authority at other times in the nation's history? When Congress attempted to legislate against child labor in the early part of the twentieth century, it ran squarely into a tradition of federalism—enforced by a conservative Supreme Court—that prohibited the federal government from regulating business matters that occurred entirely within the manufacturing stage. When congressional leadership intervened in the Terri Schiavo case nearly a century later, it was once again rebuffed for entering into a political thicket that has divided federal and state lawmakers throughout American history. In all such cases, advocates of state authority must stand strong against federal government's enhanced authority, or they risk being swept aside in the process. The United States of America has not always been the "obedient states" of America, but it is hard to imagine that the Founders would have intended the states to act otherwise.

The federal government's Marijuana Tax Act of 1937 effectively prohibited the use of cannabis as a prescription drug in the United States. Cannabis is the chemical in marijuana plants that provides the mind-altering effects which made it so popular as a recreational drug, and thus led to the 1937 law. However, cannabis has also been used for centuries for medicinal purposes. In fact, prior to the discovery of aspirin, cannabis was the most common drug used to treat headaches and other types of pain in the 19th century. The 1937 law was inspired by non-medical uses of the drug, although it had the effect of banning it for medical purposes as well. At the time the federal law was passed, many in the medical community, including the American Medical Association, opposed restricting its use for medical purposes.

BRUCE ELY/NEWHOUSE NEWS SERVICE/LANDOV

Today, the use of cannabis for medicinal purposes has become a controversial issue, debated throughout the American federal system. A number of states, including California, have recently passed laws that allow the use of cannabis for medical purposes. In 2002, Angel Raich, a Californian, was using home grown marijuana prescribed by her physician who determined that without it, Raich's high level of pain could endanger her life. Federal agents from the Drug Enforcement Administration seized and destroyed the marijuana plants that Raich was using. Raich sued, claiming that her rights were violated and that the federal government could not rely on the commerce clause to trump California law in this instance. In *Gonzales v. Raich* (2005),[26] the U.S. Supreme Court ruled in favor of the federal government, holding that Congress indeed has the authority under the commerce clause to regulate activities such as marijuana use that have a substantial impact on interstate commerce.

At http://academic.cengage.com/dautrich, find the politics interactive link for details on why the use of cannabis in medical treatment remains a point of controversy in federal-state relations. Additionally, learn how the National Organization for the Reform of Marijuana Laws (NORML) works with states and policy-makers advocating states' rights to allow the use of the drug for medicinal purposes. Consult as well the various links that relate to the "medical marijuana controversy" in historical, popular, and global perspective.

---

[26] 545 U.S. 1 (2005)

http://www.academic.cengage.com/dautrich

Chapter Summary

★ The American system of federalism links the central government in Washington, DC, to all fifty state governments. Sovereignty (the power of a government to regulate its affairs) resides concurrently in both the central government and the state governments.

★ Federal systems of government can be distinguished from confederations (a simple alliance of independent states) or unitary systems of government (in which subunits such as states subordinate their aims to those of the central government).

★ The Framers of the Constitution assigned to the national government matters of great national importance (including foreign and military affairs) and assigned to the states all local and internal matters, including those relating to the health, safety, and welfare of citizens.

★ The supremacy clause of Article VI provides that the Constitution and all federal laws override conflicting provisions in state constitutions or state laws.

★ The full faith and credit clause of Article IV requires that states respect each other's acts and official proceedings. Notwithstanding this clause, some states have attempted to prevent same-sex marriage couples from asserting their status as married couples across state lines.

★ Beginning in 1819, the Supreme Court under Chief Justice John Marshall substituted the Framers' vision of federalism (state-centered federalism) with its own national supremacy doctrine, which held that (1) states possess extremely limited sovereignty and (2) Congress was supreme within the sphere of its own constitutional powers.

★ In *McCulloch v. Maryland* (1819), Marshall applied the national supremacy doctrine to uphold the authority of Congress to create a national bank even though the Constitution did not explicitly authorize Congress to do so; congressional authority arose from a broader interpretation of the necessary and proper clause in Article I, Section 8.

★ Beginning in 1837, a system of "dual federalism," in which state authority under the Constitution served as a limit on congressional power, reigned for nearly a century until the New Deal period of the 1930s.

★ The economic hardships of the Great Depression led to an activist federal government; facing these realities, the Supreme Court eventually abandoned its dual federalism principles in favor of a more expansive view of congressional authority.

★ The era of "cooperative federalism" (1937–1990) barely limited Congress in the exercise of its powers. Through grants-in-aid and block grants, the federal government has placed huge sums of money at the disposal of states.

★ Critics of cooperative federalism note that by attaching conditions to these funds, the federal government often coerces states and state officials to administer federal laws. The National Minimum Drinking Age Amendment, for example, required states to increase their drinking age to twenty-one or risk losing national highway funds.

★ The rhetoric of the Reagan administration emphasized federal deregulation and increased state responsibilities; Reagan's Supreme Court appointees helped to usher in a period of "new federalism" (1990–present) in which state sovereignty has once again been resuscitated to prevent certain forms of congressional coercion.

★ Federalism carries with it many advantages, including the accommodation of diverse interests in a large republic, the increased protection of individual liberty, and the encouragement of states to serve as "laboratories of democracy" where they might try out new policies. Because of their smaller size, state and local governments are also more flexible in adapting to changing circumstances.

★ There are also disadvantages to a federalist system, including the problems caused by significant fiscal disparities among the states, the potential lack of accountability of officials to oversee certain undesirable programs, and the heavy reliance of federalism on unelected courts to define its boundaries and perimeters.

★ Today the American system of federalism continues to impose significant financial burdens on states. Unfunded mandates from Congress require states to perform certain regulatory tasks at their own expense; the needs of the urban poor in big cities often outstrip city tax bases, and in recent years the federal government has scaled back its support of states and cities.

Key Terms

Block grants (p. 75)

Concurrent powers (p. 65)

Confederation (p. 62)

Cooperative federalism (p. 73)

Dual federalism (p. 72)

Federalism (p. 62)

Full faith and credit clause (p. 67)

Gibbons v. Ogden (1824) (p. 71)

Grants-in-aid (p. 73)

Layer cake federalism (p. 73)

Marble cake federalism (p. 73)

Martin v. Hunter's Lessee (1819)
 (p. 67)

McCulloch v. Maryland (1819)
 (p. 70)

National supremacy doctrine
 (p. 70)

Necessary and proper clause
 (p. 65)

Preemption (p. 67)

Reserved powers (p. 65)

Sovereignty (p. 62)

Supremacy clause (p. 66)

Unfunded mandate (p. 83)

Unitary system of government
 (p. 64)

Resources

Important Books

Beer, Samuel H. *To Make a Nation: The Rediscovery of American Federalism.* New York: Belknap Press, 1993.

Conlan, Timothy. *From New Federalism to Devolution: Twenty-five Years of Intergovernmental Reform.* Washington, DC: Brookings Institution Press, 1998.

Elazar, Daniel J. *Exploring Federalism.* Tuscaloosa: University of Alabama Press, 1987.

Noonan, John T. *Narrowing the Nation's Power: The Supreme Court Sides with the States.* Berkeley: University of California Press, 2002.

Peterson, Paul. *The Price of Federalism.* New York: 20th Century Fund, 1995.

Purcell, Edward A. *Originalism, Federalism and the American Constitutional Enterprise: A Historical Inquiry.* New Haven: Yale University Press, 2007.

Walker, David. *The Rebirth of Federalism: Slouching Toward Washington.* New York: Chatham House, 2000.

Internet Sources

http://lcweb.loc.gov/global/state/stategov.html (Library of Congress web page on state and local governments)

http://www.statenews.org/ (website produced by the Council of State Governments with information about state issues and federalism)

http://www.nascio.org (National Association of State Information Resource Executives website)

4 Civil Liberties

A detainee at Guantanamo Bay

AP PHOTO/BRENNAN LINSLEY

Civil Liberties During Wartime: Now & Then

Although Congress made no formal declaration of war, calls for military action were heard throughout Washington, DC. Tyrants from the other side of the world were threatening the United States of America. For years U.S. officials had thought there was little chance of any real threat emerging from so far away; after all, the nation enjoyed the natural protection of two large oceans and had cautiously steered clear of disputes among warring entities abroad that did not directly threaten U.S. interests. But now, with an undeclared war being waged on America, Congress sought to pass legislation to consolidate and bolster the national defense. In addition to supporting the president's request for an increase in the military budget, Congress approved far-reaching measures to deal with noncitizens currently residing in America, even if there was no evidence that they posed any danger to public peace or safety. Due process rights for aliens were restricted, if not outright discarded. Presidential aides implied that anyone who spoke out against American efforts on this matter—including members of the opposing political party in particular—would be considered disloyal. Eventually the administration was forced to scale back some of these initiatives, restoring certain due process rights to criminal suspects and reducing some of its strident rhetoric on "loyalty" that had rankled so many of the administration's opponents. But at least for the time being, civil liberties would be forced to take a backseat to national security interests.

...n alien suspected of having "treasonable leanings"
... arrested in accordance with the Alien Act of 1798.

PHOTO: MULTIEDUCATOR, INC.

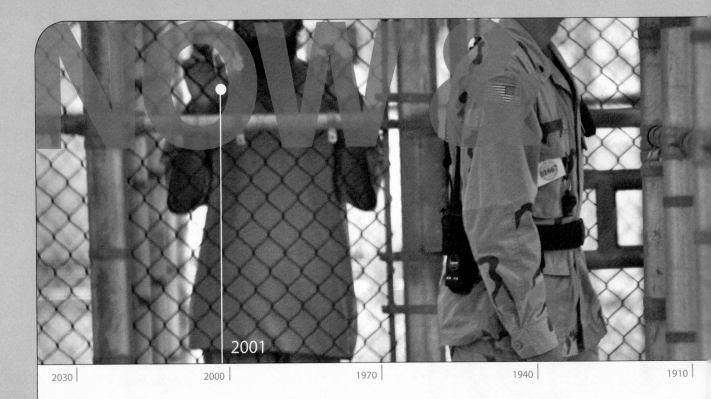

NOW

2030	2000	1970	1940	1910

2001

Now . . . Certainly many aspects of the scenario just described apply to the war on terrorism that President George W. Bush's administration launched during the late fall and early winter of 2001 in response to the September 11 terrorist attacks. Congress issued no formal declaration of war against the terrorist Al Qaeda network in Afghanistan; but it did enact the USA Patriot Act, authorizing the president to take numerous steps to prosecute the war. The Patriot Act, passed into law on October 26, 2001, gave the federal government broad new powers to detain suspects, secretly search their homes, and eavesdrop on telephone and e-mail conversations. The law targeted aliens in particular, allowing authorities to hold noncitizens suspected of terrorism for seven days without charging them. A system of military tribunals with more limited due process protections (that is, protections against arbitrary acts by the government) was established to try noncitizens. Those few congressional Democrats critical of the administration's actions were quickly labeled as "disloyal" by the attorney general. Warned of legal precedents that provided due process to all people within the United States, including aliens, the administration eventually broadened the protections afforded to defendants under the original military tribunals proposal and toned down some of its more strident rhetoric against critics as well. However, the state of civil liberties in the United States had been significantly altered by the events of September 11, 2001.

THEN

1798

Then . . . The difficult task of balancing civil liberties and national security interests during wartime is nothing new to American politics. During and immediately after World War I, some Americans considered hostile by the federal government were tried for sedition, the crime of advocating the overthrow of the existing system of government.[1] During the Civil War the federal government suspended the right of habeas corpus (proceedings that allow prisoners to question the legality of their detention) and sought to try many Confederates in military tribunals established by the federal government. All the while President Lincoln continued to claim that America was not at formal war with another nation, as the Confederate states enjoyed no formal right to secede under the Constitution.

The scenario described in the first paragraph of this chapter also harkens back to 1798, when the federal government was gearing up for hostilities against the French dictator Napoleon Bonaparte.[2] Napoleon's forces had already captured Rome and invaded Switzerland and Egypt earlier that year, and now Napoleon's aides intimated to American diplomats that a war against the United States might be next. In response, Congress passed twenty acts to help consolidate the national defense. The most controversial of these acts were the Alien Act, which authorized the president to order out of the United States all aliens suspected of "treasonable or secret" inclinations; the Alien Enemies Act, which allowed the president during wartime to arrest and imprison aliens subject to an enemy power; and the Sedition Act, which criminalized the publication of materials that brought the U.S. government into "disrepute." Together, these laws came to be known as the Alien and Sedition Acts. As the threat of war with France began to subside, these laws were applied not just against alleged French spies, but also against members of the opposition press and others critical of President John Adams and his administration. Eventually the Alien and Sedition Acts created public backlash against the same government officials who had so zealously advocated them; when he became president in 1801, Thomas Jefferson pardoned all those convicted under the controversial acts.

[1] Geoffrey Stone, *Perilous Times: Free Speech in Wartime* (New York: W. W. Norton, 2004), pp. 135–233.
[2] Ibid., pp. 15–78.

I n many other nations, restrictions on individual rights—especially during times of tension and upheaval—fail to solicit much intense resistance even from the political opposition. But the founding of the United States rested on a call for protecting the inalienable rights of all people, and the Bill of Rights, added to the U.S. Constitution in 1791, stands as a beacon against the potential tyranny of the majority. That was not always the case: the Bill of Rights has gathered true muscle only during the past seventy-five years. The challenge for so many is how to most effectively recognize the rights that are available to them. That challenge may be especially difficult during times of war, when individual rights come under the greatest threat, although perhaps with all the best intentions.

In this chapter we take up the subject of **civil liberties**—those specific individual rights that cannot be taken away by government and are guaranteed by the Constitution, such as the freedom of expression and the right of protection against self-incrimination. These individual rights, which are subject to formal interpretation from the courts and informal interpretation by those charged with their enforcement, are usually found either in the Bill of Rights or in subsequent amendments to the Constitution. Here we will focus primarily on the provision of rights guaranteed by the First, Second, and Fourth Amendments, and certain provisions within the Fifth, Sixth, Eighth, and Fourteenth Amendments.

Civil liberties may be distinguished from "civil rights" (sometimes called *equal rights*), a more modern term that refers specifically to the rights that members of various groups (racial, ethnic, sexual, and so on) have to equal treatment by government under the law and equal access to society's opportunities. This chapter deals with civil liberties, whereas Chapter 5 deals with civil rights.

The Bill of Rights: Origins and Evolution

What are rights? Strictly speaking, they are powers or privileges to which individuals are entitled. The central question is: where do rights come from, and are they absolute? *Natural rights,* which are based on the natural laws of human society, exist even in the absence of a formal government. Because natural rights theoretically transcend government entities, no authority can legitimately take them away. As Thomas Jefferson so eloquently stated in the Declaration of Independence, human beings are endowed with certain rights that are "inalienable," which means they cannot be denied by government.

Positive rights, by comparison, are granted by government authority and can usually be shaped and modified by that authority according to certain rules. An indigent person's right to a lawyer paid by the state in felony cases, for example, is a positive right. The term *liberty* refers to a right received from a higher authority, such as a government. As they articulated the basis for a new government, many of the Framers grappled with these and other terms in the nation's founding documents.

It is sometimes easy to forget that, as U.S. Supreme Court Justice Antonin Scalia once stated, individual rights are only "the fruits, rather than the roots, of the Constitutional tree."[3] The Constitution of the United States was intended to provide individuals with protection by guaranteeing a framework of limited government based on a theory of enumerated powers—the central government was allowed to exercise only those powers delegated to it by the Constitution. As James Madison wrote in Federalist No. 14, "the general government is not to be charged with the whole power of making and administering laws . . . its jurisdiction is limited to *certain enumerated objects*."[4] Thus by Madison's logic, separate provisions for the protection of individual rights were unnecessary; protection for those rights was inherent in the nature of limited government with enumerated powers. Because the government possessed no explicit power to infringe on those rights in the first place, they should never be in danger.

Yet Madison's logic ran up against an early American tradition that called for the explicit delineation of individual rights. The Declaration of Independence not only

★ Civil liberties

Those specific individual rights that cannot be denied to citizens by government that are guaranteed by the Constitution. Most of these rights are in the first eight amendments to the Constitution, known as the Bill of Rights.

[3] Antonin Scalia, "Law and the Winds of Change." Remarks made at the 24th Australian Legal Convention, Perth, West Australia, September 21, 1987.
[4] Alexander Hamilton, James Madison, and John Jay, *The Federalist Papers*, ed. Clinton Rossiter (New York: New American Library, 1971).

formally recognized that certain "unalienable rights" exist; it also stated that when a government created by "the consent of the governed" fails to protect those rights, the people have the right to "alter or abolish such government." At the time of the founding, individual rights were considered an important element of America's political culture, because they embodied the principles that justified the American Revolution. Many of the former colonists wanted those rights clearly spelled out, lest there be any doubt of their significance to the new nation.

When the U.S. Constitution was created in 1787, most state governments already maintained a bill of rights to protect citizens against government encroachment. As the final draft of the Constitution was being debated at ratification conventions in the states, it became evident to the Constitution's supporters that its approval was going to require the inclusion of a more formal bill of rights to protect citizens against the federal government. George Mason and Patrick Henry of Virginia cast votes against ratification, in part because the Constitution lacked a formal statement of rights. Thomas Jefferson was also an early proponent of a bill of rights. To Madison's fears that such a declaration of rights could never be comprehensive, and thus might leave out something important, Jefferson replied: "Half a loaf is better than no bread."[5]

Eventually it was Madison who framed the list of rights that the first Congress proposed in 1789—ten amendments to the

Bill of Rights
Congress of the United States,
Begun and held at the City of New York, on Wednesday, the fourth of March, one thousand seven hundred and eighty nine.

Constitution in all were ratified by the required three-fourths of state legislatures, but the first eight are normally regarded as the Bill of Rights. The Ninth and Tenth Amendments are more general statements describing divisions of power under the Constitution.

The provisions listed in the Bill of Rights enjoyed little influence in late eighteenth- and early nineteenth-century America, because they were understood to be restrictions on the federal government only. The Supreme Court confirmed as much in the case of *Barron v. Baltimore* (1833),[6] which pitted a wharf owner against the city of Baltimore. City officials had lowered the water level around the wharves, causing him a significant economic loss. The wharf owner thus sued the city under the Fifth Amendment's "taking clause," which stated that no private property could be taken from an individual for public use without just compensation. But the Supreme Court dismissed the suit because at that time only the federal government could be held up to the standards of the Bill of Rights. In light of the dominant role state governments played in regulating individuals' daily lives during most of this period, the *Barron v. Baltimore* decision essentially reduced the Bill of Rights to paper guarantees that only occasionally provided protection for ordinary citizens.

That all changed in the twentieth century, as the Supreme Court grew increasingly willing to protect individuals against intrusive state actions. Their instrument for doing so was the Fourteenth Amendment (ratified in 1868), which provided that no *state* could "deprive any person of life, liberty or property without due process of law." The Fourteenth Amendment had been passed immediately after the Civil War to protect freed slaves from discriminatory state laws. Yet at the beginning of the twentieth century and increasingly throughout the century, the Supreme Court by a process known as **incorporation** (or "nationalization") demonstrated a new willingness to hold state governments accountable to the Bill of Rights by utilizing the

★ Incorporation

The process by which the U.S. Supreme Court used the due process clause of the Fourteenth Amendment to make applicable to the states most of the individual rights guaranteed by the Bill of Rights. Incorporation provided that state and local governments, as well as the federal government, could not deny these rights to citizens.

---

[5] Jefferson–Madison correspondence in Philip Kurland, ed., *The Founders' Constitution* (Indianapolis, IN: Liberty Fund, 2000).
[6] 32 U.S. 243 (1833).

Table 4.1 Incorporating the Bill of Rights to Apply to the States

Provision (Amendment)	Year	Case
Protection from government taking property without just compensation (Fifth)	1897	*Chicago, Burl. & Quincy Rwy. v. Chicago*
Freedom of speech (First)	1925	*Gitlow v. New York*
Freedom of the press (First)	1931	*Near v. Minnesota*
Right to assistance of counsel in capital cases (Sixth)	1932	*Powell v. Alabama*
Freedom of assembly (First)	1937	*Delaware v. Van Arsdall*
Free exercise of religion (First)	1940	*Cantwell v. Connecticut*
Protection from establishment of religion (First)	1947	*Everson v. Board of Education*
Right to public trial (Sixth)	1948	*In Re Oliver*
Right against unreasonable search and seizure (Fourth)	1949	*Wolf v. Colorado*
Exclusionary rule (Fourth & Fifth)	1961	*Mapp v. Ohio*
Protection against cruel and unusual punishment (Eighth)	1962	*Robinson v. California*
Right to paid counsel for indigents in felony cases (Sixth)	1963	*Gideon v. Wainwright*
Right against self-incrimination (Fifth)	1964	*Malloy v. Hogan*
Right to confront witnesses (Sixth)	1965	*Pointer v. Texas*
Right to an impartial jury (Sixth)	1966	*Parker v. Gladden*
Right to compulsory process to obtain witnesses (Sixth)	1967	*Washington v. Texas*
Right to speedy trial (Sixth)	1967	*Klopfer v. North Carolina*
Right to jury in nonpetty criminal cases (Sixth)	1968	*Duncan v. Louisiana*
Right against double jeopardy (Fifth)	1969	*Benton v. Maryland*

Fourteenth Amendment's vague requirement that states respect "due process." Specifically, the Court carefully considered individual clauses from the Bill of Rights, and if the right was deemed fundamental enough, the Court held that no state could legitimately ignore the right without depriving an individual of the right to "life, liberty and property, without due process of law." By this incorporation process, states were required to live up to the dictates of the First Amendment free speech clause beginning in 1925, the Fourth Amendment right against unreasonable searches and seizures beginning in 1961, and the Sixth Amendment right to a speedy trial beginning in 1967. (See Table 4.1.) Slowly but surely the provisions of the Bill of Rights were incorporated by the Fourteenth Amendment to apply to state governments as well as to the federal government.

By 1969, nearly every provision of the Bill of Rights had been applied to state governments through the incorporation doctrine. At present, however, there are still several provisions of the Bill of Rights that theoretically provide protection against the federal government only:

★ the Second Amendment right to bear arms[7]

★ the Third Amendment safeguard against the involuntary quartering of troops

★ the Fifth Amendment requirement that defendants be indicted by a grand jury

★ the Seventh Amendment guarantee of a trial by jury in civil cases

★ the Eighth Amendment prohibition against excessive bail and fines

[7] It remains unclear whether the Supreme Court's decision in *District of Columbia v. Heller* (2008) will lead to incorporation of the Second Amendment.

Virtually all other provisions contained within the first eight amendments of the Constitution are considered applicable to all state governments and to all local governments within the states in exactly the same manner as they are applicable to the federal government.

Freedom of Religion and the Establishment Clause

THE FIRST AMENDMENT: Congress shall make no law respecting an establishment of religion, or prohibiting the free exercise thereof; . . .

Although the first words of the Bill of Rights speak to the freedom of religion, the actual rights guaranteeing religious freedom did not become widespread until the latter half of the twentieth century. In early America, Protestantism played a highly influential role in public life, and the First Amendment was intended to provide a limited barrier against its influence. In 1802, Thomas Jefferson described the First Amendment as erecting a "wall of separation" between church and state,[8] but that metaphor captured his hopes more than the reality of the time. Although there existed no official church of the United States, government aid to religion—in particular to certain Protestant sects—stood little chance of being overturned by a court on constitutional grounds. And for much of American history, minority religious groups such as Mormons, Jehovah's Witnesses, and the Amish were forced to change or abandon some of their religious practices whenever public policy conflicted with them. By the 1940s, however, American public life had grown increasingly secular, and application of the First Amendment's guarantees of freedom of religion was transformed. Even today the interest in accommodating religion continues to run up against the desire to create a "wall of separation" emphasizing government neutrality.

The Free Exercise of Religion

The **free exercise clause** of the First Amendment bans government laws that prohibit the free exercise of religion. Debate over the clause has largely focused on whether government laws can force adherents of a certain religion to engage in activities that are prohibited by their religious beliefs or prevent them from performing acts that are compelled by their religious beliefs. During the heart of World War II, the Supreme Court in *West Virginia v. Barnette* (1943)[9] ordered school officials to reinstate the children of Jehovah's Witnesses who had been suspended for refusing to salute the American flag in their public school classrooms. Yet although those children could claim legitimate religious objections to the law (the Jehovah's Witnesses' creed forbids them from saluting any "graven image"), they also could claim more generally the right of free expression—those who disagreed with the U.S. government were free to withhold displays of public support for the nation's symbol. It remained for the Court in subsequent years to sort out what rights of religious freedom might exist under the free exercise clause.

Seventh Day Adventists and the Refusal to Work. In the landmark case of *Sherbert v. Verner* (1963),[10] the Supreme Court ordered the State of South Carolina to pay unemployment benefits to a Seventh-Day Adventist who refused to work on Saturdays. Even though the state's unemployment laws required that she make herself available for work on Saturday, the Court refused to apply that law to this worker because Saturday was the Seventh-Day Adventists' sabbath. Although the state could provide legitimate reasons for refusing to pay her benefits (guarding the unemployment insurance fund against running low, for example), the Supreme Court declared that only a *compelling state interest* could justify denying her such an exception on the basis of religion. What interest counts as "compelling"? Although no precise definition is available, the Court has held that administrative convenience is not compelling; rather, the Court must be convinced that the government program (whether the draft, Social Security, unemployment benefits, and so on) would be

> ★ Free exercise clause
>
> The religious freedom clause in the First Amendment that denies government the ability to prohibit the free exercise of religion. Debate over the clause has largely focused on whether government laws can force adherents of a certain religion to engage in activities that are prohibited by their religious beliefs or prevent them from performing acts that are compelled by their religious beliefs.

---

[8] Thomas Jefferson first coined that phrase in a letter he wrote as president to the Baptists of Danbury, Connecticut, in 1802. George Seldes, ed., *The Great Quotations* (Secaucus, NJ: Citadel Press, 1983), p. 369.
[9] 319 U.S. 624 (1943).
[10] 374 U.S. 398 (1963).

The Amish at work moving haystacks. In 1972 the Supreme Court ruled that Amish children could not be forced to attend school after the eighth grade, as it would undermine the religion's emphasis on "community welfare" and "learning by doing."

significantly undermined by religious exemptions to say that the government's interest is compelling.

The Amish and Mandatory School Attendance. Continuing to accept exemptions for religious reasons, the Supreme Court in *Wisconsin v. Yoder* (1972)[11] held that members of the Amish religion were not required to send their children to school after the eighth grade. Even though Wisconsin law compelled high school attendance, the Court ruled that the enforcement of that law would undermine Amish religious principles, which include the value of "learning through doing" and support for "community welfare" over all other interests.

The Mormons and Polygamy Laws. Up until the late nineteenth century, a central tenet of the Mormon Church, also called the Church of Jesus Christ of Latter-Day Saints, required some of its adherents to practice polygamy—the act of having multiple spouses "when circumstances would permit." During the 1870s, many Mormons were prosecuted under a federal antibigamy statute that applied to federal territories, including the new Utah territory where many Mormons had settled. George Reynolds, secretary of one of the founders of the Mormon Church in America as well as the founder of Brigham Young University, brought suit in 1878, challenging the law as destructive to the Mormon Church, and thus a violation of the free exercise clause of the First Amendment.

The Supreme Court, in a unanimous decision, rejected Reynolds's argument that the First Amendment protects plural marriage. According to the Court, religious practices that impair the "public interest" do not receive constitutional protection; such practices were to be distinguished from religious "beliefs," which the government had no power to regulate. *Reynolds v. United States* [12] remains the law today, and polygamy is now banned

---

[11] 406 U.S. 205 (1972).
[12] 98 U.S. 145 (1878).

in all fifty states. Additionally, since 1890 the Mormon Church has formally renounced the practice of polygamy by its members.

Illegal Drug Use and the *Smith* Case. In 1990, the Supreme Court adopted a new approach to the free exercise of religion, which dramatically diminished the likelihood that future religious exemptions might be granted. Two Native Americans were dismissed from their jobs as drug rehabilitation counselors when it was discovered that they had ingested the illegal drug peyote as part of their tribe's religious rituals. Because their drug use violated the Oregon criminal code, the two men were subsequently denied unemployment compensation. The Supreme Court ruled in *Employment Division v. Smith* (1990)[13] that the state's legitimate interest in maintaining its unemployment insurance fund at a high level outweighed the Native Americans' religious rights and denied the two men unemployment benefits. State governments may choose to accommodate otherwise illegal acts done in pursuit of religious beliefs, but they are not *required* to do so.[14]

Today *Smith* remains the rule for judicial interpretation of free exercise cases: instead of being forced to show a *compelling* government interest (which is extremely hard to do), a government interested in applying its neutral laws over religious objections may do so based on any *legitimate state interest* it might claim. What is a legitimate state interest? The bar here is quite low; only an arbitrary or irrational objective by government will fail the test of legitimacy. The Religious Freedom Restoration Act passed by Congress in 1993 attempted to reverse the Court's holding in *Smith* and revert back to the more liberal rules established in the *Sherbert* and *Yoder* decisions. However, the Supreme Court invalidated the religious freedom law in 1997. The Supreme Court—and not the Congress—holds the lever of power in the debate over religious exemptions. And, at least for the time being, that means the courts generally will not grant such exemptions.

The Establishment Clause

Even more controversial than the debate over religious exemptions from public policies has been the battle over what role religion may play in American public life under the **establishment clause,** which prohibits the government from enacting laws "respecting an establishment of religion." Most Americans take it for granted that during the holiday season they will see Christmas decorations prominently displayed in government buildings, in front of the town hall, and in public squares. But what about nativity scenes? Menorahs? The Ten Commandments? What types of religious activities and symbols are considered acceptable in public places, and which ones run afoul of the First Amendment, whose prohibition of government "respecting an establishment of religion" has been interpreted to mean creating a "wall of separation" between church and state?

Modern debates over the proper role religion may play under the establishment clause generally divide advocates into two camps. Those who advocate a strict dividing line between church and state support a principle of "separation," which holds that government should have no involvement whatsoever with religious practices, although religion remains free to flourish privately on its own, with its own resources.[15] Opponents of strict separation argue instead for the principle of "accommodation" which holds that government neutrality toward religion requires only that it treat all religions equally. Government should be free to aid and subsidize religious activities as long as it does so fairly across different religions, and aids comparable nonreligious activities as well. In recent decades, the Supreme Court has moved from a position of especially strict separation to one that shifts back and forth between principles of separation and accommodation.

Historically Accepted Practices. Certain religious practices have been a part of political and public life for generations, and the Supreme Court has generally allowed such activities to continue. Congress opens each legislative session with a prayer from a clergy member, chaplains serve in religious capacities with the U.S. armed forces, and

★ **Establishment clause**

The clause in the First Amendment that prohibits government from enacting any law "respecting an establishment of religion." Separationist interpretations of this clause affirm that government should not support any religious activity. Accomodationists say that support for a religion is legal provided that all religions are equally supported.

---

[13] 494 U.S. 872 (1990).
[14] Carolyn N. Long, Religious *Freedom and Indian Rights: The Case of* Oregon v. Smith (Lawrence: University Press of Kansas, 2000).
[15] Noah Feldman, *Divided by God* (New York: Farrar, Straus and Giroux, 2005).

U.S. currency proclaims "In God We Trust." Even the Supreme Court opens every court session to a marshal's bellowing pronouncement: "God save this honorable court!" All of these are considered acceptable practices, products of the American historical tradition. But not all religious displays on public property will be automatically deemed as "historically accepted practices." On occasion, the Court has ordered the removal of nativity scenes and other religious displays during Christmastime.

In several Kentucky counties, versions of the Ten Commandments were posted on the walls of their respective courthouses. In Austin, Texas, a six-foot-high monolith inscribed with the Ten Commandments sits among numerous other monuments and historical markers outside the state capitol building commemorating the "people, ideals, and events that compose Texan identity." Do these public displays of the Ten Command- ments, which feature such statements as "Thou shalt have no other gods before me" and "Thou shalt not take the name of the Lord thy God in vain," violate the establishment clause of the First Amendment?

In a set of cases handed down in 2005, the Supreme Court ordered the Kentucky courthouses to remove their displays, but allowed the Texas display to remain standing. In explaining its different approach to these cases, the Court ruled that even though the Ten Commandments are inherently reli- gious, their placement in a monument outside the state capitol is an essentially "passive" act, whereas their place- ment within the courthouse had been motivated by a desire on the part of legislators to advance religion. Of course the members of the U.S. Supreme Court need not be reminded that a frieze in their own courtroom depicts Moses holding tablets exhibiting a portion of the secularly phrased Commandments in the company of seventeen other lawgivers. Perhaps the Court believes that there is little risk that such a depiction of Moses would strike an ob- server as evidence of the federal govern- ment violating religious neutrality.

A Ten Commandments monument is moved outside the Alabama Judicial Building in Montgomery, 2003.

Religious Prayers in Public School Classrooms. The public school classroom has always been viewed as a unique context in which to assess claims that the government has violated the establishment clause. Judges and politicians alike assume that students—particularly elementary school students—have not yet formed firm beliefs about religion and thus may be susceptible to even subtle forms of religious coercion. Public officials interested in promoting religion in society as a whole have focused on the school as a place to encourage religious practices; as a consequence, school policies touching on the subject of religion have undergone serious scrutiny in the courts.

In 1962, the Supreme Court in *Engel v. Vitale*[16] invalidated the New York public schools' policy of having each class recite a specified nondenominational religious prayer each day. That prayer, which proclaimed in nondenominational terms, "Almighty God, we acknowledge our dependence upon thee," was held to be a violation of the First Amendment's prohibition against the establishment of religion. In *Abington School Dist. v. Schempp* (1963)[17] the Court refused to allow spiritual Bible readings in public school classrooms and in *Wallace v. Jaffree* (1985)[18] it outlawed "moments of silence" authorized by a government officials to encourage religious prayer during those moments. The Court held that in neither of those instances was the government acting with a "secular purpose"—one not grounded in a desire to "advance religion." These decisions are especially difficult to enforce, as the closed nature of most public school classrooms allows prayer to escape the notice of those seeking to enforce these landmark decisions. And it remains unclear whether the general ban on religious prayer in public schools extends to the teaching of the Ten Commandments, among other issues.

Despite these seemingly clear rulings against school prayer, some teachers continue to lead students in prayer in public school classrooms across the country. Defiance has become widespread in some instances, forcing one court in Alabama to forbid prayer in schools throughout the state fully thirty-five years after *Engel v. Vitale*. Anecdotal evidence of violations continue to mount as well: in one highly publicized case, officials in Dekalb County, Georgia, helped lead a religious revival at a public high school in admitted disobedience of the Supreme Court. Defiance persists in part because public schools are so rarely challenged in court for their violations. Community sentiment has also played an influential role in squelching potential litigation, as dissenting parents quickly realize that only continued and expensive litigation over many years will bring a defiant school into line.

Financial Aid and the *Lemon* Test. During the last several decades, government officials seeking to promote religion as part of the educational process have expanded the variety and scope of their efforts. Many initiatives have occurred in public schools—provisions for school prayer recitations, released time programs (allowing students to visit religious schools for instruction during normal school hours), and the teaching of subjects with religious content, such as creationism. Efforts to provide religious private schools that teach students full-time with public funds have met with some recent success. In 2000, the Supreme Court approved of a program to provide government-funded computers and other teaching aids to certain parochial schools. Two years later, the Court in *Zelman v. Simmons-Harris* (2002)[19] upheld a system of private school vouchers, whereby parents are given coupons that can be used to pay tuition at private schools, including parochial schools. Such programs continue to be a source of heated policy debate between proponents of separation and accommodation.

Since 1971, issues involving the separation of church and state have often been governed by the ***Lemon* test** articulated by the Supreme Court in the landmark decision of *Lemon v. Kurtzman* (1971).[20] Under the test, government aid to public or private schools is considered unconstitutional if it fails to meet three separate criteria: "First, the statute must have a secular [that is, not religious] purpose; second, its principal or primary effect must be one that neither advances nor inhibits religion; finally, the statute must not foster 'an excessive government entanglement with religion.'" The test has been criticized by many, including a number of the Supreme Court justices, who assert that its requirements are so stringent that literally all deliberate government accommodation of religion is presumptively invalid. The Court has never renounced the test, and it continues to play a role in the consideration of various types of financial aid.

★ *Lemon* test

The legal test that determines if a government statute aiding public or private schools is an unconstitutional violation of the establishment clause. The statute is unconstitutional if: the statute has no secular purpose; its principal or primary effect advances or inhibits religion; or it fosters "an excessive government entanglement with religion."

[16] 370 U.S. 421 (1962).
[17] 374 U.S. 203 (1963).
[18] 472 U.S. 38 (1985).
[19] 536 U.S. 639 (2002).
[20] 403 U.S. 602 (1971).

Group prayer before a high school football game in Austin, Texas.

Prayers at Graduation Ceremonies and Football Games. In recent years, some school officials have attempted to facilitate student prayers in school contexts outside of the classroom. Those efforts have met with little success. In *Lee v. Weisman* (1992)[21] the Supreme Court ordered a Providence, Rhode Island, middle school to stop its practice of permitting prayers to be read at the school's graduation ceremony, even though attendance was voluntary. Eight years later, in *Santa Fe v. Doe* (2000)[22] the Court ruled that a student-led prayer before a football game at a Texas public high school violated the separation of church and state. The Court believed that both practices forced all of those present to participate in an act of religious worship. In addition, these practices could have been interpreted as state endorsements of prayer, which is unconstitutional.

The debate over the role religion should play in American public life remains a highly charged topic. Public schools especially will continue to be a focus of intense interest, as the proponents of a greater role for religion seek ever more creative ways to combine the educational process with efforts at spirituality and religious participation.

Free Expression Rights

THE FIRST AMENDMENT: Congress shall make no law . . . abridging the freedom of speech, or of the press; . . .

Among the many civil liberties guaranteed by the Bill of Rights, the First Amendment rights of free speech and press enjoy especially revered status. That wasn't always the case. The Sedition Act of the late 1790s egregiously restricted speech that negatively reflected on the Federalists who were in power; during the Civil War too, the Lincoln administration took harsh action against those who sought to undermine the Union's cause. Today, nearly all politicians openly celebrate rights of free expression, at least in the abstract. For many, these rights of free expression serve as a cornerstone for all other individual rights, facilitating the more effective realization of such freedoms as the right to vote and participate in the democratic process.

What accounts for the lofty status of free expression rights in the American political system? Several theories have been offered to justify this high level of respect:

★ **"The marketplace of ideas,"** a phrase coined by Supreme Court Justice Oliver Wendell Holmes in 1919, is a metaphor for the premise that the best test of truth is the free trade of ideas; only through such free exchange and presentation of all arguments, valid and invalid, can the truth prevail. To ensure a robust "marketplace of ideas," government restrictions on speech must be kept to a minimum.

[21] 505 U.S. 577 (1992).
[22] 530 U.S. 290 (2000).

★ **Self-governance** is another frequently cited justification for protecting free expression. Speech is considered essential to representative government, because it provides the mechanism by which citizens deliberate on important issues of public policy. Free speech also serves as a means for ordinary citizens to check the abuse of power by public officials.

★ **Self-fulfillment.** Some philosophers have emphasized the importance of free speech and expression as a means of achieving individual self-fulfillment. The human capacity to create ideas and express oneself is thus considered central to human existence; government restrictions on free speech invariably threaten that human capacity. Such a justification of free speech rights extends as well to the protection of music, pictures, and other forms of artistic expression.

★ **A "safety valve."** Free speech also serves a critical role in encouraging adaptability and flexibility according to the changing circumstances in society. If the suppression of free speech forces citizens to adopt more extreme means of enacting change such as violence, the promotion of free speech provides an essential mechanism for balancing the need for order with cries for reform.

Each of the above justifications for free speech protection may be subject to legitimate criticisms as well. But for better or worse, the First Amendment's protection of free expression today enjoys a special status in our constitutional system, even though that was not always the case.

Free Speech During the Early Twentieth Century: "The Clear and Present Danger Test"

The modern status of free expression rights is a far cry from the low level of protection the First Amendment afforded to free speech nearly a century ago. Many of the earliest cases that came before the Court pitted dissenting speakers against the government when tensions were great—either during wartime or at the height of the Cold War when fears of communist infiltration in American society gripped many ordinary Americans. In neither instance did free speech fare well.

The Supreme Court gave birth to the clear and present danger test in *Schenck v. United States* (1919).[23] In 1917, with the United States readying for active participation in World War I, Charles Schenck, a general secretary for the American Socialist Party, was tried and convicted for distributing leaflets arguing that the military draft was immoral. Although the pamphlet posed little danger of interfering with the draft, the Supreme Court refused to release Schenck from jail. Writing the majority opinion for a unanimous court, Justice Oliver Wendell Holmes stated that there was in fact "a clear and present danger" that the pamphlet could bring about the damage being claimed by the government.

In practice, the clear and present danger test soon became a hammer on speakers' rights rather than a shield against government suppression. Under the doctrine, members of the Socialist and Communist parties were tried and punished for participating in organizational meetings or declaring allegiance to their party's principles. Justice Holmes was clearly alarmed by the legacy his *Schenck* decision had wrought; in subsequent decisions he modified his earlier view by insisting that the present danger must relate to an "immediate evil" and a specific action. But Holmes was now in the minority, and there was little he could do to stop the momentum. During the late 1940s and early 1950s, when the fear of communism in the United States was reaching a fever pitch, members of the Communist Party were convicted for their advocacy of sedition. In *Dennis v. United States* (1951),[24] the Supreme Court gave a measure of credibility to this red scare when it upheld the convictions of numerous communist defendants for "teaching and advocating the overthrow and destruction of the Government of the United States."

---

[23] 249 U.S. 247 (1919).
[24] 341 U.S. 494 (1951).

The Warren Court and the Rise of the "Preferred Freedoms" Doctrine

By the late 1950s, fears of subversion and communist infiltration in the United States were beginning to subside. However, it was the ascension of former California Governor Earl Warren to the position of chief justice of the United States in 1953 that eventually changed the Court's free speech doctrine from one that offered little protection to dissenting speakers into one that protected even the most unpopular speakers against suppression by the majority. The Warren Court brought about this change by embracing a doctrine first articulated by Justice Harlan Fiske Stone in 1938. In a footnote to the otherwise unnotable case of *United States v. Carolene Products* (1938),[25] Justice Stone declared that various civil liberties guaranteed in the Bill of Rights, including the right of free expression, enjoyed a "preferred position" in constitutional law. Stone's explicit support for this preferred freedoms doctrine did not take immediate hold. Yet in the 1960s, when new social tensions such as the battle over civil rights and resistance to the Vietnam War threatened to wreak havoc on civil liberties, the Warren Court issued several key decisions that shattered any possibility the government might be able to suppress the exercise of free speech rights under the Constitution, as it had in the earlier part of the century.

In 1969, the Supreme Court abandoned the clear and present danger test and replaced it with a test that was much more protective of free speech in *Brandenburg v. Ohio* (1969).[26] A Ku Klux Klan rally in Cincinnati, Ohio, featured numerous

American Government . . . in Global Perspective:
One Russian Writer Asks: Is the American Press Truly Free?

Although no longer a communist country, pockets of Russia remain committed to the communists, and the Communist Party of the Russian Federation (CPRF) remains a viable entity in Russian national politics today, garnering one out of every eight votes cast in the 2003 national elections. The implementation of glasnost (the policy of political openness instituted by Soviet Premier Mikhail Gorbachev in the 1980s), though inconsistent at times, gives CPRF at least some voice in national newspapers and periodicals. For a dose of perspective that seems reminiscent of the old Soviet regime's attitudes, consider what one leftist Russian writer, David R. Hoffman, wrote in 2005 about American press freedoms in *Pravda OnLine*, the first web-based newspaper in the Russian language:

> There, of course, are those who claim the "great lie theory" cannot work in democratic countries like America, because, unlike nations

with government-controlled media, there is "freedom of the press." But this criticism is easily muted by the events that occurred a little over fifty years ago. . . . In 1950, a politically ambitious senator named Joseph McCarthy, during a speech in Wheeling, West Virginia, held up a piece of paper that allegedly contained the names of communists who were employed by America's State Department. This bold announcement helped to usher in an era of hysteria, fear, censorship and blacklisting that only began to wane four years later. . . . The legacy of McCarthyism demonstrates that, despite popular myth, America does not truly have a "free press." While the Bill of Rights guarantees that "Congress shall make no law . . . abridging freedom of the press," it is usually nongovernmental factors—fear of losing readers, viewers and/or advertising dollars—that actually control the decisions made by corporate-controlled news media.

Source: David R. Hoffman, "Great Lies of the American Free Press," *Pravda,* May 23, 2005, republished in Worldpress.org.

[25] 304 U.S. 144 (1938).
[26] 395 U.S. 444 (1969).

figures in white hoods uttering phrases that demeaned African Americans and Jews. The principal speaker had argued that some form of vengeance be taken against both groups. The group's leader was convicted under a law criminalizing the advocacy of violence. The Supreme Court overturned his conviction. In the process, it declared a new "imminent danger" test for such speech: first, is the speech "directed to inciting or producing imminent lawless action" and second, is the advocacy *likely* to produce such action? Few of the speakers jailed in the previous half century for seditious speech could have been convicted under this new standard.[27]

The preferred freedoms doctrine also offered protection to those exercising their rights of free expression in other contexts—to writers and publishers, filmmakers and protesters. Indeed, it provided a foundation for the protection of such modern activities as the dissemination of information on the Internet. Even speakers and publishers of certain categories of speech that have not traditionally enjoyed First Amendment protection—obscenity and libel, for example—soon discovered that the preferred freedoms doctrine provided protection for their activities.

The Freedom of the Press, Libel Laws, and Prior Restraints

Freedom of the press enjoys a long and storied tradition in the United States. Well before the American Revolution or the drafting of the Constitution, the trial of newspaper publisher John Peter Zenger in 1734 on charges of libel laid the foundation for robust press freedoms. **Libel** is the crime of printing or disseminating false statements that harm someone. Zenger was accused of attacking the corrupt administration of New York's colonial governor in his weekly newspaper. When he was acquitted on the basis of his lawyer's argument that he had printed true facts, Zenger's case helped to establish the legal principle that truth would serve as a defense to any libel action. In the late 1790s, after many Republican editors and publishers had been jailed under the highly controversial Sedition Act, public distaste for the act helped to catapult Thomas Jefferson and his Republican Party into power in the election of 1800.

Despite the general recognition of the importance of the press, newspapers traditionally enjoyed few special privileges under the law. Specifically, individuals whose reputations were harmed were free to bring libel suits—akin to the type brought against John Peter Zenger—against newspapers and other publications without any implications for the First Amendment. That all changed in 1964 with the landmark decision of *New York Times v. Sullivan*.[28] A Montgomery, Alabama, police commissioner sued the *New York Times* in March 1960 for an advertisement the newspaper had published. The ad—charging the existence of "an unprecedented wave of terror" against blacks in Montgomery—had been signed by several black clergymen. In its description of events that had transpired, the ad also contained some minor inaccuracies. Although the police commissioner was unable to prove that he had suffered any actual economic harm, he still sought a $500,000 judgment against the *Times*. But the Supreme Court refused to allow the official to claim damages, and in the process articulated a much more stringent test to be met by public officials suing for libel: they must prove that the newspapers had published false facts with malice (bad intentions) or reckless disregard for the truth (they ignored clear evidence of contrary facts).[29]

In subsequent years, the *New York Times v. Sullivan* decision has applied to public figures as well as public officials; today a libel lawsuit brought by any famous person—whether it's the president of the United States, Tiger Woods, or Julia Roberts—must prove that the newspaper or magazine in question not only printed false facts, but did so either with "malicious intent" or in "reckless disregard" for the truth. Of course, an important question remains: Who is a public figure? This was the question raised in the case of Richard Jewell, a security guard suspected of

★ **Libel**

Printing or disseminating false statements that harm someone.

[27] Harry Kalven, *A Worthy Tradition: Freedom of Speech in America* (New York: Harper & Row, 1988).
[28] 376 U.S. 254 (1964).
[29] Anthony Lewis, *Make No Law: The Sullivan Case and the First Amendment* (New York: Vintage Books, 1992).

setting off a bomb in Centennial Park in Atlanta, Georgia, during the 1996 Summer Olympics. Two people died in the explosion. Jewell was initially portrayed as a hero for his role in discovering the bomb, alerting authorities, and evacuating bystanders from the immediate vicinity. But when Jewell's status changed from hero to suspect, the resulting media coverage of the criminal investigation caused Jewell and his family considerable anguish. Although the investigation ultimately cleared Jewell of any involvement in the bombing, his reputation had been harmed enough that he decided to sue the *Atlanta Journal-Constitution,* which had rushed to judgment against him.

Jewell's entire lawsuit rested on the premise that he was (and continued to be) a private figure. Unlike public figures who had to prove the libeling newspaper had demonstrated a "reckless disregard for the truth," private figures seeking monetary damages need only show that the newspaper was "negligent." Immediately following the bomb explosion, but before he became a suspect, Jewell granted one photo shoot and ten interviews to the media, including *Larry King Live* and the *Today* show. During the course of these interviews, Jewell repeatedly stated that he had spotted a suspicious bag after a group of rowdy, college-aged men had left the park, and announced that he had matched one of the men to a composite sketch. These interviews proved Jewell's undoing, as both a trial judge and the Georgia Court of Appeals ruled that his media activities meant he had "voluntarily assumed a position of influence in the controversy," and thus was a public figure for purposes of his lawsuit. Jewell never received any monetary relief from the *Atlanta Journal-Constitution.*

★ Prior restraint

The government's requirement that a story be approved by government before it can be published.

Whereas libel laws punish publications after the fact, a **prior restraint** imposes a limit on publication *before* the material has actually been published. Securing a prior restraint is very difficult for government to accomplish. In the *Pentagon Papers Case* (1971),[30] the Supreme Court refused the U.S. government's request to stop the *Washington Post* and the *New York Times* from publishing a classified study of U.S. decision making about the Vietnam War. The courts have made it very difficult for government to implement a prior restraint of expression. In only the rarest of cases, such as the publication of information about troop movements during wartime, has government been able to block the publication of a story.

Obscenity and Pornography

Despite the exalted status free expression rights enjoy under the Constitution, obscenity has long been recognized as an exception to the rule. Even through the so-called sexual revolution of the 1960s and 1970s, the Supreme Court continued to adhere to the premise that truly obscene speech—words or publications that tend to violate accepted standards of decency by their very lewdness—may under certain circumstances be regulated. When asked how he would define obscene pornography, Justice Potter Stewart in 1964 uttered his now celebrated phrase: "I can't define it, but I know it when I see it." Stewart's statement captures the often confusing state of obscenity law in the United States. The First Amendment does not allow governments simply to ban all sexually explicit materials. But what types of materials can be banned? Is all pornography to be considered "obscene"?

In *Miller v. California* (1973)[31] the Supreme Court created the modern legal test for determining what sexually explicit materials may be legitimately subject to regulation under the Constitution. According to the Court, a work is obscene if *all* of these three conditions are met:

1. The average person applying contemporary community standards would think that the work (taken as a whole) appeals to the "prurient" (that is, lustful) interest.

2. The works depicts sexual conduct in a patently offensive way.

3. The work taken as a whole "lacks serious literary, artistic, political or scientific value."

[30] 403 U.S. 713 (1971).
[31] 413 U.S. 15 (1973).

With regard to obscenity, the First Amendment has often provided a measure of protection against attempts by communities to impose the majority's tastes on the minority. As social mores have evolved—and the bounds of tastelessness have been stretched—the courts have required governmental entities to go beyond oversimplified pleas for decency and good taste in their efforts to regulate sexually explicit material. At the same time, courts remain unwilling to ban any and all forms of regulating obscenity. As a consequence, court rulings attempt to find the fine line between tasteless speech and social mores.

In the late 1950s, a New York State licensing agency denied a movie company a license to show the film *Lady Chatterley's Lover* in the state. Although the movie's depiction of sexuality would be considered tame even by 1950s standards, the film focused at its core on an adulterous relationship, accompanied by the suggestion that adultery may be "right and desirable" for certain people under certain circumstances. The state banned *Lady Chatterley's Lover* as an "immoral film" that portrayed sexual immorality as "desirable, acceptable or proper." But in 1959, the Supreme Court reversed the licensing decision as a violation of free speech rights. At the same time, the Court distinguished the mere concept or idea of "sexual immorality" from "obscenity" or "pornography," both of which could still be regulated under certain circumstances.

Controversial disc jockey Howard Stern.

In 1973 during a midafternoon weekday broadcast on contemporary attitudes toward the use of language, a New York City radio station aired satirist comedian George Carlin's twelve-minute monologue titled "Filthy Words." Immediately before the broadcast, the station had advised listeners that it would include sensitive language that might be offensive to some. In the monologue, Carlin provided his thoughts about "the words you can't say on the public airwaves, um, the ones you definitely wouldn't say ever," especially the "original seven dirty words." Carlin then repeated the outlawed words in a variety of colloquialisms. When the Federal Communications Commission (FCC) threatened to impose formal sanctions on the radio station, it sued. In 1978, the Supreme Court narrowly upheld the FCC's authority to impose sanctions. The Court took pains to say that in this particular case, context was all-important: "Broadcasting is uniquely accessible to children, even those too young to read." At the same time, the Court hinted that occasional expletives, including even those in Carlin's monologue, might never justify a full criminal prosecution or some more serious sanction.

In 1995, the Infinity network paid over $1.7 million to the FCC to clear more than a hundred indecency claims made against the Howard Stern radio show. Stern, self-nicknamed "the King of all media," regularly describes in graphic detail oral, anal, and other forms of sex during his morning radio show, at a time when children may be part of the listening audience. As a consequence, Stern's lawyers have had little success getting the fines dismissed in court. Driven by his especially high ratings, Stern's radio station continued to back him even as his program lost more than eight thousand advertisers during the 1990s. Stern departed from commercial radio in 2006 to begin a pay-for satellite broadcast on Sirius Satellite Radio, where his material is not subject to FCC fines.

NOW YOU CAN SEE IT!

The most whispered about book in the world becomes the MOST TALKED ABOUT PICTURE OF THE YEAR!

THE FILM WITHOUT FALSE MODESTY!

D.H. LAWRENCE'S CONTROVERSIAL MASTERPIECE

"Lady Chatterley's Lover"

DANIELLE DARRIEUX

LEO GENN

and Introducing ERNO CRISA

A Kingsley International Release

EVERETT COLLECTION

Poster advertising *Lady Chatterly's Lover.* The film was based on a book which was the target of a New York state ban during the 1950s.

★ SLAPS test

A standard that courts established to determine if material is obscene based in part on whether the material has serious literary, artistic, political, or scientific value. If it does, then the material is not obscene.

★ Symbolic speech

Nonspoken forms of speech that might be protected by the First Amendment, such as flag burning, wearing armbands at school to protest a war, or camping out in public parks to protest the plight of the homeless.

This third condition has come to be known as the **SLAPS test** (derived from taking the first letter of each word). In theory, adherence to the SLAPS test allows a jury to apply its own conception of "contemporary community standards" and thus ban relatively innocent sexual materials. In practice, however, courts have found very few materials able to survive the SLAPS test (after all, who is to say what possesses "artistic value"?). None of the above rules apply to child pornography, which enjoys no First Amendment protection whatsoever under the Constitution.

The rise of the Internet as a medium of communication in recent years has caused even more confusion as to what types of obscenity and/or pornography can be regulated. In *Reno v. ACLU* (1997)[32] the Supreme Court invalidated a federal law passed to protect minors from "indecent" and "patently offensive" communications on the Internet. The Court feared that in denying minors access to potentially harmful speech, the law had suppressed a large amount of speech that adults have a constitutional right to receive. Still, the question of how to restrict sexually explicit speech on the Internet will remain an issue for years to come.

Symbolic Speech and the Flag-Burning Controversy

When school officials in Des Moines, Iowa, suspended two students for wearing black armbands in protest of the Vietnam War in the 1960s, they claimed they were not restricting free speech rights at all—rather, the students were engaging in conduct that could be regulated by authorities.[33] The Supreme Court in 1969 disagreed and the students were vindicated;[34] but the line between speech and conduct remains difficult to draw. Protesters often engage in disruptive activities that make powerful statements about important issues of public policy. They may camp out in public parks overnight to bring attention to the plight of the homeless, or burn their draft cards as a statement of opposition to a war. Are such forms of **symbolic speech** protected by the First Amendment?

In 1968, the Supreme Court in *United States v. O'Brien*[35] refused to allow a Vietnam War protester to burn his draft card in violation of federal law. That case introduced three criteria for determining whether the regulation of symbolic speech may be justified:

1. The government interest must be valid and important.

2. The interest must be unrelated to the suppression of free speech.

3. The restriction should be no greater than is essential to the furtherance of that interest.

In *United States v. O'Brien,* the key was motive: the Court believed the government actions were motivated by the need to operate a military registration system during wartime, rather than simply to suppress the ideas and message of this particular protester. Similarly, protesters do not have the right to violate federal park service rules and sleep in parks after closing—those rules were established for one

American Government: Historical, Popular, and Global Perspectives

[32] 521 U.S. 844 (1997).
[33] John W. Johnson, *The Struggle for Students' Rights:* Tinker v. Des Moines *and the 1960s* (Lawrence: University Press of Kansas, 1997).
[34] *Tinker v. Des Moines* (393 U.S. 503 (1969)).
[35] 391 U.S. 367 (1968).

reason: to prevent damage to public property. By contrast, students were granted the constitutional right to wear black armbands in school to protest the Vietnam War—their "conduct" was considered the equivalent of "pure speech," and school officials' arguments about the maintenance of order and discipline were given little credibility.

The constitutionality of flag burning has been a source of considerable debate in recent years. To many the American flag is a symbol of nationhood and national unity, and thus must be preserved at all costs. For that very reason, protesters seeking to attract publicity for their ideas have burned or desecrated the flag in public places. The Supreme Court ended the legal debate over flag burning with its decision in *Texas v. Johnson* (1989).[36] In 1984, Gregory Lee Johnson was arrested and convicted for "desecrating a venerated object" at a political demonstration in Dallas, the site of the Republican National Convention. Johnson had been leading a protest against the Reagan administration; he eventually set an American flag on fire, after which he and the other protesters chanted: "America, the red, white and blue, we spit on you." But the Supreme Court threw out Johnson's conviction because the "government may not prohibit the expression of an idea simply because society finds the idea itself offensive or disagreeable."[37]

Man arrested for flag burning on the steps of the United States Capitol.

AP PHOTO/CHARLES TASNADI

---

[36] 491 U.S. 397 (1989).
[37] Robert Justin Goldstein, *Flag Burning and Free Speech: The Case of* Texas v. Johnson (Lawrence: University Press of Kansas, 2000).

American Government ... in Popular Perspective:

Varying Levels of Support for the First Amendment

A 2008 book, which presented a comprehensive national study of American adults, high school students, teachers, and principals, explored the depth of support that exists for First Amendment free expression rights. The study found that students are less likely than adults to think that people should be allowed to express unpopular opinions or that newspapers should be allowed to publish freely without government approval of stories. The study also revealed that when it comes to situations more relevant to students' own lives and concerns, students agree at higher rates than adults that certain forms of expression should be allowed (that is, musicians singing songs with offensive lyrics, students reporting controversial issues in their papers without approval, and so on).

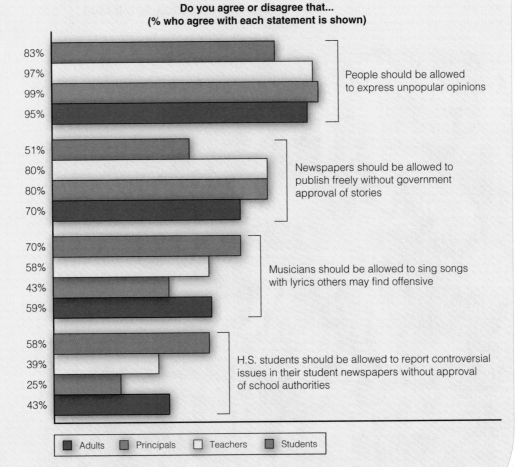

Do you agree or disagree that...
(% who agree with each statement is shown)

83%	
97%	People should be allowed to express unpopular opinions
99%	
95%	
51%	
80%	Newspapers should be allowed to publish freely without government approval of stories
80%	
70%	
70%	
58%	Musicians should be allowed to sing songs with lyrics others may find offensive
43%	
59%	
58%	
39%	H.S. students should be allowed to report controversial issues in their student newspapers without approval of school authorities
25%	
43%	

■ Adults   ■ Principals   □ Teachers   ■ Students

Source: Kenneth Dautrich, David Yalof, and Mark Hugo Lopez, *The Future of the First Amendment* (Lanham, MD: Rowman & Littlefield, 2008).

Despite the Supreme Court's apparent resolution of the matter, heated feelings on both sides of the flag-burning issue have kept it alive. After an initial attempt by Congress to pass flag-burning legislation failed to withstand judicial scrutiny in 1990, some members of Congress proposed passage of an amendment to the Constitution that would make flag burning unconstitutional. Although that proposed amendment has on several occasions achieved the necessary level of support in the House of Representatives, the U.S. Senate has so far failed to approve it, thus preventing it from being promulgated to state legislatures for ratification.

Hate Speech Codes

Since the 1970s, communities have sought to prevent speakers preaching hatred for certain groups—whether racial, religious, or some other classification—from exercising their rights of free speech in certain specified neighborhoods or other places where the perceived harms may be great. Such efforts have not always passed constitutional muster. In one instance during the late 1970s, the courts refused to deny Nazis the right to march in a parade in Skokie, Illinois, home to a large number of Holocaust victims.[38] By contrast, efforts to ban cross burning and other controversial forms of expression have sometimes been upheld. In *Virginia v. Black* (2003)[39] the U.S. Supreme Court ruled that the state of Virginia could prohibit cross burning with the "intent to intimidate any person or group," because the law applied only to intimidation and not to cross burning in general. The law also applied to all groups, not just racial or ethnic groups.

It is a considerable challenge for school officials to restrict hate speech by students at public colleges and universities, even when that speech proves disruptive to the school's mission of providing a constructive environment for learning.[40] In 1988, the University of Michigan passed a regulation subjecting individuals to discipline for "behavior, verbal or physical" that stigmatized or victimized an individual on the basis of race, ethnicity, religion, sex, or a host of other criteria. Stanford University similarly attempted to prohibit "discriminatory harassment," which was defined to include speech intended to stigmatize or insult on the basis of sex, race, and so on. Lower courts invalidated both of these "hate speech codes" on grounds that they violated the First Amendment.

The Second Amendment Right to Bear Arms

THE SECOND AMENDMENT: A well regulated militia, being necessary to the security of a free State, the right of the people to keep and bear Arms, shall not be infringed.

The Second Amendment "right to keep and bear arms" remains something of a puzzle for Americans. On one hand, the second part of the amendment appears to trumpet the "people's" right to own firearms at their discretion, and has taken its place as a central tenet in the platforms of interest groups such as the National Rifle Association (NRA), which opposes nearly all government attempts to restrict gun ownership. On the other hand, the first part of the amendment speaks directly of a "well-regulated militia," and implies that some relationship must exist between the private gun owner's rights and more formal state activities. The U.S. Supreme Court finally weighed in on the subject in 2008. In *District of Columbia v. Heller* (2008),[41] the Supreme Court by a 5–4 vote held that the Second Amendment forbids the government from banning all forms of handgun possession in the home for purposes of immediate self-defense. However, this Second Amendment right is not absolute: the Court noted that government can still regulate the commercial sale of handguns, and it can prohibit their possession by felons and the mentally ill, or in sensitive places such as school buildings.

GABRIEL BOUYS/AFP/GETTY IMAGES

A man buying a handgun at a gun shop in California. The 2008 Supreme Court decision in *District of Columbia v. Heller* ruled that the Second Amendment protects a person's right to own a handgun.

Congress has been reluctant to regulate gun ownership—only rarely are the sponsors of gun control able to overcome fierce lobbying efforts by the NRA and others in opposition. Advocates of gun control scored some success following the attempted assassination of President Ronald Reagan in 1981. Reagan was wounded

---

[38] Philippa Strum, *When the Nazis Came to Skokie: Freedom for Speech We Hate* (Lawrence: University Press of Kansas, 1999).
[39] 528 U.S. 343 (2003).
[40] Milton Heumann and Thomas W. Church, eds., *Hate Speech on Campus* (Boston: Northeastern University Press, 1997).
[41] 554 U.S. _____ (2008).

in the attempt, as was James Brady, his press secretary. Although the president fully recovered from his injuries in a matter of weeks, Brady sustained serious head injuries because a bullet tore into his temple and lodged in the base of his brain. He ultimately experienced a partial recovery, losing the permanent use of his left arm and left leg, as well as suffering from slurred speech patterns.

In 1985 Brady and his wife, Sarah, became spokespersons for gun control measures. Their efforts resulted in the Brady Handgun Violence Prevention Act, signed by President Clinton in 1993. The "Brady Law" required a five-day waiting period and a background check on handgun purchases from licensed firearms dealers to ensure that felons, drug users, fugitives, and other specified categories of individuals not be permitted to purchase guns. Gun advocates, including the NRA, lined up in opposition to the new law; publicly, they charged that the law violated citizens' Second Amendment "right to bear arms." But the NRA avoided any direct court challenges on this ground, hammering instead at more peripheral aspects of the law, such as the requirement that local sheriffs conduct these checks as part of a federal regulatory scheme. In 1997, the Supreme Court struck down this aspect of the Brady Law as a violation of federalism, although leaving the substance of the law in place. Congress has also attempted to restrict the carrying of firearms near schools, even though some of these efforts have been invalidated by the Supreme Court on the grounds that the federal government cannot commandeer the states to enforce federal legislation.

The Rights of the Criminally Accused

★ **Bill of attainder**

An act of a legislature declaring a person (or group) guilty of some crime, and then punishing them without a trial. The Constitution denies Congress the ability to issue a bill of attainder.

A few rights for the accused may be found in the language of the original Constitution. Article I prohibits Congress from passing a **bill of attainder,** which is an act of a legislature declaring a person (or group) guilty of some crime and then punishing them without a trial. It also prohibits **ex post facto laws,** which are new criminal laws retroactively applied to those who engaged in activities when they were not yet illegal. But the vast majority of constitutional rights for those accused of crimes are contained in the Fourth, Fifth, Sixth, and Eighth Amendments to the Constitution. Despite the seemingly explicit protections found in those four amendments, accused individuals enjoyed only limited substantive protection from arbitrary violations of criminal due process for better than a century and a half of this nation's history, as they protected defendants primarily only against intrusions by the federal government.

★ **Ex post facto laws**

A law that punishes someone for doing something in the past, at a time when the act was not illegal. The Constitution denies government the ability to write laws ex post facto.

Much of that changed in the 1960s with a number of decisions handed down by the Warren Court. During that period the Supreme Court applied many of the provisions of the Bill of Rights against state governments by incorporating most of the protections given accused persons in the federal judicial system. In addition, the Warren Court gave increased substance to these rights, holding government officials accountable under the Bill of Rights for their actions at highway road stops, during the interrogation of witnesses at the police station, and elsewhere.[42] Even the right to counsel was broadened to extend to far more of those accused of committing crimes. During the late 1980s and 1990s under Chief Justice William Rehnquist, the Court scaled back some of these protections. Nevertheless, defendants forced to weave their way through the criminal justice system today still enjoy numerous rights protections that were guaranteed for only the first time during the Warren Court era.

Fourth Amendment Rights

THE FOURTH AMENDMENT: The right of the people to be secure in their persons, houses, papers and effects, against unreasonable searches and seizures, shall not be violated, and no Warrants shall issue, but upon probable cause. . . .

The right of citizens to be free from unreasonable searches and seizures has a long history in America. Before the American Revolution, colonists loudly protested Eng-

[42] Lucas A. Powe Jr., *The Warren Court and American Politics* (Cambridge, MA: Belknap Press of Harvard University, 2002).

lish abuses of the power to inspect merchants' goods through the use of an unlimited "general warrant." Although the Fourth Amendment had been in place for nearly two centuries, the Warren Court modernized the rules governing police searches with its decision in *Katz v. United States* (1967).[43] The Court's ruling created the **Katz test,** which requires that the government attain a warrant demonstrating "probable cause" for any investigative activity that violates a person's reasonable expectation of privacy, whether or not the person is at home. A **warrant** is a document issued by a judge or magistrate that allows law enforcement to search or seize items at a home, business, or anywhere else that might be specified.

Perhaps the most controversial aspect of the Fourth Amendment is the mechanism by which it is enforced. Although no specific provision for enforcing civil liberties is provided in the amendment, since its 1961 decision in *Mapp v. Ohio*[44] the Supreme Court has demanded that the states adhere to the **exclusionary rule,** by which all evidence obtained by police in violation of the Bill of Rights must be "excluded" from admission in a court of law, where it might have assisted in convicting those who have been accused of committing crimes. Complaints about the exclusionary rule focus on its most likely beneficiaries: those who are guilty of committing some wrongdoing. They are the ones with the most potential evidence against them and thus have the most to gain from such exclusion. Detractors also complain about the "injustice" of the rule—whenever evidence is thrown out because of a warrantless search by police, "the criminal is to go free because the constable has blundered." Defenders of the rule counter that without a means of excluding such evidence, the government could violate the rights of guilty and innocent individuals alike by conducting the equivalent of fishing expeditions.

Since the 1960s, the Court has modified application of the exclusionary rule somewhat, although it has refused to back down from its central requirements. The most significant of these modifications is the **good faith exception** to the rule, which was first instituted in 1984: if a search warrant is invalid through no fault of the police (for example, the judge puts the wrong date on the warrant), evidence obtained under that warrant may still be admitted into court. Police may also under certain circumstances conduct warrantless searches of a defendant's premises. The allowable circumstances for a warrantless search include (1) the search is incidental to a lawful arrest; (2) the defendant has given consent to be searched; (3) the police are in "hot pursuit" of the defendant; and (4) the evidence is in "plain view" of police standing in a place where they have the legal right to be. Police may also briefly stop individuals driving in their cars, or conduct a "pat down" of suspicious individuals for weapons—in neither case is a warrant required. Nevertheless, police should conduct such warrantless searches with caution, as the good faith exception may be relied on only when conducting searches under the authority of a warrant.

Advances in technology and new innovations in police work have invited new types of Fourth Amendment civil liberties claims, and a potential reinterpretation of those rights by the U.S. Supreme Court. The testing of defendants for drug or alcohol use through breathalyzer tests and the taking of blood samples may require the police to jump through a series of procedural hoops imposed on them by the state, but no warrant is generally required in either instance when the defendant is in the legitimate custody of the police. Similarly, the DNA testing of defendants has provided a significant breakthrough in the prosecution of difficult cases that lack eyewitnesses or other "hard" evidence of the crime. The use of thermal imaging scans, which expand police investigative tactics from afar, has also been tested in the courts. A thermal imaging scan detects infrared radiation, which then converts radiation into images based on relative warmth, operating somewhat like a video camera showing heat images. In the mid-1990s, police forces began to employ the device to detect the presence of indoor halide lights used to grow marijuana plants inside large buildings; police are able to conduct these scans from vehicles parked across the street from the buildings in question. Do such scans violate a person's reasonable expectation of privacy? "Yes," said the Supreme Court, in a narrow 5–4 decision handed

★ *Katz* test

The legal standard that requires the government to attain a warrant demonstrating "probable cause" for any "search" that violates a person's actual and reasonable expectation of privacy.

★ Warrant

A document issued by a judge or magistrate that allows law enforcement to search or seize items at a home, business, or anywhere else that might be specified.

★ Exclusionary rule

The legal rule requiring that all evidence illegally obtained by police in violation of the Bill of Rights must be "excluded" from admission in a court of law, where it might have assisted in convicting those accused of commiting.

★ Good faith exception

An exception to the exclusionary rule that states if a search warrant is invalid through no fault of the police, evidence obtained under that warrant may still be admitted into court.

---

[43] 389 U.S. 347 (1967).
[44] 367 U.S. 643 (1961).

PHOTO: AP PHOTO/GARY TRAMONTINA

A thermal imaging instrument used by police to detect intense heat emissions. The Supreme Court banned its use without a warrant in 2001.

down in 2001:[45] "Where the Government uses a device that is not in general public use, to explore details of the home that would previously have been unknowable without physical intrusion, the surveillance is a 'search' and is presumptively unreasonable without a warrant."

Recently, some communities have posted cameras at stoplights that produce photographic evidence of traffic violations. Other communities have installed cameras on street corners in busy areas. When used in conjunction with computer databanks of convicted criminals, these cameras can provide surveillance capable of instantly detecting the presence of such figures on the street. Officials in Tampa, Florida, have recently turned to closed-circuit television systems to assist police departments in performing surveillance. Specifically, face recognition software programmed to identify certain wanted individuals has been employed on the streets of Tampa as well as in certain airports; an extensive network of cameras deployed throughout those areas can theoretically identify the faces of wanted individuals, and alert authorities quickly and efficiently of their presence.

Reviews of this technology have so far been mixed: Critics complain that the system often makes false matches in the same way that humans so often are mistaken. Civil libertarians further complain that the use of surveillance cameras in general violates many citizens' privacy rights, which they believe extend beyond the privacy of their own homes. Tampa abandoned the face recognition system in April 2001, but other cities continue to rely on closed-circuit cameras in general as a means of detecting crime—or if possible, preventing it from taking place.

To date, none of these modern police tactics have been successfully challenged on Fourth Amendment grounds. But as the use of these techniques is broadened—perhaps to facilitate racial profiling or other controversial forms of police investigation—it is certain that legal challenges will be waged.

Fifth Amendment Rights

THE FIFTH AMENDMENT: . . .No person shall be held to answer for a capital, or otherwise infamous crime, unless on a presentment or indictment of a grand jury ... nor shall any person be subject for the same offense to be twice put in jeopardy of life or limb; nor shall be compelled in any criminal case to be a witness against himself. . . .

Under the Fifth Amendment, the accused enjoy an assortment of rights that may prove crucial to their defense. The requirement that a grand jury, a jury that meets to decide whether the evidence is sufficient to justify a prosecutor's request that a case go to trial, be convened for serious crimes is theoretically significant; it forces prosecutors to convince an initial jury that a defendant should rightfully be forced to go to trial. (Grand juries do not decide on a defendant's guilt or innocence.) In practice, however, the grand jury requirement is rarely much of an obstacle to a skilled prosecutor, who can selectively present evidence to the jury members outside the view of the defendant or the defendant's lawyer. Moreover, because the grand jury requirement was never incorporated, it applies only to federal prosecutors in federal court.[46] The **double jeopardy clause** is a source of much greater protection for defendants: it provides that

★ **Double jeopardy**

The constitutional protection that those accused of a crime cannot be tried twice for the same crime.

American Government: Historical, Popular, and Global Perspectives

---

[45] *Kyllo v. U.S.* 533 U.S. 27 (2001).

[46] It should be noted, however, that a majority of states have chosen to use grand juries, even without being compelled to do so by the U.S. Constitution.

©DAVID R. FRAZIER/THE IMAGE WORKS

"You have the right to remain silent. Anything you say will be used against you in a court of law. You have the right to an attorney during interrogation; if you cannot afford an attorney, one will be appointed to you."

Miranda warning,
Miranda v. Arizona

no defendant may be tried twice for the same crime. Prosecutors must weigh carefully their probability of success at trial and bring forth all the relevant resources at their disposal. If the jury acquits the defendant, the prosecutor cannot try the defendant again. Still, the double jeopardy clause does not stop an altogether different government from retrying the defendant for violating that government's own laws. This occurred in the high-profile case of several white Los Angeles police officers who were accused in 1991 of beating Rodney King, an African American motorist whom they had stopped for a traffic violation. The acquittal of the police set off a series of race riots in Los Angeles. Later, federal charges were brought against the police for violating King's civil rights. At the federal trial, the officers were convicted.

Another provision of the Fifth Amendment is the so-called self-incrimination clause, which prevents individuals from being compelled to testify against themselves. Although originally interpreted to provide protection for defendants only in the courtroom, the self-incrimination clause today offers substantial protection to defendants being questioned by police at the station house or elsewhere. Certainly the clause protects defendants from being coerced or tortured into confessing to crimes. But the Warren Court truly changed this area of the law in the now famous case of *Miranda v. Arizona* (1966).[47] In that ruling, the Supreme Court announced the requirement that **Miranda warnings** be read to all defendants in custody before they are questioned by police.

Ernesto Miranda was convicted of the March 1963 kidnapping and rape of an eighteen-year-old girl in Phoenix, Arizona. Soon after the crime, the police picked up Miranda, who fit the description of the girl's attacker. Officers immediately took him into an interrogation room and told him (falsely) that he had been positively identified by his victim. After two hours of questioning, Miranda confessed. At trial, the defense counsel prodded one of the detectives into admitting that Miranda had never been given the opportunity to seek advice from an attorney prior to his interrogation. Miranda was nevertheless convicted and sentenced to forty to sixty years in prison. On appeal, the U.S. Supreme Court in 1966 set aside Miranda's conviction. Chief Justice Warren wrote: "Prior to any questioning, the

★ Miranda warning

The U.S. Supreme Court's requirement that when an individual is arrested he or she must be read a statement that indicates the person's right to remain silent and the right to an attorney.

[47] 384 U.S. 436 (1966).

person must be warned that he has a right to remain silent, that any statement he does make may be used as evidence against him, and that he has a right to the presence of an attorney, either retained or appointed. . . ."

Miranda was retried, this time without his confession being introduced into evidence at the trial, and again convicted. Although his original confession could not be used, a former girlfriend testified that Miranda had told her about the kidnapping and rape. After Miranda was paroled in 1972, he spent time in and out of prison before being stabbed fatally in a bar at the age of thirty-four. Thanks to police drama shows and movies, the Miranda warnings are better known to citizens today than are any other constitutional protections: police must routinely tell suspects being questioned that they have the right to remain silent and the right to a court-appointed attorney, and confirm that the suspects understand these rights. Perhaps that's why a more conservative Supreme Court conceded in the case of *United States v. Dickerson* (2000) that Miranda has become so "embedded in routine police practice" that the warnings have become "part of our national culture." Thus a failure to read the list of Miranda rights to witnesses may still result in any subsequent confession to the police being thrown out of court by virtue of the exclusionary rule.[48]

Sixth Amendment Rights

> *THE SIXTH AMENDMENT: In all criminal prosecutions, the accused shall . . . have the Assistance of Counsel for his defense.*

Images of beleaguered and confused defendants trying desperately to defend themselves against experienced and well-seasoned prosecutors are now mostly a thing of the past. In 1963, the Supreme Court in *Gideon v. Wainwright*[49] ordered a new trial for an indigent defendant who had been ordered by the State of Florida to defend himself in a criminal trial, even though he possessed no legal training. Under prevailing Sixth Amendment standards today, no indigent criminal defendant can be sentenced to jail unless the defendant has been provided with a lawyer at no cost. This constitutional right to the assistance of counsel even extends beyond the trial: a court-appointed lawyer must assist the defendant in preparing the case and in all other hearings and meetings before trial. Some critics of the criminal justice system cite the disparity that often exists between the quality of court-appointed counsel and of paid counsel for well-off defendants. Nevertheless, public defenders' offices have been established all over the country in response to the requirement that indigent defendants be provided with lawyers.

Eighth Amendment Rights

> *THE EIGHTH AMENDMENT: Excessive bail shall not be required, nor excessive fines imposed, nor cruel and unusual punishments inflicted.*

★ Bail

An amount of money determined by a judge that the accused must pay to a court as security against the defendant's freedom before trial.

The Eighth Amendment deals in a limited way with defendants being held for trial: according to its language, **bail,** which is an amount of money paid to the court as security against a defendant's freedom before trial, may not be excessive. In practice, that provision applies only when bail is proper in the first place; many high-risk defendants are held either to prevent flight or to ensure that they do not cause more harm while on release. In those instances, bail may be denied altogether without any violation of the Constitution.

Far more significant are the concluding words of the Eighth Amendment with respect to "cruel and unusual punishment." No government may impose a cruel and unusual punishment on an individual, but there remains heated debate over what is "cruel and unusual." Traditionally, the clause prohibited only those punishments that even the drafters of the Bill of Rights would have disapproved of—drawing and quartering, beheading, and other forms of extreme torture. In recent times, the Court has added to the mix the requirement of "proportionality," in which serious punishments

[48] Gary Stuart, *Miranda: The Story of America's Right to Remain Silent* (Tucson: University of Arizona Press, 2004).
[49] 372 U.S. 335 (1963).

may not be imposed for relatively minor offenses. Thus, for instance, the Court has struck down imprisonment for the offense of narcotics addiction.

The Supreme Court has never held the death penalty to be inherently cruel and unusual. Most modern lawsuits by prisoners on "death row" focus on the manner by which the death sentence has been imposed. Any judge or jury that imposes capital punishment must have the opportunity to consider mitigating circumstances that might generate some sympathy for the accused. Nor can a jury impose a death sentence at the same time that it finds the defendant guilty; the defendant's lawyers must be given a chance to argue against imposition of the death penalty without also having to prove the defendant is innocent. Finally, certain defendants may not receive the death penalty. In 2002, the Court in *Atkins v. Virginia* ruled executions impermissible in the case of mentally retarded defendants.[50] Then in 2005, the Court also ruled executions impermissible for defendants who committed their crimes while under the age of eighteen.

Critics of the system claim that so many death penalty cases are held up on appeal that bad luck and misfortune are inevitable in the process.[51] Furthermore, advances in DNA testing technology have revealed that some prisoners on death row were innocent of the crime for which they had been sentenced to death. Even in the face of unrelenting popular support for the death penalty, governors in Illinois and Maryland recently announced a "moratorium" on executions in their respective states, to be continued as long as the process by which death sentences are determined remains so riddled with errors.

The Modern Right to Privacy

Perhaps no single constitutional right garnered more controversial attention during the second half of the twentieth century than the right of a woman to have an abortion. Unlike all the other rights mentioned so far in this chapter, however, neither the specific right to abortion, nor the more general right to privacy, are explicitly referred to in the Constitution or in the amendments to the Constitution. The right to privacy is thus often referred to as an unwritten or "unenumerated" right. The Ninth Amendment counsels against dismissing such rights offhand. It reads: "The enumeration in the Constitution of certain rights, shall not be construed to deny or disparage others retained by the people." In other words, the fact that other rights such as freedom of speech are written down in the Bill of Rights does not mean that the Constitution doesn't also recognize certain unwritten rights.

The recognition of unstated rights in the Constitution raises difficult questions, such as how to justify recognizing certain unenumerated rights but not others. In 1965, the Supreme Court stepped into this controversy with its decision in *Griswold v. Connecticut*,[52] when it invalidated an 1879 Connecticut law prohibiting the dissemination of information about and the sale of contraceptives. Seven of the nine justices ruled that although the right to birth control is not explicitly mentioned in the Constitution, several provisions of the Bill of Rights (the First, Third, Fourth, and Fifth) and the Fourteenth Amendment suggest that, taken together, these provisions create a "zone of privacy" that includes within it the right to decide whether or not to bear a child. Although the Supreme Court's methods were considered highly speculative, widespread acceptance of birth control devices allowed the Supreme Court to avoid controversy in the years following the decision.[53]

No such sidestepping of heated controversy was possible in 1973, when the Supreme Court formally recognized the constitutional right of a woman to an abortion in *Roe v. Wade*.[54] By the early 1970s, nearly fifteen states had passed liberal abortion laws, but lawyers for Norma McCorvey (she used the pseudonym of "Jane Roe" for purposes of her lawsuit) argued that the decision to end a pregnancy was a constitutional right that *all fifty states* must adhere to. McCorvey herself had been unable to

50 536 U.S. 304 (2002).
51 Austin Sarat, *When the State Kills* (Princeton, NJ: Princeton University Press, 2002).
52 381 U.S. 479 (1965).
53 John W. Johnson, *Griswold v. Connecticut: Birth Control and the Constitutional Right of Privacy* (Lawrence: University Press of Kansas, 2005).
54 410 U.S. 113 (1973).

secure a legal abortion in Texas and so eventually gave birth and put her baby up for adoption. The Supreme Court agreed to take her case and rule on the general constitutionality of abortion restrictions.

In ruling in McCorvey's favor, the Supreme Court affirmed that the Constitution recognizes a woman's right to privacy in general—and thus a right to abortion more specifically—even though neither of those rights is ever spelled out explicitly. Such a right is not absolute throughout the term of the pregnancy, however. The author of the opinion, Justice Harry Blackmun, divided the pregnancy into three stages as part of a highly controversial *trimester framework*. During the first trimester, a woman's right to end her pregnancy is absolute. During the second trimester the right is nearly absolute, although the government has the right to restrict abortions that might pose threats to a woman's health. Finally, in the third trimester (when the fetus is potentially viable), the state government is allowed to

CHECKtheLIST

Three "Might Have Beens" on the Road to the Rights Revolution

In his *Book of Legal Lists* (1997), the late scholar Bernard Schwartz identified what he termed "The Ten Greatest Supreme Court 'Might Have Beens.'" Of those ten, three would have had a direct impact on the rights revolution, which enjoyed unprecedented encouragement from the Supreme Court during the 1960s and 1970s.

✔ **Earl Warren as Chief Justice**. President Eisenhower did not want to name California Governor Earl Warren, who had no judicial experience whatsoever, to be the next chief justice of the U.S. Supreme Court. But he had promised Warren the "first available Supreme Court vacancy" to earn his support at the 1952 Republican convention, and when sixty-three-year-old Chief Justice Fred Vinson died unexpectedly in 1953, Warren insisted that President Eisenhower live up to his promise. Warren's subsequent leadership of the Supreme Court gave birth to the rights revolution of the 1960s.

✔ *Roe v. Wade*. Justice Harry Blackmun's first draft of a majority opinion in this famous case was unremarkable, avoiding altogether the critical issue of whether a pregnant woman had an absolute right to an abortion. Rather, the draft actually supported state substantive power over abortion, but ruled that the laws presented to the Court (those in Texas and Georgia) were too "vague" to be constitutional. Had that draft been handed down as the official Court opinion, the "subsequent schism that has been a major factor in American life" might well have been postponed or avoided. But Chief Justice Warren Burger ordered reargument in the case, and Blackmun's later draft became the controversial law of the land.

✔ *Mapp v. Ohio*. Called the most radical decision of its time, the 1961 Mapp decision ensured that in every state of the country, whenever the police blunder, the criminal goes free and society pays the price. But the decision truly came out of nowhere—the briefs and arguments in the Supreme Court were all devoted to the First Amendment issue of whether Ohio's law barring obscene material (which the police found in Mapp's possession) was constitutional. The Court's discussion of the case at conference even proceeded that way. But in the elevator after leaving the conference room, three justices decided this would be a good case to use to overrule the exclusionary rule, and they found two more allies within the next few days, including Justice Tom Clark, who agreed to reverse his position on the exclusionary rule. "I was shocked," wrote Justice Potter Stewart later about the events that had transpired. As Bernard Schwartz notes, had the elevator meeting and Clark's switch not occurred, "the Warren Court's most important criminal law holding would have been stillborn."

Source: Bernard Schwartz, *A Book of Legal Lists* (New York: Oxford University Press, 1997).

impose any abortion restrictions on the mother, so long as they do not limit efforts to protect the life or health of the mother.[55]

The number of legal abortions that occurred in the United States rose dramatically in the years immediately following *Roe v. Wade*. The decision also unleashed a fury of controversy from antiabortion interest groups and conservative lawmakers. The election of Ronald Reagan to the presidency in 1980 and his re-election in 1984 set the stage for *Roe v. Wade*'s weakening; as a candidate for high office, Reagan had specifically targeted *Roe v. Wade* as a case of illegitimate judicial activism and had promised to nominate Supreme Court justices who would overturn the controversial decision. Reagan's more conservative Supreme Court appointments began to make their presence known during the late 1980s, when increasingly severe restrictions on abortion were upheld by the Court.

In 1992, the Supreme Court overhauled *Roe v. Wade's* controversial trimester framework in *Planned Parenthood v. Casey*.[56] Although the Court did not specifically overturn *Roe*, the justices replaced the trimester framework with a less stringent *undue burden test:* does the restriction at issue—regardless of what trimester it affects— *unduly burden* a woman's right to privacy under the Constitution? One example of this new constitutional test at work can be found in the Court's approach to state-mandated twenty-four-hour waiting periods for abortion. Under *Roe v. Wade*, the requirement that a woman wait for an abortion in either of the first two trimesters would have been unconstitutional. Yet in *Casey*, the Court held that such a waiting period does not unduly burden the woman's right to privacy. Other regulations that have been upheld under the *Casey* framework include the requirement that minors seek permission from a parent or a court before having an abortion, and the requirement that women be provided information about the specific medical effects an abortion will have on the fetus.

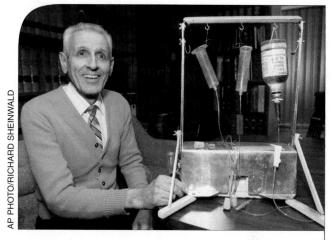

Jack Kevorkian, with his euthanasia machine, in 1991.

Not all abortion restrictions are allowed under this new framework. In *Casey*, the Supreme Court invalidated a requirement that women notify their spouses of their intention to have abortions. Yet many more provisions restricting abortion have been upheld since 1992 under the less restrictive *Casey* doctrine. In *Gonzales v. Carhart* (2007)[57] the Supreme Court upheld the Partial Birth Abortion Act of 2003, which effectively banned the use of the "intact dilation and extraction" abortion procedure, most often performed during the second trimester of pregnancies.

Once the unwritten right to privacy became a reality in constitutional law, it seemed inevitable that citizens might try to claim other unwritten rights implicating privacy in the same fashion. Although most efforts to expand the right to privacy beyond abortion and birth control have met with limited success, the Court has not always shut the door on these claims. In 1986, the Court held that a Georgia law that criminalized acts of sodomy by homosexuals was constitutional. Seventeen years later in the case of *Lawrence v. Texas*,[58] the Court reversed itself, holding that a Texas law making it a crime for two people of the same sex to engage in certain types of intimate sexual conduct did in fact violate the individual's right to due process.

The highly visible prosecutions of Dr. Jack Kevorkian for helping terminally ill patients end their lives has brought added attention to the issue of physician-assisted suicide in recent years. On April 13, 1999, Kevorkian, a retired pathologist, was sentenced to jail in Michigan for helping a terminally ill man die by direct injection, a form of voluntary euthanasia. Kevorkian, labeled by many of his opponents as "Dr. Death," had already acknowledged publicly that he had helped at least ninety other people to die by assisted suicide in Michigan between 1990 and 1997. Indeed, when enforcement authorities in Michigan initially refused to charge Kevorkian with

[55] N. E. H. Hull and Peter Charles Hoffer, Roe v. Wade: *The Abortion Rights Controversy in American History* (Lawrence: University Press of Kansas, 2001).
[56] 505 U.S. 833 (1992).
[57] 550 U.S. ___ (2007).
[58] 539 U.S. 558 (2003).

killing his most recent patient, he took a tape of the incident to CBS television and aired it in the widely watched news program *60 Minutes*. On the program, Kevorkian challenged the state to act: three days later he got his wish.

Questions remain about Kevorkian's tactics—do terminally ill patients have the right to end their life, and if so, can a licensed physician assist them in doing so? Although the Court has been willing to recognize a right of terminally ill patients to end their medical treatment, it has steadfastly refused to extend that privilege to the active termination of one's life. In 1997, the Supreme Court held that no such constitutional right exists, although the justices were significantly divided as to the specific reasons why that is so. But the Court also indicated that states are free to legalize physician-assisted suicide. Since then, only one state (Oregon) has enacted an assisted suicide law. As for Kevorkian, after serving eight years of his prison sentence for second-degree murder, he was granted parole and released from prison on June 1, 2007.

Now & Then: Making the Connection

Passionate debates over constitutional rights are hardly a new phenomenon. With a tradition of robust press protections in America dating back to John Peter Zenger's acquittal in the early eighteenth century, the Sedition Act of 1798 stood little chance of long-term success; America's policy of openness to immigrants from abroad similarly doomed the Alien Act passed that same year. (Both were effectively repealed just three years after their passage.) President George W. Bush and the members of his administration expected criticism when they attempted to circumvent some of those same protections in prosecuting a war on terrorism; still, they vigorously defended those initiatives as necessary for national security. Although the Adams and Bush administrations' respective initiatives could have been loosely defined as "wartime measures," not all Americans proved equally willing to sacrifice their rights toward this greater cause. Of course their stories ended quite differently: John Adams suffered the public's wrath at the polls in 1800, whereas George W. Bush's prosecution of the war on terrorism earned him some resistance, but did not prevent his re-election to the presidency in 2004. Ultimately a balancing act between the interests of national security and the integrity of these constitutional rights is required—of course not all presidents are able to strike that balance with the same degree of political success.

Notwithstanding the enduring value conflict between national security and individual liberty, it is quite clear that during the past half century the Bill of Rights has been transformed from a set of mostly paper guarantees with only limited impact on the daily lives of Americans into a truly formidable arsenal of rights that have revolutionized government practices in the public square, at police stations, and in the nation's criminal courts. Certainly the Warren Court of the 1960s was responsible for much of this transformation. But the seeds of change were planted much earlier, first through ratification of the Fourteenth Amendment to protect individuals against state intrusion on their rights, and then later, when Justice Harlan Fiske Stone offered a theory of preferred freedoms in 1938 that trumpeted the freedom of speech and other rights that gave citizens their voice in the democratic process. Chief Justice Warren took Justice Stone up on this offer nearly a quarter of a century later, and the rights revolution was subsequently born.

In recent decades, the Supreme Court has attempted to return some authority to state governments to manage their own affairs. It has also scaled back some of the more controversial Warren Court decisions. In particular, the Rehnquist Court loosened many of the restrictions on government imposed by the two religious clauses of the First Amendment: the establishment clause and the free exercise clause; it also diluted a woman's right to abortion under *Roe v. Wade* in the 1990s. At the same time, many of the sweeping changes introduced by the Warren Court have been left untouched. And some constitutional protections have even been broadened in the past fifteen years—the right to free speech, for example, now encompasses the right to burn a flag as a statement of political protest.

CAPITAL PUNISHMENT

The death penalty is the ultimate punishment for those convicted of crimes—it cannot be reversed once carried out, and it effectively trumps the exercise of all other rights. And yet capital punishment remains a staple of the American criminal justice system, sustained by public opinion polls which have long shown a clear majority of Americans in its favor. An ABC News survey in July 2006 found 65 percent in favor of capital punishment, consistent with many other polls taken in recent years. Moreover, according to a Gallup poll from two months earlier, nearly half the American public thinks the death penalty isn't imposed frequently enough, and fully 60 percent believe it is applied fairly in its current form. Since 1976, the Supreme Court has consistently held that with proper safeguards, the application of the death penalty to competent adults does not violate the Eighth Amendment's prohibition against "cruel and unusual punishment."

AP PHOTO/MICHAEL CONROY

What may seem surprising to many is the degree to which Americans' support for the death penalty defies worldwide trends which have moved consistently in the opposite direction since World War II. By 1977, 16 countries had become "abolitionist" regarding the death penalty; by 2006, 89 countries worldwide had abolished capital punishment for all offenses, including all but one European country (Belarus is the exception), many Pacific area states (including Australia and New Zealand), and Canada. In 2005, just 25 countries carried out executions, with the United States ranking sixth (53 executions), behind only China, Iran, Pakistan, Iraq, and the Sudan. To a nation that prides itself as a beacon of light for freedom, this seems like unusual company. And yet the movement to abolish the death penalty in the United States has not made much headway in recent years. Supporters of capital punishment argue that it deters crime and prevents recidivism. Opponents counter that it does not deter criminals more than life imprisonment, risks the execution of the wrongfully convicted, and discriminates against minorities.

At http://academic.cengage.com/dautrich, find the politics interactive link for details on the current state of the death penalty in the United States, the factors that have contributed to its continued support, relevant statistical information, and death penalty studies. Consult as well the various links that help place the current debate over the death penalty into historical, popular, and global perspectives.

http://academic.cengage.com/dautrich

Chapter Summary

★ Civil liberties are those specific individual rights that cannot be denied to citizens by government that are guaranteed by the Constitution. Most of these rights are in the first eight amendments to the Constitution, known as the Bill of Rights.

★ The original Constitution did not include a bill of rights, and the way the Framers guaranteed ratification of the Constitution was to promise that the first Congress would take up as its first task the passage of these amendments.

★ Civil liberties are subject to formal interpretation from the courts, and informal interpretation by those charged with their enforcement. The courts' interpretation of these rights has evolved greatly over the past two centuries. Originally, these rights were protected from intrusion by the federal government, not necessarily state or local government. However, beginning in the mid-twentieth century, the U.S. Supreme Court, through a process known as incorporation, used the Fourteenth Amendment to extend most of these protections from state and local encroachment as well.

★ The free exercise clause bans government laws that prohibit the free exercise of religion. Debate over the clause has largely focused on whether government laws can force adherents of a certain religion to engage in activities that are prohibited by their religious beliefs or prevent them from performing acts that are compelled by their religious beliefs.

★ The establishment clause prohibits the government from enacting any law "respecting an establishment of religion." In recent decades, the Supreme Court has moved from a position of especially strict separation to one that shifts back and forth between principles of separation and accommodation.

★ The First Amendment rights of free speech and press enjoy especially revered status in the United States because free expression promotes the marketplace of ideas, acts as a watchdog on government, and advances the capacity for individuals to create ideas and improve society.

★ The press is afforded a great deal of latitude because the courts have made libel suits very difficult to prosecute, and under very few conditions may government issue a prior restraint on the publication of a story. Speech is not just the spoken word—it also includes such things as flag burning, referred to as symbolic speech, and also enjoys high protections by the courts.

★ The right of citizens to be free from unreasonable searches and seizures has a long history in America, and is the subject of the Fourth Amendment. Although there are some exceptions to the exclusion of evidence based on a warrantless search, the basic notion that probable cause is a requirement for a warrant and that a warrant is necessary for a search holds true.

★ Modern technologies have given the police and investigators new methods of search and surveillance. Some of these modern police tactics have been successfully challenged on Fourth Amendment grounds. But as the use of these techniques is broadened—perhaps to facilitate racial profiling or other controversial forms of police investigation—it is certain that legal challenges will be waged.

★ Additional rights of the accused are articulated in the Fifth Amendment, including the double jeopardy clause, the grand jury requirement, and the self-incrimination clause. The U.S. Supreme Court has ruled that police must read the "Miranda rights" to anyone who is arrested, which indicates not only the right to remain silent, but also the right to an attorney—a right protected by the Sixth Amendment. The failure to read the Miranda rights may lead to a confession being excluded as evidence at trial.

★ The Ninth Amendment indicates that just because an individual right is not explicitly spelled out does not mean that the right is not protected. Two such high-profile rights are the subject of much national debate: the right to privacy and the right to die. The former served as the basis for *Roe v. Wade*—the case that provided women with abortion rights. A more recent conservative Supreme Court has allowed the states to place more restrictions on abortion rights of late. And although the Court has been willing to recognize the right of terminally ill patients to end their medical treatment, it has steadfastly refused to extend that privilege to the active termination of one's life.

Key Terms

Bail (p. 114)

Bill of attainder (p. 110)

Civil liberties (p. 92)

Double jeopardy (p. 112)

Establishment clause (p. 97)

Ex post facto laws (p. 110)

Exclusionary rule (p. 111)

Free exercise clause (p. 95)

Good faith exception (p. 111)

Incorporation (p. 93)

Katz test (p. 111)

Lemon test (p. 99)

Libel (p. 103)

Miranda warning (p. 113)

Prior restraint (p. 104)

SLAPS test (p. 106)

Symbolic speech (p. 106)

Warrant (p. 111)

Resources

Important Books

Amar, Akhil Reed. *The Constitution and Criminal Procedure.* New Haven, CT: Yale University Press, 1997.

Brigham, John. *The Constitution of Interests: Beyond the Politics of Rights.* New York: New York University Press, 1996.

Graber, Mark. *Transforming Free Speech.* Berkeley: University of California Press, 1991.

Irons, Peter. *The Courage of Their Convictions.* New York: Penguin Books, 1988.

Lewis, Anthony. *Gideon's Trumpet.* New York: Vintage, 1989.

Lewis, Anthony. *Make No Law: The Sullivan Case and the First Amendment.* New York: Vintage, 1991.

O'Connor, Karen. *No Neutral Ground? Abortion Politics in the Age of Absolutes.* Boulder, CO: Westview Press, 1996.

O'Neil, Robert M. *Free Speech in the College Community.* Bloomington: Indiana University Press, 1997.

Ravitch, Frank. *School Prayer and Discrimination.* Boston: Northeastern University Press, 1999.

Stone, Geoffrey. *Perilous Times.* New York: W. W. Norton, 2004.

Internet Sources

http://www.aclu.org (the home page of the American Civil Liberties Union; features coverage of a wide range of developments in civil liberties, as well as links to resources and other relevant websites)

http://www.cfa-inc.org/ (the website of the Citizens Flag Alliance, which is dedicated to fighting for a constitutional amendment to ban flag desecration)

http://www.fac.org/ (the website of the First Amendment Center, which works to preserve and protect First Amendment freedoms in America through information and education)

http://www.eff.org/ (the website of the Electronic Frontier Foundation, founded to protect rights and promote freedom on the electronic frontier, including the Internet)

http://www.rfcnet.org/ (the website of the Religious Freedom coalition)

5 Civil Rights, Equality, and Social Movements

Shannon Faulkner in 1995

Slow Going for a Pioneer in Equal Rights: Now & Then

After fighting a landmark legal battle with the help of civil rights groups, she had finally secured the right to attend this famous southern institution of higher education. The Fourteenth Amendment, the courts had ruled, prohibited the school from excluding her. Bracing for the worst, she expected resentment and hostility from fellow students once she arrived on campus. The torments and continuous taunting were worse than she anticipated. After receiving numerous death threats, she needed an armed escort to accompany her to classes. Soon the isolation proved unbearable, and in less than a week this landmark experiment in equal rights had reached its premature conclusion. While detractors cheered, the woman packed her bags and left the school she had fought so long and hard to enter. Although equal rights did not prevail at that moment in time, her overall cause was not lost—within a few years many other students like her would successfully enter that same institution under more favorable conditions, and many of them would go on to graduate. Although her efforts to strike a blow at the backward traditions of the institution had failed for her personally, those efforts had not been in vain.

Autherine Lucy in 1956

PHOTO: ©BETTMANN/CORBIS

NOW &

2007 | 1997 | 1987 | 1977 | 1967 |

1995

Now . . . In 1995, Shannon Faulkner became a modern-day pioneer in equal rights. The institution Faulkner challenged was The Citadel in Charleston, South Carolina. The Citadel was a 152-year-old male-only military academy that prided itself on producing "citizen-soldiers," men uniquely prepared for leader-ship in military service and in civilian life. Faulkner had been accepted to The Citadel in 1993 after submit-ting an application that had failed to reveal her gender. When the school found out Faulkner was a woman, it immediately withdrew her acceptance, sparking a lawsuit filed on her behalf. Eventually a federal district court ordered The Citadel to admit Faulkner in 1995 on the grounds that no public school could discrimi-nate on the basis of sex. She moved into the barracks on August 12, 1995, accompanied by federal mar-shals because she had received so many death threats. Although Faulkner began "hell week" with the rest of her classmates, the emotional toll of the death threats and her isolation—combined with the physical toll of intense physical training—eventually proved too much for her. After only a day of training she was admitted to the infirmary with heat-related symptoms, and on her fifth day at The Citadel Faulkner dropped out of the school. When the news of her withdrawal got out, the male cadets let out a roar of celebration around campus. But their "victory" was short-lived: taking advantage of the court order that Faulkner had secured, four more women enrolled at The Citadel the following year. By 1999, 83 women were among the 665 incoming freshmen at the once all-male Citadel.

1956

1957 | 1947 | 1937 | 1927 | 1917 |

Then . . . Faulkner was hardly the first pioneer to face such trying circumstances at an institution of education steeped in tradition. The hypothetical also describes the experience of Autherine Lucy, the first African American student to win admission to the University of Alabama. On June 29, 1955, lawyers from the National Association for the Advancement of Colored People (NAACP) secured a court order restraining the university from rejecting Lucy's application on the basis of race; seven months later, on February 3, 1956, the twenty-six-year-old Lucy enrolled as a graduate student in library science at the university's main campus in Tuscaloosa. That's when her personal nightmare began. Immediately upon her arrival she faced mobs of students yelling "Kill her! Kill her!" wherever she walked on campus. She needed a police escort to get her to class and to protect her in the classroom, where she could hear the crowds chanting epithets at her from outside. Just three days after Lucy enrolled, the university's board suspended her, defending its action as necessary "for her safety and that of other students." Although the NAACP's attempts to overturn Lucy's suspension were unsuccessful, within a decade many more African American students would follow in her footsteps, using a series of court orders to force the integration of the University of Alabama. The battle Autherine Lucy waged against University of Alabama officials was played out over and over again at other educational institutions in the late 1950s and early 1960s as part of a civil rights movement that brought national and international attention to issues of racial discrimination and inequality.

The Eleven Largest Political Demonstrations Ever Held in Washington, DC

Demonstration	Date	Number of People
✔ **March for Women's Lives** (favoring abortion and reproductive rights)	April 24, 2004	1,150,000 people
✔ **Vietnam Moratorium Rally**	November 15, 1969	600,000 people
✔ **Vietnam "Out Now" rally**	April 24, 1971	500,000 people
✔ **National Organization for Women March for Women's Lives**	April 5, 1992	500,000 people
✔ **Million Man March**	October 16, 1995	400,000 people
✔ **March on Washington II**	August 20, 1983	300,000 people
✔ **Pro-Choice Rally**	April 9, 1989	300,000 people
✔ **Lesbian and Gay Rights Rally**	April 25, 1993	300,000 people
✔ **Solidarity Day Labor Rally**	September 19, 1981	260,000 people
✔ **Solidarity Day for Labor**	August 31, 1991	250,000 people
✔ **March on Washington**	August 28, 1963	250,000 people

List does not include routine events such as presidential inaugurations or Fourth of July festivities.

Just as Autherine Lucy challenged the white-only traditions of the South, Shannon Faulkner dared to rock the foundations of a well-entrenched male-only institution. Neither of these two women was able to stay in her school long enough to see the institution transformed. Both women, however, made significant contributions to the cause of equal rights. Traditions die hard, and those who battle such institutions in the name of equality must prepare themselves for slow going. Even when court opinions and legislation have transformed the political landscape in favor of equality, social and cultural landscapes often remain products of a stubborn past.

Types of Equality

In the abstract, the word *equality* sits alongside terms such as *liberty, freedom,* and *justice* as lofty values that underlie American political culture. Unfortunately, when it comes to settling on a formal definition of equality, no consensus exists. "All men are created equal," Thomas Jefferson wrote in the Declaration of Independence of 1776. But Jefferson never intended that document to extend to African American slaves, at least not in the short run. When Abraham Lincoln warned in 1859 that "those who deny freedom to others, deserve it not for themselves," the future president of the United States did not consider the lot of women in American society, who at that time enjoyed no freedom to vote or own property, among other rights. As with any other abstract ideal, we must fully define *equality* in order to understand all that it encompasses.

References to different types of equality tend to appear again and again in discussions of American politics:

Political equality generally refers to a condition in which members of different groups possess substantially the same rights to participate actively in the political system. These rights include voting, running for office, and formally petitioning the government for redress of grievances. In a democracy, the rights to free speech, to free press, and (at least arguably) to a quality education may also be considered necessary elements of political quality, as those who are denied such rights often are less able to exercise influence over the political process in any meaningful way. In the years immediately following the Civil War, some moderates in Congress argued that if freed slaves were simply given formal political equality, other benefits and privileges would inevitably follow. Reality quickly proved otherwise, as even African Americans in the North who were able to exercise their right to vote were generally unable to influence the political process.

Social equality extends beyond the granting of political rights; it refers additionally to equality, and fair treatment within the various institutions in society, both public and private, that serve the public at large. Social equality calls for a sameness of treatment in stores, theaters, restaurants, hotels, and public transportation facilities among many other operations open to the public. Jim Crow Laws passed in the South during the late nineteenth century segregated many of these institutions, thus denying social equality to African Americans.

Economic equality remains the most controversial form of equality—indeed, its very mention often touches off heated debate among political officials. To some, society's responsibility to promote economic equality requires only that it provide equality of economic "opportunity," by which different groups enjoy substantially the same rights to enter contracts, purchase and sell property, and otherwise compete for resources in society. To others, economic equality extends beyond equality of economic opportunity to something approaching an "equality of results." Whichever meaning one gives to the term, economic equality has been exceedingly difficult to achieve. Although the government has introduced a graduated income tax and other resource-leveling measures during the past century to improve economic opportunities for the poor, large variances in the quality of education afforded to different groups continue to render economic equality an elusive ideal.

The term **civil rights** has traditionally referred to those positive rights, whether political, social, or economic, conferred by the government on individuals or groups that had previously been denied them. What type of equality does the guarantee of civil rights promote? Immediately after the Civil War, civil rights legislation that would have provided for extensive social equality (equal accommodations in hotels, restaurants, trains, and other public facilities) was struck down as unconstitutional by the U.S. Supreme Court. As a result, the package of civil rights granted to freed slaves included only limited political rights, including the right to vote. In the late 1950s and 1960s, renewed efforts to guarantee equality in all areas of American life led to the civil rights movement.[1]

Many civil rights battles in American history have been waged by African Americans, but other ethnic groups, women, the physically disabled, the aged, and homosexuals have also sought the political, social, and economic equality denied them. The Constitution of the United States and the amendments to it have provided a framework for these groups to use to win equality. As a result, the meaning of civil rights has been significantly expanded both in the scope of its protection and in the variety of groups who seek its guarantees.

The Struggle for Equality: Approaches and Tactics

The methods and tactics various groups use to achieve equality have evolved since the end of the Civil War. Initially, the battle over what constituted the most

★ **Political equality**

A condition in which members of different groups possess substantially the same rights to participate actively in the political system. In the United States, these rights include voting, running for office, petitioning the government for redress of grievances, free speech, free press, and the access to an education.

★ **Social equality**

Equality, and fair treatment of all groups within the various institutions in society, both public and private, that serve the public at large, including in stores, theaters, restaurants, hotels, and public transportation facilities among many other operations open to the public.

★ **Economic equality**

May be defined as providing all groups the equality of opportunity for economic success, or as the equality of results. In the United States, the latter has been the more common understanding of economic opportunity.

★ **Civil rights**

Those positive rights, whether political, social, or economic, conferred by the government on individuals or groups.

[1] Juan Williams, *Eyes on the Prize: America's Civil Rights Years, 1954–1965* (New York: Penguin, 1988).

effective means of fostering change—at least in the context of challenging racial discrimination against African Americans—pitted two competing philosophies against each other. Booker T. Washington, who founded Tuskegee Normal and Industrial Institute (today Tuskegee University) in Alabama in 1881, advocated a philosophy of *accommodation*, which promoted vocational education for African Americans and opposed confrontation with the mostly white power structure in place in post–Civil War America. Washington urged his fellow African Americans to accept existing conditions, even to the point of tolerating racial segregation and all but surrendering the newly won right to vote. According to his philosophy, only by engaging in law-abiding practices and standing by their former white oppressors would African Americans become prepared for the exercise of the franchise. Washington's philosophy of accommodation fit comfortably within the dominant conservative political and economic structure of his time. Although some critics charged him with accepting second-class citizenship for his race, Washington was perhaps the most powerful and influential figure in African American affairs until his death in 1915.[2]

Washington's passive approach contrasted with the philosophy of *agitation*, which challenged racial discrimination and injustice through various forms of political activity. Among Washington's contemporaries, the most widely recognized proponent of this alternative approach was W. E. B. Du Bois. At the beginning of the twentieth century, Du Bois and his associates proposed a specific platform of legal, political, and social reforms to achieve social, economic, and political equality for African Americans.[3] Their demands included the unfettered right to vote and an immediate end to all segregation. Agitation eventually replaced accommodation as the dominant mode by which African Americans and other groups sought equality in twentieth-century America. New debates emerged, however, over what would be the most effective means and methods for achieving these reforms. Tactics that various groups have used to seek their civil rights include:

★ **Work within the Political System.** Some groups have used the political process to implement reforms to end discrimination. In recent decades, for example, African Americans have used their substantial power as a voting bloc to

Members of the Congressional Black Caucus at the August 2008 Democratic National Convention in Denver, Colorado.

PAUL J. RICHARDS/AFP/GETTY IMAGES

[2] Louis R. Harlan, *Booker T. Washington: The Making of a Black Leader* (New York: Oxford University Press, 1975).
[3] David Levering Lewis, *W. E. B. DuBois, 1868–1919: Biography of a Race* (New York: Owl Books, 1994).

American Government: Historical, Popular, and Global Perspectives

influence the outcome of some elections. Various groups have expanded their influence more directly over public policies and programs by lobbying and petitioning government officials; in some cases members of these groups have been elected to high public office, giving them a place at the table of political power.

★ **Litigation.** When the political arena fails to provide adequate remedies to discrimination, a lawsuit brought before a court may afford a better opportunity for success. Founded in 1909 for the purpose of ensuring the political, educational, social, and economic equality of rights of all Americans, the NAACP focused its efforts on legal challenges to discrimination and segregation because the political arena had offered inadequate remedies. Civil rights legislation in particular had proven ineffective, with southern state legislatures either ignoring or circumventing the laws. The NAACP won a string of legal battles that gradually broke down racial barriers in education and elsewhere. These efforts culminated with the U.S. Supreme Court's decision in ***Brown v. Board of Education* (1954),**[4] which ordered desegregation of public schools. In subsequent years women's groups, disabled Americans, and other victims of discrimination have similarly turned to the courts for remedies to discriminatory practices.

★ **Legal Boycotts.** The organized refusal to buy, sell, or use certain goods or to perform certain services has long been a tool in economic battles waged between employers and unions. Adopting this tactic for use in the war on racial discrimination, African American citizens of Montgomery, Alabama, refused to ride the city's buses for more than a year in the mid-1950s; their efforts drained the city's public transportation budget and ultimately forced city officials to desegregate the bus system. In 2003, women's rights organizations discouraged some companies from sponsoring the Masters Golf Tournament held at the all-male Augusta National Golf Club in Augusta, Georgia.

★ **Civil Disobedience.** Sometimes citizens resort to passive resistance to what they see as an unjust government policy or law by openly refusing to obey it. Such a tactic may result in arrests, fines, or even jail time for those who practice it. Still, civil disobedience may also call attention to a group's plight in an especially effective way. Reverend Martin Luther King Jr., who had studied the methods used by Mohandas Gandhi of India and other nonviolent protestors, applied these methods to the civil rights movement in the American South.

★ *Brown v. Board of Education* (1954)

The 1954 U.S. Supreme Court decision that declared school segregation to be unconstitutional.

The African American Struggle for Equality and Civil Rights

Colonists who supported the American Revolution trumpeted the notion of equality as a means of justifying their war with England. Yet when the U.S. Constitution was drafted in 1787, the document said nothing about such a call to equality, nor did the Bill of Rights (ratified in 1791) guarantee to all citizens "equal protection of the law." The period following the Revolution offered equality primarily to property-owning white men. Nowhere did Jefferson's call for equality, as stated in the Declaration of Independence, seem more hollow than in the area of racial discrimination. Throughout the North, African Americans were denied the right to vote and numerous other economic and social privileges enjoyed by white citizens. And in the South, the institution of slavery thrived for more than a half century after the Constitution was ratified.

---

[4] 347 U.S. 483 (1954).

Racial Discrimination: From Slavery to Reconstruction

The organized antislavery movement in the United States began in the late eighteenth century as an effort to eradicate slavery through progressive elimination. Advocates of gradual emancipation believed that by preventing the extension of slavery to new areas and relocating emancipated slaves to areas outside the United States, slavery would eventually die out. Opposed to gradual emancipation were the abolitionists, who sought the immediate emancipation of all slaves. A leader of the abolitionist movement was William Lloyd Garrison, who founded the antislavery periodical, *The Liberator,* in 1831. It is noteworthy, however, that among even extreme abolitionists such as Garrison the "fatal characteristic" of slavery was that it denied African Americans the basic legal rights to own property, enter into contracts, or testify in court. Many abolitionists at the time did *not* believe that emancipation automatically entitled freed slaves the right to vote or serve on juries. Even among some of the most ardent advocates of equality before the Civil War, a sharp distinction was often drawn between economic rights—which they felt African Americans were entitled to—and basic political rights including suffrage, which were somehow not viewed as natural entitlements.

Neither conception of civil rights for slaves gained much favor in the South, where the economy of the plantation system depended on slave labor. The Southerners' approach to racial equality was perhaps best summed up by Chief Justice Roger Taney of Maryland, who in the landmark Supreme Court case of *Dred Scott v. Sandford* (1857)[5] wrote that blacks were "so far inferior that they had no rights which the white man was bound to respect." The initial rhetoric surrounding the outbreak of the Civil War in 1861 focused on issues such as states' rights and territorial expansion in addition to slavery. The Emancipation Proclamation issued by President Lincoln in 1863 declared the freedom of all slaves in states fighting the Union and allowed blacks to enlist in the Union Army. By the end of the struggle in 1865, the war was essentially transformed into a battle over the end of the institution of slavery.

With the Union victory in the Civil War, the complete emancipation of African Americans after the war was a foregone conclusion. Former slaves were able to legally marry, worship as they wished, and migrate to different parts of the country. But the years following the Civil War—normally referred to as the Reconstruction Era (1865–1877) in American history—proved a mixed blessing for the newly freed slaves.[6] The **Civil War Amendments** to the Constitution did grant African Americans the rights of citizenship. The Thirteenth Amendment (ratified in 1865) banished slavery from all states and U.S. territories. The Fourteenth Amendment (ratified in 1868) granted full U.S. and state citizenship to all people born or naturalized in the United States and guaranteed to each person "the equal protection of the laws." Finally, the Fifteenth Amendment (1870) forbade the denial or abridgement of the right to vote by any government on account of race. The Republican-controlled Congress hoped that these three amendments would institutionalize freedom for the former slaves and protect their rights from being undermined by future generations.

During the Reconstruction era, many freed slaves were successful in getting on ballots in the former Confederate states—in all, twenty-two African Americans were elected to the House and one (Hiram Revels of Mississippi) was elected to the Senate during the latter part of the nineteenth century. African American participation in Congress tailed off at the beginning of the twentieth century, however, because restrictions on the franchise curtailed the political viability of most black candidates. No African American served in either house of Congress for most of the first three decades of the twentieth century, and just four served in the House up to 1954. After George Henry White (R-NC) left Congress in 1901, no African American would be elected from a southern state again until 1973, when Barbara Jordan (D-TX) and Andrew Young (D-GA) were each elected to serve in the Ninety-third Congress.

Although African Americans achieved some gains during Reconstruction, the Reconstruction-era generation posed the greatest threat to those civil rights victories.

★ Civil War Amendments

The Thirteenth Amendment (ratified in 1865) banished slavery from all states and U.S. territories. The Fourteenth Amendment (ratified in 1868) granted full U.S. and state citizenship to all people born or naturalized in the United States and guaranteed to each person "the equal protection of the laws." The Fifteenth Amendment (1870) forbade the denial or abridgement of the right to vote by any government on account of race.

---

[5] 60 U.S. 393 (1856).
[6] Eric Foner, *Reconstruction: America's Unfinished Revolution* (New York: Harper, 2000).

The Fourteenth Amendment had been proposed in part to negate the infamous *Black Codes* passed by the Southern states, which denied African Americans numerous economic and social rights. However, in *The Slaughterhouse Cases* (1873),[7] a conservative U.S. Supreme Court narrowly defined the scope of rights protected by the Fourteenth Amendment, holding that the great body of civil rights still lay under the protection of state governments, not the U.S. Constitution. The Civil Rights Act of 1875 attempted to ensure the social and political rights of freed slaves by, among other provisions, prohibiting discrimination in public accommodations. The Supreme Court invalidated the act in *The Civil Rights Cases* (1883),[8] ruling that whereas the Constitution prohibits the states from discriminating by race against certain civil rights, it does not protect the invasion of such civil rights by private individuals unaided by state authority. Therefore, privately owned restaurants and hotels could freely discriminate on the basis of race without violating the Constitution.

This judicial gutting of federal civil rights guarantees opened the way for numerous abuses of freed slaves once the federal government's military occupation of the South ended in 1877. Although the Fifteenth Amendment had given African American men the right to vote, the Southern states imposed new barriers to disenfranchise the former slaves. They levied *poll taxes,* which a voter had to pay before being allowed to vote; they required potential voters to pass *literacy tests;* they demanded some form of property-owning and residency documentation; they issued a grandfather clause requirement, which stated that to be eligible to vote one's grandfather had to have voted; and they restricted blacks from participating in crucial party primaries. Discrimination against African Americans in all areas of public life soon became the norm. Terrorist groups like the Ku Klux Klan intimidated or threatened African Americans to keep them under control, sometimes backing up their threats with beatings, arson, or murder. White vigilante groups resorted to lynching in an effort to restore white supremacy and deny blacks their rights. Post–Civil War blacks might no longer be slaves, but they could hardly be considered fully equal citizens under the law.

Racial Segregation and Barriers to Equality

In the period immediately following the Civil War, some African Americans were able to use public accommodations as long as they could afford to pay for them. By the turn of the twentieth century, however, growing racial tensions, exacerbated by urbanization and industrialization, led to racial segregation throughout America. The Southern states enacted **Jim Crow laws,** which required segregation of blacks and whites in public schools, railroads, buses, restaurants, hotels, theaters, and other public facilities. The laws excluded blacks from militias and denied them certain education and welfare services. When Homer Plessy (described in court filings as being "seven-eights Caucasian and one-eight African blood") was arrested on a Louisiana train for refusing to leave a seat in a coach section designated for whites, he challenged the Louisiana law requiring segregated railroad cars, arguing that the law violated the equal protection clause of the Fourteenth Amendment. In **Plessy v. Ferguson (1896),**[9] the Supreme Court upheld the Louisiana law on the theory that as long as the accommodations between the racially segregated cars were equal, the equal protection clause was not violated. The Court's ruling established the constitutionality of racial segregation according to the *separate but equal* doctrine. To the argument that such an enforced separation of the two races stamps the colored race with a "badge of inferiority," the Supreme Court replied matter-of-factly: "If this be so, it is not by reason of anything found in the act, but solely because the colored race *chooses* to put that construction upon it."

African American leaders responded to the spread of segregation in different ways. Initially, Booker T. Washington's accommodationist philosophy prevailed. W. E. B. Du Bois, by contrast, advocated direct and militant challenges to segregation. Perhaps the greatest breakthrough against segregation occurred through the legal arm of the organization that Du Bois helped found: the NAACP. Beginning

★ Jim Crow laws

Laws used by some southern states that required segregation of blacks and whites in public schools, railroads, buses, restaurants, hotels, theaters, and other public facilities. The laws excluded blacks from militias and denied them certain education and welfare services.

★ *Plessy v. Ferguson* (1896)

The 1896 Supreme Court case that upheld a Louisiana segregation law on the theory that as long as the accommodations between the racially segregated facilities were equal, the equal protection clause was not violated. The Court's ruling effectively established the constitutionality of racial segregation and the notion of "separate but equal."

---

[7] 83 U.S. 36 (1872).
[8] 109 U.S. 3 (1883).
[9] 163 U.S. 537 (1896).

Table 5.1 Tracking the NAACP's Legal Assault on Racially Segregated Education

U.S. Supreme Court Case	Description
Missouri Ex. Rel. Gaines v. Canada (1938)	Invalidated the exclusion of black students from the University of Missouri's School of Law absent some other provision for their legal training.
Sipuel v. Okla. State Regents (1948)	Rejected Oklahoma's attempt to create a separate law school for blacks by roping off a section of the state capitol for black law students and assigning three law teachers to them; such a form of separation failed to comply with the constitutional requirement of "equality."
Sweatt v. Painter (1950)	Invalidated Texas's attempt to create an alternative to the University of Texas law school for blacks, because any such alternative would be inherently different in the reputation of its faculty, the experience of its administration, the position and influence of its alumni, its standing in the community, and so on.
McLaurin v. Okla. State Regents (1950)	Rejected as "unequal" Oklahoma's attempt to provide graduate education to a black student by making him sit in a classroom surrounded by a railing marked "reserved for colored," assigning him a segregated desk in the library, and requiring him to sit separately from whites in the cafeteria.
Brown v. Board of Education (1954)	Rejected the "separate but equal" doctrine altogether, declaring that in the field of public education, "separate educational facilities are inherently unequal."
Cooper v. Aaron (1957)	Condemned the attempts of the Little Rock, Arkansas, school board to postpone desegregation efforts, ruling that no scheme of racial discrimination against black schoolchildren can stand if "there is state participation through any arrangement, management, funds, or property."

in the late 1930s, NAACP lawyers Charles Houston and Thurgood Marshall began attacking the legal basis for segregation in the courts.[10] They won their first battles against state-mandated segregation in institutions of higher education, as the Supreme Court in 1950 recognized that separate accommodations in law schools and colleges had failed to meet the essential requirements of equality mandated by the Fourteenth Amendment (see Table 5.1).

The NAACP's incremental approach to eliminating segregation in education reached its climax in 1954, with the Supreme Court's landmark decision in *Brown v. Board of Education.* Chief Justice Earl Warren, writing for a unanimous Court, held that racial segregation in any facet of public education constituted a denial of equal protection by the laws. Recognizing the psychological harms of segregation on African American children, the Court declared that segregated schools were "inherently unequal."

The *Brown* decision also confirmed that in all future cases related to racial (and ethnic) discrimination, the Court would apply a standard of **strict scrutiny,** a level of judicial review that requires the government to prove that the racial classification of the law or practice in question is "narrowly tailored" to meet a "compelling state interest." What precisely does this mean? At a minimum, there should be no less restrictive alternative means available for achieving the government's objectives, and those objectives should stand among the most necessary that may be pursued by any government. Many legal scholars and judges say the

★ Strict scrutiny

A legal standard set in *Brown v. Board of Education* for cases related to racial discrimination that tends to invalidate almost all state laws that segregate racial groups.

American Government: Historical, Popular, and Global Perspectives

[10] For a comprehensive account of the NAACP's strategy, see Richard Kluger, *Simple Justice* (New York: Vintage Books, 1975).

strict scrutiny standard tends to invalidate nearly all government laws and programs. In the years following *Brown*, the courts would apply the standard of strict scrutiny in decisions on segregated public swimming pools, police forces, and laws banning interracial marriages.

A year after handing down the *Brown* decision, the Supreme Court declared that its implementation should proceed "with all deliberate speed." Despite that decree, many local school boards resisted desegregation. The school board of Little Rock, Arkansas, adopted a plan for "phased integration" over a ten-year period, spurring more lawsuits to speed up the process. Undeterred, Arkansas Governor Orval Faubus declared that no "*Brown* decisions" enjoyed "the force of law" in his state. In one famous instance, he placed soldiers of the Arkansas National Guard at Little Rock's Central High School to stop African American students from entering the school. Governor Ross Barnett of Mississippi refused to comply with court desegregation orders on so many occasions that a federal court held him in contempt and committed him "to the custody of the Attorney General of the United States." Alabama Governor George Wallace blocked a University of Alabama doorway, refusing to allow black students to pass through in 1963. As discussed in the chapter opening, Autherine Lucy was turned back in her attempt to remain a student at the University of Alabama. One hundred members of Congress signed a "Southern Manifesto" declaring their intention to use "all lawful means" to reverse the *Brown* decision. On several occasions, the Supreme Court was forced to reassert its authority over state governments. In *Cooper v. Aaron* (1957),[11] for example, the Court held that the rights of African American students could "neither be nullified openly and directly by state legislatures or state executive officials . . . by evasive schemes for segregation."

African American students are escorted through the doors of Little Rock's Central High School by the U.S. National Guard on September 25, 1957.

Despite the Supreme Court's increasingly clear edicts against segregation, many school districts in the South and North continued to drag their feet.[12] Significant and widespread change would not occur until after passage of civil rights legislation in the mid-1960s, which gave the executive branch of the government increased power to enforce school desegregation in local districts. Additionally, a sudden influx of federal money into local schools gave extra bite to court desegregation decrees. As scholar Gerald Rosenberg remarked: "Put simply, courts could hold up federal funds." Many school districts in the Deep South where less than half of all blacks were being educated alongside whites as late as 1967 were almost fully integrated by 1971.

In urban areas where whites and blacks lived largely apart, strict adherence to a neighborhood school system meant indefinitely perpetuating a racially unmixed setting; thus massive court-ordered "busing" in the late 1960s and 1970s became a controversial feature of efforts to integrate these schools. Many such court orders were issued in both northern and southern cities, as the Supreme Court required communities to cease both *de jure discrimination* (segregation sanctioned by the law), which was found mostly in the South, and *de facto discrimination* (segregation in reality, such as that which occurs when different racial groups voluntarily choose to live in different neighborhoods or attend different schools), which was found in both the North and the South. Yet busing was a remedy limited to a single

---

[11] 358 U.S. 1 (1957).

[12] Jennifer Hochschild, *The New American Dilemma: Liberal Democracy and School Desegregation* (New Haven, CT: Yale University Press, 1984).

metropolitan area, and comprehensive efforts to integrate schools were further hindered by white flight to suburbia, which left inner-city school districts in many large northern cities predominantly black and Hispanic. Today, fully 70 percent of the nation's African American students attend schools that are predominantly black. Thus more than fifty years after the *Brown* decision, de facto discrimination in public education remains a reality in many parts of America.

The Beginnings of the Civil Rights Movement

Although *Brown* signaled the end of state-sponsored segregation, the Supreme Court took pains to note that its holding applied only to discriminatory acts by the government. The extension of civil rights protections to all public accommodations did not occur until the civil rights movement began to gather momentum in the late 1950s and early 1960s. In December 1955, Rosa Parks, an African American seamstress in Montgomery, Alabama, was arrested for refusing to give up her seat at the front of a city bus. Her arrest sparked a racial boycott of the city's bus system. Leading the boycott was Martin Luther King Jr., pastor of the Dexter Avenue Baptist Church. King's eloquent speeches and his methods of nonviolent civil disobedience brought national attention to the boycott. King had been introduced to these tactics of nonviolent protest when he was a student at Crozer Theological Seminary in Chester, Pennsylvania, and studied the pacifist philosophy of Mohandas Gandhi of India, whose unshakable belief in nonviolent protest and religious tolerance helped secure independence for his country from Great Britain.

In 1957, King and other African American ministers in the South formed the Southern Christian Leadership Conference (SCLC), which encouraged Ghandian practices of nonviolent civil disobedience as a way to gain equal rights for blacks and spur white politicians into action. African American and white college students in numerous cities across the South eventually became the engine for pressing such change. One early tactic the students used was the sit-in. On February 1, 1960, four freshmen from the black North Carolina A&T College in Greensboro sat down at a whites-only lunch counter and refused to move after being denied service. The next day more students—black and white—joined them. Angry mobs harassed the students verbally and physically. Committed to nonviolence, the students endured the abuse. The episode brought considerable publicity to the civil rights movement. In 1961, interracial groups of students sponsored "Freedom Rides," boarding public buses together to test court decisions prohibiting segregation on interstate buses and in bus terminals; departing from Washington, DC, many within the groups of interstate travelers of mixed races were beaten when their buses arrived in Alabama. Eventually President John F. Kennedy was forced to nationalize the Alabama police to help assure the freedom riders safe passage.

In 1948, a nineteen-year-old student named Martin Luther King Jr. was first introduced to the pacifist philosophy of Mohandas Gandhi. By seeking a nonviolent confrontation with the segregation laws, King's students practiced Gandhi's philosophy in a way that sent shockwaves throughout the South and eventually the entire nation. King would continue to preach Gandhi's call for nonviolent protest up until his assassination in 1968.

Birmingham 1963:
The Turning Point of the Civil Rights Movement

The civil rights movement's strategy of nonviolent civil disobedience reached a climax between 1963 and 1965.[13] 1963 will long be remembered as the "Year of Birmingham." Tension was growing between King's SCLC and new civil rights groups that favored more radical and militant action, including the use of violence. Looking for a site where nonviolent demonstrations might succeed and draw national attention to the civil rights movement, King and his followers settled on Birmingham, Alabama. Birmingham was an obvious target, for several reasons. First, as an industrial city (unlike most southern cities), it had a sizable concentration of workers. Also, during the 1930s and 1940s, the labor movement had introduced to the city a tradition of organized protest unusual throughout most of the South. And finally, the city was a stronghold of segregation; city leaders included the notoriously racist Public Safety Commissioner Eugene "Bull" Connor, who ruthlessly enforced segregation laws throughout the city.

In Birmingham, King led other demonstrators in a nonviolent march downtown, where he was arrested and placed in solitary confinement. While confined, he wrote his famous "Letter from Birmingham City Jail," addressed to the white Alabama clergymen who had criticized King's campaign. In the letter, King explained his philosophy and defended his strategy of nonviolent protest. Despite King's arrest, the demonstration in Birmingham continued. The marchers, including more than a thousand black schoolchildren, were met by attack dogs, cattle prods, and fire hoses. Pictures of children being attacked flashed across the nation's television sets and the violence was covered by newspapers and magazines across the world. The nation would be forever aroused by these events; the civil rights movement had finally been transformed into a truly national cause.

Birmingham businessmen, fearing damage to their downtown stores, hastened negotiations with King and his fellow civil rights leaders. An accord was eventually reached on May 10, 1963, with merchants agreeing to desegregate lunch counters and hire more black workers for clerical and sales positions. Yet the agreement did not bring peace to Birmingham: On the night of May 11, a Ku Klux Klan rally outside the city was followed by the explosion of bombs at the motel where King was staying. Riots erupted and some stores were set ablaze. This time, however, the federal government got involved; specifically, President Kennedy dispatched soldiers to Fort McClellan, thirty miles outside of Birmingham. Nevertheless, in September a bombing at the city's Sixteenth Street Baptist Church killed four African American schoolgirls.

The events in Birmingham were not the last of the civil rights demonstrations, nor the end of violence in response to those activities. In August 1963, more than 250,000 people participated in the March on Washington where King delivered his memorable "I Have a Dream" speech from the steps of the Lincoln Memorial. In 1964, the murder of three civil rights workers and a local NAACP leader in Mississippi revealed the depth of continuing opposition to racial equality. In 1965, King and other civil rights leaders organized a march from Selma, Alabama, to the state capital in Montgomery to bring attention to harsh political realities in the South, where African Americans had been denied the right to vote by illegitimate tests and in some instances outright intimidation.

President Lyndon Johnson and the U.S. Congress were eventually prodded into action. Johnson signed into law the **Civil Rights Act of 1964,** which banned racial discrimination in all public accommodations, including those that were privately owned; it also prohibited discrimination by employers and created the Equal Employment Opportunity Commission to investigate complaints of discrimination; and it denied public funds to schools that continued to discriminate on the basis of race.[14] The **Voting Rights Act of 1965,** enacted the following year, invalidated

Mohandas Gandhi. of India, whose unshakable belief in non-violent protest helped secure independence of his country from Great Britain.

★ Civil Rights Act of 1964

The federal law that banned racial discrimination in all public accommodations, including those that were privately owned; prohibited discrimination by employers and created the Equal Employment Opportunity Commission to investigate complaints of discrimination; and denied public funds to schools that continued to discriminate on the basis of race.

★ Voting Rights Act of 1965

The federal law that invalidated literacy tests and property requirements and required select states and cities to apply for permission to the Justice Department to change their voting laws. As a consequence, millions of African Americans were effectively re-enfranchised in the South.

---

[13] See Taylor Branch, *Pillar of Fire: America in the King Years, 1963–65* (New York: Simon & Schuster, 1999).

[14] Charles Whalen and Barbara Whalen, *Longest Debate: A Legislative History of the Civil Rights Act* (Santa Ana, CA: Seven Locks Press, 1984).

★ Civil Rights Act of 1968

The federal law that banned race discrimination in housing and made interference with a citizen's civil rights a federal crime.

★ Twenty-fourth Amendment

A 1964 constitutional amendment that banned poll taxes in federal elections.

literacy tests and property requirements and required select states and cities to apply for permission to the Justice Department to change their voting laws. As a consequence, millions of African Americans were effectively re-enfranchised in the South.

The **Civil Rights Act of 1968** banned race discrimination in housing and made interference with a citizen's civil rights a federal crime. Even the state legislatures played a role in this civil rights transformation by ratifying the **Twenty-fourth Amendment** in 1964, which banned poll taxes in federal elections.

The focus of the civil rights movement began to shift in the mid- to late 1960s with the rise of "black nationalism," which was grounded in the belief that African Americans could not effectively work within the confines of a racist political system to produce effective change. Malcolm X, a leading advocate of black nationalism, sought to turn the characteristic of being black-skinned into a source of strength, and he urged African Americans to shun white culture and the values promoted by white society. He and other black nationalists criticized the civil rights leaders who advocated integration into white society rather than building separate black institutions. Following the assassination of Martin Luther King Jr. in 1968, the influence of black nationalism in the civil rights movement reached its peak during the late 1960s and early 1970s. Epitomizing a revolutionary vision of society that replaced the strategy of nonviolence with confrontational tactics, the Black Panther Party became a controversial militant presence in some cities.

Although the Black Panther Party had all but faded as a significant entity by 1972, black separatist organizations continue to maintain a strong presence. For example, the Nation of Islam (Black Muslims), led by Louis Farrakhan, preaches class consciousness and the concept of black self-rule. In 1995, Farrakhan's Nation of Islam led the Million Man March in Washington, DC, which far outdrew the 1963 March on Washington. This Million Man March garnered

Table 5.2 The Effect of the Voting Rights Act on Registration Rates in the South.

The following table compares black voter registration rates with white voter registration rates in seven Southern states in 1965 and 1988. All numbers are percentage rates.

State	March 1965			November 1988		
	Black	White	Gap	Black	White	Gap
Alabama	19.3	69.2	49.9	68.4	75.0	6.6
Georgia	27.4	62.6	35.2	56.8	63.9	7.1
Louisiana	31.6	80.5	48.9	77.1	75.1	-2.0
Mississippi	6.7	69.9	63.2	74.2	80.5	6.3
North Carolina	46.8	96.8	50.0	58.2	65.6	7.4
South Carolina	37.3	75.7	38.4	56.7	61.8	5.1
Virginia	38.3	61.1	22.8	63.8	68.5	4.7

Source: Bernard Grofman, Lisa Handley, and Richard G. Niemi. *Minority Representation and the Quest for Voting Equality.* (New York: Cambridge University Press, 1992). Reprinted with permission of Cambridge University Press.

In 1963, firefighters in Birmingham, Alabama, sprayed civil rights demonstrators with fire hoses.

international attention for Farrakhan's movement. Four years later, African American women responded with their own million women march.

Clearly Barack Obama's historic election as the first African American president in U.S. history has fundamentally changed the relationship between African Americans and their national government. Still, African Americans as a whole face immense challenges in making their voices heard in other institutions on the national political scene. Obama left a Senate chamber in which he had the distinction of being the only African American then serving and where he was just the third African American senator to serve since Reconstruction. Meanwhile, thirty-nine African Americans served in the House of Representatives during the 110th Congress. Finally, African Americans have been mostly absent from the highest levels of state government: In 2006, Deval Patrick of Massachusetts became only the second elected African American governor in history.

Continuing Struggles over Racial Equality

Two contemporary and hotly debated topics related to racial equality are affirmative action and racial profiling.

Affirmative Action. Some observers have called the civil rights movement a "Second Reconstruction," because it eliminated most of the vestiges of racial discrimination and segregation from the books. But would this successful legal revolution translate into real change? Various civil rights leaders in the 1970s and 1980s shifted their focus to affirmative action as a means of promoting African American gains in education and the workplace. **Affirmative action** programs are generally laws or practices designed to remedy past discriminatory hiring practices, government contracting, and school admissions. The women's movement too has benefited from affirmative action programs in the workplace and elsewhere. Although "quotas" (specifically defined numerical goals for hiring or admitting members of certain groups) have been used in the past, more often such programs involve giving some form of preferential treatment, whether by adding points to a mathematical score due

★ Affirmative action

Programs, laws, or practices designed to remedy past discriminatory hiring practices, government contracting, and school admissions.

Students at the University of Michigan rally in support of affirmative action. In 2003 the U.S. Supreme Court upheld the use of affirmative action by the University of Michigan's Law School but struck down the affirmative action program utilized in undergraduate admissions.

to a person's status as a member of a particular racial group, or by creating economic or other incentives for administrative bodies to increase the diversity of their incoming workforce and/or educational institutions.

Proponents of affirmative action argue that past discriminatory practices have deprived certain racial groups and women of opportunities to get the skills or experiences they need to compete for jobs or college admissions on an equal footing with those who have not experienced such discrimination. The issue of affirmative action reached the U.S. Supreme Court in the case of *Regents of the University of California v. Bakke* (1978).[15] In 1973, Alan Bakke, one of 2,664 applicants for one hundred seats at the University of California–Davis Medical School, interviewed with one of the school's officials, Dr. Theodore West. At that time, West told Bakke that he was a "very desirable applicant to the medical school." Thus Bakke was quite surprised when he was denied admission. Bakke in fact was rejected not once but twice for admission: in 1973 and again in 1974. In both instances, sixteen applicants with lower grade point averages and MCAT (Medical College Admission Test) scores than Bakke's were admitted to the school under a special minority admissions program. Bakke challenged the program as a violation of the Fourteenth Amendment's equal protection clause. In previous years, the courts had dismissed most lawsuits because they were quickly rendered "moot," a legal term that indicates that circumstances have removed the practical significance of deciding the case. (By attending some other school, those unsuccessful applicants had essentially prevented their cases from ever being decided.) But Bakke was determined to go to University of California–Davis Medical School and thus his case eventually reached the U.S. Supreme Court.

In deciding the case, the Supreme Court ruled that a university could take into account race and ethnicity when making decisions about the admission of students, as long as it did not utilize specifically assigned numerical goals. To the Court, no

[15] 438 U.S. 265 (1978).

constitutional infirmity exists where "race or ethnic background is simply one element—to be weighed fairly against other elements—in the selection process." In his majority opinion, Justice Lewis Powell also heralded the benefits of a diverse student body, noting that students with particular racial backgrounds may bring to a school "experiences, outlooks and ideas that enrich the training of its student body."[16]

Five years after he was first denied admission, Bakke got what he wanted: on June 28, 1978, the U.S. Supreme Court directed that he be admitted to the university's medical school. Opponents of affirmative action thought they had received the victory they were looking for; after all, the Court held that the university could not use fixed racial quotas in this instance. But schools and universities took refuge in the Court's statements favoring the consideration of racial criteria more generally, and in the quarter century that followed, countless schools of higher education utilized race-conscious admissions programs. Thus although Alan Bakke won his personal battle for admission, the war over affirmative action would continue to be waged in the years that followed.

Opponents of affirmative action complain that such programs punish white applicants who played no role at all in the original discriminatory practices. They also claim that a racial divide that currently exists in this country may be exacerbated by affirmative action, because members of racial groups who benefit from such programs may be stigmatized by the perception that they are not fully deserving. Finally, affirmative action programs are explicit racial classifications, and thus may be thought to violate the principle of a "color-blind Constitution" that was celebrated by the Supreme Court's decision in *Brown v. Board of Education*.

A string of Supreme Court decisions in the late 1980s and 1990s have effectively brought an end to explicit affirmative action programs in public employment and contracting. The final nail in the coffin for affirmative action in contracting may have been the Court's decision in *Adarand v. Pena* (1995),[17] which held that any racial classification may be considered unconstitutional unless it meets the test of strict scrutiny: that it must be "narrowly tailored" to further a "compelling governmental interest," a standard that has proved nearly impossible for the government to meet. In fact, no affirmative action employment plan has been upheld as constitutional since the early 1990s.

By contrast, affirmative action in education remains steeped in controversy; the confusion over what is legal in this context was only partially resolved by two University of Michigan cases in 2003 that essentially reaffirmed *Bakke's* finding that diversity constitutes a "compelling state interest" under certain circumstances. In *Grutter v. Bollinger* (2003),[18] the Court upheld the university's law school admission program because it only considered race as a positive factor in a review process where all individual applications were carefully reviewed and analyzed on their own merits. Yet that same day in *Gratz v. Bollinger* (2003),[19] the Supreme Court struck down the same university's undergraduate admissions program because instead of providing such careful, individualized review, it automatically awarded twenty points to all students from underrepresented groups, greatly enhancing their chances of being admitted. The Court declared that such a blanket award of benefits was not "narrowly tailored" enough to promote diversity.

In an attempt to balance the interests of having a diverse student body with frequently heard criticisms of affirmative action, state governments in Texas, Florida, and California have enacted alternative programs that would guarantee a place at the state's top universities for every student who finishes in the upper tier (normally the top 5 or 10 percent) of his or her high school class. Given that racial minorities tend to predominate at high schools both in the inner city and in especially poor rural neighborhoods in the South, these percentage plans tend to guarantee seats at major state universities to minority students who would otherwise have been denied admission. Critics of the plans charge that they capitalize on patterns of segregation in housing and geography.

---

[16] Howard Ball, *The Bakke Case: Race, Education and Affirmative Action* (Lawrence: University Press of Kansas, 2000).
[17] 515 U.S. 200 (1995).
[18] 539 U.S. 306 (2003).
[19] 539 U.S. 244 (2003).

Racial inequality remains a fact of life in twenty-first-century America. According to a 2000 U.S. Census Bureau report, the mean and median income of African American workers is just 64 percent that of similarly situated non-Hispanic whites, and the mean net wealth of African Americans is 17 percent of what it is for non-Hispanic whites.[20] Meanwhile, the *Journal of Blacks in Higher Education* recently reported that almost 37 percent of non-Hispanic white Americans aged thirty to thirty-four hold at least a bachelor's degree, as compared to just 21 percent of all African Americans in that same age group.[21]

Racial Profiling. Statistics of the criminal justice system also testify to continuing racial inequality, and racial tensions. For instance, although African American youth at the end of the twentieth century represented just 15 percent of the nation's total youth population, they made up 26 percent of the youth arrested, 31 percent of the youth referred to juvenile court, and 44 percent of the youth detained by the police.[22] African American males in particular comprise a disproportionate number of those imprisoned. Critics of the system charge that it is racially biased, especially in how it metes out capital punishment. A study conducted by social scientist David Baldus in the early 1990s concluded that the victim's race was a significant factor in predicting which convicted murderers receive the death penalty. Specifically, killers of whites were 4.3 times more likely to be sentenced to death than killers of African Americans.

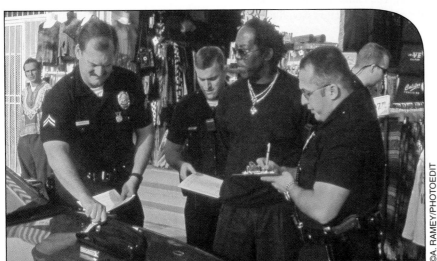

©A. RAMEY/PHOTOEDIT

Officers of the Los Angeles Police Department stop an African American on suspicion of possession of illegal drugs. Racial profiling became a subject of heated controversy in the 1990s.

Racial discrimination may also characterize the initial phases of gathering information about a crime. For example, some law enforcement officials admit to using **racial profiling**—the practice of taking race into account when investigating crimes. African Americans may be stopped, questioned, and even held in custody not because there is specific evidence that links them to a particular crime, but because they fit a "profile" of the perpetrator that includes the characteristic of race.

Even in the wake of the civil rights revolution of the 1960s, little objection was raised against the practice, provided that it was done for purposes of "bona fide law enforcement" and not racial harassment, and so long as race was one of several factors that police officers considered when investigating crimes. But racial profiling became a source of considerable controversy in the 1990s. During the spring of 1999, victims of the New Jersey State Police force's allegedly overaggressive racial profiling testified at hearings held by the Black and Latino caucus of the state's legislature. President Bill Clinton publicly condemned racial profiling as a "morally indefensible, deeply corrosive practice." Finally, in March 2003, New Jersey became the first state in the nation to enact an "Anti-Profiling Law," which made any profiling by police punishable by five years in prison and a $15,000 fine.

Are criticisms of racial profiling exaggerated? Statistics overwhelmingly confirm that African American young men commit a disproportionate share of street crime in the United States. Thus not all racial profiling may be driven by an animus against that race—civil rights leader Jesse Jackson admitted in 1993 that he was less fearful of white strangers than black strangers on dark streets, if only because statistically

★ Racial profiling

The law enforcement practice of taking race into account when identifying possible suspects of crimes.

American Government: Historical, Popular, and Global Perspectives

20 Edward N. Wolff, "Racial Wealth Disparities: Is the Gap Closing?" Public Policy Brief No. 66 (Annandale-on-Hudson, NY: Levi Economics Institute of Bard College, 2001).

21 "Vital Signs: Statistics That Measure the State of Racial Inequality," *Journal of Blacks in Higher Education,* No. 44 (Summer 2004).

22 Michael Jones and Eileen Poe-Yamagata, *And Justice for Some* (Washington, DC: Building Blocks for Youth Press, 2000).

speaking, he stands a greater risk of being robbed by a black person than a white person. At the same time, defenders of racial profiling (as one of many factors in the investigative process) tend to minimize the extent to which the practice adds to the sense of resentment of law enforcement felt by rich and poor blacks alike. No court has ever banned the practice outright. Moreover, even if a court did take such a bold action, it would be difficult to disprove an officer's claim that nonracial factors were in fact the primary consideration in his or her decision-making process.

Controversies surrounding affirmative action and racial profiling highlight a vexing challenge in modern society. Even if all vestiges of formal racial classifications under the law are eliminated, calculations of racial differences inevitably enter into the subjective judgments of those in positions of authority. Thus for all the successful challenges launched against the racist legal and political structures that prevailed in American society during much of the twentieth century, the greater challenge of winning over the "hearts and minds" of individuals still remains.

The Women's Movement and Gender Equality

The process by which women achieved their own degree of equality during the course of the 20th century took a circuitous route. In the early part of the twentieth century, women's rights leaders linked their calls for equality to other social movements of the same period, including those calling for child labor laws and increased literacy for immigrants. Initially, the women's rights movement pressed for protective laws, arguing that such legislation was necessary because of women's otherwise inferior legal status. For example, in *Muller v. Oregon* (1908),[23] the Supreme Court upheld an Oregon law that prohibited women laundry workers from being required to work more than ten hours a day; similar laws applied to male workers had been invalidated as beyond the government's authority. Yet the reason for the holding could hardly have cheered advocates of women's equality: according to the Court, "a woman's physical structure and the performance of maternal functions place her at a disadvantage in the struggle for subsistence."

Woman Suffrage and the Equal Rights Amendment

After ratification of the Nineteenth Amendment in 1920 guaranteed women the right to vote, women's rights groups began to alter their strategy for pursuing gender equality through the courts. In attempting to expand women's legal rights, these groups now argued that men and women should be treated equally. Their efforts met with only limited success at first. Although the NAACP achieved a string of successful challenges to racial discrimination in the 1940s and 1950s, the Supreme Court refused to view gender discrimination as similarly deserving of suspect scrutiny. In *Goesaert v. Cleary* (1948),[24] the Court upheld an Oklahoma law that banned women from tending bar unless they were the daughter or wife of the bar owner. Thirteen years later, the Court accepted as legitimate a Florida law that gave only women the right to excuse themselves from jury duty. In both cases, the Court continued to accept sex-role stereotypes of women as weak, and as dedicated above all else to taking care of the children at home. As the Court pointed out in *Hoyt v. Florida* (1961), "despite the enlightened emancipation of women from the restrictions and protections of bygone years . . . woman is still regarded as the center of home and family life."[25]

The women's rights movement did not achieve any significant breakthroughs in this regard until the early 1970s. Although the National Women's Party had first proposed an equal rights amendment to the Constitution in 1923 and in nearly every session of Congress since then, the amendment never got very far. In 1966, the newly formed *National Organization for Women* (NOW) became a new and forceful

---

[23] 208 U.S. 412 (1908).
[24] 335 U.S. 464 (1948).
[25] 368 U.S. 57, 61 (1961).

The belief that "all men are created equal" has become part of the American ideology. Yet reality hasn't always kept up with theory. In the early years of the republic, the eligible electorate consisted primarily of white, male property owners. For everyone else, the road to suffrage remained fraught with legal and political struggles.

In 1841, the state of Rhode Island became the last of the United States to liberalize suffrage requirements so that even white males with little or no property enjoyed the right to vote. During the late 1820s and 1830s, the Whig Party had resisted suffrage for all white males, trumpeting the principle of a "hierarchical society" in which voting was treated as a privilege rather than an entitlement. But the rival Democratic Party, worried less about civic virtue and more about government tyranny, called for universal white male suffrage to put electoral pressure on the Whigs. The Democrats converted state after state to their cause. Rhode Island's requirement that a man outright own land worth $134 in order to vote seemed increasingly restrictive once the Rhode Island economy shifted from the emphasis on agriculture to industry. Only after the state held a constitutional convention in 1841, and then a special gubernatorial election that same year, did Rhode Island join the rest of the union in championing suffrage for all white males.

In 1920, following decades of intense struggles dating back even before the Civil War, the requisite number of states finally ratified the Nineteenth Amendment, granting women the right to vote. Meeting in 1848 in Seneca Falls, New York, some three hundred male and female reformers issued a Declaration of Sentiments (modeled on the Declaration of Independence), which included a demand for the right of women to vote. As the movement for women's suffrage grew, it encountered especially well organized resistance from the liquor industry (which feared female support for prohibition) and the textile industry (which feared female support for restrictions on child labor). The sudden triumph of progressive reforms at the turn of the century, which helped to clean up industrial workplace abuses, made the women's suffrage movement seem less radical by comparison. In 1916, both the Republicans and the Democrats embraced female enfranchisement, and four years later, it became a constitutional reality.

In 1965, the newly passed Voting Rights Act established a foundation for the mass registration of African Americans throughout the South. Their realization of the right to vote should not have had to wait so long; the Fifteenth Amendment, ratified in 1870, had formally guaranteed the right to vote to all U.S. citizens regardless of race. But racial intimidation at the polls, the use of poll taxes and literacy requirements, and the manipulation of election laws by local registrars all combined to render the right to vote for African Americans a hollow promise at best. Only when the civil rights movement started making significant headway in the late 1950s did national politicians begin seriously to reconsider the issue of voting rights. The key moment in this struggle came in March 1965, when police in Alabama assaulted marchers making their way from Selma to Montgomery. President Lyndon B. Johnson then demanded passage of an effective voting rights act, and in August 1965 Congress passed and he signed into law the Voting Rights Act. The new act, combined with ratification of the Twenty-fourth Amendment in 1964, which prohibited poll taxes, spelled the effective end to nearly a century of systematic disenfranchisement.

advocate for the Equal Rights Amendment and other equal rights in education, employment, and political opportunities for women. NOW and other women's groups vigorously pressed for passage of the Equal Rights Amendment, which stated simply that "equality of rights under the law shall not be denied or abridged by the United

States or any state on account of sex." In 1972, Congress passed the amendment and sent it to the state legislatures for ratification. Even after the deadline for ratification was extended to June 1982, the amendment failed to achieve the approval of the three-fourths of state legislatures necessary for passage, falling just three states shy.

Although the Equal Rights Amendment failed, women have recently achieved some noteworthy victories in politics. For example, women made political history in 2003, when Democrat Nancy Pelosi of California was elected minority leader in the House, the first woman ever to hold that high a position in either branch of Congress. When Democrats won control of Congress after the 2006 midterm elections, Pelosi was elected Speaker of the House, again the first woman to hold that exalted position. Pelosi's ascension to such high congressional leadership positions contrasts with the way women in Congress were often relegated to lesser committees and noninfluential positions in the past. When the 110th Congress began in 2007, there were seventy women serving in the U.S. House of Representatives and sixteen in the U.S. Senate.

Legal Challenges to Gender Discrimination

Ironically, some attributed the failure of the Equal Rights Amendment to other legal developments that may have rendered it unnecessary. The American Civil Liberties Union (ACLU), an organization traditionally dedicated to protecting the First Amendment rights of political dissidents and labor unions, turned its attention to women's rights in the late 1960s. Led in court by board member Ruth Bader Ginsburg (who was later appointed by President Clinton to the U.S. Supreme Court), the ACLU brought suit on behalf of women who charged that they had been victims of gender discrimination. Although the Court refused to accord gender discrimination the strict scrutiny normally reserved for racial discrimination, the ACLU achieved several victories in cases brought before the Supreme Court. In *Reed v. Reed* (1971),[26] the Court invalidated an Idaho law that gave males preference over females as administrators of estates. In *Frontiero v. Richardson* (1973),[27] the Court struck down a federal law requiring only female members of the armed forces to show proof that they contributed more than 50 percent to the income of their household in order to receive certain fringe benefits. And in the landmark case of *Craig v. Boren* (1976),[28] the Court invalidated an Oklahoma law that prohibited the sale of 3.2 percent beer to males under the age of twenty-one and to women under the age of eighteen.

Since *Craig*, the Supreme Court has applied *intermediate scrutiny* in all gender discrimination cases, a standard requiring the government to show that the gender classification is "substantially related to an important state interest." This level of scrutiny is less than that of strict scrutiny, which tends to invalidate all racial classifications. But under intermediate scrutiny, *nearly* all laws that discriminate against women will be invalidated. That fact alone distinguishes intermediate scrutiny from *rational basis (or "minimum") scrutiny,* which asks only whether the law is "rationally related to a legitimate state interest"—a question to which courts can readily answer "yes" in nearly every instance.

In fact, in the modern era the Court has upheld only a handful of gender classifications as constitutional. For example, in 1981 the Court upheld a challenge to federal laws that required selective military service registration for males, but not for females. That same year the Court upheld a statutory rape law in California that punished men for having sex with underage females, although not vice-versa. In each of those two instances, perceptions of real and relevant differences between men and women persuaded the Court to allow the discrimination to stand.

The highest-profile lawsuits charging gender discrimination targeted two all-male southern military academies, The Citadel in Charleston, South Carolina, and the Virginia Military Institute (VMI) in Lexington, Virginia. Both were classified as state institutions because they accepted significant funds from their respective states'

---

[26] 404 U.S. 71 (1971).
[27] 411 U.S. 677 (1973).
[28] 429 U.S. 190 (1976).

University of Tennessee women's head basketball coach Pat Summitt giving instructions to one of her players. Thanks to Title IX, colleges and universities have been forced to provide as many sports teams for women as they do for male athletes.

★ Title IX

The section of the Federal Educational Amendments Law of 1972 that prohibits the exclusion of women from an educational program or activity receiving financial assistance from the federal government. Courts have interpreted those provisions to force colleges and universities to provide as many athletic teams for women as they do for men.

budgets; thus each was hard-pressed to continue excluding women in violation of the Fourteenth Amendment's equal protection clause. Shannon Faulkner's frustrating experience as the first female cadet at The Citadel paved the way for future women to apply and be accepted to the institution in subsequent years. In an attempt to fend off gender integration of its own student body, VMI contracted with nearby Mary Baldwin College to create a parallel military program for women called the Virginia Women's Institute for Leadership (VWIL). But in 1996, the Supreme Court ruled that VWIL did not approximate VMI in terms of student body, faculty, course offerings, facilities, or opportunities for its alumni and ordered VMI to accept women. The issue of "separate but equal" that was resolved by the Supreme Court for racial classifications in 1954 was still being litigated for gender classifications well into the 1990s.

As with race discrimination, discrimination against women has been mostly eliminated in the formal sense. **Title IX** of the Federal Educational Amendments of 1972 prohibited the exclusion of women from an educational program or activity receiving financial assistance from the federal government. Courts have interpreted those provisions to force colleges and universities to provide as many athletic teams for women as they do for men. Title VII of the Civil Rights Act of 1964 extended to women's protection against discrimination in private and public businesses alike. Armed with equal rights to education and to entry in the workforce, women have made considerable occupational gains during the twentieth century.

Women have also benefited from affirmative action programs, especially in the workplace and in admission to professional and trade schools. To rectify long traditions of excluding women from certain occupations, scores of businesses and firms have aggressively recruited women. The period of most striking change occurred over the two decades between 1970 and 1990, when the proportion of women physicians doubled from 7.6 percent to 16.9 percent, and the percentage of women lawyers and judges nearly quadrupled from 5.8 percent to 22.7 percent. The percentage of women who are engineers also rose over that same period from 1.3 percent to 8.6 percent. Still, complaints remain that in some occupations women continue to be clustered in low-paying positions. Thus women still comprise only 3 percent of the nation's firefighters, 8 percent of state and local police officers, 1.9 percent of construction workers, 11.8 percent of college presidents, and 3 to 5 percent of senior-level positions in major companies. Some observers contend that a "glass ceiling" exists in many businesses, whereby women are prevented from receiving raises and promotions due them because of the subjective biases of their male bosses.

The securing of formal equality under the law and the proliferation of affirmative action programs have not always translated into actual equal opportunities to succeed. At the turn of the twenty-first century, women continue to earn less than men in comparable positions—calls for "equal pay for equal work" have not always generated substantive changes in the pay structures of private companies or even the government. When women's salaries are compared with those of equally qualified men, the differences remain dramatic. Although Congress passed the Equal Pay Act in 1963 to ensure that women would be paid the same as men for work that is "substantially equal" (that is, almost identical unless the pay difference is based on seniority, experience, or other legitimate factors), even as late as the year 2000 women earned only 73 cents for every dollar a man received.

American Government . . . in Global Perspective:
Muslims' Attitudes on Gender Equality

In the United States, citizens take some degree of gender equality for granted. Although the Equal Rights Amendment failed to gather the necessary support for passage, many legal scholars today believe the ERA has been rendered unnecessary by the eradication of gender discrimination in so many different walks of American life. Not all nations around the world see this aspect of American democracy as positive. In 2003, the Pew Global Attitudes Project showed just how world opinion differs on gender equality, as Muslim populations in particular appeared to wholeheartedly reject this particular aspect of American democracy. The survey results, however, revealed some notable differences between Muslim men and Muslim women on some of these issues:

Women Should Be Permitted to Work Outside the Home	Men %	Women %	Diff.
Bangladesh	36	57	+21
Lebanon	58	75	+17
Pakistan	24	41	+17
Uzbekistan	64	77	+13
Turkey	60	72	+12
Senegal	60	68	+8
Nigeria	32	38	+6
Mali	51	56	+5
Indonesia	20	24	+4
Jordan	13	16	+3
Tanzania	47	47	0

Percent "completely agree" within each category.

Question based on Muslim respondents only.

Separation of the Sexes in the Workplace	Men %	Women %	Diff.
Bangladesh	20	36	+16
Turkey	21	30	+9
Nigeria	32	40	+8
Tanzania	15	21	+6
Pakistan	35	36	+1
Indonesia	5	6	+1
Lebanon	25	23	-2
Uzbekistan	48	42	-6
Senegal	17	11	-6
Jordan	18	14	-4
Mali	44	32	-12

Percent "completely agree" within each category.

Question based on Muslim respondents only.

Source: Nicholas Spuelda and Mary McIntosh, "Global Gender Gaps," (Released May 13, 2004), Pew Global Attitudes Project (see http://pewglobal.org/commentary/display.php?AnalysisID=90).

A recent study conducted by the AFL-CIO revealed the salary discrepancies by gender for several different occupations:

★ Female lawyers' median weekly earnings are nearly $500 less than those of male attorneys.

★ Female clericals receive about $100 a week less than male clericals.

★ Female doctors' median earnings are nearly $500 less each week than male doctors.

★ Although 95 percent of nurses are women, they earn $100 less each week on average than the 5 percent of nurses who are men.

★ Women elementary school teachers receive $70 less a week than men.

★ Waitresses' weekly earnings are about $50 less than waiters' earnings.

Sexual harassment, normally in the form of unwelcome sexual advances by superiors, continues to pose a threat to working women in America. Since the mid-1980s the Supreme Court has considered such harassment—which includes any and all actions that create a hostile working environment such as putting up provocative posters, making lewd comments, and so forth—to be a form of sexual discrimination actionable under Title VII of the 1964 Civil Rights Act. Still, many such sexual advances in the workplace continue despite the law, either because women remain unclear about the bounds of permissible conduct or because they fear reprisals for reporting the legal violations of superiors. Indeed, more than four in ten women employed in federal agencies say they have experienced some form of harassment.[29] For all the legal equality that is now afforded to women, some discrimination continues on a level that falls under the radar screen of the legal and judicial process.

Other Struggles for Equality

The political and legal systems in the United States directed increased attention during the late nineteenth and twentieth centuries to the plights of African Americans and women. The hardships suffered by these two groups inspired the passage of five constitutional amendments in all (the three Civil War Amendments, the Nineteenth Amendment granting women the right to vote, and the Twenty-fourth Amendment banning poll taxes) as well as many federal and state antidiscrimination laws. But both these groups' continuous quests for equal privileges under the law comprise only part of the equal rights landscape. American history is replete with accounts of discrimination against other underrepresented groups as well. In recent years, these additional groups have begun to see their own claims to fairness and equal treatment recognized and vindicated within the American political system.

Native Americans protest federal policies by temporarily occupying Alcatraz Island in San Francisco Bay.

Native Americans

One of the nation's most unfortunate tales of mistreatment concerns Native Americans. For much of the eighteenth and nineteenth centuries, vast numbers of white Americans migrated west, pursuing what they viewed as their manifest destiny to settle across the continent. Consequently, millions of Native Americans were herded onto reservations according to a removal policy backed by the federal government. By a federal law passed in 1871, the government no longer agreed to recognize Native American tribes or nations as independent powers capable of entering treaties with the United States—all future tribal affairs were to be managed by the federal government without tribal consent. With passage of the Dawes Severalty Act in 1887, the U.S. government divided tribal lands still in existence among individual Indians who renounced their tribal holdings, further undermining tribal cultures and structures.

Although certain Native American tribes received piecemeal U.S. citizenship beginning in the 1850s and the Dawes Act granted citizenship to those who ceded their tribal holdings, the class of Native Americans as a whole was not admitted to full citizenship until 1924, nearly sixty years after freed slaves had been afforded that same privilege. The federal government's attempt to undo the tribal structure did not produce widespread assimilation of Indians into American society as proponents of the Dawes Act intended; many chose to remain on reservations in an attempt to protect their culture from outside influences. Beginning in the middle of the twentieth century, some Native Americans turned to activism to protest their mistreatment by government authorities. From November 1969 until June 1971, seventy-eight

[29] U.S. Merit Systems Protection Board, "Sexual Harassment in the Federal Workplace: Trends, Progress, Continuing Challenges" (Office of Policy Evaluation, U.S. Merit Systems Protection Board Document).

members of one tribe occupied Alcatraz Island in San Francisco Bay, demanding that it be made available as a cultural center to the tribes. Members of the American Indian Movement (AIM), an organization founded in 1968 to promote civil rights for Native Americans, occupied the Washington, DC, offices of the Bureau of Indian Affairs in 1972, demanding that they receive the rights and privileges that had been promised them under the original treaties entered into by the federal government. This activism drew public attention to Native American causes and spurred action by Congress, which formally terminated its policy of assimilation and began to recognize the autonomy of Native American tribes to administer federal programs on their own lands. In the past quarter century, the U.S. government has settled millions of dollars in legal claims pressed by Native American tribes and has returned nearly half a million acres of land to the Navajo and Hopi tribes alone.

Asian Americans

Immigrants from East Asia—especially Japan and China—supplied much of the labor building U.S. railroads in the nineteenth century. Even so, many were excluded from labor unions and denied other civil rights. The government has enacted several immigration acts specifically designed to limit or prevent Asian immigration. For example, the Chinese Exclusion Act passed in 1882 prohibited Chinese laborers from immigrating and denied U.S. citizenship to Chinese living in the United States. The 1907 Gentleman's Agreement with Japan prohibited the immigration of Japanese laborers. The National Origins Act of 1924 banned all Asians from further immigration to the United States.

Discrimination was especially rampant on the West Coast, where many Asian American populations were concentrated. Asian children were segregated into separate public schools in San Francisco and the state of California restricted Japanese immigrants' rights to own farmland. Perhaps the most notorious incident of discrimination against Asian Americans occurred in 1942, when the U.S. government in response to the Japanese bombing of Pearl Harbor forcibly relocated 110,000 Japanese Americans to inland internment camps and seized their property. The Supreme Court upheld the internment policy in 1944, perpetuating an especially egregious brand of racial discrimination committed against legal residents of the country, including more than sixty thousand legal U.S. citizens. National security concerns used to justify the policy at that time have been exposed in later decades as baseless claims.

In the post–World War II period, Asian Americans enjoyed increased economic prosperity and made significant civil rights gains as well. The ban on Asian immigration was officially lifted in 1952, and provisions of federal law encouraging the immigration of professionals helped attract to the United States large numbers of educated and highly skilled Asian professionals. The end of the Vietnam War in 1975 brought a great influx of immigrants from Vietnam, Laos, and Cambodia to the United States. With increasing numbers of immigrants from South Korea and the Philippines, the Asian American population today stands at approximately 4 percent of the American population as a whole.

Muslim Americans

The events of September 11, 2001, had a profound impact on America's foreign policy priorities and its approach to international terrorism. Those events have also taken a toll on citizens' perceptions of Muslim Americans, a group already set apart by its members' distinct religious practices and forms of dress. The stereotype that associates the Islamic religion with terrorism is hardly applicable to the vast majority who practice the faith, but post–September 11 initiatives sanctioned by Congress under the USA Patriot Act targeted many Muslim Americans for questioning, and in some cases temporary detention. Of course African Americans have long suffered from racial profiling in criminal law enforcement, but the level and degree to which Muslim Americans have been singled out has created a special source of worry for civil rights groups.

Hispanic Americans

Hispanic Americans are defined as those of Spanish-speaking descent. A majority descended from Mexicans who were living in the Southwest when it became part of the United States in the 1840s. Even after immigration laws were tightened in the 1890s, hundreds of thousands of Mexicans continued to enter the United States illegally, drawn by opportunities in farming, mining, and other industries. Segregation of Mexican students from white students began in California in 1885 and continued through the 1950s; beginning in the 1960s, many Mexican Americans moved from rural areas to cities. Public schools in California, Texas, and elsewhere were forced to assimilate this growing population, including the children of illegal aliens, into overcrowded school districts.

Today with more than fourteen hundred miles of border in common between the two nations, the United States and Mexico continue to be at odds over some important issues, including immigration. Meanwhile, more than 35 million people of Hispanic descent currently live in the United States, forming the nation's largest language minority. Cubans, Puerto Ricans, and numerous immigrants and refugees from other Central American countries contribute to the ranks of Hispanic Americans today. Some of the Cubans who left their native land hailed from privileged socioeconomic conditions; fleeing Castro's communistic agenda, their move to the United States was at least in part an effort to save their standard of living. Still, most immigrants from Hispanic countries such as Mexico and Cuba come from adverse economic circumstances in those nations. The crime linked to Mexican immigration in particular may be directly related to the impoverished conditions many of them live under in the United States.

Of course discrimination against Hispanics also contributes to the overall disproportionate levels of poverty and unemployment in this group. And despite there being such a large number of Hispanic Americans, the group's political power has yet to have its due influence on public policy, perhaps because many Hispanics are not yet citizens, and thus do not always enjoy the right to vote.

As governor of Texas in the late 1990s, and then later as president, George W. Bush has continually regarded the Hispanic community as a potential source of growth within the more conservative Republican party. Yet in the 2006 midterm elections, exit polls showed Hispanics voting in favor of the Democrats by a wide margin, helping them to defeat Republican incumbents in Texas such as Rep. Henry Bonilla (R-TX). As the fastest growing ethnic minority in the country, Hispanic Americans should see their political clout only increase in the coming years.

Older Americans

Today approximately 13 percent of Americans are over the age of sixty-five, compared with just 4 percent of Americans who were at that age at the beginning of the twentieth century. With their increased numbers has come increased political power; older Americans are among the most politically active of all citizens, and groups such as the American Association of Retired Persons (AARP), with more than 33 million members on its rolls, have become especially influential players on the political scene. This increased influence has been used to counteract incidents of age discrimination in the workplace and elsewhere. The Age Discrimination in Employment Act, passed in 1967 and broadened in 1986, makes it unlawful to hire or fire a person on the basis of age. Older Americans have also been at the forefront of lobbying efforts to protect Social Security trust funds and to ensure the continuation of cost-of-living adjustments to their payments. Ironically, older Americans' success at wielding influence within the political system has given credence to the suggestion that age classifications do not require suspect scrutiny by courts; at least in this instance, the political system appears to protect the civil rights of this particular subset of Americans.

Disabled Individuals

As with age classifications, discrimination against Americans with physical and mental disabilities has never received heightened scrutiny from the courts. Misperceptions about the nature of certain disabilities have on occasion led to discriminatory treatment of disabled individuals. In the 1920s, some states passed laws authorizing the sterilization of institutionalized "mental defectives"—Justice Oliver Wendell Holmes callously dismissed all legal challenges to such laws with the statement that "three generations of imbeciles are enough." Today,

thanks to significant technological and medical advances, a more enlightened social understanding, and a more sophisticated approach to educating citizens about the nature of these limitations, millions of disabled Americans have been mainstreamed into society, attending school, going to work, and living otherwise normal lives. The Americans with Disabilities Act of 1990 established a national commitment to such mainstreaming efforts and extended to those with disabilities protection from discrimination in employment and public accommodations comparable to that afforded women and racial minorities under the 1964 Civil Rights Act.

Activists for the rights of disabled individuals at a rally advocating broader enforcement of the Americans with Disabilities Act of 1990.

Gays and Lesbians

Of all the groups that have claimed to be discriminated in the United States, homosexuals stand among the least successful in having their claims to equal treatment vindicated under the law. Gays and lesbians have traditionally suffered discrimination in society, whether from those whose religions frown on homosexuality in general or from those who are simply uncomfortable with this lifestyle. In the period immediately following World War II, a movement for gay rights emerged with generally integrationist goals, encouraging homosexuals to conform to most existing social standards. Gays and lesbians assumed a more activist quest for equality beginning in the late 1960s, marching for "gay power," urging reluctant gays to "out" themselves by openly admitting their sexual orientation, and interrupting government meetings to draw attention to their cause of equal treatment and non-discrimination. Although homosexual activists made some advances, no significant antidiscrimination legislation followed. Some communities reacted by passing laws that prohibited the granting of "any special rights or privileges" to homosexuals. The Supreme Court in *Romer v. Evans* (1996)[30] struck down such a provision of the Colorado Constitution in 1996. Perhaps the biggest court victory of all for gays and lesbians occurred in 2003, when the Supreme Court in *Lawrence v. Texas* struck down a Texas law that forbade same-sex partners from engaging in certain types of intimate relations. Despite these victories, the Supreme Court has still never recognized homosexuals as a protected class on a par with women or African Americans.

The issue of homosexuals in the military first drew intense national attention when Army Colonel Margarethe Cammermeyer was discharged from the armed forces in June 1992 when, during a routine security clearance interview, she acknowledged that she was a lesbian. Cammermeyer hinged her hopes for restatement on a promise made to her by candidate Bill Clinton during his successful presidential campaign that fall. At one campaign stop, Clinton reportedly told the twenty-seven-year Army veteran and winner of a bronze star in Vietnam that he "absolutely"

[30] 517 U.S. 620 (1996).

American Government . . . in Popular Perspective:

Recognizing the Legitimacy of Same-Sex Marriage

When New Hampshire became the fourth state in the union to offer civil union status to same-sex couples in June 2007, some interpreted the event as a sign of a growing trend in favor of increased rights for gays and lesbians. Soon thereafter, Oregon joined several other states in electing to recognize same-sex "domestic partnerships." Yet there are other indications that many in the public may have embraced civil unions in some states as a way of fending off other measures such as civil rights laws that afford "special rights" or "special status" to homosexuals, as well as the far more controversial institution of same-sex marriages. At the time this book went to press, Massachusetts, Connecticut, and California were the only three states to have formally recognized same-sex marriage, although voters in California sent their state's law into flux in November 2008 when they approved a constitutional amendment to ban the right. Nor has the public offered much support for recognizing gay or lesbian couples who are married elsewhere. In 1996, the Defense of Marriage Act—which attempts to ensure that each state retain the option of deciding whether or not to recognize same-sex marriage—was passed overwhelmingly by

Congress (85-14 in the House and 342-67 in the Senate) before being signed into law by President Bill Clinton, considered a supporter of gay rights in other contexts.

Eight years later, the issue of whether the states must recognize same-sex marriages and civil unions sanctioned in other states was thrown into the spotlight once again when eleven states voted on ballot measures that either defined marriage as between a man and a woman (three states), refused to recognize same-sex civil unions or domestic partnerships from other states (eight states) or banned civil unions outright. All these ballot measures were held at the same time as the November 2004 presidential election. And all eleven states passed the measures, with eight of the eleven ballot measures receiving at least two-thirds public support, and four measures topping the 75 percent mark (see the figure below). Then, on election day 2008, voters in Arizona and Florida joined Californians in passing measures to ban same-sex marriage in their respective states. Gay rights advocates know that so long as these measures retain their overwhelming popularity, an uphill fight for the cause remains.

November 2, 2004: Same-Sex Ballot Measures

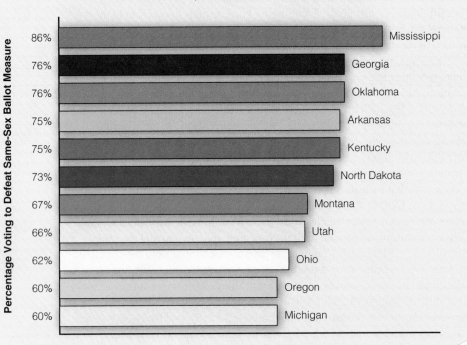

Percentage Voting to Defeat Same-Sex Ballot Measure

State	Percentage
Mississippi	86%
Georgia	76%
Oklahoma	76%
Arkansas	75%
Kentucky	75%
North Dakota	73%
Montana	67%
Utah	66%
Ohio	62%
Oregon	60%
Michigan	60%

would carry out his promise to end the ban against homosexuals in the military. Yet what Clinton the candidate viewed as a "simple civil rights issue" became much more complicated for Clinton the president. Even before his inauguration, Republicans in Congress made clear that they had the votes to reverse any executive order Clinton might issue to allow gays in the military. The Senate Armed Services Committee Chairman, Sam Nunn (D–GA), became infuriated when the new administration began communicating with the Joint Chiefs of Staff while ignoring and taking for granted the support of Senate Democrats. Quickly the president began to backtrack on his promise: at his first televised news conference two weeks into his presidency, he indicated he might go along with a supposed compromise that would segregate gays within the military. The ultimate compromise reached was a "don't ask, don't

AP PHOTO/SCOTT COHEN

Gay marriage supporters at a Seattle rally in March 2006.

tell" policy that would allow gays still in the closet to stay in the military, so long as they never publicized their status. Questions such as those posed to Margarethe Cammermeyer about sexual orientation would no longer be asked. Yet for Cammermeyer, Clinton's compromise provided little solace, as her dream of returning to the military was effectively over. The "don't ask, don't tell" compromise provided little consolation to frustrated gay activists. Though some European countries have actively recruited gays and lesbians for military service, the U. S. military continues to oppose open homosexuality in the armed services.

The federal government has also reaffirmed its prohibition against gay marriage for purposes of receiving marital benefits under federal law. Meanwhile, limited strides have occurred within some states. Vermont's sanctioning of "civil unions" between gays under state law attracted considerable nationwide attention, and a handful of other states soon followed suit. Then, in February 2004, the Massachusetts Supreme Court cleared the way for gay and lesbian couples in that state to marry, ordering the legislature to rewrite the state's marriage law to benefit same-sex couples, which it did on May 17, 2004. Since then, licenses have been issued to same-sex couples in that state. Four years later, California and Connecticut joined Massachusetts as the only other states to sanction same-sex marriages.

However, efforts to nationalize same-sex marriages have also been dealt numerous setbacks in recent years. On Election Day 2004, constitutional amendments that in some way denied same-sex marriages, civil unions, or the recognition thereof were approved in all eleven states where they were under consideration. Further, in the 2006 elections, ballot initiatives in seven states rejected the idea of same-sex marriages. Only in Arizona did voters outright reject a ban on same-sex unions.

Meanwhile, antigay violence continues. The 1998 murder of college student Matthew Shepard brought new calls for hate crime legislation directed at such criminal activity. Despite suffering countless setbacks, gays and lesbians continue to enjoy a significant presence in the political system, forging alliances with more liberal administrations and even electing some openly gay politicians. The attention paid to the Log Cabin Republicans—members of that party who actively promote gay and lesbian rights—provides some indication that homosexuals represent a political force in America today that cannot be so easily ignored.

Now & Then: Making the Connection

A form of the civil rights movement continues to be waged in modern-day courts and legislatures. Despite all the gains of the past, battles are still being taken up by racial, ethnic, and religious groups, as well as by other traditionally disadvantaged groups, to attain equal rights under the law. Just as Autherine Lucy walked a lonely path to achieve admission for African Americans at the University of Alabama in the 1950s, Shannon Faulkner walked a similar path to achieve admission for female applicants at the all-male Citadel in the 1990s. Both Lucy and Faulkner quickly learned that formal recognition of their rights would not suffice to transform many people's minds and hearts. But their actions provided a foundation for future aspirants to build on their accomplishments and present those stubborn minds with alternative perspectives on equality.

Even today, groups such as Native Americans, gays and lesbians, and Muslim Americans continue to walk this path, seeking recognition of rights traditionally denied to them by authorities acting on behalf of "the political majority." For every one or two steps they take forward, they are just as likely to take one other step backward. The hearts and minds of the majority are not so easily transformed. Fortunately, the openness of the American political system encourages some form of dialogue between the majority and underrepresented groups, and it shows no sign of stifling that dialogue anytime soon.

The midterm congressional elections of 2006 resulted in a Democratic Party sweep of both houses of Congress. Lost at first in the headlines about the elections was a smaller event that occurred during that same election season: Keith Maurice Ellison, an American lawyer and politician running as a Democrat and member of the Farmer-Labor Party, became the first African American elected to the House from Minnesota when he won the right to represent Minnesota's fifth congressional district. Yet Ellison's race was not as much an issue as his religion: he was also the first Muslim elected to the federal government in American history and became only the fourth elected Muslim official in the United States as of December 2006. Of course all this occurred during a period when the federal government's war on terrorism has raised questions within the general public about the loyalty of Muslim Americans, many of whom have done nothing illegal or even suspicious.

Ellison's religion made national news when he was first elected. Yet media coverage of Ellison went through the roof when words of intolerance were directed at him by one of his future colleagues, Congressman Virgil Goode (R–VA). After his victory, Ellison indicated that he planned to use the Koran for his unofficial swearing-in ceremony. This led Goode to send a letter to constituents in which he wrote the following:

I do not subscribe to using the Koran in any way. The Muslim Representative from Minnesota was elected by the voters of that district and if American citizens don't wake up and adopt the Virgil Goode position on immigration, there will likely be many more Muslims elected to office and demanding the use of the Koran.

Ellison criticized Goode about the letter, noting that he was not an immigrant and that Goode does not understand Islam. He has also offered to meet with Goode to discuss the matter. Rather than defusing the issue, Goode went on to state publicly that he was in favor of decreasing legal immigration to the United States, and that he hoped to eliminate diversity immigration visas, which go to applicants from countries that do not normally provide many individuals to the United States. Goode argued that such visas might allow people "not from European countries" or from "some terrorist states" to enter America.[31]

On http://www.academic.cengage.com/dautrich, find the "Politics Now" link for details about Ellison's political and religious background, as well as statistics about religious diversity in the current and past congresses. Consult these and other links that relate to religious diversity in American government institutions, and incidents of current discrimination directed against Muslim Americans, including those who are U.S. citizens.

ROGER L. WOLLENBERG/UPI/LANDOV

Congressman-Elect Keith Ellison, being sworn in to the House of Representatives in January 2007.

---

[31] See http://www.cnn.com/2006/POLITICS/12/21/quran.congress/index.html.

http://academic.cengage.com/dautrich

Chapter Summary

★ Civil rights are those political, social, or economic rights conferred by the government to individuals in groups that had previously been denied those rights. The battle for civil rights in American history has focused primarily on African Americans and other ethnic groups (Hispanics, Asian Americans, Native Americans, Muslim Americans), women, older Americans, the physically disabled, and gays and lesbians.

★ The tactics used by groups seeking to achieve civil rights include working within the existing rules and political process, litigation, boycotts, and civil disobedience.

★ The long and hard-fought African American struggle for equality included heated debate as early as the Constitutional Convention. The Civil War and the amendments that passed in its aftermath (Thirteenth, Fourteenth, and Fifteenth) ended slavery, granted citizenship to former slaves, guaranteed all Americans "equal protection under the laws," and denied states the ability to prevent voting rights on the basis of race.

★ Despite these amendments, states have used many means to prevent African Americans from obtaining political, social, and economic equality, including black codes, literacy tests, poll taxes, and Jim Crow laws. A number of U.S. Supreme Court decisions, along with congressional legislation and constitutional amendments, have served to bring America closer to the goal of equality for African Americans.

★ The *Brown v. Board of Education* decision of 1954 eliminated the "separate but equal" doctrine. The movement toward civil rights to minority groups in all public accommodations began in the later 1950s and emerged as a major force under the leadership of Martin Luther King Jr. and his use of nonviolent civil disobedience tactics.

★ King's legacy was memorialized through sweeping civil rights legislation including the Civil Rights Act of 1964 (which banned racial discrimination in all public places), the Voting Rights Act of 1965 (which effectively re-enfranchised millions of African Americans by eliminating the literacy test and property requirements for voting), and the Civil Rights Act of 1968 (which prohibited discrimination in housing and made it a federal crime to deny individuals their civil rights).

★ Two contemporary issues relating to civil rights include affirmative action and racial profiling. The courts have struck down many affirmative action programs, but many states continue to try to find ways for government to level the playing field in hiring and college admissions.

★ The seeds were sown for the movement for gender equality in the early twentieth century with the ratification of the Nineteenth Amendment, guaranteeing women the right to vote. But it would not be until after the formation of the National Organization for Women (NOW) and its emergence as a significant political force that the march for women's equality would capture national attention.

★ Some of the most heated contemporary debates over equality relate to discrimination against Muslim Americans (and how to protect their civil rights in the post-9/11 era), Hispanic Americans and immigration policy, and the rights of gays and lesbians, particularly as they relate to marriage.

Key Terms

Affirmative action (p. 137)

Brown v. Board of Education
   (1954) (p. 129)

Civil rights (p. 127)

Civil Rights Act of 1964 (p. 135)

Civil Rights Act of 1968 (p. 136)

Civil War Amendments (p. 130)

Economic equality (p. 127)

Jim Crow laws (p. 131)

Plessy v. Ferguson (1896) (p. 131)

Political equality (p. 127)

Racial profiling (p. 140)

Social equality (p. 127)

Strict scrutiny (p. 132)

Title IX (p. 144)

Twenty-fourth Amendment (p. 136)

Voting Rights Act of 1965 (p. 135)

Resources

Important Books

Bowen, William, and Derek Bok. *The Shape of the River*. Princeton, NJ: Princeton University Press, 2000.

Branch, Taylor. *Parting the Waters: America in the King Years, 1954–1963*. New York: Simon & Schuster, 1988.

Gerstmann, Evan. *The Constitutional Underclass: Gays, Lesbians, and the Failure of Class-Based Equal Protection*. Chicago: University of Chicago Press, 1999.

Hochschild, Jennifer. *The New American Dilemma: Liberal Democracy and School Desegregation*. New Haven, CT: Yale University Press, 1984.

Kluger, Richard. *Simple Justice*. New York: Vintage Books, 1975.

McWhorter, Diane. *Carry Me Home Birmingham, Alabama: The Climactic Battle of the Civil Rights Revolution*. New York: Simon & Schuster, 2001.

Strum, Phillippa. *Women in the Barracks: The VMI Case and Equal Rights*. Lawrence: University Press of Kansas, 2004.

Washington, Booker T. *Up from Slavery*. New York: Airmont Publishing, 1967.

Woodward, C. Vann. *The Strange Career of Jim Crow*. New York: Oxford University Press, 1955.

Internet Sources

http://www.civilrights.org (the official site of the progressive coalition for equal opportunity and justice, which is made up of more than 180 civil rights organizations from around the country; up-to-date civil rights news and information can be found here)

http://www.naacp.org (the National Association for the Advancement of Colored People's home page; contents include information about the organization, its programs, and its activities, as well various links to other sites of interest)

http://www.noi.org (the official website for the Nation of Islam)

http://www.feminist.org (the Feminist Majority Foundation On-line, which features coverage of global feminist news, issue highlights, links to issues about women in sports, and so on)

http://www.hrc.org (the website of the human rights campaign, which works on behalf of lesbian, bisexual, gay, and transgender equal rights; features extensive coverage of issues related to gay and lesbian interests, including a comprehensive review of legislation in all fifty states)

http://www.usdoj.gov/crt/ada/adahom1.htm (the U.S. Department of Justice's Americans with Disabilities Act [ADA] home page)

Congress

6

Senator Patrick Leahy (D-VT), Chairman of
the Senate Judiciary Committee

TOBY TALBOT/AP PHOTO

The U.S. Senate Plays the Role of Disloyal Opposition: Now & Then

Once a regal and powerful lawmaking body, the United States Senate—like so many other institutions in Washington, DC—had learned to defer to the reality of the modern presidency. An elite group of ambitious politicians sporting their own independent political agendas proved little match for a president determined to make strategic use of the bully pulpit. Still, when the president reached a bit too far in a policy area where the Senate had traditionally exercised significant control, something unexpected happened: the U.S. Senate pushed back. Suddenly the president had to deal with a revitalized institution prepared to stymie the president's objectives by exercising its own considerable tools of political power, including the power wielded by Senate committee chairs to control committee procedures and the ever-present threat of a filibuster. Just when the political system appeared to be under the president's thumb, the upper house of Congress served notice that it remained a vibrant and stubborn obstacle to efforts at presidential steamrolling . . . at least when it wanted to be.

Senator Henry Cabot Lodge of Massachusetts

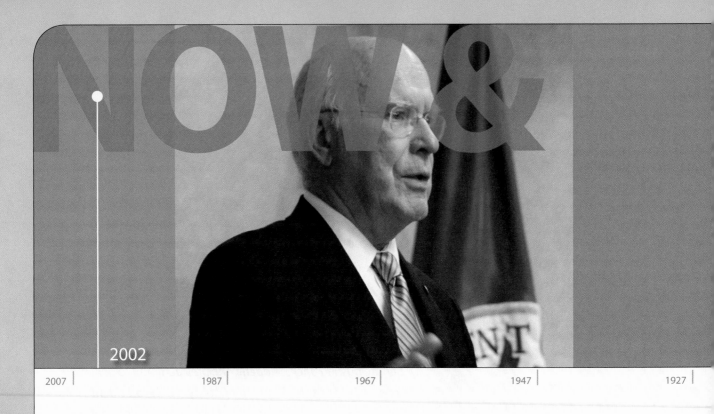

2007 | 1987 | 1967 | 1947 | 1927 |

Now . . . President George W. Bush arrived in office in January 2001 with both houses of Congress under his own Republican Party's control. That changed in part on May 24, 2001, when Senator Jim Jeffords (R-VT) announced that he was leaving the party to become an independent, but would caucus with the Democrats. Jeffords's decision swung control of the Senate to the Democrats by a narrow 51-49 margin. Democratic control of the Senate would have negative implications for many aspects of George W. Bush's agenda, but it would have perhaps the most devastating and immediate effect on his plans to pack the federal courts with ideologically conservative judges—those who, in Senator Charles Schumer's (D-NY) words, lay outside the "judicial mainstream." Notwithstanding the "advice and consent" provisions of the Constitution, with his judicial nominations President Bush had paid little heed to the practice of senatorial courtesy, which traditionally respected the wishes of both parties' senators. In response, the new Senate Judiciary Committee Chairman, Senator Patrick Leahy (D-VT), announced that some of Bush's judicial nominees would be denied an up-and-down vote in his committee; by exercising this prerogative against the most conservative nominees, the Democrats prevented those nominations from being passed to the full Senate, where a handful of more conservative Democrats might give Bush's nominees the margin for victory. Even after Republicans recaptured the Senate in 2002, ending the committee bottleneck, those controversial nominations that made it to the floor of the full Senate now faced a second obstacle: the threat of a filibuster. That tool of the Senate minority, which stops Senate business based on the vote of just forty-one senators, had rarely been used against judicial nomination in the past. Now, it would serve as a central threat in the Democratic senators' war on judicial nominations: If President Bush did not agree to withdraw his most controversial judicial nominees, Senate Democrats would continue to tie up many of his less controversial choices as well. President Bush was eventually forced to adjust to this new reality, as moderate senators from both parties brokered a deal in the spring of 2005 to allow some, but not all, of the president's controversial nominees through to confirmation.

1919

THEN

1917 | 1907 | 1897 | 1887 | 1877 |

Then . . . Nearly a century earlier, another president ran head-first into an emboldened U.S. Senate whose leaders were equally unwilling to defer to the chief executive on issues where its power and authority were constitutionally grounded. Article II, Section 2 of the Constitution affords the Senate a clear role in overseeing treaties—the president can make treaties, but only "by and with the advice and consent of the Senate" and only so long as "two thirds of the Senators present concur." As the first sitting president to travel to Europe, Woodrow Wilson participated in the 1919 peace negotiations after World War I, and he worked tirelessly to incorporate a proposed league of nations (the precursor to the modern United Nations) into the Treaty of Versailles that ended the war. But Wilson, a Democrat, was not willing to seek advice from the Senate, especially after control of both houses of Congress went to the Republicans after the 1918 midterm elections. The new Senate Majority Leader, Senator Henry Cabot Lodge (R-MA), was especially irked by Wilson's refusal to afford senators any kind of voice in the treaty negotiations; he and his Republican colleagues already detested Wilson, and they now feared that U.S. membership in the League of Nations would tie the hands of future Congresses over whether to enter international conflicts. Lodge's official "reservations" to the treaty would have allowed passage of the agreement only so long as the U.S. Congress maintained its full autonomy to act at its discretion in the future. As a member of the Senate Foreign Relations Committee, Lodge slowed the treaty approval process down to a trickle: he took two weeks to read aloud every page of the 268-page treaty and then solicited testimony from scores of witnesses. The treaty would win approval only if Wilson accepted the "reservations," a path that he refused to take. Wilson was awarded the Nobel Peace Prize in 1919, but the League of Nations itself was formed without U.S. participation, and Wilson left office several months later. He never adjusted to the reality of a Senate willing to stand up to the twentieth-century presidency and reject his peace treaty. Biographer Robert Caro put the battle this way: "Woodrow Wilson was defeated by a body he considered both unrepresentative and oligarchical. He was right . . . [b]ut it had the power."

While lower court judicial nominations and international peace treaties were two very different issues debated at markedly different moments in the nation's history, the characteristics of Senate resistance in opposing the president proved remarkably similar in each instance. Senators with considerable power in their branch of government dug in, used Senate Committee and floor procedures to their own benefit, and then let the slow pace of the Senate work its will to frustrate the chief executive. The separation of powers—a provision that gives Congress a significant role—was never designed to run quickly, and in both cases described here, that pattern of slow movement was readily apparent. This chapter discusses the complex organization, structure, and processes of both houses of Congress that underlay the often slow and difficult manner in which this important institution does its work. It shows how particular members achieve disproportionate power and influence in the legislative process and offers the rationale for why Congress plays such a central role in the dealing with issues of paramount importance to the nation.

CALEB JONES/AP PHOTO

AP PHOTO/MANNIE GARCIA

AP PHOTO/MEL EVANS

Daniel Akaka (D-HI), an Asian-American, Barack Obama (D-IL), an African-American, and Bob Menendez (D-NJ), a Hispanic American, were all elected to the U.S. Senate and served in the 110th Congress.

American Government: Historical, Popular, and Global Perspectives

Article I and the Creation of Congress

Article I of the U.S. Constitution created Congress; and the fact that it came first was no accident. The Father of the Constitution, James Madison referred to Congress as the "first branch of government," and as a graduate student, Woodrow Wilson (later the twenty-eighth president of the United States) wrote in his book *Congressional Government* (1885) that "anyone who is unfamiliar with what Congress actually does and how it does it . . . is very far from a knowledge of the constitutional system under which we live."[1] As the legislative branch of the federal government, Congress has ultimate authority for enacting new laws. Because this authority is central to any system of government, the Founders took considerable debate and care in building this first branch.

There was little question that a congress of some type would be the central institution in the new political system—a congress had been a central feature in all attempts to organize the states up through and including the Constitutional Convention of 1787. The Albany Congress of 1754 was the first attempt to unite the colonies—at the time for common defense against the French in the pending French and Indian War. The Albany Plan of Union called for the colonies to organize through the vehicle of a "congress." The first official government of the United States, created under the Articles of Confederation, again used a congress as its organizing principle. It is not surprising, then, that Article I, Section 1 of the U.S. Constitution states: "All legislative powers herein granted shall be vested in a Congress of the United States."

The Founders engaged in plenty of debate, negotiation, and compromise in defining the powers, functions, and structure of the U.S. Congress. The complexity

---

[1] Woodrow Wilson, *Congressional Government* (Baltimore: Johns Hopkins University Press, 1981; originally published in 1885).

of this institution continues today. Congress is filled with paradoxes. On one hand, it is a highly democratic institution in which senators and representatives are selected in free and open elections; on the other hand, Congress often is responsive to an exceedingly narrow set of specialized interests. Citizens and journalists frequently criticize the institution as being too slow to act responsively; yet voters return more than nine in ten of their elected members to office. At times, such as in the weeks following the terrorist attacks of September 11, 2001, Congress can show enthusiasm for tackling large issues expeditiously. Within days of the attacks it passed the USA Patriot Act featuring numerous antiterrorism measures. At other times, it seems to avoid taking positions on important issues, such as campaign finance reform and abortion rights.

Most significantly, Congress is the branch of the U.S. government that ensures representation of the people through the direct election of members of the House and in more recent times, of members of the Senate as well. Through its 535 members, Congress provides representation of many groups throughout the country, such as women, African Americans, Native Americans, and Hispanics.

In 1916, Jeannette Rankin, a Republican from Montana, became the first woman elected to Congress. After one term in the House, she ran for the Senate and lost. She was re-elected to the House in 1940. An ardent pacifist, she was the only member to vote against American entry into both World War I and World War II.

Joseph Rainey of South Carolina was the first African American elected to Congress. He took office in 1870 and was re-elected four times.

Table 6.1 How "Representative" Are Our Representatives?

A Demographic Profile of the 110th (2007–2008) Congress Compared to the Nation

	Congress	US Adults
Median age	58	38
Religion		
Protestant	63%	50%
Catholic	29%	20%
Gender		
Men	84%	48%
Women	16%	51%
Race (Non-exclusive categories)		
African American	8%	13%
White	86%	80%
Hispanic	5%	14%

The Structure and Organization of Congress

★ Bicameral legislature

A legislature composed of two separate chambers.

A fundamental characteristic of Congress is that it is organized into two separate chambers, the Senate and the House of Representatives, and is thus termed a **bicameral legislature.** At the time the U.S. Constitution was written, ten of the thirteen states featured this type of legislature. Creating a bicameral legislature enabled the Founders to reach a compromise between two factions at the Constitutional Convention—those who represented large states and wanted congressional representation according to population, and those from small states who favored the model of the Articles of Confederation: that each state, regardless of population, would be equally represented in Congress. The "Great Compromise" reached by the convention delegates allowed for equal state representation in the Senate, and representation based on population in the House. These two chambers have shared lawmaking responsibilities since 1789.[2]

This nearly equal sharing of legislative power between the two chambers is significant. Many other nations in the world have bicameral legislatures, but the two legislative houses are rarely equal in power and usually do not share power. In the British Parliament, for example, the House of Lords has little power and serves a mostly symbolic function in that nation's politics, whereas the House of Commons wields the most authoritative power. Legislatures in other nations, such as Canada, France, Germany, Israel, and Japan, are also heavily dominated by one house. By contrast, in the U.S. Congress, the Senate and House are coequal chambers, each enjoying about as much power as the other. Similar to the United States, the national legislatures in Italy and Mexico include two houses with nearly equal power. Many nations have *unicameral* legislatures that consist of only one body, such as the 275-member legislature elected to govern the democracy established in Iraq in 2005.

Bicameralism has important implications for the legislative process in American politics—passing new laws is difficult because the two chambers, constructed so differently, must come to absolute agreement before a new law is enacted. The slowness that so often characterizes lawmaking in Congress is, in part, a product of this reality. The sharing of power and the "checks" that each chamber has on the other are no mistake. Indeed, the Founders intentionally built a Congress that would move slowly and carefully in the adoption of new laws, a process that, although often characterized as gridlock, ensures that change is well contemplated before it is adopted.

American Government: Historical, Popular, and Global Perspectives

---

[2] For a good discussion of the Constitutional Convention and issues related to Congress, see Charles Stewart III, "Congress and the Constitutional System" in Paul J. Quirk and Sarah A. Binder, eds., *Institutions of American Democracy: The Legislative Branch* (New York: Oxford University Press, 2005).

The House of Representatives: The "People's House"

The Founders intended the House of Representatives to be the "people's house," or the institution through which ordinary people would be represented in government. At the time the Constitution was adopted, the only federal officials directly elected by the people were members of the House of Representatives. Senators were chosen by state legislatures; the president and vice president were selected by electors in the Electoral College; and judges, ambassadors, and high-ranking officials in the executive branch were nominated by the president and approved by the Senate. In Federalist No. 51, James Madison admonished, "As it is essential to liberty that the government in general should have a common interest with the people, so it is particularly essential that the branch of it under consideration [the House] should have an immediate dependence on and an intimate sympathy with, the people."[3] The House of Representatives thus directly connects voter sentiment with popular representation.

To ensure that members of the House would be accountable to voters, Article I, Section 2 sets the term of a House member at two years, keeping members constantly attentive to the currents of public opinion. Indeed, because of their relatively brief term of office, members of the House are typically consumed with concerns about winning re-election. This preoccupation has been well documented by scholars such as Thomas Mann, who argues that incumbent House members are in campaign mode most of the time, feeling "unsafe at any margin" of victory.[4]

Article I also ensures that the House of Representatives reflects the popular will by requiring that the number of representatives from each state be proportional to each state's population. States are not equally represented in the House of Representatives; rather, the population of each state is proportionately represented, at least to a large degree. This means that a more populous state has greater representation than a less populous one. The state of Texas, for example, now has thirty-two seats in the House of Representatives, compared to Wyoming, which has only one.

The first Congress in 1789 included sixty-five members, consistent with the Article I requirement that the number of House members should not exceed one for every thirty thousand people in a state. As the nation grew in both the number of states and number of people, the number of members of the House of Representatives also grew. If the thirty thousand people to one representative ratio persisted to today, there would be nearly ten thousand members of the House of Representatives! By the mid-1800s, Congress began enlarging the population size of a congressional district to keep the membership of the House from getting too large. Public Law 62-5, passed in 1911 to take effect in 1913, capped the total number of House seats at 435.[5]

Today there are still 435 **congressional districts,** each represented by one House member. The number of people who are represented in a congressional district is tied to a number that changes after every census. Since fixing the number of seats at 435, Congress has struggled to find an equitable way to allocate House seats to the states—a process known as **reapportionment.**

Several U.S. Supreme Court decisions in the early 1960s[6] established the basic principle that guides the process of reapportionment after every census—the "one man, one vote" principle. According to this principle, the population size of congressional districts must be as equal as possible. Currently, that amounts to roughly 646,000 people per district. The requirement that each state maintain at least one House district causes some variance among the population sizes of each district. The single congressional district for Wyoming, for example, has a population of less than five hundred thousand because that is the number of people who live in that state. Consequently, Wyoming's population is proportionately "overrepresented," compared to most other congressional districts. Because congressional districts cannot cross state boundaries, the population size of congressional districts across states also varies. Yet once congressional districts are officially allocated to states based on the U.S. Census, the size of each district within a state must be as close to equal as possible.

The Constitution requires that a new census of the population be taken every ten years, which is used to reapportion seats in the House of Representatives to each

★ Congressional district

A geographic region (either a state itself or a region located entirely within one state) whose residents select one member to represent it in the House of Representatives.

★ Reapportionment

The allocation of a fixed number of House seats to the states.

[3] Hamilton, Madison, and Jay, *The Federalist Papers* (Chicago: The New American Library of World Literature; reprinted in 1961).
[4] Thomas Mann, *Unsafe at Any Margin: Interpreting Congressional Elections* (Washington, DC: Brookings Institution Press, 1978).
[5] Paul Finkelman and Peter Wallenstein, *The Encyclopedia of American Political History* (Washington, DC: CQ Press, 2001), pp. 55–56.
[6] See, for example, *Baker v. Carr* 369 U.S. 186 (1962); *Reynolds v. Sims* 377 U.S. 533 (1964); *Wesberry v. Sanders*, 376 U.S. 1 (1964).

American Government . . . in Popular Perspective:
Confidence in Congress

Compared to its perceptions of the other two main branches of government, the American public has consistently expressed lower levels of confidence in Congress. The figure below shows the Gallup Poll's results for confidence levels in Congress, the presidency, and the Supreme Court from 2001 through 2007. While confidence in all three branches has declined over the past seven years, confidence in Congress has consistently lagged behind the other two branches.

An important book on the topic of public confidence in Congress is *Congress as Public Enemy* by John Hibbing and Elizabeth Theiss-Morse (New York: Cambridge University Press, 1995). The authors argue that the openness of Congress to public scrutiny is responsible for its lower confidence ratings. Despite the low regard for Congress as an institution, Americans have a much higher opinion of the particular members who represent them in Congress. When national polls ask people to rate their own senator and representative, the average ratings tend to be twenty points higher than those that people give to the rating of the institution as a whole (*The Public Perspective,* 1998). Why do people "love their congressperson, but hate Congress?" Individual members' visibility in their home states and districts and the constituent services provided to those they represent tend to promote favorable ratings. In contrast, news about the institution tends to revolve around conflict, debate, and gridlock in the legislative process.

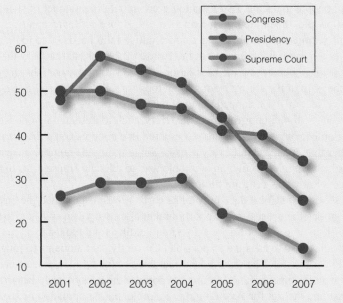

Gallup Poll's Rating of Public Confidence in Institutions

% saying that they had either "a great deal" or "quite a lot" of confidence in the institution

★ Redistricting

The act of redrawing congressional boundaries to achieve equal representation in each of the congressional districts.

state. The states are then responsible for **redistricting** congressional boundary lines to achieve equal representation in each of the congressional districts; that is, redrawing congressional district lines to achieve the "one man, one vote" principle within the borders of the state.

In addition to equalizing the size of congressional districts, parties in each state try to optimize the partisan characteristics of each district to their advantage. This drawing of district boundaries to favor one party over the other is referred to as **gerrymandering,** a term named for Elbridge Gerry, who was a signer of the Declaration of Independence, a Massachusetts delegate to the Constitutional Convention, a U.S. congressman, governor of Massachusetts, and vice president under James Madison. While governor, he endorsed legislation that redrew districts in Massachusetts, resulting in huge advantages for his political party, the Democratic-Republicans. The map of one of the new districts took on an odd shape, that of a salamander. Gerry's political opponents, the Federalists, dubbed the plan the "gerry-mander plan." The political fallout for Gerry was significant—he lost his next bid for governor. But the legacy of gerrymandering continues. Every decade or so, parties in states with more than one House member must ultimately negotiate a redistricting plan based on gerrymandered district boundaries that each party hopes will optimize its electoral successes.

Article I requires that all members of the House of Representatives be at least twenty-five years of age, have been a U.S. citizen for a minimum of seven years, and live in the state (though not necessarily the congressional district) from which they are elected. These requirements are somewhat less restrictive than those for the Senate (see below)—another indication of the Founders' intention to give the people a greater role in deciding on who members of the House should be.

The Senate: A Stabilizing Factor

Whereas the Founders wanted to make the House of Representatives highly responsive to the people, their idea for the Senate was quite different. The Senate was to represent the states—with each state having two senators, thus being equally represented. As adopted, the Constitution specified that senators were to be elected not by the people of the state, but by the state legislatures, another way to recognize states' importance. Not until passage of the Seventeenth Amendment to the Constitution in 1913 were senators elected directly by the people of the state they represented.

The Founders were also concerned that the "people's house" might be too prone to radical changes in membership resulting from swift changes in popular opinion. James Madison in particular regarded the U.S. Senate as "a necessary fence against this danger,"[7] able to resist fast changes in federal legislation because it was less accessible to the people. In fact, during the first five years of our constitutional government, the U.S. Senate met in closed session. By sharing legislative power with the House of Representatives, the Senate, a slower, more deliberative body, would be the mechanism for protecting against the potential tyranny of the masses. Thus the creation of new laws would be forced to proceed at a more thoughtful pace.

The Constitution sets the term of a U.S. senator at six years, three times the length of that for a House member. The Founders staggered the terms of senators. Every two years, only one-third of the seats in the Senate are up for re-election, as compared to all of the seats in the House. So although in theory all of the seats in the House can change every other year, the Senate may change only by a maximum of thirty-four seats every two years and is thus less prone to drastic changes in membership.

The qualifications for becoming a U.S. senator are also tighter. The minimum age is thirty, five years older than in the House, with the idea being that older people were less likely to endorse radical change. Also, a U.S. senator must be a citizen for at least nine years (rather than seven for the House) and be a resident of the state that he or she represents.

Article I requires that there be two senators from each state. The total number of senators grew from twenty-six in 1789 to one hundred in 1959, the year Alaska and

★ Gerrymandering

The drawing of House district boundaries to the benefit of one political party over another. The term is named for Elbridge Gerry, a Massachusetts delegate to the Constitutional Convention, who (as governor) redrew districts in this fashion to favor the Democratic-Republicans.

[7] See James Madison, Federalist No. 63.

Hawaii became the forty-ninth and fiftieth states, respectively, to join the union. Although the size of the Senate has grown, it still remains small, at least relative to the size of the House of Representatives. The smaller size of the Senate is often cited as the primary reason why debate in the Senate tends to be more civil and camaraderie between individuals more important.

Leadership in Congress

Unlike the executive branch of American government, which is headed by the president, no one person or office leads Congress. Leadership is distinct in the Senate and the House of Representatives. Though both chambers must work together to pass new laws, each chamber maintains its own leadership structure to work on bills, pass laws, and conduct its other business. Cooperation between the House and Senate is necessary to accomplish legislation.

The principal factor driving leadership in each chamber is the political party system, which, interestingly, is not mentioned in the U.S. Constitution.[8] The two-party system in America typically generates a majority of members from one of the two major parties, in both the Senate and House of Representatives. Since 1851, the majority party in each house has been either the Democratic Party or the Republican Party. Members of the party that has the majority of seats comprise the **majority caucus,** whereas those who are members of the party with a minority of seats comprise the **minority caucus.** The majority caucus in the House and the majority caucus in the Senate use their respective majorities to elect leaders and maintain control of their chamber. The larger any one party's majority, and the more discipline and unity among party members, the stronger is the power of the majority party's leadership ability.

★ Majority caucus

The members of the party that has the majority of seats in a particular chamber.

★ Minority caucus

The members of the party that has a minority of seats in a particular chamber.

Over the past thirty years, party control of the Senate has changed hands quite a few times. The 1980 elections gave Republicans control of the Senate for the first time since 1954, and they held at least a narrow margin of control up until the 1986 elections, when Democrats won back a majority. The 1994 elections swept the Republicans once again back into the majority, and they maintained control over that body until 2001, when Vermont Senator James Jeffords's switch from lifelong Republican to independent threw a 50–50 split chamber back into Democratic hands. The Republicans regained control after the 2002 midterm elections, but then forfeited it once again in 2007, when fifty-one senators caucused with the Democrats and placed them back in control.

The Senate Democrats' slender 51–49 working margin at the outset of the 110th Congress in 2007 was made possible by the votes of two Independent senators—Bernie Sanders (I-VT) and Joe Lieberman (I-CT)—who aligned themselves with the Democrats. Still, in December 2006, the Senate Democratic leadership received a reminder of just how precarious their pending hold on the Senate chamber truly was when Senator Tim Johnson (D-SD) suffered a rupture in his brain and had to be hospitalized. Democrats feared the possibility that were Johnson to become permanently incapacitated and forced to resign, the Republican governor of South Dakota would replace him with a Republican, thereby returning control of the chamber back to the GOP.[9] As it turned out, Johnson's surgery was successful, and he returned to the Senate in September. As a result of the 2008 elections, the Democratic majority in the Senate increased significantly.

By contrast, the House of Representatives has enjoyed a bit more stability, undergoing fewer changes in party control of the majority caucus since 1954. Up through 1994, the Democratic Party had maintained a seemingly iron grip of control over the House. Finally after forty years, the 1994 elections transformed a Democratic majority to a Republican majority. The Republicans continued to dominate the House until the 2006 midterm elections, at which point the Democrats once again regained leadership of the people's chamber and then increased their majority as a result of the 2008 elections.

American Government: Historical, Popular, and Global Perspectives

[8] For a discussion of leadership in Congress, see Burdett A. Loomis, *The Contemporary Congress*, 3rd ed. (Boston: Bedford St. Martin's, 2000), chap. 6.
[9] If Johnson or any other Democratic senator had been replaced by a Republican in the 110th Congress, Republican Vice President Dick Cheney would have been empowered to break a 50–50 Senate tie in favor of his own party.

Leadership in the House of Representatives

The only guidance the Constitution offers regarding House leadership is contained in Article I, Section 2: "The House of Representatives shall choose their Speaker and other officers." The **Speaker of the House** is the title given to the leader of this chamber. Every two years, when a new Congress takes office, the full House of Representatives votes to determine who the Speaker will be from among its 435 members. In practice, the selection of Speaker is made by the political party in the House that holds the majority of seats. Members in the majority caucus meet prior to the vote for Speaker and agree on their leader, who receives virtually all the votes from the majority party members, thus guaranteeing that the majority party will occupy the Speaker of the House post.

As presiding officer, the Speaker of the House is the most powerful member of the House of Representatives, though that was not always so. Throughout the first century of the American political system, the Speaker acted mostly as procedural leader, or presiding officer, of the House, and had little more than power than committee chairs. However, with the accession of Joe Cannon to Speaker in 1903, this post became much more powerful. Cannon, a Republican from Illinois, served in the House for more than fifty years and was Speaker from 1903 to 1911. As Speaker, Cannon used the House Rules Committee to amass a tremendous amount of power.[10] Known as "Uncle Joe," he arbitrarily recognized who could speak in the House chamber and required that any measure passing the Rules Committee would have to be personally approved by him. Cannon also made a practice of filling important committee posts with those who were loyal to him. A coalition of Democrats and insurgent Republicans eventually unseated Cannon, but Uncle Joe permanently changed the visibility and power of the Speaker position.

The Speaker remains powerful today for a variety of reasons. First, as the person responsible for assigning new bills to committees, the Speaker can delay the assignment of a bill or assign it to a committee that is either friendly or hostile to its contents, a power that gives the Speaker control over much of the House agenda. Second, the Speaker has the ability to recognize members to speak in the House chamber. Because an important part of the legislative process involves members debating bills on the House floor, the Speaker's authority over this process is significant.

Third, the Speaker is the ultimate arbiter and interpreter of House rules. The ability to cast final judgment on a rule of order can make or break a piece of legislation. For example, Republican Speaker Newt Gingrich's decision in 1998 to assign impeachment authority over President Bill Clinton to the House Judiciary Committee rather than to a select committee on impeachment was significant. Gingrich may

CHIP SOMODEVILLA/GETTY IMAGES

After the Democrats won control of the House of Representatives in the 2006 elections, the new Congress elected Nancy Pelosi as the first woman Speaker of the House. Pictured above, Pelosi takes the gavel in her historic first day on the job as Speaker on January 4, 2007.

★ Speaker of the House

The leader of the House of Representatives, responsible for assigning new bills to committees, recognizing members to speak in the House chamber, and assigning chairs of committees.

Chapter 6: Congress

---

[10] See Eric Schickler, "Institutional Development of Congress," in Quirck and Binder, eds., *Institutions of American Democracy: The Legislative Branch* (New York: Oxford University Press, 2005), chap. 2.

JIM YOUNG/REUTERS/LANDOV

The leadership in the House of the 110th Congress, which began work in January 2007. Pictured from left are Majority Leader Steny Hoyer (D-MD), Speaker Nancy Pelosi (D-CA), and Minority Leader John Boehner (R-OH).

have surmised that the makeup of the existing Judiciary Committee was inclined toward impeachment. Indeed, the Judiciary Committee ultimately recommended the impeachment of Clinton to the full House. Fourth, the Speaker appoints members to serve on special committees, including conference committees, which iron out differences between similar bills passed in the House and Senate. The Speaker's influence is thus felt in the final changes made to a bill before Congress completes work on it. Fifth, the Speaker plays an influential role in assigning members to particular permanent committees. Some committees, as we will see later in this chapter, are more important than others. Being on the "good side" of the Speaker helps in getting a good committee assignment. In addition, the Speaker hand picks the nine members of the all-important Rules Committee. Finally, the Speaker has ultimate authority

Table 6.2 Leaders in the 110th Congress

110th Congress (January 2007 to December 2008)		
House of Representatives		
Speaker of the House	Nancy Pelosi	Democrat of California
Majority Leader	Steny Hoyer	Democrat of Maryland
Minority Leader	John Boehner	Republican of Ohio
Majority Whip	James Clyburn	Democrat of South Carolina
Minority Whip	Roy Blunt	Republican of Missouri
Senate		
President of the Senate	Richard Cheney	Republican Vice President of the United States
President Pro Tempore	Robert Byrd	Democrat of West Virginia
Majority Leader	Harry Reid	Democrat of Nevada
Minority Leader	Mitch McConnell	Republican of Kentucky
Majority Whip	Richard Durbin	Democrat of Illinois
Minority Whip	Trent Lott/John Kyl	Republican of Mississippi/ Republican of Arizona

to schedule votes in the full House on a bill, an authority that allows the Speaker to speed the process or delay it, using timing to either enhance or subvert a bill's chances of being passed.

Partisan control of the House is the key factor regarding how that body is organized to do its work. Because the party that holds a majority of seats selects the Speaker, the majority party controls the legislative agenda through members serving in other leadership posts, including chairs of committees. The current Speaker is Nancy Pelosi, a Democrat from California. As of 2007, Pelosi became the first woman in American history to hold a top leadership position in any of the three branches of government. Pelosi was chosen as speaker-elect by the House Democratic caucus when it convened in mid-November 2006; she assumed the formal constitutional title of Speaker of the House during the first week of January 2007.

To promote partisan leadership, the majority caucus in the House votes for a House **majority leader,** and the minority caucus for a House **minority leader.** These leaders oversee the development of their party platforms and are responsible for achieving party coherence in voting. Other important party leadership positions in the House are the House minority and majority **whips.** Whips report to their respective party leaders in the House and are primarily responsible for counting up the partisan votes on bills—that is, they contact members of their party caucus and try to convince them to vote the way their party leadership wants them to vote. The whips spend much of their time on the floor of the House, on the phone, or in the offices of their party colleagues, counting votes and urging their members to vote the party line on bills.

Leadership in the Senate

The Constitution prescribes that the presiding officer of the Senate is the vice president of the United States. In this capacity, the vice president also holds the title of president of the Senate. Unlike the Speaker of the House, who is necessarily a member of the House of Representatives, the president of the Senate is not a member of the Senate. She or he cannot engage in debate on the floor of the Senate and has no legislative duties in the Senate, with one notable exception: the vice president casts a vote in the Senate in the event of a tie. John Adams, the first vice president of the United States, was the most frequent tiebreaker in U.S. history, casting a vote twenty-one times in the Senate.

The leadership in the Senate of the 110th Congress, which began work in January 2007. Pictured with their Senate colleagues are Minority Leader Mitch McConnell (R-KY), left, and Majority Leader Harry Reid (D-NV).

★ Majority leader

In the Senate, the controlling party's main spokesperson who leads his or her party in proposing new laws and crafting the party's platform. The Senate majority leader also enjoys the power to make committee assignments. In the House, the majority leader is the controlling party's second in command, who helps the Speaker to oversee the development of the party platform.

★ Minority leader

The leader of the minority party in each chamber.

★ Whips (majority and minority)

Member of Congress elected by his or her party to count potential votes and promote party unity in voting.

American Government . . . in Historical Perspective:

Important Tie-breaking Votes Cast by Vice Presidents in the Senate

The Constitution specifies only two formal functions for the vice president of the United States: to be the presiding officer of the U.S. Senate and to cast a vote in Senate in the event (and only in the event) of a tie. A number of tie-breaking votes by vice presidents have been quite consequential . . .

In 1790, Vice President John Adams's second tie-breaking vote in the Senate was responsible for moving the capital of the United States from New York City to Washington, DC. The decision to find a permanent capital for the new country was a divisive issue. New York City was the early temporary home of the capital, but southerners feared that the location of the national capital in the North would give that region an unfair advantage on important regional issues, such as slavery and urban development, at the expense of farmers and rural areas. In the House, a deal had already been struck to support moving the capital to a plot of land on the Potomac River bordering Virginia and Maryland. A move by several senators to block the move by supporting a bill that would keep the capital in New York resulted in a 13–13 tie. Adams's tie-breaking vote in favor of moving the capital paved the way for passage of a new bill to move the capital to Philadelphia for ten years, while the land that would become Washington, DC, was prepared to be the nation's capital.

In 1881, on March 18 the Senate met to begin its session by selecting a slate of committee leaders and members. For twenty years, the Senate had been controlled by the Republicans, making

such votes quite predictable. But in the 1880 elections, Americans sent thirty-six Republicans and thirty-six Democrats to the U.S. Senate, along with two independents. The Senate vote on this day would determine whether the Democrats or the Republicans would control the Senate and thus hold the power to confirm or deny Republican President Garfield's patronage appointments. The initial vote was 37–37, giving Republican Vice President Chester Arthur the all-important deciding vote. Arthur's tie-breaking vote allowed the Senate Republicans to ward off a significant Democratic threat to their power.

In 1993, newly elected President Bill Clinton placed at the cornerstone of his new presidency a budget proposal that included tax increases and new federal spending to stimulate a sluggish economy. Much was riding on this budget proposal, as Clinton had won the election of 1992 over George H. W. Bush based on his criticism of Bush's lack of concern for bringing the nation out of economic recession (made famous by the Clinton campaign slogan "It's the economy, stupid"). Clinton argued that the budget plan was essential not only to economic recovery, but ultimately to eliminating the federal budget deficit. Though passed by the House of Representatives, the vote in the Senate ended in a 50–50 tie, setting the stage for Vice President Al Gore to cast the deciding vote to pass the budget. A most remarkable economic development of the 1990s was, in fact, the elimination of federal deficits.

★ **President pro tempore**

In the absence of the vice president, the senator who presides over the Senate session. By tradition, this is usually the senator from the majority caucus who has served the longest number of consecutive years in the Senate.

In practice, the vice president rarely shows up on the Senate floor to preside over its session. The presiding officer, in the absence of the vice president, is the **president pro tempore** ("pro tempore" is Latin, meaning "for the time being"). By custom, the official president pro tempore is the senator in the majority caucus who has served the longest number of consecutive years in the Senate. Again, however, in practice the president pro tempore rarely excises the authority to preside over the Senate. With fewer rules and a greater culture of respect to fellow members than in the House, the presiding officer of the Senate serves what is largely a ceremonial role.

Leadership in the Senate is principally a function of partisanship, with the majority and minority caucuses organizing through leadership posts similar to those of the House of Representatives. As in the House, the majority party exercises tremendous power by controlling the agenda and mobilizing majority votes on important issues for the party. The majority caucus elects a Senate majority leader, and the minority caucus a Senate minority leader. These leaders are the main party spokespersons in the Senate, lead their party caucuses in proposing new laws, and are the chief architects of their party's platform. As leader of the majority, the Senate majority leader enjoys special power in making assignments to leadership of committees.

As in the House, the Senate majority and minority leaders are supported by whips, majority and minority. The whips in the Senate serve the same function as those in the House—they keep track of how caucus members are planning to vote on upcoming bills, and they communicate the positions of party leaders on upcoming legislative votes.

Leaders in the Senate generally have far less power than their counterparts in the House. The smaller number of senators requires less discipline in membership, and the culture of the Senate includes a greater amount of deference from one senator to another. Because there are fewer rules and formal procedures in the Senate, leaders and rule-making members have less power to control debate in that body.

The Committee System

The work of a member of Congress can be classified into four categories: (1) running for re-election, (2) serving constituents, (3) working on legislation, and (4) providing oversight of federal agencies. Working on legislation involves two activities—working on bills in committees and voting on proposed bills.[11] The bulk of work on legislation consists of what members do in committees, which includes generating ideas for new laws, debating the merits of those ideas, holding hearings, conducting investigations, listening to the testimony of experts, offering modifications and additions to proposed bills, and giving important advice to all House and Senate members regarding how they should vote on a new bill. Committee work also is the means through which members fulfill their role of oversight of federal agencies. Voting, on the other hand, is a rather simple and straightforward process. Members show up on the House or Senate floor and cast a vote of either "aye," "nay" or "present," indicating their support for or opposition to a proposed piece of legislation.

Every year about ten thousand bills are introduced into Congress. A **bill** is a formally proposed piece of legislation, and many bills are long, complex documents with much legal and technical information. It is not practical to assume that each senator and House member reads and digests every bill that is introduced. As a way to manage the workload, both chambers of Congress rely heavily on a committee system. In both the House and Senate, each member is assigned to a few committees and becomes an expert in the subject area of the committee. Most of members' legislative work revolves around the committees to which they are assigned.

Congressional committees also include subcommittees, providing for even more specialization and division of labor. Currently there are more than ninety subcommittees in the House alone. Each of the subcommittees is also assigned a chair, so many members in the majority party of the House are chairs of either a committee or subcommittee. In the Senate, with fewer members, all members of the majority are usually the chair of at least one committee or subcommittee. A House member sits on an average of five different committees, whereas a senator sits on an average of seven committees.

What makes the committee system so powerful a force in legislation? It is the deference that most members give to the work of their colleagues in committees. Recognizing specialized knowledge, respecting the need for division of labor, and protecting one's own authority in the committees in which one serves all lead senators and House members to vote on the basis of a committee's recommendation on a bill.

★ Bill

A proposed law presented for consideration to a legislative body.

---

[11] A classic work on congressional committees is Richard F. Fenno Jr., *Congressman in Committees* (Boston: Little, Brown, 1973).

Types of Committees in Congress

There are four general types of congressional committees: standing committees, select committees, conference committees, and joint committees.

Standing committees are permanent committees that exist in both the House and Senate. Most standing committees focus on a particular substantive area of public policy, such as transportation, labor, foreign affairs, and the federal budget. A few focus on procedural matters of the House and Senate, such as the House Rules Committee and the Senate Rules and Administration Committee. The most significant power of the standing committee is that of **reporting legislation**—which means that the full House or Senate cannot vote on a bill unless the committee votes to approve it first. No other type of congressional committee has the power to report legislation. Table 6.3 lists the standing committees of the House and Senate.

Standing committees have been the heart and soul of congressional organization since the very early 1800s. Just like today, standing committees then were divided into substantive policy areas and had plenty of authority to determine the future of a bill within its jurisdiction. For example, in 1802 the House of Representatives established the Ways and Means Committee to set policies for America's federal tax system. Any bill dealing with changes in the tax system had to pass through this

★ **Standing committee**

A permanent committee that exists in both the House and Senate; most standing committees focus on a particular substantive area of public policy, such as transportation, labor, foreign affairs, and the federal budget.

★ **Reporting legislation**

The exclusive power of standing committees to forward legislation to the full House or Senate. Neither chamber can vote on a bill unless the committee votes to approve it first.

Table 6.3 The Standing Committees in Congress

Committees in the House	Committees in the Senate
Agriculture	Agriculture, Nutrition, and Forestry
Appropriations	Appropriations
Armed Services	Armed Services
Budgets	Banking, Housing, and Urban Affairs
Education and the Workforce	Budget
Energy and Commerce	Commerce, Science, and Transportation
Financial Services	Energy and Natural Resources
Government Reform	Environment and Public Works
Homeland Security	Homeland Security and Governmental Affairs
House Administration	Finance
Intelligence	Foreign Relations
International Relations	Health, Education, Labor, and Pensions
Judiciary	Indian Affairs
Resources	Judiciary
Rules	Rules and Administration
Science	Small Business and Entrepreneurship
Small Business	Veterans Affairs
Standards of Official Conduct	
Transportation and Infrastructure	
Veterans Affairs	
Ways and Means	

committee, as it still does today. The House Ways and Means Committee remains the primary author of tax bills, including the tax cuts approved by Congress and signed into law by President Bush in 2001 and 2003.

Though most standing committees focus on a substantive area of public policy, such areas of focus are often broad and complex. In order to further divide labor and provide for even greater levels of specialization, most standing committees include subcommittees. For example, the House Transportation and Infrastructure Committee includes the following subcommittees: Aviation; Coast Guard and Marine Transportation; Economic Development, Public Buildings, Hazardous Materials, and Pipeline Transportation; Ground Transportation; Oversight, Investigations, and Emergency Management; and Water Resources and Environment.

Before the House of Representatives or the Senate can vote on any bill, it must first be approved by a majority of members on the committee. A number of factors can affect a committee's consideration of a bill, which can seriously slow down the process of a bill becoming law and create a sense of "legislative gridlock." When a committee gets a new bill, the chair usually directs the bill to a subcommittee. The subcommittee discusses the bill, holds hearings, and makes changes, additions, or deletions to the bill. Usually, after a successful subcommittee vote, the bill moves back to the full committee, where additional debate and hearings might occur. Only after a successful committee vote is the bill ready to be considered by the full House and/or Senate. This process occurs in both the House and the Senate. There are, therefore, many opportunities for standing committees to slow the policy-making process, or bring it to a grinding halt.

A second general type of committee in Congress is the **select committee,** a special committee established to examine a particular issue of concern. Select committees do not have the power to report legislation, and they are not permanent. Once their work on a particular issue of the day is complete, the select committee is dissolved. Select committees are often formed to deal with a particularly serious national problem—a problem for which legislation may not be considered but rather a recommendation might be made. Recently, for example, select committees have been established to investigate the problem of illegal immigration and the national drug problem. House or Senate leaders may choose a select committee to deal with an issue for political reasons as well. If leaders suspect that a standing committee might have trouble reporting a bill to the full chamber, they might appoint a select committee, which does not have reporting power.

A third type of committee found in Congress is the **conference committee.** As described earlier in this chapter, the House and Senate are equal players in the legislative process. This means that both chambers debate, hold hearings on, comment on, and vote on individual pieces of legislation. A bill, then, is considered, modified, and voted on by both the House and the Senate. Assuming that a bill survives both chambers and passes, it is likely that the changes made to the bill during the standing committee process will differ between the House and Senate. Conference committees consist of both House members and senators, who work together to iron out differences in the House and Senate versions of a bill.

A fourth type of committee is the **joint committee,** which consists of members from both chambers. Joint committees do not propose legislation and have no reporting power, but rather are investigative in nature, focusing on issues of general concern, such as oversight of programs that are administered by the executive branch of the federal government. Unlike select committees, which are temporary and focus on a narrower topic, joint committees are typically permanent and focus on broader policy areas. An example is Congress's Joint Economic Committee. This committee keeps tabs on the performance of the nation's economy and provides oversight to the Federal Reserve Board, the unit that, among other things, has authority to adjust the federal prime interest rate.

★ Select committee

A committee established by a resolution in either the House or the Senate for a specific purpose and, usually, for a limited time.

★ Conference committee

A joint committee of Congress appointed by the House of Representatives and the Senate to resolve differences on a particular bill.

★ Joint committee

A committee comprised of members of both the House and the Senate which is investigative in nature.

Leadership of Congressional Committees

Although there are a handful of broad leadership positions such as "presiding officers" and "party leaders" in the House and Senate, the vast majority of leaders are the chairs of the many committees and subcommittees in the two chambers. The power of the majority caucus is fully felt in the committee and subcommittee chairs, as all chairs are members of the majority caucus. Committees are where Congress gets most of its work done, and the chairs of committees have a great deal of power in determining what gets done and when it gets done.[12]

CHECKtheLIST

The Six Most Prolific Congressional Dynasties

With Hillary Clinton establishing herself as a powerful force within the Democratic Party, and former Florida governor Jeb Bush eyeing a possible presidential bid in 2012, one might think political dynasties are once again in vogue. Yet according to scholars who have studied this issue, political dynasties—at least as measured by family membership in Congress—are actually in decline. Still, strong family ties in politics offer more than just connections and a measure of credibility...they offer all-important name recognition. Below is a list of the six most prolific Congressional dynasties, as measured by the number of members the families have placed in one of the two major branches of government:

The three most famous Breckinridges: U.S. Senator and Attorney General John Breckinridge (1760-1806); U.S. Representative and Vice President John C. Breckinridge (1821–1875); and U.S. Representative and diplomat Clifton Rodes Breckinridge (1846–1932).

✔ **The Breckinridge family** (17 members in 72 different Congresses). Its most notable member was John C. Breckinridge, who served as a U.S. Senator from Kentucky, 14th Vice President of the United States, and Democratic candidate for President in 1860.

✔ **The Harrison family** (8 members in 24 Congresses). Its most notable member was President William Henry Harrison, a former U.S. House member and Senator from Ohio.

✔ **The Kennedy family** (6 members in 37 Congresses). Its most notable member was President John F. Kennedy, a former U.S. House member and U.S. Senator from Massachusetts.

✔ **The Lodge family** (4 members in 37 Congresses). Its most notable member was Henry Cabot Lodge, a U.S. House member and U.S. Senator from Massachusetts.

✔ **The Adams family** (3 members in 16 different Congresses). Its most notable member was President John Quincy Adams, a former U.S. Senator and future U.S. House member from Massachusetts.

✔ **The Bryan family** (3 members in 15 Congresses). Its most notable member was William Jennings Bryan, three-time Democratic party nominee for President and a former U.S. House member from Nebraska.

Source: "Political Dynasties" by Ernesto Dal Bo (University of California, Berkeley), Pedro Dal Bo (Brown), and Jason Snyder (Northwestern) in *The Atlantic Monthly,* June 2007, p. 32

---

[12] See Stephen S. Smith and Christopher Deering, *Committees in Congress,* 2nd ed. (Washington, DC: CQ Press, 1990).

American Government: Historical, Popular, and Global Perspectives

For example, the chairs decide how much time, if any, to spend on a new bill; they choose the people who will testify before the committee; and they allot the time to be spent on testimony and committee discussion. House and Senate leaders choose committee chairs from members of the majority caucus, a selection generally based on seniority and party allegiance. For each committee, the majority party's ranking, or senior, member is typically the person who becomes the committee chair, although the Speaker of the House ultimately determines the chairs for House committees and the Senate majority leader does the same for Senate committees.[13] Though seniority remains important, congressional reforms in 1974 and 1994 have somewhat reduced the power of seniority in the determination of committee chairs. More recently, the selection of chairs and the chairs' adherence to party leadership has provided a strong basis for party influence in congressional leadership. For example, on December 1, 2006, Nancy Pelosi confirmed her plans to bypass for chair of the House Intelligence Committee the senior member of that committee, Jane Harman (D-CA), opting instead for Silvestre Reyes (D-TX).

Partisan Nature of the Committee System

The large number of standing committees and subcommittees, along with the significant power of the committee given its expertise in the policy area, disperses legislative power. It is in the interest of the majority party, however, to control what bills are given priority, how bills are written, and what bills get passed. Thus, the primary organizational characteristic of most committees in Congress is partisanship. To control the committee agenda and the committee votes, the majority caucus ensures that all committees have a majority of members of their party.[14] Furthermore, the chair of each committee is from the majority caucus. In addition, the majority caucus typically reserves a "supermajority" of seats on the most powerful committees, such as the Rules and Appropriations Committees.

Congressional Staffing

The 435 House members and 100 senators are supported by a large professional staff, many of whom are young, recent college graduates. Staffers perform a variety of support functions related to the roles of members of Congress. They conduct background research on bills, help generate new ideas for bills, provide services to constituents, and aid in the oversight of executive agencies. There are three categories of congressional staff.

First is the member's **personal staff.** Each member of Congress is given a budget to support a group of staffers to assist them. They typically have a staff in their Washington, DC, office and one in their home district office. The personal staffers serve a number of legislative support functions, including tracking bills that the member has introduced and conducting research on ideas for new bills. They also work with the local media in the member's home district, answering journalists' questions and providing information on the member's legislative activities. Perhaps the personal staffers' most important responsibility is responding to constituents in the district. House and Senate members receive many kinds of communications from constituents, ranging from requests for information about bills and explanations of why they voted a particular way, to letters expressing opinions on various issues and requests for speaking engagements. The personal staffers are responsible for dealing with these myriad constituent inquiries.

Another form of support for members of Congress comes in the form of **congressional agencies.** The volume of legislative work has grown substantially over the years, as has the complexity of the federal budget and the policy issues

★ **Congressional personal staff**

A group of workers who assist an individual member of Congress in performing his or her responsibilities.

★ **Congressional agencies**

Government bodies formed by and relied on by Congress to support members of Congress in performing their functions.

AP PHOTO/RUSTY KENNEDY

Congressman Patrick Murphy (D-PA) is congratulated by his wife (immediate left) and staff after his re-election victory in 2006.

---

[13] See Roger Davidson and Walter Oleszek, *Congress and Its Members*, 4th ed. (Washington, DC: CQ Press, 1994).
[14] A classic piece on the topic is John Manley, "Wilbur Mills: A Study of Congressional Influence," in *American Political Science Review* 63 (1969), 442–464.

The Library of Congress,
Washington, DC.

that Congress deals with. One way that Congress has dealt with problems of growth and complexity has been to delegate authority to executive agencies of government, a consequence of which was that Congress began to lose control of the ability to keep tabs on what those agencies were doing. The explosion of budget deficits in the 1970s and suspicions about the administration that were inspired by the Watergate scandal also left Congress feeling that it lacked necessary information for effective monitoring of executive agencies under presidential control. Through the 1970s, Congress relied on budget data from the Office of Management and Budget (OMB), which reports to the president. Congress suspected that the budget figures produced by OMB were compiled with an eye toward supporting the president's point of view. In response, in 1974 Congress created a new congressional agency, the Congressional Budget Office (CBO), to monitor the nation's economic situation and provide objective projections of the national budget. It reports directly to Congress. With the CBO, Congress no longer needs to depend exclusively on the executive branch to gather economic data and produce information to help Congress oversee the budget process.

At the same time, Congress also substantially expanded the size and funding of the Government Accountability Office (GAO; formerly called the General Accounting Office) and the Congressional Research Service (CRS). Congress uses the GAO to monitor executive agency expenditures. Essentially, the GAO audits the spending of federal organizations to find and remove any abuses. The CRS is Congress's information and statistical data archive. It provides members with information they might need in preparation for writing a bill, conducting a hearing or investigation, or making a speech. Other important agencies of Congress include the Library of Congress, which acts both as the de facto national library of the United States as well as a research arm for congressional members; and the Government Printing Office, which prints and provides access to documents produced by and for all three branches of the federal government.

A third type of staffing resource at Congress's disposal is the congressional committee staff. Each standing committee of Congress employs a professional staff, many of whom are policy or legal experts in the policy area of the committee.

How a Bill Becomes a Law

It is not easy for a bill to become a law. Though most work on bills occurs in committees, there are numerous other points at which a bill might be "killed." The Speaker of the House, the Senate majority leader, and the president all have means at their disposal to kill a bill. There are other points, as well, when bills might be stopped dead in their tracks. Not surprisingly, of the ten thousand or so bills introduced annually in Congress, only about 5 to 10 percent end up becoming law. And rarely does a bill, as originally introduced, become law without significant revision in the process. An important book on the process of a bill becoming law by is *The Dance of Legislation*, by Eric Redman.[15] As the title suggests, the lawmaking process involves many people and much politicking; the process is difficult and often follows no regular or consistent path. The steps to a bill becoming law are also highly influenced by partisan politics, lobbyists and special interests, public opinion, and powerful voices in and out of government. Even though the actual dance of legislation typically follows no neat pattern or order, we describe here the general way in which a bill becomes a law.

Step 1: A Bill Is Introduced

With the exception of tax or revenue proposals, which must originate in the House of Representatives, a bill can be first introduced into either the Senate or the House. The revenue exception, as stipulated in the Constitution, is a product of the American colonial experience with England, and the famous cry, "no taxation without

Figure 6.1 The Steps in a Bill Becoming a Law

---

[15] Eric Redman, *The Dance of Legislation* (Seattle: University of Washington Press, 1974).

representation." Because the House provides popular representation, and representation is the philosophical basis undergirding taxation, the Founders gave the House sole authority to originate tax and revenue bills.

Whereas the Constitution requires that only a House member or a senator can introduce a bill, the ideas for new bills come from a variety of sources. Many come from the president of the United States or someone in the president's office or executive branch of government. Others come from lobbyists. Because House members and senators depend on lobbyists for information, and lobbyists represent groups who support candidates for congressional office, those with access to members are an important source of ideas for new legislation. Business leaders, educators, journalists, and regular constituents may also generate ideas for new bills. The next step for those with a suggestion for a new law is to find a sponsor in the House or Senate to introduce the idea in the form of a bill.

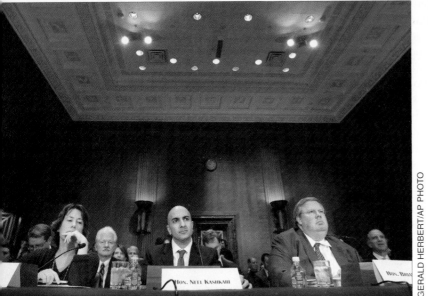

FDIC Chair Sheila Blair, Assistant Treasury Secretary Neel Kashlari, and Assistant HUD Secretary Brian Montgomery attend an October 2008 hearing of the Senate Banking Committee, which was meeting to address the U.S. financial crisis.

Whether the idea for a law comes directly from a member of Congress or from some other source, the first official step in the process is for the sponsoring member to submit the bill to the House or Senate clerk, who issues a unique number to the bill. The clerk in the House sends the bill to the Speaker of the House; the Senate clerk forwards the bill to the Senate majority leader.

Step 2: The Bill Is Sent to a Standing Committee for Action

The next step in the process requires the bill to be assigned to the standing committee that has policy jurisdiction over the topic the bill addresses. A bill introduced in the Senate to raise the minimum wage, for example, would likely be sent to the Senate Labor and Human Resources Committee; a bill proposing increased criminal penalties for mail fraud introduced into the House might be assigned to the House Judiciary Committee.

Most bills die during their initial consideration by the committee. In some cases, the committee chair simply sits on the bill and ignores it. In other cases the full committee, without deliberation, votes to kill the bill. If the committee decides to give the bill serious consideration, the committee chair usually assigns it to a subcommittee. The subcommittee may hold hearings, conduct investigations, and deliberate on the merits of the bill. Often the subcommittee will make amendments to the bill before sending it back to the full committee.

When a bill is back in full committee, the recommendations of the subcommittee may be accepted, rejected, or further revised. The full committee may conduct additional hearings, call more witnesses and experts to testify, and debate the bill. At the end of this process, a "markup," or final version of the bill is prepared. The markup is the proposed legislation on which the full committee will vote. If a majority of committee members vote against the bill, the bill goes no further, so here is another point in the process where a bill might be stopped. If a majority of committee members vote in favor of the bill, it moves forward in the process.

Step 3: The Bill Goes to the Full House and Senate for Consideration

At this next stage, the full House or Senate debates the bill and proposes amendments. The start of this process differs between the House and Senate. In the House, a bill that makes it through the committee is immediately assigned to the House **Rules Committee.** The Rules Committee decides when the bill will be debated, the amount of time that will be allotted for debate, and the extent to which amendments may be added from the floor of the House. The ability to control the timing and amount of time for debate is significant, thus making this committee one of the most important ones in the House. The ability to control the amendment process is even more powerful. If the Rules Committee issues a **closed rule,** House members are severely limited in their ability to amend the bill. An **open rule** order, on the other hand, permits amendments to the bill.

In the Senate, there are no rules set up ahead of time for debate. The Senate majority leader decides when to bring a bill to the floor. But, in theory, there are no limits on the amount of time the bill will be debated, and all senators are given the courtesy of speaking on any bill, if they so wish. The fact that the Senate includes far fewer members than the House allows for less structured debate. With no rules about how long a senator might speak, there is a possibility that a minority of senators—or even one senator—might try to block a bill from passage by refusing to end discussion, a process known as a **filibuster.**[16]

In 1917, a group of senators successfully filibustered to thwart a bill that would have armed American ships in anticipation of the nation's entry into World War I. In response to this event, the Senate adopted a **cloture** rule, which permitted the Senate to end debate and force a vote on a bill by approval of a two-thirds vote. The Senate left a loophole in place, however: if any senator, once properly recognized, refuses to concede the floor, he or she can exercise the equivalent of a one-person filibuster for as long as his or her voice will hold out. Accordingly, in 1957 South Carolina Senator Strom Thurmond spoke for more than twenty-four hours in an attempt to block the Senate from passing civil rights legislation. For many years, Senate filibusters successfully blocked legislation supported by a majority of senators. Then in 1975, the Senate modified the cloture requirement, so that currently a less stringent three-fifths vote of the Senate (sixty out of one hundred senators) is required to end debate.

At the end of the debate and amendment process, the House and Senate take a vote on the proposed bill. Passage of a bill must achieve a majority of votes (half of all present for voting, plus one) from members on the floor. A majority of votes must be achieved in both the Senate and House for the bill to survive to the next step in the legislative process.

How any one member of the House or Senate makes his or her decision to vote "aye" or "nay" on a given proposed bill differs from one bill to another, and from one member to another. But there are at least six common explanations, which vary in importance, depending on the situation:

1. **Personal opinion and judgment.** Many members of Congress have strong personal opinions and convictions on issues, and cast their votes on bills on the basis of those opinions. Rep. Henry Waxman (D-CA), for example, is an ardent environmentalist and consistently votes this position on environmental bills. Similarly, Rep. Chris Smith's (R-NJ) pro-life stance on abortion leads him to vote that position on bills.

2. **Constituent opinion.** Members of Congress want to be liked by their constituents, and most want to be re-elected. In voting on particular bills, members often use results of polls, editorial commentary in local media,

★ **Rules Committee**

A committee in the House of Representatives that determines the rules by which bills will come to the floor, be debated, and so on.

★ **Closed rule**

A rule of procedure adopted by the House Rules Committee that severely limits the ability of members of Congress to amend a bill.

★ **Open rule**

A rule of procedure adopted by the House Rules Committee that permits amendments to a bill.

★ **Filibuster**

The action by a single senator or a minority of senators to block a bill from passage by refusing to end discussion.

★ **Cloture**

A Senate debate procedure that permits that body to end debate and force a vote on a bill by a vote of sixty senators.

---

[16] For a discussion of the motivations for senators to filibuster, see Sarah A. Binder and Stephen S. Smith, *Politics or Principles? Filibustering in the United States Senate* (Washington, DC: Brookings Institution Press, 1997).

and letters written to them by their constituents to help them make up their minds in voting on a particular bill.

3. **Interest groups and lobbying.** As a way of achieving their goals, interest groups exert influence on congressional voting in a number of ways, including making contributions to congressional campaigns and hiring lobbyists to provide arguments to members regarding why they should vote a particular way on a bill. So members use both information provided by lobbyists to aid in their voting, and the campaign support from interest groups to prompt how they will vote.

4. **Political parties.** The party of a member often conveys quite a bit about their political positions and ideology, with Democrats tending to be more liberal on social and economic issues, and Republicans tending to be more conservative on these issues. So party membership is an important cue. In addition, the leadership of each party is organized to influence party members to vote the "party line" on bills. Members voting with their party tend to be rewarded with better committee assignments and greater campaign funding, thus making party a very important factor in voting on legislation.

5. **The president.** Presidents are the focus of national attention and have, as President Teddy Roosevelt once said, a "bully pulpit" to make their case and influence others, including members of Congress. Presidents are quite influential in directing congressional members of their own party how to vote, but often exert influence on members of the opposition party as well. Particularly in times of international crisis, presidents can effectively make appeals to put partisanship aside and convince members to vote in the interests of the country.

6. **Logrolling.** Members often enter into an agreement with other members to vote a certain way on one bill in exchange for a favorable vote on another bill. This process is known as **logrolling.** Members vote on thousands of bills every term. Giving up a vote on less important bills in exchange for favorable votes on more important bills is a common practice, and one that often guides congressional voting behavior.

★ Logrolling

The trading of influence or votes among legislators to achieve passage of projects that are of interest to one another.

Step 4: Conference Committee Action

Often the version of a bill that passes the Senate differs from that passed by the House. To iron out any differences between Senate and House bills, Congress has two options. The first and most common route is to work out the differences informally. Of course the ability to do this depends on the extent of differences in the two versions of the bill and the closeness of the votes in committee and in the full chambers. When the versions are not far apart in content and when the margins of approval are large, informal discussions between House and Senate leaders and committee chairs are usually sufficient to strike a deal. When the prospects for informal agreement are less likely, then House and Senate leaders select a conference committee to work out the kinks. The conference committee consists of House and Senate members—usually drawn from the standing committees that worked on the bills.

Step 5: Presidential Action

The president plays both an informal and a formal role in the passage of new laws. The president's informal role is to develop new ideas for laws and urge members of Congress to introduce them. The president also lobbies Congress, attempting to persuade members to support or oppose certain bills. The president's strong presence in the American political system, along with attention from the national media, offers the president a unique platform to lobby on behalf of or against certain legislation.

Surrounded by members of the U.S. Senate, President Bush signs into law the Intelligence Reform and Terrorism Prevention Act.

The formal constitutional role that the president plays in legislation is the fifth step in the process by which a bill becomes law. Once both chambers of Congress have agreed to a bill, the bill is sent to the president for action. The president has three options for dealing with the congressionally approved bill. First, the president can sign the bill, which officially makes it new law. Second, the president can **veto** (or refuse assent to) the bill, which stops the bill from becoming law. If the bill is vetoed, Congress has one more opportunity to pass the bill, by **overriding** the presidential veto. This requires a two-thirds vote in favor of passage in both the Senate and the House, a margin substantially more difficult to achieve than the simple majority vote required prior to a presidential veto. Third, the president can decide not to act on a bill (that is, neither sign it nor veto it), in which case the bill automatically becomes law after it has sat on the president's desk for ten days. If Congress passes a bill and sends it to the president within ten days of the end of a congressional session and the president does not act on the bill, then the bill does not become law, a process known as a **pocket veto.**

Oversight and Personnel Functions of Congress

In addition to creating new laws, Congress performs four other important constitutional functions: oversight of federal agencies, approval of top federal executives and judges, impeachment of top federal executives and federal judges, and approval of treaties.

Congressional Oversight

Congress's principal responsibility is to enact new laws to deal with national problems and concerns. But given the complexity of many issues (nuclear and toxic waste disposal, creating new sources of energy, promoting the role of high technology, and enhancing the performance of a multi-trillion-dollar economy that has become highly integrated in the global economy, to name just a few), Congress often lacks the scientific and technological expertise needed to enact laws. In addition,

★ Veto

The constitutional procedure by which the president refuses to approve a bill or joint resolution and thus prevents its enactment into law.

★ Overriding a veto

The power of the Congress to enact legislation despite a president's veto of that legislation; requires a two-thirds vote of both houses of Congress.

★ Pocket veto

The indirect veto of a bill received by the president within ten days of the adjournment of Congress, effected by the president's retaining the bill unsigned until Congress adjourns.

American Government ... in Global Perspective:
World Views on the Sincerity of the United States in Fighting Terrorism

Following the lead of President George W. Bush, and with initially strong support from the American public, the U.S. Congress voted to prosecute the war on terrorism with large-scale military operations in both Afghanistan and Iraq. Opinion about the sincerity of U.S. intervention to fight the war on terrorism, which Congress continues to fund, is not universally positive around the globe. The *2004 Pew Global Attitudes Survey* conducted in February and early March of 2004, for example, found that in six of nine countries surveyed, the public described the United States as not being sincere in its efforts to reduce terrorism:

COUNTRY	% saying not sincere	% saying sincere
United States	25%	67%
Britain	41%	51%
Russia	48%	35%
France	61%	35%
Germany	65%	29%
Turkey	64%	20%
Morocco	66%	17%
Jordan	51%	11%
Pakistan	58%	6%

Source: The Pew Research Center for the People and the Press, Pew Global Attitudes Project: Nine Nation Survey *(March 2004), Q. 11, p. 32* (http://people-press.org/reports/questionnaires/206.pdf).

for political reasons, sometimes Congress prefers not to deal with issues on its own, but rather to "pass the buck" to a bureaucratic agency. Defining the limits of genetic cloning is one such political hot potato. Whether the reason is technical capability or politics, Congress often delegates more specific legislative authority to the executive branch, which has the resources and expertise to make more highly technical policy decisions. The delegation of congressional power to the executive branch has become more frequent as our society has become more complex.

This delegation of authority, however, is not carried out blindly or without accountability. When Congress delegates its authority, it generally monitors the activities of agencies and administrators who are given this power through congressional oversight. One agency to which Congress has delegated considerable authority is the Federal Reserve Board (known as "the Fed"). Established by the Federal Reserve Act of 1913, it has authority over credit rates and lending activities of the nation's banks. Congress created the agency because it recognized that specialized monitoring of the economy and the technical expertise of economists were necessary to make decisions about credit rates and lending activities in order to maintain a viable economy. The act gave the Fed the authority to adjust the supply of money to banks and to shift money from where there is too much to where there is too little. The Fed also has the power to take means to ensure that banks do not overextend themselves in lending so that a sudden economic scare will not cause a sudden run on banks for money. For more than ninety years, Congress has given this agency the power to set important economic and fiscal policy for the nation. But Congress retains its authority to exercise oversight of the Fed. The Joint Economic Committee in Congress carefully monitors the Fed's performance and regularly holds hearings to inquire about its policies and decisions. In addition, newly appointed members of the Federal Reserve Board must be approved by Congress.

In his book on Congress titled *Congress: The Keystone of the Washington Establishment*,[17] political scientist Morris Fiorina notes other important reasons for congressional delegation of power to executive agencies, including garnering political rewards while shifting blame to the executive branch, enabling Congress to blame federal agencies for failing to fulfill legislative intent, and taking credit for problem solving by holding oversight and investigative hearings.

Confirmation of Presidential Nominations and Approval of Treaties

The U.S. Senate plays a pivotal role in the selection of cabinet officers, other agency and executive branch heads, federal judges, and foreign ambassadors. The president nominates individuals for these posts, but the Senate must consent to the nomination with a majority vote in favor of the candidate. This function is one performed solely by the U.S. Senate, and not the House of Representatives.

At the beginning of a new presidential administration, the U.S. Senate is typically quite busy reviewing the president's nominations for high executive office positions.[18] Although the Senate usually endorses most nominees, there have been a number of high-profile instances when the Senate has been unwilling to confirm the nominee, typically occurring during eras of divided government when the political party of the president is different from the majority party in the Senate.

When there is a vacancy on the U.S. Supreme Court, a situation that often draws considerable interest from both the press and the public, the president nominates a new justice, whom the Senate also must confirm with a majority vote. Conflict between the Senate and the president over Supreme Court nominees goes all the way back to the first U.S. president, George Washington, and his choice of John Rutledge for chief justice of the Supreme Court. Although Rutledge appeared eminently qualified for the post (he was associate justice on the Supreme Court from 1789 to 1791 and chief justice of the South Carolina Court of Common Pleas from 1791 to 1795), he had openly criticized the highly controversial Jay Treaty with Britain (backed by Washington and the Federalists), which reneged on the terms of America's 1778 treaty with France. Rutledge's criticism was directed as much at its chief negotiator, John Jay, as at the treaty itself, which reassured Britain of American neutrality. Apparently, Rutledge still harbored a grudge against Jay, who had edged him out to become the nation's first chief justice in 1789. Although Washington stood behind his nominee and gave him a temporary recess appointment as chief justice, Federalist senators argued that confirmation of Rutledge would be an extreme embarrassment to their party and denounced him publicly. One called him a character "not very far above mediocrity." On December 15, 1795, the Senate rejected Rutledge's nomination by a 14–10 vote.

A more recent example of Senate opposition to a Supreme Court nominee occurred in the case of Clarence Thomas, nominated for the Court by President George H. W. Bush in 1991. The Democrat-controlled Senate opposed Thomas, an African American who held conservative views on numerous issues. Thomas's problems mounted further when a law professor and former employee of Thomas's at the EEOC, Anita Hill, testified that he had sexually harassed her while he was her boss. Thomas ultimately won confirmation by a close 52–48 vote and currently sits on the Supreme Court.

Sometimes presidents find themselves at odds over judicial appointments with members of their own party. During the fall of 2005, Senate Republicans led the opposition to Harriet Miers, President George W. Bush's second nominee to the Supreme Court. Miers had spent most of her legal career in private practice in Dallas and was well known in Texas legal circles. During the 1990s she established a close professional relationship with then–Texas governor George W. Bush, assisting him

---

[17] Morris P. Fiorina, *Congress: Keystone of the Washington Establishment*, 2nd ed. (New Haven, CT: Yale University Press, 1989).
[18] For a discussion of the presidential nominating process, see David A. Yalof, *Pursuit of Justices* (Chicago: University of Chicago Press, 2001).

on his presidential campaign; as a lawyer in the Bush administration, she eventually rose to become White House counsel during Bush's second term. Yet critics argued that Miers lacked sufficient credentials and that she had no judicial experience. Moreover, little in her background indicated with any certainty how she might vote on the hot-button issues of the day: abortion, school prayer, and homosexual rights, to name just a few. This uncertainty was of special concern to more conservative Senate Republicans, who feared that Miers would not vote conservative on all such issues. Meanwhile a more moderate Republican, Senate Judiciary Committee Chairman Arlen Specter (R-PA), complained that some of Miers's answers to a questionnaire submitted to his committee were "inadequate," because she had failed or refused to answer questions with acceptable accuracy or sufficient detail. Eventually President Bush bent to political reality and withdrew Miers's nomination even before Senate confirmation hearings took place.

Under certain circumstances, Congress may also become involved in the selection of president and vice president of the United States. When no candidate receives a majority of electoral votes, the House of Representatives chooses the president and the Senate chooses the vice president. This has happened three times in the history of the nation—in 1801 when the House chose Thomas Jefferson as president, in 1825 when the House chose John Quincy Adams, and in 1877 when the House appointed a commission to resolve the controversial 1876 election (it chose Rutherford B. Hayes).

In the event of a vacancy in the vice presidency, the Twenty-fifth Amendment to the Constitution stipulates that the president's nomination of an individual to fill that position is subject to the approval of both the House and Senate by majority vote. This has happened twice since adoption of that amendment: in 1973 when Vice President Spiro Agnew resigned and Nixon's nomination of Gerald Ford was quickly approved, and in 1974 when Ford became president due to Nixon's resignation and Congress approved Ford's nomination of Nelson Rockefeller as vice president.

Finally, the Senate has the power to approve treaties that the president negotiates with foreign countries. The Constitution stipulates that approval of a treaty requires the consent of two-thirds of the Senate. Even though the standard for treaty approval is much higher than a simple majority, most treaties do obtain the necessary two-thirds approval. In fact, only twenty-one times in the nation's history has the Senate rejected a treaty; perhaps, the most important rejection concerned the Treaty of Versailles following World War I. The relatively low number of rejected treaties may be due to presidents' reluctance to negotiate treaties that they are not reasonably certain will pass. President Woodrow Wilson's failure to consult with the Senate and consider their objections to the Treaty of Versailles led to the treaty's twice being rejected by the Senate, once in 1919 and again in 1920. More recently, the House also plays an important role in approving treaties because most of them involve financial issues that require the approval of that chamber.

Impeachment and Removal of Federal Judges and High Executives

Congress also has the authority to impeach and remove federal judges, cabinet officers, the president, the vice president, and other civil officers. The removal process requires an impeachment action from the House and a trial in the Senate.

Impeachment is the formal process by which the House brings charges against federal officials. A judge, president, or executive official who is "impeached" by the House is not removed; he or she is charged with an offense. In this sense, the House acts as an initial forum that makes the decision about whether a trial is warranted. An impeachment occurs by a majority vote in the House of Representatives. An official may be impeached by the House on more than one charge, each of which is referred to as an article of impeachment.

Assuming the House passes at least one article of impeachment, the official must then stand trial in the Senate. The prosecutors in the trial are members of the House of Representatives and are referred to as House "managers." Selected by the House leadership, the House managers present the case for removal to the full Senate. If the defendant is the president, the chief justice of the U.S. Supreme Court presides over the trial; otherwise the vice president of the United States (who is president of the Senate) or the president pro tempore of the Senate presides. Other than in the impeachment of a president or vice president, the Senate in recent times has usually designated a committee to receive evidence and question the witnesses. The impeached official provides lawyers in his or her own defense. A two-thirds vote of the full Senate is required for removal of an official.

Constituent Service: Helping People Back Home

Much of what has been discussed thus far in this chapter pertains to what members of Congress do in Washington. As the people's representatives, members are sent to Washington to develop new laws and deliberate on important issues. They are expected to safeguard the nation's security, act as watchdogs against fraud, and ensure that judges and high-ranking executive officers are qualified for office. An integral part of the way members serve their constituents is by reflecting the opinions and input of those whom they represent while carrying out these legislative functions.

However, the service of members of Congress does not stop with the work they do in Washington. Often constituents will call upon a House member or senator to provide information about federal programs, to render assistance in getting benefits from federal programs, or to prepare a talk or visit with a community group to educate them about the political system or on a specific legislative or policy topic. Members are often asked by officials in state or local government to facilitate federal help for a local or state issue. The direct assistance that a member provides to a constituent, community group, or a local or state official is referred to as **casework.** A now classic book by Richard F. Fenno, titled *Home Style: House Members in Their Districts*, provides a rich description of this role played by members of Congress.[19]

Casework is important for a number of reasons. First is its electoral importance to members of Congress. Casework raises the visibility of members in their home state or district, which reflects positively on how well the member is regarded and gives members an advantage over their opponents in elections. More than nine in ten House and Senate members who run for re-election are returned to office, and effectively managing casework is an important reason for this high return rate.

It has also become an implicit responsibility of members to help their constituents navigate the complex federal bureaucracy. Federal programs are varied and complex, and constituents are often overwhelmed in their efforts to obtain the benefits for which they are eligible. For example, under the Workforce Development Act, the federal government has programs that provide assistance to "displaced workers," defined as those who have lost their jobs due to technological or broad trends in the workplace. Many workers in the manufacturing industry in the United States have lost their jobs over the past decade as the national economy has shifted away from manufacturing and toward technology and information services. A variety of programs are available for these displaced workers to help them obtain training in new skills necessary to adapt to the new workforce. Finding these programs is often difficult, and members provide information to connect constituents with available programs.

Third, casework provides a direct connection between members and their constituents. Casework requires members to keep in touch with those whom they represent.

★ Casework

The direct assistance that a member of Congress provides to a constituent, community group, or a local or state official.

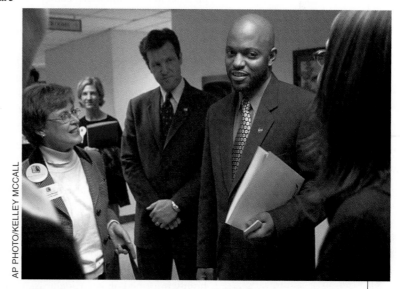

AP PHOTO/KELLEY MCCALL

Missouri Congressmen Russ Carnahan (left) and Rodney Hubbard (right), both Democrats, visit with some constituents back home.

[19] Richard F. Fenno Jr., *Home Style: House Members in Their Districts* (Boston: Little, Brown, 1978).

Giving a speech to a local Rotary club or League of Women Voters organization, showing up to "cut the ribbon" at an opening of a new local school building or park, and coming to speak to a group of students or employees all provide face time between the members and their constituents. The experiences that members have and the type of work they do in Washington can shelter them from the real-life concerns of their constituents back home. Casework provides a constant reminder of the needs and interests of those whom members represent.

Another aspect of constituent service involves what is known as "pork-barrel" politics. The federal budget includes a great deal of money for local projects, such as parks, dams, or road improvements. Members secure federal funds to support these projects in their states and districts through what is often referred to as **pork-barrel legislation.** The pork-barrel reference is based on the idea that members are "bringing home the bacon." Members use their influence on congressional committees and leadership positions to add amendments to bills that authorize pork-barrel spending on projects back home. Though many observers of the political system decry the unfairness of pork-barrel legislation, it has been an important aspect of constituent service since the beginning of our political system and promises to remain so in the future.

Now & Then: Making the Connection

This chapter began with examples of Senate resistance in two issue areas at two very different points in American history—the approval of the League of Nations provisions of the Treaty of Versailles following World War I, and lower court judicial nominations in the first decade of the twenty-first century. In both instances, the Senate moved at a glacier pace, frustrating an impatient president at every turn. When Senate leaders offered the president compromises that might speed up the process, he was reluctant to give up any of what he viewed as "executive prerogative" and so the stalemates continued. Putting these two instances of Senate resistance in the context of the information presented in this chapter, what conclusions can we draw about the way the Congress as a whole, and the Senate in particular, tend to work?

First, and most apparent, when Congress is dealing with major problems or issues of the day, the process of creating new laws, approving new treaties and approving presidential appointments can be very slow indeed—many observers use the word "gridlock" to describe congressional inaction. Congress's actions are slow and deliberate; there are many points at which the process may be halted, and many actors with the capacity to hinder progress. Second, the compromises necessary to achieve success in Congress rarely prove entirely satisfactory to everyone involved. In the case of the Treaty of Versailles, Senator Henry Cabot Lodge's reservations to the treaty, which rejected any advance U.S. obligation to enter international conflicts to defend the autonomy of another country, were considered unacceptable to President Wilson, and so the Senate rejected the treaty and U.S. membership in the League of Nations. In the case of George W. Bush's judicial nominations, Senate Democratic leaders proposed to speed up the nomination process for some nominees, only if his more controversial nominees were withdrawn.

Both these conflicts also highlight the power and significance of individual actors in the legislative process. Strong individuals such as Senator Henry Cabot Lodge and Senator Patrick Leahy dominated the debate over these issues. Congress is not simply two houses of 535 individuals who vote, with a majority obtaining victory. Those in leadership positions can exert a disproportionate influence on the process. Those with special communication skills enjoy more power, as do those who are highly informed on a particular issue. The better part of a century separated Senate debate and action on the treaty of Versailles and President Bush's judicial nominations. However, in both instances the same principles guided Senate activity and worked to produce similar approaches to resisting the chief executive.

★ Pork-barrel legislation

A government project or appropriation that yields jobs or other benefits to a specific locale and patronage opportunities to its political representative.

Senator Tim Johnson's (D-SD) sudden hospitalization in December 2006 threw a potential wrench in the Senate works as that body approached the start of the 110th Congress in January 2007. Even without Johnson's vote in favor of the Democrats' organizing the Senate, the Democrats still enjoyed a 50–49 margin of control following the November 2006 midterm election results. Yet would the Democrats stay in control if the senator remained hospitalized indefinitely? Johnson hailed from a state that—like many others—authorized its governor to fill any Senate vacancies with a replacement until a Senate election could be conducted. In 2007, South Dakota's governor was Mike Rounds, a Republican. Most expected that if Senator Johnson was incapacitated or otherwise unable to complete his term, Rounds would replace Johnson with a Republican, thereby deadlocking the Senate 50–50. With Vice President Cheney ready to cast his tie-breaking vote in favor of the Republicans, Senator Johnson's health watch thus took on serious political ramifications. (On April 27, 2007, Johnson was discharged from the hospital. He eventually returned to his duties on Capitol Hill in September 2007.)

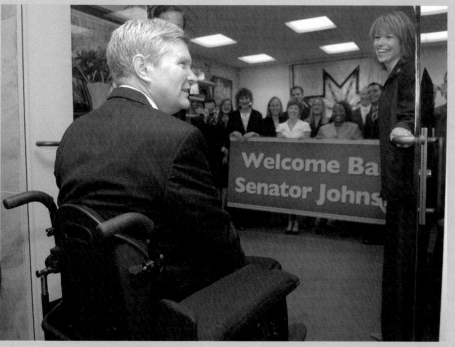

KEVIN DIETSCH/UPI/LANDOV

Certainly this was not the first time a senator had become ill in American history. And if Johnson had been forced to resign, it would not have been the first time a death or illness of a member of Congress had threatened to swing a house of Congress in another political direction. With Congress preparing to address the war in Iraq in early 2007, much of the world was also watching with interest what was going on in Washington. Finally, Johnson's illness raised another issue that had been simmering in Washington, DC, since the terrorist attacks of September 11, 2001: are the procedures for replacing ill or deceased members of Congress effective enough in the event of an attack that harms many members of Congress at the same time?

On http://academic.cengage.com/dautrich, find the politics interactive link for details on Johnson's illness, the South Dakota state procedures for replacing an ill senator, and a list of states with similar procedures. Consult as well the various links that relate to the process of replacing ill or deceased members of Congress. Historical, popular, and global perspectives on the issue are also presented.

http://academic.cengage.com/dautrich

Chapter Summary

★ Congress, the legislative branch of the government, was the central institution in America's new political system at the beginning of the republic. Congress consists of two houses, a "people's house" apportioned by population (the House of Representatives), and a Senate in which the states, regardless of population, have equal representation.

★ To ensure the principle of "one person, one vote" in the House, the population of congressional districts must be made as equal as possible based on the results of a federal census conducted every ten years. Parties try to maximize their advantage in the House of Representatives by "gerrymandering," which means that they draw district boundaries in order to favor their party on election day.

★ The relative strength of political party membership determines leadership in each legislative chamber. The Constitution designates that the leader of the House carry the title Speaker of the House. The Speaker is responsible for assigning new bills to committees and recognizing members to speak in the House chamber. The Constitution also prescribes that the vice president is to be the presiding officer of the Senate. Unlike the Speaker, the president of the Senate can vote only to break ties. When the vice president is absent from the Senate chamber (as is quite often the case), the presiding officer is the president pro tempore ("for the time being").

★ There are four types of congressional committees: standing committees (permanent), select committees (established to look at a particular issue for a limited time), conference committees (reconcile differences between House and Senate versions of a bill), and joint committees (includes members from both houses, investigative in nature). Most members defer to committee recommendations on a bill.

★ The lawmaking process is often slow, and bills that survive frequently receive significant revisions along the way. After a bill is introduced by a member of Congress, it is usually sent to a committee for consideration (often in the form of hearings) and possible action. If the bill is endorsed by a majority of the committee, it then goes to the full House and Senate for consideration. Finally, if it is endorsed by a majority of each chamber, a conference committee reconciles differences in versions between the chambers, and then after a vote on the bill's final version, it goes to the president for signature.

★ If the president vetoes the final bill, Congress can override the presidential veto by a two-thirds vote of both houses of Congress.

★ Congress delegates considerable legislative authority to the executive branch, whether because it lacks the expertise of bureaucrats or because it wishes to shift blame for policies to the executive branch. Still, Congress may exercise oversight to ensure that the implementation of laws and regulations is consistent with national problems and concerns.

★ The U.S. Senate plays an important role in consenting to the president's selection of cabinet officers, other executive branch officials, and judges. Senate confirmation of Supreme Court nominees in particular has been the subject of considerable controversy

★ If a majority in the House of Representative impeaches a president, federal judge, or other executive official, the official must stand trial in the Senate. A two-thirds vote of the full Senate is required for the removal of an official from office.

★ Members of Congress also play an important role doing casework for local constituents, whether assisting them in getting federal benefits, educating them on policy issues, or performing some other service on their behalf. Casework provides a direct connection between members and their constituents.

Key Terms

Bicameral legislature (p. 162)

Bill (p. 171)

Casework (p. 185)

Closed rule (p. 179)

Cloture (p. 179)

Conference committee (p. 173)

Congressional agencies (p. 175)

Congressional district (p. 163)

Congressional personal staff
  (p. 175)

Filibuster (p. 179)

Gerrymandering (p. 165)

Joint committee (p. 173)

Logrolling (p. 180)

Majority caucus (p. 166)

Majority leader (p. 169)

Minority caucus (p. 166)

Minority leader (p. 169)

Open rule (p. 179)

Overriding a veto (p. 181)

Pocket veto (p. 181)

Pork-barrel legislation (p. 186)

President pro tempore (p. 170)

Reapportionment (p. 163)

Redistricting (p. 164)

Reporting legislation (p. 172)

Rules Committee (p. 179)

Select committee (p. 173)

Speaker of the House (p. 167)

Standing committee (p. 172)

Veto (p. 181)

Whips (majority and minority)
  (p. 169)

Resources

Reference Works

Barone, Michael, and Richard E. Cohen, eds. *The Almanac of American Politics.* Washington, DC: The National Journal, 2006. The *Almanac* is published biannually with each new Congress and contains in-depth profiles of the 535 members of Congress along with the states and congressional districts that they represent.

The *Congressional Record* is the official proceeding of Congress. It contains a record of all the proceedings of the House and Senate.

Important Books

Davidson, Roger H., Walter J. Oleszek, and Frances E. Lee. *Congress and Its Members.* Washington, DC: CQ Press, 2007.

Fenno, Richard F., and Richard F. Fenno, Jr. *Congressmen in Committees.* Boston: Little, Brown, 1973.

Fenno, Richard F., Jr. *Home Style: House Members in Their Districts.* Boston: Little, Brown, 1978.

Fiorina, Morris. *Congress: Keystone of the Washington Establishment.* New Haven, CT: Yale University Press, 1979.

Hall, Richard. *Participation in Congress.* New Haven, CT: Yale University Press, 1996.

Hibbing, John R., and Elizabeth Theiss-Morse. *Congress as Public Enemy: Public Attitudes Toward American Political Institutions.* New York: Cambridge University Press, 1995.

Mayhew, David R. *Congress: The Electoral Connection*, 2nd ed. New Haven, CT: Yale University Press, 2004.

Rohde, David W. *Parties and Leaders in the Post-House Reform.* Chicago: University of Chicago Press, 1991.

Smith, Stephen S., Jason M. Roberts, and Ryan J. Vander Wielen. *The American Congress.* New York: Cambridge University Press, 2007.

Internet Sources

http://www.thomas.gov (offers links to the *Congressional Record*, which provides the text of bills, floor debate, committee hearings, and reports)

http://www.lcweb.gov (offers links to information and statistics about Congress, including demographic characteristics of members, current leaders in both houses, and e-mail addresses of members)

http://www.whitehouse.gov (offers links to the official pages of the Senate and the House of Representatives; the site also provides links to the pages of all 535 members and to congressional agencies)

7 The Presidency

MARTIN H. SIMON/CORBIS SABA

President George W. Bush in 2001

Leadership During a Crisis: Now & Then

It arrived like a bolt of lightning from the sky on a clear blue morning—and in a just a few short hours it produced thousands of American casualties. Enemies of the United States had launched an attack on American territory, inflicting immense damage not only on the immediate victims and their families, but on the American psyche as well. Amid the confusion and anger that boiled over in the days following the attack, one individual, the president of the United States, offered Americans a strong voice in an atmosphere of fear and uncertainty; he instilled a sense of confidence that those responsible would pay the price. The president declared war on the attack's perpetrators; he emphasized that the war would be hard and difficult and that it might take years to pursue. He resolved that America would pass the "great test" before it. Of the many thousands of officials who work in Washington, DC, only the president could respond so effectively to this unexpected threat to America's national security, and he alone shouldered the awesome responsibility of rallying the nation around a difficult cause.

President Franklin D. Roosevelt in 1941

2001

Now... On September 11, 2001, nearly three thousand Americans perished when jet airliners were hijacked and deliberately steered into the World Trade Center towers in New York City and the Pentagon in Washington, DC, by members of Al Qaeda, a band of fanatic fundamentalist Muslims led by the wanted international terrorist, Osama Bin Laden. In the days following the attacks, President George W. Bush asserted immediate control over America's response, visiting the sites of the tragedy and formulating plans to invade Afghanistan, home base of the Taliban organization, which had lent support to Bin Laden. Addressing the U.S. Congress and the millions of Americans watching on television, Bush declared a "war against terrorism," and warned that the American people must be prepared for a difficult road ahead, but that the nation would endure:

> *Great harm has been done to us. We have suffered great loss ... freedom and fear are at war. The advance of human freedom, the great achievement of our time and the great hope of every time, now depends on us. Our nation, this generation, will lift the dark threat of violence from our people and our future ... We will not tire, we will not falter and we will not fail.*

Just nine months after the president had secured a controversial election victory that divided the American people, citizens of all political stripes quickly rallied around the commander-in-chief. By a wide margin, Congress approved the president's demands for increased resources and administrative mechanisms to fight this war against terrorism.

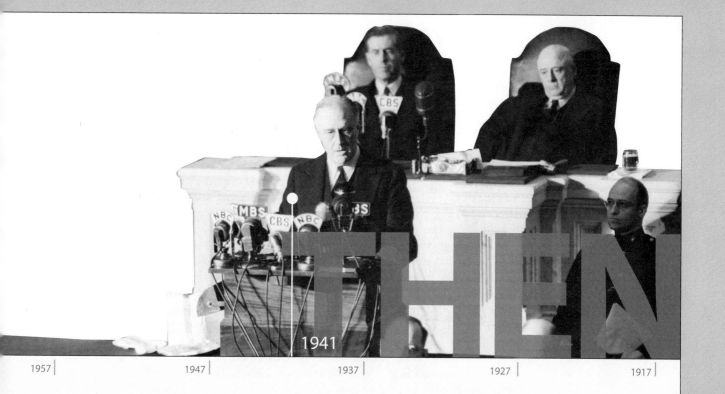

THEN

1941

1957 | 1947 | 1937 | 1927 | 1917 |

Then. . . George W. Bush did not have to look far back in history to find a model of presidential success in confronting unexpected crises. On December 7, 1941, the United States lost a large part of its Pacific fleet when the Japanese imperial navy launched a surprise assault on Pearl Harbor, Hawaii. Approximately twenty-four hundred Americans were killed in the attack, most of them military personnel. President Franklin Delano Roosevelt (FDR), then in the ninth year of his presidency, was presiding over a country whose citizens had been deeply conflicted over American involvement in foreign wars. All such hesitancy collapsed in the wake of the Japanese attack—referring to December 7 as "a day of infamy," Roosevelt called for a war on the empire of Japan, a sentiment that Congress confirmed with its own overwhelming resolution of war. "No matter how long it may take us to overcome this premeditated invasion, the American people in their righteous might will win through to absolute victory," said FDR. Nearly all Americans rallied around this patrician president as the ideal voice for the United States in conducting this second world war.

There were some key differences in the challenges facing Presidents George W. Bush and Franklin Delano Roosevelt. Whereas Roosevelt could target particular warring nations as enemies, Bush was confronting an attack by terrorists who had acted without the specific authorization of any foreign state. In response to the two attacks, the presidents urged the nation's citizens onto markedly different courses: Roosevelt introduced a draft and called on Americans to make numerous sacrifices in their daily lives; President Bush encouraged citizens to carry on as normal with their daily routines. Still, their calls were treated similarly at the beginning, as Americans temporarily put aside their partisan preferences and rallied around the commander-in-chief. In times of crises such as these, only the president can command the nation's attention, direct its spirits, and employ the resources to act on that command quickly and effectively.

Where Do Presidents Come From? Presidential Comings and Goings

What career experiences have provided the most effective launching pads for the forty-two individuals who have attained the presidency? Many vice presidents have gone on to become president, including most recently George H. W. Bush, vice president under Ronald Reagan, who in 1988 won election to the White House in his own right. Yet that form of promotion is actually quite rare. Although five of the last thirteen vice presidents have become president, only Bush won election as a sitting vice president. In fact, in the 132-year period between Vice President Martin Van Buren's presidential victory in 1836 and former Vice President Richard Nixon's election in 1968, every vice president who rose to the presidency did so initially as a consequence of the president's untimely death in office.

Although the U.S. Senate has been aptly described as a body of one hundred individuals who all think they should be president, only sixteen senators have gone on to the White House, including Senator Barack Obama, who won election to the White House in 2008. By comparison, nineteen governors and nineteen members of the House of Representatives have served as president. Three presidents—William Henry Harrison, John Tyler, and Andrew Johnson—actually served in all three of those jobs. Another nine presidents formerly served in another president's Cabinet, although none have held that distinction since Herbert Hoover, who was commerce secretary before he was elected president in 1928. The military has also been something of a breeding ground for presidents: twenty-nine had some military experience, and twelve served as generals. Fully twenty-seven of the forty-three chief executives have been lawyers, but the cohort of presidents also includes among its ranks a mining engineer (Hoover), a peanut farmer (Carter), a baseball team executive (George W. Bush), and even a hat salesman (Truman).

As a formal matter, the adage that "anyone can grow up to be president" is not literally true. Article II of the Constitution imposes three prerequisites on those who aspire to the Oval Office. Every president must be (1) a "natural born" citizen, (2) thirty-five years of age or older, and (3) a resident within the United States for at least fourteen years. Although the Constitution poses no other formal obstacles to the presidency, as a practical matter the first forty-three holders of the office have tended to fall into several clearly identifiable categories. All but one of these forty-three chief executives have been white males (Barack Obama is the lone African American president) between the ages of forty-two and seventy-seven. All were born Christians, and nearly all identified themselves as Protestants at one point or another in their lifetimes. (John Kennedy was Catholic; Lyndon Johnson was mostly nonobservant in his adulthood.) Twenty-four were firstborn males in their families, and all but nine attended college (since 1897, every president except Harry Truman received some form of higher education). Some states have served as birthplaces for a disproportionate share of presidents including Virginia (eight), Ohio (seven), Massachusetts (four), and New York (four). Although presidents are not royalty and none are entitled to serve for life, on several occasions birthright has played a role in helping an individual reach the Oval Office. Twenty-six presidents have been related to other presidents; these relationships encompass two father–son combinations (John and John Quincy Adams; and George H. W. and George W. Bush), a grandfather–grandson combination (William Henry Harrison and Benjamin Harrison), and cousins (James Madison and Zachary Taylor were second cousins; Theodore Roosevelt and Franklin Roosevelt were fifth cousins).

When George Washington, after serving two terms as the nation's first president, declined to run again, he established an unwritten two-term precedent. No president challenged that precedent until Franklin Roosevelt sought a third term in 1940. FDR's successful election to four consecutive terms (he won in 1932, 1936, 1940, and then again in 1944) led to passage of the **Twenty-second Amendment** in 1951, which restricts any one person from being elected to the presidency "more than twice," or from acting as president for longer than two and a half terms. Four chief

★ Twenty-second Amendment

Passed in 1951, this constitutional amendment restricts any one person from being elected to the presidency "more than twice," or from acting as president for longer than two and a half terms.

Changing images of FDR, seen here in 1932, 1936, 1940, and 1944.

executives were assassinated while in office, and four others died of natural causes while still serving as president including Franklin Roosevelt, who died in 1945, only a few months into his unprecedented fourth term.

The constitutional means of removing a president from office is by **impeachment** and subsequent conviction. Article II, Section 4 of the U.S. Constitution provides that the president may be removed from office upon impeachment by a majority vote of the House and conviction by two-thirds of the Senate of "Treason, Bribery, or other high Crimes and Misdemeanors." Just what type of offense qualifies as a "high crime and misdemeanor"? It's difficult to say. Just two presidents, Andrew Johnson and Bill Clinton, have ever been impeached under these provisions, and both were impeached for primarily political reasons: Johnson was charged with illegally firing a Cabinet member, pardoning traitors, and impeding ratification of the Fourteenth Amendment; Clinton was accused of lying to a grand jury about his sexual relationship with an intern and for obstructing justice. Both men were acquitted on all charges by the U.S. Senate and served out their respective terms.

The only president to resign was Richard Nixon, who was accused of obstructing justice in the now infamous Watergate burglary and political scandal. Nixon left office less than halfway through his second term in 1974 under the looming threat of impeachment. In practice, unpopular presidents are usually turned out of office not by the real threat of removal, but by more routine political procedures. In recent times, three sitting presidents (Gerald Ford, Jimmy Carter, and George H. W. Bush) lost their bids for re-election because of public disapproval with their presidencies; Lyndon Johnson chose not to run for re-election in 1968 when frustration with his unpopular Vietnam War policy undermined his prospects for victory in the November election.

★ Impeachment

The first step in a two-step process outlined in Article II, Section 4 of the U.S. Constitution to remove a president or other high official from office. The House of Representatives, by majority vote, may impeach if the official has committed "treason, bribery, or other high crimes or misdemeanors." The second step requires a conviction in the Senate by a two-thirds vote.

William Henry Harrison was a born military leader. His victories made him a national hero and earned him the Whig Party nomination for president in 1840, and then the presidency. Yet for all of his strengths as a war leader and later a candidate, he was ultimately a victim of his own stubbornness. Inauguration Day on March 4, 1841, proved to be one of the coldest and most blustery days of the year in Washington, DC. Not only did Harrison refuse to wear a hat and coat; he also gave one of the longest inaugural addresses in history, lasting nearly two hours. One month later, Harrison died of pneumonia, probably contracted during his inaugural address. He was the first president to die in office, although perhaps the last not to bundle up warmly for his own inauguration day celebration.

American Government . . . in Historical Perspective:
Presidential Sex Scandals

In 1802, rumors that President Thomas Jefferson had secretly fathered children by his slave Sally Hemings were published by one of Jefferson's political rivals, James Callender. Hemings herself was the daughter of Jefferson's father-in-law and another female slave. Such personal attacks were not unusual in the early politics of the republic, and historians dismissed the rumors as scurrilous for the better part of two centuries. Finally in 1998, the British journal *Nature* published the results of DNA tests that suggested Jefferson was the "probable father" of at least one of Sally Hemings's descendants. Recent reunion celebrations that included both the descendants of Jefferson as well as descendants of Sally Hemings may have put this issue to rest once and for all.

In 1922, President Warren Harding entertained a mistress, Nan Britton, in the White House. Three years earlier, while Harding was still a U.S. senator, Britton gave birth to Harding's child.

The Republican Party effectively buried evidence of the relationship during the 1920 presidential campaign, but once elected Harding resumed the relationship. Four years after Harding's death in 1923, Britton wrote a tell-all bestseller disclosing details of her relationship with the president, including intimate acts performed in an anteroom near the White House.

Between 1995 and 1997, President Bill Clinton had a series of sexual encounters with White House intern Monica Lewinsky. The affair became public when an independent counsel investigating Clinton's activities with respect to another alleged affair came across evidence of his affair with Lewinsky. Clinton was ultimately impeached for lying to a grand jury and obstructing justice with respect to the Monica Lewinsky affair. The Senate eventually acquitted him of both charges, but the scandal would occupy the Clinton presidency for more than a year.

When President John Adams was defeated for re-election in 1800 and turned over the White House to arch-rival Thomas Jefferson, he helped establish a precedent of peaceful transition between chief executives that has held firm to this day, despite the hostile feelings that sometimes exist between successive presidents. In the case of the president's removal by death, resignation, or inability to serve, the Constitution requires that the powers and duties of the president "devolve" on the vice president. When William Henry Harrison died barely a month after becoming president in 1841, Vice President John Tyler took over all the powers, duties, and responsibilities of the presidency, rejecting any notion that he was simply there to serve as a more limited "acting president" until the next election. Since Tyler, seven vice presidents have become chief executive in this manner, including most recently Lyndon Johnson, who assumed office after John Kennedy was assassinated in November 1963. Four of the last six vice presidents thrust unexpectedly into office—Theodore Roosevelt, Calvin Coolidge, Harry Truman, and Lyndon Johnson—eventually secured election as presidents in their own right.

The Evolution of the American Presidency

The U.S. Constitution appears to place as many limitations on the office of the presidency as it does grant the president specific powers and duties. Wary of the excessive authority wielded by the king of England, most of the Founders rejected Alexander Hamilton's radical suggestion that the president should be elected for life; instead, the Founders designed a chief executive who would be powerful enough to respond quickly when necessary, but also would be limited by lack of lawmaking power and the need to gain congressional approval for most long-term commitments, whether foreign or domestic.

As a review of the history of the presidency reveals, the institution has evolved over the past two centuries not so much because of any constitutional expansion of the chief executive's powers, but rather through practice, tradition, and the personal energy of some presidents. The changing dynamics of policy making in the United States from a mostly local concern to a national phenomenon has given presidents the opportunity to exert unprecedented influence over the process, and many have done exactly that. In many ways, the growth of power of the presidency has paralleled the growth of the United State.

The President as "Chief Clerk of the United States": 1789–1836

The earliest presidents established the office as a forceful power in the national gov ernment. Still, even the most popular presidents of the period were careful to avoid interfering with the clear legislative prerogatives of Congress. Several played a major role in helping steer America away from or toward war, despite the inclinations of Congress. But the truly dominant chief executive would not emerge until many years later.

When George Washington, the immensely popular former general of the Continental Army, agreed to be nominated as the nation's first president, widespread public confidence in his abilities helped secure immediate respect for this new office. Serving as the first chief executive from 1789 to 1797, Washington established various precedents that helped preserve a republican form of government in the nation's infancy. Washington rejected entrapments of royalty such as being referred to as "your majesty," preferring instead to be called "Mr. President." As a practical matter, Washington consulted constantly with the other branches—at one point he even asked the Supreme Court for an advisory opinion about his own interpretations of a foreign treaty. (The Court declined his invitation for comment.) Washington also established the executive's influential role in crafting public policy, siding with his Secretary of Treasury Alexander Hamilton's plans for industrialization and the creation of a national bank, and striving to maintain an isolationist foreign policy. Often serving as a mediator between differing positions in his administration, Washington rejected the less interventionist, farmer-friendly policies favored by his Secretary of State, Thomas Jefferson.[1] For better or worse, most subsequent presidents would be forced to work within the framework of a divided party system that originated as an intramural fight within the Washington administration.

During the four decades after Washington's retirement, most presidents of the United States served more as chief "clerks" than chief "executives," doing Congress's bidding and performing mostly administrative duties on behalf of the federal government. Upon winning the presidency in 1800, Thomas Jefferson (1801–1809)[2] put into practice his own theory that "government is best which governs least." Accordingly, the Jefferson administration abolished many judgeships, trimmed government economic planning efforts, and scaled back the armed forces. The one crucial exception to such downsizing occurred in the area of land acquisition: Jefferson personally arranged for the purchase of the vast Louisiana territory from France, more than doubling the physical size of the country.

A presidency characterized by limited executive powers soon confronted unexpected challenges. When tensions between Great Britain and the United States erupted into the War of 1812, President James Madison (1809–1817) found himself hampered both by the small size of the federal army and by the lack of a powerful national bank capable of funding the government's prosecution of the war. This war with Britain revealed the limited powers of the president to influence national matters without strong institutional resources at his disposal. Madison's successor, James Monroe (1817–1825), exercised most of his influence in foreign affairs. Monroe's Secretary of State John Quincy Adams, who himself was president from 1825 to 1829, helped craft

[1] Joseph Ellis, *His Excellency: George Washington* (New York: Knopf, 2004).
[2] Dates provided after a president's name refers to year(s) of service as president of the United States.

the "Monroe Doctrine," which declared that the United States would thereafter regard as an "unfriendly act" any attempt by a European nation to increase its possession or otherwise intervene on the American continent. Meanwhile, Congress led the way in domestic matters, crafting key compromises over slavery and paying off much of the public debt incurred during the War of 1812.

Andrew Jackson, who served as president from 1829 to 1837, remade the presidency into an office of tremendous political power. The military hero of the Battle of New Orleans in 1815, Jackson came to the White House as a political outsider but with overwhelming popular support. Capitalizing on this resource, Jackson wielded presidential power in a way that few of his predecessors had, dismissing hundreds of officeholders, forcing out cabinet members who angered him, using his constitutionally authorized power to veto Congress's bill to recharter the Second National Bank of the United States, and introducing the so-called spoils system of doling out federal offices to individuals as rewards for political service.[3]

The Weakened Presidency in the Wilderness Years, 1837–1900

Andrew Jackson raised the profile and authority of the presidency to unprecedented heights, but its ascendancy was largely a product of his own popularity and energetic personality. The pre–Civil War presidents who followed Jackson also proved to be much weaker. The model of president as chief clerk seemed once again alive and well.

Perhaps the only effective president during this antebellum period was James K. Polk (1845–1849), who presided over a period of incredible westward expansion. Polk exercised his powers as commander-in-chief to instigate a successful war with Mexico over the Texas territory; his foreign relations successes included the acquisitions of the California and Arizona territories after the Mexican-American War, and the acquisition of the Oregon territory (including current-day Oregon and Washington state) from the British.[4] More typical were Presidents Franklin Pierce and James Buchanan during the 1850s; the failures of both of these men to address growing sectional tensions over slavery left pro-slavery and abolitionist interests alike bitterly frustrated.

The presidency of Abraham Lincoln (1861–1865) thrived due to a rare combination of factors. Frequently underestimated as a great political mind, Lincoln was confronted with the single greatest threat in the history of the republic—the secession of eleven southern states and the great battle between North and South to restore the Union. Although Lincoln proceeded carefully in his prosecution of the war against the South for fear of alienating crucial border states, those acts he did undertake were bold and unprecedented. At the outset of the war in April 1861, with Congress not even in session, Lincoln proclaimed a blockade of southern ports and called on the northern states to provide 75,000 soldiers for battle. He (at least in one court's opinion[5]) unconstitutionally suspended the writ of habeas corpus, by which anyone arrested is to be brought before a judge or court to determine if there is sufficient reason to hold the person for

Portrait of General Andrew Jackson, later the seventh president of the United States.

©MARY EVANS PICTURE LIBRARY/THE IMAGE WORKS

American Government: Historical, Popular, and Global Perspectives

[3] H. W. Brands, *Andrew Jackson: His Life and Times* (New York: Random House, 2005).
[4] John Seigenthaler, *James K. Polk, 1845–1849* (New York: Times Books, 2003).
[5] See *Ex Parte Merryman*, 17 Fed.Cas. 144 (1961).

President Abraham Lincoln delivering the Gettysburg Address in 1863.

trial. Suspending the writ allowed Lincoln to hold some criminal defendants indefinitely. The president also spent freely from the U.S. Treasury without congressional approval. Although Congress ultimately ratified all his actions after the fact, Lincoln's bold exercise of authority essentially reinterpreted Article II into a source of executive authority during emergencies.

Following Lincoln's assassination in April 1865, Congress, dominated at that time by radical Republicans determined to punish the former Confederate states, quickly reasserted its control over the nation's agenda. For the remainder of the century, Congress would determine domestic policy. Indeed, after the former Civil War hero Ulysses Grant left office in 1877, no sitting president won election to a second term until William McKinley accomplished the feat in 1900.

The Birth of the Modern Presidency and Its Rise to Dominance, 1901–1945

The beginning of the twentieth century marked the onset of a new era for the American presidency. In an increasingly global and interconnected world, the power of the presidency grew disproportionately. By the time two world wars had concluded, the presidency had emerged as the premier institution in American politics.

American Government ... in Global Perspective:

A Nominee with African Roots, As Viewed by a Writer in Kenya

In securing the Democratic nomination for the presidency in 2008, Barack Obama became the first major party nominee with direct roots to Africa, as his father was from Kenya. One foreign journalist asked: How might that connection affect Obama's policy on U.S.-African relations as president of the United States? John Harbeson wrote as follows in the August 16, 2008, edition of the *Daily Nation*, an English-language newspaper serving the East African areas of Kenya and Nairobi:

Obama needs to align himself as both a "black" politician and an exemplar of post-black politics, keeping alive the civil rights agenda while crowning the success of the civil rights generation by merging it with the agendas of mainstream liberal American politics. But what has all this to do with African politics? The connection is between building on the achievements of the civil rights generation in America and those of the generation that has spearheaded African political liberation from colonial rule.

Neither agenda has been completed. America has made real civil rights progress over the past half-century, and African nationalism has largely expelled colonial political oppression over the same period. But affirmative action in the US is still needed, and Nepad (New Partnership for Africa's Development) has in many ways only just begun. So here's the question, common to both the American and African contexts.

How possible, indeed how legitimate and politically viable, will it be for Obama to continue the civil rights agenda while crowning its success by moving beyond it, and for post-independence generations of African leaders to maintain continuity with the political liberation agenda while building on its successes to embrace new and wider issues? There are many parallels between Obama's challenge and analogous challenges for Africa's political leaders. . . .

Senator Barack Obama of Illinois in the attire of a Somali Elder during a visit to Kenya, the homeland of his father.

AP PHOTO

Source: John Harbeson, "Harbeson's Dreams and the African Agenda," *Daily Nation*, August 16, 2008 (http://www.nation.co.ke/News/world/-/1068/457288/-/rx0emi/-/index.html; accessed on August 19, 2008).

In the fall of 1901, William McKinley was assassinated during the first year of his second term, thrusting into office his young and ebullient vice president, forty-two-year-old Theodore Roosevelt (TR). Roosevelt's presidency (1901–1909) ushered in a new era of presidential authority. He injected a forceful energy and enthusiasm into the office, using his position as "a bully pulpit" (Roosevelt's own words). As one observer noted, "He wanted to be the bride at every wedding; the corpse at every funeral." Unlike many of his predecessors, Roosevelt was willing to gamble political capital on bold assertions of presidential power: his efforts to break up corporate monopolies were narrowly upheld by the Supreme Court and forced

Congress to enact new antitrust legislation. Roosevelt, through the creative use of executive orders, increased the acreage of national parks fivefold. When Roosevelt became president, foreign affairs were assuming an ever-more significant place in the nation's list of priorities. In less than two full terms in office, Roosevelt encouraged a Panamanian revolution, initiated the building of the Panama Canal, won a Nobel Peace Prize for mediating war settlements between Japan and Russia, and sent the nation's naval fleet around the world as a demonstration of American military authority.[6] The first president to travel to foreign lands, Roosevelt expanded the Monroe Doctrine by advancing the "Roosevelt Corollary," which declared that the United States would serve as a police power to maintain stability in the Western Hemisphere by opposing any European interference in the affairs of Latin American nations but justifying any U.S. intervention. Certainly in foreign affairs, where force of personality is so important, Congress proved little match for this charismatic president.

PICTURE HISTORY

President Woodrow Wilson being welcomed by crowds in Paris following the Allied victory in World War I.

As president from 1913 to 1921, Woodrow Wilson achieved some significant successes and suffered some great failures: his aggressive industrial reform agenda marked a mostly well-received first term in office; during his second term he eventually led the United States into World War I and received accolades at the Paris Peace Conference following the war. But Wilson's hopes for a stable international order based on a system of collective security ultimately confronted political reality, as spurned Senate leaders whom Wilson had excluded from the peace talks rejected U.S. membership in the League of Nations. Still, Wilson's presidency illustrated just how much more powerful the presidency had become since the mid-nineteenth century. In the early part of the twentieth century, the president began to dominate the political landscape.

The onset of the Great Depression during Herbert Hoover's presidency (1929–1933) and the looming threat of a second world war in the late 1930s called for a new and innovative approach to the office. Franklin Delano Roosevelt placed his own indelible stamp on the nation by transforming the presidency into an institution marked by permanent bureaucracies and well-established repositories of power. FDR tackled the Great Depression with **New Deal** policies that tied the economic fate of millions of Americans to the fate of the American government: a social security program of old-age insurance and unemployment insurance would provide income for workers who retired or lost their jobs; the government would guarantee deposit accounts in commercial banks through the Federal Deposit Insurance Corporation (FDIC); and the government would provide federal jobs to the unemployed to perform various public works. Roosevelt communicated extensively with the American people through the media—millions listened to his "fireside chats" on the radio. By restoring public confidence with his energetic support for New Deal programs, FDR redefined the presidency as a source of national leadership. Future presidents would enjoy significant resources of power simply by taking the helms of the formidable institution FDR established.

★ New Deal

An aggressive set of federal domestic policies proposed by President Franklin Roosevelt in the 1930s and passed by Congress as a response to the Great Depression, which ultimately transformed the presidency into an institution marked by permanent bureaucracies and well-established repositories of power.

[6] Edmund Morris, *Theodore Rex* (New York: Random House, 2001).

CHECKtheLIST

The Ten Greatest Presidents of All Time

In late 1996, historian Arthur M. Schlesinger Jr. polled thirty-two historians to rank the "great," "near great," and "high average" presidents of the United States. Two years later, the Intercollegiate Studies Institute countered with a poll of its own members of historians, social scientists, and political philosophers. Among the most significant differences between the two polls are Franklin Roosevelt's relative downgrading, Ronald

Reagan's emergence, and the absences of Harry Truman and Woodrow Wilson on the latter poll. (Ronald Reagan was ranked twenty-fifth on Schlesinger's poll, and Truman and Wilson dropped down to fifteenth and twenty-eighth, respectively, on the Intercollegiate Studies Institute Poll.) While Washington and Lincoln usually top most lists, there remains disagreement regarding who the great presidents have been.

Schlesinger Jr. Poll 1996	Intercollegiate Studies Institute Poll 1998
Great:	**Great:**
✔ Lincoln	✔ Washington
✔ Washington	✔ Lincoln
✔ F. D. Roosevelt	
Near Great:	**Near Great:**
✔ Jefferson	✔ Jefferson
✔ Jackson	✔ Jackson
✔ T. Roosevelt	✔ Reagan
✔ Wilson	✔ T. Roosevelt
✔ Truman	✔ F. D. Roosevelt
✔ Polk	✔ Eisenhower
High Average:	**High Average:**
✔ Eisenhower	✔ J. Adams
	✔ J. Q. Adams

Like Theodore Roosevelt and Woodrow Wilson, FDR felt especially at home in foreign affairs. Although adhering to popular sentiment that the United States should maintain strict neutrality as to foreign wars, in the early days of World War II, Roosevelt met with British royalty and the British prime minister as a show of support, initiated a "lend-lease" policy by which Britain could purchase war supplies from the United States as long as it paid cash and transported the supplies in its own ships, and traded Britain fifty destroyers in exchange for rights to build military bases on British possessions in the Western Hemisphere—all without the consent of Congress. When America did enter the war in 1941 after being attacked at Pearl Harbor, presidential power in this international context was put on full display. FDR met personally with British and Soviet leaders to craft military plans; then, near the end of the war, the Allied leaders literally carved up Europe and the Middle East into "spheres of influence" that would establish an American presence in those parts of the world for the remainder of the century. With the president playing a dominant role in both national and world affairs, the imperial presidency that took root at the beginning of the twentieth century came to fruition by the close of World War II.

The Imperial Presidency Comes Under Attack, 1945–1980

By the end of World War II, the presidency had emerged as a very powerful office. FDR's fireside chats on the radio linked average Americans to the occupier of the White House in a fashion that was unimagined by the Founders. In the late 1940s, television would become a central influence in American life, and presidents honed their skills with this new medium to further nurture their relationship with the public.

Now recognized as powerful chief executives, those who followed in the footsteps of FDR confronted a new and unprecedented threat to American national security: the presence of a second world military superpower—the Soviet Union. With presidential authority greatest in the area of national security, waging the Cold War that began in the late 1940s consumed much of these presidents' energies. Harry Truman, FDR's immediate successor, proclaimed the "Truman Doctrine" in foreign policy, by which the United States pledged military and economic aid to any nation threatened by communism or the Soviet Union. Like Truman, Presidents Eisenhower and Kennedy also focused their administrations' energies on containing the Soviet communist threat. As long as the Soviet Union challenged American interests, the presidency would remain the focus of attention in the American political system.

Not until the presidency of Lyndon Johnson (1963–1969) was a president able to enact a sweeping domestic agenda similar to FDR's New Deal. Johnson's **Great Society** program featured more than sixty reform measures, including increases in federal aid to education, the enactment of Medicare and Medicaid, and a voting rights act for African Americans. But Johnson's domestic policy success was offset by his failures in foreign policy. Exercising his authority as commander-in-chief, Johnson sent more than half a million troops to Vietnam to fight an increasingly unpopular war. The failure to stop the Communists from taking over South Vietnam was laid squarely at the feet of Johnson, just as earlier foreign policy successes had been credited to his predecessors.

The presidents who followed Johnson came under increasing attack in the 1970s. Richard Nixon achieved foreign policy success by improving America's relationship with the Soviet Union and China, but in 1974 he became the first president in history to resign from office before the end of his term when the Watergate scandal enveloped his presidency. Jimmy Carter's presidency (1977–1981) was beset with hardships, as the nation's economy faltered in the 1970s. Carter's failure to resolve an Iranian revolution that included the taking of fifty American hostages further cemented his image as an inept commander-in-chief. Carter thus became the first elected president since 1932 to lose a re-election bid. By the end of the 1970s, the modern presidency created by Theodore Roosevelt and brought to new heights by Franklin Delano Roosevelt found itself increasingly under attack from an emboldened Congress and a frustrated public.

President Lyndon Baines Johnson.

★ Great Society

A set of aggressive federal domestic policies, proposed by President Lyndon Johnson and passed by Congress in the 1960s, which further enhanced the role of the presidency.

Redefining the Presidency in an Era of Divisiveness, 1981–2008

The election of Republican Ronald Reagan to the White House in 1980 marked the return of the chief executive as an unmatched force over American politics. No president in the twentieth century (save perhaps FDR) could match Reagan's prowess as a "great communicator"; by speaking directly to the American people in terms they could understand, Reagan bypassed Congress and enjoyed early victories with passage of an economic program marked by tax cuts, decreased social spending, and a marked increase in defense spending. Reagan's legislative success was all the more remarkable given that he was working with a divided-party government. The Democrats controlled the House of Representatives in every year of Reagan's presidency; his legislative success thus contrasted favorably with that of previous presidents who had struggled to get legislation passed by a Congress controlled by the opposite party. In foreign policy, Reagan's aggressive program of military buildup

American Government . . . in Popular Perspective:
The Best of Times and the Worst of Times

The presidential job approval rating is an important indicator of the amount of political power and influence at the president's disposal. Presidents with high ratings speak with the authority of popular support and have greater influence over the policy agenda and election campaigns.

Presidents typically experience significant ups and downs in their public job approval rating over the course of their tenure in office. For more than a half century, the Gallup Poll has been tracking presidential approval ratings. Most presidents since Harry Truman have experienced ups and downs in their ratings—but none more so than President George W. Bush. Bush was the recipient of the highest Gallup approval rating of 90 percent in 2001. In April 2008, however, Bush scored the highest ever disapproval rating of 69 percent. The average job approval rating for all presidents since Truman is 55 percent. The average for President Bush across his eight years in office is 52 percent.

The following chart shows the average approval ratings for President Bush during each of the eight years of his presidency:

Percent Approving George W. Bush's Performance as President

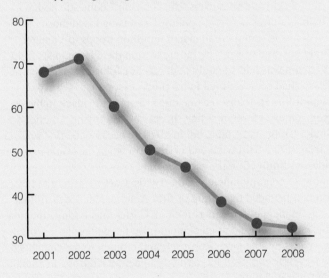

combined with his own hard-line position against the Soviet Union is credited with helping bring about the fall of Communist regimes in eastern Europe, the breakup of the USSR, and the end to the Cold War. In addition, Reagan's immense popularity allowed him to weather numerous crises and scandals in a way that few of his predecessors had.

Reagan's two immediate successors also faced the reality of divided-party government. George H. W. Bush took the lead in foreign policy, overseeing the dismantling of the Soviet Union and forging international alliances prior to mounting a successful war against Iraqi aggression in Kuwait. However, by compromising with the opposition Democrats on tax legislation, he frustrated some of his more conservative constituencies and undermined his efforts at re-election. In the mid-1990s, Bill Clinton became the first Democratic president in a half century to serve two full terms by co-opting the opposition's domestic program—Clinton's three main legislative successes (free-trade agreements, budget cutting, and welfare reform) were all programs that had been more closely associated with Republicans than Democrats at the time Clinton took office.

After securing a controversial election victory in 2000, Republican President George W. Bush focused his efforts at the outset on passing numerous economic reforms. During his first six months in office, the Bush administration secured passage of a tax cuts package and the "No Child Left Behind" Education Bill, which favored greater accountability of school performance through testing of students. With the Congress narrowly split between the two parties, each of those bills required a degree of bipartisan support.

In the aftermath of the terrorist attacks of September 11, 2001, Bush moved quickly to position his administration as the eminent world leader in an emerging "war on terrorism." His early efforts to fight terrorism at home and abroad enjoyed congressional support from both parties: his aggressive military intervention against the Taliban-controlled government in Afghanistan in late 2001 proved extremely popular and helped cement his administration's image of toughness and resolve. Yet when the Bush administration expanded the war on terrorism to include military intervention in Iraq, justified on the basis of inaccurate reports that Iraq possessed weapons of mass destruction, these same policies became much more divisive. Bush won a second term in office in 2004, but his victory was no landslide: Bush captured just 51 percent of the national vote, and a switch of just seventy thousand votes in Ohio would have given the Electoral College victory to his Democratic opponent, Senator John Kerry of Massachusetts.

Bush's second term got off to a rocky start. His nomination of Judge John Roberts as chief justice of the United States to replace William Rehnquist who died in September 2005 was generally well received, but in other matters he encountered opposition and criticism. More Americans began to question the war in Iraq as U.S. casualties continued to climb. The president's controversial plan to alter the Social Security program stalled in Congress, with many Republicans distancing themselves from the proposal. Then in early September 2005, Republicans and Democrats alike in Congress criticized what they perceived as the Bush administration's slow response to the human tragedy wrought in Louisiana and other Gulf Coast states by Hurricane Katrina, and President Bush's approval ratings dropped below 40 percent, the lowest of his presidency up until that point. During the remainder of his term, Bush's approval rating would fall even lower, to below 30 percent in some polls. This further decline in Bush's approval rating was the consequence of problems in the economy, exacerbated further by the Wall Street crisis of September 2008.

Presidents in the modern era have proven most successful when they've been able to navigate bipartisan waters, bringing members of both parties to compromise and agreement. In his first term, President George W. Bush often resorted to the traditional presidential hammer of party politics, attempting to win congressional approval of his domestic policies and controversial appointments by enforcing compliance among Republicans and grinding the opposition party into submission. With Democrats at the helm in Congress beginning in 2007, President Bush encountered increasing barriers to advancing presidential initiatives. Indeed, his final two years in office were marked by dissension from members of his own party in Congress, undermining his efforts to enact widespread immigration reform, among other initiatives.

Express Powers and Responsibilities of the President

Article II of the Constitution provides that the president of the United States holds executive power, but it is not very detailed about what constitutes executive power. In fact, the Constitution lists only four specific powers of the president: (1) commander-in-chief of the armed forces, (2) power to grant reprieves or pardons, (3) power to "make" treaties (subject to Senate approval), and (4) power to make certain appointments, including those of ambassadors and justices of the Supreme Court (again subject to Senate approval). Despite this limited number of constitutionally expressed powers, presidents serve many important functions in the American political system. Noting these varied roles, political scientist Clinton Rossiter referred to the many different "hats" that the president must wear during the course of a week, or even during just one day.[7] Some of these are specified in the Constitution and laws of the United States, which conceive of a limited executive, but one who possesses the authority to react quickly and energetically to unexpected crises.

Head of State

The office of the presidency combines the political and symbolic functions that are often divided in other countries. As the nation's head of state, the president fulfills numerous formal duties and obligations on behalf of the country. Most visiting foreign heads of state meet directly with the president; sometimes those visits include an official "state dinner" at the White House hosted by the president and attended by key political leaders from throughout Washington. Article II of the Constitution also carves out a more formal role for the president in foreign affairs; the president's role in receiving ambassadors and other public ministers has often been interpreted as granting the president the discretion to give or deny official recognition to foreign governments. Although such a power may seem mostly honorary, it can have a real political impact in some circumstances. President Woodrow Wilson's refusal to recognize the new government of Mexico in 1913 caused considerable consternation among American supporters of the Mexican revolution, and led to growing tensions between the two neighbors. More recently, American presidents during the 1970s and 1980s refused to recognize the Palestine Liberation Organization as the legitimate representative of the Palestinian people, buttressing Israel's own hard-line stance against that organization.

Chief Executive and Head of Government

In his *Second Treatise of Government*, the political theorist John Locke argued that executive power was so fundamental that it predated civil society.[8] According to Locke, legislatures were ill-equipped to enforce their own laws because they need "perpetual execution" and legislatures sit only infrequently. Moreover, if the same entity both made and enforced the laws, it might be tempted to "suit the law to their own particular advantage," regardless of the law's language. Another political theorist, Baron de Montesquieu, also advocated the separation of legislative and executive powers—specifically, he decried the tendency of legislatures to exert too much influence over the executive, increasing the opportunity for abuse.[9]

Influenced in part by these arguments, the Framers of the Constitution vested all executive power in the president alone. Unfortunately, they failed to define that power with any specificity. At a minimum, the Constitution grants presidents alone the responsibility to execute laws of the United States, which encompasses the implementation and enforcement of measures passed by Congress; in other words, to see that Americans actually abide by those laws in practice. A president's failure to "take care that the laws be faithfully executed"—whether intentionally or due to negligent administration of his subordinates—can have obvious implications for the effectiveness of such laws. Actual levels of execution sometimes lie squarely within the discretion of the chief executive. Presidents Reagan and Clinton, for example, defined antitrust laws in markedly different ways simply by offering contrasting approaches to the execution of those laws. During the 1980s, Reagan's lack of enthusiasm for government intervention in the marketplace translated into the prosecution of far fewer antitrust

[7] See Clinton Rossiter, *The American Presidency* (Baltimore: Johns Hopkins University Press, 1987).
[8] See John Locke, *Two Treatises of Government and a Letter Concerning Toleration,* ed. Peter Laslett (Cambridge: Cambridge University Press, 1963).
[9] Baron de Montesquieu, *The Spirit of the Laws* (Anne M. Cohler et al., eds.) (Cambridge: Cambridge University Press, 1989).

President George W. Bush greets Australian Prime Minister John Howard at a state dinner in May 2006. Also pictured to the right are Janette Howard (the prime minister's wife) and First Lady Laura Bush.

actions than had been brought by previous administrations. By contrast, under President Clinton the Justice Department applied the antitrust laws enthusiastically, such as when it brought suit against the Microsoft Corporation in 1997 for monopolistic practices that stifled competition in the software industry. More recently, Republican President George W. Bush and the Democrats in Congress sparred not just over the written terms of the USA Patriot Act, but also over the Bush administration's aggressive enforcement of those provisions against some individuals, which gave the laws far more teeth than some had originally anticipated.

The president's power to see that laws are faithfully executed also implies some power to hire and fire those charged with administrative authority to help execute federal laws. The **power of appointment** thus stands among the president's most important executive powers.[10] The Constitution specifically authorizes the president to appoint ambassadors and other public ministers, judges of the Supreme Court, and all other federal officers under his charge. Additionally, the president appoints all federal judges. Most of these appointments require the consent of the Senate. In recent years, senators have subjected the president's nominees to intense scrutiny, occasionally even rejecting the president's choices. President George W. Bush's second choice for the Supreme Court, White House Counsel Harriet Miers, was withdrawn from consideration before even receiving a formal Senate vote in October 2005.

Although Supreme Court nominees often receive the most intense investigation, the Senate may occasionally question other executive appointments. In 1989, the U.S. Senate rejected President George H. W. Bush's choice for Defense Secretary, John Tower, due to allegations that Tower had a drinking problem. President Bill Clinton withdrew several of his more controversial nominees including his first

★ Power of appointment

The president's constitutional power to hire and fire those charged with administrative authority to help execute federal laws, including ambassadors, federal judges including those on the Supreme Court, and all other federal officers under the president's charge. Most of these appointments require the consent of the Senate.

Chapter 7: The Presidency

[10] Michael J. Gerhardt, *The Federal Appointments Process: A Constitutional and Historical Analysis* (Durham, NC: Duke University Press, 2003).

choice for attorney general, Zoe Baird, who was charged with hiring undocumented immigrants and failure to pay Social Security taxes on the wages of her household help.

The president's removal power has proven a source of controversy as well. The Supreme Court's decision in *Myers v. United States* (1926) established that chief executives have the power to remove "purely executive officers" without congressional consent. Although federal judges and independent agency heads can be removed only by congressional action, Cabinet heads and military officials can be terminated by the president alone. In one famous instance during the Korean War, President Truman decided in 1951 to fire the extremely popular General Douglas MacArthur, commander of the UN forces in Korea. Of course political pressures may hamper the president's ability to fire executive branch officials. President Clinton was certainly frustrated by Attorney General Janet Reno's decision in late 1997 to authorize independent counsel Kenneth Starr's investigation into allegations of sexual harassment by Clinton. But removing Reno from office would have invited charges of evasion and cover-up, leading to even greater political problems for Clinton. Consequently, Reno survived as attorney general for the duration of Clinton's presidency.

Not only is the president responsible for the enforcement of all federal laws, he is also authorized by the Constitution to grant reprieves and pardons to individuals who violate those laws. The Founders vested this power in the chief executive because they believed that the prerogative of mercy, on which the pardon power is based, is most efficiently and equitably exercised by a single individual, as opposed to a body of legislators or judges. A **reprieve** reduces the severity of a punishment without removing the guilt; a full **pardon** relieves an individual of both the punishment and the guilt. A president's decision to exercise the pardon power can invite considerable negative comment and political backlash. Not surprisingly then, most presidents wait until the end of their presidential terms to grant pardons. Less than two months after being denied his bid for re-election in 1992, President George H. W. Bush pardoned six officials for their involvement in the Iran-Contra scandal from 1987, including former Defense Secretary Casper Weinberger. President Clinton issued 140 pardons on his last day in office in 2001, including one to Marc Rich, who had previously fled the country for tax evasion and whose wife was a major contributor to Clinton's

★ Reprieve

The president's constitutional authority to reduce the severity of a punishment without removing the guilt for those who have violated the law.

★ Pardon

The president's constitutional authority to relieve an individual of both the punishment and the guilt of violating the law.

President Richard Nixon and Vice President Gerald Ford conferring on August 9, 1974, the day Nixon resigned from office.

HULTON ARCHIVE/GETTY IMAGES

political campaigns. No president received more criticism for granting a pardon than the late Gerald Ford, who as vice president succeeded to the presidency when Richard Nixon resigned in 1974. Ford's pardon of his former boss for involvement in the Watergate scandal helped undermine his prospects for election to the White House in his own right two years later.

Chief Diplomat

As chief diplomat of the United States, the president has the power to negotiate treaties and appoint diplomatic representatives to other countries, including ambassadors, ministers, and consuls. The president's power over treaties is limited to negotiation and execution—enactment of any treaties requires approval by two-thirds of the Senate. Still, the power to negotiate and execute the terms of treaties affords the president immense authority in the field of foreign affairs. John F. Kennedy used this power to negotiate an end to the Cuban Missile Crisis in 1962;[11] Jimmy Carter personally presided over the negotiation of the Panama Canal Treaty of 1977–1978, which relinquished U.S. control over the canal by the year 2000. Every president during the latter stages of the Cold War conducted arms control negotiations with the Soviet Union, working to check the spread of nuclear weapons to other nations. More recently, Bill Clinton surprised many in his own party when he completed negotiations on the North American Free Trade Agreement, an economic treaty with Canada and Mexico that was favored primarily by Republican presidents who came before him.

Chief Legislator

Although Congress is the branch of government authorized to make laws, modern presidents are involved in nearly every stage of federal lawmaking.[12] The Constitution's express provision that the president recommend for the consideration of Congress "such measures as he shall judge necessary and expedient" barely hints at the president's real role in this context: major legislation is often the product of a give-and-take process between the president and congressional leaders. Indeed, the president plays a critically important role in helping to set the lawmaking agenda for Congress, especially when the president's party is also in control of the legislative branch of government. While campaigning for the White House, the future president will lay out a policy agenda; once elected, he will claim a legislative mandate to follow through on those campaign proposals. In the **State of the Union address,** an annual speech made to Congress laying out the status of the nation, the president typically proposes suggestions for legislation. The legislative programs of FDR's New Deal and Lyndon's Johnson's Great Society were both influenced heavily by the executive branch. Similarly, Congress's reorganization of various executive branch agencies into a unified Department of Homeland Security in 2002 was based on a plan drafted by officials within the Bush administration. According to social scientist Paul Light, recent presidents have tended to offer fewer legislative proposals than presidents of the mid-twentieth century, consistent with the modern administrations' increased emphasis on reducing the size of the federal government.[13]

The **White House Office of Legislative Affairs** serves as a liaison between the president and Congress and helps develop the strategy used to promote passage of the president's legislative agenda. Administration officials often testify before congressional subcommittees on behalf of legislation, and presidents meet with congressional leaders frequently throughout the lawmaking process to negotiate details and discuss strategy. Many bills have the president's imprint squarely upon them, even though the power of lawmaking rests formally with Congress. The president's legislative authority also includes the constitutional power to veto, or reject, legislation that he opposes. While Congress can technically override a veto by a two-thirds vote of both houses, barely 4 percent of presidential vetoes have been overridden in history.

★ State of the Union address

An annual speech that the president delivers to Congress laying out the status of the nation and offering suggestions for new legislation.

★ White House Office of Legislative Affairs

A presidential office that serves as a liaison between the president and Congress. This office helps the president develop the strategy used to promote passage of the president's legislative agenda.

[11] Robert F. Kennedy Jr., *Thirteen Days: A Memoir of the Cuban Missile Crisis* (New York: W. W. Norton, 1999).
[12] Mark Peterson, *Legislating Together: The White House and Capitol Hill from Eisenhower to Reagan* (Cambridge, MA: Harvard University Press, 1990).
[13] Paul Light, *The President's Agenda: Domestic Policy Choice from Kennedy to Clinton* (Baltimore: Johns Hopkins University Press, 1999).

During the twentieth century, vetoes became a routine form of political exercise for presidents, especially those confronting Congresses controlled by the opposite political party. For Richard Nixon, Gerald Ford, and George H. W. Bush, the only three presidents during this span to never enjoy unified party rule, the veto became something of an art form. Nixon and Bush vetoed forty-three and forty-four bills, respectively. (Only eight of those vetoes were overridden.) Gerald Ford vetoed sixty-six bills in just two and a half years, but more than one in five were overridden, a clear sign of the limited power Ford held during his brief term as president. With Republicans controlling the House during George W. Bush's first six years in office, he did not need to veto any bills during that time—in fact, Bush did not veto his first bill until July 19, 2006, when he vetoed the Stem Cell Research Enhancement Bill, legislation that would have eased restrictions on federal funding for embryonic stem cell research. However, since the Democrats' takeover of Congress in 2007, Bush has become increasingly willing to exercise this authority, vetoing eleven more bills sent to him by the Democratic Congress. The Democratic-controlled Congress, in turn, has overridden four of President Bush's vetoes in all.

Commander-in-Chief

One of the defining features of the American political system is its firm commitment to civil control of military, embodied in the president's status as head of the nation's armed forces. As commander-in-chief, the president is the nation's principal military leader, responsible for formulating and directing all military strategy and policy. Although the Constitution awards to Congress the formal power to "declare war," the balance of war-making power has shifted overwhelmingly from Congress to the president during the past century, as modern executives have assumed the nearly unlimited power to send troops into combat.[14] Terming it a "police action," President Harry Truman sent troops to Korea in June 1950 without even asking Congress for a formal declaration of war. In 1973, Congress passed over President Nixon's veto the War Power Resolution, which theoretically limits the power of the president to unilaterally commit troops to battle. Ignoring its provisions, Presidents Reagan, George H. W. Bush, and Clinton have deployed U.S. troops to invade Grenada (1983), Panama (1989), and Haiti (1994), respectively. Of course presidents are not entirely immune from public pressures in this context. In the two most recent Gulf War conflicts, the weight of popular opinion led both President Bushes to seek congressional authorization for the invasions of Iraq in 1991 and 2003.

Implied Powers and Responsibilities of the President

Article II of the Constitution does not specifically spell out all the powers that a president may exercise; during the past two centuries presidents have assumed the right to exercise some "implied" or "inherent" powers not listed in the Constitution, and the Supreme Court has for the most part acceded in their right do so. These implied powers allow the president to act quickly in crisis situations, to serve as leader of his political party, and to issue executive orders and make executive agreements that do not require congressional approval.

Crisis Manager

More than any other official in government the president is in a unique position to respond quickly and effectively to unexpected crises. Consequently, Americans look immediately to the president under such circumstances to provide assurances, comfort, and where appropriate, a plan to address the difficulties. When a natural disaster strikes, the president will often visit the scene, meet with family members, and in many cases

[14] Lee Hamilton and Jordan Tama, *A Creative Tension: The Foreign Policy Roles of the President and Congress* (Washington, DC: Woodrow Wilson Press, 2003).

Table 7.1 Vetoes Issued by Modern Presidents (through July 1, 2008)

President	Congresses	Regular Vetoes	Pocket Vetoes	Total Vetoes	Vetoes Overridden
Theodore Roosevelt	57th–60th	42	40	82	1
William H. Taft	61st–62nd	30	9	39	1
Woodrow Wilson	63rd–66th	33	11	44	6
Warren G. Harding	67th	5	1	6	....
Calvin Coolidge	68th–70th	20	30	50	4
Herbert C. Hoover	71st–72nd	21	16	37	3
Franklin D. Roosevelt	73rd–79th	372	263	635	9
Harry S Truman	79th–82nd	180	70	250	12
Dwight D. Eisenhower	83rd–86th	73	108	181	2
John F. Kennedy	87th–88th	12	9	21	....
Lyndon B. Johnson	88th–90th	16	14	30	....
Richard M. Nixon	91st–93rd	26	17	43	7
Gerald R. Ford	93rd–94th	48	18	66	12
James Earl Carter	95th–96th	13	18	31	2
Ronald Reagan	97th–100th	39	39	78	9
George H. W. Bush	101st–102nd	29	15	44	1
William J. Clinton	103rd–106th	37	1	38	2
George W. Bush	107th–110th	11	1	12	4

provide aid from the Federal Emergency Management Agency (FEMA). Domestic and international terrorism has posed special challenges for presidents in this regard. Even President Clinton's most bitter critics praised his efforts in 1995 when he led the nation in mourning the loss of 168 lives from a truck bombing at a federal building in Oklahoma City. In the days following the September 11 attacks, George W. Bush redefined his presidency as a fight against terrorism—his visits to "Ground Zero," the site of the attacks on the World Trade Center, and his address to a joint session of Congress created indelible images in the media and won him widespread public support.

Party Leader

Once elected, the president of the United States assumes the position of de facto leader of his own political party. Not surprisingly, presidents are normally well attuned to how their political decisions will reflect on the party as a whole. A popular president is often expected to campaign for the party's congressional candidates, and if possible, help secure control of Congress for the party. Any assistance the president provides to congressional candidates seeking election may have an important side effect: the president may now have the leverage to demand support from those members

Senator Barack Obama of Illinois and his running mate, Senator Joseph Biden of Delaware, greet the crowd after Obama's speech accepting the presidential nomination of the Democratic Party at the party's national convention in August 2008.

of Congress for his own legislative programs. Similarly, the "coattail effect," by which congressional candidates and state and local officials benefit at the polls from the votes of the president's supporters, may strengthen the president's position with party members during the upcoming term.

Executive Orders and Agreements

★ Executive orders

Rules or regulations issued by the chief executive that have the force of law and do not require the consent of Congress.

On their own, presidents can issue **executive orders,** which are rules or regulations issued by the chief executive that have the force of law. Once thought to be an unconstitutional exercise of Congress's lawmaking power, executive orders have now become a routine feature of American government.[15] Since the beginning of the twentieth century, presidents have issued more than thirteen thousand executive orders regulating all manner of topics including affirmative action, civil service, federal holidays, the classification of government documents, public land designations, and federal disaster relief. Many executive orders deal with the nation's armed services: Truman used an executive order to end segregation in the armed forces in 1948; Clinton's "don't ask, don't tell" policy, which allowed homosexuals to serve in the military as long as they did not reveal their sexual orientation, was similarly established by an executive order (albeit one that Clinton modified in response to congressional and public uproar). President George W. Bush issued more than 150 executive orders during his first term in office alone.

Presidents may be reluctant to issue executive orders on especially controversial topics that may elicit a negative response from Congress, as any executive order can be partially or fully revoked by an act of Congress. FDR strategically issued executive orders to create agencies that Congress refused to establish; eventually, however, he was frustrated by the legislature's refusal to fund those agencies near the end of his presidency. Similarly, Richard Nixon's efforts to dismantle by executive order certain agencies created by his Democratic predecessors, such as the Office of Economic Opportunity, were often stymied, because the courts refused to allow the elimination of an agency established with the approval of Congress.

★ Executive agreement

A pact reached between the president and a foreign government that does not require the consent of Congress.

An **executive agreement** is a pact, written or oral, reached between the president and a foreign government. As with executive orders, these agreements do not require the consent of Congress, although Congress does have the power to revoke them.

American Government: Historical, Popular, and Global Perspectives

[15] Kenneth Mayer, *With the Stroke of a Pen: Executive Orders and Presidential Power* (Princeton, NJ: Princeton University Press, 2001).

Executive agreements have become important tools by which presidents conduct foreign affairs. FDR agreed to trade U.S. destroyers for British military bases in 1940, more than a year before the United States formally declared war on Germany, thus implicitly supporting the British military cause against Germany. In recent years, the U.S. government's military alliances with Great Britain and other countries in response to Iraqi aggression have not been spelled out in any treaties that required the advice and consent of the Senate; rather, those alliances came in the form of executive agreements between President Bush and the British government.

Presidential Resources

Nearly a half century ago, Professor Richard Neustadt defined the central problem that all presidents face from the moment they are sworn into office: how do presidents mobilize the powers of the office to work for them? The federal bureaucracy has grown so vast that presidents cannot simply "command" the bureaucracy to do their will. So what exactly can presidents do to make their will felt within the executive branch, and to carry out their choices through that "maze of personalities and institutions called the government of the United States"?

In his landmark book, *Presidential Power: The Politics of Leadership,* Neustadt argued that the president's most fundamental power is the "power to persuade."[16] Presidents use this power most effectively by keeping themselves informed, employing a system of information that allows them to be at the center of the decision-making apparatus, and carefully cultivating the image of a powerful president. Modern presidents have tended to emphasize certain individuals and offices under their control that play critical roles in the success of their administrations.

The Vice President

After Vice President Martin Van Buren's successful election to the White House in 1836, few vice presidents rose to the presidency by running and winning on their own accord. In fact, after Van Buren no sitting vice president even emerged as a serious contender for the presidency until the Republicans nominated Richard Nixon in 1960. And the next sitting vice president after Van Buren to be elected president was George H. W. Bush in 1988.

Next in line for succession and thus "only a heartbeat away" from the presidency, vice presidents have often been relegated to the very fringes of presidential power.[17] FDR barely communicated with John Nance Garner, who was vice president during FDR's first two terms in office. Of course, Garner did not have a very high opinion of the vice presidency either, referring to the position (in a sanitized version of his remarks) as not worth "a bucket of warm spit." When asked toward the end of his presidency what ideas Vice President Richard Nixon had offered within his own administration, President Dwight D. Eisenhower quipped: "If you give me a week, I might think of one." In fact, up through the 1950s, vice presidents maintained their principal offices on Capitol Hill near the Senate Chamber, where they occasionally performed their one clearly defined constitutional responsibility: to preside over the Senate and to cast a vote in the event of a tie.

LUKE FRAZZA/AFP/GETTY IMAGES

Former Vice President Al Gore, speaking about the environment while campaigning for the presidency in 2000.

[16] The updated version of this work is Richard Neustadt, *Presidential Power and the Modern Presidents: The Politics of Leadership from Roosevelt Through Reagan* (New York: Free Press, 1991).

[17] Jules Witcover, *Crapshoot: Rolling the Dice on the Vice Presidency* (New York: Crown, 1991).

Vice President Dick Cheney speaking to U.S. troops in 2006.

The vice presidency, however, has undergone a transformation in recent decades. Modern-day vice presidents have assumed roles as key advisers and executive branch officials working on behalf of the president. Walter Mondale developed U.S. policy on South Africa and was one of President Jimmy Carter's most trusted advisers. Al Gore was an active participant in most critical policy meetings conducted during the Clinton administration, and he headed the National Performance Review, which recommended ways to increase the federal government's efficiency and reduce its costs. Perhaps no federal official is more influential with President George W. Bush than Vice President Dick Cheney. According to journalist Bob Woodward, Cheney was the driving force behind President Bush's controversial decision to invade Iraq in March 2003.[18]

Constitutionally, the vice president is also the first in line to succeed the president in the event of the death or incapacitation of the president. By statute, if the vice president is not available to serve, succession falls in turn to the Speaker of the House, the President Pro Tempore of the Senate, and then to Cabinet-level officials in the order of each department's creation.

The Cabinet

★ Cabinet

The collection of the principal officers in each of the executive departments of the federal government who serve as key advisers to the president.

The Constitution specifically affords presidents the power to solicit the advice of the principal officers in each of the executive departments. Thus in addition to running their own executive departments within the large federal bureaucracy, principal officers also serve as key advisers. Together, they form the president's **Cabinet.** Today's Cabinet consists of fifteen heads of departments and six other important officials considered of "Cabinet rank." In reality, such a large body of individuals with different areas of expertise can serve only limited functions for a president, and recent chief executives have convened their full Cabinets to serve more as a sounding board and a communications device than as a significant instrument of policy making. Nevertheless, in individual meetings Cabinet-level officials may still provide critical input to the president on issues related to their own departments.

The Executive Office of the President and the White House Staff

Created in 1939 to bring executive branch activities under tighter control, the Executive Office of the President (EOP) and its two thousand federal employees consists of numerous agencies that assist with the management and administration of executive branch departments. Some of these agencies, such as the Office of Management and Budget, the President's Council of Economic Advisors, the National Security Council, and the Office of the U.S. Trade Representatives, have near permanent status. Other EOP agencies come and go, depending on the policy priorities of the current administration. Thus during the height of the Cold War, the EOP included agencies that focused on preparedness and civil defense in the event of a nuclear attack.

★ White House Chief of Staff

The manager of the White House staff, which serves the president's organizational needs, including speechwriting, advance work for presidential appearances, scheduling, congressional relations, public relations, and communications.

The EOP also includes an expanded White House staff. Until 1939, this staff consisted mostly of assistant secretaries and clerks who helped the president with correspondence; the White House staff today consists of nearly six hundred employees and runs on an annual budget of almost $730 million. In charge of this bureaucracy is the **White House Chief of Staff,** who manages and organizes the staff to serve the president. Some modern presidents, including Ronald Reagan and George H. W. Bush, have adopted management styles that rely

[18] Bob Woodward, *Plan of Attack* (New York: Simon & Schuster, 2004).

heavily on the chief of staff to control access to the president. Others, such as President Clinton, have utilized a "spokes-of-a-wheel" arrangement in which five or six different advisers have direct access to the president.[19] Regardless of the arrangement chosen, the White House Chief of Staff will have a significant hand in the success of the modern presidency. The principal duties of the White House staff include, but are not limited to, speechwriting, advance work for presidential appearances, scheduling, congressional relations, public relations, and communications.

The First Lady

All but one president (James Buchanan) have been married at some point in their lifetimes, and the spouses of sitting presidents, now referred to as first ladies, have come to assume an important role in the affairs of the nation. Until recently, presidents mainly relied on their spouses to help them perform social obligations, such as hosting state dinners. Woodrow Wilson's two wives broke somewhat with this mold: his first wife, Ellen, took public positions on bills being considered for Congress, and his second wife, Edith, served as an intermediary between the president and other government leaders while Wilson was recovering from a massive stroke in the fall of 1919. Eleanor Roosevelt, wife to Franklin Delano Roosevelt, marked a course for first ladies as aggressive public advocates. Mrs. Roosevelt launched one of the earliest civil rights organizations, the Southern Conference on Human Welfare; she actively supported the building of model communities; and she lobbied for refugees fleeing Nazi persecution. Occasionally, Mrs. Roosevelt even disagreed publicly with some of FDR's policies in foreign affairs.

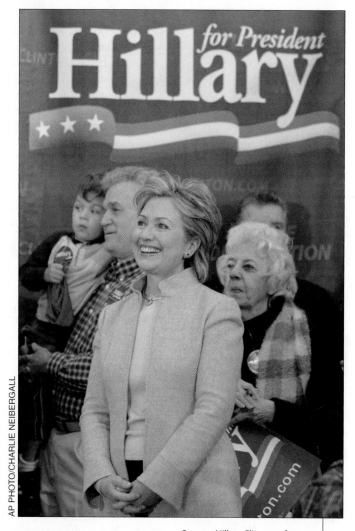

AP PHOTO/CHARLIE NEIBERGALL

Senator Hillary Clinton, a former First Lady, waiting to talk at a town hall meeting during her presidential campaign in 2007.

Although none of the first ladies after Eleanor Roosevelt were willing to so boldly challenge their husbands' policies in the media, many did stake out policy areas where they could contribute, and some have become active members of their husband's administrations.[20] They have been assisted in this regard by a formal Office of the First Lady, now staffed by more than twenty aides. Rosalynn Carter lobbied Congress for mental health initiatives; Nancy Reagan became the public voice of the "Just Say No" to drugs campaign; and Barbara Bush (wife of George H. W. Bush) campaigned widely against the problem of illiteracy. A distinguished lawyer, Hillary Rodham Clinton led a task force in 1994 charged with reforming the nation's health care system; Mrs. Clinton's complex plan ultimately proved too ambitious, and it was rebuffed by Congress. In another unprecedented move, Hillary Clinton ran for and won a seat in the U.S. Senate in 2000 and was re-elected to the Senate in 2006. Most recently, Laura Bush epitomized to many the more traditional role of the first lady, attending to matters outside of the administration's central policy-making apparatus. Regardless of what roles first ladies may assume, modern presidents have increasingly come to rely on their wives as advisers on a range of issues.

Although no woman has ever been nominated as a major party's candidate for the presidency, the day when that happens may be rapidly approaching. In 1984, Geraldine Ferraro, a member of Congress from New York, was the Democratic

---

[19] For a comprehensive discussion of the various ways that modern presidents have organized the White House, see Stephen Hess, *Organizing the Presidency* (Washington, DC: Brookings Institution Press, 1988).
[20] Bill Adler, *America's First Ladies* (New York: Taylor, 2002).

Party's candidate for vice president, a historical breakthrough to be sure. More recently, in 2008 the Republicans nominated Alaska governor Sarah Palin as the party's vice presidential candidate. Although she fell just short of capturing the Democratic presidential nomination, Senator Hillary Clinton (D-NY) was the instant front-runner for the nomination from the time she first threw her hat into the race in early 2007. When a woman not only captures her party's nomination, but goes on to win the presidency, a dilemma will be raised for the new chief executive in the event she is married: what role, if any, should be played by her spouse, who will become the first "first gentleman" in American history?

In other countries where the heads of government have been women, the male spouse was only rarely seen and almost never heard. Perhaps the most famous example was Denis Thatcher, the husband of former British Prime Minister Margaret Thatcher. Mr. Thatcher was commonly portrayed by the British media as a reactionary interested in only golf and gin. He often referred to his wife as "the Boss," and few gave him credit for influencing policy in any meaningful way. It's hard to imagine Hillary Clinton's husband, former President Bill Clinton, laying so low if he were to one day become the "first gentleman."

Important Presidential Relationships

The power of the president is influenced by the relations that a president develops and cultivates with three important constituencies: the public, Congress, and the news media.

The President and the Public

Catering to the needs and demands of the public mattered little to presidents prior to 1824, when presidential nominees were chosen by congressional leaders in secret caucuses. By contrast, the presidency today is a truly public institution that depends heavily on its public popularity for political effectiveness. Modern presidential nominations and elections are won on an arduous campaign trail in which aspiring chief executives must reach out, communicate with, and ultimately gain acceptance from large segments of the public. Once in office, presidents must remain constantly attentive to the sentiments of the public at large. FDR was the first president to rely on public opinion polls, and his administration utilized them to monitor support for his New Deal policies. Through his fireside chats, he reached into the living rooms of millions of Americans, winning their support for and confidence in his domestic and foreign policies.

Most modern presidents continuously engage the public to support administration policies, whether through the annual State of the Union address to Congress and other special televised messages, staged events, or interviews and press conferences with the media where they attempt to promote the benefits of their programs. Presidents Richard Nixon and Ronald Reagan preferred the "set piece" speech presented from the Oval Office during prime time; Presidents Jimmy Carter and Bill Clinton occasionally held "town meetings" to discuss issues in open forums with concerned citizens. In bypassing legislators and appealing directly to their constituents, modern presidents have perfected the art of what social scientist Samuel Kernell calls "going public."[21]

Some recent presidents have come under criticism for being too dependent on public opinion polls. President Clinton's critics charged that he too quickly withdrew support for some of his more controversial appointments when public opinion swung against them. But presidents may find themselves in even greater political trouble when they refuse to heed public opinion. President Johnson's escalation of troops in Vietnam during the late 1960s ignored growing public opposition against that war and undermined his hopes for re-election. Just as the Watergate scandal began to engulf Richard Nixon's presidency, his decision to hold press conferences less frequently only fed the impression that he was hiding from the public and fueled

[21] Samuel Kernell, *Going Public: New Strategies of Presidential Leadership* (Washington, DC: CQ Press, 1992).

Left: President Ronald Reagan giving a "set speech" from the Oval Office in 1986. Right: President Bill Clinton interacting with the public at a "town meeting" in 1993.

even more calls for his resignation. Whereas high levels of public support increase a president's chances to get legislation passed, precipitous drops in public support may stop a president's program in its tracks.

The President and Congress

The history of the American political system is marked by the ebb and flow of power between the president and Congress. For much of the nineteenth century, a form of "congressional government" prevailed, with most presidents acting as dutiful administrators of the laws passed by Congress. Buoyed by advances in communications technology that placed modern presidents at the center of American politics, presidents today play far more influential roles in the legislative process, at times even prodding Congress forward to meet their administrations' goals. Since the 1970s, the frequency of divided-party government, with the executive and the legislature controlled by opposing political parties, has placed the two branches in a near continuous battle over the nation's domestic policy agenda. Because credit for a program's success is rarely spread evenly among the two branches, tensions are inevitable and compromises often difficult to come by. President Reagan managed to get the Democrat-controlled House of Representatives to pass his program of tax decreases and spending cuts in 1981; when the economy rebounded a few years later, Reagan and the Republican Party benefited politically far more than did the Democrats. President Clinton's willingness to sign a welfare reform bill in 1996 aided him in that year's election, when he claimed to have lived up to his earlier promise to "end welfare as we know it." The Republican Congress that actually drafted and passed the welfare bill received far less credit for its accomplishments. In foreign policy, presidents continue to act nearly independent of Congress.

Presidents have many tools at their disposal to influence Congress. As party leader, the president can campaign for congressional candidates, and then leverage that assistance into support. Personal contacts by the president with members of Congress can be effective as well. The White House Office of Congressional Relations (OCR) serves as a liaison to Congress, rounding up support and monitoring events on Capitol Hill. Still, the most effective lobbying for a president's policies comes from members of Congress friendly to the administration, who persuade other members of Congress to vote in favor of the policies. The rewards for such service often come in the form of future appointments, pork-barrel projects for home districts or states, or financial support from the political party for future election bids. FDR rewarded at least one key Senate supporter (Hugo Black) of the president's controversial 1937 court-packing plan to increase the size of the Supreme Court with an appointment to the Court; Bill Clinton was prepared to reward Senate Majority Leader George Mitchell with the same prize in 1994, but held back because he needed Mitchell's support in Congress for a pending health care bill. (Despite Mitchell's efforts, Clinton's health care bill went down to defeat.)[22]

The President and the Media

The relationship between presidents and the media that cover their administrations is important. The media provide perhaps the most effective channel through which the president can communicate information about their policies to the public. At the same time, the media's desire for interesting headlines to attract greater numbers of readers, listeners, viewers, and online observers leaves them to rely heavily on the executive branch for information. Effective media management has been a hallmark of the most successful modern presidents. Much of the responsibility rests with the **White House Press Secretary,** who plays an especially important role in briefing the press, organizing news conferences, and briefing the president on questions he may be forced to address.

The administration that ignores media management does so at its own peril. Social scientists Kathleen Hall Jamieson and Paul Waldman revealed how the mainstream media today does not so much report the news about presidents as create it, transforming "the raw stuff of experience into presumed fact" and "arranging facts into coherent stories" that can prove crucial to presidential success.[23] The media's focus on President George W. Bush talking with recovery workers at Ground Zero and issuing warnings to terrorists through a megaphone emphasized his toughness and compassion in dealing with the terrorist attacks of September 11, 2001. Yet nearly four years later that same press corps emphasized perceptions of President George W. Bush's aloofness aboard Air Force One after Hurricane Katrina killed thousands in and around New Orleans, Louisiana.

Today the president also relies on the White House Director of Communications to articulate a consistent and effective message to the public.[24] But even before that office came into being, chief executives felt the need to craft a message and hone their public images. Though known best for his fireside chats and effective public speeches, Franklin Roosevelt worked hard to cultivate good relations with the media, allowing his administration to set the news agenda and influence the content of the news. Many of his press conferences included "off-the-record" commentary that fed the media's appetite for information, yet allowed the president to change his position as circumstances changed. John F. Kennedy perfected the modern press conference in the East Room of the White House; his colorful banter with reporters played well as sound bites on the evening television news. Ronald Reagan's reputation as the "great

★ White House
Press Secretary

The person on the White House staff who plays an especially important role in briefing the press, organizing news conferences, and even briefing the president on questions that may be asked.

American Government: Historical, Popular, and Global Perspectives

[22] Elizabeth Drew, *On the Edge: The Clinton Presidency* (New York: Touchstone, 1995).

[23] See Kathleen Hall Jamison and Paul Waldman, *The Press Effect: Politicians, Journalists, and the Stories That Shape the Political World* (New York: Oxford University Press, 2002).

[24] John A. Maltese, *Spin Control: The White House Office of Communications and the Management of Presidential News* (Chapel Hill: University of North Carolina Press, 1992).

communicator" was enhanced by positive media coverage. His administration perfected the use of "staged" or "pseudo" events, which presented the president in a positive light—perhaps visiting flag factories or reading Shakespeare to children at elementary schools—all packaged in time for the evening newscasts. Even when scandals rocked Reagan's second term in office, his mostly friendly relations with the press paid off when they painted him as the unwitting victim of his own administration's follies.

Borrowing from Reagan's playbook, President George W. Bush has similarly avoided live press conferences wherever possible, preferring controlled situations that could be molded to fit his message. The Bush administration's communications operation's attention to detail has been meticulous. During a speech in Indianapolis to support his tax cuts, White House aides insisted that the people sitting in the crowd behind the president remove their ties so they would look more like the "common folk" his tax cuts were supposed to benefit. In an even more striking example of using the background of a speech to great effect, during a speech at Mount Rushmore Bush's aides moved the speaking platform so TV cameras would picture Bush's profile among the four great presidents carved in stone behind him. The Bush administration also worked hard to cultivate the image of a president working hard for the American people—even while vacationing at his ranch in Crawford, Texas, the president was often pictured clearing brush and performing various chores, rather than simply relaxing.

Although presidents and their staffs take great care to present a positive public image through the media, the glare of the spotlight can sometimes catch off-the-cuff commentary or statements from chief executives that would have best been left unsaid. Some of the more notable gaffes spoken by recent presidents include these remarks:

President John Kennedy held many press conferences. He is pictured above, taking questions at a press conference in June 1963.

★ "I am not worried about the deficit. It is big enough to take care of itself."
　—President Ronald Reagan.

★ "At breakfast, she was complaining that it is impossible to get a decent bagel in Washington."
　—President Bill Clinton, on wife Hillary's run for a U.S. Senate seat from New York.

★ "We see nothing but increasingly brighter clouds every month," referring to an improving economy.
　—President Gerald Ford, speaking to a group of businessmen about the economy.

★ "I don't see what's wrong with giving Bobby a little experience [as attorney general] before he starts to practice law."
　—President John Kennedy, reacting to critics who argued that his brother Robert was too young to be attorney general.

★ "When I need a little free advice about Saddam Hussein, I turn to country music."
　—President George H. W. Bush, at a country music awards ceremony.

★ "I would have made a good pope."
　—President Richard Nixon. [25]

[25] Ted Rueter, *The 267 Stupidest Things Republicans Ever Said/The 267 Stupidest Things Democrats Ever Said* (New York: Three Rivers Press, 2000).

Chapter 7: The Presidency

Now & Then: Making the Connection

When unexpected crises confront the nation—the December 7, 1941, attack on Pearl Harbor and the tragedy of September 11, 2001, are just two examples—leadership must come from the president of the United States. As head of state, the president plays a symbolic role in helping the nation heal from tragedy. As commander-in-chief of the armed forces, the president is in a position to strike back militarily if needed. As the nation's chief legislator and executive, the president can effectively propose legislation to address the crisis and can implement that legislation in the best interests of the nation. And as chief diplomat, the president can work with other foreign leaders to find common solutions and solicit support from allies.

Two other aspects of the presidency give the office an elevated place among American political institutions. Unlike the Congress, the president is just one person and thus can act quickly and decisively. Additionally, the president and the vice president are the only two officials elected by the entire nation—thus, the president alone can claim a mandate to act on behalf of the American people as a whole, rather than on behalf of a state, a district, or one political party. In times of crisis, citizens look to presidents for strength because they alone are in a position to provide it. For that reason more than any other, presidents only rarely have to demonstrate their continued relevance in the modern political system.

With his victory in the 2008 presidential election behind him, President Obama could look forward to a "honeymoon period" with the press and the public during his first few months in the White House. The question was not whether that honeymoon would occur, but how, if at all, the newly elected president would take advantage of it.

Past U.S. presidents have found that during this honeymoon period, even Congressional opposition is likely to support some of the new president's more controversial initiatives. Ronald Reagan, for example, was able in 1981 to win support from the Democratic-controlled House of Representatives for some of the largest tax cuts in American history. FDR in 1933 was able to pass a record number of bills during his administration's first 100 days. Of course these honeymoons may be cut short by presidential missteps. Gerald Ford enjoyed high approval ratings in 1974 when he took over the presidency following Richard Nixon's resignation; but when he pardoned the ex-president just a month into his own presidency, Ford suffered an immediate 30-point drop in his approval ratings and was never able to get back into the public's good graces. Bill Clinton rode a wave of high hopes into the White House in 1993. Yet when during his first week in office he announced his plans to allow gays in the military, even some Democratic support for his administration began to diminish.

The presidential honeymoon may be a reality, but even the most careful presidents know that it doesn't last forever. By the summer of a president's second year in office, the nation begins to turn its attention to the midterm Congressional elections; the following year, the president is usually gearing up to run for reelection.

On http://academic.cengage.com/dautrich, find the politics interactive link for details on presidential agenda-setting and the short "honeymoon period" presidents work with during their first term in office. Consult as well the various links that relate to how different presidents began their administrations with ambitious policymaking agendas. Historical, popular, and global perspectives on the issue are also presented.

AP PHOTO

President Gerald Ford announced on September 8, 1974, that he granted Nixon a "full, free and absolute pardon" for "all crimes committed against the United States" during Nixon's presidency. His presidency's "honeymoon period" ended that day.

http://academic.cengage.com/dautrich

Chapter Summary

★ Though theoretically any American who is at least thirty-five years old, a "natural born" citizen, and has lived in the United States for fourteen years is eligible to be president, in fact the forty-three individuals who have held the office have been mostly older, well-educated Protestant men who have prior political experience.

★ The office of the president has evolved over the nation's history. Over time, the office has accumulated more power. For the century after George Washington's term, Congress dominated the federal government, with only a few exceptions—namely during the presidencies of Andrew Jackson and Abraham Lincoln.

★ The birth of the modern presidency occurred with the ascension of Theodore Roosevelt to office in 1901. His strong personality forced itself on the office. Taking strong pro-American positions in foreign policy and aggressive antimonopoly positions during the industrialization period, Roosevelt promoted power in the executive office.

★ FDR's New Deal policies, in response to the failing economy of the 1930s, cemented a large role for the president in the American constitutional system. The growth of the federal bureaucracy under FDR significantly changed the role that the president would play and the power that office would yield.

★ The emergence of the United States as a superpower after World War II cemented the role of the U.S. president as a dominant player in world and national politics. Contemporary presidents find themselves as the focal points of American politics, setting the political and legislative agenda and leading American foreign and domestic policy.

★ The powers of the president, as expressly stated in the Constitution, are (1) to be commander-in-chief of the armed forces, (2) to grant reprieves or pardons, (3) to "make" treaties (subject to Senate approval), and (4) to make certain appointments, including those of ambassadors and justices of the Supreme Court (again subject to Senate approval).

★ Beyond the express powers granted to the president in the Constitution, presidents today also play a key role in setting the legislative agenda, managing national and international crises, and serving as leader of their political party.

★ The singularity of leadership in the executive branch affords the president a unique position in the American political system, giving the president the power to command the attention of the nation's people, Congress, and the media—thus enhancing the president's ability to persuade others what to do.

★ The Cabinet, the Executive Office of the President, and the White House staff provide large organizational support for the president to administer federal programs and agencies and lead the national government.

Key Terms

Cabinet (p. 214)

Executive agreement (p. 212)

Executive orders (p. 212)

Great Society (p. 203)

Impeachment (p. 195)

New Deal (p. 201)

Pardon (p. 208)

Power of appointment (p. 207)

Reprieve (p. 208)

State of the Union address (p. 209)

Twenty-second Amendment
(p. 194)

White House Office of Legislative
Affairs (p. 209)

White House Chief of Staff (p. 214)

White House Press Secretary
(p. 218)

Resources

Important Books

Beschloss, Michael. *Presidential Courage: Brave Leaders and How They Changed America,
1789–2007*. New York: Simon & Schuster, 2007.

Dallek, Robert. *Hail to the Chief: The Making and Unmaking of American Presidents*. New York:
Oxford University Press, 2001.

Greenstein, Fred. *The Hidden-Hand Presidency: Eisenhower as Leader*. New York: HarperCollins,
1982.

Greenstein, Fred. *The Presidential Difference: Leadership Style from Roosevelt to Clinton*.
New York: Free Press, 2000.

Gregg, Gary L., and Mark Rozell. *Considering the Bush Presidency*. New York: Oxford University
Press, 2004.

Jones, Charles O. *The Presidency in a Separated System*. Washington, DC: Brookings Institution
Press, 1994.

Kernell, Samuel. *Going Public: New Strategies of Presidential Leadership*. Washington, DC: CQ
Press, 1993.

Neustadt, Richard. *Presidential Power*. New York: John Wiley & Sons, 1980.

Peterson, Mark. *Legislating Together: The White House and Capitol Hill from Eisenhower to
Reagan*. Cambridge, MA: Harvard University Press, 1993.

Internet Sources

http://www.whitehouse.gov/ (the home page of the White House including information on broader
aspects of the presidency, a virtual library, and so on)

http://www.americanpresidents.org (C-SPAN-sponsored site on the presidency, including life
portraits and a video archive of all American presidents)

http://www.archives.gov/presidential_libraries/index.html (the official National Archives site
on presidential libraries, featuring links to all the individual libraries, a digital classroom, a
research room with a searchable index, and so on)

http://www.archives.gov/federal_register/electoral_college/ (the National Archives guide to the
Electoral College, including frequently asked questions, voting resources, and so on)

http://whitehouse.gov/firstlady (the official White House home page for the First Lady, including
information about her initiatives, transcripts of remarks, and so on)

The Federal 8 Bureaucracy

AP PHOTO/J. SCOTT APPLEWHITE

President Bill Clinton and Vice President Al Gore in 1993

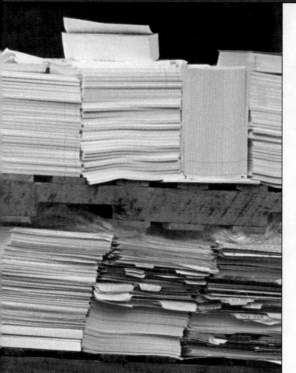

Reinventing the Way Government Works . . . Again . . . and Again. . . .: Now & Then

Government tends to develop in a sprawling fashion. As the need for the performance of new functions arises, new agencies, offices, rules, and regulations are created that frequently have little relation to other parts of government performing similar or related functions. Even more frustrating, shifts in the state of the nation and technological breakthroughs are rarely reflected in government, which continues to work under past conditions and within the confines of past structures. The result? The government remains confined by outdated infrastructure, archaic rules, and outdated regulations. Reacting to this state of affairs, this president of the United States, like others before him, authorized a commission to recommend fundamental changes in the way government works. The result was a long and detailed document chock full of proposals. While much symbolic change would occur, real and lasting change would occur much more slowly than the president and his administration desired.

Louis Brownlow

1993

2007   1997   1987   1977   1967

NOW. . .
Bill Clinton's presidential campaign in 1992 was successful in part because it capitalized on a pervading feeling in Washington, DC, and elsewhere in the nation that it was time for a change in the federal government. Incumbent President George H. W. Bush was the quintessential establishment candidate; Clinton, by contrast, had spent the previous decade in the statehouse of Arkansas. But how could the new president get a handle on the growing federal bureaucracy that had come to frustrate so many Americans? His administration's answer was to create an inter-agency task force charged with reforming the way the federal government works. Originally titled the National Performance Review (NPR), and later renamed the National Partnership for Reinventing Government, this body began its work on March 3, 1993, less than six weeks after Clinton's inauguration. Headed by Vice President Al Gore, the NPR went well beyond similar past efforts in two ways: (1) the NPR involved itself in the implementation of its many proposals beginning in 1994; and (2) the NPR conducted a second round of reviews in 1995. Gore went on talk shows to parody the federal government's bloated hardware costs, such as a $436 hammer at the Pentagon. Still, while Gore hoped to cause a fundamental culture change in government, the real test of the NPR's impact will come only in future years, as technologies change once again. Will the federal government be able to adjust to these changes?

THEN

1937

THEN. . .Those who followed the NPR during the Clinton Administration should be excused if they thought it had never been tried before. In fact, the NPR was the eleventh federal government reform effort in the twentieth century alone. Perhaps the most well-known instance of government review occurred in 1937 under President Franklin Roosevelt. FDR's Brownlow Committee, headed by public administration consultant Louis Brownlow and formally titled the President's Performance on Administrative Management, recommended sweeping changes to the executive branch of government. Perhaps its most lasting effect came with the Reorganization Act of 1939, which authorized the president to make various changes to agencies and government corporations under his control. Pursuant to these powers, FDR created the Executive Office of the President, an organization that brings together in one office the personnel who directly support or advise the president, including the White House Press Secretary, the Office of Presidential Communications (including senior media relations personnel and presidential speechwriters), and White House-based presidential policy and legal advisors. Unfortunately, the Reorganization Act of 1939 incorporated only two of the many recommendations included in the fifty-three-page report of the Brownlow Committee. The remaining recommended reforms would succeed in streamlining the increasingly bloated federal bureaucracy only if future presidents proved as willing as FDR to use the power at their disposal to tinker with government mechanisms and create more efficient structures. As future presidents would learn, this task would be easier said than done.

What Is Bureaucracy?

Bureaucracy is a term that usually conjures up negative images. It often refers to overgrown government, excessive rules and paperwork, or a burdensome process for getting something done. Political candidates extol the vices of "the unresponsive, fat bureaucracy" to strike a sympathetic chord with voters, as did Bill Clinton in his bid for the presidency.[1]

Despite the negative connotations of the term, bureaucracy is necessary for any government. Laws must be enforced, programs must be administered, and regulations must be implemented. Without a federal bureaucracy, the government could not function. To be sure, there are many problems with bureaucracy. It is often hard to get things done in an efficient manner, or to fire workers who do not perform well, or to reward deserving workers. The buck often passes from one desk to another, and silly or irrelevant rules often dictate the actions of the bureaucrats. Despite its problems and the "bad rep" that the term often conjures up, bureaucracy is absolutely essential for any government to implement and carry out its laws and public policies.[2]

A **bureaucracy** is an organization set up in a logical and rational manner for the purpose of accomplishing specific functions. Sociologist Max Weber (pronounced VAY-ber), an early student of bureaucratic organizations, identified six characteristics of effective bureaucracies:[3]

1. Bureaucracies are organized on the basis of specialization, expertise, and division of labor. The organization is divided into subunits based on function, and subunits are staffed by employees who are qualified to administer those tasks.

2. They are organized in a hierarchical manner with an identifiable "chain of command" from top to bottom.

3. A common set of rules for carrying out functions characterize the operation. These rules are often referred to as standard operating procedures (SOPs). Employees are trained to know and use these SOPs so that functions are performed smoothly and consistently.

4. Bureaucracies maintain good records, or a "paper trail" of actions taken and decisions made. Good record maintenance enables periodic review, efficiency of operation, and proof of action.

5. Bureaucracies are characterized by an air of professionalism on the part of employees.

6. The hiring and promotion process within effective bureaucracies is characterized by merit-based criteria and insulated from "politics."

Bureaucracies are created within many types of organizations. Organizations typically exist to carry out a function, or set of functions. Bureaucracies are what actually carry out these functions. Large private companies typically have bureaucracies that divide labor functions into categories or departments such as sales, accounting, human resources, MIS (management information systems), and other divisions. Colleges and universities have bureaucracies that usually include an admissions department, a registrar's office, an academic counseling center, an athletics department, and so on. Even small organizations such as physicians' offices feature a bureaucracy that includes medical support staff (e.g., nurses), a front-office staff (receptionist and secretary), and business offices (accountant and medical insurance specialist).

Most governments maintain bureaucracies to carry out specific governmental functions, and the federal government is no exception. As with political parties, there is

---

★ Bureaucracy

An organization set up in a logical and rational manner for the purpose of accomplishing specific functions.

American Government: Historical, Popular, and Global Perspectives

---

[1] See *Washington Monthly*, a periodical that regularly reports on the excesses and waste in the federal bureaucracy.
[2] For a comprehensive discussion of the virtues of contemporary bureaucracy, see Charles T. Goodsell, *The Case for Bureaucracy* (Chatham, NJ: Chatham House Publishers, 1994).
[3] Max Weber, chapters 11 and 12 in *Economy and Society*, ed. by Guenther Roth and Claus Wittich (New York: Bedminster Press, 1968).

American Government . . . in Popular Perspective:
Mixed Views on Bureaucracy

Public opinion surveys about the federal bureaucracy tend to provide mixed reviews. People generally support the idea of government addressing important problems, but many are of the opinion that when government does act it tends to waste money and act inefficiently. As the following figures show, Americans, after the Hurricane Katrina disaster that destroyed much of New Orleans and surrounding areas, supported federal involvement but questioned waste in spending.

Do you approve or disapprove of the 62-billion dollar relief effort President Bush and Congress have passed to help rebuild after Hurricane Katrina?

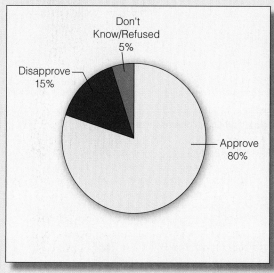

Don't Know/Refused 5%

Disapprove 15%

Approve 80%

In the long run, which concerns you more?

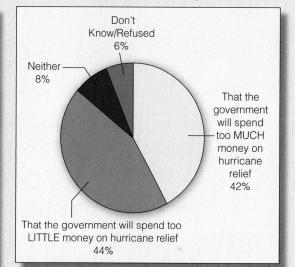

Don't Know/Refused 6%

Neither 8%

That the government will spend too MUCH money on hurricane relief 42%

That the government will spend too LITTLE money on hurricane relief 44%

Which of the following, if any, concerns you MOST about the government's hurricane relief effort?

Don't Know/Refused 12%

That we are spending too MUCH money on hurricane relief 26%

Neither 17%

That we are spending too LITTLE money on hurricane relief 45%

Which concerns you more?

Don't Know/Refused 3%

Multiple 6%

None 2%

The money will be wasted on unnecessary things 32%

The money will add too much to the budget deficit 6%

The money won't go to the people who really need it 51%

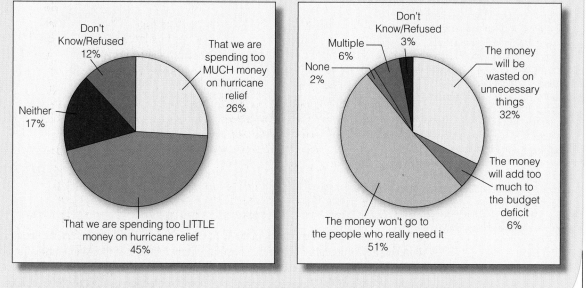

Source: National survey of American adults conducted by Pew Center for People and the Press, October 2005, N=1,500.

Figure 8.1 The Organization of the Federal Bureaucracy

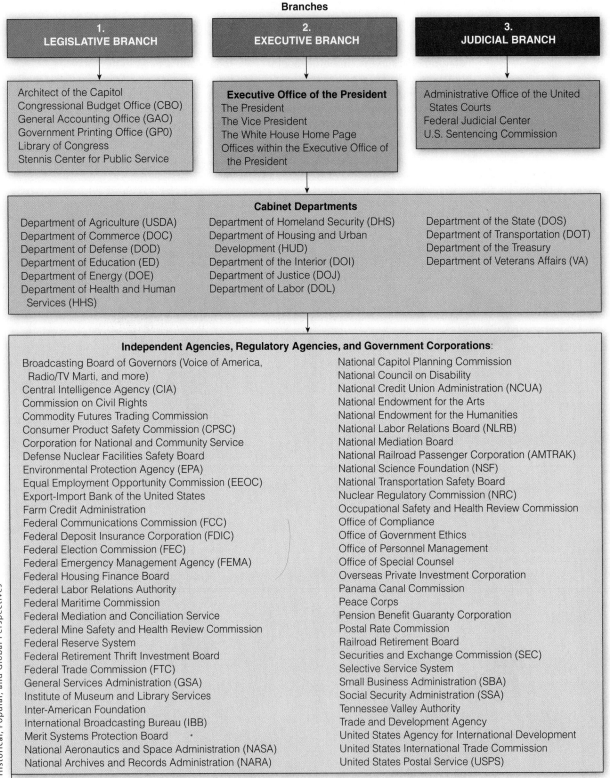

Branches

1. LEGISLATIVE BRANCH	2. EXECUTIVE BRANCH	3. JUDICIAL BRANCH
Architect of the Capitol Congressional Budget Office (CBO) General Accounting Office (GAO) Government Printing Office (GPO) Library of Congress Stennis Center for Public Service	**Executive Office of the President** The President The Vice President The White House Home Page Offices within the Executive Office of the President	Administrative Office of the United States Courts Federal Judicial Center U.S. Sentencing Commission

Cabinet Departments

Department of Agriculture (USDA)
Department of Commerce (DOC)
Department of Defense (DOD)
Department of Education (ED)
Department of Energy (DOE)
Department of Health and Human Services (HHS)

Department of Homeland Security (DHS)
Department of Housing and Urban Development (HUD)
Department of the Interior (DOI)
Department of Justice (DOJ)
Department of Labor (DOL)

Department of the State (DOS)
Department of Transportation (DOT)
Department of the Treasury
Department of Veterans Affairs (VA)

Independent Agencies, Regulatory Agencies, and Government Corporations:

Broadcasting Board of Governors (Voice of America, Radio/TV Marti, and more)
Central Intelligence Agency (CIA)
Commission on Civil Rights
Commodity Futures Trading Commission
Consumer Product Safety Commission (CPSC)
Corporation for National and Community Service
Defense Nuclear Facilities Safety Board
Environmental Protection Agency (EPA)
Equal Employment Opportunity Commission (EEOC)
Export-Import Bank of the United States
Farm Credit Administration
Federal Communications Commission (FCC)
Federal Deposit Insurance Corporation (FDIC)
Federal Election Commission (FEC)
Federal Emergency Management Agency (FEMA)
Federal Housing Finance Board
Federal Labor Relations Authority
Federal Maritime Commission
Federal Mediation and Conciliation Service
Federal Mine Safety and Health Review Commission
Federal Reserve System
Federal Retirement Thrift Investment Board
Federal Trade Commission (FTC)
General Services Administration (GSA)
Institute of Museum and Library Services
Inter-American Foundation
International Broadcasting Bureau (IBB)
Merit Systems Protection Board
National Aeronautics and Space Administration (NASA)
National Archives and Records Administration (NARA)

National Capitol Planning Commission
National Council on Disability
National Credit Union Administration (NCUA)
National Endowment for the Arts
National Endowment for the Humanities
National Labor Relations Board (NLRB)
National Mediation Board
National Railroad Passenger Corporation (AMTRAK)
National Science Foundation (NSF)
National Transportation Safety Board
Nuclear Regulatory Commission (NRC)
Occupational Safety and Health Review Commission
Office of Compliance
Office of Government Ethics
Office of Personnel Management
Office of Special Counsel
Overseas Private Investment Corporation
Panama Canal Commission
Peace Corps
Pension Benefit Guaranty Corporation
Postal Rate Commission
Railroad Retirement Board
Securities and Exchange Commission (SEC)
Selective Service System
Small Business Administration (SBA)
Social Security Administration (SSA)
Tennessee Valley Authority
Trade and Development Agency
United States Agency for International Development
United States International Trade Commission
United States Postal Service (USPS)

Source: From http://www.firstgov.gov.

American Government: Historical, Popular, and Global Perspectives

no reference to the bureaucracy in the U.S. Constitution. But like parties, the federal bureaucracy is arguably one of the most important features of the American political system, because Americans have come to depend on it for many important things such as the defense of U.S. interests around the world, protection against terrorist attacks, cleaning up the destruction caused by natural disasters, a financial safety net for those who are unemployed or retired, the maintenance and expansion of the nation's roads and airways, and research for cures to such health problems as heart disease, cancer, and AIDS. In American government, the federal bureaucracy has traditionally come under the authority and jurisdiction of the president and the executive branch. As we will see, however, the modern federal bureaucracy is a complex set of agencies and organizations, parts of which are accountable to the legislative and judicial branches as well.

Citizens are more likely to come into direct contact with the bureaucracy than any other part of government, and so for many Americans the bureaucracy comes to symbolize what government is. A visit to an unemployment office to register for unemployment benefits, a check in the mail from the Social Security Administration, a trip to the Department of Motor Vehicles to renew a driver's license, or a visit to the website of the Consumer Protection Agency to inquire about the safety of a child's car seat—these are just a few of the many ways citizens interact with the bureaucracy.

The federal bureaucracy, in fact, is a huge set of organizations that is expected to serve many different functions. It includes hundreds of departments, offices, agencies, bureaus, councils, foundations, commissions, boards, services, and authorities. Each of these units, as Weber's analysis of bureaucracies suggests, specializes in an area of public policy, is hierarchically organized to carry out its particular duties, conducts its operation on the basis of a set of standard operating procedures, maintains records of its actions and decisions, is trained to carry out functions in a professional manner, and engages in hiring practices that are based on merit. The vast size and level of responsibility that these units have make the federal bureaucracy a complex and often confusing system to study.

People wait in line to speak to a clerk at a U.S. Social Security office.

What Does the Federal Bureaucracy Do?

Most of the federal bureaucracy is contained within the executive branch of government, and ultimately reports to the president of the United States.[4] Article II of the Constitution states that "the executive power shall be vested in a President of the United States of America." The executive power, or the power to carry out, administer, and enforce specific laws, then, falls mainly under the purview of presidential responsibility. The president uses the federal bureaucracy to exercise executive authority.

Policy Implementation

The full range of activities in which the federal bureaucracy engages is known as **policy implementation.** Policy implementation is the process of carrying out a law. Laws that are passed by Congress often include the development of new or modification of existing federal programs or services. In order to carry out the specific programs or services outlined in a law, the federal bureaucracy is assigned the task of implementation. For example, in 1935 Congress passed the Social Security Act to provide older Americans with a stable source of income during their retirement years and to offer support for the children of deceased workers. The Act created the Social Security Administration as the agency in the federal government that had the authority to carry out the provisions of the Act. Today, the Social Security Administration remains the unit in the federal bureaucracy responsible for maintaining records and authorizing benefits to those eligible for Social Security payments.

★ Policy implementation

The process of carrying out laws, and the specific programs or services outlines in those laws.

[4] For a good discussion of organizational issues in the federal bureaucracy, see James Q. Wilson, *Bureaucracy: What Government Agencies Do and Why They Do It* (New York: Basic Books, 1989).

★ Regulations

Rules or other directives issued by government agencies.

★ *Federal Register*

The journal that publishes draft regulations that implement a federal program.

★ Administrative discretion

The freedom of agencies to decide how to implement a vague or ambiguous law passed by Congress.

★ Delegation of congressional power

Congress's transferring of its lawmaking authority to the executive branch of government.

★ Administrative law

A law that relates to the authority of administrative agencies and the rules promulgated by those agencies.

Implementation of a law requires translating the congressional legislation into action. Bureaucratic units begin the process of implementation by developing **regulations,** or a set of rules that guide employees of the agency in carrying out the program or service. These rules are supported by the force of law. The Social Security Administration, for example, has written a detailed set of regulations defining who is and who is not eligible for Social Security retirement benefits. The rules include a schedule for the amount of monthly payment benefit based on a person's age, the number of years he or she contributed to the Social Security system while working, and other criteria. Regulations are useful not only because they translate laws into actions, but because they are written down and are usually very specific, they also provide a basis for employees in the bureaucracy to consistently apply them from one case to the next.

Once an agency drafts a set of regulations to implement a program, they are published in the *Federal Register.* This federal government publication is widely accessible to elected leaders, interest groups, corporations, the media, and regular citizens. The agencies authoring the regulations have an open period where they accept comments on the proposed rules and decide whether to redraft based on the commentary they receive. If the agency refuses to redraft based on an objection, the objector can ask Congress to require the agency to modify the regulations; or the objector might take the matter to court on the basis that the agency was acting outside of Congress's intentions in the law.

Bureaucratic Legislation

The types of laws passed by Congress are many and varied, and thus policy implementation encompasses many different bureaucratic activities. Some laws are very vague and offer agencies very little guidance about implementation. Other laws can be very specific in directing the agency how to implement it. When laws are vague, agencies are said to have **administrative discretion,** which gives them considerable freedom in deciding how to implement the law. Vague laws require an agency to spend more time and effort in developing regulations.

Two policy areas where congressional legislation tends to be vague and where agencies have much latitude in making rules and regulations are environmental quality and workplace safety. Important pieces of legislation, such as the Clean Air Act and the Occupational Safety and Health Act, have given agencies such as the Environmental Protection Agency (EPA) and Occupational Safety and Health Administration (OSHA) much discretion in setting specific standards for car emissions, pollution, and workplace safety standards. This discretion usually is the product of at least one of two conditions. First, Congress often does not have the technical expertise to define how to achieve clean air or workplace safety, and so it gives agencies that have such technical capabilities the discretion to set standards. Second, Congress sometimes chooses not to deal with politically difficult issues such as how to clean up toxic-waste dumps, and so it "tosses the ball" to the bureaucracy, forcing an agency to resolve the problem. When an agency makes an unpopular decision as a result of Congress's "passing the buck," the agency's action contributes further to the negative image of bureaucracies.

When Congress writes vague legislation and thus transfers legislative authority to an agency, it gives that agency the effective power to make laws, a constitutional power that is supposed to rest with the Congress alone. When Congress does this, it is said to have **delegated congressional power.** Laws that relate to the authority of administrative agencies and the rules promulgated by those agencies are referred to as **administrative law.** Congress has delegated considerable legislative authority to the EPA and OSHA to craft both environmental and workplace safety laws. Similarly, Congress has delegated a substantial amount of authority to the Federal Reserve to manage the nation's economy. The "Fed" has the power to adjust the prime interest rate in response to economic conditions to encourage investments and ward off inflation.

CHECKtheLIST

Senator Proxmire's Top Ten Golden Fleece Awards

Stories of waste in bureaucratic spending always become good fodder for calls to cut federal spending and eliminate unnecessary federal programs. Much of this "wasteful" spending is rooted in congressional "pork-barrel" spending, that is, congressional spending on projects that benefit individual members' home districts. Perhaps no one took better aim at wasteful pork-barrel spending in the federal bureaucracy than former U.S. Senator William Proxmire (D-WI). In 1975, Proxmire began what he called the "Golden Fleece Awards" as a way to target bureaucratic agencies that spent money on wasteful programs. Proxmire announced 150 awards in all. Asked to identify the top ten most egregious spending wastes, Proxmire provided the following list:

✔ **Tequila Fish:** The National Institute on Alcohol Abuse and Alcoholism for spending millions of dollars to find out if drunken fish are more aggressive than sober fish, if young rats are more likely than old rats to consume alcohol in order to reduce anxiety, and if rats can be turned into alcoholics.

✔ **The Great Wall of Bedford:** The U.S. Department of Commerce for spending $20,000 to build an 800-foot limestone replica of the Great Wall of China in Bedford, Indiana.

✔ **Buying Worcestershire Sauce:** The Department of the Army for spending $6,000 to prepare a seventeen-page document that told the federal government how to buy a bottle of Worcestershire sauce.

✔ **The New Jersey Sewer Museum:** The Environmental Protection Agency for spending $1 million to preserve a Trenton, New Jersey, sewer as a historical monument.

✔ **Lessons in Watching TV:** The Office of Education for spending $220,000 to develop a curriculum to teach college students how to watch television.

✔ **Tennis Cheating:** The National Endowment for the Humanities for a $25,000 grant to study why people cheat and act rudely on tennis courts in Virginia.

✔ **Tailhook:** The Department of the Navy for using sixty-four planes to fly 1,334 officers to the Hilton Hotel in Las Vegas for a reunion of the Tailhook Association.

✔ **$2 Million Patrol Car:** The Law Enforcement Assistance Administration for spending $2 million on a prototype police car that was never completed.

✔ **Basketball Therapy:** The Health Care Financing Administration for Medicaid payments to psychiatrists for unscheduled meetings with patients who were attending basketball games, which cost the federal government between $40 million and $80 million.

✔ **Surfing Subsidy:** The Department of Commerce for giving the Honolulu city government $28,000 to study how to spend $250,000 for a good surfing beach.

Source: Taxpayers for Common Sense website: http://www.taxpayer.net.

Delegation of power from Congress to bureaucratic agencies, however, is not typically open-ended. Congress may cede law-making authority to the bureaucracy, but it does not relinquish all power. **Congressional oversight** is the term used to describe Congress's regular monitoring of bureaucratic agency performance for the purpose of achieving accountability. Although the vast bulk of bureaucratic agencies ultimately report to the president as chief executive, Congress through its oversight function

★ Congressional oversight

Congress's exercise of its authority to monitor the activities of agencies and administrators.

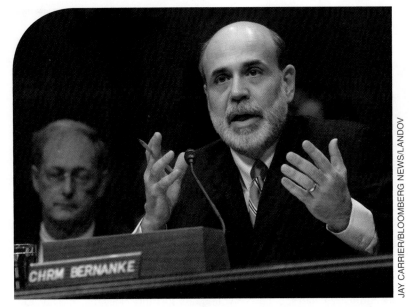

Ben Bernanke, Chairman of the Federal Reserve Board, testifies before a Senate Budget Committee hearing.

commands a significant amount of accountability from executive agencies.[5]

If Congress is not satisfied with an agency's performance, it has a variety of means to coerce change: it can reduce or eliminate an agency's budget; it can refuse to confirm presidential appointments to that agency; it can eliminate the agency; it can conduct investigations into the activities and performance of the agency; or it can establish a new agency and shift resources and powers to it. This strong system of checks often renders the federal bureaucracy just as (if not more) responsive to Congress as to the president.

Specific congressional oversight functions may be carried out in a number of ways. Particular committees (or subcommittees) in Congress hold hearings, on either a regularly scheduled or ad hoc basis, to review agency performance. For example, the House Armed Services Committee meets with the secretary of defense and Joint Chiefs of Staff to review Pentagon programs. The Senate Environment and Public Works Committee holds regular meetings with the administrator of EPA to review that agency's activities. The House Science and Technology Committee reviews the activities of NASA. In addition, the House Appropriations Committee is divided into a number of subcommittees, each of which regularly reviews pending authorizations for funding individual agencies. These subcommittees often scrutinize agency spending.

Two bureaucratic agencies under the direct control of Congress (rather than the president) that support the oversight function of congressional committees are the Congressional Budget Office (CBO) and the Government Accountability Office (GAO). These offices compile data on federal programs and are staffed with program review and accounting professionals who comply with members' and committees' requests for information on agency performance and cost. Congress uses the GAO to investigate the actions or inactions of an agency, and it uses the CBO to conduct research, such as program effectiveness studies.

Bureaucratic Adjudication

★ Bureaucratic adjudicating

Determining the rights and duties of particular parties within the scope of an agency's rules or regulations.

Just as policy implementation sometimes includes the writing of legislation, it also may involve **bureaucratic adjudicating,** or determining the rights and duties of particular parties within the scope of an agency's rules or regulations. Such adjudication might include ruling on whether an individual is eligible to receive Social Security payments, or whether a company has violated an air pollution rule. Most adjudication takes place in the court system. However Congress, which has the authority to create federal adjudicating agencies, has placed judicial power in some bureaucratic agencies as well. For example, the Equal Employment Opportunity Commission (EEOC) has the authority to adjudicate cases where an individual(s) charges that a company has violated federal laws preventing discrimination in hiring or promotion practices in the workplace. The EEOC can try a case against a company, and if the finding is that the company violated federal law, the EEOC is authorized to prescribe a punishment or corrective action.

The EEOC and other agencies such as the EPA, the National Labor Relations Board (NLRB), and the Federal Communications Commission (FCC) employ the personnel, procedures, and case law more typically seen in the judicial branch. Bureaucratic judicial personnel and powers include "administrative judges,"

[5] See Joel Aberbach, *Keeping a Watchful Eye: The Politics of Congressional Oversight* (Washington, DC: Brookings Institution Press, 1990).

appellate courts within the agency, and administrative hearings that resemble a trial. Ultimately, any administrative court decision may be appealed to the federal court system, because the power of adjudication ultimately rests in the hands of the judicial branch. In reality, however, federal courts routinely uphold cases appealed from administrative courts.

The Development of the Federal Bureaucracy

The executive branch of government during the first four years of George Washington's presidency was extremely small. Congress created just three departments to aid the first president in executing the law: the Department of State to oversee foreign affairs, the Department of Treasury to oversee fiscal affairs, and the Department of War to oversee military affairs. Washington selected and the Senate confirmed Thomas Jefferson, Alexander Hamilton, and Henry Knox to lead these departments, respectively. Shortly after these departments were created, the president was authorized to hire an attorney general and a postmaster general. During the first year of the Washington administration, the federal bureaucracy employed only about fifty individuals.

As the role of government expanded, and as the United States added new territories, there was a need to expand the size of the federal bureaucracy. Military operations, such as those conducted during the War of 1812, required increased support services and agencies to support military operations. Westward expansion brought with it the need for federal services to settle the new areas. A centralized national bank required federal agencies to centralize the economic and monetary system. By the mid-1800s, Congress saw the need to create a new Cabinet department, the Department of the Interior, to manage federally owned lands and to aid in the westward expansion of the nation. The important role of farming in the nation's growth and development led to the establishment of the Department of Agriculture in 1862 to support and promote farming and farm product commercialization. The Department of Justice was established in 1870 to aid the attorney general in the post–Civil War era in prosecuting violators of federal law and representing the federal government in the courts.

In 1884, a Bureau of Labor was created to address the concerns of the labor force that arose with the growth of the industrial economy. Large-scale industrialization and economic development led to the development of a Commerce Agency in 1888 to help regulate interstate and foreign trade. These agencies were elevated to Cabinet status in the early 1900s to reflect the growing role they played in the federal government. The Great Depression set the stage for the election of Franklin Delano Roosevelt in 1932. The FDR administration advocated an activist role for the federal government in responding to the economic crisis. Consequently, FDR's New Deal created a myriad of new federal agencies to deal with the nation's fiscal woes, including the Social Security Administration, the Securities and Exchange Commission, the Civilian Conservation Corps, and a host of public works programs to provide jobs for the large number of unemployed. In 1936, Roosevelt established the Brownlow Committee (named for its chair Louis Brownlow) to investigate how to make the growing bureaucracy more efficient and more responsive to the president.[6] The committee unanimously agreed that the president's power should be enhanced to give the president greater authority as manager of the bureaucracy. The Brownlow Committee's recommendations led to the consolidation of presidential authority over the bureaucracy.

By 1940, the federal government accounted for 10 percent of the nation's gross domestic product (GDP), with $9.5 billion spent on federal programs, including the employment of about seven hundred thousand Americans in the federal bureaucracy. The increased role of government led to greater demands for federal services, which

---

[6] Beverly Cigler, "The Paradox of Professionalization" in Camilla Stivers, ed., *Democracy, Bureaucracy and the Study of Administration* (Boulder, CO: Westview Press, 2001).

American Government . . . in Global Perspective:
One Italian Writer Experiences American Bureaucracy

Americans tend to think that our bureaucracy is far too large, complex, and difficult for most average citizens to navigate. Of course the Italian bureaucracy can more than hold its own in a battle with the American version; it is renowned by its own citizens for its size, power, and grip on Italian government, as well as for its overall complexity for Italians. In his book *Ciao, America!: An Italian Discovers the U.S.,* writer Beppe Severgnini of Italy offers a dose of perspective to Americans by chronicling the relatively pleasant experience an Italian recently had with the bureaucracy in Washington, DC:

For Italians coming to live in the United States, the greatest satisfaction . . . is grappling with American bureaucracy. Why is that? It's because, having trained on the Italian version, we feel like a matador faced with a milk cow. It's a pushover… After sorting everything out, an Italian has a craving for a few more phone calls to make, some last-minute problem to unravel, or another clerk to convince. What now follows is the story of one short but exciting morning in action against the bureaucratic legions of Washington:

The "battle station" was a phone booth at Sugar's, a Korean coffee shop on the corner of P and Thirty-fifth streets. Weapons and ammunition—five quarters, paper, pen, passport, map of the city, a good command of English, and a moderate degree of optimism. The first thing, in a country where everything is done over the phone, was to get a telephone. All this took was a call to C&P (the local—private and therefore efficient—equivalent of the Italian Telecom) to ask for a number. The clerk asked a few questions of the kind that any student on a beginner's English language course could answer—name, surname, age, address. At the end of the conversation, the same clerk told me, "Get your pen and write. This is your number. You'll be connected in twenty-four hours." Total time required for the transaction—ten minutes. Cost—twenty-five cents.

At this point, it is necessary to connect your new phone to a long-distance carrier. Competition among AT&T, MCI, and Sprint is ruthless. Each provider offers special conditions, such as discounts on numbers you call frequently, on calls to a foreign country of your choice, at particular times of day or on certain days of the week. Time required to decide—fifteen minutes. Cost—nothing. Each company has its own free phone number (which in the USA begin with 1-800).

But to apply for a Social Security number, which is the de facto equivalent in the United States of an identity card, the phone is not enough. You need to go to the appropriate office, where a clerk asks you questions and types your answers straight into a computer. Queue (sorry, line)—none. Forms—ditto. Interview time—five minutes.

Then we made a visit to the police for a temporary parking permit. (Time—fifteen minutes. Cost—nothing.) After which to open a bank account, all you need to do is turn up with the money (essential), and proof of domicile. The address on a letter is okay. A photocopy of your rent contract is even better. A temporary checkbook is issued on the spot and you can choose the definitive version from a catalog. There's the classic model, the old-fashioned type, and one with Sylvester the cartoon cat on every check. My wife, of course, insisted on Sylvester. That was perhaps the most trying moment of the entire morning.

Source: Beppe Severgnini, *Ciao, America!: An Italian Discovers the U.S.* (New York: Broadway Press, reprint edition 2003), pp. 13–14.

in turn necessitated growth in the federal bureaucracy. Between 1940 and 1975, the federal bureaucracy experienced an unprecedented growth spurt. During this period, the number of federal employees more than tripled to 2.2 million; the federal budget increased to $332 billion; and the federal budget as a percentage of the gross domestic product reached 22 percent.[7]

Two factors accounted for this massive growth in the bureaucracy. First was President Lyndon B. Johnson's Great Society program of the 1960s. The Great Society encompassed numerous new laws aimed at social and economic improvements to American society through a highly activist role of the federal government. The post–World War II prosperity of the American economy allowed Johnson to convince a Democratic Congress that programs to promote social justice, a safety net for the impoverished, improvements to urban life, guaranteed health care for the elderly, and greater access to educational opportunities should be guaranteed to all Americans and funded by the great wealth of the American economy. These programs had a large influence on growth of the bureaucracy through the 1970s.

A second factor contributing to the massive growth in the bureaucracy was the Cold War. World War II resulted in two superpowers, the United States and the Soviet Union, vying against each other for global influence. From 1945 to 1991, these superpowers developed expensive nuclear and other war technologies in search of military superiority. The federal budget for defense programs grew dramatically, as did the programs to support intelligence operations and aid to foreign nations for diplomatic purposes.

Getting Control of the Growing Bureaucracy

During the mid- to late 1970s, the American economy began to slump. Whereas the prosperity of the 1960s facilitated the creation of a larger-size government to accomplish a number of policy goals, the sluggish economy of the late 1970s was unable to support the by now very large federal bureaucracy. Federal budget deficits began to accumulate, and the United States could no longer afford the huge federal bureaucracy that it had created. Ronald Reagan was elected president in 1980 with an agenda to scale back the federal bureaucracy. The Reagan administration targeted domestic programs to achieve the reduction in government. Since the 1980s, various administrations have attempted to reduce the size of the federal bureaucracy. The methods they have used include the following:

★ **Privatization: Privatization** means replacing government-provided services with services provided by the private sector. The theory of privatization is that if private companies compete to provide services, the cost of those services will be less than if government provides those services directly. Additionally, some contend that private corporations can more flexibly adapt to changing circumstances because they are not weighed down by civil service restrictions and government red tape. Accordingly, a number of federal programs were privatized during the 1980s. For example, the U.S. Department of Labor frequently provided job training services to the unemployed during the 1960s and 1970s. Federal laws passed in the 1980s eliminated much of the federal management of job training and contracted out these services to private companies. More recently, the federal government has used a number of private contractors, including Halliburton (the company Vice President Dick Cheney formerly ran) to help rebuild Iraq after the second Persian Gulf War, under the idea that the costs would be even greater if the federal government played a more direct role.

★ Privatization

The process of replacing government-provided services with services provided by the private sector.

Chapter 8: The Federal Bureaucracy

---

[7] For a good discussion of the growth of the federal bureaucracy during the FDR years, see Brian J. Cook, *Bureaucracy and Self-Government: Reconsidering the Role of Public Administration in American Politics*, chapter 5: "Serving the Liberal State" (Baltimore: Johns Hopkins University Press, 1996).

The United States contracted with a number of private firms to repair damage caused by the war in Iraq. Here, Iraqi men rebuild a house in Baghdad destroyed by a bomb.

MARIO TAMA/GETTY IMAGES

★ **Deregulation:** The development of rules and regulations to achieve a policy goal requires units in the bureaucracy to ensure that such rules and regulations are followed. **Deregulation,** that is, eliminating government oversight and regulation of certain activities, results in less government to do the regulating. Prior to the mid-1970s, the trucking and railroad industries, long-distance telephone service, prices for air flights, and the activities of savings and loan institutions were regulated by the federal government. Deregulation of these and other activities resulted in the abolition of a number of federal agencies, including the Civil Aeronautics Board and eventually the Interstate Commerce Commission.

★ **Devolution:** A central question in our federal system of government is which level of government—national or state—should have the authority to provide programs and services to citizens. The New Deal and Great Society programs gave the national government increased responsibility and authority for such services. In response to extensive growth of the national government, the 1980s witnessed a **devolution** of power and responsibility back to the states, mainly to shrink the size of the national government. For example, welfare reform in the mid-1990s shifted much responsibility for welfare from the federal to the state governments.

★ **"Reinventing Government":** When Bill Clinton was elected president in 1992, he promised to "reinvent government." This promise translated into

★ Deregulation

The elimination of government oversight and government regulation of certain activities.

★ Devolution

The transfer of power and responsibilities for certain regulatory programs from the federal government back to the states.

238

an eight-year effort to promote bureaucratic accountability. The Clinton administration instituted mechanisms such as customer satisfaction research with those who received federal services and freedom of information policies that gave the public and the news media access to government documents to help promote accountability. In addition, the Government Performance and Results Act, passed in 1997, required that agencies establish goals and set out a plan for achieving those goals. In the book *Reinventing Government,* David Osborne and Ted Gaebler describe how bureaucracy and other aspects of the public sector in the United States have undergone a transformation.[8] They contend that the "entrepreneurial spirit" brought to bear on government performance, which includes market-driven and business-oriented planning, has improved the effectiveness and efficiency of bureaucracy at all levels of government.

In addition to implementing these strategies for reducing the size of the federal bureaucracy, the Cold War, which concluded in 1991 with the collapse of the Soviet Union, put an end to escalating annual budgets to support the arms race with the Soviets.

The end of the Cold War and the implementation of strategies that contain, if not reduce, the size of the federal bureaucracy do appear to have reversed the decades-long trend toward increasing the size of government. From 1990 until 2000, the number of civilian employees in the federal government declined by about five hundred thousand,[9] and the percentage of the GDP accounted for by federal spending dropped from 21.9 percent to 18.2 percent. Despite these efforts, however, federal spending on the bureaucracy continues to increase annually at a pace that exceeds inflation. In particular, defense spending to fight the war on terrorism and the war in Iraq in recent years have increased federal spending. Also, the Department of Homeland Security, created in response to the terrorist attacks of September 11, 2001, required increased federal dollars to protect the nation within its own borders.

The Organization of the Federal Bureaucracy

The federal bureaucracy is made up of a variety of different types of agencies that are empowered to carry out laws and federal programs. Some of these organizations have broad authority over a public policy area, whereas others have a narrow focus; some are empowered to implement laws and programs established by Congress, whereas others have the added responsibility of creating rules and policies, and adjudicating. Some report directly to the president, whereas others answer to both the president and Congress. Also, though most organizations in the federal bureaucracy are part of the executive branch, some are part of the legislative and judicial branches. Units of the federal bureaucracy include Cabinet departments, independent agencies, regulatory agencies, government corporations, and the Executive Office of the President.

Cabinet Departments

Amid the complex web of bureaucratic units is a select set of fifteen organizations called **Cabinet departments,** which are the major administrative organizations of the executive branch. These departments vary in terms of both size and importance. The Department of Defense, for example, employs nearly 1 million civilian workers, and another 1.5 million military personnel. By contrast, the Department of Education has only about five thousand employees.

★ Cabinet departments

Those federal agencies that qualify as the major administrative organizations of the executive branch.

[8] David Osborne and Ted Gaebler, *Reinventing Government: How the Entrepreneurial Spirit Is Transforming the Public Sector* (New York: Penguin Books, 1993).
[9] Harold S. Stanley and Richard G. Niemi, *Vital Statistics on American Politics, 2005–2006* (Washington, DC: CQ Press, 2006), p. 266.

Table 8.1 The Cabinet Departments

The Cabinet Departments

Department of State

The Department of State has been the leading U.S. foreign affairs agency since 1789, and the secretary of state is the president's principal foreign policy adviser. The State Department engages in the following activities: it leads in the coordination and development of U.S. foreign policy; it manages the foreign affairs budget and other foreign affairs resources; it represents the United States abroad, conveying U.S. foreign policy to foreign governments and international organizations through U.S. embassies and consulates in foreign countries and diplomatic missions to international organizations; and it negotiates agreements and treaties on issues ranging from trade to nuclear weapons.

Department of Treasury

The Treasury Department, also established in 1789, is entrusted with a broad range of duties and functions. It is responsible for paying all the bills of the federal government, collecting federal taxes, borrowing money for the federal government, printing money, and overseeing the operations of national banks. In addition to these monetary functions, the Department of the Treasury also oversees critical functions in enforcement and economic policy development. The Internal Revenue Service and the U.S. Mint are part of the Treasury Department.

Department of Defense

First called the Department of War in 1789, the Department of Defense (DOD) currently employs nearly 1 million civilians far more than any other agency in the federal bureaucracy. These employees, for the most part, work at military bases around the United States. In 1947, the separate Departments of the Army, Navy, Air Force, Marines, and Coast Guard were reorganized into the new Department of Defense to achieve greater efficiency and coordination. In addition to its large civilian workforce, the Department is responsible for 1.5 million active-duty military personnel, and another 1.2 million in the Guard and Reserve.

Department of Justice

The Office of Attorney General was created in 1789 as an adviser to the president, and in 1870 was elevated to cabinet department status. The role of the Department of Justice (DOJ) is to prevent and control crime, to punish those who are guilty of unlawful behavior, to enforce the nation's immigration laws, and to administer the justice system. DOJ employs U.S. attorneys who prosecute offenders and represent the U.S. government in court. It also oversees the Federal Bureau of Investigation (FBI), the Drug Enforcement Administration (DEA), the Bureau of Prisons, and the United States Marshals Service (USMS), which protects the federal judiciary, apprehends fugitives, and detains people in federal custody.

Department of the Interior

The Department of the Interior (DOI), created in 1849, is responsible for maintaining and managing federally owned land, which includes about 20 percent of the nation's landmass. It maintains 900 dams and reservoirs that provide water to more than 30 million Americans. The department also handles federal relations with Native American tribes. Located within the department, the Bureau of Indian Affairs manages nearly 60 million acres of land held in trust by the United States. Finally, the DOI manages the national park system, which includes 388 parks and 540 wildlife refuges.

Department of Agriculture

The U.S. Department of Agriculture (USDA) was created in 1862 by Congress at the request of President Abraham Lincoln. At the time, nearly half of all U.S. workers were employed in farming. The USDA originally was created to provide farmers with seeds and information for improving farm production and services. Today, the USDA runs the school lunch, school breakfast, and food stamp programs; brings housing, telecommunications, and safe drinking water to rural farmland areas; is responsible for the safety of meat, poultry, and egg products; and provides research on farm technologies and safe food-handling practices.

Department of Commerce

Originally part of the U.S. Department of Commerce and Labor created in 1903, the independent Department of Commerce (DOC) was established in 1913. Today, the DOC provides comprehensive statistical analysis of economic conditions in the United States, manages patent and trademark protection programs, and is responsible for conducting the U.S. Census. The department also provides grants to economically distressed areas for business and job development, promotes exports of U.S. manufactured goods, promotes the growth of minority-owned businesses, and runs the National Oceanic and Atmospheric Administration, which forecasts weather and environmental conditions.

Table 8.1 The Cabinet Departments (*continued*)

The Cabinet Departments (*continued*)

Department of Labor

The mission of the Department of Labor (DOL), created in 1913, is to promote the welfare of the job seekers, wage earners, and retirees of the United States by improving their working conditions, advancing their opportunities for profitable employment, protecting their retirement and health care benefits, helping employers find workers, strengthening free collective bargaining, and tracking changes in employment, prices, and other national economic measurements. The department administers a variety of federal labor laws including those that guarantee workers' rights to safe and healthful working conditions; a minimum hourly wage and overtime pay; freedom from employment discrimination; unemployment insurance; and other income support.

Department of Housing and Urban Development

The Department of Housing and Urban Development (HUD), created in 1965, is the federal department primarily responsible for dealing with the nation's housing needs. It administers programs that help cities and communities develop and rehabilitate. Many of HUD's activities focus on the nation's urban areas, providing housing assistance and public housing projects in many cities.

Department of Transportation

The Department of Transportation (DOT), established in 1966, sets federal transportation policy and works with state and local governments along with private-sector partners to promote a safe, secure, efficient, and interconnected national transportation system of roads, railways, pipelines, airways, and seaways. DOT is responsible for managing more than a dozen agencies, including the Federal Aviation Administration, the Federal Highway Administration, the National Highway Traffic Safety Administration, and the Federal Railroad Administration.

Department of Energy

The Department of Energy (DOE) was created in 1978 in response to an energy crisis spawned by a reduction in the production of oil from the Middle East. Today DOE helps protect national security by applying advanced science and nuclear technology to the nation's defense, manages programs to promote diverse energy sources, and is responsible for disposal of the nation's high-level radioactive waste.

Department of Education

The U.S. Department of Education, created in 1978, was originally one part of the Department of Health, Education and Welfare. The department is responsible for administering a variety of federal programs supporting aid to local public schools and college tuition loan programs. The Office of Civil Rights within this department is responsible for administering Title IX of the Education Amendments of 1972 to the Civil Rights Act of 1964, which requires that educational institutions receiving federal funds maintain policies, practices, and programs that do not discriminate on the basis of sex. In accordance with Title IX, colleges must provide the same opportunities for sports team participation for women as they do for men.

Department of Health and Human Services

Created in 1978, the Department of Health and Human Services (HHS) administers more than three hundred federal programs, covering a wide range of health and human services topics. These programs focus on medical and social science research, preventing the outbreak of infectious disease, immunization services, assuring food and drug safety, financial assistance and services for low-income families, improving maternal and infant health, preventing child abuse and domestic violence, substance abuse treatment and prevention, services for older Americans, including home-delivered meals, and comprehensive health services for Native Americans. HHS has the largest of the cabinet department budgets, over $500 billion for 2006.

Department of Veterans Affairs

This department, created in 1988, is charged with overseeing programs that promote the interest and general welfare of veterans of the U.S. military. The department operates the Veterans Health Administration and the Veterans Benefits Administration.

Department of Homeland Security

Created in 2002, the Department of Homeland Security (DHS) is the newest of the cabinet departments. It was created in response to the terrorist attacks of September 11, 2001. The department's main role to protect the nation against further terrorist attacks within the nation's borders.

President George W. Bush meets with his Cabinet in February 2007 in the White House Cabinet Room.

At the head of each Cabinet department is a secretary (with the exception of the Justice Department, which is headed by the attorney general) who reports directly to the president. Along with a few other high-level presidential advisers and the vice president, these secretaries comprise the president's Cabinet, a set of high-level administrators who report directly to the president. Cabinet heads and their deputies are nominated by the president and must be confirmed by the Senate. Typically, a secretary shares the same views as the president on policy matters and often is a loyal political supporter (if not close friend) of the chief executive. The "inner cabinet" is a term used to describe the secretaries of the most important departments in the cabinet—State, Defense, Treasury, and Justice. Whereas the Cabinet once served as the president's primary advisory panel, the growth in the Executive Office of the President, discussed later in this chapter, has shifted primary advisory responsibilities to that office.

Cabinet departments (sometimes referred to as executive departments) generally have a broad scope of authority over a particular policy area, such as the nation's military (the Department of Defense), federal law enforcement (the Department of Justice), the federal road and highway system (the Department of Transportation), and protecting the nation from terrorism and responding to emergency situations (Department of Homeland Security). The scope of activities in any one department tends to be so broad that most departments are best viewed as a collection of many different agencies and sub-agencies, each with a narrower policy focus.

The U.S. Department of Labor, for example, is charged with promoting the American labor force and the interests of labor. It is organized into a large array of agencies and offices, each of which focuses on a particular aspect of labor issues. The Occupational Safety and Health Administration (OSHA) develops standards to promote safe workplace environments, and implements regulations to ensure that employers live up to these standards. The Bureau of Labor Statistics (BLS) is responsible for compiling data on the labor force on a regular basis. The Office of Labor-Management Standards (OLMS) sets policies for the conduct of negotiations between employers and employees.

Likewise, the U.S. Department of Defense manages the armed forces, and is organized into a number of subunits, including the Army, Navy, Air Force, and the National Guard. The hierarchical organization of departments facilitates the bureaucratic goals of area specialization, division of labor, and chain of command.

Although the head of a cabinet department advises and reports directly to the president, only Congress has the authority to create a new department or eliminate an existing one. The power to define the scope, authority, and indeed the very existence of a specific major department in the federal bureaucracy is an important "check" that Congress exercises over the president.

Special situations, and particularly crises, have led the U.S. government to create cabinet-level departments to deal with large-scale national problems. The creation

of the Department of Defense in 1947, for example, was in response to large and costly inefficiencies in military operations during World War II. The Department of Energy was established in 1977 in response to the severe energy crisis and gasoline shortage that plagued the country during the 1970s. President Reagan successfully pressed for the creation of a Veterans Affairs Department in 1988 in order to promote his administration's appreciation of those who served in the U.S. military. The newest cabinet department is the Department of Homeland Security (DHS), established in 2002.

ALEX WONG/GETTY IMAGES

Michael Chertoff, pictured above at a press conference, was the second secretary of the newest cabinet department, the Department of Homeland Security.

The Department of Homeland Security

The terrorist attacks of September 11, 2001, led to President George W. Bush's request to Congress to create the new department. At first, Bush resisted calls for another large unit in the federal bureaucracy. But given strong support in Congress and in the public for a unit to be in charge of the nation's security, he became an advocate of its creation. DHS represents a reorganization of twenty-two existing federal agencies into one Cabinet department. The reorganization was intended to improve the coordination and operations of these agencies in protecting the nation against threats to the homeland.

The primary units of DHS are the following:

★ **Border and Transportation Security:** This unit includes the U.S. Customs Service (previously part of the U.S. Department of Treasury) and the former Immigration and Naturalization Service (previously part of the U.S. Department of Justice).

★ **Emergency Preparedness and Response:** This unit includes the Federal Emergency Management Agency (FEMA), formerly an independent agency, and the National Domestic Preparedness Office (previously in the FBI).

★ **Science and Technology:** This unit includes a variety of scientific research offices formerly part of the U.S. Departments of Energy, Defense, and Agriculture.

Presidents choose the leaders of their cabinets, and those chosen are most often high-level political supporters and friends of the president, as well as those who agree with the chief executive on key issues of public policy. Even though the president makes all these high-level appointments, conflicts between department heads are not uncommon. Substantive differences of opinion on important policy matters are often the source of the conflict. Discord among high-ranking officials may sometimes play out in the media and become a source of embarrassment to presidents. Yet Cabinet leaders' differences of opinion on key policy matters may not always be a bad thing, because they give the president a variety of perspectives from which to make a choice.

From 1789 through 1793, President George Washington's Cabinet included Secretary of State Thomas Jefferson and Secretary of the Treasury Alexander Hamilton. Washington's desire for his Cabinet officers to work closely with each other and provide coordinated advice to him was soon dashed as severe conflicts broke out between these two men. Their primary disagreement was over Hamilton's proposal to create a central national bank. Hamilton believed that the federal government had the authority to establish such a bank, which he saw as necessary to solve the nation's economic problems. For Jefferson, the creation of a central bank exceeded the authority of the central government. The conflict between these top two Cabinet officials reflected a battle between Jefferson's "state's rights" beliefs and Hamilton's "strong central government" views. In the end, Washington sided with Hamilton, and a central bank was created.

From 1977 through 1979, President Jimmy Carter's foreign policy team included Secretary of State Cyrus Vance and National Security Advisor Zbigniew Brzezinski. Brzezinski was a close adviser to the president and over time came to take on more and more of the responsibilities normally under the purview of the secretary of state. For example, Carter in 1978 sent Brzezinski to Beijing to help normalize China–U.S. relations. As an emissary for Carter, Brzezinski assumed state functions beyond those of a policy adviser. The role Brzezinski played caused mounting friction between himself and Vance. This friction came to a head in 1979 over the U.S. response to the Iranian hostage crisis. Vance favored a policy of recognizing the Ayatollah Khomeini and negotiating with him, whereas Brzezinski favored U.S. military action to remove Khomeini. When Brzezinski convinced Carter to approve a plan to rescue the hostages by force (which failed), Secretary of State Vance resigned.

In 2003, George W. Bush found two of his inner-circle Cabinet secretaries locked in a profound battle over the question of whether or not the United States should militarily intervene in Iraq. Iraqi leader Saddam Hussein had continuously defied UN resolutions regarding inspections to locate sites used for the development of weapons of mass destruction. Secretary of State Colin Powell advocated a diplomatic solution, threatening the use of the U.S. military only if the UN would endorse such action. Secretary of Defense Donald Rumsfeld argued for U.S. military action even without UN approval (France, Germany, and Russia, and members of the UN Security Council had refused to support military intervention). In the end, President Bush sided with Rumsfeld, and the United States went to war with Iraq without the UN's full support. These conflicting positions between the president's top two foreign policy advisers reflect Rumsfeld's "hawkish" military perspective and Powell's more "realist" perspective. Powell resigned after President Bush's re-election in 2004; meanwhile, Rumsfeld remained defense secretary until December of 2006, resigning soon after the 2006 midterm elections.

NASA/GETTY IMAGES

* **Information Analysis and Infrastructure Protection:** Parts of this unit include the Federal Incident Computer Response Center, which was previously part of the General Services Administration (GSA), and the National Incident Protection Center (formerly in the FBI).

* **The Secret Service**, which was previously in the Treasury Department.

* **The U.S. Coast Guard.**

In addition to maintaining the authority to carry out many of the nation's laws, the Cabinet also plays a symbolic role in the political system. Many interest groups provide input to the president through leaders in the Cabinet, and the voices of community and business leaders are often heard first by Cabinet department officials. As the highest-level units in the bureaucracy, Cabinet departments theoretically represent the most important policy areas. Increasingly, presidents have used their Cabinet secretary appointments to demonstrate diversity in government. For nearly two centuries, Cabinet secretaries were almost exclusively white men, but over the last twenty years presidents have used race and gender as factors influencing their appointments. President Clinton made history by naming women to the inner cabinet for the first time: Janet Reno as attorney general in 1993, and Madeleine Albright as secretary of state in 1997. President George W. Bush similarly made history by appointing the first African American to the inner cabinet: Colin Powell as secretary of state in 2001. In 2005, Bush appointed an African American woman, Condoleezza Rice, as Powell's replacement; he also appointed the first Hispanic to the inner cabinet when he named Alberto Gonzales as the nation's attorney general during his second term in office.

NASA is an independent agency with a highly trained technical and scientific staff. Pictured above is the NASA control room in Houston, Texas, during the flight of the Columbia space shuttle mission in 2003.

Independent Agencies

A number of units in the federal bureaucracy do not have the high status of a Cabinet department, but at the same time they report directly to the president. Whereas Cabinet departments tend to concentrate on broad areas, such as labor, energy, defense, or education, these **independent agencies,** which are not part of any executive Cabinet department, tend to focus on a narrower scope of issues. NASA, for example, focuses on the U.S. space program, whereas the Small Business Administration (SBA) concentrates on low-cost loans and support to encourage the development of small businesses. Independent agencies tend to be smaller than Cabinet departments. The heads of these agencies are appointed by and report to the president.

★ Independent agency

A department that focuses on a narrower set of issues than do higher-status Cabinet departments.

Regulatory Agencies

Regulatory agencies are responsible for implementing rules and regulations with respect to individual or corporate conduct related to some aspect of the economy. Such agencies are supposed to be staffed by nonpartisan individuals who are entrusted to make sound decisions that promote fairness and weed out corrupt practices on fiscal matters. To accomplish this, regulatory agencies (unlike Cabinet departments and independent agencies) are not under the control of the president. They are created by Congress and are run by independent boards or commissions that are not supposed to exert partisan influence.

The first regulatory agency was the Interstate Commerce Commission (ICC), created by Congress in 1887.[10] As with the creation of most regulatory agencies, the ICC was the federal government's response to widespread corruption. In the

★ Regulatory agency

A government body responsible for the control and supervision of a specified activity or area of public interest.

Chapter 8: The Federal Bureaucracy

---

[10] Robert H. Wiebe, *The Search for Order: 1877–1920* (New York: Hill and Wang, 1967).

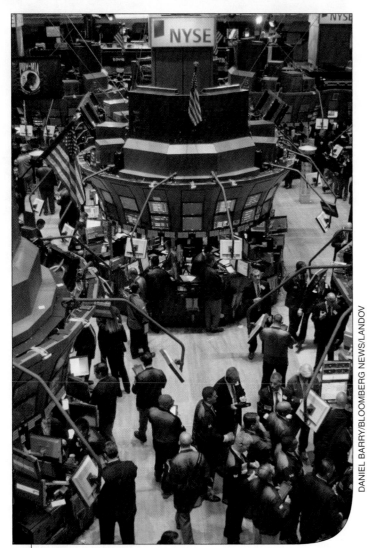

The SEC, a regulatory agency, regulates the activities of traders on the busy floor of the New York Stock Exchange, pictured above in May 2007.

DANIEL BARRY/BLOOMBERG NEWS/LANDOV

case of the ICC, the target was corruption in the railroad industry, which led to the high cost of railroad transportation. The ICC's scope of responsibility extended to regulation of commerce not only via railroad, but also via pipeline, barge, automobile, and aircraft. The ICC established a complex set of rates for both passenger and freight transportation via the various modes of transport. ICC rules were intended to guarantee that transportation companies pay a fair fee on the value of property they used in carrying out their services. Congress abolished the ICC in 1995 because it determined that it was overregulating and thus stymieing growth in certain business sectors.

Today's federal bureaucracy includes a number of important regulatory agencies:

★ **The Federal Trade Commission (FTC):** The FTC was established in 1914 and has the authority to develop and implement rules and regulations to encourage competition in industry. Over the years, the FTC has played an instrumental role in preventing "price fixing" policies of corporations.

★ **The Federal Communications Commission (FCC):** The FCC was established in 1934 with the authority to regulate radio, television, and interstate telephone companies. Unlike newspapers, which are not regulated, radio and TV stations use public airwaves, making them subject to regulations developed and administered by the FCC.

★ **The Securities and Exchange Commission (SEC):** The SEC is responsible for rule making with respect to the stock market and corporate bookkeeping practices. It was created in 1934 in response to the stock market crash of 1929.

★ **The Equal Employment Opportunity Commission (EEOC):** Created by Congress to help administer the Civil Rights Acts of 1964, the EEOC is charged with investigating violations of the act.

★ **The Environmental Protection Agency (EPA):** The EPA was created in response to the environmental protection movement of the 1960s and 1970s. Concerns about air and water quality, as well as hazardous waste materials, led Congress to pass a number of important laws that addressed antipollution measures and empowered the EPA (in 1970) to implement environmental regulations. The EPA is the largest of the regulatory agencies.

★ **The Consumer Product Safety Commission (CPSC):** Consumer advocacy was also a movement that gained steam in the 1960s and 1970s. Efforts to make manufacturers produce products that were safer for consumers were an important feature of that movement. The CPSC was created in 1972 to protect the public against risks associated with consumer products.

Government Corporations

A small number of units in the federal bureaucracy are set up to run like private companies even though they serve an important public purpose. These are called **government corporations.** The idea behind a government corporation is that there is a market of customers who are willing to pay individually for the services provided by the corporation. The revenue on which the government corporation relies comes primarily from citizens paying for the service provided by the corporation. Unlike private corporations, government has a special interest in the solvency of government corporations because they serve an important public purpose. Consequently, when the revenue of a government corporation falls short of meeting expenses, government often will intervene to keep the unit in business.

The most widely known and used government corporation is the U.S. Postal Service (USPS), which employs nearly 1 million workers. The primary source of funds for the USPS comes from the sale of U.S. postage stamps. Similar to a private business, the USPS has a product to offer (mail delivery) and charges a fee (the cost of postage) for use of that service.

Another government corporation is the Tennessee Valley Authority (TVA), which serves the power needs of seven states in the Tennessee Valley and operates the system for navigation and flood control of the Tennessee River. Users of TVA's generated power pay for service, as do those who navigate on the Tennessee River. Another well-known government corporation is AMTRAK, a railroad service operated by the National Railroad Passenger Corporation. AMTRAK maintains more than twenty thousand miles of track and operates five hundred stations across the nation. Its revenue is largely derived from the sale of passenger tickets; however, in recent years low ridership has forced Congress to subsidize AMTRAK from the general revenue fund.

★ Government corporations

Units in the federal bureaucracy set up to run like private companies that depend on revenue from citizens to provide their services.

The Executive Office of the President

The president of the United States has an office staff that reports directly to the president, provides advice and counsel, and helps the president manage the rest of the federal bureaucracy. The **Executive Office of the President** is managed by the White House Chief of Staff and includes a Communications Office, a press secretary, a Council of Economic Advisors (to provide advice and management of the bureaucratic agencies responsible to the economy), a National Security Council (to provide advice on foreign and military affairs), an Office of Management and Budget (to coordinate and provide data on the national budget), a White House Counsel (to provide legal advice to the president), an Office of Science and Technology, an Office of the U.S. Trade Representative, and an Office of National Drug Control Policy, among others.

★ Executive Office of the President

The staffers who help the president of the United States manage the rest of the federal bureaucracy.

The Federal Workforce

The federal bureaucracy encompasses an immense workforce. Currently it employs approximately 2.7 million civilian personnel.[11] This number excludes the 1 million U.S. postal workers, and the 1.5 million U.S. military personnel.

Political Appointees and Career Professionals

About eight thousand members of this federal workforce are presidential appointees, some of whom must be confirmed by the Senate. Those requiring Senate confirmation include Cabinet secretaries and the attorney general, heads of independent agencies, ambassadors, U.S. attorneys, and other high-level officers who have administrative responsibility. When a president's term of office expires, the new

---

[11] Harold S. Stanley and Richard G. Niemi, *Vital Statistics on American Politics, 2005–2006* (Washington, DC: CQ Press, 2006), p. 266.

Many of the federal bureaucracy's "alphabet soup" agencies were created as New Deal programs during the administration of President Franklin Delano Roosevelt. Pictured above are workers at one such agency, the Tennessee Valley Authority, seen here assembling a new power generator at the Cherokee Dam on the Holston River in east Tennessee.

★ Senior Executive
   Service (SES)

Since the late 1970s, a defined group of approximately seventy-five hundred career professionals in the federal bureaucracy who provide continuity in the operations of the bureaucracy from one presidential administration to the next.

president generally fills these positions with new appointees. Presidential appointees are frequently referred to as "political" appointees because the job often represents a political reward for past service to the president or the president's political party.

Another seventy-five hundred of the 2 million plus civilian federal employees are part of what is called the **Senior Executive Service (SES).** These are senior officers in the federal bureaucracy who are career professionals. Those in the SES do not leave their positions when a new president takes office but work closely with presidential appointees and provide continuity in the operations of the federal bureaucracy from one presidential administration to the next. Congress established the SES in the late 1970s as a means of providing this continuity in leadership. Congress also spelled out a nonpartisan process for hiring SES officers based on educational background, work experience, and other qualifications.

Presidential appointees are largely selected to reflect the political orientation of the president, and senior executives are selected primarily to find highly qualified career professionals who maintain stability in the operations of the bureaucracy. Together, these groups of employees provide leadership and senior management of the units in the federal bureaucracy.

The Civil Service

The vast majority of the federal bureaucracy workforce is known as the **civil service.** Similar to the SES, civil service workers in the federal bureaucracy are theoretically hired for their position based on their qualifications, and remain employees beyond the term of a particular president. Thus they are supposed to be immune from partisan political maneuvering. Civil service jobs were not always insulated from partisan politics, as they are today. To understand the rules and processes for employment in the federal bureaucracy, it is useful to examine how employment in the federal workforce has changed over the years.

During the early years of the American republic, continuous recruitment of well-educated upper-middle-class men who tended to come from "higher society" characterized the development of the federal bureaucracy. Presidents Washington, Adams, and Jefferson hired political, business, and social elites to carry out the activities of the federal bureaucracy. With the exception of top posts in government such as Cabinet secretaries, those in federal jobs usually remained from one presidential administration to the next. This tradition ensured an able and effective federal workforce, albeit a nondiverse one.

President Andrew Jackson, elected to office in 1828, undertook a massive restructuring of the federal workforce. Jackson ran for the presidency as a populist advocating for the interests of the "common man." Upon taking office, he chose to remove individuals in the bureaucracy who were not at all "common," and who found themselves politically at odds with the new president. Resistance among many in the bureaucracy to follow Jackson's orders, along with the president's own desire to see that the bureaucracy more closely reflected the demographics of American society, led Jackson to undertake a major overhaul of the bureaucratic workforce.

Jackson replaced the long-term, upper-middle-class bureaucrats with political supporters and friends who came from many walks of life. This **spoils system** of hiring federal workers quickly became a steadfast American tradition. To the victors of presidential elections went the spoils of jobs in the federal government. Under this system of **patronage,** campaigning, political party activities, and governing became intertwined. Political parties enticed people to work on political campaigns by promising the payoff of a good federal job with an electoral victory. Often, those who were given a job were expected to return a percentage of their salary to the political party—a very clever fund-raising strategy. Strength of partisan support became the key criterion for landing and maintaining a good job.

Needless to say, this system of hiring workers produced a number of problems. Because qualifications to do the job were not important in the hiring decision, the bureaucracy became inefficient. Bureaucrats were more concerned about campaigning and supporting the political party than they were about doing their job. Further, the bureaucracy lacked any sort of continuity—for when the partisan control of the presidency changed hands, federal workers were fired en masse and replaced by a new set of underqualified political appointees.

By the time of the Civil War, the spoils system was entrenched and the bureaucracy was thoroughly corrupt. A civil service reform movement arose in the post–Civil War era, advocating an end to the spoils system and the development of a "professionalized" bureaucracy. Strong resistance from the political party bosses stalled the reform movement's agenda. But the 1881 assassination of President James Garfield by a disgruntled party worker who did not receive the federal job he thought he deserved gave strength to the movement. In 1883, Congress passed the **Pendleton Civil Service Reform Act,** which did the following:[12]

★ Civil service

The system whereby workers in the federal bureaucracy are supposed to be immune from partisan political maneuvering.

★ Spoils system

The postelection practice of rewarding loyal supporters of the winning candidates and party with appointive public offices.

★ Patronage

The act of appointing people to government positions.

★ Pendleton Civil Service Reform Act

The 1883 law that created a merit system for hiring many federal workers, protected them from being fired for partisan reasons, and set up a Civil Service Commission to oversee the hiring and firing process.

---

[12] See Ari Hoogenboom, *Outlawing the Spoils: A History of the Civil Service Reform Movement, 1865–1883* (Champaign: University of Illinois Press, 1961).

A system of appointing and promoting civil service personnel based on merit rather than political affiliation or loyalty.

★ It created a **merit system** for hiring many federal workers based on qualifications for the job, including educational background, related job experience, and performance on civil service tests.

★ It prevented employees from losing their federal jobs when the presidency changed hands.

★ It set up a Civil Service Commission to oversee federal hiring and firing practices.

Initially, the Pendleton Act applied only to a limited portion of the federal workforce, but it provided the basis for Progressive Era reformers of the early 1900s to develop a more professional bureaucracy through additional reform legislation. Today job qualifications in federal hiring and federal worker immunity from patronage are firmly rooted in the federal bureaucracy's employment practices. These principles now apply to more than 90 percent of federal workers.

★ Hatch Act of 1939

The 1939 law that insulated the civil service from partisan politics by prohibiting employee dismissals for partisan reasons and by prohibiting federal workers from participating in political campaigns.

The **Hatch Act of 1939** further insulated the civil service from partisan politics by (1) prohibiting the dismissal of an employee for partisan reasons (with the exception of certain high-level political appointments) and (2) prohibiting federal workers from running for office or actively campaigning for a political candidate. In the early 1990s, revisions to the Hatch Act relaxed some of the more stringent requirements of the law and allowed federal workers more flexibility in engaging in political activities. Those in the civil service can now participate in campaigns outside of their work hours, contribute money to a candidate or party, express partisan opinions, and wear campaign buttons, among other activities. However, under the current law, federal workers still cannot be candidates in a partisan election or use their official position to raise money or influence votes.

★ Civil Service Reform Act of 1978

The federal act that replaced the Civil Service Commission (the agency that oversaw federal hiring and firing practices) with the Office of Personnel Management (OPM) and the Merit Systems Protection Board (MSPB).

The **Civil Service Reform Act of 1978** replaced the Civil Service Commission with the Office of Personnel Management (OPM) and the Merit Systems Protection Board (MSPB). OPM and MSPB, bureaucratic agencies themselves, manage the civil service system today. Their functions include administering the system of federal hiring, protecting the rights of federal employees, conducting hearings and deciding cases where there are charges of wrongdoing in hiring and firing of employees, evaluating the effectiveness of federal hiring and retention practices, and regulating the ways in which federal workers can participate in politics.

Getting a Job in the Federal Government

Applying for a job in the federal government is much different than applying for a job at a company. For one thing, most federal jobs require that the applicant take and pass a civil service examination. And once you have a federal job, you may find that the job itself is much different than a job in the private sector. In his book *Insider's Guide to Finding a Job in Washington,* Bruce Maxwell lists four primary advantages of having a job in the federal bureaucracy:[13]

★ "The federal government is the nation's largest employer, and has lots of jobs. In January 1999, in the Washington area the executive branch employed 293,584 people—and that's just civilians. Between January 1998 and January 1999, federal agencies and departments together hired an average of 3,272 new employees each month in the Washington area."

★ "Federal jobs provide excellent job security. It's true that the federal government has been on a downsizing kick in recent years, but the vast majority of the job cuts have occurred through attrition and buyouts, not layoffs. The downsizing trend has now largely tapered off. In fact, between January 1998 and January 1999, the number of executive branch employees in the Washington area grew by 4,254."

[13] Bruce Maxwell, *Insider's Guide to Finding a Job in Washington* (Washington, DC: CQ Press, 2000), pp. 74–75.

★ "In general, federal wages and benefits are good, and are comparable to those in the private sector. Federal workers in the Washington area got a 3.68 percent pay hike in January 1999, raising the salary of the average white-collar employee to $59,307."

★ "Workers who retire from the federal government receive excellent pension benefits."

Job openings in the federal bureaucracy are advertised in what is known as a "vacancy announcement," which includes job title, pay grade level, application submission deadlines, where the job is located, a description of the job duties, a description of the requirements for the job, and procedures for applying for the position. The Office of Personnel Management (OPM) is the federal agency responsible for coordinating and distributing information on hiring and vacancy announcements in the federal government. OPM provides updated information on jobs at the following website: http://www.usajobs.opm.gov.

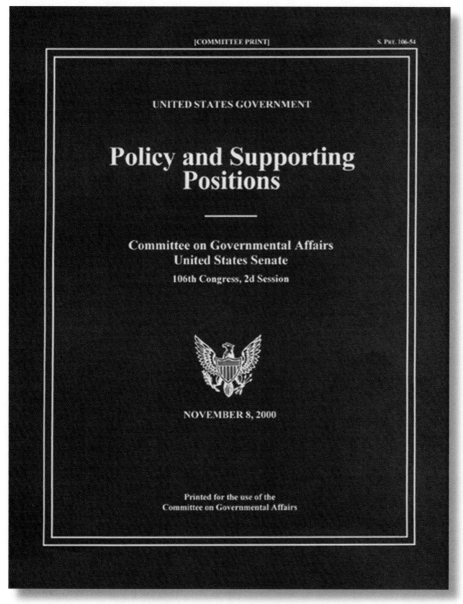

Pictured above is the "plum book," which provides a listing of all job openings in the federal bureaucracy.

Now & Then: Making the Connection

The federal bureaucracy has grown dramatically since the George Washington administration. As new presidents seek to advance new policy goals, federal departments and agencies have been created and expanded. These agencies have aided presidents in accomplishing new feats and bringing the United States to world "superpower" status. Unfortunately, the growth of government is only rarely accompanied by efforts to streamline government or to make it run more efficiently. As a consequence, bureaucracy designed to aid and support the president's goals may do as much to hinder those goals as to further them.

After President Franklin Roosevelt was reelected in 1936, he was determined to search for more logical ways to structure government. Some of the Brownlow Committee's recommendations were incorporated into the Reorganization Act of 1939, which in turn led to the creation of the Executive Office of the President. President Bill Clinton was determined to "reinvent government" by getting rid of archaic rules and regulations and increase government accountability. Both of these presidents accomplished their goals to a degree. And yet a visitor to the federal government today would find just as much waste and inefficiency, and as many archaic rules as ever before.

Over the centuries, presidents, with the support of the American people, have used the bureaucracy to accomplish important policy goals. The bureaucracy has also served as the "whipping boy" in rhetorical campaigns for political office. In many instances the bureaucracy has earned its reputation as wasteful, inefficient, and bloated. But without the federal bureaucracy, the most important national initiatives could not have been realized. Even those presidents who campaigned on a platform to cut the bureaucracy ended up using it to advance important initiatives. The federal bureaucracy is an easy target of criticism, yet there is no denying the fact that it has contributed as much to the development of the American political system as any other part of the political system.

The failure of the federal intelligence agencies to thwart the September 11, 2001, terrorist attacks spawned calls for a total reorganization of the federal government's intelligence agencies. Critics claimed that bureaucratic fighting among agencies resulted in a lack of communication about potential terrorist activities. Calls for changes to the federal intelligence capability became deafening when it became apparent that Saddam Hussein's Iraqi government did not have weapons of mass destruction, undermining Bush administration claims that had been used to justify the 2003 invasion of Iraq.

The Intelligence Reform and Terrorist Prevention Act of 2004 (IRTPA) was the federal government's response to failures within intelligence community. The Act created the White House Office of the Director of National Intelligence (ODNI). The ODNI is responsible for coordinating the work of a number of pre-existing intelligence agencies, and facilitating communication between them. The ODNI director is the point person for the president in terms of budget recommendations and national strategic planning for the country's intelligence needs.

On http://academic.cengage.com/dautrich, find the politics interactive link for details on the ODNI and its current activities. Consult as well the various links that relate to the process of gathering intelligence for national security purposes. The website offers historical, popular, and global perspectives on the issue.

OFFICE OF THE
DIRECTOR
OF NATIONAL INTELLIGENCE

AP PHOTO/KEVIN WOLF

Mike McConnell, Director of National Intelligence.

http://academic.cengage.com/dautrich

Chapter Summary

★ Though the term *bureaucracy* often conjures up negative images, the government could not function effectively without bureaucratic organizations.

★ Most units in the vast federal bureaucracy are located within the executive branch of government, and most engage primarily in policy implementation. Such implementation begins with the development of regulations that guide employees of the agency in carrying out particular programs or services.

★ Because Congress lacks technical expertise, it often gives agencies wide administrative discretion to decide how to implement laws. Sometimes Congress also delegates important programs to agencies because it wants to avoid thorny political issues.

★ Congressional oversight of executive agencies may occur through legislative hearings or through the use of congressional agencies such as the CBO and GAO. Congress may threaten poorly performing agencies with reduced funding, a refusal to confirm appointments to the agency, or (in some extreme cases) the elimination of the agency altogether.

★ Congress has placed judicial power in some bureaucratic agencies to help determine the rights and duties of parties within the scope of an agency's authority.

★ The size of the federal bureaucracy exploded as the federal government played an increasingly active role in regulating the U.S. economy, overseeing new territories, and conducting overseas military operations. After FDR's New Deal was enacted during the 1930s, the federal government accounted for a sizeable portion of the nation's economy as a whole. The bureaucracy continued to expand in the 1960s and beyond to meet the needs of President Lyndon Johnson's Great Society program and to compete with the Soviet Union in the Cold War.

★ Beginning in the 1980s, some administrations attempted to reduce the size of the federal bureaucracy through (1) the privatization of certain government-provided services, (2) the deregulation of some federal activities, (3) the devolution of various powers and responsibilities back to the states, and (4) efforts to promote greater bureaucratic accountability through initiatives such as the Government Performance and Results Act.

★ The federal bureaucracy is organized into fifteen Cabinet departments including the recently created Department of Homeland Security, numerous independent agencies that focus on a narrower scope of issues, regulatory agencies that implement rules and regulations of private conduct, government corporations, and the Executive Office of the President.

★ The federal workforce includes eight thousand presidential employees who received their positions through political patronage, a Senior Executive Service consisting of approximately seventy-five hundred senior career professionals, and a vast number of civil service workers whose jobs are immune from partisan politics. Today most lower-level federal workers are hired through a merit system, rather than through the spoils systems that prevailed throughout much of the nineteenth and early twentieth centuries.

Key Terms

Administrative discretion (p. 232)

Administrative law (p. 232)

Bureaucracy (p. 228)

Bureaucratic adjudicating (p. 234)

Cabinet departments (p. 239)

Civil service (p. 249)

Civil Service Reform Act of 1978 (p. 250)

Congressional oversight (p. 233)

Delegation of congressional power (p. 232)

Deregulation (p. 238)

Devolution (p. 238)

Executive Office of the President (p. 247)

Federal Register (p. 232)

Government corporations (p. 247)

Hatch Act of 1939 (p. 250)

Independent agency (p. 245)

Merit system (p. 250)

Patronage (p. 249)

Pendleton Civil Service Reform Act (p. 249)

Policy implementation (p. 231)

Privatization (p. 237)

Regulations (p. 232)

Regulatory agency (p. 245)

Senior Executive Service (SES) (p. 248)

Spoils system (p. 249)

Resources

Important Books

Cook, Brian J. *Bureaucracy and Self-Government.* Baltimore: Johns Hopkins University Press, 1997.

Johnson, Ronald N., and Gary D. Libecap. *The Federal Civil Service System and the Problem of Bureaucracy.* Chicago: University of Chicago Press, 1994.

Maxwell, Bruce. *Insider's Guide to Finding a Job in Washington.* Washington, DC: CQ Press, 2000.

Neiman, Max. *Defending Government: Why Big Government Works.* Upper Saddle River, NJ: Prentice Hall, 2000.

Osborne, David, and Ted Gaebler. *Reinventing Government: How the Entrepreneurial Spirit Is Transforming the Public Sector.* New York: Plume Books, 1993.

Osborne, David, and Peter Plastrik. *Banishing Bureaucracy.* New York: Plume Books, 1997.

Stivers, Camilla, ed. *Democracy, Bureaucracy, and the Study of Administration.* Boulder, CO: Westview Press, 2001.

Wildavsky, Aaron. *The New Politics of the Budget Process.* 2nd ed. New York: HarperCollins, 1992.

Wilson, James Q. *Bureaucracy: What Government Agencies Do and Why They Do It.* New York: Basic Books, 1989.

Internet Resources

http://www.firstgov.gov (the U.S. government's official web portal, this site provides links to all units and subunits of the Executive Office of the President, the fifteen Cabinet departments, and most of the independent agencies, regulatory agencies, and corporations of the federal government)

The Judiciary

9

Supreme Court nominee Clarence Thomas, testifying in 1991

A Future Justice Sits on the Firing Line: Now & Then

The president's choice for the vacancy on the U.S. Supreme Court hailed originally from a small rural town in the deep South. From modest beginnings he had risen to find a place among the powerful elite in the nation's capital. Now partisans from the president's party were celebrating his nomination to a seat on the nation's highest court; protests against his nomination from the other side of the political spectrum were just as passionate. The press relentlessly lambasted the young nominee for his limited judicial experience and for shows of extreme partisanship that they felt were ill-suited to a future jurist. Then, near the end of the confirmation process, new revelations emerged that threw his future as a Supreme Court Justice into further peril. To save his appointment, he was forced to make a publicly broadcasted appeal on his own behalf that was heard by millions of Americans. Ultimately, the nominee survived Senate scrutiny to take his place on the Court. His tenure would reflect little timidity as a result of the episode; as a justice he would become a passionate advocate of what he believed.

Justice Hugo Black in 1937

1991

2007   1997   1987   1977   1967

NOW... No politically aware American over the age of thirty-five will soon forget the controversy that surrounded President George H. W. Bush's nomination of Judge Clarence Thomas to the U.S. Supreme Court during the summer of 1991. Born in the five-hundred-person town of Pinpoint, Georgia, on June 23, 1948, Thomas went on to attend Yale Law School, work as a legislative aide to Senator John Danforth (R-MO), and then land a term as chairman of the Equal Employment Opportunity Commission (EEOC) in the Reagan administration. Because Thomas was African American and had finished in the middle of his law school class, he was plagued by accusations that he was a beneficiary of affirmative action—the same policy that he opposed as head of the EEOC. Doubts about his qualifications did not stop Thomas from being appointed to a federal appeals court in 1990; nor did they prevent his nomination one year later to the U.S. Supreme Court. During the initial Senate hearings on his nomination, Thomas fended off criticisms that he was both underqualified and too overtly partisan for such an honor. Then, just before the Senate was to vote on his appointment, charges of sexual harassment brought by University of Oklahoma Law Professor Anita Hill, who had worked for Thomas at the EEOC, threw his Supreme Court nomination into serious jeopardy. In televised testimony viewed by millions of Americans, Thomas indignantly denied any wrongdoing, calling the Senate proceedings "a high-tech lynching of an uppity black man."[1] The Senate eventually confirmed Thomas by a narrow margin (52–48). Undaunted, Thomas as a Supreme Court justice consistently and ardently championed the conservative position in high-profile cases.

[1] Jane Mayer and Jill Abramson, *Strange Justice: The Selling of Clarence Thomas* (New York: Plume Books, 1995).

1957   1947   1937   1927   1917

THEN...The Supreme Court appointment process has undergone a significant transformation during the past century: it has been increasingly politicized by the significant role the Court plays in numerous policy issues, as well as the heightened media attention that now follows nominees from initial selection through confirmation. Still, Clarence Thomas's experience in 1991—when he was suddenly greeted by serious allegations concerning earlier events in his career—harkened back to a similar episode from decades earlier. Like Thomas, Hugo Lafayette Black was also the product of an impoverished rural upbringing—born in Harlan, Alabama, on February 27, 1886, he was the youngest of eight children and was raised by a small-town storekeeper. Black rose quickly through the ranks of Alabama politics; after brief stints as a police court judge and county solicitor, Black won election to the U.S. Senate in 1926. During the mid-1930s Black became a trusted foot soldier for President Franklin Roosevelt's legislative program. FDR rewarded Black for his loyalty by nominating him to the Supreme Court in 1937. Having served as a highly partisan champion of Democratic causes, Black was depicted by his foes as unqualified for the position. Later, as the Senate's vote on his confirmation neared, charges surfaced that Black had been an active member of the Ku Klux Klan while rising up the ladder of Alabama politics in the 1920s. Black survived the scrutiny and was confirmed by a 63–13 margin. Still, new revelations emerged even after the final vote—one press report charged that Black remained a KKK member in good standing to that day. Hounded by reporters, the new justice eventually gave a national radio address in which he reaffirmed his decision to resign from the KKK twelve years earlier; Black's address was heard by the second-largest radio audience to that point and ended any speculation that Roosevelt might pressure him to leave the Court. Black went on to a highly influential thirty-four-year career on the Supreme Court, establishing himself as an apostle for liberalism and an unapologetic advocate of a literal reading of the Bill of Rights.

The U.S. Supreme Court building in Washington, DC.

How was the nomination of a single justice to the U.S. Supreme Court able to capture the rapt attention of the American public in each of the two instances described above? Whenever the current composition of the Supreme Court appears split on the most controversial issues of the era, the selection of even one justice may tip the balance in one direction or another—court observers predicted that Hugo Black would solidify an emerging judicial bloc willing to uphold the constitutionality of the New Deal; Thomas's appointment would help to fortify a conservative majority favoring a more restrictive view of defendants' rights and federalism, among other areas of the law. The stakes were high indeed.

Because justices serve for life, they are not normally accountable for judicial decisions rendered while on the bench. Thus Senate hearings on Supreme Court appointments have been transformed into public forums where legislators, interest groups, and the public get their only chance to weigh in on the Court's activities. Although many such hearings are uneventful, a nominee with expressed views on hot-button issues may generate considerable interest. The personal background of the nominee often becomes part of the political fight—as happened in the cases of Black and Thomas—and the powder keg becomes even more likely to explode.

Article III of the U.S. Constitution vests in the Supreme Court the power to decide legal cases or controversies that come before it. As one of the three primary branches of the federal government, the judiciary enjoys a special status in our constitutional system. Many scholars have suggested that courts enjoy heightened prestige over other actors in government as a result of their own conscious efforts to foster the perception that they somehow stand "above the political fray." The solemn formalities that pervade so many judicial proceedings conducted by "high priests of the law"—donning black robes, the prohibition of cameras in the U.S. Supreme Court, and the general reluctance of judges to seek out publicity—contribute to a mythology about courts in general, and a "cult of the robe" that carries credence with many Americans.[2]

---

[2] For an account of the ways in which the Supreme Court's methods contribute to its image and status as an institution, see John Brigham, *The Cult of the Court* (Philadelphia: Temple University Press, 1987).

This chapter explores the nature of the federal judiciary and the specific role it plays in the U.S. political system by examining types of law and the manner in which the legal system in the United States is organized. It also explores the role state courts play in the political system and how individuals come to occupy all types of judgeships. The chapter then focuses on the U.S. Supreme Court more closely, with an eye toward learning how cases come to and are resolved by the nation's highest tribunal, and how that court is confronting some of the great issues of the day.

Types of Law

The concept of law defies simple understanding. Although law is normally defined simply as "authoritative rules made by government," the philosopher John Locke argued that certain laws precede society and government. These natural laws are god-given, exist within human beings from the time they are born, and are intrinsic to the nature of individuals. Locke's notions of natural law (as distinguished from human-made or government-issued law) have influenced the legal systems of many nations, including the United States. Prior to the Civil War, opponents of slavery challenged its legitimacy with the claim that it ran counter to natural law. During the 1960s, civil rights advocates seeking to overhaul discriminatory practices presented similar arguments.

Still, even the foremost advocates of natural law concede that the rules imposed by sovereign governments enjoy some measure of legitimacy in most instances. Those rules and laws may be created and passed down in different ways. **Civil law** (also called "statutory law") refers to legislative codes, laws, or sets of rules that are enacted by authorized lawmaking bodies such as Congress, state and local legislatures, or any executive authority entrusted with the power to make laws.[3] **Common law** refers to judge-made law handed down through judicial opinions, which establish slowly evolving precedents over time. Many European legal systems, such as those in France, Germany, and Italy, are characterized as primarily "civil law systems" due to their extensive reliance on detailed legislative codes. The legal system in Britain, by contrast, is recognized as mainly a common law system. The modern U.S. legal system features a combination of these two approaches: although the common law held sway for most of the nation's history, legislatures in all fifty states and Congress during the past century have replaced many traditional common law rules with detailed legislative codes on a number of important topics, including commercial law, probate law, and various aspects of criminal law. Other categories of law include the following:

★ **Criminal law:** The body of rules and regulations that declare what types of conduct constitute an "offense against society," and that prescribe the punishment to be imposed for those offenses. Criminal laws against murder, rape, and burglary can be found in almost any legal system. The body of non-criminal law—which includes the law of property, contracts, and other issues dealing with the private rights of citizens—is sometimes referred to as "civil law" (Be careful not to confuse references to "civil law" in this context with the "civil law" referenced earlier, which primarily concerns the enactment of statutes and codes.) Serious criminal offenses may lead to jail time; by contrast, those who violate non-criminal laws can be fined, but not imprisoned. Of course criminal law and civil law may touch on the same events—for example, a person alleged to have killed someone may be criminally prosecuted for murder and also separately sued in a "wrongful death action" for the same action. The two sets of proceedings are distinct and separate: O. J. Simpson was acquitted of murder charges brought against him by the Los Angeles County district attorney, but that did not prevent subsequent civil suits being successfully brought against him by the victims' families.

★ Civil law

There are actually two meanings to this term: (1) Legislative codes, laws, or sets of rules enacted by duly authorized lawmaking bodies such as Congress, state and local legislatures, or any executive authority entrusted with the power to make laws; (2) the body of non-criminal laws of a nation or state that deal with the rights of private citizens.

★ Common law

Judge-made law handed down through judicial opinions, which over time establish precedents.

---

[3] John Merryman, *The Civil Law Tradition* (Palo Alto, CA: Stanford University Press, 1985).

★ **Constitutional law:** The body of rules and judicial interpretations of rules found in the fundamental law of the nation or state, such as the Constitution of the United States. Normally constitutional law is considered "supreme" and overrides any statutes or executive decisions with which it comes into conflict.

★ **Administrative law:** The body of rules, regulations, orders, and decisions issued by administrative agencies of a government such as the Federal Trade Commission, the Environmental Protection Agency, the state department of health, and so on.

★ **Public law:** A term used more by academics than practitioners, this refers to the laws and rules that govern disputes and issues involving the government directly acting in its official capacity. Constitutional, administrative, and criminal laws are all subcategories of this general rubric of public law.

★ **Private law:** Refers to all parts of the law concerned with the definition, regulation, and enforcement of rights in cases where either (1) all the parties directly implicated are private individuals (such as a divorce settlement) or (2) the government is acting like any other private citizen when it sues or is being sued. For example, when a private person crashes his car into a government mail truck, the government's lawsuit against that person is usually a matter of private law rather than public law.

Significant overlap exists among all these categories of law. Knowing something about the different types of law is useful in helping to understand courts and the functions they serve in the American political system.

The Structure of the American Legal System

Every court occupies a unique position within the larger hierarchy of state and federal courts. As a result, each court performs a variety of specific roles dictated by where it happens to be situated within the larger court structure.

State Legal Systems and State Courts

Most criminal and civil law matters in the United States first find their way into one of the fifty states' legal systems. Together, the state governments process nearly 35 million cases per year, a number that amounts to more than 95 percent of the nation's litigation. About a third of the cases in state legal systems involve criminal matters. Each state system features its own set of unique characteristics and different nuances, an outgrowth of their different historical origins, and the wide variety that exists in the number of cases each state system may be responsible for due to significant population differences. Still, some common elements exist across all states.

Every state maintains trial courts, which do the bulk of work processing cases at the lower levels of the state legal system. These trial courts (often called "district courts" or "circuit courts" depending on the state or locality) may hear appeals from subordinate courts such as traffic courts; they also serve as sites for trials of more significant crimes. Thirty-nine of the fifty states have intermediate appellate courts, to which all appeals from trial courts must first be directed. All fifty states maintain at least one high supreme court. (Texas and Oklahoma have separate supreme courts for criminal and civil cases.) State supreme courts (or their equivalent of a different name) generally provide the final source of appeal for each state legal system.[4] To appeal beyond the state supreme court directly to the U.S. Supreme Court, a losing

---

[4] G. Alan Tarr and Mary Cornelius Porter, *State Supreme Courts in State and Nation* (New Haven, CT: Yale University Press, 1988).

Figure 9.1 Common Features of a State Court System

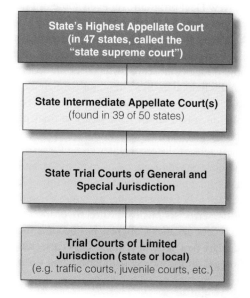

party must first exhaust all the remedies available at the state level, including losing his or her case at the state system's court of final appeal.

In theory, state courts must comply with pronouncements from the U.S. Supreme Court over the meaning of the federal Constitution. The reality is much more complicated. During various periods of American history, rebellious state courts tried to evade certain Supreme Court pronouncements by distinguishing or limiting the Supreme Court ruling, and on occasion even by denying the Supreme Court's jurisdiction over the matter. The Virginia Supreme Court resisted various pronouncements of the U.S. Supreme Court in the early part of the nineteenth century; more than a century later, state courts sometimes ignored U.S. Supreme Court decisions protecting the accused. Although the Supreme Court can usually exert its will over defiant state courts, it must be willing to expend key institutional resources and prestige to do so.

Development of the Federal Court System

Article III of the Constitution establishes a Supreme Court and any "inferior courts" that Congress may wish to create. Accordingly, Congress provided at the nation's outset for the creation of district and circuit courts, the latter of which bear little resemblance to modern circuit courts. Specifically, these early federal circuit courts were staffed by Supreme Court justices and district court judges, and they performed both trial and appellate functions. Thus in addition to their formal duties on the high court, Supreme Court justices in the early days of the Republic were also required to "ride circuit," traveling to their assigned circuits on a regular basis. (This practice formally ended when Congress reestablished the U.S. Courts of Appeals in 1891.)

During the nation's early history, the Supreme Court was seen as a weak third branch of government, with limited enforcement powers. With his ruling in *Marbury v. Madison* (1803),[5] Chief Justice John Marshall established the Court's power to review all acts of Congress for their constitutionality; even so, just one act of Congress was struck down as unconstitutional during Marshall's thirty-four-year reign as chief justice.

The Constitution makes no reference to the specific size of the Supreme Court. Thus Congress during the eighteenth and nineteenth centuries altered the size of the Court to consist of one chief justice and anywhere from five to nine associate justices serving on the Court at one time. Occasionally the issue of Court size comes up as a matter of strategic politics: In 1937 President Franklin Delano Roosevelt's ill-fated plan to expand the size of the Court (to up to fifteen members depending on the

---

[5] 1 Cranch (5 U.S.) 137 (1803).

age of the sitting justices) was driven by the president's desire to appoint new justices who would support his New Deal program. Yet even some of President Roosevelt's own Democratic supporters opposed the plan. Since 1869 the Court's composition of nine members (one chief justice and eight associate justices) has remained essentially unchanged. Meanwhile, Congress has been active in creating, disbanding, and modifying the number of other judges that serve throughout the federal court system.

Cases today begin in the federal court system, rather than the state court system, only when they fit into one of three categories: (1) the lawsuit requires interpretation of the U.S. Constitution, a federal law, or a treaty of the United States; (2) the federal government is suing or prosecuting someone, or is itself being sued; or (3) the lawsuit is between two citizens of different states suing for an amount of more than $75,000. Many of the highest-profile legal cases in recent years have become federal cases because they featured defendants accused of committing federal crimes. Included on this list were the trial of Oklahoma City bomber Timothy McVeigh and the prosecution of some of the terrorists involved (directly or indirectly) in the attacks of September 11, 2001. In recent decades Congress has become increasingly active in passing legislation to declare new federal crimes. Thus carjacking, the sale or possession of many types of illegal drugs, money laundering, and various other offenses are

Figure 9.2 The Federal Court System[6]

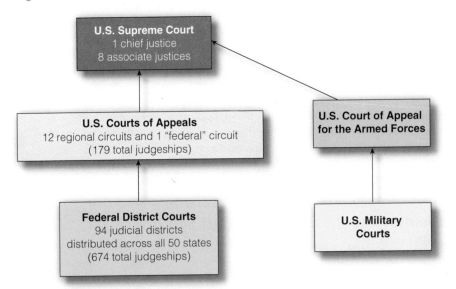

now considered federal crimes, and defendants who commit such offenses may face prosecution in federal courts.

The federal judicial system today also features a number of specialized courts, including tax courts, bankruptcy courts, and military courts. Most parties to a federal case start out in one of the ninety-four federal district courts located throughout the country. Federal district court judges have original jurisdiction (the power to rule in the first instance) over criminal and civil trials, and along with federal magistrates, they provide the initial sources of potential legal relief available in the federal judicial system.

After the federal district court has rendered its judgment, appeal is available to one of thirteen federal appeals courts (also referred to as "circuit courts of appeals") across the country. With some exceptions, federal appeals are normally decided by a panel of three judges selected at random from the pool of ten or more judges authorized to serve on that court. In some cases, litigants can appeal from the three-judge panel to the full circuit court, which may contain twenty or more judges—this type of hearing is called "en banc." Because the San Francisco–based Ninth Circuit maintains a roster of forty-seven judges (spread out from Hawaii and California in

[6] Chart doesn't include specialized courts including courts of international trade, tax courts, claims courts, etc.

the west, to Arizona, Nevada, Montana, and Idaho in the east), the phrase "en banc" on that court refers to eleven-judge panels that perform essentially the same function as en banc panels in other circuits.[7]

Litigants may petition for a writ of certiorari from an adverse judgment in the federal appeals court, seeking to be heard in the U.S. Supreme Court. Currently the Supreme Court enjoys near absolute discretion over its docket, and so it remains a long shot (less than 1 percent) that it will even grant the writ of certiorari in the first place.

Petitioning the U.S. Supreme Court for review is the final option available to state court litigants who suffer adverse decisions in the highest state court, and to federal court litigants who suffer adverse decisions after exhausting all forms of appeal in the federal court system. In a normal year, approximately half of the cases heard by the Supreme Court come from federal appellate courts and the other half from any of the fifty state court systems.

The United States' Adversarial System of Justice

Some European legal systems are based on an *inquisitorial system* of justice, in which judges, working on behalf of the government, are responsible for gathering information relevant to the disposition of a particular case. For example, in France—which adheres to the inquisitorial model—judges may initiate a criminal investigation against an individual, commission experts to investigate and report on special aspects of the crime, and even call witnesses and question them intensely. By contrast, the American legal system is primarily an *adversarial system* of justice, in which opposing parties contend against each other for a result favorable to themselves. In jury trials judges act merely as independent referees overseeing the contest; in so-called bench trials where no jury is present, judges must still remain objective arbiters as they prepare to make final decisions on the merits.[8] In an adversarial system, the judge is entrusted only with ensuring that the litigants achieve procedural fairness and plays no active role in evidence gathering or in the advocacy of one side over the other. Supporters of this system contend that adversarial proceedings pitting zealous representatives of parties against one another offer the best prospect of allowing the judge or jury to determine the truth. Critics counter that inquisitorial systems tend to be free of the many strategic "maneuvers" parties so frequently practice in U.S. courtrooms, such as the withholding of crucial evidence or the presentation of evidence that bears only a minimal relationship to the actual facts at issue.

Elements of Civil Litigation

Countless disputes among individuals or entities are resolved quietly, long before the threat to litigate is even invoked. Still, whenever one private party contests another over the definition or enforcement of certain legal rights or the legal relationship that may exist between them, the disagreement may wind up in the form of a lawsuit brought before a judge in a court of law. Any such judicial contest, including all the events that lead up to a possible court event, is referred to as **litigation.** Although the procedural rules governing such private disputes vary widely from state to state and system to system, some elements of civil litigation are common among all systems. Normally the complaining party who chooses to initiate formal legal proceedings (usually called the **plaintiff**) does so by filing a **complaint,** which is a written document justifying why the court is empowered to hear the case and explaining why he or she is entitled to some form of relief (usually an amount of money) under the current law. The target of the complaint, the **defendant,** normally must respond to the complaint with a formal written defense, in which he or she either admits to or denies what the plaintiff has said.

★ Litigation

Any judicial contest, including all the events that lead up to a possible court event.

★ Plaintiff

The party that chooses to initiate formal legal proceedings in a civil case.

★ Complaint

A document written by the plaintiff arguing why the court is empowered to hear the case and explaining why he or she is entitled to some form of relief under the current law.

★ Defendant

The target of a plaintiff's complaint explaining why he or she is entitled to some form of relief under the current law.

---

[7] Arthur Hellman, *Restructuring Justice: The Innovations of the Ninth Circuit and the Future of the Federal Courts* (Ithaca, NY: Cornell University Press, 1991).
[8] One rare exception to the strict use of the adversarial approach in the American legal system comes in the form of "structural reform litigation," a term which describes certain types of lawsuits brought against bureaucracies such as prisons, school systems, welfare systems, etc. Judges in these types of cases often assume a more active "managerial approach" in the process, overseeing the implementation of remedies and occasionally taking a proactive role to ensure that the lawyers are properly representing their client's interests. For comprehensive analysis of one example of structural reform litigation in action, see Malcolm Feeley and Edward Rubin, *Judicial Policymaking and the Modern State: How the Court Reformed America's Prisons* (Cambridge: Cambridge University Press, 2000). Of course the more traditional adversarial system still tends to predominate in most other forms of civil litigation.

If the defendant convinces the judge either that the court has no power to hear the case (perhaps it was filed in the wrong court) or that there is no law that provides a remedy to the plaintiff, the case may be dismissed. If the defendant's argument is unsuccessful, the case then moves forward to the stage of pretrial litigation normally referred to as "**discovery.**" During discovery, each side has the right to find out what information the other side has about the case by requesting documents or materials, access to property, and/or examinations, or by offering answers to questions about the litigation either in written form or verbally at a deposition. Although the judge may play some role in supervising discovery at pretrial conferences, almost all such discovery occurs outside of the courtroom. Following the discovery stage of the proceedings, each side may file new written documents to the court contending that it now has overwhelming evidence in its favor or that the other side has discovered no evidence to prove its own contentions.

The vast majority of civil disputes never make it to trial. In some cases, one party may succeed in convincing the judge that no trial is necessary and that the judge should rule in that party's favor immediately. Far more often, the sides agree to a legally binding "settlement" of claims made against each other, in which one side pays money to the other side, or agrees to cease and desist a certain practice in order to avoid the costs and uncertainties of trial. In civil litigation, judges often play an active role in encouraging the two parties to settle their differences out of court, saving resources for them and the judicial branch that would have been wasted in a long, drawn-out trial.

In some instances, the parties are not able to reach an out-of-court settlement, and a formal trial becomes necessary. In a "bench trial," the parties present evidence to a judge, rather than a jury of citizens. A jury trial usually takes far longer than a bench trial because of the many procedures required to prevent undue prejudice of the jury. Even if a jury trial is necessary, the judge still plays a role in the courtroom by ensuring that the jury is properly selected and that fair procedures are adhered to during the trial. One of the most crucial roles played by a judge in either type of trial is to rule on the admissibility of evidence that may be used to reach a decision. Only relevant evidence, which logically tends to prove or disprove a disputed fact, may be admitted into the trial proceedings. In civil cases, the complaining party is obligated to prove its allegations by a "preponderance of the evidence," which is generally thought to be anything greater than 50 percent. Although there is widespread disagreement on what this standard exactly means, it is clearly well below the high standard imposed on prosecutors in criminal cases to prove guilt "beyond a reasonable doubt."

Once the judge or jury has reached a final decision on the case, normally called the "verdict" in the case of a jury trial or the "judgment" in a bench trial, and the judge or jury has settled on a monetary amount to be awarded, the trial stage of the process comes to an end. Some post-trial motions may be available, and a dissatisfied party is also free to appeal the decision to a higher court.

The Criminal Justice System at Work

Although the rules of criminal procedure also vary widely, most criminal prosecutions begin with the arrest of a suspect by some law enforcement official at the federal, state, or local level. Once he or she is formally accused, the suspect is also referred to as the "defendant." Because some criminal charges may be later revealed as groundless or unsubstantiated, the government must quickly demonstrate the charges are valid against

★ Discovery

A stage of pretrial litigation in which the plaintiff and defendant have the right to learn what information the other side has about the case by requesting documents or materials, access to property, and/or examinations, or by offering answers to questions about the litigation either in written form, or verbally at a deposition.

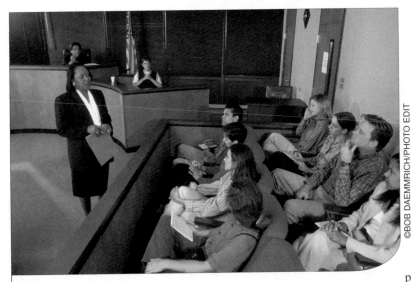
©BOB DAEMMRICH/PHOTO EDIT

A jury listens to an attorney present her case.

the defendant in one of two ways. Some prosecutors elect to present initial evidence at a preliminary hearing held before a magistrate or trial judge, where they must demonstrate that there is probable cause to proceed to trial against the suspect. Far more often the prosecutor convenes a **grand jury,** whose duty it is to receive complaints, hear the evidence offered by the prosecutor, and determine whether a trial is justified. Grand juries comprise a greater number of jurors than an ordinary trial jury. Unlike regular juries, which hear only one case, grand juries may be asked to hear evidence on numerous cases over a period of several weeks or even months. Because the grand jury process is supervised entirely by the prosecutor, he or she maintains a distinct advantage—some say a prosecutor could get the grand jury to "indict a bologna sandwich." In the overwhelming majority of cases the grand jury does indeed return a bill of **indictment** authorizing the government to proceed to trial against the defendant.

Whereas discovery is far-ranging and extensive in civil litigation, it is far more limited in criminal trials. Defense attorneys are usually under little or no obligation to provide any evidence at all to prosecutors; as a general matter, prosecutors are under an obligation to provide defense attorneys only with evidence that tends to "clear" the accused from alleged fault or guilt, although some states and localities provide additional discovery rights to the accused.

Most criminal prosecutions in the United States are resolved through a negotiated **plea bargain** between the defendant and the prosecutor.[9] Indeed, over 90 percent of convictions are the direct product of negotiated plea bargains. Many defendants seek to reduce their jail sentences by entering plea agreements that lead to lesser punishments. Much of the negotiation that occurs between prosecutors and defense attorneys is over the appropriate charges that will be formally filed, as most courts have adopted the equivalent of "going rates" for particular crimes.[10] Prosecutors willingly trade down penalties for crimes either because they are seeking that defendant's cooperation at another trial or because they wish to avoid the uncertainty and huge expenditure of resources that come with a trial.

In criminal cases that do go to trial, the burden rests squarely on the prosecutor to prove that the defendant committed the crime "beyond a reasonable doubt." Defendants, by contrast, do not have to prove their innocence. Unless a defendant waives the right to a jury trial, she or he must be tried by a jury of peers. State courts require anywhere between six and twelve jurors, whereas the federal court system require twelve jurors in all cases where a jury is present. Defendants, shielded by the Fifth Amendment privilege against self-incrimination, are under no obligation to testify. Numerous other constitutional safeguards are available to the defendant, including the right to a public and speedy trial and the right to directly confront witnesses. If the jury renders a "not guilty" verdict, the double jeopardy clause of the Fifth Amendment generally forbids the government from trying the defendant again for the same crime. A defendant who is convicted has a constitutional right to appeal the conviction or the resulting sentence to a higher court.

Although the burdens at trial appear to favor the accused, prosecutors generally have the benefit of experience in prosecuting many other defendants in the same court and can draw on a relatively large pool of resources (such as government investigators or medical examiners) to aid them in securing a conviction.

The Sixth Amendment has been interpreted to guarantee each indigent defendant the right to a government-provided lawyer in any instance where they face the possibility of jail time. Unfortunately, many public defenders' offices are overworked and underfunded, placing defendants at a relative disadvantage. By comparison, wealthy or well-connected defendants who do enjoy access to top legal talent and other resources at trial often fare much better. For example, in 1995 former pro football star O. J. Simpson was acquitted of charges of murdering his wife and a male friend of hers, thanks in no small part to the efforts of some of the nation's most well-known and highly regarded lawyers (nicknamed "the Dream Team" at that time by reporters). Clearly the American legal system does not always offer the same types of outcomes to those who are not similarly

★ Grand jury

A jury whose duty it is to hear the evidence offered by a prosecutor and determine whether a trial is justified.

★ Indictment

A decision by a grand jury authorizing the government to proceed to trial against the defendant.

★ Plea bargain

A pretrial negotiated resolution in a criminal case in which the defendants seek to reduce their jail sentences by pleading guilty and in return prosecutors are willing to trade down the severity of the punishment.

---

[9] See George Fisher, *Plea Bargaining's Triumph: A History of Plea Bargaining in America* (Palo Alto, CA: Stanford University Press, 2003); Milton Heumann, *Plea Bargaining: The Experiences of Prosecutors, Judges, and Defense Attorneys* (Chicago: University of Chicago Press, 1981).
[10] James Eisenstein, Roy Flemming, and Peter Nardulli, *The Contours of Justice* (New York: Addison-Wesley Publishing, 1988).

Former football star O. J. Simpson (left) confers with his "dream team" of high-priced legal talent at his murder trial in 1995.

situated or well-connected. For the vast majority of defendants, "justice" in the courtroom is meted out at lightning speed, with judges and prosecutors running through multiple criminal trials in a matter of hours with little opportunity provided to understand all the facts of a particular case. Public defenders only rarely have the chance to contest these trials with witnesses and evidence, lest they ignore all the other defendants under their charge. In sum, the picture of drama-filled trials seen so often on television or in the movies hardly depicts the reality of what goes on in this nation's criminal courtrooms.

©POO/AFP/GETTY IMAGES

Judicial Review and Its Implications

Courts in general, and judges in particular, serve in a variety of capacities: supervising the disposition of legal controversies between private parties, overseeing preliminary hearings or trials of criminal defendants, and ruling on important issues concerning the procedures to be followed or the evidence to be introduced at trial. Indeed, the role many judges play as "independent magistrates" is fundamental to the effective functioning of the American legal system. But courts and judges also play a significant and far-reaching role in overseeing the operations of the other branches of government, both by supervising conflicts between those branches and by protecting citizens against government action that may violate the Constitution.

This judicial authority has been magnified by the general recognition that American courts enjoy the added power of **judicial review,** by which they may declare acts of the other branches of the federal or state governments unconstitutional and thus invalid. This dimension of judicial authority is not mentioned anywhere in the U.S. Constitution. Although Article VI of the Constitution declares the Constitution of the United States to be the "supreme law of the land . . . anything in the Constitution or laws of any state to the contrary notwithstanding," nowhere does the document explicitly vest any specific court (including the U.S. Supreme Court) with the authority to determine whether state laws are unconstitutional. Nor does the Constitution authorize the Supreme Court to serve as the authoritative interpreter of the document over the president, Congress, and other federal officials, all of whom are equally sworn to uphold the Constitution. In fact, scholars of the early constitutional period believe the drafters of the Constitution were unable to reach any consensus at all on this issue. How then did the power of judicial review arise?

It was the fourth chief justice of the United States, John Marshall, who established the power of judicial review for the Supreme Court in the highly controversial case of *Marbury v. Madison* (1803).[11] With Thomas Jefferson's victory in the presidential election of 1800 and the Jeffersonian Republicans' rise to power in both houses of Congress the following year, nearly all of the nation's most powerful Federalists, including John Adams, Alexander Hamilton, and John Jay, were soon to be relegated to outsider status in the federal government. In his final hours as president, however, Adams appointed sixteen circuit court judges and forty-two new justices of the peace for the District of Columbia (all loyal Federalists); these positions were fully authorized by the Congress, and each of the individuals chosen for the posts was confirmed by the

★ Judicial review

The power of a court to declare acts of the other branches of government or of a subordinate government to be unconstitutional and thus invalid.

American Government: Historical, Popular, and Global Perspectives

[11] R. Kent Newmyer, *The Supreme Court Under Marshall and Taney* (Arlington Heights, IL: Harlan Davison, 1968).

Five of the Most Famous Twentieth-Century Trials

These five trials may have garnered more media attention than any others that were held in the United States during the twentieth century.

✔ **The Sacco-Vanzetti Trial (1921)**—The trial of two Italian anarchists for the murders of a local paymaster and his bodyguard sharply divided the public. Many thought two innocent men were being scapegoated in order to issue a more general warning against rising anarchist sentiment in the United States after World War I; others felt the trial of these two murderers had been fairly conducted in every respect. Both men were executed in 1927, six years after their respective convictions.

✔ **The Scopes "Monkey" Trial (1925)**—The prosecution of a high school biology teacher (John Scopes) for violating a state law that prohibited the teaching of evolution theory to students encapsulated a larger showdown being waged across the country between traditionalist forces grasping for the values of the past and modernists encouraging intellectual experimentation in education and elsewhere. The trial's carnival atmosphere (featuring lemonade stands outside the courtroom and chimpanzees performing in side shows) did not help Scopes—he was ultimately convicted and fined $100 by the court. Scopes's ordeal was eventually immortalized in the play *Inherit the Wind* (it also became a popular 1960 movie). The issue of whether public school teachers should teach evolution, creationism, or both continues to be a matter of debate in American politics today.

✔ **The "Lindbergh Baby" Trial (1935)**—The trial of German-born Bruno Hauptmann, accused of kidnapping the child of aviator Charles Lindbergh, seized the attention of the nation during the Great Depression. The trial raged on for a month as nearly 162 witnesses were called before a courtroom packed with such celebrity observers as writer Walter Winchell and entertainer Jack Benny. The jury returned a guilty verdict against Hauptmann after less than twelve hours of deliberation. A year after the verdict, Hauptmann was executed by electrocution.

✔ **The Rosenbergs' Trial (1951)**—With the Cold War raging between the United States and the Soviet Union and the American public's fear of Communists on the rise, the trial of Julius and Ethel Rosenberg for conspiracy to commit espionage was certain to draw intense national attention. Although both defendants had been members of the Communist Party in the 1950s, evidence of espionage existed only against Julius; prosecutors charged his wife Ethel on much weaker evidentiary grounds in hopes of convincing her husband to talk. In fact, neither defendant ever confessed, and both were convicted and sentenced to death in the electric chair. The sentences were carried out in 1953.

✔ **The O. J. Simpson Murder Trial (1995)**—The investigation and trial of former football star O. J. Simpson for the murders of his wife, Nicole, and her friend, Ronald Goldman, provided the nation with an especially gripping drama that played out in the courtroom and on television over many months. What writer Dominick Dunne termed "the Super Bowl of all murder trials" pitted an all-star cast of defense attorneys (including F. Lee Bailey and Alan Dershowitz) against a Los Angeles District Attorney's office determined that Simpson not receive special treatment for his celebrity status. After a series of prosecution gaffes, including the infamous "glove incident" (paraded before the jury, Simpson was unable to fit on his hand the glove he allegedly wore the night of the murder), the celebrity defendant was ultimately acquitted on all charges. Months later, at a civil trial initiated by the families of the victims, Simpson was found "responsible" for the murders and was ordered to pay $33.5 million for his actions.

Chapter 9: The Judiciary

lame-duck Federalist Congress that remained loyal to Adams. President Adams also named John Marshall as chief justice of the United States. Although surrounded by partisan opposition in Washington, Marshall made the Supreme Court into the Federalist Party's beachhead, from which that party's judicial holdovers, enjoying the benefit of life tenure, could continue to espouse their vision of a powerful central government.

Immediately after Thomas Jefferson and his secretary of state James Madison formally took office in March 1801, they learned that several of the commissions for the new justices of the peace appointed by Adams had never been delivered—including one for William Marbury. When Jefferson ordered Madison to withhold the commissions, Marbury asked the Supreme Court to issue a *writ of mandamus,* a judicial order commanding an official (in this case, Madison) to perform a ministerial duty over which his discretion is limited (namely, the formal delivery of a duly signed and sealed commission). As authority for the Supreme Court's power to issue such a writ, Marbury cited the Judiciary Act of 1789, which appeared to give the U.S. Supreme Court exactly that authority.

Marbury was seeking to have the Supreme Court decide the case immediately, without first having to suffer a loss in a lower court. Because Chief Justice Marshall was an ardent Federalist, Marbury further assumed the Court would be sympathetic to his plight. In truth, it was Marshall who was really at fault in the case—as Adams's secretary of state, he had failed to properly mail the commission. Indeed, given his intimate knowledge of the facts, Marshall should have recused himself from the case, refusing to participate as a judge in the first place. Yet Marshall's Supreme Court rejected Marbury's request. Recognizing the tense political situation that surrounded the case—and all too aware that Jefferson might not abide by court order—Marshall lambasted the Jefferson administration for its refusal to perform their statutorily mandated duty, but denied that the Supreme Court possessed the power to issue the writ as requested.

Why the refusal to help his fellow Federalist? Marshall acknowledged that the 1789 law did in fact authorize the Court to issue such a writ in "original jurisdiction." But, Marshall ruled, that law was in explicit violation of Article III, Section 2, Clause 2, which did not specifically list "writs of mandamus" among the types of cases over which the Supreme Court had original jurisdiction. Nor could Congress extend the Court's original jurisdiction by mere statute. Thus, Marshall decided, the 1789 law was repugnant to the Constitution and was therefore null and void. With this decision, Marshall seized for the Court a power of judicial review over congressional laws that is unmentioned in the Constitution. The Supreme Court exercised this power only once more before the Civil War, although it has struck down well over 150 acts of Congress since then.

Two rulings more than a decade later further established the Supreme Court's authority in interpreting the Constitution. In *McCulloch v. Maryland* (1819), the Court upheld the constitutionality of the Bank of the United States, thereby establishing the precedent that congressional power extends beyond those powers specifically listed in Article I of the Constitution. In *Martin v. Hunter's Lessee* (1816),[12] the Supreme Court ruled that the power of federal courts to review government actions for their constitutionality was not just applicable to other federal institutions; the supremacy clause ("The Constitution … shall be the Supreme Law of the Land") meant that the Supreme Court could also invalidate any actions of state governments that it believed to be in conflict with the U.S. Constitution. During his thirty-four years as chief justice, Marshall wrote 519 opinions, many of which remain influential commentary on constitutional power and authority. Under Marshall's leadership, the Court consistently rejected claims of state sovereignty that conflicted with federal interests. It was the special duty of the Supreme Court, Marshall believed, to make difficult judgments on the Constitution that either limited or affirmed the exercise of federal authority. In doing so, Marshall's court defined a strong role for the federal government, which was more clearly realized beginning in the twentieth century.

In the two centuries since Marshall served as chief justice, the Supreme Court has invalidated more than 1,200 state laws. In 1958, it once again reaffirmed the principle of judicial supremacy in *Cooper v. Aaron*[13] in response to official defiance of a lower court's desegregation rulings: governors and state legislatures were bound to uphold decisions of the Supreme Court just as they were bound by oath to uphold the Constitution.

[12] 1 Wheat (14 U.S.) 304 (1816).
[13] 358 U.S. 1 (1958).

At times the exercise of judicial review has been extremely controversial. For example, the Supreme Court in *Dred Scott v. Sandford* (1857)[14] ruled that slaves were forever the property of their owners, even when they are brought temporarily into free states. The decision overturned a congressional law regulating the extension of slavery in the territories and may have helped to precipitate the Civil War four years later. During the Great Depression, the Supreme Court's rulings that many of President Roosevelt's New Deal proposals were unconstitutional instigated another constitutional crisis. Despite the uncertain beginnings that led to this practice and the tense moments in the nation's history that it has given rise to, judicial review of federal and state laws has become an unchallenged dimension of judicial power within the U.S. political system.

Limitations on Courts

In Federalist No. 78, Alexander Hamilton deemed the judiciary "the least dangerous" branch because it had "no influence over either the sword or the purse … and can take no active resolution whatsoever." Despite Hamilton's opinion, courts have played a critically influential role in the American political system. When the Supreme Court aggressively interposes itself between aggrieved citizens and the government, as it did when it ordered desegregation of public schools in *Brown v. Board of Education* (1954);[15] or when it helps resolve some great political crisis, as it did when it ordered President Richard Nixon to hand over controversial tapes of White House conversations in *United States v. Nixon* (1974),[16] the judiciary appears more like an all-powerful branch than one that is weak and inconsequential.

The power of American courts is great, but the method by which courts participate in the political system is far more circumscribed than that of the other two branches. The limitations that courts must adhere to include the following:

1. **Courts cannot initiate or maintain lawsuits.** Unlike legislatures, which can propose and pass bills on their own initiative, judges in the United States cannot decide issues that are not currently before them in a legitimately filed lawsuit. If none of the actors in a controversy elect to involve the courts directly, the court has no role whatsoever in resolution of the conflict.

2. **Courts can hear only those lawsuits that constitute true "cases" or "controversies."** Article III imposes on the Supreme Court and all federal courts the same type of limitation that applies to nearly all other courts: judges may hear and resolve only those lawsuits that amount to legitimate "cases" or "controversies" and must ignore mere "hypothetical" or "theoretical" conflicts. Although most of these terms are fuzzy enough to give courts room to maneuver, in practice courts tend to refuse to decide lawsuits that are moot (that is, it is too late to provide any effective remedy), including lawsuits involving affirmative action programs and policies brought by applicants to educational institutions who have since matriculated (and in many cases, graduated) from another institution. Courts are equally reluctant to decide cases that are not yet ripe (that is, the actual conflict is still sometime in the future). Accordingly, courts are reluctant to provide executives with what amounts to "legal advice" about future controversies that have not yet occurred. Courts similarly refuse to hear cases that were contrived by the parties in the form of collusion, or cases in which jurisdiction has not been properly invoked.

   The courts have also maintained a long-standing tradition of refusing to decide cases where the Constitution has explicitly entrusted the issue to be decided by one of the other branches of government; such issues are generally referred to as "political questions." Of course when attempting to justify its

[14] 60 U.S. 393 (1857).
[15] 347 U.S. 483 (1954).
[16] 418 U.S. 683 (1974).

refusal to take on a political question, the court often engages in such extensive analysis of the underlying issues that it is hard to distinguish those opinions from analysis of the merits of the case itself. Thus in *Nixon v. United States* (2003),[17] the Supreme Court explained its refusal to reconsider the Senate's process of trying the impeachment of a federal judge, Walter Nixon, by issuing a lengthy opinion that reviewed in considerable detail the constitutional provisions entrusting the Senate with the "sole power" of trying impeachments. Related to the "case or controversy" rule is a requirement that courts impose on the parties themselves: courts will hear lawsuits only from parties that have proper **standing,** meaning that they are "uniquely" and "singularly affected" by the controversy. For example, courts usually reject lawsuits brought by individuals who are frustrated with the allotment of their tax dollars, because those individuals are not "singularly affected." Nor are individuals with a mere academic or political concern in a conflict allowed in court as parties to a case unless they have suffered some unique economic or physical burden related to the issue being decided. In the mid-twentieth century, Congress and many state legislatures have loosened these harsh standing requirements by authorizing lawsuits brought by large numbers of people with clearly defined common interests. Such **class action lawsuits** can proceed through the legal system even when not every member of the class has formally signed on. High-visibility class action lawsuits in recent years include those brought by tobacco users across the country and those by people who have suffered from the effects of asbestos.

3. **Courts must rely on other branches for enforcement.** Unlike the other branches of government, courts rely on other political institutions to put their opinions or orders into direct effect—police officers, marshals, and executive branch officers, among others, must carry out the courts' mandates. Whereas Congress can cut off funding to executive agencies that ignore its dictates, no similar tool is available to the judiciary. In the vast majority of instances, disobedience of the court is not in question. Yet when a court makes a controversial pronouncement, officials may be reluctant to adhere to the court's decision. In some rare cases, a court's decisions may be met with outright disobedience. Sometimes even courts may react negatively to another court's rulings: In July 2001, Chief Justice Roy Moore of the Alabama Supreme Court authorized the installation of a monument to the Ten Commandments in the Alabama state judicial building. Even after a federal district court ruled that the monument violated the separation of church and state, Moore refused to remove it; more than two years after installation of the monument, Moore was removed from office for defying the federal court's order.

In 1832, President Andrew Jackson declined to enforce the Supreme Court's decision in *Worcester v. Georgia,*[18] ordering that a white Christian missionary be freed from a Georgia prison. Chief Justice Marshall had ruled that the Georgia law imprisoning the missionary for residing on Cherokee Indian property without permission violated a U.S.–Cherokee treaty; yet President Jackson declared—perhaps apocryphally—that "John Marshall has made his decision . . . now let him enforce it." (The missionary served his entire four-year mission in jail.) Sometimes even popular Supreme Court decisions face the threat of resistance. President Richard Nixon considered refusing to comply

American Government: Historical, Popular, and Global Perspectives

[17] 506 U.S. 224 (1993).
[18] 6 Pet. (31 U.S.) 515 (1832).

American Government . . . in Popular Perspective:

Is the U.S. Supreme Court Too Liberal or Too Conservative?

Although thousands of judges are appointed or elected to judicial seats every year, the handful of U.S. Supreme Court appointments that occur receive the lion's share of public attention. Even more important, they tend to greatly influence the public's views of the high court. Consider these findings from the ABC News/*Washington Post* Polls: in September 1987, less than one in five Americans thought the Supreme Court was too conservative. Four years later, after Republican presidents had appointed three straight Supreme Court justices, 31 percent then thought the Court was too conservative. More recently, in July of 2005, once again less than one in five thought the Supreme Court was too conservative. Yet a mere two years later, President George W. Bush's appointment of Justices John Roberts and Samuel Alito had once again shifted public opinion about the court's ideological direction.

Do you think the U.S. Supreme Court tends to be too conservative or too liberal in its decisions, or is it generally balanced in its decisions?

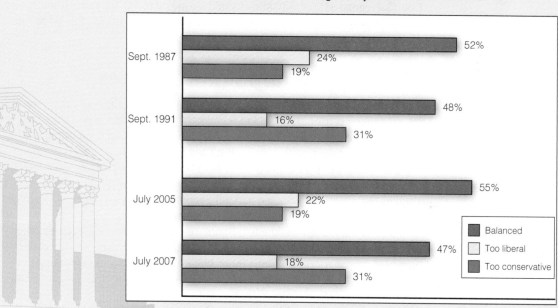

with the Supreme Court's 1974 decision in *United States v. Nixon* ordering him to hand over the secret tapes he made of conversations in the Oval Office.[19]

Controversial Supreme Court decisions in the 1950s and 1960s occasionally led to significant resistance on the part of ordinary citizens as well.[20] The landmark decisions in *Brown v. Board of Education,* which first held that segregated public schools violated the equal protection clause and then commanded that public schools be desegregated "with all deliberate speed," met with violent reaction in the South. Ultimately President Dwight Eisenhower sent U.S. marshals to the South to enforce the desegregation decrees; otherwise, there might have been even greater resistance to the Court's controversial decisions. The Supreme Court's 1962 decision invalidating school-sponsored religious prayer in public schools *(Engel v. Vitale)*[21] goes ignored in many parts of this country even today—in one instance, a federal district court in Alabama was forced to prohibit prayer in public schools throughout the state in response to reports of widespread defiance.

---

[19] See Bob Woodward and Carl Bernstein, *The Final Days* (New York: Simon & Schuster, 1994).
[20] Bradley Canon and Charles Johnson, *Judicial Policies: Implementation and Impact,* 2nd ed. (Washington, DC: CQ Press, 1999).
[21] 370 U.S. 421 (1962).

★ Appellate jurisdiction

The authority of a court to review decisions handed down by another court.

★ Original jurisdiction

The authority of a court to be the initial court in which a legal decision is rendered.

In addition to these limitations on courts just described, courts must also adhere to limitations that arise from the constitutional or statutory law. For example, Congress can by statute alter the Supreme Court's **appellate jurisdiction,** which is the power to review prior decisions handed down by state and lower federal courts. However, it cannot change the Court's **original jurisdiction,** which is the power to hear a lawsuit at the outset. Article III authorizes the Court's original jurisdiction in cases involving ambassadors and cases in which states are the only parties. Thus Congress could in theory declare that federal courts as a whole are not empowered to hear abortion cases. In fact, foes of the Supreme Court's abortion decisions proposed such a bill in the 1980s, but it was never passed.

One final limitation on courts is harder to see, but is no less significant. Because retiring judges and justices are normally replaced in office by politically accountable entities such as executives and legislatures, or in some states by the public itself, courts in general rarely stray too far from the reigning political majority. Social scientist Robert Dahl affirmed this hypothesis in his landmark 1957 article, "Decisionmaking in a Democracy."[22] Dahl's study of Supreme Court opinions revealed that although the Supreme Court often defies public opinion in the short run, its opinions usually fall in line with the dominant national majority coalition in the long run. The Court's eventual adaptability to shifts in the national mood, though much more subtle and slow-moving than the more political branches of government, has helped sustain it as a vital force in the American political system.

Electing and Appointing Judges

The state and federal court systems differ dramatically in the way judges are selected. State court judges tend to be selected in one of five ways. Partisan elections are utilized in some states, with prospective and sitting justices required to campaign for their party's nomination and then to run in a general election. Nonpartisan elections, held in many other states eliminate party designations from the election process. The "Missouri Plan" or merit plan selection process features a three-step process by which a judicial nominating commission initially screens candidates and then submits a list of three potential nominees to the governor, who then selects the judge from the list. Shortly thereafter, the new judge must then secure voter approval in a nonpartisan retention election.[23] Several other states authorize gubernatorial appointment of judges, in which the governor appoints judges, subject to approval of the state senate. Finally, a handful of states require that the state legislature appoint judges.

The selection of federal judges follows a more universal formula: all federal district court judges, federal appeals court judges, and Supreme Court justices are appointed by the president, subject to confirmation by a majority vote in the U.S. Senate. Whereas the Constitution dictates this formula for appointment of Supreme Court justices, Congress in its discretion authorized the appointment of lower federal court judges to require the Senate's advice and consent as well. Because all federal judges and Supreme Court justices hold their offices during "good behavior"—the functional equivalent of life tenure—they are thought of as more independent than those state judges who must run for re-election. In fact, the retention rate for state judges is often so high (due to low voter turnout and other factors) that even elected state judges tend to enjoy a large degree of independence in rendering decisions.

The Nomination Process

During a single term in office a president can expect to make hundreds of federal judicial appointments. In practice, a tradition of deference to home-state senators (often called "senatorial courtesy") provides legislators in the upper chamber—especially those hailing from the president's party—with considerable influence over the selection of district court judges in their own states. (Senatorial courtesy also has

[22] Robert Dahl, "Decisionmaking in a Democracy: The Supreme Court as a National Policy-Maker." *Journal of Public Law,* Vol. 6 (1957), pp. 279–295.
[23] Philip DuBois, *From Ballot to Bench: Judicial Elections and the Quest for Accountability* (Austin: University of Texas Press, 1980).

a more limited impact on the selection of court of appeals' judges, as circuits cross individual state boundaries.) In recent decades, presidents have not only relied on senators' recommendations to generate nominees for judgeships; they also consider ideological factors and the personal characteristics of potential nominees.

Some modern presidents have sought to place their own ideological stamp on the lower courts (whether liberal or conservative) by utilizing a committee of White House and Justice Department attorneys to screen and suggest candidates.[24] The Reagan and George W. Bush administrations were especially active in seeking to use the appointment of lower court judges as a means of moving the constitutional landscape in a conservative ideological direction. When the presidency and the Senate are held by different parties, battles over judicial nominees may become especially fierce. In 2002 and 2007–2008, the Democrat-controlled Senate Judiciary Committee gave heightened scrutiny to President George W. Bush's more conservative nominees.

Given its place atop the U.S. legal system, vacancies on the U.S. Supreme Court tend to draw far more political attention than do other judicial vacancies. Because the president, the U.S. Senate, and the media follow personnel changes on the Supreme Court far more closely, the process by which justices are nominated and confirmed is a major news event. A president may have the opportunity to appoint several Supreme Court justices—Presidents George H. W. Bush and Bill Clinton appointed two justices each, whereas President Ronald Reagan appointed three associate justices and promoted one associate to chief justice (the justice responsible for administering the Court's affairs and heading the federal justice system as a whole) during his eight years in office. President George W. Bush appointed no justices during his first term, but filled two vacancies (including the chief justiceship) during the latter half of 2005. Bush's re-election helped him escape the fate suffered by President Carter, whose lone term in office witnessed no Supreme Court vacancies at all.

AP PHOTO/LAWRENCE JACKSON

Supreme Court nominee Harriet Miers, meeting with Senate Majority Leader Bill Frist in October 2005. President Bush withdrew her nomination in response to conservatives' complaints.

If a vacancy occurs in the position of chief justice, the president may choose to promote one of the eight associate Supreme Court justices to this prestigious position, as President Reagan did when he promoted William Rehnquist to the Court's center seat in 1986. More often, presidents reach outside the confines of the current Supreme Court for someone to take the position of chief justice. Chief Justice Earl Warren, for example, served as governor of California immediately prior to becoming chief justice in 1953. President George W. Bush also named an outsider, Judge John Roberts of the U.S. Court of Appeals for the D.C. Circuit, to succeed Rehnquist.

In choosing nominees to the high court, presidents in recent decades have considered several factors:

★ **The nominee's ideological and policy preferences.** This factor has enjoyed a place of special importance in presidential calculations. A nominee's views on abortion, school prayer, and other hot-button issues may well tip the balance of the Court in favor of the president's stated views. Certainly there exists little

---

[24] Sheldon Goldman, *Picking Federal Judges* (New Haven, CT: Yale University Press, 1997).

evidence that presidents employ "litmus tests" on nominees, by which they might refuse to appoint individuals unless they explicitly state their views on such issues to the president in advance. President Dwight Eisenhower allegedly referred to his appointments of Chief Justice Earl Warren and Justice William Brennan as the "two biggest mistakes" of his presidency, because both men decided cases in a far more liberal direction than Eisenhower would have preferred. More recently, the elder George Bush may have been frustrated by the pro–abortion rights opinions of Justice David Souter, his first appointment to the Supreme Court. Still, most modern presidents have mobilized White House and Justice Department resources to conduct extensive research on each candidate's past writings and opinions in hopes of eliminating any surprises.

★ **Judicial competence.** Most presidents have an interest in appointing especially qualified candidates for the high court, if only because it assists in speeding along the confirmation process. The American Bar Association (ABA), an interest group of lawyers, rates candidates for every federal judicial vacancy on a scale from "highly qualified" to "not qualified" on the basis of their legal background and accomplishments. Ethical considerations may also be considered, because the ABA may be reluctant to approve candidates who have previously been convicted of crimes, for example. Although a negative rating from the ABA does not always eliminate a candidacy, it may present significant obstacles in the Senate confirmation process. Early in his first term, President George W. Bush announced that he would no longer vet judicial candidates through the ABA prior to their formal nomination. Still, the ABA continued to rate those candidates after their nominations were submitted to the Senate. Two of President Bush's first three nominees for the high court, John Roberts and Samuel Alito, received the highest rating of "well qualified" just prior to their appearance before the Senate Judiciary Committee. (Bush's other nominee, Harriet Miers, withdrew her name from consideration before the ABA released its rating of her candidacy.)

★ **Political loyalty.** Although loyalty has diminished somewhat as a priority in recent years, presidents still occasionally practice old-fashioned politics in the selection of Supreme Court nominees, choosing a justice based on a background of service to the president's party or to the president. During the twentieth century, well over 90 percent of all Supreme Court nominees were members of the president's political party. Of these, many emerged from the president's Cabinet, from the members of Congress loyal to the president's legislative program, or from other positions close to the chief executive or his subordinates at the time the appointment was made. Certainly the former president of the United States, William Howard Taft, was well-positioned to tout his own appointment as chief justice of the United States; President Warren Harding placed Taft on the high court just seven years after Taft had left the White House.

★ **Demographic factors.** A president may choose a candidate for the diversity the nominee adds to the demographics of the current Supreme Court.[25] Lyndon Johnson appointed Thurgood Marshall as the first African American to the Court in 1967; Ronald Reagan appointed Sandra Day O'Connor as the first female justice in 1981 and Antonin Scalia as the first Italian American justice in 1986. The selection of nominees who can diversify the Court may pay political dividends for the White House as well: the president may be counting on such nominations to build support among certain groups. Yet with his first two

[25] Barbara Perry, *A Representative Supreme Court* (Westport, CT: Greenwood Press, 1991).

The current members of the U.S. Supreme Court. Top row, left to right: Stephen Breyer, Clarence Thomas, Ruth Bader Ginsburg, and Samuel Alito. Bottom row, left to right: Anthony Kennedy, John Paul Stevens, John Roberts (chief justice), Antonin Scalia, and David Souter.

Table 9.1 Current Membership of the U.S. Supreme Court

Member	Gender	Position	Date Born	Year Appointed (President)	Law School	Party	Religion
John Roberts	M	Chief Justice	1-27-55	2005 (Bush II)	Harvard	Republican	Roman Catholic
John Paul Stevens	M	Associate Justice	4-20-20	1975 (Ford)	North-western	Republican	Protestant
Antonin Scalia	M	Associate Justice	3-11-36	1986 (Reagan)	Harvard	Republican	Roman Catholic
Anthony Kennedy	M	Associate Justice	7-23-36	1988 (Reagan)	Harvard	Republican	Roman Catholic
David Souter	M	Associate Justice	9-17-39	1990 (Bush I)	Harvard	Republican	Episcopalian
Clarence Thomas	M	Associate Justice	6-23-48	1990 (Bush I)	Yale	Republican	Roman Catholic*
Ruth Bader Ginsburg	F	Associate Justice	3-15-33	1993 (Clinton)	Harvard/ Columbia	Democrat	Jewish
Stephen Breyer	M	Associate Justice	8-15-38	1994 (Clinton)	Harvard	Democrat	Jewish
Samuel Alito	M	Associate Justice	4-1-50	2006 (Bush II)	Yale	Republican	Roman Catholic

*Clarence Thomas was a declared member of the Episcopal faith at the time of his appointment in 1991; he later converted to Roman Catholicism.

appointments, John Roberts and Samuel Alito, George W. Bush confounded predictions that he might appoint the first Hispanic American to the Supreme Court. Moreover, the eventual selection of Alito to replace O'Connor actually *decreased* gender diversity on the court, reducing the number of female justices to just one for the first time in over a decade.

★ **The current political environment.** Supreme Court vacancies do not occur in a vacuum; presidents are well aware of the political conditions that surround a particular court vacancy, and more often than not they respond to it through their nomination choices. Such factors as low presidential approval ratings, a Senate controlled by the political opposition, or the need to achieve other legislative proposals may convince the president to select a more moderate or less controversial nominee. Thus President Bill Clinton—facing a challenging political environment during his first two years in office—chose two Supreme Court nominees during that period (Ruth Bader Ginsburg and Stephen Breyer) who were deemed acceptable by the ranking Republican member of the Senate Judiciary Committee, Sen. Orrin Hatch (R-UT). Similarly, a president who enjoys a strong political position may decide to name a more controversial Supreme Court nominee.

The Confirmation Process

Although Hugo Black found himself embroiled in a controversy over his nomination in the late 1930s, most confirmation processes up to that point tended to be little noticed events, drawing little public attention or press coverage. Beginning in the mid-twentieth century, however, with the growth of federal regulatory schemes placing more and more cases in the federal courts, presidents began to routinely utilize judicial appointments as a means of shaping public policy. The confirmation process for those nominees was simultaneously opened up to unprecedented high levels of public scrutiny. All hearings for Supreme Court nominees have been televised live on C-Span during the past quarter century. Interest groups have become increasingly active in confirmation proceedings, lobbying senators directly and testifying in favor of or against particular nominees. With the ideological stakes raised, presidents and their aides have become increasingly active in lobbying for their nominees.[26]

The Senate confirms the vast majority of Supreme Court nominees; since 1900, fifty-seven of the sixty-one Supreme Court candidates who came up for a Senate vote on the merits were confirmed. Nevertheless, controversial nominees in recent

John Roberts, nominee for chief justice of the United States, testifying before the Senate Judiciary Committee in September 2005.

American Government: Historical, Popular, and Global Perspectives

AP PHOTO/PABLO MARTINEZ MONSIVAIS

[26] John Maltese, *The Selling of Supreme Court Nominees* (Baltimore: Johns Hopkins University Press, 1995).

decades have experienced their share of public scrutiny—and in some cases, humiliation—when subjected to the glare of the confirmation process. One of Richard Nixon's nominees to the Supreme Court in 1970, Court of Appeals judge G. Harrold Carswell of Florida, was rejected by the Senate in part because of his alleged links to white supremacist groups. Carswell was also dogged by charges that he was not competent

American Government . . . in Global Perspective:
The Risks of American-Style Criminal Justice . . . to Foreign Companies

Americans take pride in a justice system that they believe should be the envy of the rest of the world. The reality, however, is a bit more complicated. Many foreign corporations, for example, live in fear that actions they take, which may be legal elsewhere, might nevertheless ensnare them in a legal trap under U.S. law. Writing in the *London Times*, journalist William Rees-Mogg laments the dilemma that the American legal system tends to create for even law-abiding entities in the United Kingdom:

Americans are well aware of the horrid faults of their legal system, but they still like to think that it is the best in the world. Its abuses include plea bargaining, class actions, Guantanamo Bay, racism, elected district attorneys looking for votes, hick justice in states such as Arkansas, federal patronage of prosecutors and judges, the politicisation of the Supreme Court, the squalor and brutality of big federal and state prisons and the aggressive ruthlessness of tax and regulatory authorities. In the United States, you can be ruined by the cost of doctors if you get sick and by the cost of lawyers if you get into court.

There are, of course, honourable lawyers and distinguished judges, some of whom are among the best in the world. It is the downside of US law that terrifies Americans and should terrify foreign businessmen. A treaty with the United States was signed in 2003 and came into effect in 2004. It is an unequal treaty in that the required proof of an offence is quite high in extradition from the United States but virtually nonexistent in the British case. It is often difficult for defendants to organise their defence effectively after they have been extradited.

That puts them under pressure to enter the US plea-bargaining negotiations on unequal terms.

The United States Justice Department has been anxious to extend American regulation of business to the rest of the world, particularly in the areas of price fixing and of fraud. . . . In all these cases, the British authorities have decided not to prosecute and the potential penalties in the US are higher than they would be here. About ten British citizens are currently in jeopardy, but there are more to come. In several of these cases plea bargaining is an important factor.

The risk of a miscarriage of justice is inherent in the US plea-bargaining system. Two competitors, such as Sotheby's and Christie's, or British Airways and Virgin, may confer together to fix prices; their action might, at the time, have been legal in Britain, but might have been an offence in the US. . . .We do not want to tell the Americans that the defects of their justice system have become notorious. Yet the 2003 treaty invades human rights and, in European terms, may well be illegal as well as unjust.

Source: London Times, May 28, 2007.

to serve on the bench; to that came the deadly retort of one Senate supporter that "even the mediocre deserve some representation on the Supreme Court too." Despite all these obstacles, Carswell nearly survived Senate confirmation anyway—he was rejected by a mere 51–45 margin, with 17 Democrats voting to confirm the controversial nominee. Frustrated by his defeat, Carswell resigned from the bench a few months later and ran unsuccessfully for the U.S. Senate in 1972.

Ronald Reagan's nomination of Judge Robert Bork to the Supreme Court in 1987 was defeated in the Senate amid a cloud of interest group cries that Bork would reverse liberal precedents on free speech and abortion.[27] Bork, a former Yale law professor, sported a record of opposition to many Supreme Court doctrines supported by political liberals, including the doctrine of constitutionally protected abortion rights that the Court articulated in *Roe v. Wade* (1973). In his award-winning book, *The Selling of Supreme Court Nominees* (1994), University of Georgia Professor John Maltese notes that liberal interest groups determined to defeat Bork employed "a wide variety of tactics, including advertising, grass roots events, focus groups and polling" to increase public awareness of Bork's controversial positions.

The Reagan White House was caught off guard by the groundswell of opposition to Bork's nomination generated by the intense interest group–driven media campaign. By the time Senate confirmation hearings were held at the end of the summer, the campaign had taken its toll on Bork's candidacy: several senators, including Joseph Biden (D-DE), chairman of the Senate Judiciary Committee, had already been persuaded to oppose the appointment. The Senate eventually defeated Bork's nomination by a 58–42 vote. Presidents since then have come to understand the new politics of judicial confirmations, working closely with interest groups to mount their own campaigns in favor of judicial nominees. The Bork nomination gave rise to a new term in Washington's political lexicon—"to Bork," which defines the act of challenging a president's nominee through well-financed and organized interest group opposition.

The Bork confirmation fiasco also encouraged subsequent presidents to favor nominees who either possess no paper trail at all, or who would be far more circumspect than Bork in their willingness to engage the Senate on constitutional issues. Accordingly, in 1990 the first Supreme Court vacancy of George H. W. Bush's presidency went to David Souter, a little known federal appeals judge who had logged most of his judicial career on the New Hampshire Supreme Court deciding technical issues of state law. Souter's position on issues such as abortion and the establishment clause were never really tested in the state court system, and senators on both ends of the political spectrum thus had little to work with when interrogating Souter. (He was confirmed easily by a 90–9 Senate vote.)

In recent years, the confirmation process for lower court nominees has been politicized as well, with battles being waged with extra ferocity over appointments to the U.S. courts of appeals. During the Clinton administration, Senate Republicans in control of that chamber often delayed nominees they felt were too liberal; Senate Democrats did the same to President George W. Bush's nominees in 2001. Before the Democrats regained control of Congress in the 2006 midterm elections, Senate Democrats opposed to some of George W. Bush's nominees on ideological grounds began to take advantage of Senate rules to stop votes on contested nominees. Specifically, they utilized the filibuster to block ten of President Bush's appellate court nominees during his first term in office. Bush renominated nine of those blocked nominees at the start of his second term, and a frustrated Republican Senate leadership began to consider rule changes to foreclose the use of filibusters against future nominees. Senate Democrats referred to any such rule change as the "nuclear option," because they were prepared to respond by shutting down Senate business through use of the filibuster rule in all other instances. On May 24, 2005, this growing crisis was averted, as a group of fourteen moderate senators (seven Republicans and seven Democrats) settled on a plan to allow several of Bush's most controversial nominees to be confirmed, in return for the promise that the filibuster would be reserved for use against judicial appointments when there are "extraordinary circumstances."

[27] Ethan Bronner, *Battle for Justice: How the Bork Nomination Shook America* (New York: W. W. Norton, 1989).

How a Case Proceeds within the U.S. Supreme Court

The vast majority of cases that come before the U.S. Supreme Court arrive by a **writ of certiorari,** the formal term for an order by which the court acts in its discretion to hear a case on appeal. Losing parties in the highest state court, a federal circuit court, or (in extremely rare cases) a federal district court can properly file a "cert petition" with the Supreme Court, asking the Court to hear its case. Decisions to grant a writ of certiorari generally follow the *Rule of Four*—if four of the nine justices vote to hear the case, it is placed on the Court's official docket of cases that it will hear during the coming year. Of the many thousands of cert petitions that arrive at the Court during a given year, barely more than 1 percent (fewer than ninety overall) are normally granted.

In theory, the justices decide to hear only those cases that are considered so important that they justify intervention at such a high level. Two other factors may also increase the likelihood that the Supreme Court will grant a writ of certiorari: (1) when the federal government intervenes in the case; or (2) when there is a split among two or more of the U.S. circuit courts of appeals on a similar issue. Additionally, some justices as a matter of strategy may vote to deny the petition for cert, even when they

★ Writ of certiorari

The formal term for an order by which the Supreme Court acts in its discretion to review a case from a lower court.

Figure 9.3 From Cert Petition to Final Judgment in the U.S. Supreme Court

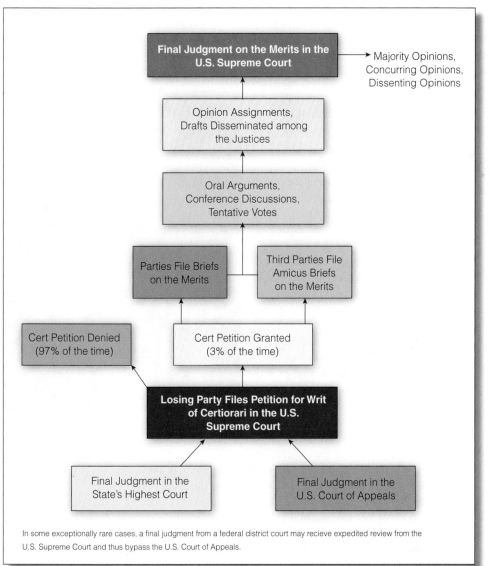

In some exceptionally rare cases, a final judgment from a federal district court may recieve expedited review from the U.S. Supreme Court and thus bypass the U.S. Court of Appeals.

think the lower court case was wrongly decided, because they do not want their colleagues to transform the lower court precedent into a Supreme Court edict applicable throughout the land. Regardless of the justices' many motives, denial of a cert petition theoretically casts no aspersions whatsoever on whether a case has been wrongly or rightly decided, although it does allow the lower court decision to stand as the controlling legal decision for the parties in that case. For example, the Supreme Court's 1997 denial of a cert petition in a case concerning affirmative action at the University of Texas did not necessarily imply high Court dissatisfaction with affirmative action; rather, it simply left intact a U.S. Court of appeals decision rejecting affirmative action as unconstitutional that applied to just three states: Texas, Mississippi, and Louisiana. Meanwhile, the U.S. Supreme Court waited until six years later to articulate rules for affirmative action that would become applicable in all 50 states.

If the Court elects to issue a writ of certiorari and hear a case, both the losing and winning parties in the lower court file written documents called **briefs** arguing why constitutional or federal statutory law weighs in favor of their respective positions. Outside parties with an interest in the litigation may also elect to file briefs, known formally as **amicus curiae briefs** ("amicus curiae" is Latin for "friend of the court"), expressing their own views on how the Court should decide a particular case. Interest groups frequently file amicus briefs in Supreme Court cases that affect their members; in doing so, they offer a version of "expert testimony" on the law, albeit with their own strategic bent on the issue in question. The American Medical Association, for example, routinely files amicus briefs in abortion cases; the American Trial Lawyers Association may express its opinion in cases interpreting rules of trial procedure through amicus briefs as well. In some of the more high-profile cases, literally hundreds of such briefs may be filed, offering the court an admittedly informal tally of the state of public opinion on the issue.

The **solicitor general** argues on behalf of the U.S. government in most cases where the federal government is a party. That office also stands among the most influential "friends of the court," filing amicus briefs on behalf of the federal government in approximately a quarter of all cases heard by the Supreme Court each year. Acting through the solicitor general, the U.S. government has enjoyed a disproportionate share of success in affecting Supreme Court case discretionary grants of review and case outcomes.[28]

After all party and amicus briefs have been filed, the Supreme Court justices normally hear oral arguments from opposing counsel in the Supreme Court's chamber. Attorneys licensed to practice before the Supreme Court present their client's view of the law and facts within an allotted period of time (normally 30 minutes); most of that time is actually spent answering questions and inquiries from the justices. If a justice is truly undecided, he or she may be affected in the margins by the positions of advocates at oral arguments; the give-and-take with the lawyers may also suggest ways to more effectively draft the final opinion. Still, there remains little evidence that the oral arguments actually shift the votes of most justices. Regardless, the

MPI/GETTY IMAGES

Justice Oliver Wendell Holmes Jr.

★ Briefs

Written documents filed by parties in an appealed case arguing why constitutional or statutory law weighs in favor of their respective positions.

★ Amicus curiae briefs

Written documents filed by outside parties in the case with an interest in the outcome of the litigation expressing their own views on how the Court should decide a particular case.

★ Solicitor general

The lawyer representing the U.S. government before the U.S. Supreme Court.

28 Richard Pacelle, *Between Law and Politics: The Solicitor General and the Structuring of Race, Gender, and Reproductive Rights Litigation* (College Station: Texas A & M University Press, 2003).

hearings in the Supreme Court chamber can still offer moments of high drama, such as when Richard Nixon's attorneys argued for an especially broad interpretation of executive privilege in the 1974 Watergate tapes case. Their argument was ultimately rejected, and Nixon resigned just days after the Court's decision was handed down.

Shortly after the oral arguments are completed and the case has been formally submitted, the justices meet in conference to discuss the case, offer initial votes, and assign opinions. The chief justice presides over all conferences, which culminate in the assignment of opinions to be researched and written by individual justices in accordance with the conference discussions. Each justice employs four clerks—selected from a pool of the top law school graduates from across the country—who work behind-the-scenes researching the law and creating initial drafts of written opinions according to the justice's specific wishes. In some cases clerks enjoy even more influence over the justices they work for, assisting them as they sort through competing legal arguments.

A **majority opinion** requires agreement of at least five of the Court's nine members; only a majority opinion carries the force of law. The chief justice has just one vote like his colleagues, but if he is in the majority, the chief justice also has the crucial power to choose who will write the Court's main opinion. (If the chief justice is not in the majority, the senior-most justice in the majority retains that power of assignment.) Individual justices may choose to write other opinions either on their own or on behalf of a minority of justices. A **concurring opinion** agrees with the end result reached by the majority but disagrees with the reasons offered for the decision. A **dissenting opinion,** on the other hand, disagrees with the result reached by the majority. Justices write concurring and dissenting opinions both to register their differences with the majority and to lay the groundwork for the future, when those alternate grounds may one day secure the support of a Court majority.

The dissents written by Oliver Wendell Holmes Jr., who served as an associate justice on the U.S. Supreme Court from 1902 to 1932, established him as one of the most important legal thinkers in American history. When President Theodore Roosevelt appointed Holmes to the U.S. Supreme Court in 1902, the Court majority at the time appeared to be favorably disposed to protect the rights of big business. Armed with his own "realist" view of law that emphasized the "necessities of the time," Holmes dissented vigorously from the Court's majority opinions invalidating industrial reform laws and other progressive legislation. With speech restrictions on the rise in America during and immediately after World War I, Holmes eventually adjusted his own philosophy to promote a broader conception of free speech under the Constitution. Along with fellow Justice Louis Brandeis, Holmes dissented from the majority's opinions allowing the government to punish minority views. (Holmes also made famous the metaphor of a "marketplace of ideas" and cautioned that even liberal protections of free speech would not protect a man from "falsely shouting 'fire!' in a crowded theater.") For Holmes, "the life of law" was never logic; rather, it was "experience." Justices after Holmes came to embrace his practical, real-world approach to the law. For instance, in *New York Times v. Sullivan* (1964), the Supreme Court built on Holmes's theories about the First Amendment to apply a more protective approach to libel law, making it harder for public officials to sue newspapers that criticized their actions.

Once drafts of the justices' opinions in a case have been circulated and finalized, the decision can be announced. Occasionally the justices can shift their votes near the end of the process. For example, in 1986 Associate Justice Lewis Powell seemingly resolved his own inner struggles over the scope of privacy rights when he chose to join Justice Byron White's four-person opinion in *Bowers v. Hardwick*.[29] Powell's vote gave White the majority and determined that the right to homosexual sodomy would not receive constitutional protection until 2003, when the Court overturned *Bowers* in *Lawrence v. Texas*.[30] Powell later publicly recanted his support of *Bowers*, proving that his inner struggle had actually continued. Normally the justices issue written opinions only, but on special occasions, the justices may even decide to read from key passages of the opinion they authored.

★ Majority opinion

The opinion of a majority of members of the U.S. Supreme Court, which carries the force of law.

★ Concurring opinion

The opinion of one or more justices that agrees with the end result reached by the majority but disagrees with the reasons offered for the decision.

★ Dissenting opinion

The opinion of one or more justices who disagree with the result reached by the majority.

---

[29] 478 U.S. 186 (1986).
[30] 539 U.S. 558 (2003).

Why the Justices Vote the Way They Do

Although it is difficult to determine what causes Supreme Court justices to vote as they do on certain issues, social scientists and legal scholars have identified a number of factors that may play a role in a judge's decision making:

★ **Legal rules and precedents.** The law itself—including constitutional law, statutes, rules and regulations, and past court decisions interpreting those sources—may be unambiguous enough to counsel one particular application to the case at hand. Previous court decisions are especially hard to avoid—when judges follow the decisions of past judges ruling in similar cases, they are adhering to the long-standing doctrine of "stare decisis," which is Latin for "stand by the decision" that has already been settled. For example, though Justice Byron White dissented from the original decision in *Miranda v. Arizona* (1966) providing unprecedented rights to the accused, in later decisions he actively applied the *Miranda* holding to other cases, deferring to a high Court precedent that he personally opposed. Although the language of Supreme Court opinions suggests that stare decisis is always at work, often more than one reasonable interpretation of a law or legal opinion exists. In recent years, some judges have turned to international law and judicial opinions handed down in foreign courts as well. Most notably, Justice Anthony Kennedy in *Lawrence v. Texas* (2003) cited the European Court of Human Rights in support of the Court's protection of homosexual privacy rights. Defenders of this practice claim that because Americans share some values with the wider civilization, judges should be able to cite any and all sources of law in rendering their decisions; critics respond that there is no basis for U.S. judges to impose foreign "moods or fads" on Americans.

★ **Changes in circumstances.** Sometimes changes in real-life conditions and circumstances may influence how laws are interpreted. Prior to being appointed a Supreme Court justice in 1916, Louis Brandeis served as a public interest attorney defending the constitutionality of worker-friendly labor laws in many states. When making his arguments, he often filed with the Court what became known as a "Brandeis brief," which consisted of current statistical, sociological, economic, and physiological information about the harms these industrial laws were addressing. The strategy paid off, as Brandeis convinced some justices to uphold these laws. Similarly, in the school desegregation cases of the 1950s, the Supreme Court openly considered the harmful effects of segregation on African American children; and in 1973, the Supreme Court took into account changes in modern medicine when it formulated the definition of constitutionally protected abortion rights in *Roe v. Wade*. Some jurists and scholars believe such changes in circumstances are irrelevant—rather, they view the Constitution as fixed in time and thus limited in scope to what the Framers envisioned. The search for the Framers' original intent about the Constitution is often referred to as "originalism." By contrast, other judges and scholars advocate the more flexible view of the Constitution as a "living, breathing document," which must adapt to changing circumstances and conditions.

★ **Ideological "attitudes."** Many political scientists argue that Supreme Court justices' personal attitudes (liberal or conservative on law enforcement issues, free speech, and so forth) influence their judicial decision making. This model of understanding how justices decide cases has been labeled "the attitudinal model."

Decisions of the U.S. Supreme Court are often highly watched and frequently have a profound impact on the political system. Sometimes, a decision of the Court is characterized by both high visibility and huge consequences. Following are three points in the nation's history when all eyes were on the Supreme Court's decision:

In 1819, the nation was suffering from a financial panic brought on by intense inflation, overextended investments in manufacturing, the collapse of foreign markets, and the contraction of credit nationwide. Exacerbating these ills was the mismanagement of the Second Bank of the United States, which had been chartered by Congress in part to provide stability during just such a crisis. In fact, the national bank had also increased the hardship on state banks by offering competition for scarce resources. When several states passed laws that either taxed the national bank or restricted its operations, the very constitutionality of a national bank came under question in a case (*McCulloch v. Maryland*) that weaved its way up to the U.S. Supreme Court. The economic solvency of various state banks rested on the Court's decision, and many eagerly awaited the Court's verdict. The suspense ended in 1819, when John Marshall, speaking for a unanimous Court, upheld the national bank of the United States as constitutional and rendered it immune from inferior entities.

In 1951, Americans were gripped by a "red scare," brought on by rising tensions in the Cold War with the Soviet Union. Back at home, Senator Joseph McCarthy (R-WI) was charging that Communists had infiltrated the State Department and the U.S. Army. Two years earlier, eleven top leaders of the U.S. Communist Party, had been convicted in a high-profile trial for violating the Smith Act of 1940, which made it a crime to "knowingly and willfully advocate" the necessity or propriety of overthrowing the government. All eleven appealed their convictions to the U.S. Supreme Court, claiming that the Smith Act violated the First Amendment guarantee of freedom of speech; McCarthy's forces triumphed: the Court ruled on June 4, 1951, that the First Amendment did not bar the government from making the advocacy of violent overthrow of the government a criminal act. McCarthy's personal comeuppance would have to wait three and a half more years until December 1954, when the Senate voted to censure McCarthy for his abusive conduct by a 67–22 vote.

In 2000, more than a month after Election Day, Florida's twenty-five electoral votes remained up for grabs between presidential contenders George W. Bush and Al Gore. Although an electronic recount of the state's ballots indicated that Bush held a slim lead, Gore claimed that voter confusion had led the machine recount to inaccurately record the "intent of the voter," and his lawyers demanded a manual recount of the ballots in four counties. The Florida Supreme Court agreed with Gore's position, but the U.S. Supreme Court stopped the recount and agreed to hear the case on expedited review. With a nation of citizens left wondering if the outcome of the election would be resolved in time for the January inauguration, a narrowly divided Supreme Court issued its 5–4 decision on the evening of December 12, 2000. The Court's five more conservative justices ruled that a manual recount of the ballots in the disputed counties would violate the Constitution's equal protection clause and was thus invalid. With no time left to conduct a complete manual recount of the ballots in the entire state under a more uniform standard, Gore conceded the election the following evening to Bush. Five weeks later, Bush was sworn in as the forty-third president of the United States.

Defenders of the model cite numerous statistics which support their understanding of the way judges decide cases. For example, William O. Douglas was a New Deal liberal who voted in the liberal direction in criminal procedure cases nearly 90 percent of the time and in civil rights cases 93 percent of the time.[31]

★ **Personal traits and characteristics.** Males and females may approach political events differently; accordingly, the gender of a Supreme Court justice affects his or her reaction to legal issues and cases to some degree. Just as some demographic groups tend to be more conservative, justices who fit into those groups may be expected to vote accordingly. A justice's personal experiences may also play a role in how he or she judges. Biographers of Justice Oliver Wendell Holmes, for example, contend that Holmes's near-death experiences as a soldier in the Civil War colored his approach to judging.[32]

★ **Intracourt politics.** A justice's interest in maintaining good relations with fellow justices may push him or her to vote in a certain way; behind-the-scenes bargaining and negotiating have also been a feature of Supreme Court politics throughout its history. In the late 1950s and early 1960s, Chief Justice Earl Warren and Associate Justice William Brennan were famed for their ability to sway undecided justices in their favor; by contrast, Associate Justice Felix Frankfurter's condescending attitude toward his fellow justices persuaded few and alienated many.

★ **External political pressures.** Although Supreme Court justices enjoy life tenure and are thus theoretically immune to outside political pressures, the reality is much more complicated. Aware that the Court's prestige often rests on its ability to persuade the other branches, as well as the public, to comply with the Court's decisions, justices often react to the political environment that surrounds the Court when issuing legal opinions. *Roe v. Wade* survived its widely predicted demise in 1992 because at least two conservative justices feared its reversal would deal a blow to the Supreme Court's prestige. Public opinion may also play a role in determining the language of opinions and even the outcome of some cases.

Current Debates over the Exercise of Judicial Power

American courts often find themselves thet subject of controversy. Many of the recurring debates over the proper role of courts include the following:

★ **Judicial restraint versus judicial activism.** The Supreme Court struck down several New Deal statutes in the 1930s; a few decades later, it invalidated state laws banning the use of contraceptive devices (in 1965) and state laws restricting the right to abortion (in 1973). Critics of those decisions protested the exercise of judicial activism by the high Court. Specifically, they charged that rather than deferring to the elected branches of government as a general matter, the justices responsible for those controversial decisions had effectively turned the Court into a "superlegislature" which makes social policy. More recent cases like *Lawrence v. Texas* (2003), in which the Court struck down a state law banning homosexual sodomy, have revived those charges once again. Critics of judicial activism argue in favor of a philosophy of judicial restraint by

[31] Jeffrey Segal and Harold Spaeth, *The Supreme Court and The Attitudinal Model* (Cambridge: Cambridge University Press, 1993), p. 246.
[32] See, for example, Sheldon M. Novick, *Honorable Justice: The Life of Oliver Wendell Holmes, Jr.* (Boston: Little, Brown & Co., 1989).

which judges act more slowly and incrementally, affording the democratically elected branches considerable discretion to enact whatever laws they choose, so long as there is no clear and unambiguous prohibition against those laws in the Constitution itself. (Given the "elegant vagueness" of the Constitution's language, advocates of judicial restraint believe those instances are rare indeed.)

★ **Electing judges versus appointing judges.** Federal judges are appointed by the president with the advice and consent of the Senate and then serve for life. Many state judges are appointed as well, for either fixed or indefinite terms; others must run for election and then must seek re-election to stay on the bench. These varying methods of judicial selection may have significant implications on judicial decision making. Appointed judges no longer accountable to the public or to any political processes enjoy increased independence in their decision making. Although many judicial elections pose little or no challenge to the incumbents, these election contests have become dramatically more contested in recent decades. For instance, in 1986 conservative groups disgruntled with liberal decisions rendered by the highest state court in California campaigned successfully to defeat three of its more liberal justices in recall elections, including Chief Justice Rose Bird. What elected judges may lack in independence they make up for in accountability; unlike judges appointed for life, elected judges should be more responsive to the public as a whole. The debate over judicial selection mechanisms often boils down to a question of how to strike the proper balance between the competing interests of judicial independence and accountability to the public.

★ **Law versus politics.** Do judges sit on a court of law, or is their institution simply another political body exercising its political will? Certainly the judicial process is fashioned to trumpet the Court's role as a legal body that transcends ordinary politics. The judicial robes, magisterial courtrooms, and reliance on formality give rise to this "cult of the robe" as the "apolitical" branch. Canons of judicial ethics require that judges avoid even the appearance of impropriety by not participating in political debates and lobbying other branches on various matters. At the same time, the U.S. Supreme Court in particular often finds itself at the storm center of American politics. In some instances the other branches actually come to the court in search of legal answers to what are essentially political problems. The Court's 5–4 decision in *Bush v. Gore* (2000),[33] which ended the manual recounts for the 2000 presidential election in Florida and made George W. Bush the president-elect, illustrates just one way that law and politics can become intertwined. In extremely rare cases, the elected branches essentially abdicate their responsibility to act altogether, forcing the courts to step in by enforcing judicial decrees. For example, federal courts have on rare occasions supervised the construction of prisons and the implementation of busing programs. The highly political manner in which judges are chosen and the ambiguous nature of so many legal provisions mean that the tension between law and politics is perhaps inevitable in the U.S. political system.

Pedestrians in New York City's Times Square watch as Al Gore concedes the 2000 presidential election on December 12, 2000.

---

[33] 531 U.S. 98 (2000).

★ **Cameras in the courtroom.** The Constitution guarantees to every criminal defendant a public trial; courts can satisfy that requirement by allowing the media and some members of the public access to the trial. Many states go a step further, allowing television cameras in state courtrooms, but the federal judicial system has so far resisted any such development. Do lawyers play up to the television cameras, undermining the interests of justice? It's hard to say. When O. J. Simpson was tried for murder in a California courtroom in 1995, the trial received gavel-to-gavel television coverage. Afterward, several of the lawyers in his case became full-fledged media stars, appearing on their own talk shows.

In April 2005, Senator Charles Grassley (R-IA) introduced in Congress the so-called Sunshine in the Courtroom Act, which would allow cameras into federal courtrooms. Specifically, the bill would give the presiding federal judge in every case the authority to determine whether cameras would be permitted, and if so, for how long. Even if such legislation eventually passes, it is unlikely that cameras will appear any time soon in the U.S. Supreme Court, where the new chief justice is likely to defer to a handful of older justices who remain adamantly opposed to television coverage. Justices Stephen Breyer and Antonin Scalia have both spoken publicly against the move, and Justice David Souter noted his objection in even more stark terms, telling one congressional subcommittee: "I can tell you the day you see a camera come into our courtroom—it's going to roll over my dead body." Until then, Supreme Court observers unable to observe oral arguments in person will have to settle for audiotapes of the oral arguments a short time later.

Now & Then: Making the Connection

Alexander Hamilton's assumption that the judiciary would be "the least dangerous branch" has not been realized—at key periods in our nation's history Supreme Court justices have used the power at their disposal to exert important influence on the American political system. Even when the Court has been forced to retreat somewhat from its activism, it leaves an imprint on the political terrain by legitimating the decisions of the other branches. U.S. judges are more than just innocent "umpires" calling balls and strikes within the political system; by opening up their courtrooms to certain cases, presiding over trials, and interpreting the laws and rules that govern individuals, they play a significant role in this nation's political and legal systems.

In the modern era, presidents and senators have placed added emphasis on their respective responsibilities in the judicial appointment process. Clarence Thomas's controversial Supreme Court nomination in 1991 represented a battle of wills between the first Bush administration—eager to see a conservative African American replace arch-liberal Thurgood Marshall on the Supreme Court—and a Democratic-controlled U.S. Senate just as eager to maintain the delicate ideological balance then prevailing on the high Court. Exacerbating this already tense process were last-minute allegations of sexual harassment lodged against Thomas. Yet this was hardly the first appointment to become a political powder keg. Just four years earlier, Robert Bork's nomination to the Supreme Court was defeated amid a whirlwind of interest group activity. And fifty-four years earlier Justice Hugo Black's career on the Court seemed threatened before it had even begun, amid allegations that he remained a member of the KKK in good standing. Black and Thomas survived their public ordeals to serve on the Court, but Bork did not. This much seems certain: all future nominees to the Court must be prepared to hold the weight of the political world on their shoulders. The stakes are too high for these tensions to ever go away, much less be resolved.

Since 1973, the Supreme Court's controversial decision in *Roe v. Wade* has galvanized the nation like few other Supreme Court decisions in history. By a 7–2 vote, the Court in *Roe* struck down abortion laws in forty-six states and the District of Columbia. Opposition to *Roe* exploded from the outset, with a pro-life camp forming in heated resistance to the decision. Self-labeled "right to life" groups gained even more legitimacy when President Ronald Reagan made opposition to *Roe v. Wade* part of his litmus test for all judicial appointments. In response to *Roe v. Wade*, several states passed laws limiting abortion in various ways, such as requiring parental consent for minors to obtain abortions, twenty-four-hour waiting periods, and spousal notification, among others. Some, but not all, of these laws were upheld in *Planned Parenthood v. Casey* (1992), which upheld the basic holding of *Roe v. Wade*, while also modifying it in significant ways. Meanwhile, pro-choice groups have increased their own lobbying activities to defend the *Roe v. Wade* decision from attack. Since the early 1980s, no Democratic presidential nominee has been able to escape the requirement of professed support for the decision.

President George W. Bush's appointments of Chief Justice John Roberts and Associate Justice Samuel Alito to the U.S. Supreme Court fed the growing expectation that *Roe v. Wade* might be overturned by the increasingly conservative Supreme Court in the not-so-distant future. What effect would the overturning of *Roe v. Wade* have on the American political landscape? On http://academic.cengage .com/dautrich, find the politics interactive link for details on what life might look like if *Roe v. Wade* were overturned, including links that provide information about the issues surrounding court decisions on abortion in historical, popular, and global perspectives.

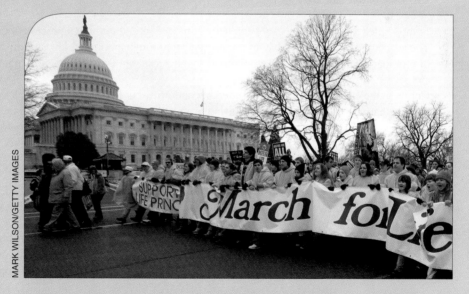

MARK WILSON/GETTY IMAGES

Pro-life protesters in Washington, DC, march in opposition to the Supreme Court's decision in *Roe v. Wade*.

http://www.academic.cengage.com/dautrich

Chapter Summary

★ Law may be defined as the authoritative rules made by government. The term *civil law* refers to the statutes and other rules enacted most often by legislative bodies; "common law" consists of the rulings handed down by judges that establish precedents over time.

★ Each of the fifty states has its own court system, which includes trial courts and appellate courts. Each state has one high supreme court, which is the ultimate arbiter of state legal controversies.

★ Article III of the U.S. Constitution established the judicial branch of the federal government and created the U.S. Supreme Court as the Unites States' supreme judicial body.

★ Chief Justice John Marshall's opinion in *Marbury v. Madison* (1803) established the Supreme Court's authority to review the constitutionality of any act passed by Congress. The power of judicial review was later expanded to cover all government acts at all levels of government.

★ Federal district courts are the trial courts of the federal government. Decisions of these courts may be appealed to the U.S. courts of appeals, whose decisions may be reviewed by the U.S. Supreme Court's grant of a discretionary writ of certiorari. The decision of a state supreme court that raises federal constitutional issues may also be brought directly to the U.S. Supreme Court by petitioning for a writ of certiorari.

★ The American legal system is an adversarial system of justice, in which opposing parties contend against each other for a result favorable to themselves, whereas judges act merely as independent referees overseeing the contest. In an adversarial system, the judge is entrusted only with ensuring that the litigants achieve procedural fairness and plays no active role in evidence gathering or in the advocacy of one side over the other.

★ In the United States, disputes between parties may be settled through a process of civil litigation. Those accused of criminal behavior are prosecuted through a criminal law system. The vast majority of criminal law procedures are settled not through a trial, but through a plea-bargaining process.

★ Courts in the United States have considerable authority, but they are also bound by particular constraints that are not imposed on the legislative and executive branches of government. Namely, courts cannot initiate lawsuits; they can only hear and rule on cases that involve true controversies; their decision affects only those parties that are part of a case; and courts have no ability to enforce their decisions but must instead rely on the other branches to do so.

★ All federal court judges are nominated by the president and must be confirmed by the U.S. Senate. Nominations and confirmation hearings for U.S. Supreme Court vacancies receive a great deal of attention.

★ In order for the U.S. Supreme Court to grant a writ of certiorari to review a case, four of the nine justices must agree that the case deserves to be taken up by the Court. Most cases that come to the U.S. Supreme Court come from state supreme courts or federal circuit courts of appeals.

Key Terms

Amicus curiae briefs (p. 282)

Appellate jurisdiction (p. 274)

Briefs (p. 282)

Civil law (p. 261)

Class action lawsuit (p. 272)

Common law (p. 261)

Complaint (p. 265)

Concurring opinion (p. 283)

Defendant (p. 265)

Discovery (p. 266)

Dissenting opinion (p. 283)

Grand jury (p. 267)

Resources

Important Books and Articles

Abraham, Henry J. *Justices, Presidents, and Senators: A History of the U.S. Supreme Court Appointments from Washington to Clinton.* Lanham, MD: Rowman & Littlefield, 2007.

Baum, Lawrence. *American Courts: Process and Policy.* Boston: Houghton Mifflin, 2007.

Baum, Lawrence. *The Supreme Court.* Washington, DC: CQ Press, 2006.

Canon, Bradley, and Charles A. Johnson. *Judicial Policies: Implementation and Impact.* 2nd ed. Washington, DC: CQ Press, 1999.

Dahl, Robert. "Decisionmaking in a Democracy." *Journal of Public Law* (1957): 279–295.

Epstein, Lee, and Jack Knight. *The Choices Justices Make.* Washington, DC: CQ Press, 1998.

Keck, Thomas. *The Most Activist Supreme Court in History.* Chicago: University of Chicago Press, 2004.

Maltese, John A. *The Selling of Supreme Court Nominees.* Baltimore: Johns Hopkins University Press, 1995.

McCloskey, Robert G. *The American Supreme Court.* 4th ed. Chicago: University of Chicago Press, 2004.

Perry, H. W. *Deciding to Decide: Agenda Setting in the United States Supreme Court.* Cambridge, MA: Harvard University Press, 1991.

Rosenberg, Gerald. *Hollow Hope: Can Courts Bring About Social Change?* Chicago: University of Chicago Press, 1993.

Segal, Jeffrey A., and Harold J. Spaeth. *The Supreme Court and the Attitudinal Model Revisited.* New York: Cambridge University Press, 2002.

Toobin, Jeffrey. *The Nine: The Secret World of the Supreme Court.* New York: Doubleday, 2007.

Yalof, David A. *Pursuit of Justices: Presidential Politics and the Selection of Supreme Court Nominees.* Chicago: University of Chicago Press, 1999.

Internet Sources

http://www.uscourts.gov (the home page of the U.S. federal judiciary, which includes information about the U.S. Supreme Court, the U.S. courts of appeals, U.S. district courts, and U.S. bankruptcy courts)

http://www.findlaw.com (the most comprehensive source of no-cost legal research available on the Internet; includes a legal search engine and links to organizations, law schools, and so on)

http://www.supremecourtus.gov (the U.S. Supreme Court's own website, which features recent decisions, briefs, and other important information about the nation's highest court).

http://www.fjc.gov (the home page of the Federal Judicial Center, which features a comprehensive history of the federal judiciary and links to publications and educational materials)

http://oyez.nwu.edu (this website features a searchable database of select Supreme Court opinions and audio excerpts of oral arguments from the Supreme Court; also includes a virtual tour of the U.S. Supreme Court building)

http://www.trutv.com (the website of truTV, formerly Court TV, which features information about major cases, including video clips, case links, and so on)

10 Public Opinion

President Bill Clinton in 1996

An Obsession with Public Opinion: Now & Then

As president, he was obsessed with how the American people viewed him. He wanted to be well respected and admired, and he wanted his policy positions to enjoy the endorsement of an enthusiastic public. He knew that public opinion was a key factor in winning many political fights, and was thus always reluctant to advocate policies that would meet with popular discontent. Ultimately, this obsession with public opinion affected the way he led the country and the decisions he made throughout his two full terms in office.

President George Washington at his inauguration in 1789

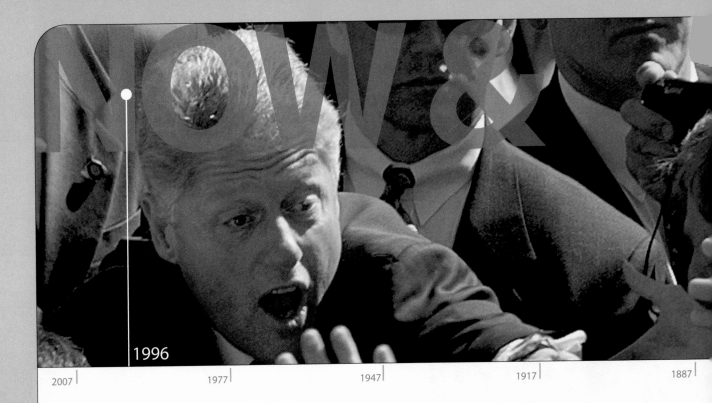

1996

2007 | 1977 | 1947 | 1917 | 1887

Now. . . Certainly the above description applied to no president more aptly than it did to President Bill Clinton. During his first year in office, Clinton spent nearly $2 million on polling. Over the course of two full terms in office, he conducted polls to determine where he should vacation, whether he should tell the truth to the American people regarding his affair with a White House intern, and whether to use ground troops in a military operation in Kosovo. His public image was important to him, and he instructed his pollsters to keep especially close tabs on his public standing. Many observers of the Clinton presidency have described it as in constant "campaign mode," even immediately after his two successful campaign bids.[1] Clinton was a consummate traveler, using his trips and public appearances around the country to stay popular and to affect positively how the public thought of him and his policies.

Though Clinton's desire to use public opinion to make both personal and policy decisions represents a particularly exaggerated obsession with public opinion, Presidents George W. Bush, George H. W. Bush, Ronald Reagan, and Jimmy Carter all made extensive use of private White House polling as well to guide their decision making. In fact, the desire to understand what the public thinks and to secure the public's endorsement of one's actions actually dates back to the nation's first presidential administration.

---

[1] David Gergen, *Eyewitness to Power: The Essence of Leadership, Nixon to Clinton* (New York: Touchstone, 2000), 330–332.

1857   1827   1797   1794   1767   1737

Then. . .

George Washington was quite attentive to public opinion even though the public's high esteem for him might have led a lesser man to act without regard for the public will. Early in his presidency he reluctantly signed into law an excise tax on whiskey, which he knew would be unpopular among western farmers. During the summer and early fall of 1794, when a group of farmers in western Pennsylvania turned to mob action to prevent federal officials from collecting the new tax, Washington grew concerned that the violent reaction to the new tax would spread.[2] Acting on his recognition of the public's growing dissatisfaction, Washington called together his Cabinet and formulated an impressive public relations campaign to deal with the possible negative ripple effects of the "Whiskey Rebellion" and to persuade the public of the legitimacy and necessity of the tax. Using military force against the rebellious farmers, a carefully crafted set of newspaper editorials published strategically around the nation, and his own presence in a tour of Pennsylvania and the southern states, Washington effectively won the battle for public opinion in 1794.

On another occasion, Washington's concern about his public standing led him to distance himself from Vice President John Adams. Early in Washington's presidency, questions arose about what would be the proper words to use in addressing the new president. In a Senate debate on the topic, Adams (acting in his capacity as president of the Senate) insisted that Washington be referred to as "His Majesty, the President."[3] Adams's insistence on a title that smacked of monarchy was greeted with considerable agitation and public apprehension, as the bitter war for independence against the tyranny of a monarch was still less than a decade old. Adams was mocked for his position on this issue, and Washington's desire not to be associated with Adams's public liability led him to distance himself from his vice president.

[2] See William Hogeland, *The Whiskey Rebellion: George Washington, Alexander Hamilton, and the Frontier Rebels Who Challenged America's Newfound Sovereignty* (New York: Scribner, 2006).
[3] Joseph Ellis, *His Excellency George Washington* (New York: Alfred A. Knopf, 2004).

For political leaders and citizens alike, the appetite for information on what the public thinks has always been hearty. Today, this appetite is fed through the large number of opinion polls whose results are disseminated through newspapers, magazines, television, radio, and the Internet. The methods of gauging public opinion have advanced quite dramatically over the nation's history, and this advancement has been driven in no small part by the obsession to know "what Americans think." The nation's democratic roots, featuring a commitment to majoritarian rule and the notion of "consent of the governed," raise public opinion to a lofty status in the workings of American politics. Indeed, the willingness of officials to heed the people's voice has become firmly entrenched in the American political culture. Presidents, like many others in the political system, have also shown an obsession with keeping tabs on public opinion. Modern presidential candidates invest heavily in conducting significant numbers of public opinion polls throughout their election campaigns. Even when they are victorious, they continue to invest in conducting polls while in office.

Scientific measurement of public opinion is a relatively recent phenomenon in American politics. But the significant role that public opinion plays in the formulation of policy is as old as American democracy itself. Understanding what public opinion is, how it is expressed, how it forms, and how it is measured in contemporary politics is critical to understanding how American government works.

The History of Public Opinion in American Politics

The concept of public opinion is central to the American system of government. But the way in which public opinion is gauged and its relevance and uses in the American political system have changed over the nation's history. The U.S. Constitution begins with the words "We the People," highlighting the important role of the *public* in the creation of the government. Nonetheless, there is no mention of the term *public opinion* in the Constitution. The word *democracy* literally translated (from its Greek roots *demos kratos*) means "rule by the people," and thus the *opinions* of the public take on a particularly important role in governing. The American system of government was founded on a set of democratic principles, first articulated by Plato and Aristotle and later popularized by political philosophers of the eighteenth-century Enlightenment, such as Montesquieu.[4] These principles herald the role of the public in governing and in consenting to what government does.

From the time of the Founders up through the present day, the virtues of public opinion and its role in American democracy have been continually extolled. James Madison argued that the "public voice" and its formal role in voting provided primary justification for adopting the proposed Constitution. Borrowing from the political theories of John Locke, Madison acknowledged that government must serve the "will of the people." Andrew Jackson's presidency encouraged and empowered the rise of the "common man" to express his opinion for the purpose of influencing government.

Political leaders recognize that public opinion plays not only a theoretically important role in our democratic form of government, but an important tactical role as well. Political scientist E. E. Schattschneider, in an influential book titled *Semi-Sovereign People*, argued that "public opinion can emerge as a key factor in any political context," and that public opinion often is responsible for determining the outcome of important political battles. Long before Schattschneider, President Abraham Lincoln expressed this idea based on his own experiences, saying: "Public sentiment is everything. With public sentiment, nothing can fail; without it, nothing can succeed."[5]

Though most scholars, elected leaders, and everyday citizens would agree that **public opinion** is and should be very important in our system of government, the concept remains hard to define and measure. Many scholars regard public opinion

★ Public opinion

The summation of individual opinions on any particular issue or topic.

American Government: Historical, Popular, and Global Perspectives

[4] Vincent Price, *Public Opinion* (Newbury Park, CA: Sage Publications, 1992), pp. 5–22.
[5] E. E. Schattschneider, *The Semi-Sovereign People: A Realist's View of Democracy in America* (New York: Holt, Rinehart and Winston, 1960).

AP PHOTO/MANUEL BALCE CENETA

as simply the summation of individual opinions on any particular issue or topic. Political scientist V. O. Key Jr., however, defined public opinion more specifically as "those opinions held by private persons which government finds it prudent to heed." As an input in the American political system, public opinion must not only exist, Key argued, but it must also be "heeded" or at least heard by those making policy decisions.[6]

Public opinion is a vague, though important, concept. It is regularly used by presidents to justify their policies, by political candidates to mount campaigns, by interest groups to promote their causes, by journalists to describe public preferences, and by scholars to understand the American government. Today public opinion polls—for better or worse—have become the yardstick through which public opinion is understood and evaluated. The barrage of polls released daily by major media organizations provides a plethora of data defining the American psyche. There are, however, numerous methods through which public opinion in America is expressed.

Protesters at an April 2006 rally in Washington, DC, calling for American intervention to stop genocide in Darfur. Protests are an important expression of public opinion in the United States.

How Is Public Opinion Expressed?

The formal constitutional mechanism by which public opinion influences the federal government is the free, open, and regular election of House members. Since ratification of the Seventeenth Amendment in 1913, the direct election of U.S. senators has served as yet another constitutional means for the expression of public opinion. Chapter 15 covers this form of expressing public opinion in detail. Voting is one important expression of public opinion and provides guarantees that officials are responsive to voters. In many state and local elections, voters are asked to respond to referendum questions, which empower the public to directly resolve policy issues. But there are a number of additional ways beyond voting in which public opinion has an influence on government. The First Amendment's guarantees that the people have the right to free speech, to peaceably assemble, and to petition their government pave the way for political rallies and protest rallies, which are important manifestations of public opinion.

[6] V. O. Key Jr., *Public Opinion and American Democracy* (New York: Knopf, 1961).

Kindergarten students in a Maryland classroom learn to appreciate the values associated with the American flag.

Supporting a candidate and engaging in attempts to elect an individual or political party to office through a monetary contribution or a contribution of time and effort is another way that public opinion is expressed. Likewise, contributing time or money to an interest group or political action committee enables individuals to express their opinion indirectly and may have a significant impact on what government does.

Public opinion is also expressed through the news media. Journalists often provide commentary on politics and public issues through talk radio shows, websites, editorial pages, and television news talk shows that provide perspectives on public opinion. Individual citizens may also use the media to express their opinion, through letters to the editor. In addition, members of the public often choose to express their opinion directly to elected officials by contacting them, via either a letter or email, a phone call, or the Internet, for their views on a particular issue. Millions of individuals also post their views in online diaries open to the public called "blogs" (short for "weblogs").

Yet perhaps the most visible and widely used expression of public opinion in contemporary politics is the public opinion poll. Most major and many smaller media organizations today regularly conduct polls on politics and policy issues, and publish the results of those polls in the form of news stories. The CNN/USA Today/Gallup Poll, the CBS/New York Times Poll, and the NBC/Wall Street Journal Poll are only a few examples of media-based polls that, on a regular basis, provide data on American public opinion.

MARK WILSON/GETTY IMAGES

The Levels of Public Opinion

Public opinion exists at three basic levels—the broad level of values and beliefs, an intermediate level of political orientations, and the specific level of preferences about particular topics.

Values and Beliefs

★ Values and beliefs

The broad principles underlying the American political culture that citizens support and adhere to.

At the highest, most abstract level are the **values and beliefs** of the American people. Values are the broad principles underlying the American political culture that citizens support and adhere to; they represent that which people find most important in life. Beliefs are the facts that derive from values that people take for granted about the world. Although there are a number of values that Americans hold dear, political scientist Samuel Huntington[7] has identified four politically relevant values that are widely accepted in the American political culture and serve as the basis for defining political beliefs on which there is great consensus in America: liberty, equality, individualism, and the rule of law.

The vast majority of Americans support the idea of basic freedoms and liberties, such as freedom of religion and freedom of speech. These liberties are embedded in our political culture and serve as the basis for many government policies. Because Americans value liberty, for example, they believe that people should have the right to choose a religion or not to choose a religion, the right to publicly disagree with the president or the party in power, and the right to publish articles or news stories without government retribution.

[7] Samuel P. Huntington, *American Politics: The Promise of Disharmony* (Cambridge, MA: Harvard University Press, 1981).

American Government . . . in Popular Perspective:
Public Support for American Values

Disagreement and dissent are ingrained aspects of the American culture—no matter the subject, conflicting views can be expected, and indeed they may even be welcome. That said, even in the United States there exist some fundamental values for which there is a "consensus." As one set of Pew Research polls indicate, these values tend to gather widespread and consistent support from Americans:

Consensus Values

	1994 %	1999 %	2004 %
Religious Faith			
Religion is a very important part of my life	n/a	75	74
Religion is not that important to me		22	24
Neither/Both/Don't know		2	2
		100	100
Personal Empowerment & Optimism			
Success in life is pretty much outside of our control	18	15	16
Everyone has it in their own power to succeed	79	80	78
Neither/Both/Don't know	3	5	I
	100	100	100
Environmental Protection			
This country should do whatever it takes to protect the environment	78	80	77
This country has gone too far in its efforts to protect the environment	19	15	18
Neither/Both/Don't know	3	5	1
	100	100	100
Perceptions of Business Power			
Too much power is concentrated in the hands of a few large companies	76	77	77
The largest companies do not have too much power	19	17	16
Neither/Both/Don't know	5	6	2
	100	100	100
Belief in Black Progress			
The position of blacks in American society has improved in recent years	72	78	73
There hasn't been much real progress for blacks in recent years	25	18	20
Neither/Both/Don't know	3	4	1
	100	100	100

Source: Pew Research Center, Trends 2005 *(Washington, DC: Pew Research Center, 2005), p. 25.*

Likewise, a majority of Americans firmly value the concept stated in the Declaration of Independence that "all men are created equal." Regardless of economic status, race, or gender, the American public on the whole subscribes to the belief that all people should be treated equally under the law and that all people should have equal opportunities for economic success.

Americans also show a strong propensity to support the value of individualism. Over the years, Americans have consistently shown a preference for rewarding individual hard work and for limiting the role of government.[8] Jefferson's maxim that

---

[8] For a good discussion of the value of individualism in the American culture, see Herbert McCloskey and John Zaller, *The American Ethos* (Cambridge, MA: Harvard University Press, 1984).

"that government is best which governs the least" presumes that society will advance by encouraging individuals to succeed and leads to a faith in capitalism and free enterprise as the optimal economic system. Also, the Puritan work ethic that served as an important value in early American society continues to be reflected in Americans' affinity for the value of individualism.

Finally, the value of the "rule of law" encourages a strong belief in the legitimacy of the U.S. Constitution, in the importance of elections as a way to configure government, and in the beliefs that the opinion of the majority should prevail, that those in the minority should have right to challenge the majority, and that those accused of a crime should be entitled to fair procedures.

Unlike other levels of public opinion, values and beliefs are unique in that they generally receive a high level of support and consensus. Whether individuals are Democrats or Republicans, from the far right or the far left, elites or more representative of the masses—the vast majority generally subscribe to these broad values. Accordingly, values are the level of public opinion that define our political culture; widespread agreement and support for them is thus critical to the maintenance of the American political system.

Political Orientations

Values and beliefs are very broad and abstract notions held by Americans that provide general guidance to people in thinking about politics. **Political orientations** are the translation of these values and beliefs into a systematic way of assessing the political environment. Although there may be broad consensus about values and beliefs among Americans, the translation of these values into an organized way of thinking about politics and issues is considerably more varied.

The two primary ways in which Americans orient themselves toward political topics and issues are partisanship and political ideology (see Figure 10.1). Partisanship, which is discussed in a later chapter, features a psychological attachment to one of the main political parties, generally either the Democrats or the Republicans.[9] A partisan identification provides an orientational mechanism for understanding how to apply one's values and beliefs to the political world. Consider, for example, the political debate over affirmative action policies. A Democratic orientation largely applies the value of equality and the belief that people of all races and creeds should enjoy equal opportunities, therefore suggesting support for affirmative action programs, which attempt to level the playing field and make corrections for policies that have historically benefited white males. A Republican orientation, on the other hand, generally places a higher priority on the value of individualism and the belief that government should not interfere with individual initiatives to succeed, thus suggesting opposition to affirmative action programs. Partisan orientation often helps people translate values into specific opinions.

Likewise, political ideology provides an orientation for translating values into specific opinions. **Political ideology** is a philosophical guide that people use to help translate their values and beliefs into specific political preferences. The dominant ideologies in America are liberalism and conservatism. The contemporary **liberal ideology,** which is more closely associated with the modern Democratic Party, prefers that government take a more assertive role in the redistribution of economic resources, but that government advocate positions that emphasize individual freedom on a range of social issues. Today's **conservative ideology,** which is more closely identified with the Republican Party, favors government activism in defense of more traditional values on social issues, but prefers government restraint in economic redistribution.

The liberal and conservative camps largely agree on the basic values and beliefs of the American political culture—in the rule of law and majority rule and minority rights and in the idea that the free enterprise system will generally guarantee the most robust economy. But liberals and conservatives often differ when seeking to translate these values and beliefs into actual policies.

★ **Political orientations**

The translation of values and beliefs into a systematic way of assessing the political environment.

★ **Political ideology**

A philosophical guide that people use to help translate their values and beliefs into political preferences.

★ **Liberal ideology**

A political orientation that favors a more assertive role in the redistribution of economic resources, but emphasizes individual freedom on a range of social issues.

★ **Conservative ideology**

A political orientation that generally favors government activism in defense of more traditional values on social issues, but also favors government restraint in economic redistribution.

[9] The concept of partisanship and controversies surrounding it over the years are presented in Warren E. Miller and Merrill Shanks, *The New American Voter* (Cambridge, MA: Harvard University Press, 1996).

American Government: Historical, Popular, and Global Perspectives

Figure 10.1 Partisanship and Political Ideology in America

The two most important and studied political orientations of the American public are political partisanship and political ideology. These orientations provide a framework through which many Americans make sense of the often complex and confusing political world. Partisanship and ideology are quite influential in helping individuals form opinions on policy preferences as well as perceptions of political leaders and candidates for office. As the graphs indicate, the distributions of partisanship and political ideology of the American public have remained relatively stable over the past fifty years.

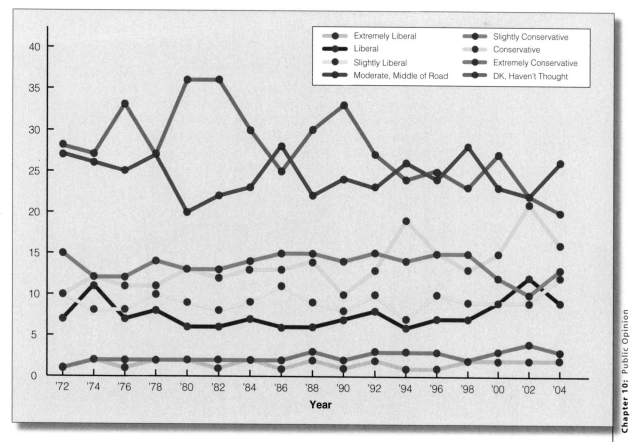

Partisanship and political ideology are two very important topics in the study of American public opinion. They provide a framework for individuals to translate broad values and beliefs into preferences for issue positions and political candidates. These orientations help people to efficiently form opinions and express those opinions. Partisanship and political ideology also enable both political leaders and scholars to better understand why Americans think what they think about particular issues and vote the way they vote in elections.

The political orientations of Americans tend to be quite stable and lasting[10]—more so than the specific preferences that people have toward policies and political actors. The stability in American political orientations provides an order and consistency to American public opinion, which ultimately promotes stability in the political system as a whole. As Figure 10.1 indicates, partisanship and political ideology have remained relatively stable over the years.

Political Preferences

★ Political preferences

The attitudes people maintain regarding the performance of political leaders and institutions, their candidate preferences in elections, and specific policy issues.

The most discussed level of public opinion is the particular **political preferences** that Americans have on policy issues, their attitudes regarding the performance of political leaders and institutions, and their candidate preferences in elections. Support for the minimum wage, gun control proposals, the use of U.S. troops in fighting terrorism, abortion policy, campaign finance reform proposals, tax increases, or tax cuts are all specific policy issues on which the American public expresses opinions. In addition to policies, Americans also hold specific opinions about the performance of their elected leaders such as the president, as well as their confidence in institutions such as Congress, the U.S. Supreme Court, and the military.

Figure 10.2 American Political Preferences and Opinions on Selected Issues

The Economy:

Opinions about the state of the economy are subject to wide fluctuations, as is demonstrated in this figure. As the economy worsened in 2001, American attitudes followed suit. Asked *"Would you describe the nation's economy these days as excellent, good, not so good, or poor?"* respondents replied as shown.

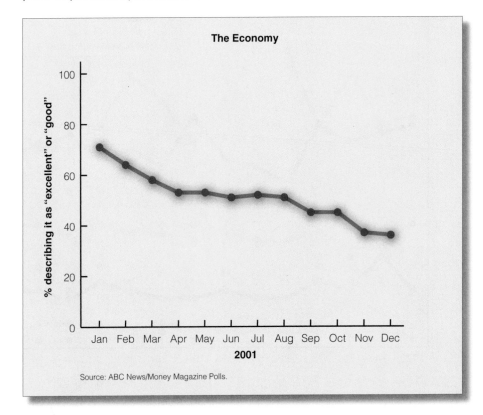

Source: ABC News/Money Magazine Polls.

American Government: Historical, Popular, and Global Perspectives

[10] See M. Kent Jennings and Richard G. Niemi, *Generations and Politics: A Panel Study of Young Adults and Their Parents* (Princeton, NJ: Princeton University Press, 1981).

Figure 10.2 American Political Preferences and Opinions on Selected Issues (*continued*)

Presidential Job Approval:

The approval rating that Americans give to the performance of the president is also subject to wide shifts. This figure shows the Gallup Poll's approval rating for first year of the George W. Bush presidency, with a "rally-around-the-flag" effect occurring immediately after the September 11, 2001, terrorist attacks.

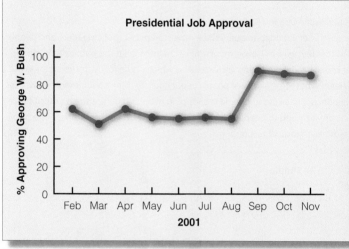

Source: The Gallup Organization. ©2001 The Gallup Organization.

Trust in the Government:

The National Election Study surveys have shown changes over the past fifty years in the number of Americans who say they trust the government in Washington to do what is right at least most of the time.

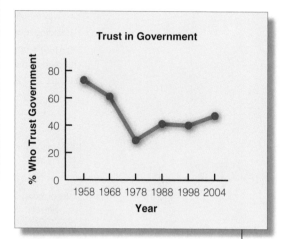

Economy as the Most Important Issue:

The Gallup Organization regularly asks the American people what they think is the most important issue facing the country. A common answer is the economy, which jumped in late 2008 as the economy tumbled.

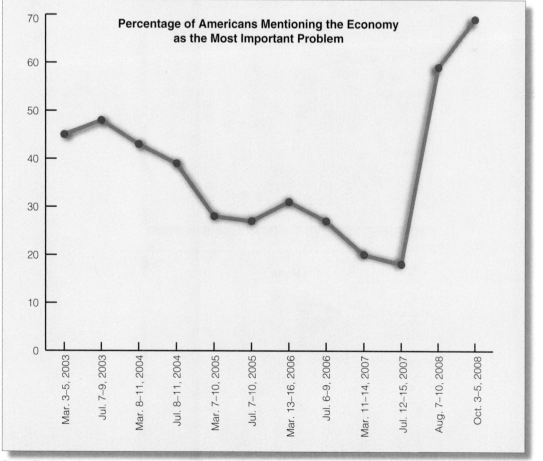

Source: The Gallup Organization. ©2003–2008 The Gallup Organization.

What Americans think about the minimum wage, the performance of the president, or the candidates in a political campaign is highly influenced by their political orientations. For example, an individual who identifies as a Republican and considers herself ideologically conservative is much more likely to say she approves of President Bush's performance than would a Democrat who considers himself to be liberal.

Figure 10.3 How Should Public Opinion Be Registered?
A survey conducted by the Kaiser Foundation queried the American public, policy leaders, and people in the news media about the best way for government officials to learn what the public thinks. These three groups were all asked the same question : "Please tell me which of the following you think is the best way for officials to learn what the majority of people in our country think about important issues? (1) holding town hall meetings, (2) talking to people in shopping malls and on the streets, (3) conducting a public opinion poll, or (4) talking to people who call, write or email the official's office." The pie charts show the results for each group of respondents.

Voters in Glendale, California, waiting to cast their ballot in the November 2006 elections.

How Informed Is Public Opinion?

As discussed earlier in this chapter, American democracy relies on public opinion to choose leaders and inform public policy. This reliance is based on an important assumption about democracy—that citizens have the necessary information and skills to be able to understand political issues and provide informed input. Since the time of Plato and Aristotle, political philosophers have dealt with questions about this important assumption: is the public capable of democracy?

In the Federalist Papers, Alexander Hamilton and James Madison expressed concerns about the fickleness of public opinion and the potential "tyranny of the masses," which could lead to instability in governance.[11] Hamilton's solution for this problem was a republican form of government, in which the public chooses leaders who run the government, rather than a direct democracy in which the public rules directly.

Suspicions about the capacity of the public for meaningful contributions to governance were also articulated quite well by Walter Lippman in the early twentieth century.[12] Lippman, a well-known public opinion scholar, delivered withering attacks on ordinary citizens' lack of knowledge regarding politics. He argued that citizens invest very little energy and effort in acquiring information about politics, and as a consequence, the public lacks the necessary knowledge for their opinions to provide value. Subsequent research in the 1960s and 1970s, most notably by Philip Converse and his colleagues in *The American Voter*, used scientific surveys to support the argument that ordinary citizens tend to be ill-informed about political issues, ill-equipped to understand politics, and quite fickle in how they stand on issues.[13]

More contemporary studies indicate that the American public today is uninformed about politics. For example, a May 2008 national survey[14] of Americans found:

★ 73 percent did not know that the Bill of Rights prohibits the official establishment of religion in the United States.

★ 79 percent could not identify the Gettysburg Address as the source of "Government of the people, for the people and by the people."

★ 50 percent could not name the three branches of the federal government.

★ 25 percent could not name any power of the federal government.

★ 35 percent could not name one country that was an enemy of the United States during World War II.

[11] James Madison, Alexander Hamilton, and John Jay, *The Federalist Papers*, Federalist No. 51 (New York: Doubleday, 1966, originally published in 1788).
[12] Walter Lippman, *Public Opinion* (New York: Harcourt Brace Jovanovich, 1922).
[13] Angus Campbell, Phillip E. Converse, Warren E. Miller, and Donald E. Stokes, *The American Voter* (New York: John Wiley and Sons, 1960).
[14] This survey was commissioned by the Intercollegiate Studies Institute and included a national adult sample of 2,500 respondents, conducted by telephone.

In addition, many surveys show that the public's level of expressed interest in politics is quite low. During the 2007 presidential primary campaign, for example, the Pew Center found that only one in five voters said that they were "very interested" in following the races—and this represented a 7 percentage point increase from interest in the race in 2003. With such little knowledge of and lack of interest in politics, should public opinion even be considered an important factor in making public policy? How much confidence should we have in the outcome of elections where the voters know little about the candidates and the issues?

Some political scientists have come to the defense of the American public in this regard. V. O. Key Jr., in his work *The Responsible Electorate*,[15] stated that although "many voters act in odd ways indeed," if one studies the electorate more carefully one would find that "voters are not fools." Key observed that "'in the large, the electorate behaves about as rationally and responsibly as we should expect, given the clarity of the alternatives presented to it and the character of the information available to it." If political leaders don't rationally discuss issues and provide a framework for voters to use to understand politics, it is not the voters who should be blamed, but rather the leaders. Considering this caveat, Key extolled the capacity of the public to form stable, responsible opinions and to contribute to the governing process.

Benjamin Page and Robert Shapiro extended Key's ideas in their book *The Rational Public*.[16] They used decades of public opinion poll data to show that over the long haul, pubic opinion on many issues does remain fairly stable, and when it does change, it moves in logical directions. The aggregate responses of the public in polls, Page and Shapiro found, make sense and demonstrate rationality. They also found that the public makes distinctions between important policy areas, and public opinion tends to form meaningful patterns, consistent with a set of underlying beliefs and values.

The link between public opinion on an issue and public policy is a difficult one to establish. Page and Shapiro report that over the long haul, there does seem to be a relationship between public attitudes on policy issues and the public policies that emerge from government. These researchers also argue that when public opinion shifts, a corresponding shift in public policy is likely to follow.

Political scientist Samuel Kernell has noted a more indirect link between public opinion and public policy:[17] political actors (most notably the president) who have high levels of public support tend to be better able to get legislation passed. President Bush, for example, in 2003 was able to get Congress to pass a new tax cut package in part because of the high job performance ratings Americans gave him at that time. High levels of public support may be translated into an officeholder's greater political power to influence the legislative process.

How Does Public Opinion Form?

Through voting, opinion polls, protest rallies, communications with leaders, and newspaper editorials, public opinion is expressed and provides an important input for public policy making. But how do individuals develop their particular political orientations, and how do they come to hold their specific political preferences? How do the more deep-seated values and beliefs form? What influences the values that people hold, their partisan and ideological orientations, and their opinions on specific issues?

Political socialization is the process by which an individual acquires values, beliefs, and opinions about politics. Political socialization is a life-long process, beginning in early childhood and continuing throughout an individual's life. The learning process that leads to the acquisition of values and opinions not only applies to politics—it also applies to other orientations of people, including their beliefs about religion and culture.

Just as there are a number of factors and influences that lead individuals to consider themselves Democrats or Republicans or supporters of gun control or gun rights, there are also numerous factors and influences that lead people to choose a particular religion, such as Protestant or Catholic, or to choose no religion at all. Socialization is important not only in the development of political learning for

★ Political socialization

The process by which an individual acquires values, beliefs, and opinions about politics.

[15] V. O. Key Jr., *The Responsible Electorate* (Cambridge, MA: Belknap Harvard, 1966).
[16] Benjamin I. Page and Robert Y. Shapiro, *The Rational Public: Fifty Years of Trends in Americans' Policy Preferences* (Chicago: University of Chicago Press, 1992).
[17] Samuel Kernell, *Going Public: New Strategies of Presidential Leadership* (Washington, DC: CQ Press, 1997).

The following is from a syndicated column, entitled "Don't Panic" written by Andisheh Nouraee, found at: http://atlanta.creativeloafing.com/gyrobase/ Content?oid=oid%3A93423. Polls often ask what Americans think about others. The Pew Global Attitudes project asks other nations what they think about Americans. Here is one author's take on the latest Pew survey about Americans:

ANDISHEH NOURAEE   Published July 5, 2006

The Pew Global Attitudes Project is an ongoing series of worldwide public opinion surveys designed to help Americans understand what the rest of the world is thinking about important issues. The [2006] survey asked 16,000 people in 15 countries what they think about several important political issues. Most important to us, the poll asked what people think about us . . . Sit back and enjoy the bad news: The world doesn't like us . . . only four [countries] had majorities who say they have a favorable opinion of the United States.

The United States' worst favorability ratings come from the Muslim countries in the survey. Only 30 percent of Indonesians and Egyptians view the U.S. favorably. In Pakistan, it's 27 percent; in Jordan, 15 percent; and in Turkey, only 12 percent of the people polled said they have a favorable opinion of the United States. Those numbers are especially disturbing when you consider that those countries are all considered friends of the U.S. And Turkey is not only a democracy, it's a member of NATO. If that's what our Muslim friends think of us, imagine what our Muslim enemies must think.

The only country with a large Muslim population whose citizens view the U.S. favorably is Nigeria. Don't cheer up just yet, though. When Pew divided the Nigerian respondents into Muslims and Christians, they found that just

32 percent of Nigerian Muslims like us. Nigeria's overall pro-America numbers were so high, it turns out, because an astonishing 89 percent of Nigerian Christians like us. According to Pew, more Nigerian Christians view the U.S. favorably than the Americans do.

The other stunner from the "How they like us now?" survey is the sharp decline of the United States' favorability rating in Spain. Only 23 percent of Spaniards view the U.S. favorably this year, down from 41 percent last year. Remember, they're not only an ally, but they actually sent troops to Iraq when we asked. Of the 14 countries surveyed, only two of the countries have majorities who say they have some or a lot of confidence in Bush's international leadership. Those two countries: Nigeria and India.

In Great Britain, our greatest ally that isn't actually touching us, 30 percent of those surveyed say that they at least have some confidence in Bush's international leadership. In France, that number dips to 15 percent; in Spain, 7 percent; and in Turkey, just 3 percent of those surveyed said they have at least some confidence in Bush's international leadership. Three percent! That's one out of every 33 people. It makes me wonder if the people who said they have confidence in Bush even heard the question correctly . . .

individuals, but also in the transmission of fundamental beliefs and values of the American political culture from one generation to the next.

Though political socialization is a life-long process, there are certain times in life when political learning is greater. For example, the political socialization that occurs early on in life has a more profound impact on political orientations than learning that occurs in adulthood. The impressions and information that are acquired while

The theory that impressions acquired while an individual is younger are likely to be more influential and longer lasting.

★ Agents of political socialization

Factors that have a significant impact on an individual's socialization to politics.

the individual is younger tend to be most influential and the longest lasting. Psychologists refer to this as the **primacy tendency.**

Though early political learning tends to be most profound, socialization to politics remains at work through a number of influences over the course of a person's life. A number of factors and institutions, known as **agents of political socialization,**[18] have been identified as having a particularly relevant impact on one's socialization to politics.

Certainly demographic factors such as race, ethnicity, gender, age, and economic status go a long way toward defining individuals' identities, and can influence their political values. But a list of the most important agents of political socialization also includes such influences as family, friends and peer groups, schools, the media, and religion. Collectively, these agents promote the acquisition of the political values, beliefs, and opinions that an individual comes to hold.

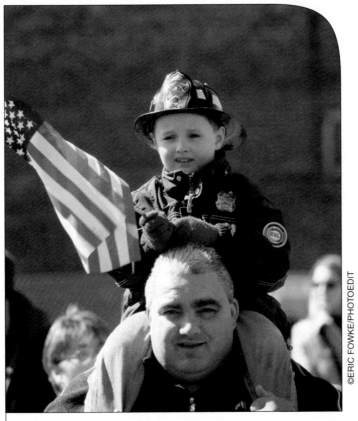

©ERIC FOWKE/PHOTOEDIT

Parents provide an important influence in socializing their children to appreciate American political values. Pictured above, a father teaches his son to appreciate the values associated with Independence Day.

Family

Because much of the early years in a person's life are dominated by experiences with the family, the primacy tendency leads many to develop values and beliefs consistent with parents' values and beliefs. Parents begin to teach their children about the political world early in the child's life. They transfer feelings about such concepts as authority, freedom, democracy, and racial prejudice to their children in both formal and informal ways. By standing at attention during the playing of the national anthem or attending a Memorial Day service, parents are informally communicating important values about politics. Telling children that skin color should not affect how to think about a particular person or explaining why it is important to vote in an election are formal ways political information is communicated.

These early formal and informal cues from parents have a long-term and lasting impact on a child's political socialization. Over the years, researchers have found that children whose parents are more involved in politics tend to be more involved in politics themselves. The transference of party identification from parent to child is also significant. Children who grew up in homes where parents regard politics as important also tend to regard politics as important throughout their lives. Because children generally want to be like their parents, the many cues, both formal and informal, that they receive from their parents are a strong influence on the formation of political orientation.

Friends and Peer Groups

As children grow older, they begin to interact with people outside of their immediate family. They seek friendships with others and show a desire to get along with social groups. Children acquire a great deal of new political learning through their friends and associates, as well as from the social groups that they seek to join. Often, the values, beliefs, and opinions of social peers are the same as or similar to those of the family, so friends and peers reinforce what was learned from parents. For example, wealthy people tend to live together in particular neighborhoods, and so as children

[18] Jack Dennis, ed., *Socialization to Politics* (New York: John Wiley and Sons, 1973).

from wealthy families find friends and peers, they are likely to find people who have been socialized by their parents in ways similar to themselves.

By the fifth or sixth grade, children become cognitively equipped to better understand the world of politics. Whereas previous learning tends to be based on unquestioned acceptance of what is being communicated, young adults have the ability to critically analyze new information. This cognitive skill development comes at a time in life (young adolescence) when friends and peer groups are particularly influential. Thus the desire to get along and to form social relationships has an important influence on political learning at this point in life.

High schools, such as this one in Austin, Texas, help to teach the values of the democratic process by providing mock trials for students to learn about how our legal system works.

The Schools

Part of the curriculum in many school systems across the United States focuses on the development of political values, such as respect for authority, legitimacy of our political institutions, patriotism, and capitalism. Classes in civic education and American government, the daily morning pledge of allegiance to the flag, and pictures of American presidents are just some of the mechanisms by which schools act as an agent of socialization.

Schools serve as an important mechanism for the positive development of attitudes about basic American democratic values, thus promoting general positive attitudes about the legitimacy of the democratic system. Research conducted by David Easton and his colleagues in the 1950s and 1960s demonstrated that schools promoted a positive affective attachment to the concept of "democracy" by the third grade.[19] During the early grades, children acquire beliefs regarding a citizen's role in politics—obeying laws, voting, and paying attention to political events.

Political socialization from the school is not limited to elementary and high school. The college experience also has an important socializing effect on citizens' political development. College graduates tend to be more likely to vote and participate in politics, they are more likely to follow news and political campaigns, and they are better able to understand the political world in which they live. The effects of formal educa-

[19] See, generally, David Easton, *A Systems Analysis of Political Life* (New York: John Wiley and Sons, 1965).

tion, even beyond the specific civics education curriculum of the earlier grades, make an important positive contribution to an individual's political socialization.

The Media

Americans spend a great deal of time accessing news information and being entertained by the mass media. It is not surprising, then, that the media act as an important agent of political socialization as well. Information that citizens glean from media news coverage about political events and political campaigns has an impact on their values, beliefs, and opinions. Research has shown that heavy users of the news media are more politically informed than lighter users;[20] they are also more supportive of basic American values, such as individualism, equality, and free speech rights.

The media's impact as a socialization agent extends beyond the provision of news information. Entertainment television, the movies, talk radio, and other media forms also inspire various types of political learning. Studies have shown, for example, that entertainment television tends to promote negative stereotypes of women and minorities, which may reinforce negative attitudes about race or affirmative action. Use of Internet websites and blogs may also help shape a person's political outlook.

DANA EDELSON/NBCU PHOTO BANK/AP PHOTO

Actress and comedian Tina Fey made several appearances on the comedy show *Saturday Night Live* impersonating Republican vice presidential nominee Sarah Palin and serving to influence how voters learned about the candidate.

Religion

Throughout American history, religious organizations have played an important role in the political socialization process. The values of individualism and hard work were important influences in establishing a capitalist economy and continue to underpin economic policy in the United States. These values, based on the Protestant work ethic, continue to influence the socialization process. More recently, the Christian-based fundamentalist movement has utilized religious teaching to influence opinions about political issues. The Catholic Church's opposition to abortion affects many Catholics' position on that issue.

How Is Public Opinion Measured?

When Americans think about the term *public opinion* in contemporary politics, they often focus on the results of public opinion polls. A **public opinion poll** is a method of measuring the opinions of a large group of people by selecting a subset of the

★ Public opinion poll

A method of measuring the opinions of a large group of people by asking questions of a subset of the larger group and then generalizing the findings to the larger group.

[20] Michael X. Delli Carpini and Scott Keeter, *What Americans Know About Politics and Why It Matters* (New Haven, CT: Yale University Press, 1996).

Stephen Colbert, of TV's popular *Colbert Report*, also uses the medium of cable television to provide political humor.

larger group, asking them a set of questions, and generalizing the findings to the larger group.

Public opinion polls are not the only way that public opinion in America is either expressed or understood, but polls have become the most obvious and important instrument for gauging public opinion. Polls provide information that elected leaders use in making public policy, thus providing an important way for public sentiment to influence public policy. Polls have also become a centerpiece of elections, used both by the candidates to shape a winning strategy and by journalists to provide news coverage of campaigns.

Polling has become a huge industry in the United States. To the public, the most visible polls are those that are regularly conducted by media organizations, asking Americans what they think about a variety of topics, such as who they plan to vote for in an upcoming election, how they rate the job the president is doing, how they feel about the condition of the economy, and many other topics. Media polls are conducted with the purpose of broadcasting results as news stories. However, the polling industry extends far beyond media polls. Candidates at all levels conduct polls to identify strategies for waging a successful election campaign. Federal, state, and local government agencies conduct polls to evaluate the successes and failures of public programs. Interest groups conduct polls to promote their agendas.

Even though polls have come to play an important and visible role in American politics, the manner in which they are conducted is often misunderstood, and questions about their accuracy are often raised. What makes a poll "scientific"? How is it possible to interview 1,000 Americans and conclude how more than 200 million Americans think? How can two polls be conducted on the same topic and produce different findings? An understanding of polling techniques can help answer these questions.

The History of Political Polling

The immediate predecessor to modern scientific polling in the United States dates back to the 1824 presidential campaign. Newspapers such as the *Boston Globe, New York Herald,* and *Harrisburg Pennsylvanian* attempted to gauge voter attitudes about the presidential candidates and predict the election outcome that year by conducting what has come to be known as the **straw poll.** A straw poll gathers the opinions of people who are conveniently available in a particular gathering place. (Today, many refer to these polls as "convenience" polls.) Back in 1824, the newspapers sent "counters" to public places (such as taverns and public meetings) to ask patrons and

★ Straw poll

An unscientific poll that gathers the opinions of people who are conveniently available in a gathering place.

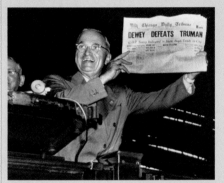

American Government . . . in Historical Perspective:
Polling Problems in Presidential Elections

"Dewey Defeats Truman"? "Gore defeats Bush"? Not so, as it turned out. Still, that didn't stop public opinion pollsters from convincing many in the media that Thomas Dewey would be elected president in 1948, and that Al Gore would be the winner in 2000. More than fifty years apart, the polls played an important role in two predictions that caused considerable confusion. Then, in 2008, the pollsters struck again. . . .

In 1948, polls leading up to Election Day predicted that New York Governor Thomas Dewey would soundly defeat President Harry S Truman. The Gallup Poll, the Roper Poll, and other opinion polling organizations consistently found Dewey ahead throughout much of the fall campaign. The scientific sampling methods they employed had been used by these same organizations in successfully calling the winner of every presidential race since 1936. The problem? All the major pollsters stopped their pre-election polling at least two weeks before Election Day. In fact, Dewey did maintain a large lead throughout the campaign, a lead that had not changed up through mid-October. So the pollsters just stopped polling. Then, in the final weeks of the campaign, Truman's furious and aggressive campaign schedule began to make a difference, and voter opinions began to shift in favor of the incumbent president. Yet the pollsters didn't pick up these changes. Thus their confident prediction that Dewey would win proved wrong, and the *Chicago Daily Tribune* became famous for running the presses with its premature headline: "Dewey Defeats Truman."

In 2000, the presidential election between Republican George W. Bush and Democrat Al Gore proved once again the pollsters could be fallible. In the last few weeks of the campaign, many respected polling organizations showed a tight race between the two candidates. The Voter

The polls projected Thomas Dewey to defeat President Harry Truman in 1948. The polls were wrong, but they led many newspapers across the country to prematurely project Truman's defeat as they went to press.

News Service or "VNS," a company that conducted polls of voters almost immediately after they exited voting booths (aptly termed "exit polls"), was supported in 2000 by ABC, CBS, NBC, CNN, FOX, and the Associated Press. On Election Day that year, VNS conducted exit polls in each of the fifty states as a way of predicting the winner in each state, thus facilitating an accurate prediction of the Electoral College outcome. For each of the fifty states in the previous seven presidential elections, network exit polling correctly predicted the presidential winners. When the polls in Florida closed at 8 P.M., VNS began tabulating its results, including its results in Florida, and sent the results to the media organizations that supported VNS. Based on the Florida exit poll data, the networks declared Gore the winner in Florida, which gave him enough Electoral College votes to win the election. Unfortunately, Florida was so close, and balloting was so complicated in that state, that the exit poll call was problematic. The flawed exit poll prediction complicated an already confusing election night for the television networks. It would take more than five weeks after Election Day, and a U.S. Supreme Court decision, to declare George W. Bush the winner in Florida, and thus the winner of the presidential election.

In 2008, pre-election pollsters struggled to accurately project the outcome of several Democratic Party primaries. Most notable were the polls associated with the New Hampshire primary. USA Today/Gallup, CBS, Fox, and a number of other organizations conducting polls in New Hampshire all concluded that Barack Obama would win the Democratic primary. Some of the polls indicated that Obama would defeat Hillary Clinton by more than 10 points. The nation and particularly the pollsters were surprised to find on election night that Clinton had defeated Obama. Clinton's surprise win in the nation's first primary came days after Obama's defeat of Clinton in the first caucus in Iowa and helped fuel a long and bitter battle for the Democratic presidential nomination.

attendees who they planned to vote for in the upcoming election. Newspaper publishers quickly found a hearty appetite among readers for stories that attempted to predict the outcome of political races—an appetite modern media executives continue to find quite strong today.

Early straw polls assumed that the accuracy of polls was based on the total number of respondents who were included in each poll. The larger the number of respondents, the more accurate the results, so it was thought. Straw polls remained the basic methodology for conducting polls for more than a century.[21]

By the early 1930s, the most famous national straw poll was the *Literary Digest* poll. In addition to conducting straw polls on policy issues, this poll correctly predicted the winner of the 1920, 1924, 1928, and 1932 presidential elections. The *Literary Digest* conducted its polls by mailing ballots to millions of people. Mailing addresses were obtained from the *Digest's* own readership lists as well as telephone directories and automobile registration lists. The *Digest* assumed its accuracy in predicting election outcomes was based on the large number of ballots that it counted from voters across the country.

In the 1936 election between Franklin Roosevelt and Alfred Landon, the *Literary Digest* collected ballots from more than 2 million people and confidently predicted that Landon would receive 55 percent of the vote, Roosevelt would get 41 percent, and the remaining 4 percent would go to Union Party candidate William Lemke. The actual election results stunned the *Literary Digest* and its many readers. Roosevelt won the election with a whopping 61 percent of the popular vote. Landon garnered 36.5 percent, whereas Lemke won less than 2 percent. The missed projection put the *Literary Digest* out of business.

This widely publicized missed call by the *Literary Digest* is explained by the faulty assumption of the straw poll methodology—the assumption that the greater the number of respondents, the more accurate the poll. The number of interviews in a poll is only one of a number of factors that affect poll accuracy. In 1936, the United States was still fighting the effects of the Great Depression, when many Americans had difficulty making ends meet. Those Americans with telephones, automobiles, and subscriptions to the *Literary Digest* (the sources of the mailing addresses for the ballots) tended to be wealthier, less affected by the Depression, and disproportionately less likely to support the liberal economic policies of FDR's New Deal.

At the time, the *Literary Digest* debacle was aptly explained by several researchers who had already begun to conduct polls with more accurate methodologies. Chief among these was Dr. George Gallup, who was applying probability sampling methods to the polls he conducted. During the 1936 campaign, Gallup argued that the *Literary Digest* methodology was producing faulty results. His cries fell on many deaf ears until after the election, when his advice sowed the seeds for a healthy polling industry based on more scientific methods.

©BILLY E. BARNES/PHOTOEDIT

An NBC News exit pollster interviews a voter in 2006 shortly after she casts her ballot. Exit polls allow the networks to project winners and losers before the polls close.

Scientific Sampling

The polling procedures popularized by Gallup in the aftermath of the 1936 election relied on the principles of probability theory, and focused on the sampling of the population under study.[22] A *sample* is a subgroup of people from a population who are studied for the purpose of learning something about the whole population. Based on the laws of probability, it is possible to draw a sample from a population, administer a set of questions to those in the sample, and understand something about the entire population, within a known level of error.

[21] Herb Asher, *Polling and the Public*, 6th ed. (Washington, DC: CQ Press, 2004).
[22] Charles W. Roll and Albert H. Cantril, *Polls: The Use and Misuse in Politics* (New York: Basic Books, 1972).

A **scientific sample** is one that uses probability theory as a guide to selecting people from the population who will comprise the sample. Random selection of respondents in the sample is key to achieving a scientific, or representative, sample. *Random sampling* is achieved by giving each possible respondent in the population a known chance of being selected in the sample. There are a number of ways of achieving a random sample.

Unscientific Polls

In a scientific poll, the results of the poll are generalizable to a population that is represented by the sample of people who are interviewed. **Unscientific polls** differ from scientific ones in that the sample of people who are interviewed is not representative of any group beyond those who register their opinion. There are many examples of unscientific polls in politics. What makes a poll unscientific is the way respondents are selected for the sample. If the vast majority of people in a population are given a chance of being sampled, then the poll is scientific. If not, then the sample represents nothing beyond itself. In an unscientific sample, some individuals in the population have no chance of being included. Many unscientific polls are conducted even today. A good example is the television call-in poll. Often television news shows that deal with political topics will offer viewers an opportunity to call an 800 or 900 number to answer a poll question. These polls are unscientific because only those people who are viewing the show have an opportunity to respond. E-mail surveys conducted by CNN.com and ESPN.com are similarly unscientific surveys. The sample of people who call in is not representative of any group beyond the callers themselves. Other examples of unscientific polls include the following:

An unscientific poll question as it appears to those who visit CNN's website.

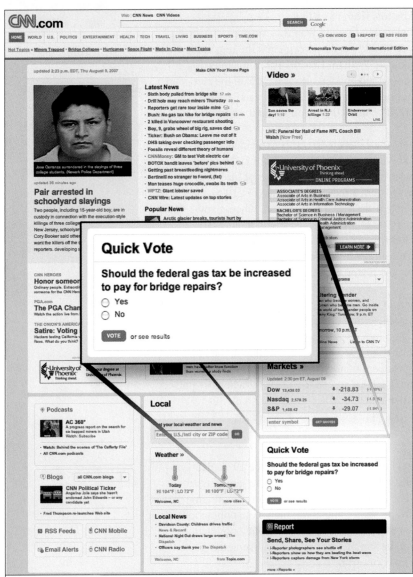

COURTESY OF CNN

★ **Log-in polls:** A poll question pops up as you enter your computer's web browser with the question: Do you think Hillary Clinton would make a good president? Click here for "yes" or click here for "no." Many services, such as Yahoo!, Netscape, and MSN, include questions such as these on their home page, and then present a tally of the results. This type of poll is an unscientific one, because only those people who click on the browser and decided to take the time to answer the question have their opinion registered. Those who don't have a computer (for example,

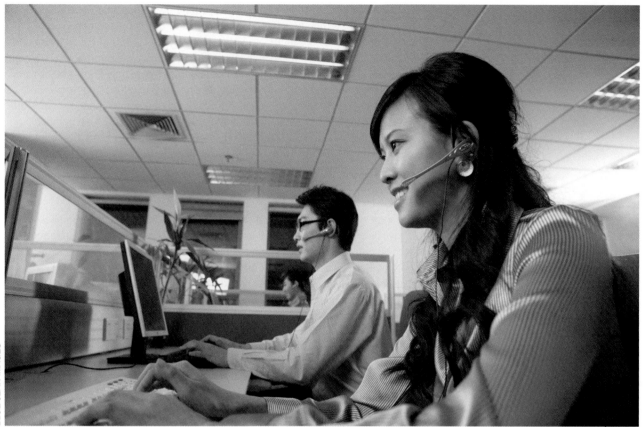

poorer and older people), those who don't have Internet access, and those who are less interested in politics have no chance or far fewer chances of being selected for such a poll. The results of those polls represent nothing more than the people who answer the question.

A telephone interviewer for a public opinion polling firm asks a randomly selected voter whom she will vote for in an upcoming election.

★ **SLOPs, or self-selected listener opinion polls:** Television and radio news/talk shows sometimes conduct polls during the course of a broadcast by offering an 800 or 900 phone number for registered listeners to call and express their opinion on some topic. SLOPs are also known as "call-in" polls. These polls are unscientific because only those people who happen to be tuned in to the broadcast have any opportunity to be included in the sample.

★ **CRAPs, or computerized response audience polling:** This kind of poll is often used by local news organizations. Telecommunications equipment places a call, and automated voice systems ask the poll questions. Respondents are asked to use the keypad of their telephone to register their answers to the questions. The extremely high rate of refusal (for example, most people hang up when they hear the automated voice) renders them highly unscientific.

★ **Intercept polls:** Have you ever been in a shopping mall when someone with a clipboard comes up to you and asks if you would answer some questions? If so, you've been solicited to participate in an intercept poll (that is, an interviewer "intercepted" you). Respondents in such polls are conveniently selected into the sample because they are spotted by the interviewer. Because people who are at shopping malls or other public places are not representative of all people, this is regarded as an unscientific type of poll.

The *Literary Digest* mishap highlights the problem with unscientific samples—those people who have no chance of being included in the sample may be very different from those who are included. Voters who had no car or published telephone number had no chance of being selected in the *Literary Digest's* sample. Even though the total number of people in the sample was quite high (more than 2 million), it was not representative of the population of voters because less-well-off people had little to no chance of being included in the sample. Today's reliance on telephone surveys to gauge public opinion has come under attack on the basis that cell phone numbers are not sampled and thus systematically exclude younger Americans from the sampling (because younger people are more likely to rely on cell phones).

Pseudo-Polls

★ Pseudo-poll

Phone calls from members of political campaigns or PACs who present themselves as pollsters for the purpose of planting messages with voters rather than measuring public opinion.

Recently, some unscrupulous political campaigns and political action committees (PACs) have been disguising themselves as pollsters for the purpose of planting messages with voters, rather than measuring public opinion. Some of these campaigns or PACs present themselves as pollsters for the purpose of fund raising as well. These phone calls have come to be known as **pseudo-polls.** As the term implies, there is no polling going on with a pseudo-poll. Pretending to be pollsters, callers often contact tens of thousands of voters and ask hypothetical (that is, untrue) questions about their political opponents—such as "Did you happen to know that John Smith is reported to have beaten his wife in the past—does this make you any less likely to support him in his race for senator?" Respondents to the call believe they are being interviewed by a legitimate polling firm and take away from the conversation a contrived and false message about a political candidate. This type of pseudo-poll is called a "push poll," because the intention of the call is to "push," or influence, people to vote a particular way.

Another type of pseudo-poll is referred to as "FRUGing," or fund raising under the guise of polling. This is an unethical practice that tricks people into thinking they are being polled by a legitimate organization, when they are really being set up for a fund-raising attempt. "SUGing," or selling under the guise of polling, is a pseudo-poll that engages in telemarketing. The individual—who will ultimately receive a sales pitch at the end of the call—believes that she or he is answering a legitimate poll.

Sample Size

A fundamental characteristic of a scientific public opinion poll is the nature of the procedures used to draw a sample from the population. The size of the sample is also a factor in poll quality. **Sampling error** is the term used to indicate the amount of error in the poll that results from interviewing a sample of people rather than the whole population under study. Sampling error is largely a function of sample size: the larger the sample size, the less sampling error with the poll. However, there is a law of diminishing returns associated with increasing the size of the sample.

For example, a national scientifically drawn sample of two hundred Americans has a sampling error of about +/–7 percent at the 95 percent level of confidence. This means that with a sample of two hundred, chances are ninety-five in a hundred that the sample will produce results within seven points above or below the survey result. By increasing the sample size by four hundred respondents, from two hundred to six hundred, the sampling error is reduced to +/–4 percent. An additional six hundred respondents in the sample, bringing the sample size to one thousand two-hundred, reduces the sampling error to +/–3 percent.

Media organizations that report poll findings often attempt to convey information about the poll to help the reader/audience understand the sampling error associated with the results. Typically, a news report on a poll will include a statement like this: "The survey was conducted by telephone with a random sample of 1,200 American adults. Sampling error for the survey is +/–3 percent at the 95 percent level of confidence."

★ Sampling error

The amount of error in a poll that results from interviewing a sample of people rather than the whole population under study; the larger the sample, the less sampling error.

What does this statement mean? Suppose the poll found that 60 percent of the respondents approved of the job that George W. Bush was doing as president. The statement indicates that there was a "random sample" of American adults. This means that the poll was a scientific poll, and the results can be generalized to the full American adult public.

With any scientific poll, there is sampling error, and probability theory allows us to calculate what the sampling error might be. This calculation is thus expressed as a "confidence interval," or range, which is reported to be +/–3 percent of the poll result (or a six-point range). The level of confidence typically reported is at the "95 percent level of confidence" (meaning that ninety-five out of one hundred similarly conducted polls would produce results in this range). Thus what the statement says, then, is that we can be 95 percent confident that the approval rating for President Bush is somewhere between 57 and 63 percent.

In addition to random selection and sample size, the quality of the sample is affected by "nonresponse" error. Once a sample is selected, it is necessary to contact and conduct interviews with those in the sample. Rarely is it possible to obtain an interview with 100 percent of those sampled. Some respondents refuse to be interviewed, some are not home when contacts are made, and others screen their phone calls through an answering machine or caller ID system. Nonresponse is problematic when those who do not respond tend to answer the questions differently than those who do respond. The goal is to achieve as high a response to the poll as possible in order to limit possible nonresponse error.

Modern-day scientific polls of Americans and voters typically use a probability technique known as **random-digit dialing (RDD)** to obtain scientific telephone samples. RDD uses known information about telephone area codes and exchanges and randomly assigns the last four digits to these. Because about 90 percent of the households in the United States have active telephone lines, almost everyone living in a house with a telephone has some chance of being selected in the sample.

★ Random-digit dialing (RDD)

A probability technique for scientific telephone polling that randomly assigns the last four digits to known information about telephone area codes and exchanges.

Asking Questions on Polls

Accurate and reliable polls require not only scientific sampling procedures, but also significant attention to the way in which polling questions are asked. The way in which a question is worded can have a large impact on the type of answers that are given by survey respondents. Consider the following example of a question asked on a national survey conducted by the Roper Organization in 1993: "Does it seem possible or does it seem impossible to you that the Nazi extermination of the Jews never happened?" More than one in five respondents to the poll indicated that they thought it was possible that the Holocaust never happened. The results from this question led to a series of news stories expressing concern that nearly one-quarter of the American public questioned the reality of the Holocaust. However, researchers noted an important problem with the wording of the question; namely, it included a double-negative. It is difficult for respondents, particularly in a telephone interview (where they are not looking at the words of the question), to interpret what it means to "seem impossible" that something "never happened." The confusing question led to the exaggerated survey result. To test the notion that the question was confusing, the Gallup organization instead asked this question in a 1994 survey: "In your opinion, did the Holocaust definitely happen, probably happen, probably not happen, or definitely not happen?" In this form of the question, only 2 percent said that the Holocaust probably did not happen, and 0 percent said that it definitely did not happen.

Another example of how wording can influence the responses to a question involves two questions, on separate surveys, intended to measure attitudes about the legality of flag burning. A CBS/New York Times poll asked: "Should burning or destroying the American flag as a form of political protest be legal or should it be against the law?" Fourteen percent said it should be legal and 83 percent said it

Items that Should be Disclosed about Any Publicly Released Poll

Many polls conducted in the United States are intended to provide information for public consumption. These polls are referred to as "public polls." The USA Today/CNN/Gallup Poll, the New York Times/CBS Poll, and the Harris Interactive Poll are just a few of the organizations that regularly conduct polling intended for public consumption.

There are so many polling organizations, people often have a hard time ascertaining the quality of a poll. The National Council on Public Polls (NCPP) is an association of organizations that regularly conduct public polls. Members of NCPP have articulated the following list of items that should be disclosed about any poll that is released publicly, as a way to help the poll consumer evaluate the quality of the poll:

✔ **The name of the organization that sponsored or paid for the poll**

✔ **The dates of interviewing**

✔ **The method for obtaining the interviews (for example, telephone, e-mail, in-person, and so on)**

✔ **A definition of the population that was sampled**

✔ **The size of the sample (that is, the number of interviews conducted)**

✔ **The size and description of subsamples, if the poll relies primarily on less than the total sample**

✔ **The complete wording of questions on which the poll results are based**

✔ **The percentages from the poll on which conclusions are based**

should be against the law. A Gallup poll asked the question this way: "The Supreme Court ruled that burning the American flag, though highly offensive, is protected under the free speech guarantee of the First Amendment to the Constitution. Do you agree or disagree?" Thirty-eight percent agreed that flag burning should be legal based on this question—fully twenty-four percentage points higher than what was found with the CBS/New York Times question. In this case, the context in which Gallup framed the question—that the Supreme Court said flag burning was legal based on the First Amendment—produced the different result.

The polling community of practitioners and scholars has, over the years, conducted a number of experiments to test how question wording can influence the results of polls. Listed here are of some of the key recommendations for guidelines in constructing good poll questions:[23]

1. Avoid double-negatives in questions (as in the Holocaust question example cited above).

2. Keep the question as simple as possible, using words that people with a limited vocabulary might understand.

3. Don't include more than one question within a question—such an error is called a double-barreled question. An example of a double-barreled question is: "Do you approve or disapprove of the job that President Bush is doing

[23] An important book spelling out the variety of problems and issues with the wording of survey questions is Howard Schuman and Stanley Press, *Questions and Answers in Attitude Surveys* (New York: John Wiley and Sons, 1981).

in handling the economic and domestic affairs of the nation?" Respondents might have different answers to the president's performance in economic versus other domestic affairs.

4. The questions should not lead the respondent to a particular answer. An example of a leading question is: "Do you approve of the job that George W. Bush is doing as president?" Because only the "approve" option is stated in the question, some respondents might likely answer "yes, they approve," when they might have answered that they "disapprove" had that option been provided as well.

5. Don't expect honest answers to socially unacceptable response questions. For example, using illegal drugs is not only illegal but regarded as socially unacceptable. So one should not necessarily expect all drug users to answer honestly a question about their own use of drugs.

Interpreting Public Opinion Data

Understanding public opinion requires attention not only to the scientific aspects of sampling and the wording of questions, but also to the analysis and interpretation of the results of a poll. In assessing results, analysts are concerned with three important characteristics of public opinion data: direction, intensity, and continuity.[23]

To understand the **direction** of public opinion, the analyst seeks to find which position or preference a majority of people hold as their opinion. On most topics, there are two possible directions in which public opinion might lean—a positive direction or a negative direction. For example, with respect to presidential approval, respondents might either approve or disapprove of the job the president is doing. Similarly, the public might either trust or distrust their political leaders; or they might support or oppose a proposal for a policy that makes it more difficult to buy a handgun. On any given opinion question, direction is a basic characteristic that the analyst seeks to gauge.

Intensity is also an important characteristic of public opinion. Often, the analyst seeks not only to find the direction of opinion but also to determine how strongly or how committed the public feels about the opinion that it holds. Consider the responses to the following question asked to a national sample of Americans in 2000: "Do you agree or disagree with this statement—companies should be allowed to advertise tobacco products on television?" Those polled were asked a follow-up question: "Do you strongly or mildly (agree/disagree) with this?" The results were as follows:

Strongly agree	24 percent
Mildly agree	27 percent
Mildly disagree	10 percent
Strongly disagree	37 percent

The direction of opinion in this case only marginally swings in agreement that companies should be able to advertise tobacco on TV. Fifty-one percent, a bare majority, agreed with this statement, and 47 percent disagreed. The direction of opinion only modestly endorses the statement. However, the follow-up question sheds additional light on the intensity of opinion. Among those who agree, they are about evenly divided, 24 percent to 27 percent, between strongly and mildly agreeing. Those who disagree are much more intense in their feelings, with 37 percent strongly and only 10 percent mildly disagreeing.

Continuity is a third important characteristic of public opinion. Political preferences may remain very stable over time, they may gradually change, or they may

★ **Direction**
(of public opinion)

A tendency toward a particular preference, usually (though not always) characterized as either positive or negative.

★ **Intensity**
(of public opinion)

The degree of strength or commitment the public feels about the opinion it holds.

★ **Continuity**
(in public opinion)

A tendency for political preferences to remain generally stable over time.

[23] For a more detailed discussion of these concepts, see W. Lance Bennett, *Public Opinion in American Politics* (New York: Harcourt Brace Jovanovich, 1980).

Chapter 10: Public Opinion

fluctuate wildly over short periods of time. Continuity (or "changeability," its opposite) is often an important dimension of public opinion. The presidential approval rating is often analyzed from the context of the continuity/change dimension. When major political events occur, we often see change.

Now & Then: Making the Connection

Public opinion plays an important role in any system of government. Even authoritarian regimes such as the French government under King Louis XVI in the late eighteenth century, Czarist Russia in the early twentieth century, and then the Soviet Union in the late twentieth century were susceptible to being overthrown by the forces of the popular will. But in a democratic society, public opinion is freely expressed and willingly heeded by those running the government. Bill Clinton sought to craft many of his actions according to popular opinion. Because of the high esteem in which the public regarded him, George Washington could have ignored public opinion throughout his presidency. But his understanding of the vital role that public opinion plays in American politics led him to deal carefully with the Whiskey Rebellion in 1794 and to plot out an effective public relations strategy for winning the battle for public opinion.

Modern technology and the advancement of social science research have enabled political scientists, journalists, political candidates, and elected leaders to measure accurately and understand better not only what public opinion is, but also how and why it changes. Modern presidents have the resources of scientific public opinion polls at their disposal and use them quite extensively. But although the scientific opinion poll is a modern phenomenon, the importance of public opinion has always been central to the life of American politics.

The 2006 Oscar-winning documentary *An Inconvenient Truth* chronicles former Vice President Al Gore's crusade to fight global warming by educating the American public about the problem. The funny, engaging, and informative film is intended to raise awareness of the global warming problem, and force government to take action to remedy the problem. It seeks to advance the issue on the political agenda through a grassroots public opinion campaign. To find out more about this tool intended to influence public opinion about global climate change, see **http://www.climatecrisis.net.**

On **http://academic.cengage.com/dautrich**, find the politics interactive link for details about the issue of global warming and the controversy surrounding how the public believes it should be addressed by public officials and the political system as a whole.

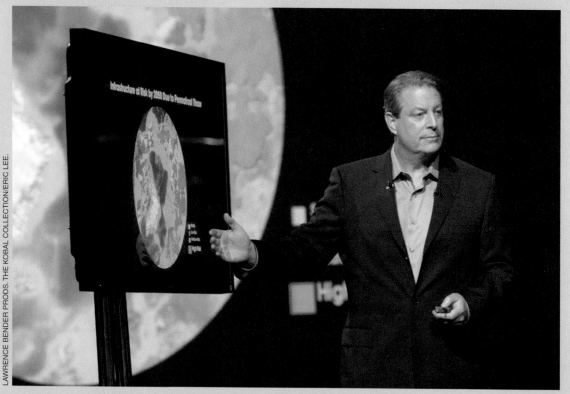

LAWRENCE BENDER PRODS. THE KOBAL COLLECTION/ERIC LEE.

Former Vice President Al Gore, now a prominent environmental activist, lecturing about global warming.

http://academic.cengage.com/dautrich

Chapter Summary

★ Public opinion plays an important role in ensuring that citizens' beliefs are embraced in a democracy; public opinion also plays a tactical role for political officials, influencing the outcome of many important political battles.

★ Public opinion may be expressed through a variety of means including public opinion polls, voting, free speech and assembly, the support of particular candidates for political office, and the contribution of time and efforts to interest groups.

★ The news media also serve as an outlet for public opinion, whether by publishing articles about important individuals' opinions or by sponsoring their own public opinion polls on politics and policy issues. Still, many members of the public prefer to express their opinions directly to elected officials through letters, phone calls, or e-mails. Weblogs (or "blogs") have become an increasingly popular way for individuals to express their views on issues.

★ Public opinion exists at its most abstract level in the form of values and beliefs; it exists in a more specific form through political orientations, which translate values and beliefs into a systematic way of assessing political realities, and in an even more specific way in the form of particular political preferences.

★ Many noted scholars in the early and mid-twentieth century argued that the public lacks the necessary knowledge for their opinions to provide value. Contemporary surveys continue to confirm that the public maintains a low interest in politics generally, and that most Americans are uninformed about basic political facts.

★ By contrast, a number of other scholars beginning with V. O. Key, Jr. in the 1960s have argued that regardless of its specific knowledge of politics, the public as a whole behaves quite rationally over the long haul, expressing stable opinions that move (if at all) in logical and meaningful directions based on their values and beliefs.

★ Individuals' opinions are shaped in part by political socialization; impressions formed during youth often last well into adulthood. Opinions are also shaped by demographics (race, ethnicity, gender, age, and so on), family members, friends and peer groups, schools, the media, and religious organizations.

★ Public opinion polls measure the opinions of a large group of people by selecting a subset of the larger group and then generalizing the findings from the small group back to the large group. To ensure that the poll is scientific, the sample must be chosen randomly using probability theory through techniques such as random-digit dialing. Unscientific polls can produce misleading results.

★ The way in which questions on a poll are worded is also an important factor in assessing the quality of a poll. Misleading questions, whether intentional or unintentional, may produce faulty results.

★ The proper interpretation of public opinion data requires attention to the direction, intensity, and continuity of the public's expressions. With regard to the latter characteristic, political preferences may fluctuate wildly over short periods of time.

Key Terms

Agents of political socialization (p. 308)

Conservative ideology (p. 300)

Continuity (in public opinion) (p. 319)

Direction (of public opinion) (p. 319)

Intensity (of public opinion) (p. 319)

Liberal ideology (p. 300)

Political ideology (p. 300)

Political orientations (p. 300)

Political preferences (p. 302)

Political socialization (p. 306)

Primacy tendency (p. 308)

Pseudo-poll (p. 316)

Public opinion (p. 296)

Public opinion poll (p. 310)

Random-digit dialing (RDD) (p. 317)

Sampling error (p. 316)

Scientific sample (p. 314)

Straw poll (p. 311)

Unscientific poll (p. 314)

Values and beliefs (p. 298)

Resources

Important Books and Journals

Delli Carpini, Michael X., and Scott Keeter. *What Americans Know About Politics and Why It Matters.* New Haven, CT: Yale University Press, 1996.

Fowler, Floyd. *Survey Research Methods.* Newbury Park, CA: Sage Publications, 1995.

Hibbing, John R., and Elizabeth Theiss-Morse. *Congress as Public Enemy.* Cambridge: Cambridge University Press, 1995.

Igo, Sarah. *The Averaged American: Surveys, Citizens, and the Making of a Mass Public.* Cambridge, MA: Harvard University Press, 2007.

International Journal of Public Opinion (quarterly journal that serves as a source of public opinion analysis for academics and polling professionals).

Key, V. O., Jr. *The Responsible Electorate.* New York: Knopf, 1960.

Key, V. O., Jr. *Public Opinion and American Democracy.* New York: Knopf, 1967.

Page, Benjamin I., and Robert Y. Shapiro. *The Rational Public: Fifty Years of Trends in Americans' Policy Preferences.* Chicago: University of Chicago Press, 1992.

Public Opinion Quarterly (quarterly journal that features important theoretical contributions to opinion and communication research, analyses of current public opinion, and investigations of methodological issues involved in survey validity).

Schattschneider, E. E. *The Semi-sovereign People.* New York: Holt, Rinehart and Winston, 1960.

Stonecash, Jeffrey M. *Political Polling: Strategic Information in Campaigns.* New York: Rowman and Littlefield, 2003.

Traugott, Michael W., and Paul J. Lavraskas. *The Voter's Guide to Election Polls.* New York: Chatham House, 2000.

Zaller, John. *The Nature and Origin of Mass Opinion.* Cambridge: Cambridge University Press, 1992.

Internet Resources

http://www.gallup.org (the website for Gallup poll data)

http://www.aapor.org (the home page for the American Association for Public Opinion Research, the association for pollsters and people who study polls)

http://www.ropercenter.uconn.edu (website for the Roper Center for Public Opinion Research, which includes the largest collection of public opinion data in the world)

http://www.umich.edu\~nes\ (includes surveys from the National Election Studies, the most extensive public opinion research on American national elections)

11 Interest Groups

Former lobbyist Jack Abramoff

ABBE LOWELL/AP PHOTO

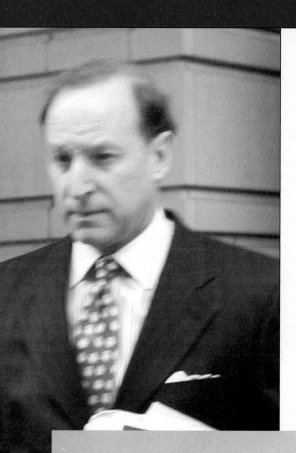

Lobbying Scandals with a Ring of Familiarity: Now & Then

The relationship between government and private interests has always been a treacherous one to navigate. Lobbying legislators to favor or oppose certain legislation may be a time-honored practice, and yet so-called legislative favors granted in return for some financial interests can quickly cross the line and betray the public trust. Interest groups that advocate their position in the halls of Congress try to straddle that line, but occasionally they fall on the side of illegality. In one instance, private financial interests hoped to capitalize on the greed of certain members of Congress, who were willing to accept rewards from these organizations in return for providing a piece of the expanding government largesse. The group's original cause may well have been noble, but once the public trust was violated, public faith in the entire operation was compromised. And because corruption knows no bounds, even the original cause was eventually undermined by those who tried to circumvent the rules of the political process.

Congressman Oakes Ames of Massachusetts

2000

2007   1987   1967   1947   1927

Now. . . During the past two decades, many Native American tribes—buoyed by passage of the 1988 Indian Gaming Regulatory Act—have undergone a rags-to-riches story that make them the envy of many other groups. Mistreated by the federal government for many years, these Native American tribes are now reaping the rewards of America's interest in gambling. Millions of Americans have visited tribe-run casinos located on reservations where gaming is now permitted. Many Native American tribes had benefited from that federal legislation, and in the 1990s tribal leaders wanted to press their advantage further. Thus several tribes, including the Mississippi Choctaw, hired lobbyist Jack Abramoff to represent them before Congress. Abramoff proved especially effective in this role, helping defeat federal legislation that would have assessed the unrelated business income tax (UBIT) on Native American casinos. House Majority leader Tom DeLay (R-TX) was one of many House members who played a role in this and other victories. It was later reported that Abramoff had done more than just "argue forcefully" on the tribes' behalf: he also spent millions of dollars to influence politicians. In addition to offering many members of Congress free meals at his restaurant, Abramoff maintained four skyboxes at major sports arenas for political entertaining at a cost of over $1 million a year. Joining Abramoff on one vacation in 2000 was DeLay, whose airfare to London and Scotland was allegedly charged to an American Express card issued to Abramoff.

Abramoff's illegal acts did not end at bribery, as he also defrauded the Native American tribes he had been hired to serve. By overbilling Indian gambling interests and orchestrating lobbying activities against his own clients, Abramoff attempted to play both sides of the fence. Accused by prosecutors of giving illegal gifts and donations, and of committing fraud and tax evasion, Abramoff eventually pleaded guilty to numerous charges and proceeded to name for prosecutors all the members of Congress who had benefited from his "generosity." The Abramoff lobbying scandal led to the downfall of House Majority leader DeLay and to charges brought against many other members of Congress and their aides. It was the sheer scope of the scandal that stunned so many in Washington. If Native Americans had wanted to be treated like any other group participating in American life, they had finally gotten their wish. Like so many others, these tribes were abused by individuals who were supposed to be acting in their interests.

1907 | 1887 | 1872 | 1867 | 1847 | 1827

Then. . .

Then. . . Immediately after the Civil War, railroads were a dominant economic interest in Washington, DC. The Union Pacific Railroad in particular exerted pressure on well-known Congressmen of the time such as Representative James Brooks (D-ME), and Senators James Harlan (R-IA) and James Willis Patterson (R-NH). Ironically, the key individual responsible for that pressure was a fellow Congressman, Oakes Ames (R-MA). As an influential member of the House, Ames obtained contracts for his family firm for the construction of the Union Pacific; he even installed his brother Oliver Ames as president of the railroad in 1866. In 1872 the railroad established a front company, known as Crédit Mobilier, as part of a financial scam to funnel money back to the railroads through their own construction contracts. Ames then allowed members of Congress to purchase railroad shares at face rather than market value; in return, the members agreed to ignore illegal corporate transactions and to help produce dividends for the railroads they now owned. Ames's scheme eventually ensnared the sitting vice president of the United States, Schuyler Colfax, as well as his successor as vice president, Henry Wilson. Ames was censured after a House investigation; Colfax was nearly impeached. In addition, Ames's actions nearly ruined the Union Pacific railroad, which went bankrupt in the 1870s. But at a time when corruption laws were still in their infancy, many politicians escaped with nothing more than "the embarrassment of public exposure."

During these two critical periods in American history, private groups and economic interests exerted their will on the public institutions of government to such a great extent that all distinctions between public and private seemingly broke down. No one could question the importance of the railways during the post–Civil War period; meanwhile Native Americans—downtrodden for so long in American society—had finally risen to a position of economic prominence in the 1990s, and their success was welcomed in many corners. Unfortunately, the aggressive lobbying on behalf of these two groups went *too* far.

Members of the well-organized and very powerful American Association of Retired Persons (AARP) at a political rally.

nterest groups today play a central role in formulating public policy, directing the regulation of certain industries, and even influencing important court decisions. Indeed, there is little doubt about the size and magnitude of their influence throughout the American political system. Of course the vast majority of interest groups are law-abiding, positive forces in government. A key issue remains, however: how far do we allow such groups to press their interests in government, before they become a negative force in democracy?

This chapter assesses the workings and performance of American politics from the perspective of interest group activity. What are interest groups? How do they work? Who belongs to them? Which ones are more and less powerful? How do they exert influence on what government does?

Pluralism and the Interest Group System

The U.S. political system provides numerous opportunities for people to influence public policy. Voting in elections to choose leaders offers one such opportunity. The guarantees of freedom of speech to speak one's mind about political issues and freedom of the press to critically assess issues and leaders' performance are others. Public opinion polls are yet another mechanism that solicits input from the masses.

But perhaps the most natural—and arguably the most influential—form of public input into government arrives by way of the activities of interest groups. James Madison, in Federalist No. 10, admonished that "the latent causes of faction are thus sown in the nature of man."[1] By faction, Madison was referring to what we now term interest groups. Madison was concerned about the potential influence of factions on the government. But at the same time, he understood that people were by nature drawn toward the organization of collective interests and the use of that organization to influence government action. Madison expected that if enough interest groups vied to influence policy, they would cancel each other out.

What Is an Interest Group?

★ Interest group

An organization of people with shared goals that tries to influence public policy through a variety of activities.

An **interest group** (also referred to as a "pressure group" or "organized interest") is an organization of people with shared goals that tries to influence public policy through a variety of activities. Every individual has interests, and interest groups are a mechanism for people with shared goals to protect or advance their own interests. People can try to influence government on their own—such as by calling or writing their elected representatives to voice their opinion, or by voting in an election. Another way that people can influence government is by joining a group that is organized to accomplish an objective.

[1] James Madison, Federalist No. 10, in *The Federalist Papers* (reprinted by Mentor Books, 1961), p. 77.

Senior citizens, for example, have a shared interest in securing cost-of-living adjustments (COLAs) in the Social Security system that disburses checks to them each month. Each year, the president and Congress determine the percentage rate increase in the COLA. The larger the increase, the higher will be an individual's monthly Social Security check. Each individual senior citizen might call his or her representatives in Congress to try to influence the vote for a larger COLA increase. Another way senior citizens may try to influence government is by joining and supporting the American Association for Retired People (AARP), an interest group that, among other activities, tries to influence government to approve large increases in the annual COLA for Social Security. AARP is large, with many resources and lobbyists to influence legislators. Though an individual citizen's call to a representative may carry some weight, it is no match for the vast resources and activities of the AARP.

Interest groups link people with government policies. The linkage created by interest groups is constitutionally protected by the First Amendment, which guarantees the people's right "to peaceably assemble and petition the government for redress of grievances." People assembling in groups that carry out activities to foster group members' goals is a common activity in Washington, in the fifty state capitals, and in thousands of local governments.

Alexis de Tocqueville, a Frenchman who toured the United States in the early 1830s and observed the early workings of the U.S. political system, was struck by the extent to which group association and activity dominated the American system. In his now-classic 1835 book titled *Democracy in America*,[2] Tocqueville praised the extent to which group activity underpins American democracy. More than his fellow French citizens and other Europeans that he observed, Tocqueville found that Americans were particularly prone to organize in groups and use their associations to influence the political process.

Pluralism refers to the theory that public policy largely results from a variety of interest groups competing with one another to promote laws that benefit members of their respective groups. By contrast, majoritarianism refers to the theory that public policy is a product of what majorities of citizens prefer. Whereas the majoritarian perspective focuses on public opinion, voting results, and mass representation to describe how democracy in America actually works, the pluralist perspective suggests that in fact "the majority rarely rules."

Political scientist Robert Dahl, an architect of pluralist ideas, suggested in *A Preface to Democratic Theory*[3] that the American people are represented in government primarily through interest group activity. The products of public policy are largely a function of support for and membership in interest groups that compete for influence through activities such as lobbying. The U.S. political system, according to Dahl, offers a number of "access points" for any given group to provide input. These access points include Congress, executive branch offices, the courts, elections, and the news media. David B. Truman, another political scientist, has advanced the notion that group activity and mobilization are natural consequences of shared concerns.[4] The free and open competition among groups advances the democratic system, just as a free and open marketplace of ideas promotes the adoption of the best ideas in society.

★ Pluralism

The theory that public policy largely results from a variety of interest groups competing with one another to promote laws that benefit members of their respective groups.

The Pros and Cons of Interest Groups

The political power that emanates from groups of people organizing for the purpose of influencing government outputs can be quite strong. "Are interest groups good or bad for American democracy?" is a question akin to the old cliché "Is the glass half full or half empty?" The answer, of course, depends on one's perspective. Madison himself recognized that interest groups were powerful and that they could be dangerous. But he also acknowledged that factions could not be eliminated. Channeling them into productive devices for promoting public input was a primary challenge his generation faced in framing the government.

---

[2] Alexis de Tocqueville, *Democracy in America* (New York: Mentor Books, reprint edition, 1956).
[3] Robert Dahl, *A Preface to Democratic Theory* (Cambridge: Cambridge University Press, 1956).
[4] David B. Truman, *The Governmental Process* (New York: Alfred Knopf, 1951).

American Government . . . in Global Perspective:
In the Words of French Political Philosopher Alexis de Tocqueville

Alexis de Tocqueville, a French observer of the American political system, praised the role that interest groups played in American politics. After touring the United States in the early 1830s, de Tocqueville wrote *Democracy in America*, published in 1835, in which he made the following observations about interest groups, or "associations" as he referred to them, in the United States:

The (citizen) of the United States learns from birth that he must rely on himself to combat the ills and trials of life. . . . If some obstacle blocks the public road halting . . . traffic, neighbors at once form a deliberative body; this improvised assembly produces an authority which remedies the trouble before anyone has thought of the possibility beyond that of those concerned . . . associations are formed to combat moral troubles; intemperance is fought in common. Public security, trade and industry, and morals and religion all provide the aims for associations in the United States. There is no end to which the human will despair of attaining by the free action of the collective power of individuals.

When a political association is allowed to form centers of action at certain important places in the country, its activity becomes greater and its influence more widespread. There men meet, active measures are planned, and opinions are expressed with that strength and warmth which the written word can never attain.

Freedom of association has become a necessary guarantee against the tyranny of the majority. In the United States once a party has become predominant all public power passes into its hands. . . . The most distinguished men of the opposite party . . . must be able to establish themselves outside of it. . . . The omnipotence of the majority seems to me such a danger to the American republics that the dangerous expedient used to curb it is actually something good. Here I would repeat something which I have put in other words when speaking of municipal freedom: no countries need associations more—to prevent either the despotism of parties or the arbitrary rule of a prince—than those with a democratic social state.

The Pros. Many observers today sing the praises of an interest group system that advances the interests of the people. Their arguments in support of interest groups include the following:

★ Interest groups provide all groups in society with an opportunity to win support for their ideas and positions. The vast number of interest groups represents a wide array of political opinions, economic perspectives, and social class differences.

★ By their very nature, humans seek out others who have ideas similar to their own. Joining groups and working for the interests of the group is a natural inclination of citizens and should be encouraged as a method of representation in our democracy.

★ The right of association is a basic right protected implicitly by the First Amendment to the U.S. Constitution, which affords individuals the right "peaceably to assemble. . . ."

★ A wide array of diverse groups in society—rich and poor, urban and nonurban, male and female, North and South, liberal and conservative—potentially may organize and attempt to influence government. The system is fair in that it gives all groups an equitable opportunity to compete.

The Cons. Many other observers of the U.S. political system are quite critical of the power exerted by interest groups. The political arms of many interest groups are called **political action committees (PACs).** As we will see in Chapter 15, PACs are a source of much controversy because many political candidates have become dependent on PAC money to wage successful campaigns. In *The Power Elite*, C. Wright Mills[5] characterizes interest groups as a tool of the political elite rather than a system that enables broad participation in influencing public policy. Along this line, many criticize the ability of wealthy corporations and individuals to exert disproportionate influence on government through well-financed interest group activities. John Heinz and his colleagues argue further that the influence of interest groups is contingent on a number of factors and that their influence may be quite limited.[6] Other criticisms of interest groups include the following:

★ Use of interest groups to make public policy is unfair because groups supported by the wealthy have far greater resources to promote their interests in the political system.

★ Large corporations exist to maximize profits. They dominate the interest group system and tend to be ruthless in achieving their policy goals. The interest group system thus promotes the advancement of interests that do not always strive for the common good.

★ The amount of interest group activity is so great that it has made it difficult to get things done in government. Too many groups are operating, slowing down the policy-making process to a state of gridlock in many arenas.

★ Interest group leaders are not elected, distinguishing them from many of the policy-making institutions that have been constitutionally ordained—such as Congress and the executive branch. Thus interest group dominance of the political system is an affront to democracy.

★ Interest groups work to concentrate benefits for the few while distributing costs to the many.

Interest Groups versus Political Parties

Political parties also link people to government policies. However, parties differ from interest groups in two important ways. First, parties today mainly focus on elections by endorsing candidates and working for their election to office. Most interest groups do not run candidates for office as parties do (although interest groups often endorse candidates). Interest groups commonly find other access points of government to accomplish their goals—access points such as the courts, the committee system in Congress, and executive agencies.[7]

A second important difference between interest groups and political parties is that groups tend to focus narrowly on special issues or sets of issues (hence the term *special interests*), whereas major parties are generally all-encompassing and are guided by broader ideological approaches to governing, rather than by a specific policy position. In short, the major parties are generalist whereas groups are focused. Consequently, there are few political parties, but many, many interest groups. Groups do not try to appeal to as many individuals as possible; rather, they appeal to those whose special interests are advocated by the group. For example, the National Rifle Association (NRA) does not try to recruit gun control advocates because they are less likely to help promote the group's interests. Conversely, parties try to appeal to as many people as possible to optimize their electoral success.

★ Political action committee (PAC)

The political arm of an interest group that promotes candidates in election campaigns primarily through financial contributions.

---

[5] C. Wright Mills, *The Power Elite* (New York: Oxford University Press, 1956).

[6] John P. Heinz, Edward O. Laumann, Robert L. Nelson, and Robert H. Salisbury, *The Hollow Core* (Cambridge, MA: Harvard University Press, 1993).

[7] David Lowery and Holly Brasher, *Organized Interests and American Government* (New York: McGraw-Hill, 2004), p. 8.

Women and children in 1890 labor at a food processing plant.

Interest Groups and Social Movements

A number of **social movements** have been identified in American history, such as the civil rights, consumer safety, women's rights, and environmental movements of the 1960s and 1970s. These large informal groupings of individuals were often spawned directly from particular interest groups. The consumer protection movement, for example, was driven by the activities of the group "Public Citizen," formed by consumer activist Ralph Nader. The American drive toward equality has produced a number of important social movements that utilized organized interests.

Movements have been political (for example, women's suffrage in the early 1900s), economic (for example, labor rights in the late 1800s and early 1900s), and social (for example, the civil rights movements of the 1960s). These movements have all been propelled by the activities of interest groups.

★ Social movement

A large informal grouping of individuals and/or organizations focused on specific political or social issues.

Interest Groups in Action

Interest groups have always played an important role in American politics. Even in the colonial period, groups such as the Sons of Liberty gathered members, collected donations, and organized protests to achieve the goal of American freedom from British taxation. The Sons of Liberty were successful in their aims because they tied their actions to the economic interests of their members. As Madison acknowledged, economic interests tend to be the type of concerns that are most salient to people and thus move them to collective action.

In 1886, the American Federation of Labor (AFL) was formed as the first broad-based national labor union. The AFL was originally established to advocate the rights of craft unions and ensure the terms of union contracts. Organized and led by Samuel Gompers for forty years, it attracted many members and successfully raised funds to promote laws benefiting organized labor. The AFL was the principal advocate for establishing a cabinet department, the U.S. Department of Labor, to administer labor programs. This department continues to serve as one of the largest executive departments in the nation. In the 1950s, the AFL merged with the Congress of Industrial Organizations (CIO) to create the AFL-CIO, an interest group still very active in promoting the labor agenda.

The National Association of Manufacturers (NAM) was organized in 1885 for the purpose of advancing the interests of the manufacturing businesses. Though setting protective tariffs was its core objective, the NAM also became a primary opponent of the AFL and other labor interest groups. The goals of organized labor (such as higher wages for workers, better working conditions, increased benefits, and job security) and the goals of business owners (maximizing profits) often came into conflict.

Tensions between labor and business interests intensified with the tremendous growth of the American economy beginning in the late 1800s and continued to mount as the economy expanded. Large companies, focusing on maximizing profits (which in turn appealed to shareholders), opposed laborers' demands for increased wages, better working conditions, and worker benefits. Today, labor and business interest groups continue to be among the largest and most powerful interest groups in the nation.

The Growth of Interest Groups

Perhaps the most significant factor leading to an increase in the number of interest groups has been the overall growth in government. Interest groups attempt to advance their agenda by influencing various aspects of government. As the number of government programs and agencies has expanded, along with their reach, opportunities for influencing what government does through interest group activities have expanded as well.

The New Deal programs of the 1930s and the Great Society programs of the 1960s led to tremendous growth in the federal government and huge increases in the federal budget. Government began to assume a more active role not only in promoting its economic policies but in promoting social policies as well. In response, a vast number of interest groups formed. Both proponents and opponents of a more active government organized interest groups to advocate their views. As the number of interest groups advocating economic issues expanded, so too did the number of groups promoting ideological perspectives, positions on single issues, and political reforms.

Though interest groups have been part of the American system since its beginning, the number of groups has increased dramatically over the past half-century. Between 1960 and 2000, the number of official associations increased by 400 percent (from 5,843 to 23,298) and the total amount of lobbying spending in Washington increased from $1.43 billion in 1998 to $2.16 billion in 2004.[8] Major political developments, such as the antiwar movement, the civil rights movement, and the Watergate scandal of the Nixon administration, mobilized a better-educated mass public to become increasingly concerned about political issues. This heightened concern about social and political issues fostered a significant amount of new interest group activity. The sophisticated use of mass-media technologies such as television, the computer, and the Internet has facilitated the ability of groups to emerge and flourish.

Another factor contributing to the increase in interest group activity has been the escalating cost of financing political campaigns. As costs have increased, interest groups have come to play a greater role in supporting political parties and the election of candidates. The Federal Election Campaign Act of 1971 placed limits on individual and corporate contributions to political campaigns. As a means of financing campaigns through alternative methods, interest groups have formed political action committees (PACs). Currently PACs can contribute up to $5,000 directly to campaigns, so long as each PAC contributes to at least five different candidates in an election year. In the 2004 election year, PACs spent more than $2 billion on political campaigning. PACs and campaign funding will receive more extensive treatment in Chapter 15.

---

[8] See http://www.opensecrets.org/lobbyists/index.asp.

American Government . . . in Popular Perspective:

American Opinion about Interest Groups

Most polls show that the public thinks interest groups have more power than they should have.

How concerned are you, if at all, about the influence of lobbyists and special interest groups in Washington these days . . . ?

Not at All Concerned 9%
Unsure 3%
Not Too Concerned 13%
Very Concerned 46%
Somewhat Concerned 29%

April 7–16, 2006

Pew Research Center for the People & the Press survey conducted by Princeton Survey Research Associates International. April 7-16, 2006. N=1,501 adults nationwide. MoE ± 3 (for all adults).

Do you think recent reports of lobbyists bribing members of Congress are isolated incidents of corruption, or do you think this kind of behavior is common in Congress?

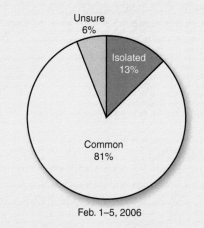

Unsure 6%
Isolated 13%
Common 81%

Feb. 1–5, 2006

Pew Research Center for the People & the Press survey conducted by Princeton Survey Research Associates International. Feb. 1-5, 2006. N=1,502 adults nationwide. MoE ± 3 (for all adults).

Do you think that YOUR member of Congress has taken bribes from lobbyists or not?

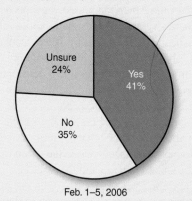

Unsure 24%
Yes 41%
No 35%

Feb. 1–5, 2006

Pew Research Center for the People & the Press survey conducted by Princeton Survey Research Associates International. Feb. 1-5, 2006. N=757 adults nationwide. MoE ± 4 (Form 1).

Iron Triangles, Issue Networks, and the Influence of Groups

The influence of interest groups is buoyed by the process in which public policy is created and modified. In any policy area, three key sets of actors interact to produce public policy: (1) congressional committees and subcommittees assigned to a specific policy area, (2) executive agencies of government that have the authority to administer policies in a particular area, and (3) private interest groups that have an interest in influencing that policy area. Members of congressional committees, managers of agencies, and leaders of interest groups all have vested interests in the specific policy area. As political scientist Theodore Lowi has noted, although these parties may not always agree on particular positions, they all seek to promote policies favorable to their interests, and they come to depend on one another for support and influence. Together, this network of actors dominates the development of public policies. This durable and seemingly impenetrable three-sided network has come to be known as the **iron triangle** of policy making.[9]

The development of U.S. defense policy illustrates how iron triangles work. The armed services and defense committees and subcommittees in Congress are responsible for appropriating funds for defense contracts (such as for the building of new military aircraft). Members of Congress on these committees are committed to maintaining a strong national defense, and they control the purse strings for developing new defense systems. Leaders in the U.S. Department of Defense are responsible for implementing defense systems under the orders of the president and rely on congressional committees to fund strong systems. Private contractors such as Pratt & Whitney (an airplane engine manufacturer) employ the engineers and researchers to design superior systems and provide valuable information to the congressional committees and the defense department.

★ Iron triangle

A three-sided network of policy making that includes congressional committees (and subcommittees) in a specific policy area, executive agencies with authority over that area, and private interest groups focused on influencing that area.

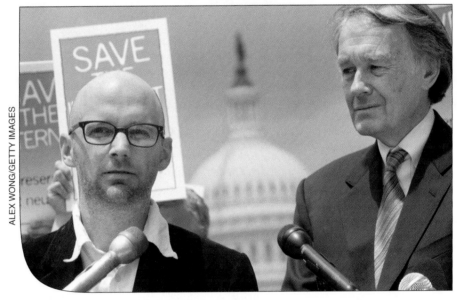

ALEX WONG/GETTY IMAGES

Musician Moby (left) with Congressman Edward Markey (D-MA) talk to the press at a news conference on Internet freedom in 2006. Moby and Markey both support limiting the influence of giant companies on the Internet.

The committees and the Department of Defense depend on Pratt & Whitney for developing advanced engine technologies, advice on aircraft design, and the capacity to produce cutting-edge aircraft engines. Pratt & Whitney benefits from winning federal contracts to produce defense systems. The congressional committees, Defense Department managers, and corporate leaders and lobbyists from Pratt & Whitney are familiar with one another, depend on one another, and use one another in the development of defense systems. The iron triangle approach to public policy making has institutionalized the role of interest groups in the exercise of American democracy.

Though an iron triangle refers to the interdependent relationship between legislators, bureaucrats, and lobbyists in a particular policy area, it is also possible to identify a broader set of actors who all have a vested interest in an area of public policy and try to collectively influence their policy area. Political scientists have used the term **issue networks** to describe this broader array of actors beyond legislators, bureaucrats, and lobbyists who try to influence a particular policy area. These include congressional staff people, journalists or other members of the media who often report on the policy area, and researchers who have done work on and are experts in the policy area.[10]

★ Issue network

The broad array of actors (beyond just the iron triangle) that try to collectively influence a policy area in which they maintain a vested interest.

---

[9] See Theodore J. Lowi, *The End of Liberalism* (New York: W. W. Norton, 1979).
[10] See William Gormley, "Regulatory Issue Networks in a Federal System," in *Polity* 18 (1986), 595–620 .

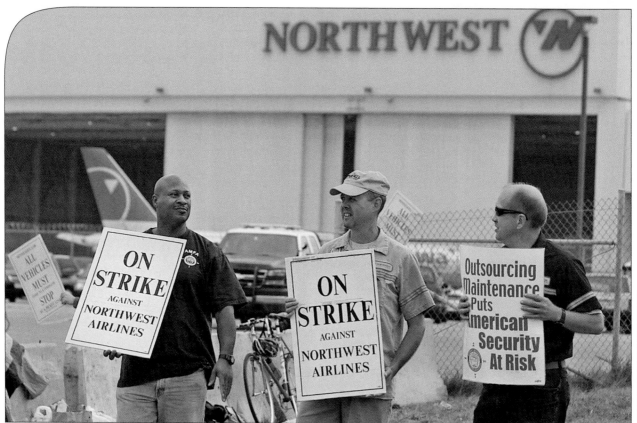

AP PHOTO/JANET HOSTLETTER

Unionized airline mechanics picket the workplace for higher wages in 2005.

Membership in Groups

Many Americans belong to interest groups, and many businesses, nonprofit organizations, and public entities belong to interest groups as well. It is estimated that about four in five citizens belong to at least one interest group. Many of the more common groups Americans belong to include labor unions (such as the AFL-CIO, which boasts a total of about 13 million members), professional associations (such as the three hundred thousand medical doctors who belong to the American Medical Association), and organizations such as the AARP to which many of the nation's senior citizens belong. As many as 3 million businesses across the United States belong to the U.S. Chamber of Commerce.[11]

Although the number of Americans who belong to interest groups is high, certain types of people are more likely than others to engage in interest group activity. Americans with higher incomes and greater resources, and those who are better educated and employed in professional occupations, are much more likely to belong to groups. Those with more financial resources tend to better appreciate the utility of group membership and interest groups' impact on the political process; wealthier individuals are also more likely to have the resources to support interest group activities. Thus many critics of interest group politics charge that the pluralist model of democracy favors the upper middle class and upper class of society. Because those with more resources can and do support interest groups, they are more likely to influence public policy to their financial advantage.

Various reasons have been proposed to explain why people or organizations might join and support certain interest groups. One is that they receive specific, tangible benefits from membership. These are referred to as **material benefits**[12] of group membership. For instance, local units of the National Education Association (NEA) work for its teacher members to win salary increases, and so the benefits of membership often produce a favorable material benefit to teachers in the form of higher wages. Many interest groups provide their members with other material benefits such as health and auto insurance discounts, magazine subscriptions, and other free products.

★ Material benefits (of group membership)

The specific, tangible benefits individuals receive from interest group membership, such as economic concessions, discounts on products, etc.

American Government: Historical, Popular, and Global Perspectives

[11] See http://www.uschamber.com.

[12] Mancur Olson, *The Logic of Collective Action: Public Goods and the Theory of Groups* (Cambridge, MA: Harvard University Press, 1971), pp. 22–35.

Another reason why interest groups are appealing are the **purposive benefits** (or expressive benefits) of membership.[13] Purposive rewards are those that do not directly benefit the individual member, but benefit society more generally. Some interest groups, for example, are committed to the goal of improving the environment and promoting policies that better protect the natural environment. The Sierra Club is one such organization that endorses these goals, and members of the Sierra Club receive purposive benefits from membership and support of the group's activities.

A third type of incentive for interest group membership is the **solidary benefits**[14] of membership, or the satisfaction that individuals receive from interacting with like-minded individuals for a cause. Solidary rewards derive less from the interest group's goals and more from the process of interacting with others to achieve a goal. For example, a union worker who attends a labor rally to support increases in a new contract may receive satisfaction from simply being with colleagues in support of a cause.

★ Purposive benefits (of group membership)

Rewards that do not directly benefit the individual member, but benefit society as a whole.

★ Solidary benefits (of group membership)

Satisfaction that individuals receive from interacting with like-minded individuals for a cause.

What Makes Some Groups More Powerful than Others?

Although there are thousands of interest groups operating in the United States, some groups are more successful than others in promoting their cause and affecting public policy to their liking. There are three general characteristics of an interest group, which may have significant bearing on how powerful that group's influence will be in Washington:

1. **The size of the membership.** There is, undoubtedly, "power in numbers." The larger the number of members of an interest group, the more powerful that group will be in affecting public policy. Large membership alone makes elected leaders responsive to a group's concerns. An interest group with a large number of members can increase its power and influence by convincing its members to vote for a candidate or candidates. The Christian Coalition of America (CCA) is a Christian political advocacy group that includes fundamentalists, Evangelicals, Pentecostals, and many members of mainline Protestant churches as well. Officials of the CCA often communicate with the organization's huge membership regarding the endorsement of candidates. Not surprisingly, the CCA attracts the attention of candidates as well as officeholders who plan on running for another term. Groups with large numbers of members also have an advantage in raising funds to support their activities. With many members, the potential for fund raising is great. And funding goes a long way in advancing the effectiveness of interest group activities. A good example of a group that exhibits strength though numbers is the American Farm Bureau Federation (AFBF), which boasts 4.7 million members and has proven especially effective at promoting policies that provide large subsidies and other benefits to American farmers. A bilateral trade agreement between the United States and Russia in late 2006 was a testament to AFBF influence, as it substantially expanded the export market for U.S. farmers.

2. **The wealth of the members.** The number of members is an important indicator of the potential amount of money that interest groups might be able to raise. But just as important is the wealth of the membership. Certain interest groups enjoy a huge advantage when it comes to the average wealth of its members. For example, the American Trial Lawyers Association (ATLA) is made up of trial lawyers who, by virtue of their occupation, are quite wealthy when compared to average Americans. Thus, whereas the

---

[13] Robert Salisbury, "An Exchange Theory of Interest Groups" in *Midwest Journal of Political Science* 13 (1969), 1–32.

[14] Peter B. Clark and James Q. Wilson, "Incentives Systems: A Theory of Organization" in *Administrative Science Quarterly* 6 (1961), 129–166.

Governor Mike Huckabee (R-AR), a contender for the Republican Party's presidential nomination in 2008, speaks at the annual Conservative Political Action Conference in Washington, DC, in March of 2007.

number of members of the ATLA is only about fifty thousand, the wealth of its membership and the consequent level of financial contributions from members provide sufficient resources to make it an especially powerful interest group in Washington.

3. **The dedication of members to the goals of the group.** In addition to the number of members and wealth of members, groups that have a loyal following based on member commitment to the cause of the group can be a powerful resource.[15] The National Right to Life Committee (NRLC) is a good example. The NRLC organized and began to solicit members and contributions in 1973, after the *Roe v. Wade* decision legalized abortion. NRLC's members tend to be dedicated to right-to-life positions and willing to contribute much time, effort, and resources to advance its pro-life agenda.

Types of Interest Groups

Although interest groups represent a wide array of interests in American society, there are two basic types of interest groups—economic groups and noneconomic groups. Many groups engage in both economic and noneconomic pursuits, but most can be classified as either primarily economic or noneconomic in nature.

Economic Groups

Although the specific goals of different interest groups vary greatly, the vast majority of groups in America have goals that are economic in nature. Two out of every three interest groups in America are **economic interest groups,** or groups that exist to promote economic conditions favorable to and economic opportunities for their members. Economic groups also tend to be the largest and most powerful groups

★ Economic interest group

An organized group that exists to promote economic conditions favorable to and economic opportunities for its members.

---

[15] For a good discussion of the influence of group member dedication to group effectiveness, see Mancur Olson, *The Logic of Collective Action: Public Goods and the Theory of Groups* (Cambridge, MA: Harvard University Press, 1971).

American Government: Historical, Popular, and Global Perspectives

The Top Ten Most Influential Interest Groups

Each year, *Fortune* magazine identifies what it views as the top ten most influential interest groups in the nation on the basis of a survey of Washington, DC, political players. One recent top ten list consisted of the following:

✔ **1. American Association of Retired Persons (AARP):** The AARP provides services for senior citizens, including consumer and policy advocacy, health care information, and tax counseling.

✔ **2. The National Rifle Association (NRA):** The NRA is dedicated to preserving the rights of law-abiding citizens to purchase, own, and use their own firearms. The Institute for Legal Action is the lobbying arm of the NRA.

✔ **3. The National Federation of Independent Businesses (NFIB):** This is the largest advocacy group in the nation that represents small businesses. Among other things, it supports a simpler tax system and lower taxes on businesses, and it opposes minimum wage increases and the expansion of the Family Medical Leave Act.

✔ **4. American Israel Public Affairs Committee (AIPAC):** AIPAC is a strong advocate of a pro-Israel foreign policy for the U.S. government.

✔ **5. The American Federation of Labor-Congress of Industrial Organizations (AFL-CIO):** The goal of the AFL-CIO is to empower working people by giving them a strong voice in the workplace and in government policy making.

✔ **6. The Association of Trial Lawyers of America (ATLA):** ATLA is the world's largest trial lawyers association, promoting policies that enhance fairness for injured persons in the judicial process and aid lawyer effectiveness in pursuing such claims.

✔ **7. The U.S. Chamber of Commerce:** This is the world's largest federation of businesses. Among other things, it lobbies to reduce government's regulation of businesses and improve trade opportunities for U.S. firms doing business abroad.

✔ **8. National Right to Life Committee (NRLC):** NRLC was formed in response to the *Roe v. Wade* decision in which the Supreme Court protected abortion under certain circumstances from government regulation. The NRLC has lobbied to make abortion laws more stringent.

✔ **9. The National Education Association (NEA):** NEA focuses on advancing public education in the United States. It lobbies to improve teacher preparation, better working conditions for teachers, and increase resources for the nation's schools.

✔ **10. The National Restaurant Association:** This is the leading business association for the restaurant industry.

because members of such groups maintain a vested personal financial stake in having the group achieve its goals.

As well as being the most numerous, economic groups also tend to be the best organized and most influential interest groups. Because economic interests are those that generally inspire more concern from businesses and citizens alike, they tend to feature greater individual involvement, commitment, resources, and organization.

There are thousands of interest groups that focus primarily on advancing the economic goals of its members. These groups include private businesses, labor unions, business and industry associations, and professional associations.

Business Groups.

The largest companies in the nation and the world typically maintain internal units that function as an interest group for the company. Very large companies, such as General Motors (GM) and IBM, for example, have their own interest groups. Such companies typically have wide and varied interests. GM, for example, is affected by environmental laws (tougher air pollution laws often require GM to spend more on technologies to reduce emissions in their cars), labor laws (increases in the minimum wage require higher pay for some workers), and product safety laws (increased safety standards might increase the cost of assembling a car). GM needs a well-staffed interest group to try to influence these and many other types of legislation.

Most businesses belong to associations, and often these associations engage in interest group activities to advocate for the interests of their members. Some associations are very broad in scope, such as the U.S. Chamber of Commerce, with its 3 million members. These businesses range from small neighborhood auto mechanics to large billion-dollar financial institutions. The Chamber seeks to broadly advance the interests of business owners.

Another type of business association is a **trade association.** A trade association typically focuses on one particular industry, and members of the association are drawn exclusively from that industry. Businesses in a particular trade often face similar types of concerns, and the trade association looks out for the specific interests of a classification of businesses. For example, the American Society of Travel Agents (ASTA) is a trade association whose twenty-four thousand member institutions include travel agencies, hotels, airlines, car rental agencies, and the like. ASTA promotes legislation and regulations favoring the travel industry.

Businesses, business associations, and trade associations have an advantage over associations and other organizations whose members are individual citizens or consumers. Businesses quickly see the advantage of joining an association, which collectively advocates for the interests of like businesses. Individuals, however, are less likely to join and contribute to an association that advocates for such things as consumer protection. Because there are so many consumers, an individual consumer is less likely to see a benefit in his or her own contribution. But because there are fewer businesses that belong to any given trade association, businesses are more likely to perceive a benefit from participating in the organization. As Mancur Olson, a well-known scholar on interest groups, has put it, smaller groups are more likely to organize and associate because members can more readily see the benefits and "logic of collective action."[16] That is, people with common interests working together in groups are more effective than the same number of people working independently.

Certainly members of smaller groups are more likely to perceive direct benefits from their membership; smaller groups are also less likely to suffer from the free rider problem. **Free riders** are those individuals who do not join or contribute to an interest group that is representing their interests. Thus, they enjoy the benefits of membership without paying for the costs. The free rider problem is more common in larger groups, which may have trouble convincing individuals to contribute due to each individual's perception that others will work to achieve the group's goal.

Labor Unions.

Whereas business groups promote the interests of companies and corporations, labor unions promote the interests of American workers. Initially, labor unions emerged from the expansion of the U.S. economy in the late 1800s and early 1900s. The new technologies that resulted from the Industrial Revolution led to the rapid growth of large-scale farming and manufacturing and created many new jobs. Many business owners exploited their laborers, providing low pay, few benefits, and often poor and unsafe working conditions. Workers then organized into unions, using the threat of a strike to improve their conditions.

---

[16] Mancur Olson, *The Logic of Collective Action: Public Goods and the Theory of Groups* (Cambridge, MA: Harvard University Press, 1971).

In the early 1940s, as many as 35 percent of workers in America were union members. Over the years, however, the percentage of union workers has declined. Today only about 13 percent of workers belong to a union. An important reason for this decline relates to changes in the type of jobs that Americans hold. Skilled and unskilled laborers are most likely to be unionized, but these types of jobs represent an increasingly smaller proportion of the workforce. Professional and service jobs, which are less likely to be unionized, now dominate the American workforce, and so union membership has declined. Rather than unionizing, professionals tend to organize and join professional associations. Some professionals, however, have unionized. The largest union in the United States today is a teachers' union, the National Education Association.

Unions differ from professional associations in that the laws provide certain bargaining rights to unions. Union membership may be required for all employees as well. State laws vary on this issue. Some states are **open shop,** which means that employees in that state maintain the option of whether or not to join a certified union. Of course in open shop states, workers who do not join the union may benefit from union activities without "paying the price"—another form of the "free rider" problem. Since 1947, the federal Taft-Hartley Act has technically banned the **closed shop,** which requires union membership as a condition of employment in a unionized workplace. Still, unions have successfully convinced some state legislatures that because all workers enjoy the benefits of union advocacy (for example, promoting pay increases and so on), all workers should at least be required to pay dues to the union. Thus many states allow so-called **union shops,** which require that employees in unionized workplaces either join the union or pay the equivalent of union dues to it after a set period of time.

Professional Associations.

Higher levels of education and advances in technology have transformed the American workforce over the past half-century. One of the major changes has been an increase in professional, technical, and service jobs,

A meeting of the Airline Pilots Association in Atlanta, Georgia, where union organizers discuss concerns of the pilots.

★ Open shop

The law that allows employees the option of joining or not joining the certified union at a unionized workplace.

★ Closed shop

The law that requires employees to become members of the union as a condition of employment in unionized workplaces.

★ Union shop

The law that requires that employees in unionized workplaces either join the union or pay the equivalent of union dues to it after a set period of time.

BARRY WILLIAMS/GETTY IMAGES

Chapter 11: Interest Groups

Table 11.1 Who Spends the Most on Lobbying?

More than $2.5 billion was spent on lobbying activities in Washington in the year 2006. This table shows the biggest spenders from 1998 through 2006.

Client	Total
U.S. Chamber of Commerce	$317,164,680
American Medical Association	$156,375,500
General Electric	$137,770,000
American Hospital Association	$129,114,026
Edison Electric Institute	$105,642,628
AARP	$105,332,064
Pharmaceutical Research and Manufacturers of America	$104,302,000
National Association of Realtors	$97,530,000
Business Roundtable	$97,060,000
Northrop Grumman	$95,682,374
Blue Cross/Blue Shield	$84,156,418
Freddie Mac (Federal Home Loan and Mortgage Corporation)	$81,884,048
Lockheed Martin	$80,206,965
Boeing Company	$77,898,310
Verizon Communications	$75,836,522
Philip Morris	$75,500,000
General Motors	$71,158,483
Fannie Mae (Federal National Mortgage Association)	$70,957,000
Ford Motor Company	$67,670,808
US Telecom Association	$65,280,000

Source: http://www.opensecrets.org, the website of the Center for Responsive Politics.

and a decrease in the number of skilled and unskilled labor jobs. Professionals have organized to promote and protect their economic interests through membership in professional organizations, which lobby on their behalf.

Two large and growing classes of professionals are lawyers and medical doctors, both of which have high-profile and powerful interest groups—the American Medical Association (AMA) for doctors and the American Bar Association (ABA) for lawyers. The medical and legal professions are regulated by state governments, and the AMA and ABA have been quite successful in influencing the regulatory process—for example, by establishing licensing requirements for doctors and lawyers.

Another large and influential professional association is the National Association of Realtors (NAR), with a total membership of over seven hundred thousand, an annual budget of over $60,000,000, and an organizational staff of more than four hundred people. The size, budget, and organization of NAR provide it with ample resources to advocate the interests of the nation's real estate agents.

Noneconomic Groups

Economic groups exist primarily to advance the commercial and financial interests of its members. Whereas economic interests dominate pluralist activities, many other interest groups advocate for primarily noneconomic concerns. Three general categories of **noneconomic interest groups** are public interest groups, issue or ideological groups, and government groups.

Public Interest Groups. **Public interest groups** promote the broad, collective good of citizens and consumers. Many public interest groups seek to promote political reforms that enhance the role of the public in the political process. The League of Women Voters is one such group. Initially formed as an interest group that promoted women's suffrage, the League has become a leading advocate for improving turnout among all citizens in elections. The League of Women Voters has also taken the lead in promoting candidate engagement on issues of importance to the voters by sponsoring campaign debates.

Fred Wertheimer, formerly the president of Common Cause.

Another highly active public interest group is Common Cause. This group's literature describes itself in the following way: "Common Cause is a nonprofit, nonpartisan citizen's lobbying organization promoting open, honest and account- able government. Supported by the dues and contributions of over 200,000 members in every state across the nation, Common Cause represents the unified voice of the people against corruption in government and big money special interests."[17]

Common Cause promotes reforming the political system in ways that enhance the role of the average citizen. Thus it supports laws limiting elected officials from taking gifts from special interests, ending the practice of providing large speaking honoraria to members of Congress, and reforming the presidential campaign finance system. Ironically, Common Cause also tries to limit the role interest groups play in the electoral process.

Ralph Nader and the various citizens' advocacy groups he helped to start (including Public Citizen and the Center for Auto Safety) are among the nation's leading public interest groups. Nader's best-selling book *Unsafe at Any Speed: The Designed-in Dangers of the American Automobile* forced the president of General Motors to publicly admit to the U.S. Senate that the company ignored automobile safety problems. Nader's Raiders, the name later given to the hundreds of young activists who arrived in Washington, DC, to help Nader investigate government cor- ruption, were highly influential in pushing automobile safety legislation in the late 1960s, which dramatically raised safety standards for cars and trucks. Their efforts effectively launched a widespread consumer movement, which remains strong. Today these groups advocate campaign finance reform, monitor the health care industry, and promote consumer safety and consumer rights, among other public interest activities.

Issue and Ideological Groups. Interest groups that focus on specific issues and ideological perspectives are known as **issue and ideological groups.** Abortion, wom- en's rights, and the environment are just a few of the policy issues that have produced interest groups such as the National Right to Life Committee (pro-life), Americans for Free Choice (pro-choice), the National Organization for Women (NOW; wom- en's rights), and the Sierra Club and the Nature Conservancy (both environmental groups). Each of these groups maintains effective lobbies on behalf of its positions.

Some groups have a broader focus than a particular issue or set of policy issues. These are known as ideological groups, and they promote a more general ideological approach on how government should deal with a host of issues. Both liberal and con- servative ideological groups operate in the American pluralist system. The Americans

★ Noneconomic interest group

An organized group that ad- vocates for reasons other than their membership's commercial and financial interests.

★ Public interest group

An organized group that promotes the broad, collective good of citizens and consumers.

★ Issue and ideological group

An organized group that focuses on specific issues and ideological perspectives.

---

[17] See http://www.commoncause.org.

Table 11.2 How Interest Groups Rate Members of Congress

The ideology of any member of Congress, or the degree to which the member represents any particular group's interests, can be discovered by flipping through the pages of the *Almanac of American Politics*. The *Almanac* provides the ratings that members receive from eleven prominent interest groups. The eleven groups are arranged from left (most liberal) to right (most conservative). The higher the rating (on a scale of 0 to 100) received by a member of Congress, the more closely that member is associated with the position of the interest group. This table shows the year 2006 scores for selected leaders in the House and Senate by two of the more liberal groups—Americans for Democratic Action (ADA) and the American Civil Liberties Union (ACLU)—and two of the more conservative groups: the American Conservative Union (ACU) and Christian Coalition of America (CCA). Note that while Senator Joseph Lieberman (I–CT) is well known for his steadfast support of President Bush's positions on foreign policy, he registers the lowest possible rating among conservative interest groups on the issues that matter most to them.

	Liberal Groups		Conservative Groups	
	ADA	ACLU	ACU	CCA
Sen. John McCain (R–AZ)	35	22	72	83
Sen. Barbara Boxer (D–CA)	95	75	4	0
Sen. Joe Lieberman (I–CT)	75	83	0	0
Sen. Joseph Biden (D–DE)	95	86	0	16
Sen. Sam Brownback (R–KS)	15	11	96	100
Sen. Mitch McConnell (R–KY)	15	0	96	100
Sen. Ted Kennedy (D–MA)	100	86	0	0
Sen. John Kerry (D–MA)	25	100	0	0
Sen. Hillary Clinton (D–NY)	95	78	0	0
Sen. Charles Schumer (D–NY)	100	78	12	0
Sen. Arlen Specter (R–PA)	45	22	75	83
Sen. Orrin Hatch (R–UT)	10	0	96	100
Rep. Nancy Pelosi (D–CA)	100	90	8	8
Rep. Jesse Jackson Jr. (D–IL)	100	100	0	15
Rep. Dan Burton (R–IN)	0	0	100	100
Rep. Barney Frank (D–MA)	100	100	4	7
Rep. John Boehner (R–OH)	0	0	100	91

Source: Reprinted with permission from *Almanac of American Politics*, 2006. Copyright 2008 by National Journal Group, Inc. All rights reserved.

for Democratic Action (ADA), for example, is an interest group that promotes government policies with a liberal orientation. Since 1947, the voting records of members of Congress on certain issues have served as the standard measure of political liberalism. The ADA supports candidates for office whose votes on key issues score a high "liberal quotient."

The American Civil Liberties Union (ACLU) is an interest group that advocates for the civil rights and liberties of American citizens. Specifically, the ACLU adamantly supports the rights of the accused, free speech rights, free press rights, religious liberty rights, and many other liberties guaranteed by the Bill of Rights. The ACLU has also become a strong advocate for students' rights, the rights of workers, lesbian/gay rights, and immigrants' rights.

The Christian Coalition of America (CCA) is another ideological group that has become a lobbying powerhouse in recent decades; it professes to offer "people of faith" a vehicle to become involved in influencing public policy. The CCA's "pro-family" agenda advocates pro-life positions, promotes the role of religion as a part of what government does, favors reducing tax burdens on families, and supports victims' rights.

Government Interest Groups. Most interest group activity organizes private concerns (of either individuals or businesses) for the purpose of influencing public policy. But private interests are not the only ones represented in the pluralist system. Groups representing the interests of governments also operate in this complex system.

Cities and states across the nation have organized to exert influence on the federal government. Most states and large cities employ their own lobbyists in Washington, DC. But states, cities, and other governments also organize collectively through a variety of interest groups, which are generally referred to as **intergovernmental lobbies.** The National League of Cities, for example, is an interest group that advocates for the broad interests of local governments. Another intergovernmental lobby advancing the cause of the nation's cities is the U.S. Conference of Mayors. The Council of State Governments and the National Governors Association lobby on behalf of the states' interests.

Not only do state and local governments lobby in Washington, DC, but foreign governments also organize and lobby. Many nations have embassies in the Washington, DC, area, and many of these embassies engage in interest group activities of their own.

★ Intergovernmental lobby

Any interest group that represents the collective interests of states, cities, and other governments.

How Interest Groups Achieve Their Goals

Interest groups engage in a number of activities to advance the goals of the group and influence public policy. These activities usually involve lobbying, supporting candidates and parties in election campaigns, persuasion campaigns, and litigation.

Lobbying

Interest groups attempt to influence elected and other public leaders to make decisions that are favorable toward the group's goals. **Lobbying** is the term used to describe how interest groups go about influencing government officials. Lobbyists are the professionals who do the lobbying.

Lobbyists provide information to public officials, with the hope that the information will convince the official to vote or act in a manner favorable to the group's interest. Lobbyists perform a valuable function to public officials by providing not only information and perspectives on issues, but expertise as well. In the iron triangle system, lobbyists seek access to members of Congress and to managers in executive agencies in a particular policy area. Public officials come to depend on the lobbyists for information and knowledge. For example, managers in the Department of Defense and members of Congress on the Armed Services Committee rely on lobbyists from Pratt & Whitney for information on emerging jet engine technologies, engine performance data, and other information, which allows the military to plan and improve the nation's defenses.

Similarly, the congressional committees responsible for workplace safety standards and the Occupational Safety and Health Administration (OSHA), the executive agency responsible for administering those standards, depend on the lobbyists

★ Lobbying

The means by which interest groups attempt to influence government officials to make decisions favorable to their goals.

Some of the most sought-after lobbyists by corporations and organizations are former elected officials, especially former senators and representatives, who are well acquainted with how government works and retain personal relationships with many of their former colleagues who remain in Congress. In 1999, the Center for Responsive Politics reported that 129 former members of Congress were registered as lobbyists in Washington. Federal law requires that a member wait one year after leaving office before lobbying. Among former members of Congress who are now highly paid lobbyists are former Congresswoman Pat Schroeder, former Senator Robert Packwood, and former Congressman Fred Grandy.

Pat Schroeder, a Democrat from Colorado, was first elected to the House of Representatives in 1972 and served there until 1997. Her quarter-century in the House included time as chair of the Congressional Caucus on Women's Issues, as a member of the Armed Services Committee, and as chair of a House select committee on children, youth, and families. She was the primary author of the Family and Medical Leave Act of 1993. Schroeder also chaired a subcommittee on intellectual property rights and became the House's foremost expert on copyright issues. Schroeder is now a successful Washington lobbyist. Putting her experience in copyrights and intellectual property rights to good use, she recently became president and chief executive officer of the Association of American Publishers, which is the main trade association for the publishing industry.

Pat Schroeder (right, seen here with Vice President Dick Cheney's wife, Lynne) as president of the Association of American Publishers in 2005.

Robert Packwood, a Republican from Oregon, served nearly three decades in the Senate. He was regarded as a shrewd, legislatively accomplished liberal on many social issues, such as abortion rights and family planning. Immediately after winning re-election to a fifth term in the Senate, a story appeared in the *Washington Post* accusing him of sexual harassment. His strong record of support for feminist issues made the charges of harassment, and Packwood's denial of them, especially controversial. Packwood resigned from the Senate in 1995 after an ethics committee recommended his expulsion for sexual misconduct. The cloud of controversy surrounding his departure from the Senate, however, did not diminish his potential for an eventual career as a lobbyist. One year to the day after his resignation, he became a lobbyist with the Sunrise Research Group. Packwood's clients include Northwest Airlines, Verizon Communications, and the National Association of Real Estate Investment Trusts, among others.

Former Senator Bob Packwood.

Fred Grandy has had at least four careers—first as "Your Yeoman Purser, Burl 'Gopher' Smith" on a popular 1980s TV show *The Loveboat*; then as Republican Congressman Grandy, representing Iowa in the House; later as president of Goodwill Industries (a large charitable nonprofit organization); and most recently as a lobbyist with the group Independent Sector (a coalition of more than seven hundred nonprofits and foundations). With extensive experience both as a former congressman and then as head of a large nonprofit corporation, Grandy was well positioned to assume a prime role as a lobbyist for charitable organizations throughout the United States.

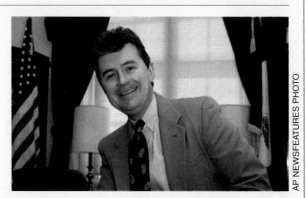

Former Representative Fred Grandy.

Today lobbyists are as important in policy making as members of Congress themselves. But this is nothing new in American politics. Lobbying has been part of the American political system since the colonial era. Some of the nation's most successful lobbyists over time include the following:

Benjamin Franklin: Most students of American history recognize Benjamin Franklin as a founding father, political philosopher, and inventor/scientist. But Franklin was also a lobbyist and quite a successful one. The colonies of Pennsylvania, Georgia, and Massachusetts hired him to lobby on their behalf before the British Parliament from 1757 to 1770. Franklin's greatest lobbying success was securing the repeal of the Stamp Act in 1766.

Tommy Corcoran: "The Cork," as he was known in Washington circles, set the mold for today's most successful lobbyists. He was a trusted friend and adviser to President Franklin Delano Roosevelt during the New Deal era, when Corcoran successfully lobbied Congress on behalf of the White House for many new government programs, including the Securities and Exchange Commission, the Tennessee Valley Authority, and the Federal Housing Administration. He also placed hundreds of attorneys in jobs to run these New Deal agencies. A well-connected insider, The Cork established a private lobbying practice in 1942, where his many connections in government proved valuable for his private-sector clients. From the 1940s until the 1960s, he was the most powerful and influential lobbyist in Washington.

Vernon Jordan: The typical lobbyist is not an African American from the Deep South who grew up poor. But Vernon Jordan is no average lobbyist. A civil rights activist in the 1960s, Jordan learned how to work within the political system. As a close personal friend of Bill Clinton, Jordan parlayed his understanding of how the system works into one of the most influential and powerful lobbying practices in Washington. Today he continues to sit on the boards of the most powerful companies and helps them advance their agenda.

Former President Bill Clinton with lobbyist Vernon Jordan.

representing labor unions and product safety groups for data and information on workplace hazards, and recommendations for remediation. Of course, these same public officials are likely to be lobbied by business interests concerned about the increased costs associated with remediation of hazards.

Lobbyists communicate with public officials in many different ways, including formal presentations, written memos and policy papers, informal e-mails or notes, face-to-face meetings, or informal discussions over a meal or a drink. The most effective lobbyists are those who provide valuable, truthful information on policy issues and who make persuasive arguments. Having a good working relationship with public officials and a quality reputation provides the lobbyist with access to officials, which is crucial to the lobbyist's success.

A common perception of lobbying is that of a lobbyist offering money, gifts, trips, or other goods in return for a favorable action, such as a congressperson's vote on a particular bill. Though such activities do take place, in modern times they have become the exception rather than the rule. The activities of lobbyists today are strictly

Table 11.3 Big Givers to Campaigns

These ten organizations were the biggest contributors to American political campaigns between 1989 and 2006.

Organization	Contributions
American Federation of State, County & Municipal Employees	$38,133,049
AT&T, Inc.	$36,992,735
National Association of Realtors	$30,298,348
National Education Association	$27,108,900
American Association for Justice	$27,107,056
International Brotherhood of Electrical Workers	$25,779,741
Laborers Union	$25,018,639
Goldman Sachs	$24,902,461
Service Employees International Union	$24,675,343
Carpenters and Joiners Union	$24,422,870

Source: The Center for Responsive Politics, June 2007.

regulated by federal and state governments. Lobbyist gift giving and bribery of public officials is illegal in most states and can be prosecuted. States require lobbyists to provide financial statements, report expenses, and maintain official registration for interest groups and individuals who provide lobbying services.

Lobbyists are regularly seen in the halls of the Capitol building and the House and Senate office buildings. They are also common fixtures in the halls and offices of the state capitol buildings. Many lobbyists own their own lobbying companies and contract with interest groups to provide services, similar to the way that an organization might hire a law firm to conduct legal work. More commonly, however, lobbyists are employed by businesses, associations, or other organizations to lobby for that employer alone. Large organizations and businesses have the resources to hire full-time lobbyists; contract lobbyists often work for smaller organizations that do not have the resources to hire their own full-time lobbying staff.

A form of lobbying that has been used more frequently in recent years is known as **grassroots lobbying.** The idea behind grassroots lobbying is that interest groups communicate with government officials by mobilizing public opinion to exert influence on government action. Because elected leaders are often quite sensitive to the opinions of voters, if a group can demonstrate that public opinion supports a particular position or the public is willing to contact officials to express their view, officeholders will respond favorably because they want to enhance their chances of being re-elected to office. Interest groups with a large number of members are particularly effective at grassroots lobbying, mainly because they can produce large numbers of potential votes in a given election. AARP, with more than 25 million members, has successfully used grassroots methods of lobbying to put pressure on Congress to protect the Social Security and Medicare systems—two primary goals of AARP.

Supporting Candidates and Parties in Elections

Interest groups are also quite active in electoral politics, providing resources for candidates and parties that support the interest groups' goals. PACs, described earlier in this chapter, are an important instrument through which interest groups provide financial support to candidates and political parties.

★ Grassroots lobbying

Communications by interest groups with government officials through the mobilization of public opinion to exert influence on government action.

In addition to providing financing to support candidates, groups can play an important role in campaigns in other ways as well. For example, a labor union might endorse a candidate and communicate that endorsement to its members, urging members to vote for the candidate. A group might also use its resources to hire a phone bank to make "get out the vote" phone calls on behalf of a candidate or slate of candidates. Groups have also provided support by drafting speeches for candidates on policy matters or hosting rallies for office seekers.

Business groups tend to support Republican candidates, largely because Republicans are more likely to agree with their goals. Similarly, labor unions tend to support Democratic candidates because Democrats are likely to support labor's positions on many issues, such as increases in the minimum wage and family leave laws. On social issues, Republican candidates tend to receive the support of conservative groups, such as pro-life groups and groups advocating stiffer crime control measures. On the other hand, groups that advocate a more liberal social agenda (such as the ACLU and Sierra Club) tend to support Democratic candidates, whose issue agenda is more consistent with the group goals.

ACLU attorney Ruth Bader Ginsburg in 1977. Today, Ginsburg is an associate justice on the U.S. Supreme Court.

Litigation

Interest groups have also become quite adept at using the court system as a means of achieving their goals. Groups regularly initiate lawsuits, request injunctions, defend members, and file briefs. Consumer product safety groups, for example, regularly file for injunctions in courts seeking to order companies to cease the sale of products that are unsafe.

Some interest groups focus primarily on the courts to achieve their goals. For example, the ACLU regularly initiates lawsuits in circumstances in which it believes the government is compromising individual civil liberties. The ACLU is very active in litigating gender discrimination cases. One of the advantages of interest group litigation is its capitalization of interest groups' financial resources; average citizens do not have sufficient resources to initiate so many lawsuits. Also, because interest groups often specialize in particular kinds of lawsuits, they are able to litigate more skillfully.

Another way interest groups use the court system to exert influence is by the filing of amicus curiae ("friend of the court") briefs, which are companion briefs supporting an argument or set of arguments in an existing Supreme Court case.[18] Although the interest group is not a direct litigant in a matter, it can use an amicus brief to further or better articulate a position and thus aid litigants in their respective case.

Interest groups have also influenced the court system by engaging in lobbying activities to influence the appointment of judges. Pro-life and pro-choice groups are very active in supporting or opposing particular judicial nominees, based on the nominees' position and past decisions on abortion cases. The American Bar Association uses a rating system to rank individuals nominated for federal judgeships that has become extremely influential in the appointment process.

Persuasion Campaigns

Many interest groups run media campaigns to persuade the public to support their position on issues. Some of this persuasion occurs during election campaigns when groups create and place ads intended to help a political candidate or political party achieve victory. But increasingly, groups have run such campaigns outside of election campaigns to persuade or educate others to the group's way of thinking.

Groups have developed sophisticated public relations operations to communicate their positions. They use tactics such as "targeted mass mailings," in which they mail a pamphlet or other document to a large list of individuals that the group is attempting to influence. For example, the Americans for Democratic Action maintains a list of voters who are not registered with any particular political party. The ADA often sends mailings to those on the list to try to persuade them to support the ADA's

[18] David Lowery and Holly Brasher, *Organized Interests and American Government* (New York: McGraw-Hill, 2004), p. 247.

position on a particular issue. In addition to mass mailings, groups regularly use television, radio, newspapers, magazines, or even billboards to communicate positions and try to persuade. They also use the Internet to send messages to the wider public.

Now & Then: Making the Connection

Interest groups have become firmly entrenched within the American political landscape. Their influence is both certain and controversial. More than two centuries ago, James Madison expressed concerns about the influence of "factions." Today, many observers of American politics continue to express concerns about the influence of groups and the value of pluralism as a mode of governance. Nevertheless, interest groups offer an important and unique linkage between American citizens' varied interests and public policy. This linkage does not diminish the importance of other linkages, such as free and open elections. But the linkage offered by interest groups is unique in that it allows citizens to exert influence by interacting with one another and collectively attempting to influence what government does.

Few would argue with the premise that interest groups have been responsible for leading the charge in promoting political and social policies that have significantly improved the lot of millions of Americans. At the same time, the relationship between interest groups and government actors can become uncomfortably close, if not downright corrupt. Nearly a century and a half apart, both the railways and the Native American tribes were interest groups that exerted a strong influence on government policymaking. Both sets of interests were well-respected for their contribution to the American landscape. Yet when Oakes Ames and Jack Abramoff, respectively, attempted to influence public policies and agreements using greed as an enticement, the democratic system suffered. Like everyone else in a democracy, interest groups must be free to press their own agenda, but not so free that they may trample the agendas of so many others.

Named after a section of the United States tax code, "527s" are a relatively new invention used by organized interests to try to influence the outcome of elections in America. 527 groups are politically oriented organizations that enjoy tax exempt status under current law, and thus are subject to no limits on the amount of soft money they can theoretically raise and spend. These groups then use the money they raise to develop and air "issue" advertisements. Although they cannot produce ads that directly tell voters which candidate or party to vote for in a particular election, 527 groups generally target positions on particular issues and craft advertisements that attempt to convince voters how they should think about those issues. Thus many 527 ads have amounted to the equivalent of negative attacks on the personality or character of particular candidates. In short, 527s have found a way to make an end run around the campaign finance system.

Spending by the 527s is significant. Through September of 2008, 527 groups spent nearly $400 million on national, state, and local election contests. This excludes the heaviest spending months of October and early November. In the full 2004 presidential election year, the 527s spent over $600 million.

In 2004, one of the 527s (The "Swift Boat Veterans for Truth") was responsible for producing and airing the so-called "swift boat" ads that attacked John Kerry's character by questioning his military record. In 2008, 527s were behind many of the negative attacks on Barack Obama that decried his association with controversial figures such as William Ayers and Rev. Jeremiah Wright.

Go to www.opensecrets.org/527s for details concerning which individuals and organizations provide the bulk of financial support to the 527s. Which industries have been most active in forming these groups? What kinds of ads have they produced? Who do you think benefits more—Democratic or Republican candidates—from 527 activities? 527 groups frequently cite the First Amendment to defend their activities. Do these groups legitimately contribute to the "marketplace of ideas," or is this an example of "free speech run amuck"?

On http://academic.cengage.com/dautrich, find the politics interactive link for details on 527s. Consult as well the various links that relate to 527 advertisements. Historical, popular, and global perspectives on the 527s are also offered.

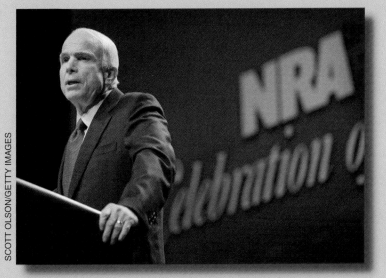

SCOTT OLSON/GETTY IMAGES

John McCain speaks at the annual meeting of the National Rifle Association, which endorsed him for president.

http://academic.cengage.com/dautrich

Chapter Summary

★ Interest groups are a popular mechanism by which groups of people attempt to influence government to advance their shared goals.

★ Pluralism is the theory that public policy largely results from a variety of interest groups competing with one another to promote laws that benefit members of their respective groups.

★ Many praise the interest group system in the United States because it provides all interest groups in society with access and a fair opportunity to compete for influence over public policy.

★ The interest group system is also criticized for allowing wealthy corporations and individuals a disproportionate influence on public policy, encouraging many groups to promote their own causes even if they run counter to the public interest, and significantly slowing down the policy-making process.

★ Unlike political parties, interest groups do not usually run their own candidates for public office, and they tend to focus more narrowly on special issues or sets of issues.

★ The growth of interest groups in the United States during the twentieth century was a product of the tremendous growth of government in general over that same period and the increased concerns about political issues that are expressed by a better-educated mass public.

★ Interest group influence over public policy is theoretically informal; in reality, interest group participation has become ingrained in the process through structures such as iron triangles and issue networks.

★ Individuals tend to join or support interest groups in order to receive material benefits, purposive benefits (those that benefit society more generally), and solidary benefits based on individuals' satisfaction from interacting with like-minded people in pursuit of a goal.

★ Large interest groups must always concern themselves with the problem of "free riders," those who benefit from interest group activities on their behalf without ever joining or contributing to that interest group.

★ The most successful interest groups tend to maintain a large membership of individuals, at least some of whom are wealthy, as well as a loyal following based on members' commitment to the cause.

★ Economic interest groups that pursue favorable monetary benefits for their members include business groups such as industry trade associations, labor unions, and professional associations. Noneconomic interest groups that pursue goals other than the commercial interests of their members include public interest groups, issue or ideological groups, and government interest groups.

★ Interest groups achieve their goals through lobbying activities, supporting candidates in election contests, litigation, and persuasion campaigns.

Key Terms

Closed shop (p. 341)

Economic interest group (p. 338)

Free rider (p. 340)

Grassroots lobbying (p. 348)

Interest group (p. 328)

Intergovernmental lobby (p. 345)

Iron triangle (p. 335)

Issue and ideological group (p. 343)

Issue network (p. 335)

Lobbying (p. 345)

Material benefits (of group membership) (p. 336)

Noneconomic interest group (p. 343)

Open shop (p. 341)

Pluralism (p. 329)

Political action committee (PAC) (p. 331)

Public interest group (p. 343)

Purposive benefits (of group membership) (p. 337)

Social movement (p. 332)

Solidary benefits (of group membership) (p. 337)

Trade association (p. 340)

Union shop (p. 341)

Resources

Important Books

Berry, Jeffrey M. *The Interest Group Society*. New York: Longman, 1997.

Birnbaum, Jeffrey. *The Lobbyists: How Influence Peddlers Work Their Way in Washington*. New York: Times Books, 1993.

Cigler, Alan, and Burdett Loomis, eds. *Interest Group Politics*, 7th ed. Washington, DC: CQ Press, 2006.

Goldstein, Kenneth M. *Interest Groups, Lobbying and Participation in America*. New York: Cambridge University Press, 1999.

Heinz, John P. *The Hollow Core: Private Interests in National Policy-Making*. Cambridge, MA: Harvard University Press, 1993.

Lowery, David, and Holly Brasher. *Organized Interests and American Government* New York: McGraw-Hill, 2004.

Olson, Mancur. *The Logic of Collective Action: Public Goods and the Theory of Groups*. Cambridge, MA: Harvard University Press, 1965.

Rozell, Mark J., Clyde Wilcox, and David Madland. *Interest Groups in American Campaigns: The New Face of Electioneering*. Washington, DC: CQ Press, 2005.

Salisbury, Robert H. *Interests and Institutions: Substance and Structure in American Politics*. Pittsburgh, PA: University of Pittsburgh Press, 1992.

Tocqueville, Alexis de. *Democracy in America*. Edited by J. P. Mayer. Garden City, NY: Harper Perennial, 1988.

Internet Sources

http://www.opensecrets.org (website of the Center for Responsive Politics, which includes facts and figures relating to lobbying activities, associations giving to political candidates, PACs, and where support for interests groups comes from)

Websites of businesses that have lobbyists:

★ http://www.ibm.com

★ http://www.generalmotors.com

★ http://www.microsoft.com

Labor unions:

★ http://www.aflcio.org (AFL-CIO)

★ http://www.aft.org (American Federation of Teachers)

★ http://www.uswa.org (United Steelworkers of America)

Trade associations:

★ http://www.nar.org (National Association of Realtors)

★ http://www.asla.org (American Society for Landscape Architects)

Governments:

★ http://www.nga.org (National Governor's Association)

★ http://www.nlc.org (National League of Cities)

Business associations:

★ http://www.uschamber.org (U.S. Chamber of Commerce)

Public interest groups:

★ http://www.citizen.org (Public Citizen, Ralph Nader's watchdog organization)

★ http://www.sierraclub.org (The Sierra Club)

★ www.lwv.org/AM/Template.cfm?Section=Home (The League of Women Voters)

The Media
and Politics

12

PHOTO: AP PHOTO/MICHAEL CAULFIELD

Matt Drudge

Could the Media Be Trusted? Now & Then

Could the media be trusted to tell the truth? That was the question on the minds of many public officials, community leaders, and average Americans. A few decades earlier, journalism had been credited with exposing corruption in government and fulfilling its role of checking the abuse of governmental power. But now confidence in the news media was eroding. Editors and owners of news organizations were sensationalizing stories as a way to "shock" audiences and increase sales of their own publications. Some journalists were even playing loose with the facts, and reports of fabricated stories were not uncommon. Those tactics worked, because profits increased. But the cost to the reputation of American journalism was great. Although the number of news outlets mushroomed, the long-term damage caused by the sensationalized news stories eroded the public's faith that the media could still act as an effective fourth branch of government.

William Randolph Hearst

NOW &

1998

Now. . . He isn't the only fly in the ointment of journalism ethics, but Matt Drudge and his *Drudge Report*[1] certainly personify many of the problems that plague the reputation of newsmakers today. Touted as an Internet "news" source, the *Drudge Report* first became famous in 1998 for its coverage of the President Bill Clinton/White House intern Monica Lewinsky sex scandal. As the first to report over the Internet the lurid sexual details of White House encounters between Clinton and twenty-one-year-old Lewinsky, the *Drudge Report* "scooped" the story. Scandal surrounding the sexual encounters between Clinton and Lewinsky provided the material that attracted Drudge's readers to his website. Yet as fast as Drudge has been to report stories, he has sometimes proven to be quite unreliable. Rumors, rather than substantiated facts, serve as the basis for many of his stories. Early in 2004, Drudge "revealed" unsubstantiated stories about the marital affairs of Democratic presidential candidate John Kerry. None of the stories proved to have any basis in fact. Critics charge that when Drudge's stories fail to materialize, he doesn't hesitate to exaggerate the facts to increase his readership.

Recent polls show that confidence in the news and newsmakers has dropped since the increase in sensationalized news that dates back at least to the 1980s.[2] Only three decades earlier, *Washington Post* journalists Bob Woodward and Carl Bernstein's careful and fact-based investigative reporting of the Watergate scandal exposed corruption in the White House and led to the resignation of President Richard Nixon. As a result of the reporters' meticulous work, the media enjoyed considerable praise and a high level of confidence from the American public. But that confidence has now waned, due to Drudge and a number of journalists even from such reputable newspapers as the *New York Times*, the *Boston Globe*, and *USA Today*, who have fabricated quotes and news sources in their stories.

---

[1] The *Drudge Report* can be found at http://www.drudgereport.com.
[2] See the 2006 General Social Survey, conducted by the National Opinion Research Center at the University of Chicago.

American Government: Historical, Popular, and Global Perspectives

1898

1907   1887   1867   1847   1827

Then. . .

The current wave of sensational coverage, inaccurate information, and questionable ethics—all in the pursuit of profits—is hardly a new phenomenon in American political journalism. American journalists in the late 1800s engaged in what has come to be known as "yellow journalism" to attract more readers and bolster the profits of newspaper owners. The yellow journalism of the late nineteenth century was marked by sensational photos, hoaxes, and even some fake interviews. A leading practitioner of yellow journalism was William Randolph Hearst, owner of several newspapers including the *San Francisco Examiner*, the *New York Journal*, and the *Chicago American*. In 1898, Hearst's newspaper coverage of the explosion of the battleship *Maine* in Havana Harbor all but suggested that Spain was responsible for the blast, even though no hard evidence existed. Many historians believe that Hearst's accounts played a role in leading the United States to war with Spain in the Spanish-American War.

Hearst used the techniques of yellow journalism to build a media empire, but at the same time his methods eroded public confidence in news reporting. There have been periods, of course, when American journalism has been held in high esteem by the public, such as when Woodward and Bernstein exposed the Watergate scandal. In both their finer and less glamorous moments, the media have always played a critical role in the American political system.

C onsider the following facts about media consumption in the United States: the average American spends more time watching television than going to work or going to school; all forms of media considered, the average person is engaged in media consumption for 3,500 hours each year—that's almost 40 percent of the 8,760 hours that exist in a year. There are even more TV sets per household than there are toilets. The media clearly have a pervasive presence in the everyday life of most Americans. From listening to radio "shock jocks" like Howard Stern, to watching popular television shows such as *American Idol*, to catching up on the latest news from around the world on CNN or a newspaper web page, Americans make ample use of media sources available to them.

The news media serve a number of important political functions in the United States and operate through a large and growing number of outlets. Political leaders constantly monitor and attempt to influence news stories printed in newspapers and broadcast on television. Voters' primary source of information about political candidates and political issues is the news media. The technologies of television and the Internet allow citizens to observe events on the battlefield, look into the eyes of presidential candidates, and watch tragedies unfold such as the devastation unleashed on New Orleans and other parts of the Gulf Coast by Hurricane Katrina in 2005—many of these events unfold live from around the world in front of viewers in their own homes. Not only do the media serve as an important information source, but they also help set the political agenda, provide perspective and commentary on issues and political candidates, and help keep government accountable to the people.

The Media in American Politics

Most news media organizations in the United States are owned by private companies, which, like most other private companies, seek to make a profit. Unlike other industries, however, the media enjoy a special constitutionally granted protection. The First Amendment to the U.S. Constitution specifically provides that "Congress shall make no law . . . abridging the freedom. . . of the press." When the First Amendment was adopted in 1791, the press was largely a small collection of newspapers and magazines. Over the years, the press, now more commonly referred to as the media, has expanded to include radio, television, book publishers, music producers, the Internet, and motion pictures.

One early event that helped shape America's perspective on freedom of the press was the trial in 1735 of newspaper printer Peter Zenger, who in the *New-York Weekly Journal* published a series of articles highly critical of the British-appointed governor of New York. Zenger was arrested on charges of criminal libel. He was defended by Philadelphia lawyer Andrew Hamilton, who won the case with his argument that Zenger had printed the truth and the truth cannot be considered libelous. Hamilton's argument thus established the principle of truth as a defense against libel.

The argument for a free press in United States today largely rests upon the concept of the "free marketplace of ideas," a phrase coined by Supreme Court Justice Oliver Wendell Holmes in his dissenting opinion in *Abrams v. United States* (1919), which suggests that allowing people to freely communicate their ideas will provide a larger variety of ideas to consider. Encouraging the publication and dissemination of a wide variety of political ideas offers citizens a diversity of opinions and perspectives and facilitates the free flow of information about local, national, and global events. Of course, for ideas to flow freely, government must be prevented from using its power to stifle perspectives with which it disagrees.

Government Regulation of the Media

Congress created the Federal Communications Commission (FCC) in 1934 to regulate the electronic media (primarily radio and eventually television) through the licensing of broadcasters and creating rules for broadcasters to follow. The FCC does not have authority to regulate the print media, such as newspapers. In fact, regulation of print media is rare, and courts have consistently treated the right of print media to publish free of government regulation. Some electronic media require broadcast frequencies that are scarce and thus need to be regulated to ensure the orderly transmission of programs.

Among the tools that the FCC may employ to regulate the activities of broadcasters are the threat of revoking a license or fining a station for violating its rules. The FCC has used these tools to limit the language and type of sexual material that broadcasters might use. For example, the FCC imposed fines on the owners of radio stations that broadcast "shock jock" Howard Stern. Stern's program often includes graphic descriptions of sexual acts and sex games, as well as language that the FCC deems unacceptable. Some of those stations fined then dropped the Stern show from their program schedule. To avoid further legal battles with the FCC, Stern moved his show to a satellite radio station in 2005, which is not subject to FCC regulations because satellite radio is purchased by users and does not rely on the public airwaves.

One of the most celebrated instances of the FCC clamping down on material in broadcast transmission involved comedian George Carlin's "Seven Dirty Words" skit, which satirized attitudes toward vulgar language. In the skit, Carlin continually repeated the seven words that you can't say on TV or radio. The piece was played on a radio station licensed to the Pacifica Foundation. Prior to playing the piece, the announcer warned the audience about its content. Nevertheless, a listener complained to the FCC, and the FCC in turn warned the radio station not to replay the piece. The station challenged the FCC's authority to regulate programming content, and the case made its way to the U.S. Supreme Court in *FCC v. Pacifica Foundation* (1978).[3] In that case the Supreme Court upheld the FCC's power to regulate the broadcast media on the criteria of indecent material.

The FCC's **equal time rule** mandates radio and TV stations to sell equal amounts of airtime to all political candidates who want to broadcast advertisements. This rule also now includes a provision requiring that if a station broadcasts the president's State of the Union message, then that station must also provide free airtime for the opposing political party to broadcast a response.

From 1950 through the late 1980s, the FCC also enforced the so-called fairness doctrine, requiring broadcasters to set aside time for public affairs programming. The proliferation of news sources and technologies for transmitting electronic messages during the 1980s effectively ended the FCC's fairness doctrine requirements. These changes in technologies also resulted in the passage of the 1996 Telecommunications Act, which shifted the emphasis of government policy from regulating to facilitating competition. This law deregulated cable television providers, eliminated monopolies held by local phone companies, and allowed local phone companies to provide long-distance phone services. The Telecommunications Act transformed the FCC from a regulator of the telecommunications industry into an aggressive supporter of competition within that industry.

★ Equal time rule

The FCC mandate that radio and TV stations sell equal amounts of airtime to all political candidates who want to broadcast advertisements.

Functions of the Media in American Politics

Throughout the history of the United States, the media have come to serve a number of functions in the political system, all of which promote the free flow of information to the public. Principal functions of the media include (1) providing objective coverage of events, (2) facilitating public debate, and (3) serving as government watchdog.

Providing Objective Coverage of Events. The media's most basic role involves monitoring events around the nation and the world and communicating those events to the public. Through modern communications technologies, the media have become proficient at reporting major events as they happen. Live coverage of presidential addresses, campaign debates, war operations, famous trials, natural disasters,

---

[3] 438 U.S. 726 (1978).

Six Lapses in Journalistic Ethics

Journalists, editors, news directors, and publishers are constantly faced with ethical dilemmas in carrying out their jobs. Deciding what kinds of stories to cover, whether a particular story is appropriate to publish, and whether a news source is reliable are just some of their responsibilities. Accuracy (making sure that what is published or aired is truthful), fairness (presenting all sides of a story), and confidentiality of sources (protecting the identity of news sources) are generally regarded as important guidelines to ethical behavior in journalism. The Society of Professional Journalists adopted a "code of ethics" in 1973 (and modified it in 1996) that provides fairly specific guidelines to help those in journalism make ethical decisions. [4]

Ethical codes, however, are merely guidelines. They are not enforceable laws. There have been a number of highlighted cases in recent years in which a serious breach of ethics led to a fair amount of criticism of organizations and specific individuals involved. Six recent examples of lapses in journalistic ethics include the following:

✔ ***Newsweek* magazine and the treatment of Iraqi detainees:** In May 2005, *Newsweek* ran a story relying on a confidential source that accused American military personnel of using unethical techniques to get Iraqi prisoners at Guantanamo Bay to talk. One such technique the magazine reported was flushing down the toilet pages of the Koran in front of the prisoners. Some observers charged that the *Newsweek* article inspired severe anti-American rioting in parts of the Muslim world, with seventeen deaths attributed to the incident. About a week after publication of the article, *Newsweek* retracted the story, indicating that the source had provided inaccurate and misleading information on which the story was based. Later, however, other prisoners corroborated the story.

✔ **Jayson Blair, *New York Times:*** The *New York Times* prides itself on being a newspaper that gives readers "all the news that's fit to print." When it discovered in 2003 that Blair, a reporter for the newspaper, had not only made up facts and quotes but had also plagiarized in thirty-six of seventy-three articles published under his byline, he was fired. Blair's ethical missteps also led the *New York Times* to fire executive editor Howell Raines for allowing the situation to happen.

✔ **Jack Kelley, *USA Today:*** In early 2004, this *USA Today* foreign correspondent resigned amid allegations that he made up stories, plagiarized, and took money from his newspaper for translation services that never happened. Kelley's ethical lapses included lifting hundreds of passages from other publications, contriving at least twenty stories, and falsely attributing information he published to "U.S. intelligence sources."

✔ ***Dateline NBC:*** In 1992, the NBC television program *Dateline* produced a segment showing how pickup trucks manufactured by General Motors had a proclivity to explode when they collided with other vehicles—but the producers of the show failed to disclose that they rigged the crash and faked the explosion. NBC was highly criticized for both faking the explosion and then not disclosing that fact to the public.

✔ **Mike Barnicle, *Boston Globe:*** In 2003, Barnicle wrote a series of articles published in the *Boston Globe* that used clever quotes and lines picked up from comedian George Carlin's book, *Brain Droppings*. Barnicle did not attribute the lines to Carlin, and the *Boston Globe* fired him for this breach of journalistic ethics.

✔ ***Dallas Morning News:*** In November 1997, this Dallas newspaper was informed that Timothy McVeigh had confessed to the April 1995 bombing of the Murrah Federal Building in Oklahoma City. The paper decided to print the story, knowing full well that the jury for McVeigh's trial had not yet been selected and that the story could jeopardize a fair trial. McVeigh's attorneys were among a crowd of critics of the *Dallas Morning News's* decision.

American Government: Historical, Popular, and Global Perspectives

[4] The Society of Professional Journalists' Code of Ethics can be found at http://www.spj.org/ethics_code.asp.

and other important world events have made their way almost instantaneously onto front-page headlines and into television's round-the-clock news coverage.

Providing information about news and events is perhaps the most basic and most important function of the media. Factual news information is an essential component of evaluating events and forming political opinions. Operating free of government control, the U.S. media can provide objective coverage of events to the American public. **Objectivity** refers to the media reporting events factually, accurately, fairly, and equitably— an important goal for many journalists. In addition to providing factual information about events, objective journalism requires signaling when important events occur and providing perspectives on all sides of an issue or policy debate. The goal of objectivity, however, is itself the subject of some debate. Objectivity is hard to operationalize, and journalists sometimes take a shortcut by trying to give equal weight to all sides without making any judgments of their own. This approach permitted Senator Joseph McCarthy to falsely but very publicly accuse people of being Communists in the 1950s; it let cigarette companies get away with denying that smoking causes cancer; and it prolonged the current national debate on global warming. Journalism professor Philip Meyer has advocated for a science-based definition of objectivity by getting journalists to seek more independent verification of facts.[5]

Numerous media formats strive to provide objective coverage of news information. Most of the content of newspapers (with the notable exception of the editorial pages) is aimed at objectively covering news events and politics at the global, national, and local levels. The twenty-four-hour cable news channels, such as CNN, Fox News, and MSNBC, provide news of events on a continuous basis. Many other formats are aimed at providing an objective look at news information to readers and viewers.

Moreover, the proliferation of cable television has broadened the role of the media as provider of information. Stations like the Biography Channel, the History Channel, local government access channels, and C-SPAN now offer programming that gives historical context to local, national, and international events.

★ Objectivity

The journalistic standard that news reporting of events must be factual, accurate, fair, and equitable.

Facilitating Public Debate. In addition to monitoring and reporting events, the media also facilitate public dialogue and debate on important political issues. By helping frame issues, offering perspectives on how a problem might be solved, and providing context and commentary on political campaigns, the media serve a vital role in a democratic system that depends heavily on voters to make informed choices in elections.

The media facilitate public debate through a variety of forms, both print and electronic. Newspaper editorials provide perspectives on policy debates and political candidates. Syndicated columnists such as David Broder, Jack Germond, and George Will publish columns in numerous newspapers around the nation on a regular basis, presenting their own perspectives on issues. Most newspapers dedicate space on their editorial pages for citizens to write opinion pieces ("op-eds") and letters to the editor offering their point of view. Many news magazines adhere to a liberal or conservative approach to discussing issues or evaluating candidates for office. *The Nation*, for example, has a liberal perspective, whereas *The National Review* presents a conservative perspective. Even magazines devoted to one perspective or another, however, usually offer a forum for readers to assess issues. Radio talk shows that offer perspectives on politics, such as those of conservative radio talk show host Rush Limbaugh or liberal political commentator Al Franken, also facilitate public debate, as do television programs like the *Capital Gang* and *Hannity and Colmes*, which feature debate-style formats in which the perspectives of the political left and the political right are contrasted.

AP PHOTO/JEFF CHRISTENSEN

Fox News conservative talk show host Bill O'Reilly maintains a very high audience for his nightly cable TV show, *The O'Reilly Factor*.

[5] See Philip Meyer, *Precision Journalism: A Reporter's Introduction to Social Science Methods* (Lanham, MD.: Rowman & Littlefield, 2002).

These media formats go beyond objectively reporting news to provide analyses of events and present arguments from varying ideological perspectives that readers and viewers can evaluate and use in forming their own opinions about public policies and political candidates.

Government Watchdog. Since the founding of the nation, American political culture has been characterized by a healthy skepticism about government. To govern is to have power, and power (in the minds of many) corrupts. The federal system that divides power between the federal government and state and local governments, the system of shared power among the legislative, executive, and judicial branches of government, and the system of checks and balances among these three branches are mechanisms that help guard against the potential abuse of government power. The news media also help prevent the abuse of government power through their role as government watchdog. In this role, the media are sometimes referred to as the fourth branch of government, or the "fourth estate," checking the power of the other branches. Rooting out corruption and abuses of power through investigative journalism is a core function of the American media, no less important today than it was two centuries ago.

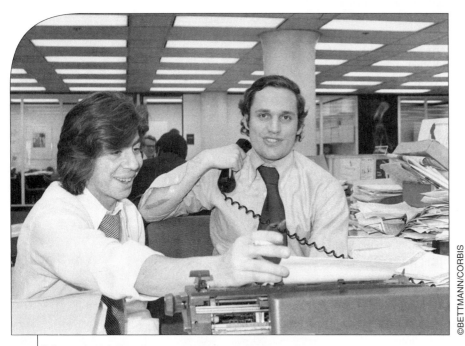

©BETTMANN/CORBIS

More than a century ago, a group of journalists, who came to be known as "muck-rakers"[6] (they were given this name by President Theodore Roosevelt), investigated and exposed corporate and political corruption in American life, including the corrupting effect of corporate contributions on presidential candidates who won office. In the late 1800s, corporate wealth was concentrated in a handful of companies in the railroad and banking industries, and those companies bought favors and influence with various presidential administrations. The muckrakers exposed the rash of influence peddling and by doing so helped spawn new laws curbing corporate contributions to federal campaigns.

Perhaps the most well-known case of the media uncovering and exposing government corruption was the investigative reporting of *Washington Post* reporters Bob Woodward and Carl Bernstein in the early 1970s concerning the Watergate corruption scandal of President Richard M. Nixon's administration. Their work led in part to the resignation of President Nixon in 1974 for his role in covering up the details of the Republican-led break-in of Democratic National Headquarters in the Watergate Hotel during the 1972 presidential campaign.[7] Woodward and Bernstein largely depended on an anonymous administration source, who came to be known as "Deep Throat," for information that ultimately exposed the White House cover-up of a number of criminal activities in Nixon's 1972 campaign for re-election. It was not until thirty years later, in 2005, that Mark Felt, who at the time of the Watergate break-in was Deputy Director of the FBI, publicly announced that he was in fact "Deep Throat."

The media also exercise their watchdog function through television programs such as *60 Minutes*, *Dateline*, and *Meet the Press* and through Internet websites set up by groups like Common Cause, which provides data on the negative influence of

Pulitzer prize-winning investigative reporters Carl Bernstein and Bob Woodward in 1973. Woodward and Bernstein investigated the Watergate scandal of the Nixon administration in 1973 and 1974 for the *Washington Post*.

[6] The word *muckrakers* is derived from the idea that this group was "raking up the mud" from scandals and corruption of government and industry.

[7] For a chronicle of the Watergate story, see Bob Woodward and Carl Bernstein, *All the President's Men* (New York: Simon & Schuster, 1974).

corporate donations on political campaigns. The media also carry out their watchdog function through books. For example, the book *Against All Enemies*[8] by Richard Clarke, a former adviser to Presidents Clinton and George W. Bush, exposed alleged weaknesses in the federal government's preparedness for the terrorist attacks of September 11, 2001.

Historical Development of the Media

Before the American Revolution, the news media consisted of a handful of newspapers that were published by printers.[9] The main job of the printer was not to publish a newspaper, but rather to prepare official documents (such as marriage licenses, deeds to land, and government documents), political pamphlets, and religious books. Newspapers of the time mostly featured notices of public events and advertisements for local merchants. These early newspapers carried little information about politics or news events.

The political events that led up to the American Revolution and the events of the Revolution itself changed the nature and functions of the colonial newspapers. Many colonists were intensely interested in the disputes with Great Britain and eager for news about the battles of the Revolution. Newspapers responded to these interests with news stories about the events. Stories about the economic turmoil of the post-Revolution period, particularly the bitter partisan fight between the Federalists and Anti-Federalists over ratification of the Constitution, also appeared in the nation's early newspapers.

The Era of the Partisan Press

The Federalist/Anti-Federalist battle ushered in the **partisan press era,** a period characterized by newspapers supporting a particular political party. This period lasted from the late 1700s through the mid-1850s. Newspapers advocating the Federalist position that favored a stronger central government included John Fenno's *Gazette of the United States* and Noah Webster's *American Minerva.* The Anti-Federalists and later the Jeffersonian-Republicans, who supported states' rights, had their own partisan newspapers, such as the *National Gazette* and the *National Intelligencer.*

Partisan newspapers appealed mostly to readers who already agreed with the political positions advocated by those publications. Partisan-oriented news eventually became big business, and government printing contracts to partisan publications became a regular part of the spoils system.

During the early nineteenth century, a number of technological developments had a significant impact on the newspaper business. The invention of the rotary press in 1815 enabled the mass production of newspapers. The invention of the telegraph and the development of the telegraph system across the United States in the 1840s provided for the widespread electronic dissemination of news information. The expansion of the railroad system across the nation facilitated the mass distribution of newspapers across the continent. These developments allowed newspapers to print news events more quickly and distribute their publications to a larger number of people in a shorter period of time. These technologies also helped reduce production costs, making newspapers affordable for most Americans. The term *penny press* aptly described the low cost of newspapers during the early to mid-nineteenth century.

By the 1850s, newspapers found that they could increase their circulation by distancing themselves from particular partisan positions. Eyeing ever-larger markets, newspapers began to appeal to all Americans. Journalists began to tout the goals of objective reporting of the facts, rather than providing a biased or partisan perspective on events. By the end of the nineteenth century, the technological innovations and the desire of newspaper publishers to reach larger numbers of readers and maximize profits through the selling of advertisements had transformed the newspaper industry from a mostly partisan press to one focused on objective reporting of the news.

★ Partisan press era

A period, from the late 1700s to the mid-1800s, when newspapers typically supported a particular political party.

[8] Richard Clark, *Against All Enemies* (New York: Free Press, 2004).
[9] For a thorough review of the history of news, see Mitchell Stephens, *A History of News: From the Drum to the Satellite* (New York: Viking, 1989).

American Government . . . in Historical Perspective:
Cartoons as Commentary on American Politics

Political cartoons have always been a popular source of entertainment in America because they provide a unique blend of humor and political commentary. A good political cartoon can often make a political statement in a way that news stories and written commentary cannot. Polls show that editorial cartoons in newspapers are more frequently read than other forms of newspaper political commentary, such as letters to the editor, political columns by syndicated columnists, and editorials.

Gary Trudeau's *Doonesbury* cartoon, a staple in hundreds of newspapers across the nation, regularly addresses controversial issues in American politics. The AIDS epidemic,

The Emergence of Electronic Media

The development of the radio in the early twentieth century provided a new means for Americans to get information about politics. Most notably, communication from the media source to the audience was instantaneous. In addition, the technology allowed political leaders to directly communicate with the American people. The first radio station was KDKA in Pittsburgh, established in 1923. The first network of radio stations, which was established in 1926 as the National Broadcasting Company (NBC), provided common programming and newscasts that were made available to the first truly mass audiences.

Franklin Delano Roosevelt (FDR), elected president in 1932, used the radio to deliver comforting and inspiring messages to the nation, then suffering in the midst of the Great Depression. FDR's weekly radio addresses, which the president called "fireside chats," represented the first significant use of this medium by a political the Vietnam War, and America in the aftermath of 9/11 have all been topics that Trudeau has dealt with in his cartoons. In 2004, he used a character named B.D. as a way of making points about the U.S. military involvement in Iraq. B.D. lost part of his left leg in Iraq, and through this character, Trudeau made a number of incisive political comments.

Trudeau is not the only, nor even the first popular political cartoonist in America. The Currier and Ives political cartoons, which appeared frequently in many publications during the Civil War years, provided important commentary during a period of great strife for the nation.

THE HERCULES OF THE UNION,
SLAYING THE GREAT DRAGON OF SECESSION

THE VOLUNTARY MANNER IN WHICH SOME OF THE SOUTHERN VOLUNTEERS ENLIST.

leader to communicate to the nation's people. In addition to FDR's fireside chats, radio commentators such as Father Charles Coughlin (Detroit's anti-Semitic "fighting priest") and Louisiana Senator Huey Long popularized radio as a medium that could provide a great deal of political commentary and debate. During World War II, Americans eager for news about the progress of the war turned to the radio for information. Edward R. Murrow's live radio reports from London during the Nazi bombings of that city and from other battle sites captivated the nation.

In the 1950s, Joe Pyne from radio station KABC hosted the first political talk radio show. Pyne challenged the status quo political views of the times, invited call-in questions from listeners, and promoted confrontation and debate.

President Franklin Delano Roosevelt, delivering one of his famous "fireside chats" in 1933.

Left: Chet Huntley and David Brinkley deliver the evening news for NBC in 1965. Right: CBS news anchor Walter Cronkite, pictured here in 1969, was a very popular and trusted newsman for CBS news.

Pyne's style and format laid the foundation for many of today's popular political talk radio shows.

A number of technological advancements have had a large impact on the scope and importance of the news media through American history, but none has had a more profound influence than the invention of television. In the post–World War II boom of the American economy, the nation quickly adopted TV as its primary medium for getting news about politics and the world. NBC and CBS developed the standard TV news show format in the early 1950s with a fifteen-minute daily news program. The program featured a news anchor reading the news, supported by film footage and supporting reporters. (This format—now modified into a half-hour format produced each evening—continues to be widely used today by all the major networks.) In the 1950s, TV networks broadcast the Army-McCarthy hearings of the U.S. Senate that exposed Senator Joseph McCarthy as a crude bully and resulted in his censure for ethical misconduct. Live television coverage of the Republican and Democratic national conventions set the standard for live broadcasts of major political events. The networks also sold advertising time to the major party candidates in the presidential election of 1952, revolutionizing the way in which candidates would wage their bids for elective office.

Presidential Debates and the Power of Television.
A defining moment in revealing the political power of electronic media was the live television broadcast of the debates between Republican Richard Nixon and Democrat John Kennedy, candidates in the presidential election of 1960. For the first time, all Americans were able to watch a live debate between the candidates. Many observers credit Kennedy's favorable TV performance as an important factor contributing to his razor-thin victory over Nixon in the November election. During the first of three televised debates, Kennedy won over the audience with his relaxed and self-assured manner before the camera; by contrast, Nixon seemed nervous and uncomfortable. He prepared for the debate by studying briefing documents, but spent little time practicing debate style. Kennedy, on the other hand, spent a great deal of time practicing answers to questions out loud. For the two days prior to the first debate, Kennedy and his inner circle of advisers didn't leave the practice session in their hotel room. On the night of the debate, a tanned Kennedy looked strong and healthy. He wore a navy blue suit that contrasted sharply with the light walls of the TV studio. Nixon, on the other hand, looked ill and underweight. Just before the debate he had been hospitalized with an infection, exhausted from a hard week of campaigning. He wore makeup to cover up his five o'clock shadow and dressed in a light gray suit that blended into the background.

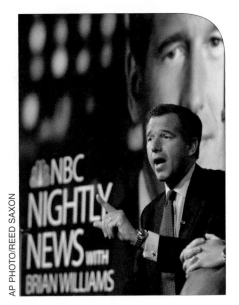

Left: Katie Couric, the first woman to become a regular solo anchor on a major network's evening news, is at *CBS News* today. Right: Brian Williams, NBC's main evening news anchor today.

The candidates debated the important issues and both did well in articulating their positions. But TV analysts reported that Kennedy won the debate. His stage presence, practice addressing the camera, tanned complexion, hand gestures, and commanding appearance compared favorably to the somber, pale Nixon. It was a lesson that no future presidential candidate would forget.

Interestingly, research on this debate[10] reveals that those who listened to the debate on the radio thought Nixon won, whereas those who watched the debate on TV tended to think that Kennedy won, proving that the medium through which events are communicated can indeed influence the way in which people evaluate those events. That the medium itself may have an important effect on the way in which people receive and perceive news was suggested by communications researcher Marshall McCluhan, who summarized this idea with his memorable phrase, "the medium is the message."[11]

Live televised debates between the candidates for president did not occur again until 1976, when Republican President Gerald Ford and Democratic challenger Jimmy Carter met. This time both candidates were well-prepared to convey the image they wanted to the American viewing audience. Dressed to coordinate with the set background, prepped with numerous practice sessions, and made up to ensure a favorable skin color tone, both Carter and Ford sought to communicate a positive image. Live broadcasts of presidential campaign debates have been a part of every presidential election contest since 1976.[12]

The first of the three debates between 2008 presidential candidates John McCain (left) and Barack Obama (right) took place at the University of Mississippi in Oxford on September 26, 2008.

Television has transformed virtually every aspect of political campaigns and government policy making. Prior to TV, the vast majority of voters never saw more than a still picture of the candidates, and most learned about them from reading newspaper accounts of their statements, speeches, and activities. Television, however, has allowed viewers to observe candidates live and in action, and to see how

[10] Kurt Lang and Gladys Lang, *Television and Politics* (Edison, NJ: Transaction Publishers, 2001).
[11] Marshall McLuhan, *Understanding Media: The Extensions of Man* (New York: McGraw-Hill, 1964).
[12] For a good review of the process and impact of presidential debates, see Alan Schroeder, *Presidential Debates* (New York: Columbia University Press, 2000).

they deliver a speech and respond to questions. Television has also given candidates the opportunity to develop an "image" through carefully planned media appearances and strategically designed political advertisements.

Presidential Press Conferences. The power of televised images has also altered the governing process. Whereas President Woodrow Wilson was the first to hold regular and formal presidential news conferences, President Dwight D. Eisenhower was the first to hold regular news conferences as we know them today, as a means of explaining his administration's policies and appealing directly to the public for support. Before Eisenhower, the news media's access to the president was primarily through appointments that the chief executive would give to favored reporters. Eisenhower opened up the press conference to reporters from all types of news organizations. The questions were not prescreened, and Eisenhower addressed whatever topics were on reporters' agendas. This format for addressing the nation, coupled with the capability of television to show Americans the event, opened up the presidency to the public.

Eisenhower's successor, President John F. Kennedy, quickly mastered the art of the presidential press conference. He made events seem even more dramatic and intriguing by allowing TV to broadcast them live. Kennedy's preparedness on issues, strong intellect, charismatic personality, and sense of humor made his press conferences interesting and successful events. President Lyndon B. Johnson continued the press conference tradition set by his predecessors, but these events came to be difficult for Johnson as America's involvement in the Vietnam War escalated, and questions frequently focused on war casualties and military ineffectiveness.

Eisenhower, Kennedy, and Johnson averaged about two press conferences every month, but Presidents Nixon, Ford, Carter, and Reagan held fewer—less than one per month. Nixon, Ford, and Carter each dealt with crisis situations (Vietnam, Watergate, a severe energy crisis, and the Iranian hostage crisis), which led to uncomfortable open questioning from journalists, and so each president cut back on the number of conferences. Reagan, despite his acting background and ease in front of a camera, had a difficult time dealing with reporters' questions in a press conference setting, and so he began a weekly radio address as a regular means of communicating with the American public. All presidents since Reagan have used this form of weekly address to speak to the nation.

The Dixie Chicks promote voter registration for young people on MTV's "Rock the Vote."

President Bill Clinton increased the number of presidential press conferences to an average of two per month, based on his ability to use this format quite effectively. However, the number of Clinton press conferences was reduced sharply during the period when he faced his biggest crisis in office over his relationship with White House intern Monica Lewinsky. President George W. Bush, who like Reagan is often ill at ease at responding to questions in a press conference situation, averaged only one press conference per year during his first term. Staged events, one-on-one interviews with reporters, televised speeches, and the weekly radio address have been Bush's preferred means of communicating to the public through the media.

With each successive presidential administration, White House staffs have become better equipped at using television to influence the public through direct communication. Press conferences, presidential addresses, and carefully staged presidential appearances (such as President Bush's visit to an aircraft carrier upon his declaration of victory in 2003 in the war against Iraq) are typical of the means by which the White House uses the media to muster support for the president's agenda.

The Mass Media Today

Today's mass media include a variety of channels of communication through which news content is disseminated to audiences. Channels of communication may be either print or electronic. Print media largely include newspapers, magazines, and books. Electronic media include television, radio, the Internet, and movies. In addition, forms of content on any medium may be classified as either news or entertainment. In newspapers, for example, the first section of most publications is entirely devoted to news stories and editorials. Subsequent sections might include other news such as sports news or business news. Typically there is an entertainment section that includes reviews of movies, comics, crossword puzzles, recipes, and so forth. Television stations also provide news programming in the forms of news broadcasts, investigative reporting shows, and political talk shows, and entertainment programming in the form of sitcoms, soap operas, reality TV programs, and drama shows.

Even media sources that are intended primarily to provide entertainment programming sometimes include content that may fall within the realm of politics. One very popular show, which combines news with comedy, is the *Daily Show* hosted by political comedian Jon Stewart. During recent presidential elections the cable television station MTV broadcast programming that attempted to increase voter turnout among young people.

The Print Media

The modern print media mostly include newspapers, magazines, and books. Use of these print media has declined in recent decades. *Time* and *Newsweek* are popular weekly magazines devoted to providing in-depth coverage of current events, though their readership too has declined as consumers of news increasingly turn to electronic sources of information. These and other news magazines often rely on photojournalism to support their longer stories to engage readers.

Books also enjoy an important place in American journalism. The 2004 book by Bob Woodward, titled *Plan of Attack,* documented the role of the Bush administration in preparing for the second Iraq War. Woodward, through interviews with top White House sources including the president and the secretary of state, concluded that the Bush administration had actively begun preparations for war long before the U.S. invasion and well before notifying Congress of its intentions. Woodward's work became an important topic during the 2004 presidential campaign. Thirty years earlier in a book called *All the President's Men,* co-written with Carl Bernstein, Woodward documented the Nixon administration's role in the Watergate affair.

Today there are only about fifteen hundred newspapers published on a daily basis, purchased by about 76 million readers. Once the prime source of news for Americans, newspapers now take a backseat to television as the nation's main news source (see

Figure 12.1). By contrast, a century ago there were about twenty-two hundred newspaper published daily, thus representing a 25 percent decline. Just as the number of newspaper readers declined following the widespread adoption of television within American households in the 1950s, today the Internet seems to be becoming a more popular source of news and as a result the number of newspaper readers is falling further.

The vast majority of newspapers are regional metropolitan and suburban publications. They range from those that cover large metropolitan areas such as the *Chicago Tribune,* the *Miami Herald,* the *Dallas Morning News,* and the *San Francisco Chronicle,* to those covering much smaller towns. A handful of newspapers such as the *New York Times, Wall Street Journal,* and *USA Today* are considered national dailies and are designed to appeal to a national readership. The *New York Times* trumpets its supposed status as the "paper of record" of events from around the world; the *Wall Street Journal* has the niche of being the nation's leading newspaper on financial markets and commerce. *USA Today*'s format featuring brief stories along with colorful graphics and pictures has helped it attract a nationwide following.

Wire services provide a clearinghouse for news as it is occurring. The largest wire service by far is the Associated Press (AP). The AP employs a large number of reporters throughout the nation and around the world to write stories on news events. Newspapers and television and radio stations that are members of the AP share the news services it produces. Using the AP as their news source allows smaller regional newspapers and local TV and radio stations to cover events from around the world in an efficient, informative, and cost-effective manner.

Figure 12.1 The News Sources That Americans Use

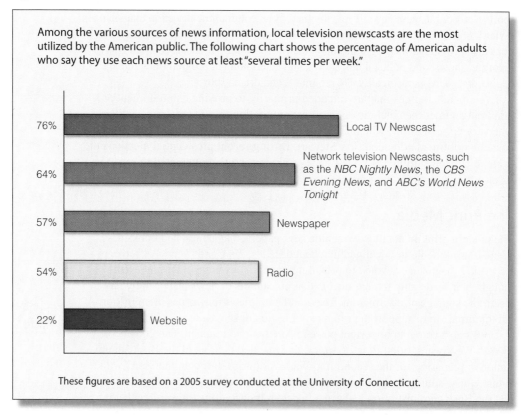

Among the various sources of news information, local television newscasts are the most utilized by the American public. The following chart shows the percentage of American adults who say they use each news source at least "several times per week."

76% Local TV Newscast

64% Network television Newscasts, such as the *NBC Nightly News,* the *CBS Evening News,* and *ABC's World News Tonight*

57% Newspaper

54% Radio

22% Website

These figures are based on a 2005 survey conducted at the University of Connecticut.

The Electronic Media

The major electronic media are television, radio, and the Internet. Television and radio have played an important role in American politics for many decades, and the Internet has been responsible for more recent changes in the news and the way in which Americans use the news. The Internet, along with other relatively new media technologies such as DVDs, fax machines, cell phones, satellites, and cable TV have

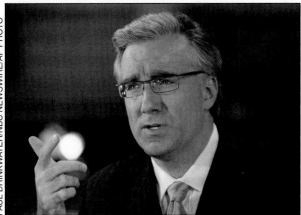

Keith Olbermann hosts the liberal-oriented news commentary program *Countdown with Keith Olbermann* on cable television station MSNBC.

Popular radio talk show host Rush Limbaugh, a favorite of conservatives across America, in 2007.

come to be known as the **new media** (or "digital media"), which have revolutionized the news business at every level.

Television. With its mass adoption by households in the early 1950s, television became and has remained the primary source of news for most Americans. More than 98 percent of households in the United States report having at least one television set. News programming on TV is provided mostly by broadcast television networks and their local affiliates. The broadcast networks include ABC, CBS, and NBC. Cable television stations, such as CNN, Fox News, and MSNBC, provide twenty-four-hour news programming as well. Other cable stations, such as C-SPAN and local public access stations, provide specialized coverage—for example, the live broadcast of congressional debates and committee meetings.

The defining characteristic of television is its visual nature.[13] The implied "reality" of seeing video of events, or live broadcasts of events, can be quite powerful. Compared to the written word, the spoken word, or even still pictures, video communicates events "as they are," and so is regarded by viewers as more trustworthy and "real." Many argue that film footage of reporters covering the Vietnam War contributed to the erosion of public support for America's involvement there. The daily barrage of video showing dead soldiers brought new meaning to Americans' understanding of war and helped influence President Lyndon Johnson's decision not to seek re-election in 1968. In 2004, video of Americans captured and mutilated by Iraqi insurgents as a protest against the U.S. military occupation of Iraq captured a great deal of attention and reduced support for the Bush administration's policy. Likewise, vivid pictures of American mistreatment of Iraqi detainees at Abu Ghraib prison did not help the Bush administration's effort to defeat the Iraqi insurgents.

New satellite technologies further facilitate the live and instantaneous coverage of events not only around every corner of the globe, but also from the moon, Mars, and Jupiter. The new high-tech satellites provide an opportunity for people to view events as they occur even from the outer reaches of the universe, such as the live pictures sent back from satellites on the 2004 U.S. spaceship mission to Mars.

Radio. Contemporary radio largely involves commercial music programming, with several minutes of each hour allotted for news, sports, traffic reports, and weather forecasts. These short news reports are an important source of information (particularly for commuters who use their cars to get to and from work or school) about news events and politics. A number of radio stations carry a specialized form of radio programming referred to as **talk radio,** in which one or more hosts provide commentary and often invite listeners to call in to the show and offer their own opinions. Talk radio steadily gained popularity in the late 1980s and early 1990s, marked by a growing interest in political talk shows, such as the Rush Limbaugh Show. Soon increasing numbers of commuters with cell phones began to take time while sitting in traffic to listen to these shows and call in to offer their own views.

★ **New media**

Media outlets that rely on relatively newer technologies for communicating, such as the Internet, DVDs, fax machines, cell phones, satellites, cable TV, and broadband.

★ **Talk radio**

A specialized form of radio programming on which one or more hosts provide commentary and often invite listeners to call in to the show and offer their own opinions.

[13] See Doris Graber, *Processing Politics: Learning from Television in the Internet Age* (Chicago: University of Chicago Press, 2001).

Chapter 12: The Media and Politics

Some of the more popular call-in shows focus on politics. The hosts often provide an ideological perspective on policies, issues, and political candidates and campaigns. Listeners of a particular ideological persuasion enjoy hearing what the host and others have to say, and a small number call in to offer their own views. Many local radio stations provide political talk radio programs, ranging from very modestly ideological debates to extremely partisan ones. Several nationally syndicated shows have also attracted a large listening audience, such as conservative commentator Rush Limbaugh's show.

A trend in ownership of radio involves smaller, local radio stations being purchased by large media organizations. Critics of this trend contend that the large corporate owners typically impose standardized programming through satellite feeds, thus depriving them of their local character.

The Internet. In 1993, a group of students at the University of Illinois developed MOSAIC, the first graphical Internet browser. MOSAIC allowed users to view pictures and color images on the World Wide Web. MOSAIC soon went commercial and became Netscape, and by the mid-1990s it was attracting tens of millions of users. Coupled with huge worldwide increases in sales of personal computers through the 1990s, the ease and user-friendliness of accessing the Internet made the medium an attractive source of news and information for people around the world.

The Internet's rise as a mass medium has many implications for news, information, and the American political system. One such effect is the way in which people use the Internet compared to other news sources. From the viewers' perspective, television watching is a passive activity. Once they've tuned into a particular channel, viewers have no other choice but to get whatever news is being presented. They cannot ask questions or seek specific answers to questions they might have. Likewise, listening to a radio broadcast is a fairly passive activity for listeners unless, of course, they choose to call in to the show. While reading a newspaper, people can pick and choose the articles they prefer to read. However, newspapers are also limited in the amount of content they can provide, and readers cannot query a newspaper to get answers on specific questions they might have.

The Internet, however, allows users to pursue exactly the kind of news and information they are interested in. Search engines such as google.com and yahoo.com allow Internet users to seek out and find whatever they are looking for. Furthermore, most news websites include a "search" feature that allows users to search the website and/or newspaper database for information relevant to a particular query.

Unlike other media, the Internet also enables individual users to be their own mass publisher. Most word processing packages include the option of "save to web page." A simple set of keystrokes enables users to place information, data, and graphics on their own web page. Web design software enables users to put a web page on a server and thus make that page available to millions of other Internet users to access. In this way, Internet users can publish material that is accessible to a mass audience.

Most newspapers and television stations maintain websites that include the organization's news content, and links to other sources, such as the Associated Press. Many of these sites also include a searchable database of archived news stories. Some of the most used news web pages are http://www.cnn.com and http://www.nytimes.com. With searchable indices to past stories, links to other sites, online forums, and audio and video files, these sites offer a broad array of content that users can easily access.

The Internet has transformed the flow of news and information about politics in other ways as well. It has become a common source of information about political campaigns, because candidates for office often create a web page and post it on a server for voters to access. A wide variety of "chat rooms" and online forums serve as venues for users to post their opinions, ask questions, and engage in dialogue on political issues. **"Blogs"** (derived from the term *weblogs*) are also becoming popular among many Internet users. In 2004, for example, the significant amount of discussion about presidential candidate John Kerry's "flip flops" on issue positions hurt the Kerry campaign's chances of success. Blogs provide a combination editorial page, personal web page, and online diary offering personal observations in real time about

★ Blogs

Derived from the term *weblogs*, these are Internet sites that include a combination of editorial page, personal web page, and online diary of personal observations in real time about news events and issues.

news events and issues. Some of the more popular blogs are published by journalists and political commentators.

About 60 percent of Americans report that they use personal computers on a regular basis, and most of these PCs are connected to the Internet. Those who use the Internet are more likely to be younger, middle- and upper-class, better educated, and nonminority—a situation that has been referred to as the **digital divide.** Greater access to the Internet facilitates access to news and information, and those who have access clearly enjoy an advantage. However, as computers and Internet access service costs decline, and as younger generations with computer skills replace older generations, the digital divide is likely to become less and less pronounced. Public libraries have provided another remedy to the digital divide. In 1996, 28 percent of all libraries had public access to the Internet. Today, 95 percent of libraries offer Internet access to patrons. Eager to gain access, the number of visitors to public libraries has increased by nearly 20 percent over the past six years.

Ownership of the Media

The Framers of the Constitution were clearly committed to the freedom of the press. Government ownership of the press was then and is today regarded as a threat to the basic freedoms that Americans enjoy. If government controls the news and the flow of information to citizens, it holds too much power. Private ownership of the media allows for the free and open exchange of ideas. Ironically, some today argue that the concentration of ownership of the news media by large non-media corporations, such as General Electric and the Disney Corporation, has stifled diversity in news content and blurred the line between what is news and what is entertainment. One large corporation that owns multiple media outlets has become the norm, whereas in the past most media outlets were independently owned. It is also argued that ownership of media organizations by a conglomerate such as GE might compromise the objectivity of the news. When NBC, which is owned by GE, reports on a story about GE, might that story be biased?

The big three television networks—ABC, CBS, and NBC—have dominated television viewership since the early 1950s. By 1956, more than nine in ten stations were affiliated with one of these networks. Over the past several decades, the growing popularity of cable and satellite TV challenged the predominant position of the three networks. With hundreds of channels now available, the three networks' share of the viewing market continues to shrink. This competition led the networks to focus on greater efficiencies in the day-to-day operation of their businesses. By the mid-1980s, all three networks had experienced a change in corporate ownership, and all three now are part of "vertically integrated" corporations that are involved in video production as well as national and local distribution. In the late 1980s, competition between the networks further increased with the addition of the Fox Network.

NBC is currently owned by the mega-corporation General Electric (GE); Viacom owns the CBS network; the Disney Corporation owns and operates the ABC network; and Fox, the newest of the major networks, is owned by the News Corporation. Table 12.1 (p. 374) suggests the extent to which these four corporate owners control the nation's media.

Not all television and radio stations in the United States are privately owned. The Public Broadcasting Act of 1967 created the Corporation for Public Broadcasting (CPB), which is responsible for distributing federal funds to support public, noncommercial radio and television stations. These stations have had a difficult time surviving economically in a marketplace dominated by commercial interests. CPB funds the Public Broadcasting Service (PBS), which was formed in 1969 to distribute programming to the nation's public television stations. CPB-funded radio programs are distributed by National Public Radio (NPR), American Public Media, and Public Radio International (PRI) to member stations.

The 1967 law provided much-needed support for noncommercial TV and radio and has established a rather impressive network of stations that provide some very popular

★ Digital divide

The term indicating the large differences in usage of the Internet between younger and older people, lower- and middle/upper-class people, lesser and better educated, and minority groups and non-minority groups.

TV network	NBC	CBS	ABC	Fox
Corporate owner	General Electric (GE)	Viacom	Disney Corporation	News Corporation
Network TV affiliates owned	13	15	10	33
Cable TV stations owned	MSNBC, CNBC, A&E, History Channel, Bravo	MTV, VH-1, BET, TVLand, TNN, Nickelodeon, Showtime	E!, Disney Channel, Lifetime, ESPN	Fox Sports, Fox Family, Fox Kids, FX, Fox News, Fox Movie Channel
Production studio	None (uses Warner Brothers, owned by AOL-Time Warner)	3—Paramount, CBS Productions, King World Productions	3—Paramount, Buena Vista, Touchstone	1—20th Century Fox
Other holdings/ manufactures	Manufactures electrical appliances, electrical power equipment	Blockbuster Video, Simon & Schuster (book publisher)	ESPN magazine, Disneyland, Disneyworld, Anaheim Angels (baseball team)	HarperCollins (book publisher), newspapers

programming. *Morning Edition* and *All Things Considered* are highly regarded radio news shows with a very loyal following; the same goes for the PBS-supported *News Hour with Jim Lehrer*. *Frontline* is a popular, award-winning investigative reporting program supported by PBS. Documentary series on such topics as the Civil War, produced by Ken Burns, have been well-received by large audiences. PBS has also supported a significant amount of children's educational programming, including *Sesame Street*.

PBS and NPR member stations do not generally engage in commercial advertising. They rely instead on funds from the CPB, as well as donations from businesses and individuals to support their broadcasting operation. For example, in 1999 General Motors provided a major ten-year commitment of support to PBS to finance productions by Burns, including the documentaries on major league baseball and on jazz music. These pledges of support are typically solicited through on-air membership drives and corporate underwriting of programming. There are nearly four hundred PBS television stations, many of which are aligned with communications departments in colleges and universities across the nation.

An important assumption underlying federal support for public broadcasting is that government is obligated to ensure diversity in what is offered and to ensure that an ample number of educational programs are developed. Federal support for public TV and radio, however, is often a political hot potato. Conservatives claim that public television has a liberal bias, and many have attempted, unsuccessfully, to curb federal funding for CPB.

The Effects of the Media

There is no doubt that Americans rely on the media for news and information about politics. What is less clear is the influence that media exposure has on citizens' opinions (Does watching a news story on the increase in crime rates make the viewer more fearful of crime?) and behavior (Does reading an article about John Kerry's heroic war experiences in Vietnam lead a reader to vote for Kerry on Election Day?).

Researchers can quite easily gauge the exposure and use of the media. It is much more difficult, however, for them to identify the impact of media exposure on opinions and behavior. Citizens are constantly bombarded by news stories from a variety of different media. Isolating how one news story, or even several stories in one medium, influences opinions or behaviors is very hard to determine.

Despite the difficulty of proving media effects, political leaders and candidates for election certainly act as though the media have powerful effects. Leaders constantly try to influence campaign stories and news stories to favor their own positions. Presidents use press conferences to send messages and attempt to win public support. Candidates buy advertising time to try to influence voters. Political parties orchestrate events at party conventions to send favorable partisan messages to voters.

Early research studies of media effects examined how citizen exposure to media content during a campaign influenced how they voted. In classic books on the subject (such as *The Voter Decides* and *The American Voter*), the media were credited with having little or no effect on voters' decisions. These studies, which led to a theory known as **minimal effects theory,** found that other factors, such as an individual's party identification, were deep-seated, long-term political attitudes that had a much greater influence on the vote decision.[14] Such enduring and pre-existing attitudes lead to selective perception and retention of news content. People evaluate news material from their own partisan perspective (selective perception) and tend to process and remember the material more consistent with their pre-existing attitudes (selection retention).[15]

Moreover, the kinds of news people choose to pay attention to in the first place are often influenced by pre-existing attitudes (selective exposure). Psychologists suggest that people's desire to achieve cognitive consistency and avoid cognitive dissonance explains why they process new information in such a way as to assimilate with existing attitudes. These early studies that found "minimal effects" were largely focused on partisan elections and attempted to evaluate the effects of media exposure on the vote decision.

Subsequent research, though not refuting the findings of the media's minimal effects on partisan behavior, examined other areas where media exposure might have an impact. **Social learning theory,** for example, argued that viewers imitate what they view on television through observational learning.[16] Television's focus on sex and violence has led to a large number of studies that try to assess whether exposure to such material leads viewers to become more violent with reduced moral standards. Some of this research suggests that viewers do learn negative, antisocial behavior from TV.

Some communications researchers have advanced the notion of *priming,*[17] which suggests that the activation of one thought also activates other thoughts, and exposure to media provides cues to people on this thought activation process. For example, watching the Road Runner beat up on Wile E. Coyote in the old Warner Brothers cartoon may make one child act violently against another child after watching the cartoon. The recent rash of injuries related to the show *Jackass* is another example of the priming theory.

Critics of media often use social learning and priming theories to advocate for government controls of the media. The Telecommunications Act of 1996, for example, required television set manufacturers to include a V-chip in new units to allow parents to block programs they did not wish their children or families to view. Another law passed in 1997 required the television industry to develop a rating system for television shows based on the show's level of sex, violence, and profanity. Studies that demonstrated a connection between TV exposure and negative behavior were important pieces of evidence used to promote support for the V-chip requirement and the TV ratings system.

The **cultivation theory** of media effects suggests that heavy television exposure helps develop an individual's overall view of the world.[18] According to this theory, the emphasis on violence and crime in both news and entertainment programming would lead the heavy viewer to overestimate and be disproportionately concerned about the extent of crime and violence.

A final theory of media effects is best known as **agenda setting.** This theory suggests that although the effects of exposure may be minimal or difficult to gauge, the media are quite influential in telling the public what to think about. For example, Monica Lewinsky's affair with President Bill Clinton was a lead story in the news throughout 1998. Daily news coverage of the number of soldiers and civilians killed in Iraq focuses public attention on the U.S. military engagement there.

★ **Minimal effects theory**

The theory that deep-seated, long-term factors, such as party identification, had much greater influence on an individual's vote decisions than did news media coverage.

★ **Social learning theory**

The theory that argues that viewers imitate what they view on television through observational learning.

★ **Cultivation theory**

The theory of media effects that suggests that heavy television exposure helps develop an individual's overall view of the world.

★ **Agenda setting theory**

The theory that holds that although the effects of television exposure may be minimal or difficult to gauge, the media are quite influential in telling the public what to think about.

[14] Mass communications researcher Joseph Klapper was a pioneer of the minimal effects (or limited effects) theory. He introduced the theory in a book titled *The Effects of Mass Communication* (New York: Free Press, 1960).

[15] For a good discussion of selection retention, see D. Sears and J. Freeman, "Selective Exposure to Information: A Critical Review," in *The Process and Effects of Mass Communication,* ed. Wilbur Lang Schramm (Chicago: University of Illinois Press, 1972).

[16] For a good discussion of social learning theory, see Albert Bandura, *Social Foundations of Thought and Action* (Englewood Cliffs, NJ: Prentice-Hall, 1986).

[17] See L. Berkowitz, "Some Effects of Thought on Anti- and Pro- Social Influences of Media Effects," in *Psychological Bulletin* 95 (1984), 410–427.

[18] A pioneer in developing cultivation theory was George Gerbner. See George Gerbner et al, "Growing Up with Television: The Cultivation Perspective," in Jennings Bryant and Dolf Zillman, eds., *Media Effects: Advances in Theory and Research* (Hillsdale, NJ: Lawrence Erlbaum, 1994), pp. 17–41.

American Government . . . in Popular Perspective:
Political Bias in the News

The American public is more likely to see a liberal bias in the news than a conservative bias, and those who describe themselves as conservative are the most likely to sense a liberal bias in reporting.

This chart shows how Americans who described themselves as liberal, moderate, or conservative answered the question asked in a 2003 poll: *"Do you think the news media favor the liberal point-of-view, the conservative point-of-view, or is news coverage pretty evenly balanced?"*

Two of the nation's leading newspapers have been accused of providing news from an ideological perspective. Specifically, the *New York Times* is sometimes seen as having a liberal bias and the *Wall Street Journal* is sometimes regarded as holding a conservative bias. This chart summarizes Americans' perception of bias in these two newspapers in a 2005 survey.

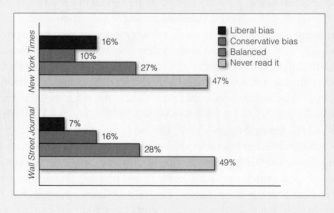

The media set the public agenda for the issues and activities that many Americans choose to think about and talk about. Prominently placed and frequently repeated headlines in newspapers, lead stories on television news shows and on talk radio, and highlighted stories on well-trafficked websites set the stage for public discourse. Citizens pick up a newspaper or flip on an all-news TV station to become informed about what is happening in their community, the nation, and the world. In this sense, the news media have a powerful impact on public debate.[19] As news media scholar Doris Graber has noted, "When media make events seem important, average people as well as politicians discuss them and form opinions. This enhances the perceived importance of these events and ensures even more public attention and, possibly, political action."[20]

Criticisms of the News Media

Though Americans rely on the media for information about what is going on in the nation and around the world, the news media are also the subject for a number of criticisms. For example, despite the vast array of news sources available, most news

[19] A number of studies have demonstrated the agenda-setting power of the media, including Maxwell E. McCombs, "The Agenda-Setting Approach," in *Handbook of Political Communication*, eds. Dan D. Nimmo and Keith Sanders (Thousand Oaks, CA: Sage, 1981), pp. 121–140; Shanto Iyengar and Donald R. Kinder, *News That Matters* (Chicago: University of Chicago Press, 1987).

[20] Doris A. Graber, *Mass Media and American Politics* (Washington, DC: CQ Press, 2002), p. 207.

Television news, too, has been charged with biased reporting. Three of the top twenty-four-hour news stations have been accused of providing biased coverage. Some analysts charge that CNN and MSNBC tilt toward the left in their coverage and that Fox News tilts right. This chart shows what bias the public perceived in coverage by the three stations.

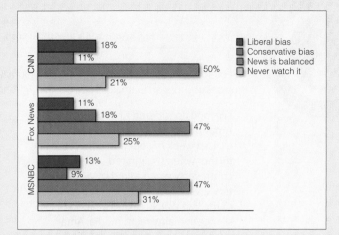

Perceptions of bias may be based on how journalists and American adults differ in their own political orientations. Among all American adults, 33 percent say they are Democrats, 32 percent claim to be Republicans, and 22 percent say they are politically independent. Among journalists, 50 percent say they are independent, 33 percent claim to be Democrats, and only 10 percent say they are Republicans.

Interestingly, 18 percent of Americans describe themselves as liberal and 18 percent of journalists say they are politically liberal. But whereas only 10 percent of journalists say they are conservative, 34 percent of Americans say they are conservative. More than half (53 percent) of journalists say they are politically moderate, whereas 40 percent of Americans describe themselves that way.

Finally, 68 percent of journalists say they voted for John Kerry in 2004, whereas only 25 percent voted for George W. Bush. Only 1 percent say they voted for Green Party candidate Ralph Nader, and 5 percent say they did not vote.

These poll results are drawn from national surveys of American adults, conducted at the University of Connecticut in October 2003 and April 2005.

programming follows a standard format that makes it appear the same to the public. A small number of companies that own large numbers of newspapers (such as the Tribune Company and Gannett) use a standard format for news. Similarly, just a few companies own many of the nation's radio stations and TV stations and employ a similar format to programming. Critics charge that this concentration in ownership could result in a handful of companies promoting their own political objectives.

Another criticism of the private ownership of the media stems from the premise that the media, like most other privately owned companies, are in business primarily to make money. For the media, increasing profits requires attracting larger audiences and more readers, and as many media companies have found, providing higher-quality news programming on politically important topics does not always guarantee increased audience ratings or numbers of readers. Rather, news that provides more entertainment tends to get larger audience shares.

Often, the result is news that is characterized by "sensationalized" content. Stories that highlight or exploit crime, violence, disasters, personal conflicts, competition, and scandals tend to be the types of stories that increase the sale of newspapers and improve the ratings of TV news programs. Thus the profit motive of private ownership drives companies in the news business to disproportionately cover events that include sensationalized content. Stories like the personal downfall of Martha Stewart, the tragic deaths of Princess Diana and John F. Kennedy Jr., O. J. Simpson's trial for his wife's murder, and the jailing of Paris Hilton for minor offenses tend to be overcovered.

American Government . . . in Global Perspective:
One Canadian's View of American Media Coverage of the War

A September 21, 2003, editorial by Canadian journalist Eric Margolis of the *Toronto Sun* provides one foreign journalist's perspective on American media coverage of the Iraqi war:

I've long considered CNN's Christiane Amanpour an outstanding journalist. Last week my opinion of her rose further when she ignited a storm of controversy when asked by a TV interviewer about US media's coverage of the Iraq War. Breaking a taboo of silence in mainstream media, Amanpour courageously replied, "I think the press was muzzled and I think the press self-muzzled. Television . . . was intimidated by the Administration and its foot soldiers at Fox News."

Christiane Amanpour is absolutely right, the US media was muzzled and censored itself. I experienced this firsthand on US TV, radio, and in print. Never in my twenty years in media have I seen such unconscionable pressure exerted on journalists to conform to the government's party line. Criticism of the wars in Afghanistan and Iraq, photos of dead American soldiers or civilians killed by bombing, were forbidden. The tone of reporting had to be strongly positive, filled with uplifting stories about liberation of Afghanistan and Iraq, and women freed from Taliban repression. Criticism, sharp questions, and doubt about US policy were hushed up.

The bloated corporations dominating US media feared antagonizing the White House, which was pushing for the bill—just rejected by the Senate—to allow them to grow even larger. Reporters who failed to toe the line were barred from access to the military and government officials, ending their careers. "Embedded" reporters in Iraq and Afghanistan became little more than public relations auxiliaries.

Critics of the administration's policies in Iraq and Afghanistan were systematically excluded from media commentary, particularly on national TV. Night after night, networks featured "experts" who droned on about Iraq's fearsome weapons of mass destruction that posed an imminent threat to the US, about Iraq's links to al-Qaeda, the urgency to invade Iraq before it could strike at America, and a raft of other fabrications.

Such "experts" echoed the White House party line and all were dead wrong. Yet amazingly, many are still on air, continuing to misinform the public, using convoluted Talmudic arguments to explain why they were not really wrong even when they were wrong. I do not exaggerate when I say that much of the US media from 9/11 to the present closely resembled the old Soviet media that I knew and disrespected during my stays in the USSR during the 1980's.

The American media, notably the sycophantic White House press corps and flag-wavers at Fox TV, treated President Bush and his entourage with the same sucrose adulation and fawning servility that Soviet state media lavished on Comrade Chairman Leonid Brezhnev. So long as Bush was riding high in the polls, the media fawned on him. The media always follows power. But now that many Americans are beginning to sense they were lied to or misled by the White House, Bush's popularity is dropping, and the media's mood is becoming edgy and more aggressive. Perhaps even vengeful. The muzzles may soon be coming off.

Source: From an editorial piece in the *Toronto Sun*, by Eric Margolis, September 21, 2003.

Michael Jackson is just one of thousands of individuals who have been accused of child molestation, but coverage of his trial attracted far more attention than all the others combined.

Sensationalism extends to coverage of elections as well. Studies of election coverage have found that most news dwells more on stories about the candidates' personal background than on their positions on the issues. Political scientists note that this emphasis on covering "character" issues rather than policy positions characterizes modern presidential election campaign news. In 2000, for example, much of the coverage of candidate George W. Bush in the final week before the election focused on a drunk-driving charge that occurred while he was young. In 2004, significant coverage targeted the military service of the candidates, including Bush's "questionable" military record in the Alabama Air National Guard and John Kerry's record as a Vietnam War soldier and protester. More recently in 2008, a significant amount of coverage focused on Barack Obama's association both with his outspoken pastor Jeremiah Wright, as well as with William Ayers, a co-founder of the radical leftist organization, the Weather Underground. Critics of election coverage also charge that there is too much focus on pre-election polls and the competitiveness of the "horse race," which crowds out the more substantive coverage of the issues and the candidates' positions on them.

Another common criticism of the news media is that they are politically biased. Some critics, for example, charge that corporate owners of media organizations are more likely to hold a conservative ideology, which is reflected in their news products. Others cite studies indicating that journalists and reporters tend to hold a more liberal philosophy, and that this orientation seeps into their stories. Certainly there is evidence to support the assertions that owners and managers are more conservative than the citizenry as a whole, and that journalists are more liberal. But the issue of whether personal ideology or partisanship is reflected in news stories is less clear. In some elections, research has demonstrated that newspaper and TV news programs have shown a pro-Republican tilt, whereas in others it has found a pro-Democratic bias.[21]

Now & Then: Making the Connection

Unlike other important political institutions in American politics, the media occupy the unique position of being privately owned. Private ownership enhances the ability of the news organizations to operate free and independent from government control. As such, the news media can provide objective information to citizens and act as a watchdog over what government does.

Private ownership, however, also makes the media sensitive to concerns of the marketplace. News organizations are not only driven by providing objective news, offering valuable context and commentary, and investigating corruption in government, but they are also motivated by the desire to increase audience shares and readership numbers to turn a profit.

At times, the value of having a free and independent media is apparent, such as with the investigative reporting that characterized the muckrakers of the nineteenth century or coverage of the Watergate scandal in the 1970s. In both these instances, the news media weeded out corruption, kept presidential power in check, and served American democracy well. The development of new technologies, from the rotary press, to radio transmissions, to television, to the Internet and satellite transmission, has enabled the media to deliver to more Americans more news and information in a more timely manner.

From time to time the downsides of a privatized media have also become apparent. The profit motive sometimes drives journalists and editors to increase audiences and readers through tactics that undermine quality news reporting, such as the focus on sensationalism, a disproportionate emphasis on crime, sex, and

---

[21] Kenneth Dautrich and Thomas H. Hartley, *How the News Media Fail American Voters* (New York: Columbia University Press, 1999), pp. 92–95.

violence, and the use of unreliable or fabricated news sources. That certainly was the case both with the yellow journalism of William Randolph Hearst as well as with the *Drudge Report*.

Despite these blemishes, however, the America media remain as important a political institution as any in our system of government. Americans' use of the media, the demand for information, the appetite of journalists to keep tabs on government performance, and political leaders' reliance on the media to communicate with citizens all serve to make the media stronger today that they have ever been.

The night of March 3, 2008, presented a crucial moment in Senator Hillary Clinton's bid for the Democratic presidential nomination. She trailed Senator Barack Obama in the delegate count, and with a dwindling number of contests remaining on the calendar, the following day's primaries in Texas and Ohio could make or break her campaign. How did she choose to spend her time, her most precious commodity, on this critical evening? Hanging out with Jon Stewart on Comedy Central network's *The Daily Show,* a half hour-long daily rundown of political satire, usually targeted at politicians such as Clinton. "It is pretty pathetic," Clinton joked via satellite from Austin, Texas, with Stewart. "I only wish you were out on the campaign trail with us ... you could make fun of us in person rather than by remote." Not to be outdone, Obama appeared on Stewart's show on April 21, the night before the crucial primary contest in Pennsylvania. Even Republican John McCain—who sewed up his party's nomination in February—could ill afford to skip Stewart's show that spring. As he explained to Stewart in a live appearance on *The Daily Show* on May 8: "You know, Ron Paul [a Republican congressman from Texas] is still in the race . . ."

America's youth increasingly rely on the award-winning *Daily Show* for their political news. The show's satirical (and often biting) commentary on politicians and political events has become the main source of news for young Americans, and candidates for high office know that all too well. Stops on *The Daily Show* have become a rite of passage for serious presidential candidates. For similar reasons, political writers have learned that a stop on Comedy Central's *The Colbert Report*—a program that satirizes personality-driven political programs such as the *O'Reilly Factor*—can do wonders for book sales and exposure among a more youthful and active class of listeners. So long as talents such as Stewart and Stephen Colbert continue to strike a chord with these prized audiences, future presidential candidates will continue to seek out appearances on these shows at every opportunity.

On http://academic.cengage.com/dautrich, find the politics interactive link for a discussion of comedy news shows. Note how *The Daily Show*'s coverage of elections in particular can affect an election campaign. Consult as well the various links that explore how the structure of the American news media has changed, and where these comedy news shows fit in the new pecking order.

JEFF CHIU/AP PHOTO

Republican presidential nominee John McCain with Jon Stewart, the host of Comedy Central's *Daily Show*, in May 2008.

http://academic.cengage.com/dautrich

Chapter Summary

★ Congress created the Federal Communications Commission (FCC) in 1934 to regulate the electronic media through licensing of broadcasters and creating rules for broadcasters to follow. The FCC does not have authority to regulate the print media, because the courts have consistently treated the right of print media to publish free from government regulation.

★ The media serve a number of important functions in the political system, all of which promote the free flow of information to the public. These functions include providing objective coverage of events, facilitating public debate, and serving as government watchdog.

★ From the nation's founding through the 1850s, news in America was largely provided by a partisan press, made up of newspapers supported by a particular political party.

★ Over the past 150 years, the standards for news reporting have become more focused on "objectivity."

★ Technological change has greatly altered the news media. The invention of the rotary press in 1815 facilitated the mass printing of papers; the railroad system provided for speedy distribution of papers; the invention of the radio provided instantaneous coverage of events as they unfolded; and television brought taped and live footage of news events into people's homes.

★ Politics and political events, such as presidential campaigns, debates, and news conferences, are widely covered by media organizations.

★ Today's mass media comprise large and varied types of news outlets, including radio, television, books, newspapers, and magazines. They also include the so-called new media facilitated by the Internet satellites, cell phones, broadband, and other newer technologies.

★ Corporate ownership of news media outlets today is characterized by large non-media corporations, such as General Electric and the Disney Corporation. Some argue that this concentration of large corporate ownership has stifled diversity in news content and blurred the line between what is news and what is entertainment.

★ Although the big three television networks—ABC, CBS, and NBC—have dominated television viewership since the early 1950s, the growing popularity of cable and satellite TV has begun to offer stiff competition.

★ The Public Broadcasting Act of 1967 created the Corporation for Public Broadcasting (CPB), which is responsible for distributing federal funds to support public, noncommercial radio (NPR) and television (PBS) stations.

★ The "effects" that exposure to news has on readers/viewers are the subject of much debate. A number of theories—including social learning, minimal effects, cultivation, and agenda setting—seek to explain how the news media influence what people think about politics.

Key Terms

Agenda setting theory (p. 375)

Blogs (p. 372)

Cultivation theory (p. 375)

Digital divide (p. 373)

Equal time rule (p. 359)

Minimal effects theory (p. 375)

New media (p. 371)

Objectivity (p. 361)

Partisan press era (p. 363)

Social learning theory (p. 375)

Talk radio (p. 371)

Resources

Important Books

Anderson, David M., and Michael Cornfield, eds. *The Civic Web: Online Politics and Democratic Values*. New York: Rowman and Littlefield, 2003.

Dautrich, Kenneth, and Thomas Hartley. *How the News Media Fail American Voters*. New York: Cambridge University Press, 1999.

Epstein, Edward. *News from Nowhere*. New York: Random House, 1973.

Goldberg, Bernard. *Bias: A CBS Insider Exposes How the Media Distort the News*. New York: HarperCollins, 2002.

Graber, Doris A. *Mass Media and American Politics*. Washington, DC: CQ Press, 2004.

Iyengar, Shanto, and Jennifer A. McGrady. *Media Politics: A Citizen's Guide*. New York: W. W. Norton, 2006.

Jamieson, Kathleen Hall, and Paul Waldman. *The Press Effect: Politicians, Journalists and the Stories That Shape the Political World*. New York: Oxford University Press, 2003.

Just, Marion, Ann N. Crigler, Dean E. Alger, Timothy E. Cook, Montague Kern, and Darrell M. West. *Crosstalk: Citizens, Candidates, and the Media in a Presidential Campaign*. Chicago: University of Chicago Press, 1992.

Meyer, Philip. *Precision Journalism: A Reporter's Introduction to Social Science Methods*. New York: Rowman and Littlefield, 2002.

Murray, David, Joel Schwartz, and S. Robert Lichter. *It Ain't Necessarily So: How the Media Remake Our Picture of Reality*. New York: Penguin Books, 2002.

Patterson, Thomas E. *The Mass Media Election: How Americans Choose Their President*. New York: Praeger, 1980.

Schroeder, Alan. *Presidential Debates: Forty Years of High-Risk TV*. New York: Columbia University Press, 2000.

Thurber, James A., Candice J. Nelson, and David A. Dulio, eds. *Crowded Airwaves: Campaign Advertising in Elections*. Washington, DC: Brookings Institution Press, 2002.

Internet Resources

http://www.bbc.co.uk (the website for the British Broadcasting Company [BBC], which is the official and publicly run news agency for Britain)

http://www.people-press.org (the site for the Pew Research Center for the People & the Press, which holds polling and other data on the news media)

http://www.mediaresearch.org (a media "watchdog" website containing a variety of reviews and research on media issues)

http://www.freedomforum.org (the site for the Freedom Forum Foundation, which includes information and analysis on news media issues and First Amendment debates)

http://www.knightfdn.org (the site for the Knight Foundation, an organization that provides programs and research on journalism topics)

13 Political Parties

Green Party candidate Ralph Nader in 2000

Third Parties as the Spoiler:
Now & Then

He was already well-known when he launched his campaign for the presidency, sporting a hard-nosed, combative approach to politics, championing the cause of working people and labor, and challenging large companies at every turn. His campaign stood little or no chance of winning, as he had few resources to match his major-party rivals. The press and most voters treated his candidacy with indifference, if not ridicule. Yet the incumbent president, who spent years warding off criticism that he had become the tool of money-grubbing wealthy interests, had to answer these charges once again from this risk-taking third-party candidate who reveled in such accusations. Indeed, the corruption of the incumbent became a centerpiece of the third-party candidate's campaign speeches. The outcome? The third-party candidate received a relatively small percentage of the popular vote. Yet the number of popular votes he attained far outpaced the margin of difference between the winning candidate and the second-place candidate. The insurgent third-party campaign had influenced the final outcome of the election. His candidacy drew plenty of attention, but in the end he failed to have any lasting impact on the dominant two-party system that prevails in American politics.

Greenback Party candidate James Weaver in 1892

PHOTO: LIBRARY OF CONGRESS, PRINTS AND PHOTOGRAPHIC DIVISION, LC-DIG-CWPBH-03668

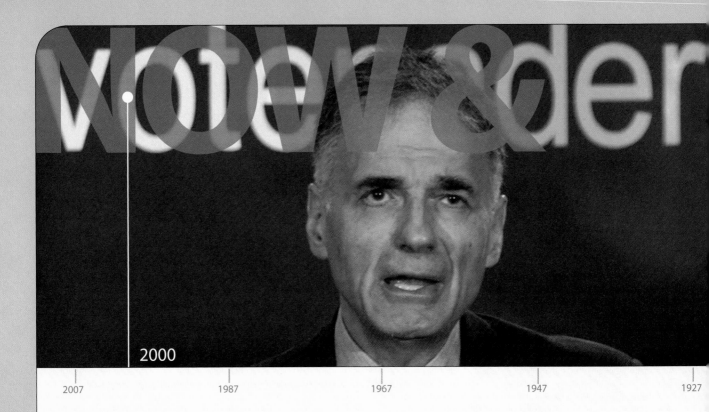

2000

2007   1987   1967   1947   1927

NOW... Who does this scenario describe? In contemporary politics, surely Ralph Nader fits the bill. The Green Party candidate in 2000 was already a well-known personality, leading the consumer protection movement against capitalist interests for decades; his candidacy for the White House that year focused on the corrupt fund-raising tactics of outgoing President Bill Clinton and Vice President Al Gore, but he was quick to remind his audiences that the Republican Party was little better. Nader, the persistent agitator of both parties in 2000, mounted an aggressive campaign despite the ridicule, lack of respect, and outright hostility that rose from the conservative ranks who opposed his policy positions, and from the liberals who feared that his presence would hand the Republicans an electoral victory. And by many accounts, that is exactly what happened.

American Government: Historical, Popular, and Global Perspectives

1892

1907   1887   1867   1847   1827

THEN... History does have a way of repeating itself. James Weaver, a "Greenback" rather than a "Green," fits the scenario above just as well. By 1892, Weaver had become a household name too, championing the causes of the labor movement and farmers against the excesses of the wealthy for well over two decades.[1] Like Nader, Weaver had a ready target for his attacks against the corruption of the system: President Benjamin Harrison. The Republican incumbent, Harrison, was pegged as sitting in the pocket of wealthy railroad and big-business interests. Like Nader, Weaver also failed to achieve a substantial percentage of the vote. But his constant calls for reforming a corrupt system helped lead to the defeat of Harrison and his administration.

The Democratic and Republican parties have long dominated the American political landscape. Still, third parties are not altogether uncommon participants in the electoral process. Although third parties rarely win major office (and have never won the presidency), they do occasionally make their presence felt, perhaps by peeling off enough votes from one of the two major parties to change the outcome of a particular election contest. In that sense, third parties enjoy influence akin to the sting of a bee: they generally bite once, then die off.

[1] See Steven J. Rosenstone, Roy L. Behr, and Edward H. Lazarus, *Third Parties in America*, 2nd ed. (Princeton, NJ: Princeton University Press, 1996).

Political parties are the lifeblood of American politics. New laws are enacted through the debate and negotiation of party leaders in government; individuals are recruited and promoted as political candidates through the apparatus of the political party structure; voters evaluate campaigns and candidates largely through a partisan looking glass. At the national, state, and local levels, the two major political parties set the tone, control the agenda, and run the government. Parties have been the dominant organizational framework through which our government has worked for over two hundred years, even though the U.S. Constitution makes no mention of parties.

More than fifty years ago, the American Political Science Association (APSA) focused the scholarly community's attention on what it referred to as responsible party government.[2] The "responsible party government" model depicts the proper role of parties as organizations that offer clear programs and policy positions to voters. Voters make choices on the basis of those programs, and when victorious in elections, the party works toward achieving those programs and policies. At the time of the next election cycle, voters hold the party accountable for what it has accomplished.

HISTORICAL PERSPECTIVE

American Government . . . in Historical Perspective:
Third Parties Play the Spoiler Role

Third parties have never won the presidency, but they have on occasion played a decisive role in determining which of the two major parties would win the presidency, sometimes even despite capturing a very small percentage of the popular vote total. Two such instances in which a third party played the spoiler role occurred more than 150 years apart.

In 1844, the Liberty Party, a party dedicated to the abolition of slavery, tallied 2.3 percent of the popular vote. Even though the party did not win the popular vote in New York State, the 15,812 votes from that state allowed Democrat James Polk to win New York by about 5,000 popular votes—and all 36 of New York's electoral votes. Had Liberal

Party candidate James Birney not been in the race, his votes would likely have been cast for Whig candidate Henry Clay. New York's 36 electoral votes would have given Clay the victory over Polk in 1844.

In 2000, Ralph Nader, the Green Party candidate in 2000, also polled less than 3 percent of the popular vote. But the number of votes cast for Nader in Florida exceeded Republican George W. Bush's margin of victory over Democrat Al Gore in that state by four to one. Most of Nader's votes would have gone to Gore had Nader not been in the race. If Florida's 25 electoral votes in 2000 had gone to Gore rather than to Bush, Gore would have been elected president.

The extent to which parties actually resemble the responsible party model has been the subject of much debate over the past half century. Moreover, despite the large role parties play in the American political system, many observers argue that parties are organizationally weak, particularly when compared to parties in other democracies around the world. Whereas most European parties have clearly defined constituencies based on social class, regional, ethnic, or religious division, American political parties are often ideologically vague, aligning with broader constituencies and gravitating toward more centrist positions on issues. And despite their prevalence in politics, there are indications that the influence of parties is on the decline.

The Founders who drafted the Constitution designed a federal system without political parties. They envisioned a system that would be run by independent-minded people who served out of a sense of civic virtue. James Madison's famous Federalist No. 10 deplores "factions," as he calls them. Madison and his colleagues

[2] "Toward a More Responsible Party System: A Report of the Committee on Political Parties, American Political Science Association," *American Political Science Review* 44, no. 3 (September 1950).

AP PHOTO/PETER NICHOLLS

AP PHOTO/KEVIN FRAYER

Parties are also important in other democracies around the globe. Left: British Prime Minister Gordon Brown of the Labour Party, in 2007. Right: Israeli Prime Minister Ariel Sharon of the Kadima Party in 2005.

largely looked upon parties (the equivalent of extremely large factions) as tools of the politically ambitious that would tend to promote corruption and bias in the political system.

Despite some of the Founders' disdain for political parties, they have become central to the American political system. E. E. Schattschneider, a well-regarded student of American politics, observed in 1942 that "democracy is unthinkable, save in terms of the parties."[3] The Democratic and Republican parties not only have become important political institutions in their own right, but they play a central role in running government at all levels, and they organize and provide context to voters.

Political parties are organizations that seek to win elections for the purpose of influencing the outputs of government. They are typically guided by a political philosophy, rooted in particular values and an ideological approach to governing. The philosophy, values, and ideological approach generally lead to specific issue positions espoused by leaders of a party and the candidates who run for office under a party's label. Some minor parties focus less on the unrealistic assumption that they might win elections and more on articulating an ideological approach to governing and supporting particular issue positions. As in any organization, parties include leaders as well as citizens. In American politics, parties provide an important link between citizens and their leaders, playing a key role in recruiting citizens and relying on them for support at election time.

★ Political party

An organization that seeks to win elections for the purpose of influencing the outputs of government.

History of Political Parties in the United States

Even though the Founders frowned on political parties and made no provision for them in the federal government they designed, not long after the first government under the new U.S. Constitution took office in 1791, a number of the architects of the Constitution became strong advocates of particular parties.[4] Perhaps more than anything else, this irony serves to highlight not only the importance of political parties to the practice of democracy, but also the necessity of parties. In the United

---

[3] E. E. Schattschneider, *Party Government* (New York: Farrar and Rinehart, 1942).

[4] See chapter 2 in John F. Bibby, *Politics, Parties and Elections in America*, 5th ed. (Belmont, CA: Wadsworth, 2002).

States, competition between the political parties has kept any one group or "faction" from becoming too powerful for too long. The Constitution provides various safeguards against the accumulation of power in the form of checks and balances. Paradoxically, though parties are not mentioned at all in the Constitution, competition between political parties has proven to be a significant check against tyranny.

The First Parties in America

The history of political parties in the United States traces back to colonial America, when supporters of the English crown aligned with the British Tory Party, and advocates of a new independent American nation aligned themselves with the British Whig Party. Benjamin Franklin and other Founders still considered themselves Tories up through the early 1770s, and during the American Revolution colonists who supported Britain were called Tories or Loyalists. The period following the war ushered in new challenges as leaders of the new American nation debated the relationship that should exist between the national government and the state governments. Ultimately this debate created two new parties (or "factions" as many still called them in the eighteenth century). The U.S. Constitution that replaced the Articles of Confederation significantly enhanced the structure, power, and importance of the national government. The debate over ratification of the new Constitution pitted the Federalists, who supported a stronger federal government, against the Anti-Federalists, who opposed a strong federal government and supported state sovereignty.[5]

More formal, identifiable political parties emerged and began to assume the critical function of supporting candidates for elective office during the first administration of George Washington. Once again, the issue that spurred the emergence of parties as vehicles for nominating candidates was the distribution of power between the federal and state governments under the Constitution. The Federalists continued to support a stronger federal government and the policies of the Washington administration, which promoted the power of the national government. Most Federalists also favored maintaining close ties with Great Britain. President Washington did not consider himself a member of the Federalist Party; he despised parties and refused to endorse their presence in the politics of the new country. Yet many of Washington's supporters, led by Alexander Hamilton, organized the Federalist Party and used the organization to recruit candidates for office.

The Federalist Party was soon challenged by the Democratic-Republican Party, which asserted that the Washington administration was assuming greater powers than those the Constitution granted to the federal government. It also criticized the federal government's favorable relations with Britain, preferring France as a closer European ally. As early as 1792, the Democratic-Republicans were organized and led by Thomas Jefferson and James Madison—the same Madison who ten years earlier had authored in Federalist No. 10 perhaps the most eloquent argument *against* factions that has ever been written. In the congressional elections of 1792, Democratic-Republican candidates won a majority of seats in the House of Representatives. George Washington was unopposed for president, but the Democratic-Republicans backed George Clinton against Federalist John Adams for the vice presidency. Adams, however, won re-election to the vice presidency by an electoral vote margin of 77 to 50.

Every presidential and congressional election since 1796 has featured some form of party competition. In this early period of American political parties, the Federalists drew most of their support from the northern states, whereas the Democratic-Republicans had greater support in the southern and mid-Atlantic states. Sectional differences in partisan support have characterized American politics for much of the nation's history. In the first competitive presidential election of 1796, the Federalists endorsed John Adams and the Democratic-Republicans endorsed Thomas Jefferson. Adams won 71 electoral votes and Jefferson won 68 votes, making Adams president and Jefferson vice president. Not anticipating

American Government: Historical, Popular, and Global Perspectives

---

[5] See Paul Finkelman and John Moore, "Political Parties," in Peter Wallenstein and Paul Finkelman, eds., *The Encyclopedia of American Political History* (Washington, DC: CQ Press, 2001).

political parties, the Constitution allowed for the election of a president and vice president who stood very far apart on critical issues of the day.

By the time of the election of 1800, the parties were highly organized. Each of the two political parties endorsed a slate of candidates for president and vice president to avoid the problem of having two separate parties occupy those offices. The party organization selected presidential electors, who dutifully cast their constitutionally granted two votes to their party's candidates. The Federalists nominated both John Adams and Charles Pinckney, whereas the Democratic-Republicans endorsed Thomas Jefferson and Aaron Burr. Jefferson and Burr each received 73 electoral votes, thus producing an Electoral College tie for the presidency. By the provisions of the Constitution, the election was then to be decided by the House of Representatives. After a fair amount of debate and politicking, the House eventually selected Jefferson on the thirty-sixth ballot. Clearly, however, the system of selecting the president needed to be modified from one that did not recognize the importance of political parties in the electoral process to one that did.

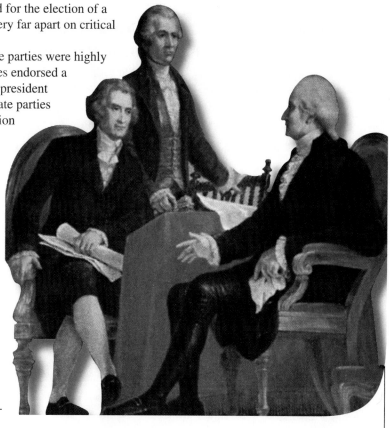

Thomas Jefferson (left) of the Democratic-Republican Party and Alexander Hamilton (center) of the Federalist Party, speaking to President George Washington (right).

The Twelfth Amendment deferred to the reality of parties in presidential elections. Ratified prior to the election of 1804, this amendment formally separated the Electoral College vote for president and vice president. Rather than having electors cast two ballots for president, electors were now to cast separate votes for president and vice president. This modification in the electoral process helped avoid the problem that had occurred in 1796 of having a president and vice president locked in partisan struggle, as well as the problem in the 1800 election that resulted in two candidates from the same party tied for the presidency.

The election of 1800 marked the beginning of the end for the Federalist Party. The Federalists would never again win a presidential election, and their strength in Congress diminished steadily over the next two decades. The Democratic-Republicans enjoyed party dominance to such an extent that the Federalists were virtually extinct after the election of 1820. Interestingly, this lack of competition from the Federalists during the first two decades of the nineteenth century had the effect of fragmenting the Democratic-Republicans. In 1824, the Democratic-Republican Party put forth several sectional candidates, but no candidate received a majority of electoral votes. (Andrew Jackson won 99 votes, John Quincy Adams took 84, and another 74 votes were scattered among other candidates.) Eventually, the House of Representatives decided in favor of Adams. The result was a Democratic-Republican Party in disarray.

A Second Party System Emerges

Disillusioned by the outcome of the 1824 election, Andrew Jackson eventually formed a new political party, the Democratic Party, which remains one of the two major parties still competing in American politics today. Jackson's support in 1824 derived from many of the new states that had been added to the union as a result of westward expansion. Many such states, including Jackson's home state

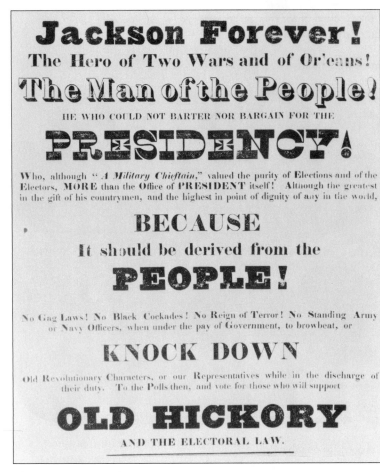

Election poster in 1828 for Andrew Jackson's presidential campaign. Jackson is the founder of today's Democratic party.

of Tennessee, allowed voters to choose presidential electors directly, rather than following the traditional practice of authorizing the state's congressional delegation (known as the "congressional caucus") to choose electors. Because he received more popular votes than John Quincy Adams in 1824, Jackson felt the presidency was rightfully his that year. However, Henry Clay, the fourth-place candidate, allied himself with Adams, thereby giving Adams enough votes for victory. When Adams became president he appointed Clay as secretary of state. Jackson and his supporters accused Clay of making a "corrupt bargain" by trading his votes to Adams in exchange for an appointment as secretary of state. Those who remained loyal to John Quincy Adams began calling themselves the National Republicans. The next presidential election would be a contest essentially between two splinter groups (Democrats and National Republicans) of the now defunct Democratic-Republicans.[6]

Jackson took his case directly to the people and ran for president again in 1828, this time as a Democrat. He ran a populist campaign, arguing that the people should have a greater say in selecting the president, and developed his campaign theme around the Adams–Clay "corrupt bargain." Jackson's theme caught fire with the voters, and the nation's continuing westward expansion, along with voting reforms and increased suffrage in eastern states, suddenly expanded the role of voters in selecting presidential electors. Thus, in a campaign that was essentially decided by the people, puritanical John Quincy Adams proved no match for the flamboyant Jackson, still revered as the general who led American forces to victory in the Battle of New Orleans, the final military engagement of the War of 1812. And Jackson's newly established Democratic Party emerged as a national force to be reckoned with.

The election of 1828 also permanently changed the nature of campaigns, and with them, the nature of parties. The precedent for a presidential election influenced by the masses was now set, and the era of congressional delegations selecting presidential electors was over. Parties quickly recognized the need to organize in states and localities to accommodate the new process of selecting presidential electors. Party organizations became larger and more powerful as they developed into critical instruments in campaigns. This era also established the tradition of holding **national party conventions.** These conventions drew together party delegates from across the states for several purposes. First, the delegates were responsible for choosing the party's presidential candidate and vice presidential candidate. Second, the delegates articulated their **party platform,** a document outlining the party's position on important policy issues. Third, the conventions coordinated the activities of parties across the states. National party conventions remain a central event both in the presidential selection process and in the organization of modern political parties in general.

The Democratic Party held its first national party convention in 1832, once again nominating Andrew Jackson for president. The National Republicans again nominated

★ National party convention

A large meeting that draws together party delegates from across the nation to choose (or formally affirm the selection of) the party's presidential and vice presidential candidates.

★ Party platform

A document outlining the party's position on important policy issues.

[6] See chapter 2 in John F. Bibby, *Politics, Parties and Elections in America*, 5th ed. (Belmont, CA: Wadsworth), 2002.

The 2004 Pew Global Attitudes Survey queried people in nine predominantly Muslim nations about a variety of democratic ideals that characterize American political culture. One of those ideals is the value of honest two-party elections. The following shows the percentage of citizens from each of the nine nations who said that "it is very important to live in a country where there are honest two-party elections":

Senegal	87%	**Pakistan**	46%
Mali	82%	**Uzbekistan**	42%
Turkey	75%	**Indonesia**	40%
Bangladesh	71%	**Jordan**	28%
Lebanon	71%		

Henry Clay, who lost to Jackson in the November election. Several years later a new political party, the Whigs, which was made up of a coalition of National Republicans and other groups, emerged as a principal competitor to the Democrats. By the 1840s, the Democrats and Whigs dominated not only election contests, but also leadership and committee assignments in Congress. Soon those two parties became the primary vehicles through which legislation was sponsored and then shepherded through the Congress.

From 1836 through 1856, the Whigs and Democrats shared the presidency and the vast majority of seats in Congress. Both parties were truly national parties, with organizations in each of the states. The issue of slavery, however, soon became the principal issue on the American political agenda. The Civil War would transform American politics forever, and a product of this transformation was the demise of the Whig Party. Within the Whigs, there were strong differences of opinion over the slavery issue, which led to the decline of the Whigs as a national force by the late 1850s. New, smaller parties emerged, such as the Free Soil and Know-Nothing parties, but none of those parties was able to attract large numbers of voters over an extended period of time. By the late 1850s, a new Republican Party had emerged to absorb these smaller parties and replace the Whigs as the major opposition party to the Democrats.

The Modern Party System in America: Democrats versus Republicans

The year 1856 marked the first presidential election when the precursors to the modern Democratic and Republican parties faced off for office. Democratic nominee James Buchanan defeated Republican candidate John Fremont by 174 to 114 electoral votes. With only one exception, every presidential election since 1856 has featured the Democrats and Republicans as the only two major political parties in serious contention for the White House. (The lone exception occurred in 1912, when former Republican President Theodore Roosevelt, the nominee of the newly formed Progressive or "Bull Moose" Party, ran second to Woodrow Wilson, the Democrat. Incumbent President William Howard Taft, the Republican nominee, finished a distant third.) In 1860,

Democratic Party support for states' rights and Republican Party support for national power and preservation of the Union divided the parties over the issue of slavery. Republican Abraham Lincoln's successful campaign that year helped his party capture the presidency and a majority in both houses of Congress. It also precipitated the Civil War. With the eventual secession of eleven Southern and Democrat-heavy states, the Republican Party came to dominate politics for the next decade.

The elephant is the symbol of the Republican Party. The donkey is the symbol for the Democratic Party.

JOE RAEDLE/NEWSMAKERS/GETTY IMAGES

RON WURZER/GETTY IMAGES

©LYNNE FERNANDES/THE IMAGE WORKS

American Government: Historical, Popular, and Global Perspectives

★ Critical election

An election that produces sharp changes in patterns of party loyalty among voters.

Like the election of 1828, the election of 1860 is considered by many scholars to be a **critical election** in the modern era of American parties. The theory of critical elections, developed by political scientist V. O. Key Jr., posits that there are certain elections that can be characterized as producing sharp changes in patterns of party loyalty among voters.[7] This occurred in 1860 when voter support for parties realigned along the issue of slavery, based primarily on a North versus South division. Until 1860, the Democratic Party had enjoyed support from urban and industrial areas in both the North and the South and the demographic and social groups associated with those regions. The Civil War shifted these alignments to a North–South division, thus rendering the 1860 contest a critical election. The theory of critical elections suggests that every such election is accompanied by some type of electoral realignment,[8] a lasting reconfiguration of how certain groups of voters align with the parties.

When the last of the former Confederate states was readmitted to the union in 1870, the Democratic Party once again began to assert itself in national politics. The Civil War had cemented a "solid South" stronghold for the Democratic Party that would continue for a century. Republicans remained the favored party in the northern and midwestern states, although some major cities in the North (including New York City) tended toward the Democratic Party. Republicans dominated the presidency for the remainder of the century, winning six of the next eight presidential contests.

[7] V. O. Key Jr., "A Theory of Critical Elections," *Journal of Politics* 16, no. 1 (1955), 13–18.
[8] See Walter Dean Burnham, *Critical Elections and the Mainsprings of American Politics* (New York: W. W. Norton, 1970).

CHECKtheLIST

Five Critical Elections in U.S. History

Scholar V. O. Key Jr. developed a theory of critical elections, which argues that certain presidential elections have produced realignments of voter groups to specific political parties. These elections tend to be ones in which voters are highly engaged and intensely involved. They are also marked by disruptions of normal voting patterns, and the new voting patterns that emerge are often lasting. Many political scientists agree that there have been at least five such critical elections in the nation's history:

✔ **1. The Election of 1828:** No candidate received a majority of electoral votes in the election of 1824. The House of Representatives awarded the election to John Quincy Adams, even though Andrew Jackson won more Electoral College votes than Adams. Jackson mounted a populist campaign in 1828 to avenge his loss in 1824, arguing for broader popular participation in the election of the president. His message caught fire, catapulting him into office and establishing a new alignment of voters, which represented in Jackson's words the "common man," for the Democratic Party.

✔ **2. The Election of 1860:** Slavery was the defining issue in the election of 1860, which saw the emergence of the Republican Party as the second major party (the Democrats being the other one) in American politics. Republican Abraham Lincoln won the support of the northern establishment, including bankers, industrialists, merchants, and laborers. Southern whites supported the Democrats, an allegiance that continued for the long haul. The Republican Party won seven of the next nine presidential races.

✔ **3. The Election of 1896:** By 1896 new problems plagued the nation, pitting the interests of the older agrarian economy against the industrialists. The realignment of voters over these problems did not result in a realignment to a Democratic majority; rather, it reinforced Republican dominance as new groups of voters were becoming aligned with the Republican Party. Farming and mining interests in the West, along with industrial worker interests in the Northeast, supported Republican initiatives to reduce corporate industrialism. Republican William McKinley won on a platform advocating a high protective tariff, a single gold standard, and an aggressive foreign policy. The Republicans would remain the dominant party up until the Great Depression of the 1930s.

✔ **4. The Election of 1932:** Economic depression was foremost on people's minds during the election of 1932. Fourteen million people lost their jobs during the time between the stock market crash in 1929 and this election. Hundreds of financial institutions failed, wiping out the life savings of millions. The gross national product fell by one-third. All this occurred during the administration of Republican President Herbert Hoover. Hoover's limited attempts to deal with the economic depression were inconsequential, paving the way for a realignment of working-class voters, immigrants, and union members to the Democratic Party under the leadership of Franklin Delano Roosevelt. FDR advocated a strong activist role for government to solve the nation's economic woes.

✔ **5. The Election of 1968:** The election of Richard M. Nixon in 1968 marked the end of Democratic domination of the presidency. The Democratic Party candidate would win only three of the ten presidential races between 1968 and 2004. In this time period, Republicans also captured majorities of both houses of Congress. The election of 1968 ushered in what many refer to as a period of "dealignment," when neither party has a lock on the electorate.

A third realigning election in the modern party era occurred in 1896. That election did not result in a clear shifting of voter preferences from one party to another; rather, it marked the rise of the Republican Party to a near total consolidation of power and voter support in the northern and western states, as well as the continued Democratic Party dominance in southern states. Republican candidate William McKinley won the 1896 election, and with it a realignment of new allegiances to the

Republican Party. Indeed, the only Democrat to capture the presidency between 1896 and 1932 was Woodrow Wilson, and Wilson's initial success was more a consequence of Theodore Roosevelt's split with the Republican Party than it was a result of an expanded Democratic base. Roosevelt, a Republican president from 1901 to 1909, formed the Progressive "Bull Moose" Party and ran as its presidential candidate in 1912. He in effect split the Republican vote across two candidates, handing Democrat Woodrow Wilson an Electoral College victory.

In 1912, the Republican Party's progressive and conservative wings split, giving the Democrats the White House and a majority in both houses of Congress. Within six years, however, Republicans regained control of Congress and were well-positioned to retake the White House in 1920. During the sixty-two-year period from 1870 to 1932, the two major parties developed their party organizations and shored up their voting coalitions. They institutionalized their power in Congress by creating the party caucuses and electing party leaders. Also, during this period the Democrats and Republicans developed party organizations so strong that the two-party Democrat–Republican system would become permanently institutionalized in American politics.

A fourth realigning election in the modern party era resulted from shifting party allegiances in the midst of the Great Depression. Republican President Herbert Hoover was elected in 1928, less than a year before the stock market crash of 1929 sent the economy into a tailspin. Hoover and the Republicans adopted some limited measures to deal with the economic disaster, but they maintained their party's traditional conservative faith in the dynamics of the market to solve economic problems. Franklin Delano Roosevelt, the Democratic candidate opposing Hoover in 1932, advocated a substantially larger and more activist role for government in dealing with the Depression. Roosevelt's pledge of a "New Deal" and an activist government won the support of the urban working class, people of lower socioeconomic status, new immigrants, and many Catholics and Jews. The shift in allegiances from the Republican Party to the Democratic Party in 1932 (FDR carried forty-two states and 60 percent of the vote) had a lasting impact on voters. Adding the "New Deal coalition" to the "solid Democratic South" resulted in Democratic Party domination of American politics for at least the next thirty-six years. The policies of Democratic Presidents Roosevelt, Harry Truman, John F. Kennedy, and Lyndon Johnson during this era, supported by large Democratic majorities in Congress, were the product of the powerful New Deal coalition established in 1932.

Since 1968, however, both the New Deal coalition and the Democrats' solid grip on the South have declined.[9] At the same time, the century-long southern hostility

President Franklin Delano Roosevelt, a Democrat, campaigning for re-election in Hartford, Connecticut, in 1936.

toward the Republican Party of Abraham Lincoln has diminished, as many conservatives in the South have become attracted to the Republican Party and its socially conservative agenda. Between 1969 and 2008, the Democrats controlled the White House for just twelve years, whereas the Republicans held the White House for twenty-eight years. During that same period, the Democrats have controlled both chambers of Congress for twenty-two years, the Republicans for ten years, and there have been eight years of split majorities in the House and Senate. No clear critical elections appear to have occurred over this time frame, and few patterns in voter realignment are obvious. Indeed, some political scientists have argued that the term **dealignment**[10] best describes the behavior of voters since the 1960s. Dealignment refers to the decline in both voter attachment to parties and clarity of party coalitions.

★ Dealignment

A decline in voter attachment to parties and in clarity of party coalitions.

The August 2006 Senate Democratic primary defeat of Senator Joseph Lieberman of Connecticut, the Democratic candidate for vice president in 2000, offers some indication that both the Democratic and the Republican parties are currently struggling with their own identities. (Lieberman went on to win that fall as an independent candidate in the general election.) The subsequent Democratic sweep of both houses of Congress in the 2006 midterm elections added further weight to the theory of dealignment: in the eyes of many, voters were expressing their displeasure with President Bush's handling of the Iraq War, rather than indicating an overall state of dissatisfaction with Republican economic and social policies.

Still, the 2008 election, in which the Democratic Party won the presidency and substantially increased its majorities in both the House and Senate, suggests the possibility that a new alignment toward the Democratic Party may be in the offing.

The Functions of Parties

Political parties serve a number of critical functions in the American political system at the national, state, and local levels of government. They give organizational coherence to both the operations of popular elections and the management of government. The functions that political parties serve have become inseparable from the principles that define how Americans choose leaders and how elected leaders formulate and administer public policies.

Contesting Elections

Free and open elections are the hallmark of the American republican form of government. With winning elections as their principal goal, political parties promote the prominence, competitiveness, and significance of elections in America. By winning elections and occupying seats in the government, members of the party can influence public policy. The larger the number of elective seats that a party controls, the greater the party's potential influence on policy outcomes. Thus contesting elections lies at the core of a political party's functions.

To contest elections most effectively, the two major parties in the United States have developed a large set of party organizations. These organizations, which operate at the national, state, and local levels, are engaged in a number of activities directed toward winning elections. These activities include fund-raising, organizing events and meetings, providing funding to candidates who are running for office, recruiting and organizing volunteers who want to work for the election of candidates, and purchasing services (for example, polling services, political advertisements, campaign materials such as bumper stickers, direct mail to homes, and so forth) to promote the election of candidates. Many election contests feature a candidate from the party currently in office (the incumbent candidate) defending his or her record against an alternative candidate from the party out of power. The fact that political parties are organized to contest elections and offer alter-native proposals for making public policy promotes the responsiveness of elected officials to the voters: by

---

[9] For a thorough analysis of how the American party system has changed since the New Deal, see Sidney M. Milkus, *The President and the Parties: The Transformation of the American Party System Since the New Deal* (New York: Oxford University Press, 1993).

[10] Paul Allen Beck, "The Dealignment Era in America," in M. N. Dalton, T. T. Flanagan, and H. Beck, eds., *Electoral Change in Advanced Industrial Democracies: Realignment or Dealignment* (Princeton, NJ: Princeton University Press, 1984).

Political parties rely on volunteers for a variety of services. Top, volunteers for 2008 Democratic presidential candidate Barack Obama meet with a staff member of Obama's election campaign to plan strategy. Bottom, volunteers working for 2008 Republican presidential candidate John McCain in California.

offering voters alternative candidates more in line with public opinion, parties provide an effective mechanism for voters to remove leaders from office through elections. The alternative candidates offered by the Democratic and Republican parties also serve to organize the process of competitive elections in the United States, because the vast majority of elections feature a Democratic candidate running against a Republican candidate. Some elections include independent or third-party candidates, and in some elections a Democratic candidate or a Republican candidate runs unchallenged. But most election contests feature some form of competition between candidates from the two major parties.

Recruiting and Nominating Candidates

Political parties are the main vehicles through which candidates for office are recruited and screened. The fact that parties exist to win elections gives them the incentive to recruit candidates to run for office under the party label. Parties want to find candidates who will represent the party well, and thus they provide a "weeding out" process resulting in higher-quality candidates.

Most recruiting and promoting of candidates begins at the local party level. Individuals interested in politics often donate their time and efforts to working for political parties by, among other things, attending and participating in party meetings, distributing campaign literature, and driving candidates to campaign events. Local organizations tend to reward this service work with nominations for local offices, such as a seat on a local school board or a planning and zoning board. Successful candidates for these local offices often move up through the ranks of the local party organization to earn the endorsement and nomination of their party for higher office.

Providing a Framework for Voters to Make Vote Choices

Political parties also provide a useful framework for voters who must choose among candidates for elective office. Without even knowing the names of particular candidates for office, voters may be cued in to those candidates' political, ideological, and policy perspectives on the basis of a candidate's party. Most voters associate the political parties with at least broad approaches to governing, if not positions on specific policy issues. For example, on the role that government should play in fixing economic problems, most voters perceive the Democratic Party to be more likely to support an active role for government, whereas Republicans are perceived as having a more "hands off" approach, preferring economic problems to correct themselves through the free market.

The organizational framework for voters to assess candidates is the political party. This framework helps voters more easily process and evaluate campaign information.

American Government . . . in Popular Perspective:

Partisan Differences on Key Issues

Voters who consider themselves Democrats tend to have different perspectives on policy issues than those who consider themselves Republicans. The following figures indicate how identifiers with each of the major parties differ in their positions on various issues.

"Overall, do you approve or disapprove of gay and lesbian couples being allowed to get married?"

Source: May 2005 survey by the *Boston Globe.*

"Would you favor or oppose allowing oil and gas drilling in the Alaskan Arctic National Wildlife Refuge?"

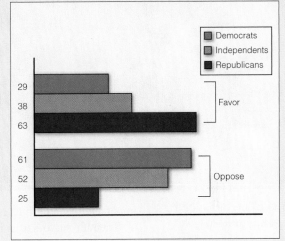

Source: Pew Center poll, March 2005.

"Do you have confidence in George W. Bush's ability to make the right decisions about Social Security, or are you uneasy about his approach?"

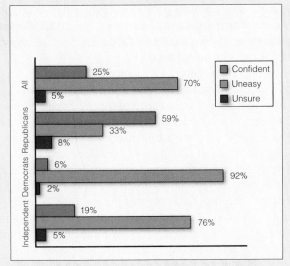

Source: CBS News Poll, April 2005. Copyright © 2005 CBS Broadcasting, Inc. All Rights Reserved. Used courtesy of CBS News.

"The United States Supreme Court handed down a landmark decision in 1973, called Roe versus Wade, *which legalized abortion. Generally speaking, are you in favor of the Supreme Court decision which permits a woman to get an abortion from a doctor at any time, or are you opposed to that, or are you indifferent on the subject—or haven't you heard enough about that yet to say?"*

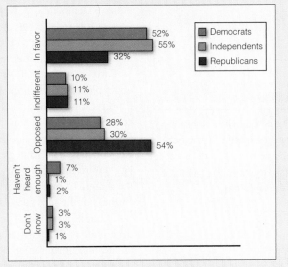

Source: Los Angeles Times poll, December 2003.

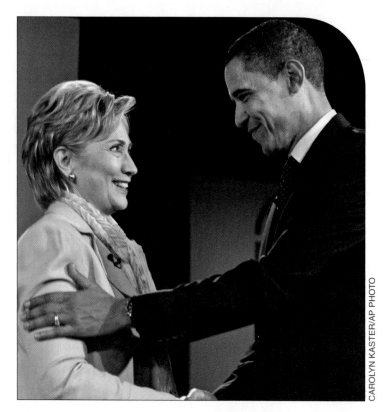

Party labels thus offer voters an efficient shortcut mechanism for choosing among candidates. For instance, the Democratic Party and candidates running under that label are often regarded by voters as being more liberal or left of center in their position on issues, whereas candidates under the Republican Party label are viewed as being more conservative or right of center. Party identification is the psychological connection that voters have with a political party that influences other attitudes (such as one's position on gun control) as well as voting behavior. **Party identification,** an individual's feeling of attachment to a particular political party, is a political attitude that begins to form early in a person's life and generally remains quite stable throughout his or her lifetime. The authors of a classic book on American voting behavior, titled *The American Voter,*[11] described party identification as "generally a psychological identification which can persist without legal recognition or evidence of formal membership." Party identification serves an

CAROLYN KASTER/AP PHOTO

Senators Hillary Clinton (D-NY) and Barack Obama (D-IL) waged a long battle for the 2008 Democratic presidential nomination.

important role in forming attitudes on particular issues and making vote decisions.

Scientific surveys usually measure party identification by asking questions such as: "Generally speaking, do you think of yourself as a Republican, a Democrat, an independent, or what?" Scholars began measuring party identification in the 1950s, and research on the concept has revealed several important findings. First, although the number of independents has grown slightly over the years, there are many more party identifiers than there are independents. Indeed, the majority of Americans today identify with a political party. Second, whereas the Democratic Party had more identifiers than the Republican Party from the mid-1940s to the 1980s, the number of Democrats and Republicans is nearly equal today. As a consequence, the two major parties enjoy pretty much equal amounts of support from the American public. Third, despite these shifts, party identification in the electorate is quite resistant to change. Thus, from one election to another, voting patterns remain remarkably stable and rarely deviate from either a Democratic or Republican victory. Fourth, party identification plays a very important role in helping voters make voting decisions: as shown in Figure 13.1, the vast majority of Republican identifiers vote for Republican candidates and the vast majority of Democratic identifiers vote for Democratic candidates.[12]

Party identification is also an important concept for candidates and party leaders in plotting campaign strategies and contesting elections. As political scientist Phillip Converse has noted, a **normal vote**[13] can be expected for any given election contest. That is, a certain percentage of voters can be expected to cast a ballot for the Democrats, whereas another predictable percentage can be expected to vote for the Republicans. The strategy designed to win an election, and the chances that the strategy will result in a victory, largely depend on the normal vote distribution. The larger the margin of one party's normal vote, the less competitive is the race. The competitiveness of the race can also be influenced by the number of the nonpartisan voters.

Though party identification is defined as a psychological attachment that an individual has to a particular political party and is regarded by political scientists as an attitude, formal membership in a political party is generally associated with the process of voter registration. In addition to making a citizen eligible to vote, the voter registration process in many states includes registering as a member of

★ Party identification

The psychological attachment that an individual has to a particular party.

★ Normal vote

The percentage of voters that can be expected with reasonable certainty to cast a ballot for each of the two major political parties.

[11] Angus Campbell, Philip E. Converse, Warren E. Miller, and Donald E. Stokes, *The American Voter* (New York: Wiley, 1960).
[12] For a thorough discussion of the concept of party identification, see Warren E. Miller and J. Merrill Shanks, *The New American Voter* (Cambridge, MA: Harvard University Press, 1996).
[13] Philip E. Converse, "The Concept of the Normal Vote" in Angus Campbell, Philip E. Converse, Warren E. Miller, and Donald E. Stokes, eds., *Elections and the Political Order* (New York: Wiley, 1966).

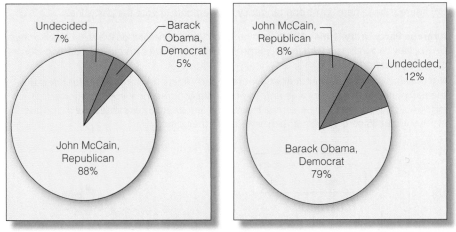

Figure 13.1 Party Identifiers Who Say They Will Support the Party Line

In the 2008 presidential election, who Republican voters supported:

- Undecided 7%
- Barack Obama, Democrat 5%
- John McCain, Republican 88%

In the 2008 presidential election, who Democratic voters supported:

- John McCain, Republican 8%
- Undecided, 12%
- Barack Obama, Democrat 79%

Source: Fox News/Opinion Dynamics Poll, September 2008.

a political party. In some states, membership in a political party is a necessary precondition for voting in that political party's primary elections to select the candidates who will represent the party in a general election. States with open primaries do not limit the nomination process to voters of one party. State laws govern how a citizen becomes a member of a political party and thus eligible to vote in the party's primary election contests. In most states, it is possible to register to vote but not be a member of any particular party. The rules for becoming a member of a party vary widely from state to state.

Providing Organization for the Operations of Government

The majority party organizes its respective institution to accomplish the task of governing.[14] The leadership organization in the House and Senate is based primarily on majority-party leadership. The top leadership position in the House of Representative is the Speaker of the House, who is always chosen by the majority-party caucus of the House. The chief leadership position in the Senate is the majority leader, who is selected by the majority-party caucus in the Senate. Members of the majority party chair committees in both houses of Congress. Leaders in Congress then try to implement the campaign pledges and platforms advocated by their party during the previous election campaigns. The executive branch, headed by the president, includes various departments and agencies that conduct the work of the federal government. Partisanship and loyalty to the president's political party are important factors that influence whom the president appoints to lead these agencies and departments.

AP PHOTO/PABLO MARTINEZ MONSIVAIS

Chief Justice of the United States John Roberts (left) administers the oath of office to the newly appointed Treasury Secretary, Henry Paulson, in 2006, as President Bush looks on. Paulson, a loyal Republican, was tapped by the Republican president to lead the Treasury department.

[14] For a discussion of governance and the parties, see John H. Aldrich, *Why Parties? The Origin and Transformation of Political Parties in America* (Chicago: University of Chicago Press, 1995), chapter 7.

Figure 13.2 Partisan Voting in Congress

The way a member of Congress votes on a bill is largely influenced by the political party to which the member belongs. No member is compelled to vote the party line, and there are many instances when a member does not use party as a voting cue. However, as the following figure shows, there is a strong tendency for members to vote the party line.

Average Party Unity, 1964–1999: *Percentage of Party Unity votes on which members voted 'yea' or 'nay' in agreement with the majority of their party. Failures to vote lowered scores for chambers and parties.*

Not only has there been a tendency to vote the party line, but over the past four decades the party line has become increasingly important in congressional voting. Whereas in 1964 slightly less than 70 percent of House and Senate members voted the party line, in 1999 about 85 percent of members voted with their party.

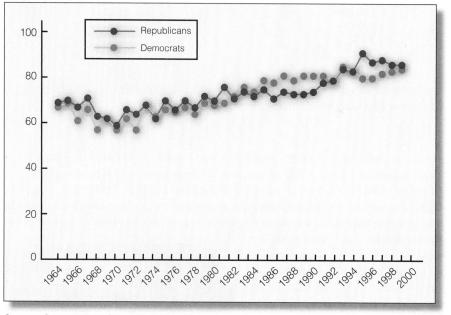

Source: Congressional Quarterly Weekly.

Average Party Unity by Region. Party line voting is strong among members across the nation. However, it is strongest among southern Republicans, who tend to be more conservative on social issues, which drives the conservative Republican agenda. Party line voting is weakest among southern Democrats, many of whom also endorse the social conservative agenda.

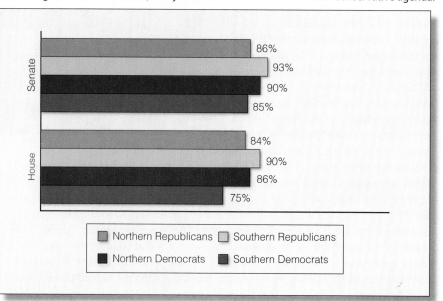

Source: Congressional Quarterly Weekly.

The policy agenda and important policy decisions are largely the result of the political party organization and partisan leadership of these key branches of government. The greater a party's control over the key governing institution, the more power that party has in influencing public policy. When the Democratic Party has a majority in both the House and the Senate and occupies the presidency, the Democratic Party has virtual control over what laws get passed. For example, the 1932 elections brought FDR, a Democrat, into the White House and resulted in increased Democratic majorities in both houses of Congress. The result of this dominance was passage of numerous laws promoting active government involvement in dealing with the Great Depression.

Divided government,[15] on the other hand, refers to split party control of Congress and the presidency. Because both houses of Congress are required for passing new laws, when the majority party in at least one house of Congress differs from the party occupying the presidency, a form of divided government exists. For example, beginning in January 2007 the Democrats controlled both houses of Congress, whereas the Republican President George W. Bush was still in the White House. The presence of divided government often makes it difficult for either party to advance its policy goals and objectives.

Whereas the first 150 years of the republic was mostly characterized by one party controlling both branches of government, the last half century has been dominated by divided government. For example, during the eight years that Republican Ronald Reagan was president, the Democrats held a majority of seats in the House of Representatives, and they continued to do so through Republican George H. W. Bush's administration that followed. During the administration of Democratic President Bill Clinton, the Republicans maintained a majority of seats in both houses for the final six of Clinton's eight years in office. For the first six months of George W. Bush's presidency, the Republicans held control of the House, while the Senate was split 50–50 among Democrats and Republicans, with the tie-breaking vote going to Vice President Dick Cheney. The defection of Vermont Senator James Jeffords from the Republican Party in mid-2001 gave the Democrats a majority in the Senate, resulting in a situation of divided government. After the 2002 elections, Republicans reasserted control over the Senate, and united government under Republican control was established for the next four years. Yet with a Democratic sweep of the House and Senate in November 2006, President Bush was forced to navigate through the perils of divided government for the remainder of his time in office.

The Democratic Party ended divided government with Barack Obama's 2008 presidential election victory over Republican challenger John McCain. In addition, the Democratic Party caucuses increased their margins in both the House of Representatives and the Senate.

Many observers of American politics question the rationality of an American electorate that so often sends one party to the presidency, yet keeps the opposite party in control of Congress. The stalemate or gridlock that may result from divided government is problematic to some. Still, many Americans believe that divided government has its benefits; certainly divided control tends to intensify the checks and balances on power envisioned by the framers of the Constitution.

Why a Two-Party System?

Political parties are an integral part of many of the world's democracies. Contemporary party systems are largely a product of the unique characteristics, history, issues, and social class structure of any given nation.

Though party systems in a democracy vary in numerous ways, they may generally be classified into one of two general types—(1) **two-party systems** and (2) **multiparty systems.** The United States features a two-party system, dominated

★ **Divided government**

Split party control of Congress and the presidency.

★ **Two-party system**

A party system dominated by two major parties that win the vast majority of elections.

★ **Multiparty system**

A political system in which many different parties are organized on the basis of political ideologies, economic interests, positions on a single issue or set of issues, religion, or geography.

Chapter 13: Political Parties

---

[15] See Richard S. Conley, *The Presidency, Congress and Divided Government* (College Station: Texas A&M University Press, 2002).

[16] For a good discussion of the rationale for America's two-party system, see Frank J. Sorauf, *Party Politics in America*, 5th ed. (Boston: Little, Brown, 1984).

Democratic presidential hopeful John Edwards speaks at Steelworker Union Hall in South Carolina while on the campaign trail in 2007.

by the Democratic and Republican parties.[16] The vast size and organizational structure of the two major parties, coupled with the fact that these two parties win the great majority of elections, appropriately classifies the United States as a two-party system. Other democracies feature as many as ten parties of relatively equal stature. The nations with multiparty systems typically include parties organized on the basis of political ideologies (such as the socialist party or conservative party), particular economic interests (such as the agricultural party or the industrial party), positions on a single issue or set of issues, religion, or geography.

In the United States, there is a wide range of ideological views, economic interests, religious orientations, ethnic groups, and geographic disparities. Other nations with such a wide diversity of interests typically rely on multiple parties to represent these different components of the population. However, in the United States a two-party model has persisted now for more than two centuries.

Reasons for the Two-Party System in the United States

What are the factors that contribute to the American two-party model? A key factor is the Electoral College system for selecting the president of the United States. In order to win the presidency, a candidate must obtain a majority, not simply a plurality, of votes in the Electoral College. Naturally, this requirement encourages groups of voters to align with one of the major political parties, lest their votes be wasted. Minority groups, such as blue-collar union members, which have no chance of achieving a majority of votes as a single unified party, have found it in their best interest to support one of the two major parties in a presidential election. Being part of a winning coalition yields more influence than being in a smaller unified group with no chance of winning.

A second important factor that promotes the two-party system is the winner-take-all process that prevails in selecting members of Congress. In U.S. congressional elections, only the candidate with the most votes in a single district wins the seat. For example, in a race for a Senate seat, if the Democratic candidate receives 40 percent of the vote, the Republican 35 percent, the Reform Party candidate 15 percent, and the Green Party 10 percent, the Democratic candidate with the 40 percent plurality is elected to Congress. By contrast, in other democracies, such as Israel, France, and Germany, forms of **proportional representation** are used. Under this system, the percentage of the vote that a party receives is reflected in the number of seats that that party occupies in the national legislature. In Israel, for example, a party that receives as little as 1.5 percent of the vote nationally is entitled to at least one seat in the 120-seat Knesset (the Israeli legislature). Whereas a proportional representation system gives minor parties representation in the legislature, the winner-take-all system does not. A third party must win the most votes in any given election contest to win a seat. The winner-take-all system promotes the two-party system and prevents smaller parties from achieving even minimal representation in the national legislature.

A third factor promoting the two-party system is the ideological nature of public opinion in American. Most Americans are ideologically centrist, or moderate, with few considering themselves strong ideologues (see Figure 13.3). The lack of strong ideological differences helps explain why only two parties dominate American politics. Neither the Democratic nor the Republican Party can afford to be too strongly ideological because to be so would risk building a winning coalition in elections.

★ Proportional representation

A system of electing a national legislature in which the percentage of the vote that a party receives is reflected in the number of seats that the party occupies.

Figure 13.3 Ideological Distribution of American Voters
Americans tend to be middle-of-the-road when it comes to describing their own political ideologies. Very few consider themselves either extreme conservatives or extreme liberals. The plurality of Americans describe themselves as being right in the middle of the ideological spectrum.

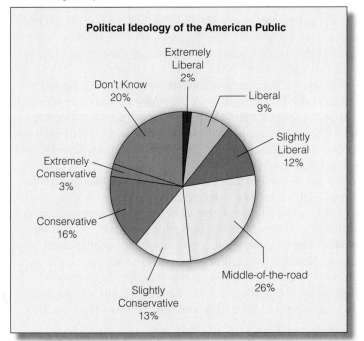

Source: 2004 American National Election Study, University of Michigan.

A fourth factor promoting the two-party system are the laws and regulations that govern campaigns in United States, which tend to benefit the major parties at the expense of third parties. For example, in order to qualify for matching federal funds for presidential campaigns and many state gubernatorial campaigns, candidates must demonstrate a minimum level of support in prior elections and/or primary elections. Most minor parties, however, are eligible to receive such funds only after the election is over. They receive public funding in federal elections, for example, if (1) they receive 5 percent of the popular vote and (2) they appear on the ballot in

Robert Barr, the Libertarian Party candidate for president in 2008.

at least ten states. Because money to finance a campaign is necessary during, rather than after, the campaign, third parties are at a serious disadvantage. The lack of a history and lack of public interest in third-party primary elections precludes most from receiving federal or state funding in these elections. For a third party's candidate to appear on election ballots in the states, the party must meet a number of criteria, including petitions supporting the candidate and often significant fees.

Minor and Third Parties

Despite the dominance of the Republican and Democratic parties over the past century and a half, a number of third parties have contested elections in the United States. The most recent third party of note was the Green Party, from which Ralph Nader launched his presidential campaign during the 2000 election.[17] Most third-party candidates fail to register even one percentage point of the popular vote in presidential elections, and few third-party candidates are found in the U.S. Congress, in state legislatures or governorships, or in local government. For the past 150 years, not one president has been elected who did not run as either a Democrat or Republican.

Even the few-and-far-between third-party candidacies that have attracted a sizeable percentage of popular votes in presidential elections have experienced only short-lived success (see Table 13.1). The Progressive or "Bull Moose" Party of Theodore Roosevelt, for example, garnered 27 percent of the vote in 1912, but failed to establish itself as a permanent threat to the two major parties. Its success was largely based on Roosevelt's stature and popularity, and by 1916 TR had returned to the Republican fold. Likewise, Ross Perot, running as an independent in the 1992 presidential race, captured nearly 20 percent of the popular vote. But his attempt to match his 1992 success met with disappointment in his 1996 bid, when he took only 9 percent of the popular vote. By 2000, Perot's Reform Party showed up as barely a blip in the vote totals.[18]

Third parties face a number of obstacles in their attempt to become viable. First, their mostly negligible chance of winning at the outset leads many voters to sense that a vote for a third party would be wasted. The strong historical and cultural institutionalization of the American two-party system is another obstacle third parties face. The sizeable number of voters who identify themselves as either a Democrat or Republican inclines most voters to support major-party candidates in elections. In addition to the legal barriers already discussed, media coverage of campaigns also plays a role; the media tend to focus most coverage on the two major parties, with little attention given to third-party candidacies.

Still, third parties persist. Despite their limited success in winning important government positions, they often have substantial influence on the outcome of elections. Third-party candidates in hotly contested presidential races have on occasion siphoned off enough votes from one of the major-party candidates to provide an Electoral College victory to the other major party. Twice since 1832 a third party has won more than 20 percent of the popular vote in a presidential race, and five times during this period a third party has won at least 10 percent of the popular vote.

Political scientist James Q. Wilson, a student of third parties, has identified four basic types of third parties. **Economic protest parties** tend to emerge in

★ Economic protest party

A party that emerges in times of economic recession to express discontent with the ruling party.

---

[17] Nader was technically the Green Party candidate for president in 1996 as well, but he was only on 22 state ballots that year, and his candidacy labored under a self-imposed spending limit of $5,000. In the 2004 presidential election the Green Party candidate was Texas attorney David Cobb; Nader ran as an independent in 2004.

[18] For a good discussion of nineteenth- and twentieth-century third-party candidacies, see Steven J. Rosenstone, Roy L. Behr, and Edward H. Lazarus, *Third Parties in America*, 2nd ed. (Princeton, NJ: Princeton University Press, 1996).

Table 13.1 Important Third-Party Candidacies in Presidential Races

Third parties are by no means a new phenomenon in American politics. Despite their tendency to be short-lived and their relative lack of success in capturing elective office, third-party movements endure, often affecting whether the Republican or Democratic Party candidate wins office.

The following is a select list of third parties and their respective candidates who registered vote totals in presidential elections:

Year	Party	Candidate	% of Popular Vote
1832	Anti-Masonic	William Wirt	8
1856	Know-Nothing	Millard Fillmore	22
1892	Populist	James Weaver	9
1912	Bull Moose	Theodore Roosevelt	27
1912	Socialist	Eugene V. Debs	6
1924	Progressive	Robert La Follette	17
1948	State's Rights	Strom Thurmond	2
1948	Progressive	Henry Wallace	2
1968	American Independent	George Wallace	14
1980	National Unity	John Anderson	7
1992	United We Stand America	Ross Perot	19
1996	Reform	Ross Perot	9
2000	Green	Ralph Nader	3
2004	Independent	Ralph Nader	1

times of economic recession. In the 1892 election, for example, the Populist Party advocated the free coinage of silver, as an alternative to the gold standard. (The Populists won 9 percent of the popular vote.) Similarly, Ross Perot's campaign in 1992 expressed strong discontent with the economic policies of the George H. W. Bush administration, including the budget deficit and trade policies. Perot won 19 percent of the popular vote.

A second type of third party is the **ideological party,** which promotes broad ideas about the purpose and role of government. In the United States, the Libertarian Party advocates an extremely minimalist role for government, whereas the Socialist Party stands at the opposite end of the spectrum, advocating a much broader and significant role for government. Third is the **issue party,** which tends to form on the basis

★ **Ideological party**

A party that promotes broad ideas about the purpose and role of government.

★ **Issue party**

A party that tends to form on the basis of a single issue.

Chapter 13: Political Parties

Former professional wrestler Jesse Ventura ran a successful independent bid for governor of Minnesota in 1998.

of a single issue. After a short period of time, issue parties generally fade away. An example is the Liberty Party, which advocated abolition of slavery. It appeared in several elections prior to 1848, when it merged with the Free Soil Party. (The Free Soil Party was a precursor to the Republican Party, which ran a candidate for president beginning in 1856.)

Finally, there are **factional parties**—pieces from one or both of the major parties that have split off to form a separate party. Theodore Roosevelt formed the Progressive Party and ran in the 1912 election after he lost the Republican Party nomination to President William Howard Taft. Roosevelt won 28 percent of the popular vote to Taft's 23 percent, helping Democrat Woodrow Wilson to win the presidency. Similarly, in 1924 Senator Robert La Follette of Wisconsin left the Republican Party to form a newer version of the Progressive Party and took 17 percent of the popular vote. In 1980, Republican Congressman John Anderson of Illinois, after failing to achieve the Republican Party's nomination for president, formed the National Unity Party; in the election Anderson received 7 percent of the popular vote.

★ Factional party

A party that has split off from one of the major parties.

Party Organizations

Political parties exist through party organizations at the national, state, and local levels. Though most elected government officials are members of the Democratic or Republican parties, political parties also exist as organizations outside of the

Table 13.2 Third Parties Today

Despite the lack of electoral success by third parties, many continue to operate in the United States today. Listed here are a few of them, along with a description of their reason for being:

1. The Natural Law Party: This party advocates "all-party" government, which it defines as "bringing together the best ideas, programs, and leaders from all political parties and the private sector to solve and prevent problems." The party argues that bringing the individual lives of people and national policies into harmony with the "natural law" will best solve the nation's problems.

2. The Constitution Party: This party bases the foundation of its political activities on religious principles of Christianity. It argues that the U.S. Constitution established a "republic under God, rather than a democracy."

3. The Reform Party: Ross Perot ran as a candidate in the 1992 presidential election under the organization called "United We Stand America." He ran to protest the leadership of both the Republican and Democratic parties and won 19 percent of the popular vote. In 1996, Perot reorganized under the Reform Party name and won 9 percent of the popular vote. Former Republican Pat Buchanan was a Reform Party candidate for president in 2000, receiving 0.5 percent of the popular vote.

4. The Libertarian Party: This party endorses the notion that government should be small and limited, interfering as little as possible with the lives of citizens. The Libertarian Party argues that "individuals have the right to exercise sole dominion over their own lives, they have the right to live in whatever manner they choose so long as they do not interfere with the rights of others." Libertarians place a premium on individual liberties and personal responsibility.

5. Socialist Party: Whereas the Libertarians support a very limited role for government, the Socialist Party supports active government involvement in providing equitable distributions of resources in society. Socialists endorse a strong government role in providing health care, jobs, housing, and education, among other public programs. Although Bernie Sanders won election in 2006 as a U.S. senator from Vermont running as a self-described "Democratic Socialist," he does not belong to the Socialist Party.

6. Green Party: The foundation of the Green Party rests on pro-environmentalist positions like "Green" parties in other democracies, such as Germany and France. In the United States, the Green Party is also identified with a number of social justice causes, including feminism, promotion of diversity, and global responsibility. Green Party candidate Ralph Nader took 2.7 percent of the popular vote in the 2000 election, finishing in third place.

---

government. These party organizations, which often count millions of volunteers among their members, articulate positions on issues, enlist members from the public at large, recruit candidates who will run under the party label for elective office, raise money from individuals, corporations, and interest groups, and provide organizational and campaign services to candidates who are running for office.

Andrew Jackson is regarded as the father of the **national party organization.** Up until the election of 1828, a party's candidates for president and vice president were nominated by the party congressional caucus. Jackson changed this process by establishing a national party convention to be held several months before a presidential election. The convention brings together state and local party leaders to nominate the party's candidates for president and vice president. In addition to party leaders, the national conventions today include delegates from the states elected by members of the party in presidential primary elections.

Since the middle of the nineteenth century, both the Democratic and Republican national party organizations have been run by a **national committee,** which oversees the conduct of the presidential campaign and develops strategy for each party's congressional elections as well. The national committees, consisting of state and local

★ National party organization

The institution through which political parties exist at the national, state, and local levels, primarily focused on articulating policy positions, raising money, organizing volunteers, and providing services to candidates.

★ National committee

The committee that oversees the conduct of a party's presidential campaign and develops strategy for congressional elections.

Barack Obama accepts the presidential nomination of the Democratic Party at that party's national convention in 2008.

★ National committee
 chair

The head of the national committee for one of the two major
parties.

party representatives, are run by a **national committee chair** chosen soon after the presidential election has concluded.

At the national level, the committees, chairs, and party organization largely provide a supportive role during the presidential campaign. Once providing a core advisory role to a presidential candidate, the national organizations today are more involved in helping their candidate raise money and campaign for office. Strategy, planning, and advising are now handled mostly by the candidate's own campaign staff, which typically includes a media consultant, a pollster, a campaign manager, and various other campaign consultants. The modern-day national party organization is also less influential in determining who the nominee will be and more responsive to the victorious candidate's personal campaign staff. They do maintain greater influence in assisting state and local party efforts to win elections by providing polling and media consulting services, campaign management services, and financial resources.

In the modern era, state and local party organizations tend to be more influential in the nomination of candidates, in developing and organizing campaigns, and in providing a cue to voters about their vote selections. Voters pay less attention to campaigns in state and local elections and therefore depend more on partisan cues in their choice of candidates. State legislative and local election campaigns generally have limited resources to mount significant image-building campaigns for candidates. Candidates are thus more dependent on the resources of the state and local party organizations for financing. Local party organizations provide "get-out-the-vote" (GOTV) services by funding phone banks to contact voters directly. State and local organizations also fund and make available polling services and media consulting services to candidates in less visible races. Benefiting from these services, candidates for local and state offices may feel the need to be more responsive to the party organizations.

Local party organizations also provide the grassroots manpower for soliciting mass participation in political activities. These activities include implementing voter registration drives, organizing political fund-raisers and rallies, and staffing phone banks to make direct contact with voters urging them to vote for their party's candidates. Local organizations also provide the mechanism for identifying and recruiting talented citizens to become candidates for elective office. They provide the "farm team" for potential candidates for higher offices, such as governor, member of Congress, and senator.

Are Parties in Decline?

Many political scientists contend that the political party is in a state of decline in America. Bolstering this claim is the dealignment thesis described earlier in this chapter, which holds that voters today are less attached to parties and tend to be more independent-minded than they were up through the 1960s. Political scientist Martin Wattenberg[19] argues that increased negativity toward the parties has contributed to party decline. Wattenberg suggests further that the mass media have contributed to this decline by neglecting to cover parties. Prior to the 1960s, voters depended mainly on parties to provide information about political issues and candidates; now voters turn to the media as the prime information source. Furthermore, the medium of television allows candidates today to bypass parties and appeal directly to the public for support. Many candidates now run campaigns that de-emphasize parties and focus primarily on the candidate's image.

Scholars have also noted a decline in the organizational linkages between officeholders and the political parties. Patronage, the practice by which victorious parties offer loyal party members jobs in government, declined substantially during the past century. Under the patronage system, parties were able to retain the strong support of many of their members by offering the prospect of a good government job if the party was victorious. The civil service and other reforms seriously limited a political party's ability to offer jobs or other favors in return for supporting the party. Although these reforms have eroded the power of parties, they have also improved the quality of government officials and reduced corruption in government affairs.

Changes in the way candidates are nominated by a party have also reduced the power of party organizations. Until recently, parties exerted powerful control over the process by which an individual becomes a candidate wearing the party label in a general election. Without endorsement of the party organization, candidates for president, Congress, and state and local office once were virtually precluded from running under the party label. However, reforms in the 1960s and 1970s reduced the party organization's role in the nomination process. The **direct primary election,** which provides for the nomination of a candidate based on an open election among all party members, has empowered rank-and-file party members rather than party leaders to choose the party's nominees. Direct primaries make it easier for candidates who are not necessarily approved by the party organization to wear the party label in a general election.

Some scholars, however, are not so convinced that parties are on the decline. They argue that although certain aspects of parties are declining, in other ways parties are showing a resurgence in relevance.[20] For example, parties have adapted quite well

★ Direct primary election

An open election, rather than an election by party leaders, to choose candidates for the general election.

[19] Martin Wattenberg, *The Decline of American Political Parties* (Cambridge, MA: Harvard University Press, 1998).
[20] See, for example, Jeff Cohen, Richard Fleisher, and Paul Kantor, eds., *American Political Parties: Decline or Resurgence?* (Washington, DC: CQ Press, 2001).

to candidate-centered campaigns by servicing candidate organizations. In 2006, the Democratic Party supported some candidates who actually de-emphasized their party identification, and thus helped forge victories for Democrats in congressional districts that were considered moderate-to-conservative.

Whether they are declining or not, at the moment parties remain alive and quite active in American politics. Even though voter partisanship may have waned, party identification still remains a strong determinant of vote choice. Although the parties may be less visible to voters, they continue to exert considerable influence over voting decisions. The Democratic and Republican Party organizations are well-funded and include millions of party workers. Party organizations provide money and expertise to candidates to help them achieve electoral success. The president remains the recognized leader of the party label he wears, and the party with a majority of seats in each house of Congress maintains clear control of the legislative agenda. Although the power of the party may have declined, it is clear that "the party" is far from over in American politics.

Now & Then: Making the Connection

Challenges from third-party candidates for the presidency, such as Ralph Nader in 2000 and James Weaver in 1892, barely threatened the two major parties, although they *did* have a hand in determining *which* of the two major parties won those presidential races. Ross Perot's success in the 1992 presidential election, when he received 19 percent of the popular vote, clearly influenced the tenor of the presidential race that year; the same could be said for Theodore Roosevelt's Bull Moose candidacy in 1912, which captured more than a quarter of the nation's popular vote.

Perhaps these third-party successes have helped to fuel arguments that the major parties' hold on the political system is tenuous. Perot's candidacy in particular led to widespread speculation in the media and elsewhere that the influence of the two major parties was on the decline. Yet on closer examination, the major parties' stronghold on American politics still appears quite impressive. All of the third-party "successes" were highly limited in important respects. Although both men certainly made a splash at the polls, neither Perot nor Nader captured even a single Electoral College vote between them in the only tally that matters to those who aspire to be president. Although he captured more than 1 million popular votes, Weaver's 22 Electoral College votes in 1892 barely registered next to the tallies of the two major candidates (Democrat Grover Cleveland won with 277 votes; Republican Benjamin Harrison ended up with 145). Even former president Theodore Roosevelt was humbled by his showing in the 1912 Electoral College vote, as Woodrow Wilson's tally of 435 was nearly five times as large as Roosevelt's 88, though considerably greater than the 8 electoral votes won by Republican candidate William Howard Taft.

Third parties clearly matter, but not in a way that shows up in the actual governance of the United States. No minor or third-party candidate has ever won the presidency, and relatively few have won gubernatorial or congressional elections. For all the talk of major-party decline and the rise of the independent, the two-party system keeps humming along, rotating seats of power in the United States among a relatively select few who have demonstrated loyalty and dedication to the cause of their respective parties.

Ever since he was elected to the U.S. Senate for the first time in 1988, Senator Joseph Lieberman of Connecticut has been something of a political enigma. In 1998, he was the first prominent Democrat to publicly challenge Bill Clinton for the poor judgment the president exercised in his affair with Monica Lewinsky. However, Lieberman then voted against removing Clinton from office by impeachment the following year. While voting as a classic liberal on social issues, Lieberman has cultivated his reputation as an extreme conservative on military and war issues. Indeed, he was one of the Senate's strongest advocates for continued prosecution of the controversial war in Iraq. And though Lieberman was tapped as the Democratic Party's nominee for vice president in 2000, the Connecticut Senator's status as a Democrat became tenuous after the party's voters in Connecticut rejected him as their nominee for the Senate in 2006. Lieberman ran for reelection that fall as an independent and coasted to victory.

Lieberman continued to caucus with the Democrats after his 2006 election victory, securing for that party a narrow, 51-49 margin of control in the Senate. Still, the Democratic leadership in the 110th Congress could no longer take his support for granted. That became clear early in the 2008 presidential campaign when Lieberman declared his support for Republican Senator John McCain's candidacy over all the Democratic contenders for the White House, including his own home state colleague, Senator Christopher Dodd (D-CT). A serious contender to be McCain's choice for vice president (McCain chose Alaska Governor Sarah Palin instead), Lieberman even received a prominent speaking position at the 2008 Republican National Convention. By contrast, the long-time Democrat was nowhere to be found at the Democratic National Convention in Denver, Colorado, held the previous week.

On http://academic.cengage.com/dautrich, find the Politics Interactive link for a discussion of the narrow working margin in the Senate, and a list of the moderate Democrats and Republicans who are most influential when no one party enjoys a large margin of control over the Senate. Consult as well the various links that relate to other famous mavericks that have confounded their own party leadership time and time again.

JOE RAEDLE/GETTY IMAGES

Senator Joseph Lieberman (I-CT), right, with 2008 Republican presidential candidate John McCain at the Republican National Convention.

http://academic.cengage.com/dautrich

Chapter Summary

★ Because many of the Founders frowned on parties and other factions, the Constitution nowhere mentions or contemplates parties. Nevertheless, the debate over ratification of the Constitution gave rise to two parties: the Federalists and the Anti-Federalists. The United States has had a two-party system ever since.

★ Every presidential and congressional election since 1796 has featured some form of party competition. National party conventions and national party organization originated during Andrew Jackson's presidency. The Democratic and Republican parties have dominated since 1856.

★ Certain elections, such as those of 1860, 1896, and 1932, are considered "critical elections" because they produced sharp and lasting changes in patterns of party loyalty among voters.

★ Some political scientists have termed the era since 1968 as a period of dealignment, characterized by a decline in voter attachment to parties and in clarity of party coalitions.

★ The two major parties have developed large organizations, and they exist at the national, state, and local levels. They assist in fund-raising for candidates, recruiting and organizing volunteers to work for candidates, and purchasing political services to promote the election of candidates.

★ Party identification develops early in a person's political life, psychologically connecting the individual to a political party, which in turn influences other attitudes and voting behavior.

★ Majority-party leadership in Congress organizes that branch to accomplish the task of governing. Partisanship also influences a president's policy positions and appointments.

★ When divided party government exists, it becomes difficult for either party to advance its policy goals and objectives.

★ The U.S. party system had been dominated by Democrats and Republicans since the election of 1856. This two-party system is perpetuated by several factors, including the need for a majority of Electoral College votes (not just a plurality) to win the presidency outright, and a winner-take-all system that makes it especially hard for third parties to succeed to any degree.

★ Third-party candidates rarely attract a significant percentage of popular votes in presidential elections because voters perceive that votes for such a candidate would be wasted and because various legal barriers make it hard for third-party candidates to receive government funding.

★ The decline of patronage and the prevalence of the direct primary election have contributed to the belief that parties are now in decline. Regardless, party identification remains an especially strong determinant of vote choice in America today.

Key Terms

Critical election (p. 394)

Dealignment (p. 397)

Direct primary election (p. 411)

Divided government (p. 403)

Economic protest party (p. 406)

Factional party (p. 408)

Ideological party (p. 407)

Issue party (p. 407)

Multiparty system (p. 403)

National committee (p. 409)

National committee chair (p. 410)

National party convention (p. 392)

National party organization (p. 409)   Party platform (p. 392)   Proportional representation (p. 405)

Normal vote (p. 400)   Political party (p. 389)   Two-party system (p. 403)

Party identification (p. 400)

Resources

Important Books

Aldrich, John H. *Why Parties? The Origin and Transformation of Party Politics in America.* Chicago: University of Chicago Press, 1995.

Beck, Paul Allen. *Party Politics in America,* 5th ed. New York: Longman, 1997.

Bibby, John F. *Politics, Parties and Elections in America.* Belmont, CA: Wadsworth, 2002.

Blevins, David. *American Political Parties in the 21st Century.* New York: McFarland & Co., 2006.

Conley, Richard S. *The Presidency, Congress and Divided Government.* College Station: Texas A&M University Press, 2002.

Green, John C., and Daniel Shay, eds. *The State of the Parties: The Changing Role of Contemporary American Parties.* New York: Rowman and Littlefield, 1996.

Keith, Bruce E., David E. Magleby, Candice J. Nelson, Elizabeth Orr, Mark C. Westlye, and Raymond E. Wolfinger. *The Myth of the Independent Voter.* Berkeley: University of California Press, 1992.

Milkis, Sydney M. *The President and the Parties: The Transformation of the American Party System Since the New Deal.* London: Oxford University Press, 1993.

Rosenstone, Steven J., Roy L. Behr, and Edward H. Lazarus. *Third Parties in America.* Princeton, NJ: Princeton University Press, 1984.

Sundquist, James. *Dynamics of the Party System: Alignment and Realignment of Parties in the United States.* Washington, DC: Brookings Institution Press, 1983.

Wattenberg, Martin P. *The Decline of American Political Parties, 1952–1996.* Cambridge, MA: Harvard University Press, 1998.

Internet Sources

Websites of various political parties:

http://www.natural-law.org (Natural Law Party)

http://www.reformparty.org (Reform Party)

http://www.constitutionparty.com (Constitution Party)

http://www.greens.org (Green Party)

http://www.dsausa.org (Democratic Socialist Party)

http://www.rnc.org (Republican Party)

http://www.democraticparty.org (Democratic Party)

Other useful websites:

http://www.fec.gov (Federal Election Commission website)

http://www.umich.edu/~nes/ (information on partisanship and party identification from the National Election Study can be found at this website)

14 Voting and Participation

★ A Young, Charismatic Campaigner Energizes

Voters and Overcomes the Weight

of History: Now & Then

★ The Legal Structure for Voting

★ Exercising the Franchise

★ Making a Vote Choice

★ Political Participation beyond

the Voting Booth

★ Now & Then: Making the Connection

CHRIS CARLSON/AP PHOTO

**Barack Obama, campaigning
for the presidency in 2008**

A Young, Charismatic Campaigner Energizes Voters and Overcomes the Weight of History: Now & Then

One of the youngest candidates ever to run for the presidency, this Democrat burst on the national political scene, sporting a remarkable talent for energizing the base of a party that had been shut out of the White House for the past eight years. Of course, the party faithful weren't the only ones looking to this new political star for answers: young people newly drawn to electoral politics were attending his political rallies in droves, hoping to see a candidate whose campaign speeches were as inspirational as they were politically strategic. Yet a significant obstacle stood in his way: Americans had never before elected to the White House someone from his demographic group, and doubts naturally followed him: Was America really ready to take this symbolic step? He incurred other attacks as well, first from his formidable Democratic Party rival from the U.S. Senate, and later from his Republican opponent, who both attempted to convince voters that this new brand of politician was in fact an intellectual elitist out of touch with mainstream America. All these attacks, however, proved unsuccessful in the end, as the young and energetic Democrat found a way to connect with large parts of middle America—including many people living in states that had overwhelmingly supported the Republican candidate in the past two elections. A majority of Americans responded to his message of change by electing him president of the United States. In connecting with voters and winning the presidential race, this new president overcame the weight of history by becoming the first candidate in his demographic group to occupy the Oval Office.

John F. Kennedy, campaigning for the presidency in 1960

PAUL SCHUTZER/STRINGER/GETTY IMAGES

Now. . . Only a state senator from Illinois, Barack Obama burst on the political scene with a fiery, impassioned keynote speech at the 2004 Democratic National Convention. Not only was he young, charismatic, and a gifted orator, but he was also African American. Though the Democrats were defeated in the 2004 presidential contest, Obama was elected to the U.S. Senate. Soon thereafter he capitalized on the popularity and fame of his keynote speech to launch his own run for the presidency in 2008. His youth and vigor attracted record numbers of new voters to the Democratic Party, raised voting turnout in Democratic primaries to record numbers, and helped him defeat well-known U.S. Senator and former First Lady Hillary Clinton for the Democratic presidential nomination. Campaigning on an agenda for "change," Obama's youth and energy contrasted sharply with the more somber personality of his eventual Republican opponent, Senator John McCain. After eight years of Republican rule from George W. Bush in the Oval Office, voters were apparently looking for something new and altogether different—and they found it in the charismatic and inspirational Obama. Ultimately voter turnout reached new highs in 2008, helped in no small part by Obama's electric candidacy. Voters from recent Republican strongholds including Colorado and Virginia—states that went for Republican George W. Bush in 2000 and 2004—helped the young Democrat make political history as the first African American to win the White House.

1960

1957 | 1947 | 1937 | 1927 | 1917

Then. . . Nearly a half century before Obama's historical run, Senator John F. Kennedy of Massachusetts exploded on the nation's political map with his own run at the vice presidency during the Democratic National Convention of 1956. He eventually lost the nod to fellow Senator Estes Kefauver of Tennessee, who became the choice of presidential nominee Adlai Stevenson. Still, the youthful and charismatic Kennedy had caught the eye of his party faithful (as well as the nation at large) with his convention appearance and narration of the keynote film. Four years later he capitalized on that stardom to mount his own successful campaign for the Democratic presidential nomination. Kennedy was young, charismatic, and a gifted and inspirational speaker, yet he had his own glass ceiling to overcome—Kennedy was Catholic, and no Catholic had ever before made it all the way to the White House. Kennedy's youthful energy proved an asset throughout the campaign, first in helping him overcome a formidable primary challenge from Senate Majority Leader Lyndon Johnson and later in his hard-fought general election contest against his Republican opponent, Vice President Richard Nixon. Kennedy generated considerable voter interest by drawing large crowds at political rallies and high turnout in primary contests. His general election campaign called for a "New Frontier" of change for America, mobilizing many new voters in the process. Kennedy's charisma contrasted sharply with the rather dull personality of his Republican opponent, Richard Nixon. Thus after eight years under Republican Dwight D. Eisenhower, voters from such Republican strongholds as Michigan and Pennsylvania—both states that twice went overwhelmingly for Eisenhower—helped Kennedy make history as the first (and so far, only) Catholic to occupy the White House.

MORRY GASH/AP PHOTO

Democratic presidential hopeful Senator Barack Obama (D-IL) and his wife Michelle at a rally in St. Paul, Minnesota, in June 2008.

American Government: Historical, Popular, and Global Perspectives

★ Majoritarianism

The principle that the choice that is supported by the most voters is the choice that prevails.

★ Voting

The political mechanism that ensures that the majority will rule.

Political participation takes many forms in American politics.[1] At the core of participation is the act of voting. Open and free elections held on a regular basis are the hallmark characteristic of a democratic government. Voting provides the critical linkage between citizens' preferences and governmental authority. The United States is not a direct democracy in which every citizen is invited to deliberate the issues and vote on public policy. Rather, the U.S. system is a representative democracy, sometimes referred to as an indirect democracy or republican form of government, in which citizens choose the individuals who are then responsible for making and enforcing public policy. The people do not directly rule, but they have the opportunity to exercise power vicariously by choosing as their leaders those whom they prefer.

The core principle underlying representative democracy is **majoritarianism,** or majority rule, which means that among the choices presented to voters, the choice that is supported by the most voters (that is, receives the most votes) is the choice that prevails. When a majority makes its choice, the consent of the governed is satisfied. Given the diversity of opinions and interests among people in our society, it is unrealistic to assume that all, or even most, voters will agree on one choice. But the will of the people is accomplished when the majority decides.

Voting is the mechanism that ensures that the majority will rule. Times change, and so do people's opinions and preferences. Therefore, representative democracy not only requires an election in the selection of leadership, but also requires that elections occur on a regular basis so that the government's authority reflects changing majority views. Regular and periodic elections allow the majority of voters to continue to exercise ultimate control over the direction of public policy.

In this chapter, we explore historical and legal factors related to who has the right to vote, how Americans exercise their right to vote, and the factors that influence the making of a vote choice. Voting, of course, is not the only way citizens participate in the political process. They also contribute time and money to parties and candidates, write letters and contact public officials, express thoughts on policy issues and political candidates in blogs, attend town meeting and rallies, and engage in protests such as sit-ins, boycotts, and marches (see Figure 14.1). We examine these forms of political participation as well.

---

[1] For a comprehensive discussion of political participation, see M. Margaret Conway, *Political Participation in the United States*, 3rd ed. (Washington, DC: CQ Press, 2000).

Figure 14.1 The Ways in Which Americans Participate in Politics

Americans participate in politics in a number of different ways. The following chart lists some of the more common methods of political participation, along with the percentage of Americans who have engaged in each type of activity.

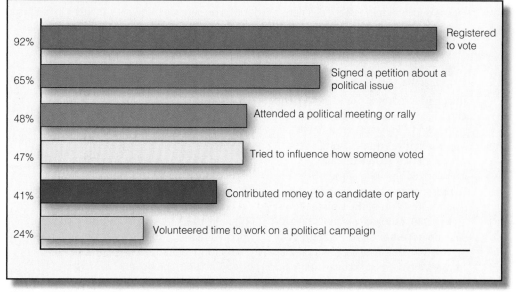

Source: 2008 national survey of 2,500 American adults, conducted by Intercollegiate Studies Institute (ISI).

The Legal Structure for Voting

The **franchise,** or suffrage, is the right to vote. When speaking about majority rule, it is important to ask, "majority of whom?" Article I, Section 4 of the U.S. Constitution assigns the system of voting, including the definition of who is granted suffrage, to the states. Voting registration, voter eligibility, methods of casting ballots, and the tallying of official results are all functions reserved for states. The original Constitution prescribes eligibility requirements for federal officeholders (representatives, senators, and the president) and lays out the system for selection of the president and vice president, but it says nothing about who can vote in the elections for these officials. Constitutional amendments have been ratified and federal laws have been passed that prevent states from discriminating in granting suffrage rights; still, technically there exists no absolute constitutional right to vote in the first place.

★ Franchise (or suffrage)

The right to vote.

Toward Universal Suffrage

The states have exercised significant authority in defining who is eligible to vote. For many years states regularly denied minorities, women, young adults, Native Americans, and the poor the right to vote for officeholders at the local, state, and national levels of government. In addition, a number of states prescribed property ownership requirements that prevented many people from being eligible to vote. Some states at various points in the nation's early history sought to broaden the right of suffrage. New Jersey, for example, allowed women the right to vote in the early 1800s, and some northern states provided for black suffrage prior to the Civil War.[2] But the goal of **universal suffrage**—or the right of all citizens to vote—has been an elusive one throughout American history. Restrictions on voting rights have systematically denied the right of particular groups of people to participate in choosing their leaders.

★ Universal suffrage

The idea that all citizens in a nation have the right to vote.

Two centuries of government under the Constitution, however, have been marked by steady progress toward the goal of extending the franchise to all Americans.

---

[2] For a discussion of the struggle for suffrage, see William H. Flanigan and Nancy H. Zingale, *Political Behavior of the American Electorate* (Washington, DC: CQ Press, 1998), chapter 2.

American Government ... in Historical Perspective:
When One Vote Made the Difference

Does your vote matter? Few elections are decided by one vote. However, there have been very important elections throughout history that prove the exception rather than the rule. In some instances, a single vote made a huge difference:

In 1776, one vote in the Continental Congress made English the official language of the United States, with German coming in a close second.

In 1801, one vote in the House of Representatives made Thomas Jefferson president of the United States.

In 1825, one vote in the House of Representatives made John Quincy Adams president of the United States.

In 1839, one vote elected Marcus Morton governor of Massachusetts.

In 1844, one vote cast by an Indiana farmer who died on the way home from the polls elected a state senator.

In 1868, one vote saved President Andrew Johnson from being removed from office.

In 1876, one vote sent an Indiana candidate to Congress, and in 1877 his one vote made Rutherford B. Hayes president of the United States.

In 1889, one vote brought the state of Washington into the Union.

In 1890, one vote brought Idaho into the Union.

In 1916, one vote in each of California's precincts re-elected President Woodrow Wilson.

In 1941, one vote saved the Selective Service System, just weeks before the attack on Pearl Harbor.

In a 1955 city election in Huron, Ohio, the mayor was elected to office by one vote.

In a 1959 city election, mayors of both Rose Creek and Odin, Minnesota, were elected to their respective offices by one vote.

In 1960, less than one vote per precinct made John F. Kennedy president of the United States.

In 1962, the governors of Maine, Rhode Island, and North Dakota were all elected by a margin of one vote per precinct.

In 1977, one vote determined the mayor for Ann Arbor, Michigan.

In 1984, one vote elected Maurice Nichols mayor of the city of Athens, Alabama.

In 1996, one vote could have elected a member of the Limestone, Alabama, County Board of Education, District Number 5. (The election was decided by a toss of a coin.)

Source: http://www.GenerationVote.com.

In the first federal elections in 1788, voting rights were limited to white men who owned property; in the most recent federal elections of 2008, all citizens of the United States aged eighteen or older (who were not otherwise prohibited from voting due to a felony conviction or some similar offense) enjoyed the legal right to vote. Enfranchisement was not achieved quickly, nor did it happen as the result of one or two events. Rather, the process of extending the right to vote to all American adults occurred over centuries of time, and with much opposition.

The Civil War presented the first major challenge to the disenfranchisement of a particular class of people, namely, African Americans. Prior to the Civil War, African American slaves not only did not have the right to vote, they had no rights at all. In the infamous U.S. Supreme Court decision, *Dred Scott v. Sanford* (1857), the Court ruled that slaves were property, that they had no rights under the law, and that they were not and could never become legal citizens of the United States. Immediately after the surrender of Confederate forces in 1865, President Abraham Lincoln gave an address suggesting that freed slaves be given the franchise. The idea met with some resistance, even among the northern states. However, the so-called Civil War amendments not only ended the institution of slavery (the Thirteenth Amendment) and granted citizenship to former slaves (the Fourteenth Amendment), but the **Fifteenth Amendment,** passed in 1870, guaranteed that "the right of citizens of the United States to vote shall not be abridged by the United States or any state on account of race, color, or any previous condition of servitude." The Fifteenth Amendment was the first formal action granting the federal government the power to enforce voting rights over the states.

The Fifteenth Amendment, however, did not deter some officials from the former Confederate states from finding ways to deny African Americans their newly won voting rights after Reconstruction ended in 1877. Threats, beatings, destruction of property, and other intimidation tactics, often ignored by local police, effectively kept blacks from coming to the polls on Election Day.[3] In addition, some states sought legal means to prevent blacks from voting. They passed laws instituting a **poll tax** that required individuals to pay a fee before being allowed to vote; they required potential voters to pass a **literacy test** to prove that they could read and write. Because most blacks were poor, they were often unable to pay the poll tax (usually about $30). Blacks also tended to have less education (in some states it had been illegal to teach slaves to read and write), so they frequently could not pass the literacy tests, which were often deliberately difficult and unfairly applied to minorities to prevent them from voting. From the late 1800s through the first half of the twentieth century, these methods posed a substantial barrier to black turnout in federal elections, which typically was about 10 percent. These laws also depressed turnout of poor people in general.

The civil rights movement of the 1960s addressed the problems associated with the disenfranchisement of blacks. Two important products of this movement were the Twenty-fourth Amendment and the Voting Rights Act of 1965. The Twenty-fourth Amendment, passed in 1964, outlawed poll taxes by making unconstitutional any law that made payment of a tax a voting eligibility requirement in federal elections.[4] The Voting Rights Act of 1965 denied states the right to use literacy tests as a requirement for voting; it also provided African Americans with protection from intimidating tactics that had been used to keep them away from the polls.

The past century also witnessed the enfranchisement of women. Though passage of the Fifteenth Amendment in 1870 granted African American men the legal right to vote, women would not receive the same constitutional guarantee until 1920 with the passage of the **Nineteenth Amendment.** In 1848, some two hundred delegates—women and men—met in Seneca Falls, New York, to issue a call for women's rights, including the right to vote. The Civil War years diverted the nation's attention from women's rights to other pressing problems.[5] Attempts to include a women's right to vote in the Fifteenth Amendment proved unsuccessful, although women began voting in some states well before passage of the Fifteenth Amendment. By the late nineteenth century, some of the new western states, such as Utah, Wyoming, Colorado, Idaho, Washington, and California, enacted women's suffrage laws. Despite continued opposition from leaders, including President Woodrow Wilson and many states in the Northeast, popular sentiment and a well-organized lobbying effort eventually led to the passage of the Nineteenth Amendment.

Three other groups have successfully won the right to vote through federal legislation and constitutional amendment. Until the early twentieth century, Native Americans had neither citizenship nor voting rights; but federal laws passed in 1924 made it illegal for states to deny Native Americans the franchise. In 1961, the **Twenty-third Amendment** to the Constitution gave residents of the District of Columbia the right to vote in presidential elections. Because the District is not a state, its residents had not been allowed to participate in presidential elections. The Twenty-third Amendment allocates electoral votes to the District using the same formula by which electoral votes are allocated to a state: the total number of representatives it would have in the House, if it were a state, plus two. Today, the District

★ **Fifteenth Amendment**

The amendment to the Constitution that guaranteed the franchise regardless of race, color, or any previous condition of servitude.

★ **Poll tax**

The requirement that individuals pay a fee before being allowed to vote.

★ **Literacy test**

The requirement that individuals prove that they can read and write before being allowed to vote.

★ **Nineteenth Amendment**

The constitutional amendment that guarantees women equal voting rights.

★ **Twenty-third Amendment**

The constitutional amendment providing electoral votes to the District of Columbia, thus giving District residents the right to vote in presidential elections.

[3] See Margaret M. Conway, *Political Participation in the United States* (Washington, DC: CQ Press, 2000), chapter 5.
[4] Some southern states continued to use the poll tax in state elections after passage of the Twenty-fourth Amendment. In 1966, the U.S. Supreme Court in *Harper v. Virginia State Board of Elections* outlawed the use of the poll tax in state elections as well as federal elections.
[5] See Nancy McGlen and Karen O'Connor, *Women, Politics and American Society,* 2nd ed. (Upper Saddle River, NJ: Prentice-Hall, 1998).

Chapter 14: Voting and Participation

★ Twenty-sixth
Amendment

The constitutional amend-
ment that lowered the
voting age to eighteen in
all local, state, and federal
elections.

of Columbia has a total of three electoral votes. In 1971, in the midst of the Vietnam War when many young Americans were dying in battle, Congress passed and the states ratified the **Twenty-sixth Amendment,** which lowered the voting age to eighteen in all local, state, and federal elections.

Although the administration of election and voting rules is largely controlled by the states, a significant number of federal laws and constitutional amendments have extended voting rights in the United States. Collectively, these laws prevent states from discriminating against particular groups of citizens with respect to their right to vote. Unfortunately, racism and other forms of discrimination continue to exist and thus continue to affect voting rights in America. Subtle forms of discrimination, including intimidation tactics by groups such as the Ku Klux Klan, may scare individuals into not voting. But more overt discriminatory tactics, supported by some state and local laws, have largely been erased. As a society the United States, over many years, has progressed toward the democratic ideal of universal suffrage. Today in the United States, the only adults legally disenfranchised are convicted felons in prison (forty-seven states), on probation (twenty-nine states), and on parole (thirty-two states).

Voter Registration Laws

Just as the extension of the franchise has evolved over the years, so has the system of voter registration. Most states today have voter registration systems in which individuals must qualify in order to become eligible to vote. The responsibility for qualifying lies with the individual. States do not compile and maintain a list of individuals who are eligible to vote. Rather, individuals must take it upon themselves to demonstrate their qualifications and file the appropriate paperwork to become eligible.

Massachusetts, in 1800, was the first state to require individuals to register to vote.[6] A handful of states followed Massachusetts's lead, but not until after the Civil War did most states adopt voter registration systems. Many of the voter registrations systems that were adopted between the 1870s and the early 1900s made it harder for immigrants, the less educated, and those less familiar with the political system to vote. A leading force behind the institution of voter registration systems was the populist movement of the late nineteenth century, which largely included white,

GLOBAL PERSPECTIVE

American Government . . . in Global Perspective:
One British Newspaper Asks: "How Can 59 Million People Be So DUMB?"

The outcome of the 2004 presidential election—with George W. Bush winning re-election—was a surprise to many in the United States and a frustration to many around the world. Many people from countries around the world had questioned the U.S. use of military force in 2003 in Iraq without UN support. When it became clear that there were no weapons of mass destruction hidden in Iraq (a primary Bush justification for the war), President Bush became even more unpopular. The headline in the November 4, 2004, issue of the *Daily Mirror* placed emphasis on world skepticism of Bush's leadership and questioned the 59 million American voters who re-elected Bush to another term as president.

[6] A thorough discussion of the development of states' voter registration systems can be found in Joseph P. Harris, *Registration of Voters in the United States* (Washington, DC: Brookings Institution Press, 1929).

middle-class, native-born Americans. In the northern states, registration laws were intended to make it more difficult for new European immigrants to vote; in the West, the intention was to make voting by new Chinese and Japanese immigrants more difficult; in the South, registration was aimed at limiting the black vote; and the source of concern in the Southwest was Mexican immigrants. Most states today still rely on some form of self-initiated voter registration, which continues to present an obstacle to voting for some people. A person must first find out how to register, remember to register in advance of Election Day, and then spend time registering. Many states require proof of age and citizenship, and many also impose a length-of-residence qualification, requiring a potential voter to prove that he or she has resided in the state for a specified period of time.[7]

A number of organizations and public interest groups have lobbied state legislatures and Congress to simplify and ease voter registration requirements in order to allow more people to vote on Election Day, including those who fail to register in advance of the election. North Dakota is the only state that does not currently require registration, and three states—Maine, Minnesota, and Wisconsin—permit voters to register on Election Day. The National Voter Registration Act of 1993, often called the **"Motor Voter law,"** mandates that when an individual applies for or renews a state driver's license, the state must also provide that individual with voter registration materials. The idea behind the law is that combining the process of registering to vote with the more routine task of obtaining a driver's license makes voter registration easier. Research suggests that although this law has increased voter registration, it has not increased actual turnout.[8]

★ Motor Voter law

The federal law that mandates that when an individual applies for or renews a state driver's license, the state must also provide that individual with voter registration materials.

Exercising the Franchise

A number of factors explain why people decide to cast a ballot on Election Day. An individual's interest in politics, for example, is one important factor. People who are more interested in politics tend to follow news about campaigns to a much greater degree than those who are less interested, and those who are more interested are more likely to vote.

Interest in politics, however, is only one factor that leads people to vote. Another is a person's sense of "civic duty," or the belief that being a good citizen requires one to vote. Many people who are not very interested in politics show up to vote nonetheless because they have a sense of civic duty.[9] From a young age, most Americans are socialized to believe that participating in elections is characteristic of the good democratic citizen, and so they feel an obligation to cast a vote even though they may not be particularly interested in elections and campaigns.

Another factor that influences some people to vote is the perception that their vote can have an impact on the outcome of an election. Individuals who feel strongly about a particular issue, set of issues, or a candidate may want to vote on the theory that if the election is close their vote might actually make a difference in the outcome. Indeed, the sense that one's vote can make a difference contributes to higher turnout in elections that are perceived to be close.

Finally, for some people social group pressure can be a motivating factor in deciding to vote. Voting is often regarded as the "right" thing to do, and some people feel that casting a ballot is expected of them by others. This sense of social pressure to do what is acceptable by society's standards can increase the likelihood that a person will vote.

Who Turns Out to Vote?

An individual's interest in politics and attentiveness to news about politics and campaigns, sense of civic duty, and sense of political efficacy (that is, the belief that one's vote can make a difference) all lead to higher rates of **voter turnout,** which is the percentage of eligible voters who show up to vote on Election Day. In addition to these "political" factors that help to distinguish between citizens who are more or

★ Voter turnout

The number of people who turn out to vote as a percentage of all those eligible to vote.

---

[7] A federal statute requires that the waiting period from becoming a state resident to being eligible to vote may not exceed thirty days.
[8] Michael D. Martinez and David B. Hill, "Did Motor Voter Work?" *American Politics Quarterly* 27 (1999), 296–315.
[9] See Lee Sigelman et al., "Voting and Non-voting: A Multi-Election Perspective," *American Journal of Political Science* 29 (November 1985), 749–765.

Many political scientists claim that the health of a democratic society may be judged by the level of political activity among its citizens. Consequently, many groups, such as the League of Women Voters and Common Cause, engage in campaigns to increase voter partici-pation. Political candidates, too, often extol the virtues of being politically active.

Why don't people vote? A 2006 poll by the Pew Center for the People and the Press asked Americans how much they agreed with the reasons people use for voting and/or not voting. The chart here lists the percentage of Americans who either "completely" or "mostly" agree with each reason.

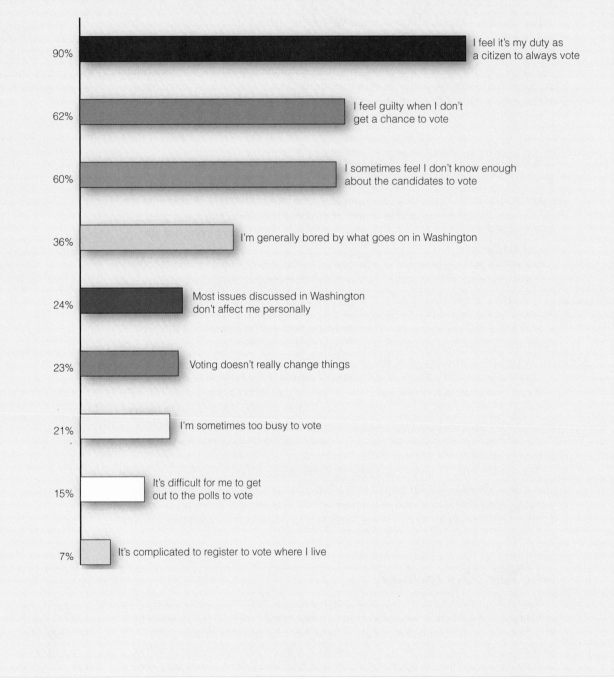

90% — I feel it's my duty as a citizen to always vote

62% — I feel guilty when I don't get a chance to vote

60% — I sometimes feel I don't know enough about the candidates to vote

36% — I'm generally bored by what goes on in Washington

24% — Most issues discussed in Washington don't affect me personally

23% — Voting doesn't really change things

21% — I'm sometimes too busy to vote

15% — It's difficult for me to get out to the polls to vote

7% — It's complicated to register to vote where I live

The 2006 Pew Poll specifically asked those who were *not* registered to vote why they were not registered. This chart lists the percentage giving each reason for not registering.

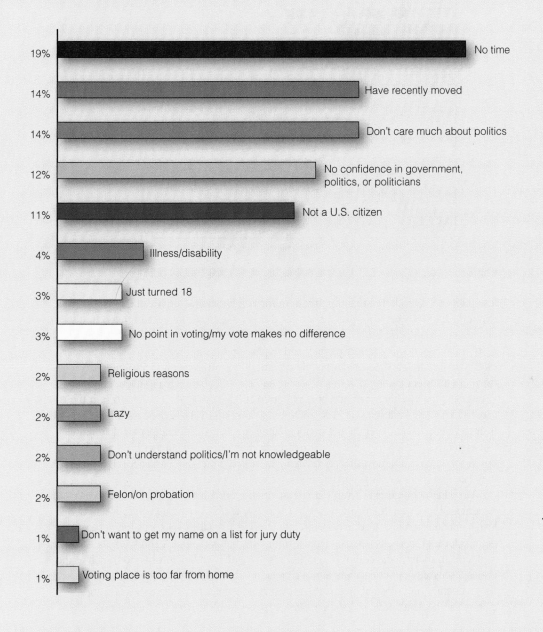

19%	No time
14%	Have recently moved
14%	Don't care much about politics
12%	No confidence in government, politics, or politicians
11%	Not a U.S. citizen
4%	Illness/disability
3%	Just turned 18
3%	No point in voting/my vote makes no difference
2%	Religious reasons
2%	Lazy
2%	Don't understand politics/I'm not knowledgeable
2%	Felon/on probation
1%	Don't want to get my name on a list for jury duty
1%	Voting place is too far from home

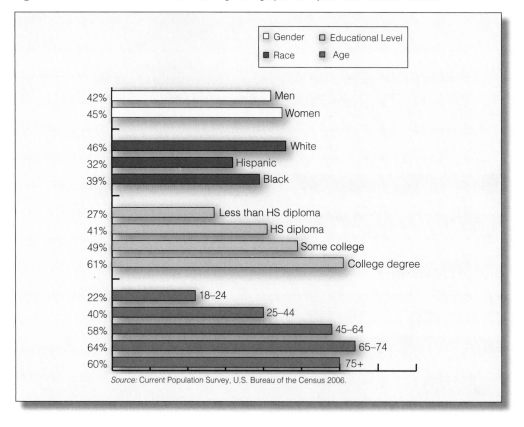

Source: Current Population Survey, U.S. Bureau of the Census 2006.

less likely to vote, there are a number of demographic characteristics that also help to explain turnout. A person's gender, age, and level of education are all related to the decision to vote (see Figure 14.2).

In many elections, younger people tend to pass up the opportunity to vote at greater rates than middle-aged and older people do. Youth nonvoting is often attributed to the more transient nature of younger people's lives.[10] At about age eighteen, many young people leave their parents' home to go to college or to take a job or to start their careers. Younger Americans are less rooted in a community, have had less time to register to vote, and are experiencing major changes in their social and personal situation. Voting tends to be less of a priority under these changing circumstances. As people age, buy a home, have a family, and reside in a particular community for a period of time, they become more socially attached and are more likely to vote.

Two other demographic groups are substantially more likely to vote—better-educated Americans[11] and wealthier Americans.[12] These two factors are related, because higher levels of education also lead to higher relative affluence and social status. The process of being educated sharpens a person's mind, improves the individual's ability to understand problems in society, and equips him or her to deal with complex information, such as the issues discussed in political campaigns. Education also enhances a person's appreciation for democracy and sense of civic duty. A better understanding of the issues and appreciation for the democratic process encourage higher levels of voter participation.

How Do They Vote? Methods of Casting a Ballot

Once a person decides to vote, there are several different ways in which a ballot can be cast. In the United States, five different methods of voting are generally used: (1) hand-counted paper ballots, (2) mechanical lever machines, (3) computer punch cards, (4) optical scan cards, and (5) electronic voting systems. Each of the fifty states has the authority to administer elections, and most states delegate most of the work to counties or other localities. In all, more than ten thousand jurisdictions at the

[10] See Raymond E. Wolfinger and Steven J. Rosenstone, *Who Votes?* (New Haven, CT: Yale University Press, 1980), pp. 44–46.

[11] Norman H. Nie, Jane Junn, and Kenneth Stehlik-Barry, *Education and Democratic Citizenship in America* (Chicago: University of Chicago Press, 1996).

[12] Todd G. Shields and Robert K. Goidel, "Participation Rates, Socioeconomic Class Biases and Congressional Elections: A Cross Validation," *American Journal of Political Science* 41 (1997), 683–691.

Clockwise from top left: the traditional paper ballot method of casting a vote, a mechanical voting lever machine, the computer punch card method of voting, the touch-screen computer ballot, and optical scanning card technology.

county level or below are responsible for carrying out the important task of collecting and tabulating votes.

Paper ballots were the only method of voting used in the United States during the first one hundred years of the nation's history. Originally the paper ballots used were produced by a political party and listed only the candidates belonging to the party that produced the ballot. On Election Day, the party would make the ballot available to the voter, who would then place it in the ballot box. In 1856, many jurisdictions began using a form of the paper ballot known as the "Australian secret ballot," which lists all the candidates for each office being contested, and voters then choose which candidate they prefer. Paper ballots are still currently used in about 3 percent of precincts, mostly in rural areas.

Each of the five methods of voting employs the characteristics of the Australian ballot: all possible choices are displayed for all offices, the voter marks choices through some mechanism, and those choices are secret.

The first real technological advance in voting technologies came with the introduction of the *lever voting machine* in 1892. A voter enters a voting booth and chooses candidates listed on a posted ballot by pulling a lever. The votes are recorded by advances in a counting mechanism that are made when the voter leaves the booth. The lever machine does not require a paper ballot and does not require (or allow) manual counting of ballots. When the polls close, poll workers simply read the numbers recorded by the counters. About 22 percent of precincts currently use lever machines.

Punch cards, which debuted in 1964, were the first computerized method of vote counting. Voters record choices by punching holes in appropriate locations on a card. These cards are computer readable. The piece of card that is punched out is called the "chad." Unlike lever machines, the punch cards may be saved as a record of the vote, and manual recounts of the actual votes are possible. The punch card system is the most widely used in the United States, with about 37 percent of precincts using this method. Much of the controversy regarding the Florida vote for president in 2000 dealt with the issue of whether a "hanging" chad (a chad that had been punched but was still clinging to the punch card by a fiber) should be counted as a legal vote.

Optical scan ballots are a method of voting based on the same technology as that used to grade standardized tests such as the SAT. Given a paper card and a pencil, voters mark their selections by filling in boxes or ovals on the card. The ballots are then scanned by a computer for vote tabulation. As with punch cards and paper ballots, a permanent record of the vote is kept and is available for manual counting. About 25 percent of precincts use optical scan voting systems.

Electronic voting is similar to lever machine voting in that it involves no paper record of the individual votes; however, the technology is much more sophisticated. Voters select candidates from a ballot, which may be posted on the voting machine or displayed on a computer screen. Typically, voters make their choices by pushing a button or touching the computer screen, then submit their selections by pushing a special button. The votes are stored in the computer. Write-in votes are entered via a keypad. About 7 percent of precincts use electronic voting systems.

In addition to these five main voting methods, several other methods are currently under development. One is Internet voting, which would allow voters to cast their ballots online using their personal computer (as long as the computer had online access) to vote. At present, the biggest obstacle to implementing Internet voting systems is the need to ensure authenticity and anonymity in the voting process.

Why Don't People Vote?

Despite the numerous factors that motivate people to vote, many in fact do not vote. Voter turnout is a measure of how engaged Americans are in voting in any given election contest. High turnout is considered a healthy sign for a democratic system. It implies that people are engaged in political issues, spend the time to contribute to the system, and take responsibility for selecting leaders. Lower turnout is often viewed as a by-product of alienation, mistrust, and lack of confidence in the political system.

Economist Anthony Downs originally offered an explanation for nonvoting based on a theory known as *rational choice*.[13] He argued that voters might decide not to vote because they reason that the costs of obtaining and understanding information about candidates and campaigns outweigh the benefits of making a vote choice. It is a rational choice, therefore, to decide not to vote, or to vote on the basis of certain "shortcuts" such as a candidate's political party.

Elections are plentiful in the United States and are held for many different offices at many different levels of government. Turnout varies from one type of election to another. Some elections draw much more media attention and thus engender more interest than others. Some feature much more political advertising and so provide more cues to voters. Some elections are inherently viewed as more important and so inspire a greater sense of civic duty among voters.

In 1966, political scientist Angus Campbell and his colleagues identified five factors that distinguish between "high stimulus" elections (in which turnout tends to be higher), and "low stimulus" elections (in which turnout is generally lower).[14] The factors that characterize a high stimulus election are: (1) greater levels of media coverage, (2) higher significance of the office, (3) campaigns in which voters assign high importance to an issue, (4) more attractive candidates, and (5) perceptions of a close race. Campbell and his colleagues argue that events external to voters may stimulate interest in elections and thus increase the likelihood that individuals will turn out to vote on Election Day. For example, when big issues such as war and peace are at stake, people are more likely to take an interest in the election and vote.

Presidential elections tend to produce the highest levels of turnout because (1) they are heavily covered by the media, (2) there is more spending on political advertisements, particularly on television, thus making the campaign more visible to voters, and (3) the presidency is the most significant office in the U.S. political system.

[13] Anthony Downs, *An Economic Theory of Democracy* (New York: Harper and Brothers, 1957).
[14] Angus Campbell, Philip E. Converse, Warren E. Miller, and Donald E. Stokes, *Elections and the Political Order* (New York: Wiley, 1966).

In presidential races where an issue important to many voters is at stake, such as problems with the economy in 1992 or the Vietnam War in 1968 or the war with Iraq and terrorism in 2004, turnout tends to be especially high. Races for higher-office typically deal with bigger issues and feature candidates who are more attractive to voters. For these reasons, turnout in presidential races, and to a lesser extent in contests for U.S. senators and state governors, tends to be higher than turnout in elections for lower state offices and local races.

A well-documented trend from 1960 through 2000 was the declining rate of voter turnout in U.S. elections. Prior to 2004, turnout hovered around 50 percent for eight presidential elections. In fact, the election of 1996 marked the first time since 1908 that turnout actually dipped below the 50 percent mark, with only 49.1 percent of Americans of voting age going to the polls. For the past two presidential elections, however, voter turnout has trended upward (at least 60 percent in both 2004 and 2008). Voter turnout is lower in midterm congressional elections (that is, the congressional elections that occur midway through a president's term). Forty-one percent of American adults cast a ballot in the 2006 elections.

Figure 14.3 Voter Turnout in U.S. Congressional and Presidential Elections
The following shows trends in voter turnout from 1960 through 2006 for presidential year elections and midterm congressional elections:

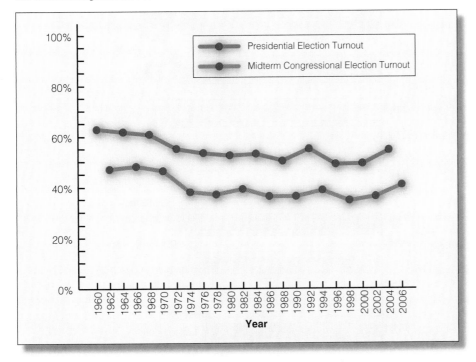

Figure 14.3 depicts the trend in voter turnout for presidential elections covering the past half century. It shows the downward trend in turnout from 1960 through 2000 has been reversed, with turnout in 2004 reaching the 60 percent level.

Voting in the United States Compared with Other Democracies

Many observers of elections note that voter turnout rates are lower in the United States than they are in other democracies. From 1992 through 2000, the average turnout rate in the United States for presidential elections was 52 percent. Over the same period, the average turnout rate in all federal elections (including midterm congressional races) was 45 percent. During roughly the same period of time, turnout in other nations, as shown in Figure 14.4 (p. 432), was much higher.

[15] For a comprehensive examination of the trends in voter turnout, see Thomas E. Patterson, *The Vanishing American Voter: Public Involvement in an Age of Uncertainty* (New York: Alfred A. Knopf, 2002).

Figure 14.4 Voter Turnout Around the World

Voter turnout varies a great deal from one country to another. This figure depicts average voter turnout from 1991 through 2000 in a number of the world's democracies. The turnout rates are expressed as the number of people who voted as a percentage of the voting age population in national elections. For the United States, the percentage includes both presidential and midterm congressional elections.

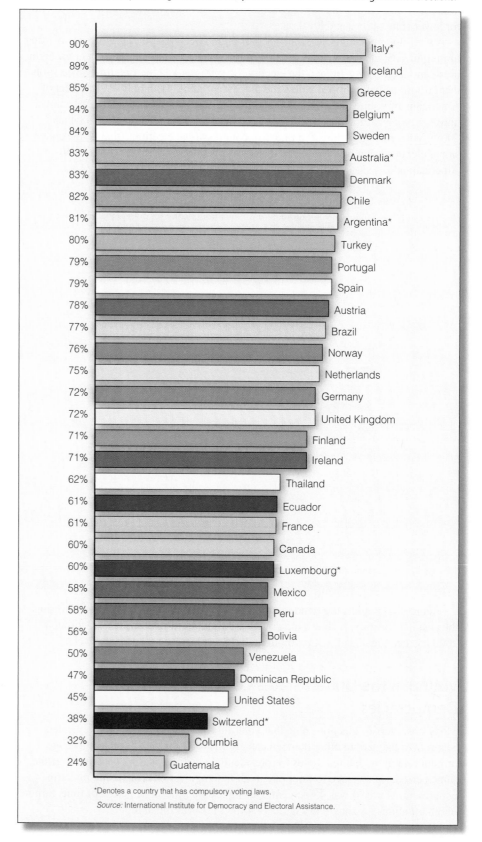

90%	Italy*
89%	Iceland
85%	Greece
84%	Belgium*
84%	Sweden
83%	Australia*
83%	Denmark
82%	Chile
81%	Argentina*
80%	Turkey
79%	Portugal
79%	Spain
78%	Austria
77%	Brazil
76%	Norway
75%	Netherlands
72%	Germany
72%	United Kingdom
71%	Finland
71%	Ireland
62%	Thailand
61%	Ecuador
61%	France
60%	Canada
60%	Luxembourg*
58%	Mexico
58%	Peru
56%	Bolivia
50%	Venezuela
47%	Dominican Republic
45%	United States
38%	Switzerland*
32%	Columbia
24%	Guatemala

*Denotes a country that has compulsory voting laws.

Source: International Institute for Democracy and Electoral Assistance.

Several explanations have been offered to account for both the lower turnout rates in the United States compared to other democracies as well as the trend toward declining rates of turnout in the United States over the past half century:

1. ***There are a large number of elections in America, making the opportunity to participate less of a novelty.*** U.S. turnout rates may be lower than those in other democracies of the world simply because there are so many elections held in the United States.[16] The U.S. system of federalism produces several layers of government—national, state, and local. At the federal level, elections are held for president, the Senate, and the House of Representatives. At the state level, there are gubernatorial races as well as elections for other statewide offices, including attorney general, state treasurer, and other state agency heads. At the local level, there may be elections for mayor, city council, sheriff, local judges, and so on. Furthermore, for many of these offices there are two elections: a primary election to elect the party candidate and a general election to determine the office winner. Also, in many states and localities there are often special elections on referendum questions and bond issues. Opportunities for participation in elections in the United States are so plentiful that they have become commonplace events. The vast number of elections may help explain lower rates of voting in any one contest. Switzerland, which also has a large number of elections, also has relatively lower turnout compared to other democracies.

2. ***Tuesdays are workdays.*** Traditionally, most elections in the United States have been held on Tuesdays. Most working people work on Tuesday, and so it may be inconvenient or difficult for many voters to find the time to vote on this day. People report having less and less free time in our society, which can account in part for declining turnout. In many other countries, elections are held on weekends or over a period of a number of days, making it easier for people to find the time to cast a vote.

3. ***Voting in the United States usually requires advance registration.*** As described earlier in this chapter, voters in most U.S. states are required to register to vote prior to Election Day. In other countries, voter registration is often automatic; that is, citizens of legal age are automatically registered to vote. Thus voters simply need to show up at the voting place on Election Day. In countries where registration is automatic, 100 percent of eligible voters are thus registered; in the United States, where registration is usually a separate process, typically about 70 percent of eligible individuals have registered to vote.

4. ***Over the past fifty years, perceptions both that participation can make a difference in what government does (that is, voters' sense of "internal efficacy") and that government is responsive to the people ("external efficacy") have declined.*** Many researchers have concluded that the decline in political efficacy,[17] which is accompanied by declines in political trust and in confidence in political institutions, has produced lower rates of voter turnout. As people come to feel that they are less able to influence the system and that the system is less responsive to them, they may become less likely to vote (see Figure 14.5).

5. ***Extensions of the franchise lead to short-term declines in turnout.*** Ironically, events that have expanded the franchise have been followed by lower rates of voter turnout. Following passage of the Fifteenth Amendment in 1870, which enfranchised former male slaves, the turnout rate dropped in 1872; passage of the Nineteenth Amendment in 1920, granting women the right to vote, led to an

---

[16] See Ivor Crewe, "As the World Turns Out," *Public Opinion* 4 (February–March 1981).

[17] For a discussion of trends in political efficacy, see also M. Margaret Conway, *Political Participation in the United States,* 3rd ed. (Washington, DC: CQ Press, 2000), pp. 51–53.

Figure 14.5 Changes in Political Efficacy in the United States

Since 1952, the National Election Study has asked voters questions that measure what political scientists call "political efficacy," or the feeling that an ordinary person can influence what government does. Questions relate to "internal efficacy," the feeling that a person can influence government, and to "external efficacy," the sense that government is responsive to an individual's input. This graph shows how responses to these two questions have changed. Levels of political efficacy have declined over the past half century, and research suggests that this decline has contributed to lower voter turnout.

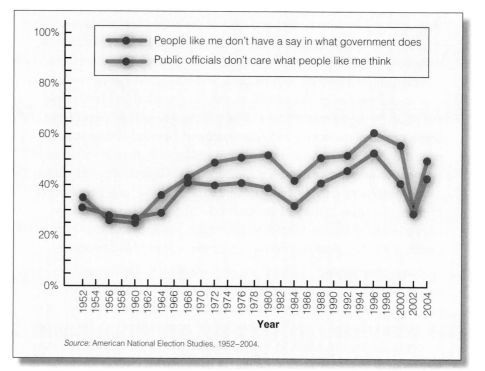

Source: American National Election Studies, 1952–2004.

overall drop in turnout; and passage of the Twenty-sixth Amendment in 1971 that lowered the voting age to eighteen led to lower turnout rates. One explanation for this phenomenon is that many newly eligible voters are not yet registered to vote and may require some time and socialization to get into the habit of voting.

6. ***Voting in the United States is not compulsory.*** Some democracies, including the United States, regard the franchise as a right. Accordingly, citizens have the opportunity to exercise their right to vote or they may choose not to vote. By contrast, some democracies have compulsory voting laws requiring citizens to vote. These nations assert that voting is a citizen's responsibility. Belgium, in 1892, was the first country to adopt compulsory voting. According to the International Institute for Democracy and Electoral Assistance, thirty-two countries have compulsory voting laws on the books. Twenty-four countries enforce these laws to some degree, and of them, nine—Australia, Belgium, Cyprus, Fiji, Luxembourg, Nauru, Singapore, Switzerland, and Uruguay—have strict enforcement policies.

Punishments for not voting in countries with compulsory voting laws include large fines, possible imprisonment (although imprisonment is generally the punishment for not paying a fine), or disenfranchisement. In Belgium, individuals who do not vote in four elections over a fifteen-year period are stripped of their voting rights. In Bolivia, voters are given vouchers after they vote, and these vouchers are needed to receive a salary from a bank during a three-month period after an election. In Greece, it is very difficult to get a passport or driver's license without showing proof of having voted.

Many arguments can be made in favor of or against compulsory voting laws, but one thing is certain: countries with compulsory voting laws have much higher turnout rates than countries without such laws. In Italy, for example, where lists of nonvoters are publicized, turnout has been around 90 percent. Though compulsory voting laws certainly increase turnout, many critics argue that the right to vote implicitly includes the right not to vote, just as the right to practice the religion of one's choice also includes the right not to practice a religion.

7. ***There has been a decline in "social capital."*** Political scientist Robert Putnam has noted a general decline in **social capital,** which is the extent to which individuals are socially integrated into their community.[18] Over the past half century, Americans have become less socially connected because they are not as likely to be members of organizations such as political parties, labor unions, civic groups, or even bowling leagues. As reasons for this decline, Putnam cites such factors as the increase of women in the workforce, technological innovations like radio, television, and the Internet, and the increase in residential mobility. People today are more likely to stay home and watch TV or surf the Internet and less likely to engage in social activities with other people. Voting is, in part, a social activity. The decline in social capital may be responsible, at least in part, for the general decline in voting.

★ Social capital

The "social connectedness" of a community, or the extent to which individuals are socially integrated into their community.

Is Nonvoting a Problem?

Although turnout has declined, the American political culture encourages people to vote. Over the years, voting has evolved from a privilege offered to a relatively few number of people to a right enjoyed by all. The League of Women Voters, Common Cause, and other groups regularly engage in campaigns to increase voter registration and stimulate turnout on Election Day. Candidates often stress the importance of voting, and the nation's educational system promotes the values of exercising the franchise, even to those not yet of age to vote. Even the music video station MTV invested time and money into the popular "Rock the Vote" campaign to encourage young people to vote. These efforts are predicated on the assumption that voting is important and that, conversely, nonvoting is problematic.

So to what extent are nonvoting, declining turnout, and lower turnout in the United States compared to other countries problems in our democracy? Two main arguments support the contention that nonvoting is problematic. The first holds that low voter turnout rates are a symptom of a weak democracy. The essence of what makes a democracy is the link between what a majority of citizens prefer and those who are given the authority to govern. Voting is the mechanism that creates this link. With low turnout, majorities of all citizens do not rule. When barely 50 percent of eligible voters cast ballots, successful candidates can hardly claim to have captured majority support. George W. Bush won the 2000 presidential election, for example, but less than 25 percent of all American adults voted for him.

The second argument contends that low turnout awards distinct advantages to the affluent, higher-socioeconomic groups in our society. As we have seen, turnout rates are lower among less educated and lower-income groups. Thus, nonvoting affords better-educated and wealthier groups of people more power in determining the winner of a political race.

There are also reasons, however, why nonvoting may not be a cause for concern. Perhaps nonvoting produces an electorate that is more informed, more aware of the important issues, and better able to make vote choices for the candidates who most deserve election to office. Former Senator Sam Ervin once said, "I don't think it's a problem that apathetic, lazy people don't vote." Voting simply for the sake of voting

---

[18] Robert Putnam, *Bowling Alone* (New York: Simon & Schuster, 2000).

may not produce good choices. Though ideally all citizens should become informed and cast a vote based on their information, many people lack the capacity or interest to cast a truly meaningful vote.

Another reason why nonvoting may not be a problem rests on the premise that voting is a voluntary right, just as the rights of free speech, religious choice, and peaceful assembly are voluntary. Our society does not compel citizens to speak out on issues, to declare a religious affiliation, or to contribute time or money to any particular cause or political party. So why should it expect people to exercise their right to vote? Furthermore, for many people nonvoting may be their expression of satisfaction with the status quo.

Making a Vote Choice

After an individual registers to vote and makes a decision to vote, the final phase of the voting decision is to make a choice among the candidates who are running for office. In covering American politics, the news media spend a tremendous amount of time and resources analyzing how voters will vote in a contest, particularly in presidential elections. For this reason, pre-election polling has become a centerpiece of American political campaign strategy as well as news coverage (see Figure 14.6). Years before a presidential election takes place, media polls query American voters on the potential candidates and assess the level of support voters offer these candidates. Months before the election, daily tracking polls monitor how voters are thinking and changing from day to day.

Likewise, political scientists' primary focus of research on American political behavior is on how voters make up their minds about who they will vote for. Research has identified a number of different factors that act as cues to individual voters in helping them make a vote decision. Collectively, these factors are referred to as "determinants of vote choice."

Candidate Familiarity

The most basic voting cue is simple name recognition and familiarity with a candidate. Many voters pay little attention to politics and political campaigns. Recognizing the name of a candidate on a ballot, then, offers an important voting cue. If voters recognize one candidate's name and no others, they are much more likely to vote for the name they recognize. Likewise, the more familiar voters are with a candidate, the more likely they are to vote for that candidate. In lower-visibility elections, such as primaries and local elections, name recognition plays a large role in the voting decision. However, even in statewide and presidential races (particularly presidential primaries), familiarity with a candidate can be an important cue to voters. High name recognition and voter familiarity propelled George W. Bush to the top of the pack in the Republican presidential primaries during the 2000 campaign. High name recognition of former first lady Hillary Clinton allowed her to gain frontrunner status early on in the race for the 2008 Democratic presidential nomination. In many congressional House races, incumbents tend to win re-election at rates in excess of 90 percent in large part because voters recognize their names and are less familiar with the challengers.

Party Identification

Political parties play many important roles in the American political system. Often voters form a psychological attachment to a party that helps them organize their political information and offers an important cue to vote choice. As discussed in Chapter 13, party identification is the term for this psychological attachment to a political party. Party identification tends to be a long-term predisposition—once it is formed, it usually remains with an individual over the course of his or her life. Party identification, then, is an important determinant of vote choice.[19]

[19] The psychological concept of party identification is developed in Angus Campbell, Philip E. Converse, Warren E. Miller, and Donald E. Stokes, *The American Voter* (New York: Wiley, 1960).

Figure 14.6 Accuracy of the Gallup Poll in Predicting Voter Behavior

Pre-election polls offer candidates, journalists, and voters detailed information on the dynamics of an election contest. How well the polls actually do in predicting vote choices is a frequently voiced concern. One of the best-known opinion polls in the United States is the Gallup Poll, which has been conducting pre-election polls since the 1936 presidential election. This figure shows Gallup's prediction for the percentage of the vote that the winner would receive in each presidential election from 1936 to the present, along with the actual percentage of the vote that the winner got on Election Day. Only once did Gallup make an incorrect prediction—in 1948, it predicted that Dewey would defeat Truman.

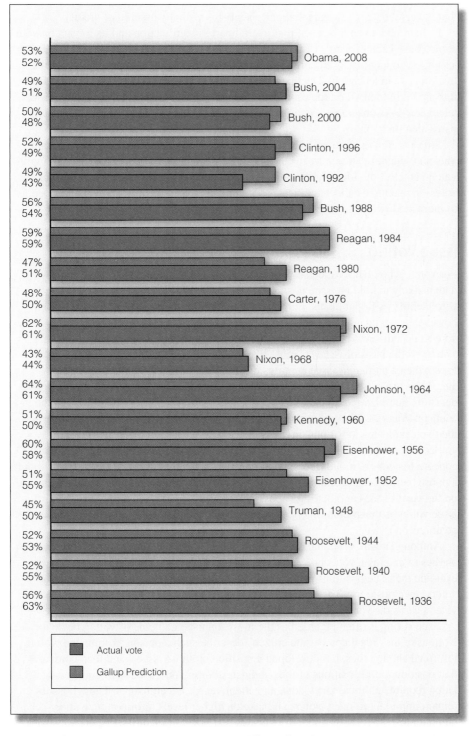

Source: The Gallup Organization. ©1936-2008 The Gallup Organization.

Party identification is particularly powerful in influencing a vote decision in lower-profile political races: those in which no particularly serious issues are at stake, the candidates are not well-known, and the news media pay little attention to covering the race. In such contests, those who identify with a political party are most likely to turn out to vote, and those who turn out usually vote for the candidate associated with their political party.[20]

For example, elections for the House of Representatives tend to be lower profile than presidential or Senate races. Among the 435 congressional districts across the country, more than 350 are considered to be "safe seats" for one of the two major parties. Safe seats are districts where the party affiliation of the voters is so one-sided that the candidate who wears that party's label is virtually assured of victory.

It should be noted, however, that overall party identification and its impact on vote choice have been in a state of decline.[21] Over the past fifty years, voters have become less likely to identify as either a Democrat or a Republican, and more likely to claim that they are independent. Decline in confidence in the political parties, campaigns that are more focused on the candidates than on the candidate's party, and increased television news coverage of campaigns are cited as primary reasons for the drop in party identification.

Still, two-thirds of voters continue to identify with one of the major parties, and thus party identification remains the single best predictor of how an individual might vote in an election. Identifying with a partisan perspective provides a shortcut for voters in making candidate choices. More broadly, party identification enables people to more readily make sense of their political world.

Issue Voting

For voters who identify themselves as Democrats, the Democratic Party's candidate is likely to hold an issue position that they favor; the same is true for voters who identify as Republicans. For voters who identify themselves as independents, however, a candidate's party does not serve as a determinant of vote choice. For these voters, a candidate's position on a particular issue or set of issues is a voting cue. Voting on the basis of issues is more likely to occur in certain types of elections.[22] First, when a particular issue captures the attention of many people in the electorate, voters are more likely to use a candidate's position on that issue to form a vote decision. For example, in the 1968 presidential race, American involvement in the Vietnam War was a central concern for many voters, and many voted on the basis of the two candidates' positions on the war.[23]

Second, issue voting occurs more often when an issue is of particular personal concern to a voter. In 2008, for example, American voters were very concerned about a poorly performing economy and the crisis on Wall Street, and thus many cast a vote on the basis of the candidates' proposals for addressing the economic crisis. Third, issue voting is much more likely to occur when the candidates hold clearly distinct positions on issues.

Anthony Downs's rational choice approach to understanding voting turnout also applies to making a vote choice. Downs suggested that in making a choice, voters examine the issue positions of the candidates and assess how close they are to the voters' own positions. The candidate whose positions on the issues are closer to the voter's earns the vote.

Issue voting is often regarded as the most sophisticated type of voting behavior. Notions of the "ideal democratic citizen" describe such a person as someone who is informed about issues, has developed a position on those issues, and then compares that position to the positions of the candidates. Voting on the basis of such a calculation requires political knowledge and attentiveness to campaigns. Though issues remain important to many voters and take on higher levels of importance under certain circumstances, most research indicates that other shortcut factors, such as party identification, are more commonly used to make choices.

American Government: Historical, Popular, and Global Perspectives

[20] For discussion of the role of party identification in forming vote choices, see Warren E. Miller and J. Merrill Shanks, *The New American Voter* (Cambridge, MA: Harvard University Press, 1996), and William H. Flanagan and Nancy H. Zingale, *Political Behavior of the American Electorate*, 9th ed. (Washington, DC: CQ Press, 1998).

[21] See Martin P. Wattenberg, *The Decline of Political Parties 1952–1996* (Cambridge, MA: Harvard University Press, 1998).

[22] Warren E. Miller and J. Merrill Shanks, *The New American Voter* (Cambridge, MA: Harvard University Press, 1996), chapter 12.

[23] See Norman Nie, Sidney Verba, and John Petrocik, *The Changing American Voter* (Cambridge, MA: Harvard University Press, 1979).

CHECKtheLIST

The Top Ten and Bottom Ten Popular Vote Winners in Presidential Elections

The ten presidential election winners who received the highest percentage of the popular votes:

✔	1. Lyndon Johnson	Democrat	1964	61.3%
✔	2. Franklin Roosevelt	Democrat	1936	60.8%
✔	3. Richard M. Nixon	Republican	1972	60.6%
✔	4. Warren G. Harding	Republican	1920	60.4%
✔	5. Ronald Reagan	Republican	1984	59.0%
✔	6. Herbert Hoover	Republican	1928	58.2%
✔	7. Franklin Roosevelt	Democrat	1932	57.4%
✔	8. Theodore Roosevelt	Republican	1904	57.4%
✔	9. Andrew Jackson	Democrat	1828	56.0%
✔	10. Ulysses S. Grant	Republican	1872	55.6%

The ten presidential election winners who received the lowest percentage of the popular vote:

✔	1. John Quincy Adams	National Republican	1824	30.5%
✔	2. Abraham Lincoln	Republican	1860	39.8%
✔	3. Woodrow Wilson	Democrat	1912	41.9%
✔	4. Bill Clinton	Democrat	1992	43.2%
✔	5. Richard Nixon	Republican	1968	43.4%
✔	6. James Buchanan	Democrat	1856	45.3%
✔	7. Grover Cleveland	Democrat	1892	46.1%
✔	8. Zachary Taylor	Whig	1848	47.4%
✔	9. Benjamin Harrison	Republican	1888	47.9%
✔	10. Rutherford B. Hayes	Republican	1876	48.0%

Retrospective Voting

★ Retrospective voting

An explanation of vote choice
that asserts that voters' evaluations of a candidate's past performance in office provides an
important cue for vote decisions.

In issue voting, a voter assesses the candidates' issue positions and casts a vote based on which candidate the voter thinks will do a better job in dealing with that issue in the future. However, a voter's past experience with a candidate or a political party also can be an important determinant of vote choice. **Retrospective voting,** a concept developed by political scientist Morris Fiorina, posits that evaluations of incumbents' past performance in office provide important cues for voters in deciding whether to vote for that incumbent.[24] Voters who believe that an incumbent has done a good job are likely to vote for the officeholder, whereas if they judge that an incumbent's job performance has been poor, they are likely to vote against the officeholder. Voter assessments of the economy and the performance of the president in handling economic conditions are especially important in a voter's retrospective evaluation of an incumbent. Bill Clinton's victory over incumbent George H. W. Bush in the 1992 presidential election was largely the result of voters' negative evaluations of Bush's handling of the nation's economy. Likewise, Ronald Reagan's defeat of incumbent President Jimmy Carter in 1980 was based on voters' perception that Carter performed poorly in dealing with economic problems and the Iranian hostage crisis.

In retrospective voting, the evaluation of the incumbent provides the determination of vote choice. In other words, a voter's assessment of the incumbent's job performance provides a shortcut decision rule on voting for or against the incumbent. Pollsters often measure this assessment through a "job approval rating" question. The percentage of voters who approve of the incumbent's job performance often reflects the percentage of the vote that the incumbent receives in a re-election bid.

Candidates for office often try to encourage voters to think retrospectively, if it is in their strategic interest to do so. In the 1980 presidential campaign, while the nation was experiencing economic problems and an extended international crisis with hostages being held in Iran, challenger Ronald Reagan defeated incumbent Jimmy Carter in part by asking the voters, "Are you better off today than you were four years ago [before Carter took office]?" Similarly, in 1992, challenger Bill Clinton questioned the integrity of President George H. W. Bush by repeating a TV clip of the president saying "Read my lips, no new taxes"—a pledge Bush had made in 1988 but did not keep.

Candidate Image Voting

The image, personal traits, and other characteristics of the particular candidates in a campaign can also influence the way people vote. Especially in higher-stimulus elections, where candidates make ample use of television advertisements to build an image, voter perceptions of candidates' qualities are important. Perceptions of candidate image include such characteristics as honesty, trustworthiness, leadership ability, concern for voters, integrity, intelligence, and sense of humor.

Candidates for office who have more favorable images than their opponents among voters tend to fare much better in election contests. In eleven of the thirteen presidential elections between 1952 and 2000, the candidate who had the higher "image score" from questions asked on the American National Election Survey won the election. The two exceptions were 1960, when John Kennedy and Richard Nixon shared an identical score in a very close election that Kennedy won, and in 1984 when Walter Mondale and Ronald Reagan shared an identical score (Reagan went on to a decisive victory).

In today's media age, candidates have found that image development is an efficient means of persuading swing voters how to vote. Thus, candidates often use television advertising to build their own favorable image or, conversely, to depict their opponents as having negative image characteristics. Visual images on television are useful in conveying symbolic, image-oriented messages. Bill Clinton in 1996 built a successful campaign around a theme that he would continue to improve the nation's economic future (his theme was captured in the slogan "building a bridge to the twenty-first century"). Ronald Reagan in 1984 cemented

---

[24] Morris P. Fiorina, *Retrospective Voting in American National Elections* (New Haven, CT: Yale University Press, 1981).

American Government: Historical, Popular, and Global Perspectives

his strong leadership image in his campaign for re-election (with the TV ad slogan "it's morning again in America").

Political Participation Beyond the Voting Booth

Though voting tends to be the most popular form of political participation in the United States, it is by no means the only way Americans participate. In a 2000 survey conducted by the National Election Study, about 1 percent of people questioned said they had themselves run for political office, about 2 percent said they had participated in a political protest, and the same percentage said they had attended a political meeting. About one in twenty Americans report having contributed money to a political candidate or party and only slightly more have displayed campaign materials on themselves (for example, worn a campaign button) or their property (for instance, put a bumper sticker on their car). More common forms of nonvoting participating include writing a letter to or contacting a public official and belonging to a political organization, with about 30 percent of Americans claiming to do each.

Though all of these forms of political participation enrich American political culture, activities that are intended to protest something often gain the most visibility. Protests can take one of three forms: legal protests in which citizens play by the "rules of the game" to speak out against a government policy, acts of nonviolent civil disobedience, and illegal protest activities that often include violence.

Marches, sit-ins, and rallies are forms of legal protests; such activities are designed to call attention to an issue that the protesters feel is not receiving adequate attention in the standard political process. Protesters are exercising their First Amendment right "peaceably to assemble and to petition the government for a redress of grievances." Many legal peaceful protests have raised awareness of an issue to a level that forces the normal legislative process to address it. A number of protest movements paved the way for substantial changes in public policy. Protests against the Vietnam War, for example, during the late 1960s and early 1970s led, in part, to American withdrawal from the Vietnam War. After World War I, protests among women's groups demanding the right of women to vote led to the adoption in 1920 of the Nineteenth Amendment granting women suffrage. Successful protests are often begun by small groups of individuals who feel strongly about an issue and are willing to spend the time and effort to make their case.

Protests make for good television because they generally feature conflict, a grievance, and individuals who are outspoken about the particular cause. Well-organized groups who engage in protests on hot-button issues, such as environmental groups, pro-life or pro-choice groups, and anti–death penalty groups, have become adept at informing the news media about the protests ahead of time and engaging articulate speakers to make their case. The media attention often provides protesters an opportunity to ensure that their causes reach the policy agenda of governing institutions.

The second type of protest behavior, *civil disobedience,* involves protesters engaged in illegal, but nonviolent activity. The goal of the protesters is to break laws that they feel are unjust, and the protesters willingly accept the consequences for breaking the law. Blacks protesting segregation laws in the southern states during the 1950s and 1960s would intentionally break those laws as a way of drawing attention to the problem of segregation.

Finally, a third type of protest behavior involves violent protests. In 1992, a number of rioters in south central Los

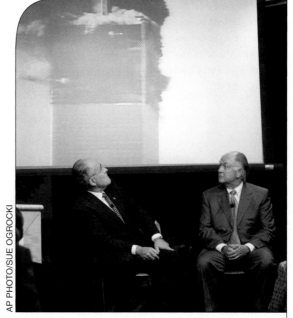

AP PHOTO/SUE OGROCKI

2008 Republican presidential candidate Rudy Giuliani (left) used images of his leadership as mayor of New York City in the aftermath of 9/11 to wage his bid for the Republican nomination for president.

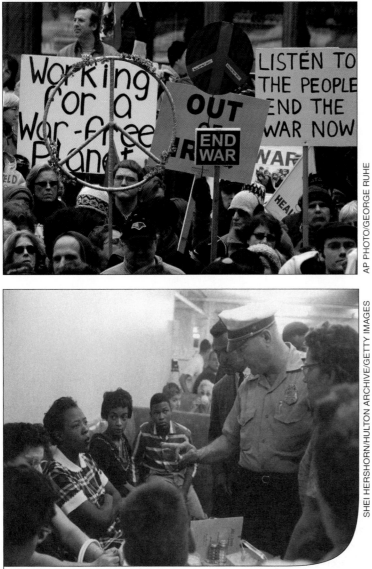

Angeles took to the streets after a jury acquitted several white police officers in a case where the officers had been caught on videotape brutally beating a black man they had stopped for a traffic violation. The rioters were protesting accusations of racial bias in the Los Angeles criminal justice system. The protesters looted businesses, stopped traffic, pulled a white truck driver out of his vehicle and severely beat him, and caused much damage to property.

Now & Then: Making the Connection

Barack Obama, like John F. Kennedy, inspired historic numbers of Americans to participate in the political process by casting their ballots. In both 2008 and 1960, these young energetic candidates mobilized millions of new and first-time voters. Their emergence on the political scene altered the political landscape by tipping the balance of the turnout among certain demographic groups (Obama's candidacy increased turnout among African Americans, while Catholics rushed to the polls to vote for Kennedy) and thus shifted the White House from one party to another. While voter turnout does not often exceed the 60 percent mark as it did in 1960 and 2008, majorities of adult Americans do regularly participate in presidential elections every four years, and in doing so they help influence decisions about the future of the country.

Americans participate not only by voting in elections. As in the historic elections of 1960 and 2008, millions of Americans regularly participate in rallies for political candidates, contribute money to interest groups and political campaigns, and donate time to political causes that are of concern to them. Outside of elections, many Americans regularly write letters to the editor, post entries on political blogs, sign petitions, and speak to their elected officials. Participation is part and parcel of the American political culture.

Above: A protest rally to end the Iraq War in 2007. Below: Oklahoma police in 1958 talking to African Americans who refuse to give up "whites only" seats at a luncheonette.

AP PHOTO/GEORGE RUHE

SHEL HERSHORN/HULTON ARCHIVE/GETTY IMAGES

For decades political scientists have used empirical methods to unwrap the mysteries of why some people participate in politics and others do not. "Rational choice" theorists have used a cost-benefit analysis to explain such participation, based on the premise that if the perceived costs outweigh the perceived benefits, an individual will "sit out" an election. Others have used social-psychological explanations such as the perceived benefits of group membership, the strength of a person's attachment to a political party or candidate, and the level of interest in the campaign or the candidates. Still others have focused on such additional factors as sense of civic duty, proximity to the polling place, and barriers to registration. Some of the research has identified patterns of participation, but no clear and convincing factors have been identified that consistently explain participation with any large degree of confidence.

Some recent research, however, may hold the key to unlock the mystery of political participation. A study released by a group of political scientists in 2008 found a strong relationship between an individual's genetic make-up and his or her propensity to participate in politics. The research found that individual genetic differences account for a significant amount of variation in political participation, even after controlling for the effects of many of the more common factors researchers have associated with participation, such as education, age, income, socialization factors, and attitudes. The researchers—James H. Fowler, Laura A. Baker, and Christopher T. Dawes—discussed the findings of their study in an article entitled "Genetic Variation in Political Participation," published in the May 2008 issue of the *American Political Science Review*. In conducting their study, the researchers examined a national panel of over 800 twins, along with nearly 400 twins in southern California. They discovered that a wide variety of types of political activity, including running for office, attending political rallies, and contributing money to candidates and parties, could be partially explained by genetic factors.

On http://academic.cengage.com/dautrich, find the politics interactive link for details on the role of genetics and political participation. Consult as well the various links that relate to biological factors and politics. Historical, popular, and global perspectives on the issue are also presented.

PHOTODISC/GETTY IMAGES

http://academic.cengage.com/dautrich

Chapter Summary

★ Citizens engage in many forms of political participation in the United States, including voting, contributing time and money to campaigns and interest groups, writing letters to elected officials and newspapers, attending political rallies, expressing their opinions on blogs, and even engaging in protests.

★ Voting is the political mechanism in a representative democracy that links the will of the majority to the outputs of government. In the United States, citizens do not rule directly. Rather, they choose the individuals who are then responsible for making and enforcing public policy. Thus, the people exercise ultimate power through their right to vote.

★ Traditionally, the states and not the federal government have had authority in running elections. However, state attempts to disenfranchise certain groups have been thwarted by constitutional amendments and federal laws. Although the goal of universal suffrage may not be fully realized today, over the centuries the United States has moved closer to this goal.

★ The constitutional amendments that have limited states' ability to disenfranchise voters include the Fifteenth Amendment (guaranteeing African American men the franchise), Nineteenth Amendment (women's suffrage), Twenty-fourth Amendment (outlawing poll taxes), and Twenty-sixth Amendment (guaranteeing the vote to those eighteen years of age).

★ States are responsible for maintaining a system of voter registration, and the systems vary widely from state to state. Only one state (North Dakota) does not require voters to register to vote as a prequalification to voting. Through the Motor Voter law, the federal government has tried to encourage higher levels of voter registration.

★ Among the factors that have been identified as relating to a citizen's propensity to vote are interest in politics, sense of civic duty, the perception that one's vote can make a difference, level of education, level of income, age, and social group pressure.

★ The nature of the times and type of political campaign can also influence turnout. High stimulus elections, in which the issues are very important or the races are more visible, tend to produce higher voter turnout. Presidential elections generally promote the highest levels of turnout, and the less visible local races inspire the lowest levels of turnout.

★ Although there has been a general declining trend in voter turnout in the United States over the past six or seven decades, the most recent presidential and midterm congressional elections have seen a modest increase in voting. This may be the result of voter concerns about U.S. military involvement in Iraq.

★ Voter turnout in the United States tends to be lower when compared with turnout in other democracies. Reasons that account for the lower U.S. turnout are the fact that there is no compulsory voting in the United States, the wide variation in states' voter registration requirements, the vast number of U.S. elections, and the tradition of holding elections on one weekday.

★ There are a number of factors that serve to explain the vote choices that voters make. These "determinants of the vote" include name recognition and candidate familiarity, party identification, the convergence between candidate issue positions and voter issue preferences, retrospective evaluations of the candidates' past performance, and voter assessment of the personal characteristics of the candidates.

★ Though voting provides the critical link between people and government output in a representative democracy, there are many other ways that citizens participate beyond voting, ranging from writing or contacting an official about a concern, to civil disobedience and protest activities.

Key Terms

Fifteenth Amendment (p. 423)

Franchise (or suffrage) (p. 421)

Literacy test (p. 423)

Majoritarianism (p. 420)

Motor Voter law (p. 425)

Nineteenth Amendment (p. 423)

Poll tax (p. 423)

Retrospective voting (p. 440)

Social capital (p. 435)

Twenty-sixth Amendment (p. 424)

Twenty-third Amendment (p. 423)

Universal suffrage (p. 421)

Voter turnout (p. 425)

Voting (p. 420)

Resources

Important Books

Alverez, R. Michael, and Thad Hall. *Electronic Elections: The Perils and Promises of Digital Democracy*. Princeton, NJ: Princeton University Press, 2008.

Conway, M. Margaret. *Political Participation in the United States*. Washington, DC: CQ Press, 2000.

Flanigan, William H., and Nancy H. Zingale. *Political Behavior in the American Electorate*, 9th ed. Washington, DC: CQ Press, 1998.

Keith, Bruce E., et al. *The Myth of the Independent Voter*. Berkeley: University of California Press, 1992.

Patterson, Thomas E. *The Vanishing Voter: Public Involvement in an Age of Uncertainty*. New York: Alfred A. Knopf, 2002.

Popkin, Samuel L. *The Reasoning Voter: Communication and Persuasion in Presidential Campaigns*. Chicago: University of Chicago Press, 1991.

Rosenstone, Steven J., and John Mark Hansen. *Mobilization, Participation and Democracy in America*. New York: Macmillan, 1993.

Tate, Katherine. *From Protest to Politics: The New Black Voters in American Elections*. Cambridge, MA: Harvard University Press, 1994.

Teixeira, Ruy A. *The Disappearing American Voter*. Washington, DC: Brookings Institution Press, 1992.

Internet Sources

http://www.nes.umich.edu/~nes/ (home to the American National Election Study, which includes survey data on voter opinion and behavior for national elections since 1952)

http://www.fairvote.org (website of the Center for Voting and Democracy; includes a host of articles, data, and information on voting rights and voting turnout)

http://www.rci.rutgers.edu/~cawp/ (website for the Center for American Women and Politics at Rutgers University; contains data, program information, and fact sheets on the role of women in elections and voting)

http://www.generationvote.com (website containing information on voting and participation geared toward younger voters)

15

Campaigns and Elections

George W. Bush, campaigning in 2000

The Stolen Election?
Now & Then

All the experts were predicting a close election. The sitting president was not running for re-election, and he did not play any visible role in the campaign. Politics, including the campaign itself, had been particularly divisive, due in part to heightened partisan tensions on Capitol Hill. Electorally, the partisan differences broke down by geography, as North and South lined up behind different candidates. But the hard-fought campaign finally ended, and Election Day drew to a close. All that was left to do was to count the votes and determine which candidate would be the next president. But Election Day came and went, and weeks passed following that first Tuesday in November without a declared winner. The Democratic Party's candidate had won the popular vote, but the Electoral College vote is what decides who wins presidential elections. The vote margins in several states were very close, particularly in Florida. Voting irregularities in that state were the subject of considerable concern. The Electoral College outcome awaited the resolution of these voting disputes and the recount of the vote in certain districts, including some key districts in Florida. Ultimately, it was the U.S. Supreme Court, and that body's Republican appointees, that decided the election: by the Court's ruling, the new president was the Republican Party candidate—and not the Democratic Party candidate who had re-ceived more popular votes. Millions of Americans were left frustrated with a process that only marginally reflected the public's will.

Rutherford B. Hayes, taking the oath of office in 1877

NOW &

A judge evaluates a questionable ballot due to a "hanging chad" after the 2000 presidential election in Florida.

2000

Now. . . George W. Bush, the Republican Party candidate for president, was not declared the winner of the November 7, 2000, presidential election until some time in December. Democrat Al Gore won the popular vote by about 500,000 votes. But on the evening of the election, with a number of states showing very close presidential races, the outcome of the electoral vote remained in question.

The campaign had been an especially hard-fought contest. The sitting president, Bill Clinton, played only a minimal role in the campaign, as the Gore campaign feared the scandals that rocked Clinton's second term might hurt Gore as well. Politically, the nation was largely divided along partisan lines, with Democrats providing the basis for Gore's coalition in the northeastern states and Republicans contributing the strongest block for Bush in the South. The vote margins were close in a number of states—New Mexico, New Hampshire, Oregon, and Pennsylvania, to name a few. But the closest race, and the one that eventually became mired in controversy regarding voting irregularities, was in Florida with its twenty-five electoral votes.

In the weeks following Election Day, as votes in that state were recounted, lawyers for both the Bush and the Gore campaigns filed suits over how to count partially punched out paper ballots that still contained confetti-like bits of paper (the so-called hanging chads). Florida's Republican Secretary of State, Katherine Harris, reported directly to Governor Jeb Bush, the brother of George W. Bush; she also had been George W. Bush's Florida campaign co-chair the year before. Despite the alleged conflict of interest, Harris formally certified the results of the Florida vote in favor of George W. Bush before the recounts were concluded. Eventually, it was the court system, and in particular the U.S. Supreme Court, that decided the controversial election. By a 5–4 decision (the five justices in the majority were all conservatives appointed by Republican presidents), the Court ruled that the vote recounts must cease and that Harris's vote certification would stand.

American Government: Historical, Popular, and Global Perspectives

Then. . .

Some 124 years earlier, the election of 1876 was similarly mired in controversy, with many observers later referring to it as the "stolen election."[1] Like the 2000 campaign, the 1876 contest was expected to be close. The sitting president, Ulysses S. Grant, whose administration was plagued by political scandals, stayed clear of the campaign. Partisan differences that lingered after the Civil War remained a source of tensions in the reconstructed United States. Northern states provided the foundation of an electoral coalition for the Republicans whereas southern states amassed a voting bloc for the Democrats. The popular vote count across the nation gave Democratic candidate Samuel Tilden a 250,000-vote margin over Republican candidate Rutherford B. Hayes. Disputes over the vote counts in several states, including South Carolina, Louisiana, and especially Florida, left the winner of the contest in doubt for more than two months after Election Day.

Each candidate claimed that he had won the popular vote in Florida; the Democratic electors sent one set of Electoral College vote counts to the U.S. Senate, and the Republican electors sent their own vote count. The Republican-controlled Senate appointed a commission, with an equal number of Democrats and Republicans, plus one "neutral" Supreme Court Justice (who happened to be a Republican). The commission, by one vote, awarded all of the disputed electoral votes to Hayes, the Republican, who was declared the winner.

---

[1] See Ari Hoogenboom, *The Presidency of Rutherford B. Hayes* (Lawrence: University Press of Kansas, 1988).

The U.S. Constitution calls for a presidential election every four years and congressional elections every two years. Without skipping a beat, the United States has met this constitutional requirement for more than two centuries. Through a Civil War, two world wars, and several major economic depressions, elections—the hallmark of American democracy—have taken place like clockwork.

In designing this representative democracy, the Founders intended a system that demanded accountability from elected officials. Elections for president and Congress provide this accountability. Regular and free elections are the lynchpin underlying democracy in America. Every year Americans are invited to cast ballots in elections for many local, county, and statewide races, but no election receives more attention than the race for the presidency.

American Presidential Elections in Historical Perspective

The U.S. Constitution says nothing about political parties or the process by which individuals become candidates for the presidency. The Founders assumed that electors, chosen by the states (and heavily influenced by the House of Representatives), would identify and evaluate potential candidates, and then the Electoral College would select the chief executive.[2] Parties, or "factions" were frowned on; the selection of president was intended to be the product of a select group of rational, wise men making choices at a lofty level above partisan politics.

Although their intentions for presidential selection were noble, the Founders' expectations about how a president would actually be chosen proved to be quite naïve. Political parties, though weaker today than in the past, provide the framework for contesting presidential elections. Each of the two major parties holds nomination contests in the fifty states to select the party's candidate in the general election; the nominees compete in the general election.

The presidential selection process that has evolved over the past two centuries of U.S. nationhood is long and complex. The manner in which the 2008 selection process occurred was not based on some elaborate constitutional design. Rather, this complicated and quirky process is the result of more than two hundred years of modification and evolution. Over the years, two distinct phases of the presidential selection process have developed: the nomination phase and the general election phase.

The Nomination Phase

In the nomination phase of the presidential election process, the political parties select specific people to run as the presidential and vice presidential candidates in the general election. This duo is referred to as the "party ticket." The Constitution did not account for a nomination phase because the Founders did not anticipate that a two-party system would emerge. The first two presidential elections did not even include political parties. Rather, the electors from the states all agreed that George Washington should be president in 1789 and again in 1792. Nevertheless, divisions within the federal government erupted and political alliances began to form during Washington's administration. These alliances resulted in the first two major political parties, the Federalists and their opponents, who eventually became known as the Democratic-Republicans. In 1796, when Washington decided not to seek a third term, each of these parties sought to win the presidency by recruiting and supporting candidates.[3]

The Federalists in Congress supported John Adams and the Democratic-Republicans threw their support to Thomas Jefferson. Electors, who were largely chosen by state legislatures, followed the cues of their partisan leadership in casting their electoral votes, and Adams, the Federalist-supported candidate, won the general

[2] See Lawrence D. Longley and Neal R. Pierce, *The Electoral College Primer* (New Haven, CT: Yale University Press, 1996).
[3] For a good discussion of the development of parties in the early Republic, see Stanley Elkins and Eric McKitrick, *The Age of Federalism: The Early American Republic 1788–1800* (New York: Oxford University Press, 1993).

American Government . . . in Global Perspective:

A Presidential Candidate Capturing the Imagination of Others...

Egyptian political scientist and former parliamentarian Mona Makram Ebeid attended the 2008 Democratic National Convention in Denver, Colorado. Upon his return to Egypt, he wrote a piece in the *Egypt Daily News* (on October 7, 2008) calling Barack Obama a charismatic leader in a nation that represents the world's "emotional centrality."

...Obama has thrived in his career by turning campaign stops into emotional experiences. He has thrived also because of big crowds and small donors. At his convention speech, he looked like a star of a rock concert and the crowd responded accordingly. Attendees chanted, danced and shook miniature American flags in unison. His speech hit the kind of emotional high notes that have thrilled his followers. I believe that this success was due to his cleverly setting himself as a breakthrough candidate who was uniquely well placed to "turn the page of history" at a moment when so many voters are frustrated with the Bush administration's record of failures and alarmed at the prospect of American decline...

The US presidential elections are watched with passion around the world not because of America's power but because of its emotional centrality....The rest of the world would certainly embrace a less fearful and more open post-9/11 America. Choosing Barack Obama, a symbol of hope, would do more to restore the image of the United States in the world than anything else. A rejection of the promise he represents would be a symptom of that nation's historical decline....

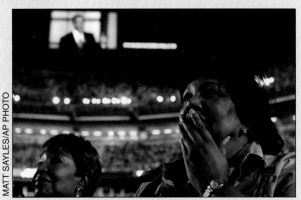

MATT SAYLES/AP PHOTO

The rapt faces of attendees at the 2008 Democratic National Convention in Denver reflect the historical moment as Barack Obama becomes the first African American to win the nomination for president from one of the nation's two major political parties.

election with seventy-one electoral votes, whereas Jefferson received sixty-eight electoral votes. The nomination process in 1796 reflected a significant level of party discipline in the casting of ballots among electors. In the elections of 1800, 1804, and 1808, both the Federalists and the Democratic-Republicans used informal meetings and discussions to choose a party nominee. Democratic-Republicans dominated electoral politics from 1812 through 1828, as the Federalist Party eventually disappeared.

In 1824, however, a significant split occurred within the Democratic-Republican Party. Andrew Jackson, who had the support of many common people, challenged party favorite John Quincy Adams. Jackson won both the popular vote and a plurality of the electoral vote, but no candidate received a majority of electoral votes. By constitutional provision, the election was sent to the House of Representatives, which voted Adams the victor. Jackson then founded a new party, the "Democratic Party,"[4] which is, of course, one of the two major parties still in existence today. Jackson and his followers believed in the enfranchisement of all white men, rather than just the propertied

---

[4] See Paul Finkelman and John Moore, "The Democratic Party," in Peter Wallenstein and Paul Finkelman, eds., *The Encyclopedia of American Political History* (Washington, DC: CQ Press, 2001).

class—during what became known as the Jacksonian era, white male suffrage was dramatically expanded throughout the country. Specifically, more and more state political parties adopted open caucuses, in which party members formally met to provide input as to who their party should nominate for elective office.

Electoral reforms during the Progressive era of the early 1900s opened participation in the nomination process to a greater number of Americans. The direct primary gave voters an opportunity to cast a ballot for delegates, who would in turn be sent to a national convention for the purpose of choosing a presidential nominee. The state of Florida in 1900 was the first to hold a direct primary in a presidential election. Although direct primaries did allow greater numbers of people the opportunity help select delegates, until the 1960s it was still the political elite of a party (governors, mayors, party chairs, and other officials) that selected most of the delegates and thus had the most input in choosing the party's presidential nominee.

The political unrest of the 1960s, spurred by anti–Vietnam War activism, led to further changes that gave voters in primaries even more weight in selecting party nominees. Benefiting from the increased percentage of convention delegates chosen through open primaries, Jimmy Carter, the little-known governor of Georgia, won the Democratic Party's nomination in 1976. A political outsider, Carter was able to appeal directly to average voters. Carter not only won the nomination, but he also went on the win the presidency that year. His victory demonstrated to candidates in both the Democratic and Republican parties that securing sufficient numbers of delegates to win the nomination requires direct appeals to voters, whether through party caucuses, or more likely, through party primary contests.

The General Election Phase

The unanticipated emergence of political parties not only established a nomination process, but it also forced a change in the Founders' design for selecting presidents. The Founders intended the state legislatures to pick well-qualified "electors," who would meet on a specified day in their state to decide who was the best choice to become president. At the end of the day, these electors would then cast votes for president. The states then sent their vote totals to the president of the U.S. Senate (the sitting vice president), who counted the votes before Congress. The candidate with a majority of votes became president, and the second-place finisher became vice president. If no one candidate received a majority of the votes, the election was to be decided by the House of Representatives with each state delegation having one vote to select the new president. The Senate was to select the vice president.

In the 1800 presidential race, nearly all of the Federalists voted for John Adams and Charles Pinckney (sixty-five and sixty-four votes, respectively) and all of the Democratic-Republicans voted for Jefferson and Aaron Burr, each of whom received seventy-three votes. Although it was generally agreed that Jefferson was the leader of the Democratic-Republican ticket, Burr challenged Jefferson in the House (because the election was a tie, the House state delegations had to choose the new president). Ultimately the House decided in favor of Jefferson, who became president, with Burr then becoming vice president. It was clear that the presidential election system needed fixing.[5]

The Twelfth Amendment to the Constitution, passed in 1804, provided for separate balloting for president and vice president by requiring that electors designate one of their two votes for president and the second of their two votes for vice president. This amendment greatly reduced the possibility that future elections would end in a tie.

Several other amendments to the Constitution have altered the presidential selection process. The Twenty-second Amendment, ratified in 1951, limits presidents to two four-year terms in office (or ten years if a vice president serves out the term of a president). The Twenty-third Amendment, ratified in 1961, provides the District of Columbia with three electoral votes. Because the District is not a state, it has no senators or voting members in the House.

---

[5] See Tadahisa Kuroda, *The Origins of the Twelfth Amendment: The Electoral College in the Early Republic 1787–1804* (Westport, CT: Greenwood Press, 1994).

American Government . . . in Historical Perspective:
The Comeback Kids of Presidential Elections

Losing a presidential election can be an enormous letdown, but it hasn't stopped a number of high-profile losers from making a comeback. Six men who lost a general election contest have come back to be elected president.

In 1796, Thomas Jefferson lost a bitter campaign to John Adams by only three electoral votes. But Jefferson came back to defeat Adams in 1800 and win re-election in 1804.

In 1808, James Monroe lost his bid for the White House in the nomination process, but then went on to win the 1816 election and ran unopposed in 1820 (the only other presidential candidate to run unopposed was George Washington).

In 1824, Andrew Jackson lost his initial bid for the presidency to John Quincy Adams in a contest that was decided by the House of Representatives (because no candidate received a majority of electoral votes). But in 1828, Jackson came back to defeat Quincy Adams and then won re-election in 1832.

In 1836, William Henry Harrison unsuccessfully ran for the presidency (he was defeated by Martin Van Buren). But like Jackson and Jefferson before him,

Harrison avenged his loss with another run at the man who defeated him and won the election of 1840. Harrison never had the opportunity to run for re-election because he died a month after taking office.

In 1884, Grover Cleveland won the election, but was defeated by Benjamin Harrison (William Henry Harrison's grandson) in 1888. Cleveland and Benjamin Harrison ran again in 1892, and this time Cleveland defeated Harrison, thus becoming the first and only chief executive to serve two nonconsecutive terms.

In 1968, the "comeback kid" was Richard Nixon, who had served eight years as vice president under President Dwight Eisenhower. In 1960, Nixon ran against John F. Kennedy and lost. Nixon then ran for governor of California, but lost that race as well. Despite Nixon's quip to the press after his gubernatorial loss that "you won't have Nixon to kick around anymore," he won the Republican nomination in 1968 and defeated Hubert Humphrey in a very close contest. Nixon won re-election in 1972 by a landslide, but midway through his term was forced to resign as a result of the Watergate scandal.

The modern presidential selection system, then, is an amalgamation of the Founders' design, modified by constitutional amendments and changes that occurred over time. This all makes for a complex system of picking a president. Although there are many caveats and exceptions to the rules, the contemporary presidential selection process generally consists of five stages:

1. **The Prenomination Campaign:** After a new president is selected, potential candidates for the next presidential election (four years hence) begin to explore the possibility of running. The ability to raise money, garner support from key leaders in the party, and attract the attention of the news media all contribute to each candidate's decision of whether to enter the race.

2. **The Nomination Campaign:** From January through June of the presidential election year, parties in each state hold either a primary or caucus in which the party delegates from the state commit to candidates. Each party has different criteria for allocating the number of delegates that a state will get. The candidate who receives a majority of delegates wins the party nomination.

3. **The National Conventions:** Each political party holds a national convention during the summer to showcase their candidate. Prior to the convention, the

President-elect Barack Obama and his wife Michelle, with their daughters Malia and Sasha, at the election night rally in Chicago's Grant Park. Thousands of supporters gathered in the park to celebrate Obama's victory.

candidates select their vice presidential running mates. Although the conventions used to play an important role in defining the party platform and selecting the party's nominee, today the conventions are largely publicity events for the ticket and other stars in the party, as well as an opportunity to critique the opposing party.

4. **The General Election Campaign:** Because national party conventions today generally affirm rather than choose party nominees, presidential candidates usually begin waging their general election campaigns before the conventions, as soon as it becomes clear who will be the two major-party nominees. (These decisions generally occur some time in spring of the election year.) Most recent campaigns have included a series of televised debates between the presidential and vice presidential candidates and a significant amount of advertising and campaigning in key states.

5. **The Electoral College Decision:** The winner of the presidential election is decided on the basis of the vote count in the Electoral College. The number of electoral votes for each state is equivalent to the state's allotment of House members plus two (for the state's two U.S. senators). In all but two states, the candidate who wins the popular vote automatically receives all of the electoral votes from that state. (Currently in Maine and Nebraska, the votes for president are counted for each congressional district; the candidate winning each district gets one elector, whereas the candidate winning the whole state gets an additional two electors.) Nationwide, the candidate who receives an outright majority of electoral votes wins the election.

The Prenomination Campaign

Although the presidential campaign officially begins with the first state contest for delegates in January of the election year, the real campaign for president actually begins much earlier, soon after the previous presidential election has concluded. As part of the **prenomination campaign,** behind-the-scenes candidates who are thinking about making a run often begin to "test the waters" by talking to party insiders, shoring up early commitments of support, lining up a campaign staff, beginning a fund-raising operation, traveling around the country making speeches and appearances, setting up "exploratory committees" to assess the feasibility of making a formal declaration of official candidacy, and then making the official announcement. Shortly after the 2004 election, Senators John McCain, Barack Obama, and Hillary Clinton established exploratory committees and began raising money for their 2008 campaigns.

The prenomination campaign also marks the beginning of the "weeding out" process. Early on, many would-be candidates find insufficient support from party insiders. Others find it difficult to raise sufficient funds to be competitive. Some tire too quickly of the arduous and time-consuming schedule necessary for launching a successful run for the presidency. These and other obstacles begin the process of narrowing the field of candidates.

In the 2008 prenomination campaign, with no incumbent president or vice president in contention, more than ten candidates from each of the two major parties seriously explored their presidential prospects during late 2006 and early 2007.

The **invisible primary** is the competition between candidates seeking the party nomination for front-runner status. A candidate gains front-runner status by winning broader support from important people within the party, raising more money than others, and achieving top position in the public polls conducted by leading news organizations. Front-runners tend to receive more coverage in the news, thus promoting their name recognition and popularity as candidates.

Within the Democratic Party, the invisible primary leading up to the 2008 primaries and caucuses began as a battle primarily among former First Lady (and U.S. Senator from New York) Hillary Rodham Clinton, former North Carolina Senator and 2004 vice presidential candidate John Edwards, Illinois Senator Barack Obama, Delaware Senator Joseph Biden, Connecticut Senator Christopher Dodd, Governor Bill Richardson of New Mexico, and Ohio Congressman Dennis Kucinich. On the Republican side, the contest for the 2008 nomination shaped up chiefly as a battle among Arizona Senator John McCain, former Tennessee Senator Fred Thompson (who is also an actor on the popular television show *Law and Order*), former Massachusetts Governor Mitt Romney, and former New York City Mayor Rudolph Giuliani. Other possible contenders included former Arkansas Governor Mike Huckabee, former South Carolina Congressman Duncan Hunter, Texas Congressman Ron Paul, and Colorado House member Tom Tancredo.

The fortunes of individual candidates can change in a hurry once the invisible primary has concluded. By the end of the invisible primary in 2007 it became clear that based on their fundraising and showing in the national polls, the major contenders for the Democratic nomination would be Senators Clinton, Obama, and Edwards. On the Republican side, the invisible primary concluded with Romney and Giuliani at the top of the pack.

The Nomination Campaign

The invisible primary may go a long way toward winnowing the field down to a handful of realistic contenders for major-party nominations; still, as Mitt Romney and Rudy Giuliani learned in 2008, money and attention can go only so far—contenders for the presidency must ultimately deliver victories in state primaries and caucuses or risk seeing their financial and volunteer support dry up in a hurry. Given

★ **Prenomination campaign**

The political season in which candidates for president begin to explore the possibility of running by attempting to raise money and garner support.

★ **Invisible primary**

The competition among candidates seeking the party nomination for front-runner status prior to the primaries and caucuses.

Left to right, former North Carolina Senator John Edwards, Illinois Senator Barack Obama, New Mexico Governor Bill Richardson, and New York Senator Hillary Rodham Clinton are seen sparring with each other during a debate among Democratic nominees early in 2008. While Edwards and Richardson struggled to win delegates, and thus bowed out of the nomination contest before it had formally concluded, Obama and Clinton continued to battle over the Democratic nomination all the way until June.

the reduced importance of party conventions in influencing nomination decisions in the modern era, success in the earliest primaries and caucuses may be crucial.

Primaries and Caucuses

The nomination of a candidate by a political party is the product of state-to-state contests in which delegates are committed to those candidates seeking the party's nomination. There are two basic methods by which states allocate delegates: presidential primary elections and caucuses.[6] A **presidential primary** is a state-wide election to select delegates who will represent a state at the party's national

★ Presidential primary

A statewide election to select delegates who will represent a state at the party's national convention.

American Government: Historical, Popular, and Global Perspectives

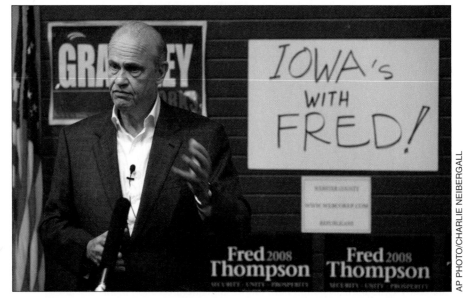

Fred Thompson, former senator from Tennessee and an actor on TV's *Law & Order*, campaigning for the Republican party's presidential nomination, in Iowa in October 2007.

---

[6] A thorough discussion of the nomination process as well as other aspects of the presidential campaign can be found in Stephen Wayne, *The Road to the White House 2008*, 8th ed. (Boston: Wadsworth Press, 2008).

Arizona Senator John McCain and former Massachusetts Governor Mitt Romney, here seen engaging in a testy dialogue during a debate among Republican presidential hopefuls in late 2007. McCain eventually defeated Romney and several other rivals to secure the 2008 Republican nomination. Once McCain's nomination was secure, Romney transformed from being McCain's foremost critic into one of his steadfast supporters and even garnered serious consideration from McCain for the vice presidential nomination later that summer.

convention.[7] In this election, voters choose among delegates who are committed to a particular candidate. The delegates who win go to the national convention and cast their vote for a party nominee to run in the general election. In 2008, more than forty-five states planned to use the presidential primary method of delegate selection. There are two types of primaries held by states. The less common approach is the **open primary**[8] in which on the primary Election Day voters can show up at the voting booth and declare whether they want to vote in the Democratic Party primary or the Republican Party primary; they then cast their vote in the primary they have chosen. A **closed primary**[9] election, by contrast, requires voters to declare a party affiliation ahead of time. When the voters show up to vote on primary Election Day, they are eligible to vote only in the party in which they are registered. Many states that use the closed primary have modified their requirements by allowing voters who have previously declared no party affiliation to show up at the polls on Election Day and declare a party, and thus vote in that party's primary.

A handful of states including Iowa, Nevada, and Maine do not hold presidential primary elections; instead they use the caucus method to select delegates for the national party convention. In the **caucus** method, party members are invited to attend local meetings at which they choose delegates who make a commitment to a candidate for the party nomination. These delegates in turn attend more regionalized meetings and select delegates from that group. Depending on the size of the state and the number of regions, this process continues until a slate of delegates attends a statewide convention, or caucus. At this statewide caucus, attendees again vote for a slate of delegates, who are committed to a candidate, to send to the party's national convention.

The first state contest for delegates, normally the Iowa caucus, launches the process by which delegates from the states commit to candidates for the party nomination. About one week after the Iowa caucus comes the New Hampshire primary,[10] which has traditionally been the first state primary election in which delegates

★ **Open primary**

An election that allows voters to choose on the day of the primary election the party in which they want to vote.

★ **Closed primary**

An election that requires voters to declare their party affiliation ahead of time.

★ **Caucus**

A method of choosing party nominees, in which party members attend local meetings at which they choose delegates committed to a particular candidate.

[7] Larry M. Bartels, *Presidential Primaries and the Dynamics of Public Choice.* (Princeton, NJ: Princeton University Press, 1988).
[8] See John F. Bibby, *Politics, Parties and Elections in America* (Chicago: Nelson-Hall, 1992), chapter 6.
[9] Ibid.
[10] For a good discussion of the relevance of the New Hampshire primary, see Dante J. Scala, *Stormy Weather: The New Hampshire Primary and Presidential Politics* (New York: Palgrave Macmillan, 2003).

commit to candidates.[11] Each of the fifty states (along with the District of Columbia, the U.S. Virgin Islands, American Samoa, and Guam) holds either a caucus or primary election, and in each of these contests delegates commit to candidates. The calendar of state caucuses and primaries, beginning in January and extending into June, is referred to as the nomination campaign. Through the **nomination campaign,** a candidate attempts to win a majority of delegates in the caucus and primary contests to lay claim to be the winner of the party's nomination.

The Traditional Importance of the Iowa and New Hampshire Contests

Iowa and New Hampshire are small states with relatively few delegates. The Iowa Democratic caucus in 2008 had a total of fifteen delegates at stake, and in the 2008 New Hampshire Democratic primary a total of thirty delegates was at stake. To win the Democratic nomination campaign that year, a Democratic candidate needed to amass support from more than two thousand delegates. In pure delegate count, larger states, such as California with 441 delegates, Florida with 201, and New York with 286, are much more important. Why, then, do Iowa and New Hampshire enjoy such disproportionately great influence in the nomination process? The answer is timing. Iowa and New Hampshire have so much influence over the nomination campaign not because of the number of delegates they offer, but because they have traditionally been the first two contests held. The news media focus a tremendous amount of attention on these initial competitions. Winners of the Iowa and New Hampshire contests receive a great amount of attention in the news, whereas losers tend to get written off as "unelectable."

The importance of the early contests has led to a phenomenon known as **frontloading,**[12] a trend that has occurred over the past five or six presidential elections in which states have moved their primary or caucus contests earlier in the year to attract greater attention from the candidates and the media. A state that holds its contest early makes itself more important in the nominee selection process. In 1988,

★ Nomination campaign

The political season in which the two major parties hold primaries and caucuses in all the states to choose party delegates committed to specific candidates.

★ Frontloading

The recent trend of states moving their primaries and caucuses earlier in the year to attract greater attention from the candidates and the media.

American Government: Historical, Popular, and Global Perspectives

©HULTON-DEUTSCH COLLECTION/CORBIS

Harold Stassen holds the record for most attempts to win a party nomination—ten. Stassen, a Republican governor of Minnesota, first attempted to win the Republican nomination in 1948. His tenth and final attempt was in 1992. In only two elections (1956 and 1972) between his first and last attempts was Stassen not a contender for the Republican nomination. Pictured here are Stassen supporters at the 1948 Republican convention.

[11] Nevada disrupted this traditional ordering in 2008 when it scheduled its Republican and Democratic caucuses for January 19, three days before the New Hampshire primary. New Hampshire then moved its primary to January 8.

[12] See William G. Mayer and Andrew Busch, *The Frontloading Problem in Presidential Nominations* (Washington, DC: Brookings Institution Press, 2003).

the time between the Iowa caucus and the date by which most states had chosen their convention delegates was more than twenty weeks.

In 2008, the majority of delegates were selected within a four-week period, from January 3 to February 5. The rush to move the contests earlier actually caused considerable confusion in the Democratic nomination race in 2008. In an attempt to ensure that New Hampshire would remain the first contest, the Democratic National Committee passed a rule that any state that moved its primary earlier than February 5 (Super Tuesday) would forfeit its delegates. Nevertheless, the states of Michigan and Florida both moved their primaries to January, disqualifying both states' primary outcomes, which had favored frontrunner Hillary Clinton. Ironically, the closeness of the ensuing race between Barack Obama and Clinton throughout the spring of 2008 meant that considerable attention would be paid to later contests held in Pennsylvania, North Carolina, and Indiana.[13]

The Nominating Conventions

The national conventions for the Democratic and Republican parties were once used to discuss the party platform and, most important, to choose the candidate who would represent the party in the general election. The images of the smoke-filled back rooms where deals were cut and delegates were lobbied to throw their support behind a particular candidate were very real. For most of our nation's history, the major parties selected candidates for the presidency in this way. Much of the brokering and deal making took place by skilled political operators at the national conventions.

The 1968 Democratic National Convention, held in Chicago, was characterized by a great deal of divisiveness and discord, much of which was captured on national

AP PHOTO/MICHAEL BOYER

Chicago has been a frequent host to national party conventions. Twenty-five national conventions have been held in the Windy City, eleven Democratic and fourteen Republican. The second most frequent hosting city is Baltimore, which has seen ten conventions. The 1968 Democratic convention in Chicago was characterized by violent protests over the Vietnam War.

[13] For an excellent preview and discussion of the 2008 presidential contest and some of its leading candidates, see Mark Halperin and John Harris, *The Way to Win: Taking the White House in 2008* (New York: Random House, 2006).

network television. Vietnam War protesters outside of the convention hall were beaten by Chicago police under the direction of Chicago mayor and "political boss" Richard J. Daley. Tension reigned inside the convention center as well, with anti-war supporters of Eugene McCarthy and George McGovern clashing with the party regulars supporting Hubert Humphrey. Television brought the negative images of the divided Democratic Party into American homes, seriously damaging the Democratic ticket. Four years later, television coverage again captured a disunited Democratic Party at the national convention in Miami, where delegates fought into the wee hours of the morning to nominate a party nominee (George McGovern finally won the nomination). At the Democratic convention in 1980, President Jimmy Carter was undermined by Senator Ted Kennedy's lack of public support for the incumbent that Kennedy had failed to defeat in the nomination campaign. The Democrats were not the only party to suffer discord and division. In 1976, grassroots support for Ronald Reagan spoiled any momentum incumbent President Gerald Ford hoped to generate at the Republican National Convention.

By the mid-1980s, both major political parties, recognizing the influential role that television was playing in election politics, had begun to adjust their agenda for the national conventions. With the frontloading process allowing candidates to capture a majority of delegates prior to the national convention, the parties began to choreograph their conventions and use them as advertisements for the party ticket. Today's conventions tend to avoid airing any intra-party differences. Instead, they are "anointing" ceremonies for the party ticket. They feature popular members of the party endorsing the nominees and include prerecorded videos highlighting the nominees' record of public service and family values.[14]

At the 2008 Democratic national convention, for example, a video of the life of Barack Obama highlighted his experience as a community organizer in Chicago and his commitment to his family. His wife and brother-in-law spoke on his behalf. Former President Bill Clinton and Senator Hillary Clinton added words of praise for the ticket, and vice presidential candidate Joe Biden delivered a "prime time" speech promoting Obama. Likewise, the Republican National Convention touted John McCain's military service. His wife, Cindy McCain, offered a brief testimonial on his behalf as well, and McCain's vice presidential running mate, Sarah Palin, gave a stirring speech that was widely regarded as the highlight of the convention.

The nominating conventions are still important events. Rather than playing a crucial role in selecting the party nominee and debating the policy positions of the party, however, the conventions now provide a week-long forum for the parties and their nominees to introduce themselves to voters and to formally kick off the general election campaign.

The General Election Campaign

A number of factors provide context for understanding general election campaigns in the American political system. These include whether or not an incumbent is running, the candidate's pick for the number two spot on the ticket, the strategy for achieving a winning coalition of states, the presidential debates, political advertisements, and finally the vote in the Electoral College.

Incumbent Race versus Open Election

General election campaigns for president are highly visible, very well funded, and among the most noteworthy of events in the American political system. Sometimes the contest is an **incumbent race,** or one between a sitting president and a challenger, such as the 2004 contest between President George W. Bush and challenger John Kerry. In an incumbent race, the focus of the campaign tends to revolve around the performance of the incumbent over the past four years. In this sense, incumbent races are often viewed as a referendum on the performance of the current occupant of the White House.

★ Incumbent race

General election race pitting a person currently holding the office against a challenger.

American Government: Historical, Popular, and Global Perspectives

[14] For a history of party conventions, see CQ Press's *National Party Conventions* 1831–2004 (2005).

In all, there have been eleven incumbents who lost their bids for another term. Five of these incumbent losses occurred over the past one hundred years: in 1912 Woodrow Wilson defeated President William Howard Taft; in 1932 Franklin Delano Roosevelt defeated President Herbert Hoover; in 1976 Jimmy Carter defeated President Gerald R. Ford; in 1980 Ronald Reagan beat President Carter; and in 1992 Bill Clinton defeated President George H. W. Bush.

In 2004, incumbent President George W. Bush touted his accomplishments and tried to convince voters that he was best able to lead in the war on terrorism, based on his response to 9/11 and military actions in Afghanistan and Iraq. Bush also claimed that the tax cuts he signed earlier in his term set the stage for a rebound to the national economy. In his campaign, Kerry harshly criticized Bush's "rush to war" in Iraq without building international support and without establishing a connection between Al Qaeda and Saddam Hussein. Kerry also blamed the policies of the Bush administration as the reason why the economy was still performing poorly. In incumbent races, the outcome often is determined on the basis of public evaluations of the incumbent. In the end, Bush's defeat of Kerry in 2004 was based on the president's ability to convince voters that he deserved another term in office.

In 1996, Bill Clinton ran for re-election against Republican nominee Senator Bob Dole. The huge economic boom of the middle 1990s along with a period of relative worldwide peace all but doomed the Dole campaign, as voters tended to reward the incumbent Clinton for the period of peace and prosperity that the nation was enjoying. Four years earlier, in 1992, President George H. W. Bush was not as fortunate, nor was President Jimmy Carter when he lost his bid for re-election in 1980. In both 1980 and 1992, consumer confidence was low and voters largely blamed the incumbents for the woes of the economy. In both of those contests, the incumbents were ousted.

In **open seat elections,** neither candidate is an incumbent. Open seat elections tend to be far less focused on the past. In 2000, for example, Democrat Al Gore was the sitting vice president, running for president. Rather than trying to take credit for being part of the Clinton team, Gore chose to distance himself from Clinton to demonstrate that he was his "own man"—and to avoid being associated with the negative baggage of Clinton's presidency (namely the Monica Lewinsky scandal and Clinton's impeachment trial). Gore was eventually able to dissociate himself from Clinton, but in the end was defeated by the Republican candidate George W. Bush.

Even less common are presidential election contests when neither the incumbent president of the United States nor the incumbent vice president is actively seeking to win the White House. Because President George W. Bush was constitutionally prohibited from seeking a third term, and Vice President Dick Cheney declined to make a bid for the White House in his own right, the 2008 presidential election was the first in eighty years to feature such an open-ended contest for the presidency. (Although neither President Harry Truman nor Vice President Alben Barkley was a major-party nominee in 1952, both pursued the Democratic nomination for a short period of time before dropping out of the race.) The last truly open-ended election occurred in 1928, when neither President Calvin Coolidge nor Vice President Charles Dawes were ever serious candidates for their party's nomination.[15]

★ Open seat election

General election race in which neither candidate is the incumbent.

The Choice of a Vice Presidential Candidate

Another important aspect of campaign strategy is the selection of the vice presidential running mate. Significant amounts of thought and fanfare go into the selection. Vice presidential candidates are quite visible on the campaign trail and can provide a boost to the ticket. The choice of running mate often attempts to balance the ticket geographically; John Edwards, for example, was from North Carolina (a southern state), a factor deemed important by the 2004 Democratic nominee, John Kerry, who was from a state in New England (Massachusetts). Vice presidential candidates

[15] The supporters of Herbert Hoover, the Republican candidate in 1928, briefly considered putting Dawes on the ticket as vice president once again, but backed down when the move was opposed by President Coolidge.

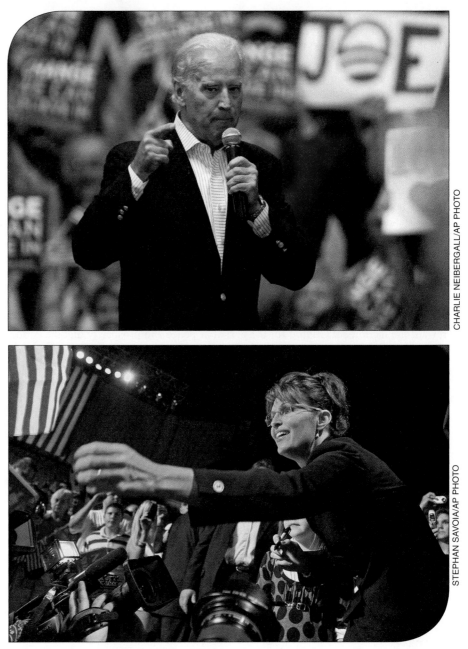

The vice presidential candidates in 2008 were Democrat Delaware Senator Joe Biden (top) and Republican Alaska Governor Sarah Palin (above).

are often chosen on the basis of their ideological fervor. Ronald Reagan selected George H. W. Bush as his running mate in part because Reagan was viewed as far to the political right and needed a running mate who was more moderate. By contrast, the more moderate Bob Dole chose the ideologically conservative Jack Kemp as his choice for vice president in 1996 to mobilize conservative Republican voters.

A fair amount of scrutiny goes into the process of selecting a vice presidential running mate, because some have turned out to be liabilities for the ticket. In 1972, when it was revealed that Senator Thomas Eagleton had been hospitalized for nervous exhaustion and had received electroshock therapy, an embarrassed George McGovern quickly replaced him on the ticket with Sargent Shriver. Similarly, it became clear in 1988 that George H. W. Bush's selection of Dan Quayle as his running mate was problematic after disclosure of Quayle's attempts to avoid the military draft during the Vietnam War. Bush kept Quayle on the ticket, however, and still went on to win the 1988 election. Many observers questioned George W. Bush's decision to keep Vice President Dick Cheney on the ticket in 2004, given the perception that Cheney was the driving influence behind the decision for early and swift American military action in Iraq, where weapons of mass destruction were never found. More recently, John McCain's selection of the relatively unknown Alaska governor, forty-four-year-old Sarah Palin, earned him plaudits from social conservatives. But the choice also led to excessive scrutiny of McCain's selection process for the vice presidential slot after Palin stumbled in several interviews with the mainstream media. Palin was also regarded by some as being too inexperienced to sit just "a heartbeat away" from the presidency.

Gathering a Winning Coalition of States

A central feature of any general election campaign is each candidate's plan to put together a coalition of states sufficient to win a majority of electoral votes. At the outset of the campaign, states may be divided into three categories: strong Republican states, strong Democratic states, and the so-called **battleground** (or "swing") **states,** which either candidate has a reasonable chance of winning. The map in the "Check the List" feature (p. 464) depicts this categorization of states for the 2008 presidential campaign. The blue states were considered safely Democratic and the red were considered safely Republican. By contrast, the gold states were the ones up for grabs.

In 2008 both the Republican nominee, John McCain, and the Democratic nominee, Barack Obama, set their sights on all twelve of the battleground states. John Kerry's narrow Electoral College loss to President George W. Bush in 2004 (Kerry fell short of the winning total by just eighteen electoral college votes) pointed Obama's way to victory: If he could hold all of Kerry's winning states, while picking up just one or two of the battleground states won by Bush, he could secure victory. Accordingly, Obama invested considerable resources in the battleground states of Ohio and Florida, either of which would provide him with the necessary margin for success. Obama's campaign also focused its attention on the three battleground states that Bush won comfortably: North Carolina, Virginia, and Colorado. Meanwhile the McCain camp was on the defensive, fighting to hold onto all these states, while looking for a breakthrough in Pennsylvania, where Kerry had won in 2004. On election day 2008, Obama's strategy reaped rewards for the Democratic ticket: Obama won a clear majority of the twelve battleground states and thus coasted to victory in the Electoral College.

The Presidential Debates

The media and the public have come to expect that a presidential campaign will feature debates between the presidential candidates, and sometimes between the vice presidential candidates as well. Candidates may not believe it is in their strategic interest to debate their opponents (for example, a candidate who is ahead in the polls might prefer to play it safe and not run the risk of losing a debate and perhaps the lead in the campaign). Still, both major-party candidates usually agree to debate so that they aren't portrayed as being "afraid" to do so. The expectation of a set of debates, however, is a relatively recent phenomenon in presidential elections. The first debates that generated a high level of interest and scrutiny were those between John F. Kennedy and Richard M. Nixon in the 1960 election campaign. Some political scientists today credit Kennedy's victory as partly the result of his strong performance in the debates.[16]

The next set of debates occurred in 1976, between Gerald Ford and Jimmy Carter. Each presidential campaign since then has included debates between the presidential candidates and sometimes also between the vice presidential candidates. The 2004 campaign, for example, featured three debates between the presidential candidates and one between the vice presidential candidates. The debates between presidential candidates George W. Bush and John Kerry included one debate on the economy with questions asked by a journalist, one debate on foreign affairs with questions posed by a journalist, and a "town meeting" debate in which the candidates were asked questions by a randomly selected group of American voters; in the vice

★ Battleground states

States identified as offering either major-party candidate a reasonable chance for victory in the Electoral College.

[16] See, for example, James Druckman, "The Power of Television Images: The First Kennedy-Nixon Debate Revisited," *Journal of Politics* 65, no. 2 (2003) , 559–571.

Top Twelve "Battleground States" in 2008

In the presidential campaign of 2008, the vast majority of states saw relatively little activity in terms of candidate appearances and television advertising. Instead, the candidates for both major parties targeted a small select number of states for concentrated activity. They spent most of their resources of time and money on these battleground states where each candidate knew well ahead of time that the election outcome would be decided.

Certainly there were some surprises in 2008. Georgia—considered a secure McCain state—ended up in the Republicans' column by a tight five-point margin. Meanwhile the battleground state of New Mexico ended up in the Obama victory column by a comfortable fifteen-point margin. But overall the twelve battleground states of 2008 held true to their status.

Popular Vote Outcomes in 2008

2008 Election		
State	**Obama (D)**	**McCain (R)**
✔ North Carolina	49.9%	49.5%
✔ Missouri	49.3%	49.5%
✔ Indiana	49.9%	49.0%
✔ Florida	50.8%	48.4%
✔ Ohio	51.2%	47.2%
✔ Montana	46.7%	50.1%
✔ Virginia	51.8%	47.3%
✔ Colorado	52.6%	45.8%
✔ New Hampshire	54.6%	44.6%
✔ Pennsylvania	54.6%	44.3%
✔ Nevada	55.1%	42.7%
✔ New Mexico	56.9%	41.8%

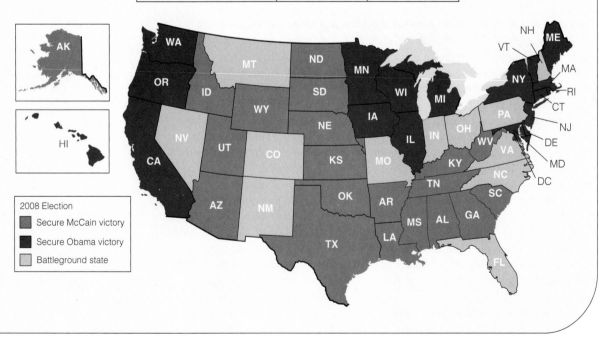

2008 Election
- Secure McCain victory
- Secure Obama victory
- Battleground state

PAUL J. RICHARDS/AFP/GETTY IMAGES

Democratic presidential nominee Barack Obama and Republican presidential nominee John McCain shake hands before their second presidential debate.

presidential debate, a journalist asked questions of the candidates. (The presidential debates are discussed in further detail in Chapter 12.)

The schedule of debates and the rules governing their conduct are the product of intense negotiation between the campaigns. In 2008, the detailed set of rules for the four debates included instructions that the candidates could not cross over a line on the stage separating them, time limits on answering questions and offering rebuttals, and a restriction for the final two debates that the candidates could not ask questions of each other.

Despite the large amount of attention both the campaigns and the media pay to the debates, the impact that debates have on the election outcome is unclear. Many researchers have documented that those who tend to watch the debates already have moderate to strong convictions regarding who they want to win, and these convictions often shape how an individual voter evaluates the candidate's performance in the debates. Though polls sometimes show that the voters tend to identify a debate "winner," there is far less evidence to show that this has any impact on voter intentions. The first of the debates often gets the most attention, and yet many of the media-dubbed "winners" of first debates, whether Walter Mondale in 1984, Michael Dukakis in 1988, Ross Perot in 1992, or John Kerry in 2004, have ended up on the short side of the electoral vote count on Election Day. In 2008 Barack Obama performed well in all three of his debates against John McCain, and while those performances did not secure his final victory, polls indicated that they helped reassure many undecided voters that the junior senator from Illinois was indeed ready to be president. Some observers of elections indicate that although debates may not have a direct impact on vote intentions, they can change the dynamics of a campaign, which in turn may influence the outcome.[17]

The Advertising

Television advertisements have become a staple of presidential campaign strategies.[18] They are used to heighten name recognition, communicate core messages to voters, and offer reasons why one should vote for (or against) a particular candidate.

[17] See Alan Schroeder, *Presidential Debates: 40 Years of High Risk TV* (New York: Columbia University Press, 1997).
[18] See Darrell M. West, *Television Advertising in Election Campaigns 1952–1996* (Washington, DC: CQ Press, 1997).

Television advertising uses a variety of different techniques to accomplish these goals. The most controversial of these techniques is the attack or "negative" ads that candidates often use to portray their opponents in a bad light.[19] Television ads can be very effective at convincing voters to support a candidate—particularly voters who are undecided on any particular candidate or who are politically independent rather than identifying themselves as a Democrat or a Republican. Whereas other forms of campaign communication (such as televised debates, political news columns, political talk shows on radio and TV, and news broadcasts) are provided in formats that appeal to voters who are interested in the campaign and have already made up their mind about who they will vote for, televised advertisements may be placed during certain shows or at certain times when independents and undecided voters are tuning in. The unsuspecting audience is captive to the short advertisement, which provides a unique opportunity for a campaign to attract votes.

The Electoral College Vote

Unlike elections for most public offices in the United States, the outcome of the popular vote does not necessarily determine who wins the presidential election. The winner of the presidential election is the candidate who receives a majority of the 538 votes in the **Electoral College.** As the opening to this chapter demonstrated, in the highly controversial 1876 and 2000 presidential elections the popular vote winner lost the presidential race. Similarly, John Quincy Adams won the 1824 election despite losing the popular vote, as did Benjamin Harrison in 1888.

How does the Electoral College work? The Constitution allocates each state a certain number of electoral votes, based on the sum of the number of senators (two) plus representatives (currently anywhere from one to fifty-three) that a state has in the U.S. Congress. The Twenty-third Amendment to the Constitution allocated three electoral votes to the District of Columbia. The number of seats a state has in the House of Representatives may change as a result of the official census conducted every ten years. Thus the number of electoral votes that a state has may change as well. The total number of electoral votes remains fixed at 538, and a candidate must receive a majority—270—to win the presidency (see Figure 15.1).

The minimum number of electoral votes possible for any one state is three because the Constitution guarantees to each state two senators and one House member. A number of states have three electoral votes: Vermont, Wyoming, North Dakota, South Dakota, Alaska, Montana, and Delaware. California currently has the largest number of electoral votes with fifty-five (fifty-three members of the House and two senators).

Even small states with as few as three electoral votes can influence the outcome of an election. In 2000, George Bush received 271 electoral votes, only 1 vote more than the 270 majority he needed to win. Had just one of the small states that gave Bush its 3 electoral votes voted for Gore, Bush would not have won the election.

Over the past sixty years, the U.S. population has shifted with the southern and western states gaining population and the northeastern and midwestern states losing. Consequently, the numbers of electoral votes in states such as Florida, California, Texas, and Arizona have grown, and the number of votes allocated to states like New York, Pennsylvania, Ohio, and Illinois has declined.

Article II of the Constitution gives the state legislature of each state the authority to appoint **electors,** one for each electoral vote that a state has been allocated. During the first few presidential elections, most states used the state legislature to select the individuals who would be the state's electors.[20] By 1860, however, states gradually shifted to using the popular vote outcome in the state to allocate electors, or the so-called **unit rule.** The unit rule (or "winner-take-all" system) means that the candidate who receives the most votes among the popular votes cast for president in a state will receive all the electoral votes from that state. At present only two states, Maine and

---

★ Electoral College

The constitutional mechanism by which presidents are chosen. Each state is allocated Electoral College votes based on the sum of that state's U.S. senators and House members.

★ Electors

Individuals appointed to represent a state's presidential vote in the Electoral College; in practice, voters in presidential elections vote for a slate of electors committed to a particular candidate, rather than voting directly for the candidate.

★ Unit rule

The system in forty-eight states by which the candidate who wins the most votes among popular votes cast for president in a state receives all the electoral votes from that state; also known as the "winner-take-all" system.

American Government: Historical, Popular, and Global Perspectives

---

[19] For an analysis of the effects of negative ads on voters, see Richard R. Lau and Gerald M. Pomper, *Negative Campaigning: An Analysis of U.S. Senate Elections* (Lanham, MD: Rowman and Littlefield, 2004).

[20] For a discussion of why the Electoral College was created and how it has changed, see Lawrence D. Longley and Neal R. Peirce, *The Electoral College Primer 2000* (New Haven, CT: Yale University Press, 1999), chapter 2.

Figure 15.1 The Electoral College Map

The following map of the states depicts the number of electoral votes each state has as a result of the 2000 U.S. census. The states shaded in red are those states whose electoral votes were cast for Republican John McCain in 2008. The blue states' electoral votes went to Democrat Barack Obama.

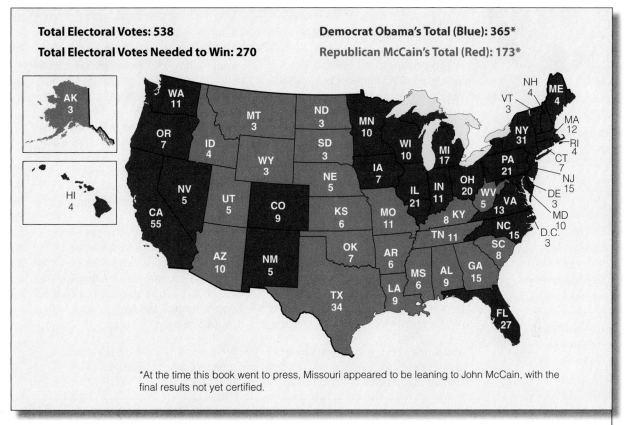

Total Electoral Votes: 538

Total Electoral Votes Needed to Win: 270

Democrat Obama's Total (Blue): 365*

Republican McCain's Total (Red): 173*

*At the time this book went to press, Missouri appeared to be leaning to John McCain, with the final results not yet certified.

Nebraska, do not use the unit rule. Rather, in those states the popular vote winner in each congressional district receives the electoral vote from that district, and the two votes that derive from the state's Senate seats are awarded to the statewide popular vote winner. In 2004, voters in Colorado defeated a referendum to allot electoral votes as Maine and Nebraska currently do.

In practice, the voters in a presidential election vote not for the actual candidate but for the slate of electors who commit to the candidate for whom the voters cast their ballots. Interestingly, the slate of electors who pledge themselves to a candidate is under no constitutional obligation to actually cast their electoral vote for that candidate. In fact, electors do sometimes break their pledge. In seven of the last fifteen presidential elections, at least one individual elector has not voted for the candidate that won the popular vote in their state. The most recent deviation occurred in 2004, when a Minnesota elector pledged to vote for Kerry cast his presidential vote for "John Ewards" [sic] rather than Kerry. That misvote may have been an accident. By contrast, in 2000 Washington, DC, elector Barbara Lett-Simmons, pledged to vote for Democrats Al Gore and Joe Lieberman, intentionally cast no electoral votes as a protest against the District of Columbia's lack of statehood. To date, however, these rare broken promises (or mistakes) have not had an impact on an election outcome—and only 9 of the 21,829 electoral votes cast since 1796 deviated from the vote that was expected of an elector.[21]

The significance of the unit rule is illustrated by the outcome of the 2000 presidential election. In Florida, which had 25 electoral votes, the popular vote distribution between Bush and Gore was very close. For nearly one month after the election, controversies surrounding the vote count and the ballot in Florida left

---

[21] See Longley and Peirce, chapter 4.

Public opinion polls are a regular feature of the American political system and no aspect of politics is more frequently polled than the presidential horse race. The presidential campaign includes a plethora of national pre-election polls and polls in the "battleground" states. Most of these polls are sponsored by major media organizations, such as the CNN/Gallup Poll, the CBS/*New York Times* Poll, the NBC News/*Wall Street Journal* Poll, the ABC News Poll, the *Newsweek* Poll, and the *Time* Magazine Poll.

Though some of these polls "test the waters" for possible candidates during the prenomination stage of the campaign, the polls kick into high gear several months before the Iowa caucus and New Hampshire primary. Once the two major-party tickets are set, most of these polling organizations keep regular tabs on voters' intentions right up to Election Day. Sometimes the polls give conflicting findings (for example, in mid-October 2008 a poll by the Pew Center showed Obama with a fourteen-point lead over McCain, whereas a poll by Gallup during the same time period showed Obama with a six point lead). For the most part, however, the national polls on voting offer consistent results.

The Gallup Poll, which has conducted pre-election polls for CNN and *USA Today*, tracks voters' intentions throughout the fall campaigns. The timeline below shows Gallup's tracking from early August through the end of October in the 2008 presidential race.

"Suppose the presidential election were being held today and it included Barack Obama and Joe Biden as the Democratic candidates and John McCain and Sarah Palin as the Republican candidates. Who would you vote for?"

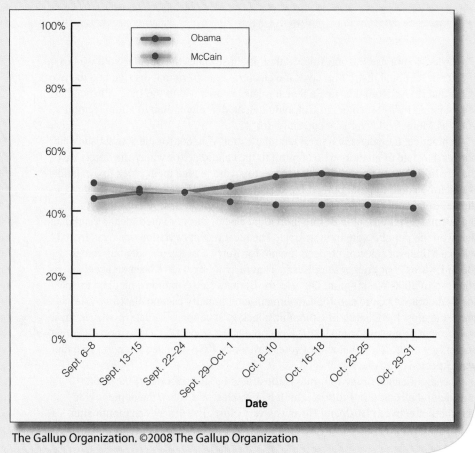

The Gallup Organization. ©2008 The Gallup Organization

uncertain which candidate won the most popular votes in the state. What loomed in the balance was all of Florida's 25 electoral votes—and the election victory. Without Florida, Gore had 267 electoral votes—just 3 votes shy of victory, whereas Bush had 246. Because the unit rule applied to Florida's 25 votes, all 25 would be allocated on the basis of which candidate received the most popular votes.

The Founders' original intent in creating the Electoral College was to keep the presidential selection process out of the direct hands of the people. They felt that the people were best represented by the House of Representatives, in which they directly voted for candidates. But the Founders questioned the ability of the general public to select the chief executive. Rather, they believed that the more knowledgeable, wise, and politically thoughtful members of each state's legislature should be empowered with the authority to appoint electors who would choose from the best of the best.

But as the meaning of democracy changed and as American politics opened up to greater political participation, states began to use the popular vote as a means of allocating their electoral votes. Why, then, do we continue to use this rather complicated, indirect system for voters to choose their president? Why not simply use the sum total of the popular vote to choose a winner? The most basic answer is explained by politics, not necessarily logic. The Electoral College system benefits smaller states. For example, Wyoming's population of approximately 494,000 represents 0.17 percent of the potential popular vote. But its three electoral votes constitute 0.56 percent of the electoral vote total. Because every state starts off with two electoral votes (for its two U.S. senators), smaller states end up with disproportionately more voting power in the Electoral College than in the popular vote. In recent years, the states that benefit from the Electoral College system have tended to be dominated by Republican legislatures. Because changing the Electoral College system requires a constitutional amendment, and because amendment procedures require approval by three-fourths of the state legislatures, any attempt to change the system is unlikely to win the support of a sufficient number of state legislatures, enough of which are small enough to benefit from the Electoral College. Despite the many proposals that have been offered to reform or eliminate the Electoral College, it seems likely, at least for the foreseeable future, that the Electoral College is here to stay.

Campaign Funding

Waging a political campaign, particularly a presidential campaign, is becoming increasingly expensive.[22] In 2004, John Kerry raised more than $326 million on his general election campaign and George W. Bush raised more than $367 million. All the candidates together raised more than $880 million in the 2004 campaign—about $300 million more than was raised during the 2000 presidential election. A front-runner for the Democratic nomination in 2008, Hillary Rodham Clinton, set a goal of raising $100 million in 2007 alone for her Democratic nomination bid. Then, in 2008, Barack Obama raised over $700 million. Campaign financing, then, is one of the most important functions of a political campaign. Hiring a professional staff to develop and implement a successful campaign, producing and airing TV commercials and radio spots, renting campaign headquarters office space, conducting polls to monitor the course of the campaign, and producing buttons, bumper stickers, and signs all cost money. Good candidates have demonstrated a high capacity for raising money to wage a campaign.

Sources of Funding

Where do campaigns find financial support? They find money from individual citizens, from interest groups and political action committees, and from political parties. Companies, groups, and individuals all have vested interests in the political system, and each may provide support (including monetary contributions)

---

[22] See David B. Magleby and Candice J. Nelson, *The Money Chase* (Washington, DC: Brookings Institution Press, 1990).

to promote candidates who advocate their own positions on issues. Our system of politics encourages people and groups to participate in the political process, and this participation includes financial contributions to campaigns. Indeed, giving money to candidates may be seen as a healthy sign that people are engaged in the political process and want to participate in making a difference.

Beginning in the 1970s, parties and candidates turned to political action committees (PACs) to address the new realities of political campaigns, particularly regarding fund-raising and limits on individual contributions. PACs are the arms of interest groups that raise and give money to political candidates. Any group that wishes to participate in financing campaigns must create a PAC and register it with the Federal Election Commission (FEC). There are more than four thousand PACs currently registered with the federal government (see Figure 15.2). Of the $1 billion raised by House and Senate campaigns in 2004, about 30 percent came from the fund-raising efforts of PACs.

In addition to individual and PAC contributions, the political parties play an important role in financing political campaigns. Both major parties have national and statewide committees, which raise money and give money to candidates to fund campaigns. In 2000, the national party committees each collected and spent about $200 million to help fund their candidates. Typically, the parties support House and Senate candidates, particularly those who have a competitive chance of winning.

Another important source of campaign funding comes from the individual candidates' House and Senate campaigns. Members of Congress who hold safe seats are very effective at raising money for their own campaigns. These campaigns, because they are for safe seats, tend not to need a great deal of funding. So the incumbents use their campaign war chests to help fund the campaigns of their colleagues in more competitive races. Often they do so through the formation of a PAC.

Though not the norm, some federal candidates for office use their own personal wealth to fund their campaigns. In 1992 and 1996, independent presidential candidate Ross Perot spent millions of dollars of his own personal fortune (Perot's personal wealth is in the billions of dollars). Similarly, Democratic Senator Jon Corzine from New Jersey spent more than $50 million of his own money to win a Senate seat in 2000 (his Republican competitor spent over $30 million of his own money).

The federal government and a handful of state governments (including Arizona, Connecticut, North Carolina, and Maine) also maintain some form of public campaign financing as well. Although candidates cannot be forced to participate in public financing schemes, which restrict their expenditures, the government may entice their participation by offering them significant public funds in return for their agreement to abide by personal campaign spending limits. The federal government's presidential election financing system allows major-party candidates to draw on funds received when taxpayers check a box on their tax returns agreeing to donate to the fund. In 2004, presidential candidates were eligible to receive approximately $70 million each if they agreed to limit their campaign expenditures. Yet neither of the two major-party candidates in 2004, George W. Bush and John Kerry, elected to participate in the federal financing scheme. By rejecting the use of such public financing, they were able to freely spend throughout the primaries and general election campaign without regard to any federally imposed limits. In 2008, John McCain accepted the $85 million he qualified for in public financing to fund his general election campaign. Barack Obama, however, declined public financing and continued to privately raise funds through the general election—a decision based on his widespread success in raising campaign money during the primaries.

In recent presidential election cycles, candidates have been able to take advantage of the Internet as yet another means of fund-raising. In 2000, Bill Bradley raised more than $2 million via the Internet for his campaign for the Democratic presidential nomination. (He ended up losing his bid for the nomination to Al Gore.) Then, in the 2004 race for the Democratic presidential nomination, a little-known former governor from the small state of Vermont, Howard Dean, waged an impressive

Figure 15.2 The Growth of Political Action Committees

The federal campaign finance legislation of the 1970s was the first vigorous attempt to monitor and regulate the money that was raised and spent on political campaigns. These laws applied to the regulation of hard money, which was money raised directly by and spent by the political candidates. They influenced the creation of political actions committees (PACs), which raised and spent money on political campaigning independent of the political candidates (soft money). In 1974, there were only 608 PACs registered with the federal government, which allowed them to engage in raising and spending money for political purposes. By 2002, there were 4,027 PACs registered with the federal government. This figure shows the total amount of receipts and expenditures of all PACs registered with the federal government from the 1975–1976 election cycle to the 2003–2004 election cycle. The growth in soft money was the primary reason for the new 2002 laws on regulating campaign finance.

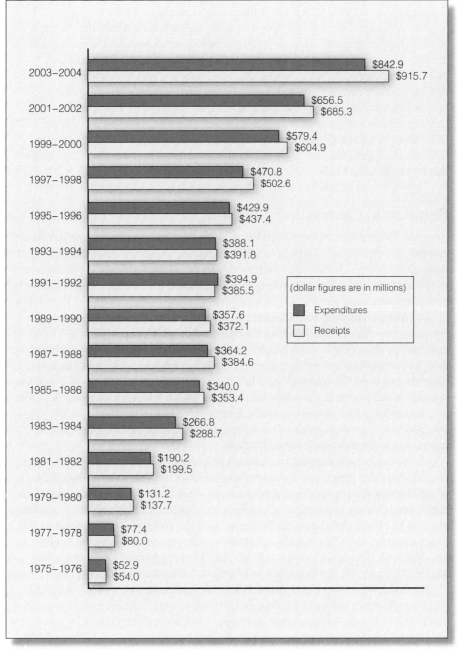

	Expenditures	Receipts
2003–2004	$842.9	$915.7
2001–2002	$656.5	$685.3
1999–2000	$579.4	$604.9
1997–1998	$470.8	$502.6
1995–1996	$429.9	$437.4
1993–1994	$388.1	$391.8
1991–1992	$394.9	$385.5
1989–1990	$357.6	$372.1
1987–1988	$364.2	$384.6
1985–1986	$340.0	$353.4
1983–1984	$266.8	$288.7
1981–1982	$190.2	$199.5
1979–1980	$131.2	$137.7
1977–1978	$77.4	$80.0
1975–1976	$52.9	$54.0

(dollar figures are in millions)

Source: Harold W. Stanley and Richard G. Niemi, *Vital Statistics on American Politics 2004–2005*, p. 103 (Washington, DC: CQ Press, 2006). Copyright ©2006 CQ Press, a division of Sage Publications.

campaign by tapping into the vast potential of the Internet and online fund-raising. His followers, who came to be known as "Deaniacs," tended to be younger Americans, a group much more inclined to use the Internet, to IM (instant message), and to blog. The Dean campaign translated this orientation of his followers into the most successful Internet fund-raising campaign that American politics ha ever seen. As *Wired.com* reported during the nomination campaign in early 2004:

> *The biggest news of the political season has been the tale of this small-state governor who, with the help of Meetup.com and hundreds of bloggers, has elbowed his way into serious contention for his party's presidential nomination...Dean has used the Net to raise more money than any other Democratic candidate. He's also used it to organize thousands of volunteers who go door-to-door, write personal letters to likely voters, host meetings, and distribute flyers.*

Dean raised an unprecedented $40 million in his campaign for the nomination. This amount exceeded that of all his competitors for the nomination, and the vast bulk of his campaign war chest was derived from small, individual donations solicited through the Internet. Although Dean's campaign collapsed after the candidate suffered unexpected losses in Iowa and New Hampshire and though most of his $40 million war chest had been depleted by the first primary contest, Dean's success at Internet fund-raising was nonetheless quite impressive. His appeal to voters through the Internet represents a significant achievement in the use of this new technology in campaign politics. As Americans increasingly come to rely on the Internet, it is likely that political candidates will follow Dean's example and harness this technology for fund-raising and other campaigning.

Regulating Campaign Financing

★ Federal Election Campaign Act (FECA)

The federal legislation passed in 1971 that established disclosure requirements and restricted individual campaign contributions.

★ Hard money

Donations made directly to political candidates and their campaigns that must be declared with the name of the donor (which then becomes public knowledge).

★ Soft money

Money not donated directly to a candidate's campaign, but rather to a political advocacy group or a political party for "party building" activities.

★ Federal Election Commission (FEC)

The agency created in 1974 to enforce federal election laws.

Congress and the states have passed many and varied laws to regulate the conduct of campaign contributions. These laws are not intended to prevent individuals or groups from giving money. Rather, they attempt to prevent a "quid pro quo," or a donation in return for an elected official voting or acting in a certain way in direct response to accepting the campaign gift.

The first significant piece of federal legislation aimed at regulating campaign financing was the **Federal Election Campaign Act (FECA),** passed in 1971 and amended in 1974. The law required that all federal candidates accurately disclose campaign contributions and document all campaign expenditures. Subsequent amendments to FECA imposed legal limits on campaign contributions by individuals ($1,000 to each candidate per election cycle; $5,000 to PACs per year; and $20,000 to national party committees per year). Additionally, FECA imposed an outright ban on certain campaign contributions by corporations, unions, national banks, and foreign nationals, among others.

All these provisions targeted so-called **hard money** contributions that go directly to candidates and their campaign committees. FECA did little to stem the influx of **soft money** funds to political parties and political advocacy groups that are not contributed directly to candidate campaigns and that do not expressly advocate the election of a particular candidate. In the two decades following FECA, the two major political parties have strategically spent soft money on administrative and party building activities, as well as on issue ads that do not specifically promote an individual candidate, but that nevertheless attempt to affect the election outcome.

The **Federal Election Commission (FEC)** was established in 1974 to enforce all campaign financing rules and regulations, including limits on campaign contributions. Today, the FEC is the federal agency in charge of enforcing election laws. Provisions for public funding of presidential campaigns were subsequently passed in 1976 and 1979.

Critics have voiced a number of complaints about the system of campaign finance regulations. For one thing, the original limits on individual contributions—fixed by legislation in the 1970s—were never indexed to inflation. This oversight was

addressed in legislation in 2002 which mandated that limits be indexed for inflation every two years. For example, in 2005–2006 individuals were able to give
up to $2,100 to candidates and up to $26,700 to national party committees.

Another complaint concerns the failure of the system to adapt to modern campaign dynamics. As a result of frontloading, presidential primary elections are now
bunched up earlier and earlier in the general election campaign; yet the strict limits
on expenditures imposed on those who accept public financing do not really account
for these new campaign realities, which compel candidates to spend a considerable
amount of their money during a relatively short period of time.

In recent years, advocates of campaign finance reform have focused their greatest criticism on soft money in the form of **independent campaign expenditures.**
These are monies that PACs or individuals spend to support political campaigns but
that do not directly contribute to them. FECA banned the unlimited use of independent expenditures to directly support the election of one candidate or the defeat of
another candidate, but those funds could still be used to build the party as a whole.
For example, a PAC can produce and support a political advertisement that endorses a particular party's position on an issue and pay for the airtime to broadcast
that ad on television. The money for the ad is not donated to a campaign per se,
but instead is spent on services that support the campaign; thus, the money spent is
considered an "independent" expenditure. The U.S. Supreme Court in **Buckley v.
Valeo (1976)**[23] ruled that Congress could limit campaign contributions consistent
with the First Amendment, but that it could not limit independent campaign expenditures or personal money spent by candidates on behalf of their own campaigns.
Twenty years later in *McConnell v. F.E.C.* (2003),[24] the Court extended that ruling
to apply to spending by political parties as well. Thus political parties themselves
often sponsor television ads that talk more generally about issues facing the country
without mentioning any individual candidate or race; of course most political experts
acknowledge that these ads may have a significant impact on individual campaigns.

The most recent reform attempts have focused on soft money and independent
campaign expenditures. Senators John McCain (R-AZ) and Russell Feingold (D-WI)
were particularly critical of the loopholes in campaign financing that have allowed soft
money to go unregulated by the Federal Election Commission. They co-sponsored legislation designed to better regulate the way campaigns are financed and how the money
is spent. In 2002, Congress passed the **Bipartisan Campaign Reform Act (BCRA),**
popularly known as the McCain-Feingold Act, which included the following new rules:

1. The national parties and candidates for federal office cannot accept soft
   money (for example, that which is not subject to regulation by the FEC).

2. Corporations, unions, and other groups may not pay for radio or TV advertisements within two months of the general election (or within one month of a
   primary election) if the ad refers to a candidate. PACs can continue to pay for
   such ads, but these expenditures are now considered hard money and thus
   subject to FEC regulation.

3. The limits on hard-money contributions that may be made to campaigns have
   increased. The limit on contributions to a particular candidate for federal office was raised from $1,000 to $2,000. Furthermore, in each two-year election
   cycle, an individual may contribute up to $95,000 to federal candidates, politi-
   cal parties, and political action committees. The previous limit was $50,000.

Congressional Campaigns and Elections

Although presidential elections typically receive the most attention from the media
and the public, many other elections also occur regularly, including those that send
members to the two houses of Congress. In each presidential election year, all

★ Independent campaign
expenditure

Political donations that PACs or
individuals spend to support
campaigns, but do not directly
contribute to the campaigns.

★ *Buckley v. Valeo* (1976)

The 1976 Supreme Court opinion that held that spending
money to influence elections
is protected First Amendment
speech, and that prohibited
limitations on independent expenditures or personal money
spent by candidates on their
own campaigns.

★ Bipartisan Campaign
Reform Act (BCRA)
of 2002

Also called the McCain-Feingold
Act, the federal legislation that
(1) restricted soft money
spent by political parties,
(2) regulated expenditures
on ads that refer to specific
candidates immediately before
an election, and (3) increased
limits on hard money donated
directly to candidates and their
campaigns.

[23] *Buckley v. Valeo*, 424 U.S. 1 (1976).
[24] *McConnell v. F.E.C.*, 540 U.S. 93 (2003).

435 seats in the House of Representatives are contested, as are one-third of the seats in the Senate. Midway between successive presidential elections are the **midterm congressional elections,** in which all 435 House seats are contested again and another one-third of the Senate seats are voted on (senators serve six-year terms, and the one hundred Senate elections are staggered so that about one-third of the seats are contested every two years).

Midterm elections for Congress differ from presidential year elections in important ways.[25]

Democratic leaders Nancy Pelosi and Harry Reid (along with Senator Charles Schumer of New York) celebrating the victories of Democratic candidates who won new majorities in the House and Senate on election night 2006. Pelosi later became Speaker of the House, and Reid became Senate majority leader.

KAMENKO PAJIC/UPI/LANDOV

★ Midterm congressional elections

Congressional elections held midway between successive presidential elections.

★ Coattail effect

The potential benefit that successful presidential candidates offer to congressional candidates of the same political party during presidential election years.

First, voter turnout tends to be lower in the midterm contests. Without the large-scale attention the presidential race receives, voter interest and engagement in the midterm elections are lower, and thus turnout tends to suffer. Even in the highly charged midterm elections of 2006, voter turnout was just 41 percent, almost fifteen percentage points below voter turnout figures for the preceding presidential election.

Second, midterm elections fail to offer congressional candidates what has come to be known as the **coattail effect.** In a presidential election year, the names of candidates for Congress typically are listed below the name of their party's candidate for president on the ballot. Thus, voters' selection of congressional candidates may be influenced by their choice for president. The congressional candidates, in effect, ride the coattails of the presidential candidate.[26] For the coattail effect to be apparent, the outcome of the presidential race typically needs to be a landslide victory for the winner, such as in 1984 when President Ronald Reagan soundly defeated Democrat Walter Mondale. For the first time in decades, the 1984 elections ushered in a Republican majority to the U.S. Senate. By contrast, George W. Bush's narrow victory in 2004 did not appear to produce a coattail effect.

Third, in midterm elections there has been a discernible trend—though often not very strong—that favors congressional candidates in the party opposite the president's party in midterm contests. When a president wins, especially by a large margin, the coattail effect distorts what would normally occur in any given congressional race. Yet in midterm elections, without the president's name at the top of the ballot, the absence of the coattail gives the advantage to the opposing party. In the modern era, the party in opposition to the president has managed to regain control of Congress only in the midterm elections when the president's popularity is waning. Thus in 1946 and then in 1994, the Republicans wrestled both houses of Congress back from the Democrats at midterm elections during the presidencies of Democrats Harry Truman and Bill Clinton, respectively. More recently in 2006, voters upset about the state of the war in Iraq dealt a devastating blow to the Republicans' control of Congress: though many Republican incumbents in the House and Senate were ousted from office that year, not one Democratic House member or Senator lost a seat in the 2006 midterm elections. The Democrats successfully rode the public's antiwar sentiment to regain control of both houses of Congress midway through the second term of Republican President George W. Bush.

American Government: Historical, Popular, and Global Perspectives

[25] For a thorough discussion of congressional elections, see Paul S. Herrnson, *Congressional Elections: Campaigning at Home and in Washington*, 2nd ed. (Washington, DC: CQ Press, 1998).

[26] For a complete discussion of the coattail effect, see Gary C. Jacobson, *Electoral Origins of Divided Government 1946–1988* (Boulder, CO: Westview Press, 1990).

More important than presidential coattails or any other factor in congressional elections, however, is the **power of incumbency.** Incumbent members of Congress, particularly those in the House, are returned to office by voters at amazingly high rates. In a normal year of House races, an incumbent who is running for re-election stands a better than 90 percent chance of being returned to office.[27] What accounts for such a high return rate? First, name recognition of the candidate is a significant factor in lower-profile congressional races, and incumbents, because they have been in office, tend to have higher name recognition than do challengers. Second, the vast majority of congressional districts and thus the vast majority of seats in Congress are dominated by either the Republican Party or the Democratic Party. Congressional seats from districts that include either a high percentage of Democratic voters or a high percentage of Republican voters are dominated by their respective majority party and are referred to as **safe seats.** A far smaller number of districts tend to have similar numbers of Democratic and Republican voters and are known as **marginal seats.** In the redistricting of congressional districts that periodically takes place, the political parties try to configure districts to their own partisan advantage. This maneuvering tends to create a large number of safe seats and often very few marginal seats (see Table 15.1).

Table 15.1 "Safe Seats" in Congress

The vast majority of the 435 seats in the House of Representatives, each of which are contested every two years, and the 100 U.S. Senate seats, each of which is contested every six years, are safe seats for incumbents who are running for re-election. Even if there is not an incumbent running for re-election, most of these seats tend to be safe for one of the two major political parties. In the 2006 midterm congressional elections, Republican incumbents suffered significant electoral setbacks, losing to Democratic challengers in six Senate races and twenty-two House races. Meanwhile, not one Democratic incumbent was defeated.

The table below shows the number of incumbents defeated and the number of seats that switched from one party to another in each congressional election since 1980. **Keep in mind that in each election year, 435 House races and 33 or 34 Senate races are usually contested.**

Year	Incumbents Defeated	Open Seats Where Party Changed	Total Changes	Incumbents Defeated	Open Seats Where Party Changed	Total Changes[28]
	House of Representatives			Senate		
1980	30	11	41	9	3	12
1982	23	8	31	2	2	4
1984	16	6	22	3	1	4
1986	6	15	21	7	3	10
1988	6	3	9	4	3	7
1990	15	6	21	1	0	1
1992	24	19	43	4	0	4
1994	35	26	61	2	6	8
1996	21	14	35	1	3	4
1998	6	11	17	3	3	6
2000	6	12	18	6	2	8
2002	4	8	12	3	1	4
2004	5	5	10	1	7	8
2006	22	8	30	6	0	6

Source: Harold W. Stanley and Richard G. Niemi, *Vital Statistics on American Politics 2005–2006,* pp. 48–49. (Washington, DC: CQ Press, 2006). Copyright ©2006 CQ Press, a division of Sage Publications.

[27] See Gary C. Jacobson, *The Politics of Congressional Elections,* 5th ed. (New York: Longman, 2001), chapter 3.
[28] Figures include only shifts from one major party to the other party.

Finally, incumbent members of Congress enjoy financial advantages, such as the **franking privilege,** which allows members to mail materials to their constituents without paying postage.

Now & Then: Making the Connection

Elections and campaigns are central features of the republican form of government in the United States. The number of elections is many, the cost of campaigns is high, and the process for selecting the nation's chief officeholder, the president of the United States, is long and complex. Several times in the nation's history the complicated procedure for selecting a president has resulted in considerable controversy, as in the elections of 1876 and 2000. Yet through these controversies and many others, the U.S. political system has maintained free, open, and regular elections since George Washington was unanimously chosen as the nation's first president in 1789. U.S. presidential elections evoke a great deal of passion, engage the interest of millions of voters; persuade vast numbers of citizens and groups to contribute large amounts of money, and focus attention on the great issues of the day. Thus campaigns and elections duly serve their purpose in providing an important connection between Americans and their government.

One significant development in the financing of the 2008 presidential primaries and caucuses was the success Democratic candidate Barack Obama enjoyed in raising many small donations using the Internet. According to the non-partisan Campaign Finance Institute, Obama raised $101 million in small individual contributions of $200 or less through March 31, 2008. The vast majority of these small donations were made through the Internet. As compared to larger donations solicited directly from individuals, these Internet donations offered Obama numerous advantages: (1) they provided his campaign with broad-based funding at no cost, as compared to more expensive methods such as events, telemarketing, and direct mail; (2) they required little time or effort on the part of the candidate himself; and (3) they filled the campaign's coffers without the risk of influence buying that accompanies larger contributions from a smaller number of individuals. Howard Dean, a candidate for the Democratic nomination in 2004, became the first presidential candidate to tap funds so successfully in this way—his campaign raised $50 million in the third quarter of 2003 with an average donation size of $80. In 2008, Obama refined and built on Dean's model, helping Obama secure his party's presidential nomination.

On http://academic.cengage.com/dautrich, find the politics interactive link for information about the Internet campaign financing phenomenon, including analysis of which candidates have benefited the most from Internet donations in recent election cycles. Historical, popular, and global perspectives on the issue are also presented.

BLOOMBERG NEWS/LANDOV/PHOTOSHOT, INC.

http://academic.cengage.com/dautrich

Chapter Summary

★ The system for choosing U.S. presidents includes two distinct phases: a nomination phase (during which major-party nominees are chosen) and a general election phase (in which a new president is selected).

★ From 1796 up through the 1830s, the nomination process was dominated by officials of the two major parties who chose party nominees based on informal discussions. Andrew Jackson and the Democratic Party he founded gave the "common man" increased influence in choosing nominees; by the twentieth century, electoral reforms such as the direct primary gave voters in many states a formal opportunity to cast a ballot for delegates, who would in turn choose their party's nominees at a national convention.

★ Modern presidential elections begin with a prenomination campaign waged by potential candidates to raise money and gain the support of key party leaders. A candidate's failure to raise sufficient funds in this "invisible primary" may cause him or her to drop out of the race before any formal primaries or caucuses have been held.

★ Nomination campaigns focus on attaining victories in presidential primaries and caucuses. The Iowa caucus and the New Hampshire primary have traditionally come at the beginning of the nomination calendar, and so they tend to disproportionately influence the final outcomes. In recent elections, many states have attempted to move their primaries and caucuses up on the calendar in a process known as frontloading.

★ National party conventions used to play an important role in helping choose party nominees; today they are mostly made-for-television affairs, anointing the party ticket with speeches offering testimonials to the nominees.

★ General election races may be either incumbent races (pitting a sitting president against a challenger) or open elections (with no incumbent in the race). In the former, the election often amounts to a referendum on the performance of the president over the previous four years.

★ Presidential candidates choose their running mates (the vice presidential candidates) strategically to address specific weaknesses of the presidential candidate or to boost the ticket's prospects in certain geographical areas.

★ To win the presidency, a candidate must put together a coalition of states sufficient to win a majority of the 538 Electoral College votes, which are allocated to each state based on the sum of the number of senators and the number of representatives. The candidate who does well in "battleground states" will normally win the 270 or more votes necessary to secure a majority.

★ Televised presidential debates between major presidential candidates occurred for the first time in 1960 and have been held in every presidential election since 1976. These debates tend to receive a large amount of attention from the press and the public, but their impact on the final election outcome remains unclear.

★ Campaign funding is critical to the success of individual candidates. Election laws since 1974 have limited the amount individuals or organizations can give to candidates (hard money). The Bipartisan Campaign Reform Act (BCRA) of 2002 went a step further, restricting expenditures to political parties or advocacy groups that are theoretically independent of specific candidates or campaigns (soft money). The Federal Election Commission enforces all such limitations.

★ In congressional elections, the power of incumbency is more important than any other factor. Unlike the case in midterm elections, congressional elections that coincide with presidential elections tend to produce greater voter turnout, and members of the successful presidential candidate's party sometimes benefit from the coattail effect.

Key Terms

Battleground states (p. 463)

Bipartisan Campaign Reform Act (BCRA) of 2002 (p. 473)

Buckley v. Valeo (1976) (p. 473)

Caucus (p. 457)

Closed primary (p. 457)

Coattail effect (p. 474)

Electoral College (p. 466)

Electors (p. 466)

Federal Election Campaign Act (FECA) (p. 472)

Federal Election Commission (FEC) (p. 472)

Franking privilege (p. 476)

Frontloading (p. 458)

Hard money (p. 472)

Incumbent race (p. 460)

Independent campaign expenditure (p. 473)

Invisible primary (p. 455)

Marginal seat (p. 475)

Midterm congressional elections (p. 474)

Nomination campaign (p. 458)

Open primary (p. 457)

Open seat election (p. 461)

Power of incumbency (p. 475)

Prenomination campaign (p. 455)

Presidential primary (p. 456)

Safe seat (p. 475)

Soft money (p. 472)

Unit rule (p. 466)

Resources

Important Books

Abramson, Paul R., John H. Aldrich, and David W. Rohde. *Change and Continuity in the 2000 Elections.* Washington, DC: CQ Press, 2002.

Edwards, George. *Why the Electoral College Is Bad for America.* New Haven, CT: Yale University Press, 2004.

Magleby, David B., ed. *Financing the 2000 Election.* Washington, DC: Brookings Institution Press, 2002.

Mayer, William G., and Andrew Busch. *The Frontloading Problem in Presidential Nominations.* Washington, DC: Brookings Institution Press, 2003.

Wayne, Stephen J. *The Road to the White House 2008*, 8th ed. Boston: Wadsworth Press, 2008.

Internet Resources

http://www.electoral-vote.com (a website that takes the polls in each state and classifies a state as likely to provide electoral votes to each of the major-party candidates; this site estimates the Electoral College vote outcome and provides other historical data on Electoral College outcomes and statewide polls)

http://www.ammi.org/livingroomcandidate (the University of Oklahoma and the American Museum of the Moving Image produce this valuable site, which contains televised campaign advertisements of candidates since the 1952 election)

http://www.opensecrets.org (this site, maintained by the Center for Responsive Politics, contains a wealth of information about PACs, campaign finance, and links to the Federal Election Commission's data)

http://www.democrats.org (this is the site for the Democratic National Committee and provides information on the schedule for primaries, caucuses, and the Democratic National Convention, among other details about the party)

http://www.rnc.org (this is the site for the Republican National Committee and provides information on the schedule for primaries, caucuses, and the Republican National Convention, among other details about the party)

American Economic Policy

16

President George W. Bush with two of his economic advisors, Edward Lazear (left), chair of the Council of Economic Advisors, and Al Hubbard (right), director of the National Economic Council, in 2006.

MANDEL NGAN/AFP/GETTY IMAGES

British economist John Maynard Keynes

Making Good Use of Economic Theories: Now & Then

The president of the United States was no economist, so he kept economists on his White House staff to help him make sense of detailed economic data. He understood politics and the way that economic forces could make or break his administration. He also knew that certain economic theories justified the fiscal policies he was now advocating as president—he hoped these policies would win him a large degree of support, and if all went well, ensure that his administration would leave a successful economic legacy. Thus the president stood fast by his economic policies and the theories on which they were based, even in the face of some harsh criticism from adherents of competing theories. In the short term, his faith was rewarded; it wasn't until later in his presidency that those same policies were once again criticized, this time for creating economic deficits that would be difficult to tame for the foreseeable future.

NOW &

STRENGTHENING

AMERICA'S

ECONOMY

2001

Now. . . As president, George W. Bush often cited the theory of "supply-side economics" as the way to increase productivity and lower unemployment. This theory, also referred to as "trickle-down" economics, favors cutting tax rates as a means of putting more money in the hands of people and businesses; the money in turn trickles down into the economy and stimulates an increase in overall spending and production. Citing supply-side theory, President Bush successfully pressed for tax cuts in 2001. During Bush's first year in office Congress passed three major tax cuts, and after a short recession in late 2001 and 2002, the economy quickly stabilized, increasing the president's re-election prospects significantly. Re-elected in 2004, Bush advocated making his tax cuts permanent and pushed for additional tax cuts in 2005 and 2006. Unfortunately, the combination of tax cuts, the 2001 recession, and extensive outlays for national defense combined to produce an average annual deficit of $374 billion during Bush's first term in office; by 2005 the debt had reached a record level of $7.9 trillion, and by 2008 it stood at a record $9.5 trillion. Congress was thus wary of passing more tax cuts during Bush's second term, although in early 2008 it approved a $168 billion economic stimulus plan that issued tax rebate checks to most Americans. Moreover, Bush's supply-side philosophy continued to hold favor among the Republican faithful; in addition to supporting efforts to make Bush's tax cuts permanent, 2008 Republican candidate John McCain proposed $650 million in tax cuts of his own during the presidential election contest.

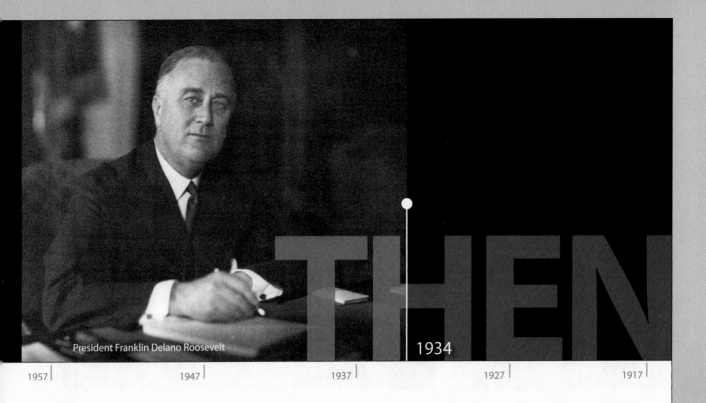

President Franklin Delano Roosevelt

THEN

1934

PHOTO: TIME LIFE PICTURES/GETTY IMAGES

1957 1947 1937 1927 1917

Then. . . Quite a different economic theory held sway among key policy makers in Franklin D. Roosevelt's administration of the mid-1930s. During a visit to the White House in 1934, British economist John Maynard Keynes urged Roosevelt to forget about the steep deficit that arose when tax revenues dried up during the Great Depression and instead engage in even more government spending to create jobs, build the nation's infrastructure, and assist struggling industries. Keynesian economic theory, named for the economist, is based on the principle that taxation, government spending, and other forms of intervention can help spur the economy forward, even during bad economic times. The Roosevelt administration relied on these tools of fiscal policy to minimize unemployment and increase productivity. Ignoring the protests of Treasury Department officials who advocated greater fiscal responsibility by tightening the government's belts, Roosevelt all but abandoned his efforts to balance the budget and eventually launched a $5 billion spending program in the spring of 1938 in an effort to increase mass purchasing power. Though few recognized it at the time, Keynesian economic theory was transforming the economic policy making of the U.S. government. Of course the deficit also mushroomed; only the onset of World War II curbed the out-of-control budget shortfalls that resulted from the implementation of economic policies based on Keynes's theory.

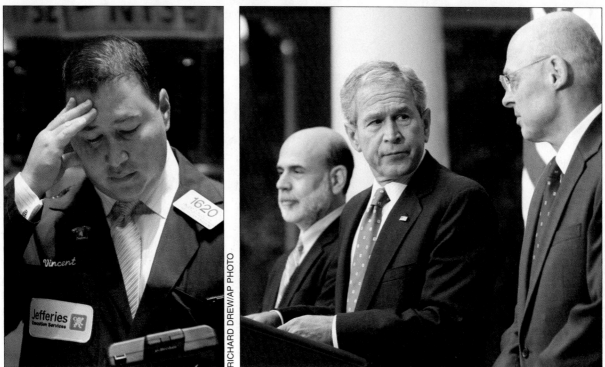

Left: A trader on the floor of the New York Stock Exchange on September 17, 2008. Right: Left to right, Federal Reserve Chairman Ben Bernanke, President Bush, and Treasury Secretary Henry Paulson deliver a statement about the government's plans to address the nation's financial crisis of September 2008.

E conomic theories may come and go, but that doesn't diminish their influence on economic policy in the United States. Until the 1930s, the leading fiscal theory was the so-called classical (or "laissez-faire") view of economics. According to this view, the economy is a self-adjusting mechanism that works best without government interference of any kind. From the late 1930s through the late 1960s, Keynesian theory held sway with presidents and lawmakers alike, and economic policies reflected this new Keynesian "tax-and-spend" mentality. Then in the 1980s (and later revived by George W. Bush during the first decade of the twenty-first century), supply-side economic theory guided economic policy making under Republican presidents. Trillions of dollars can change hands based on policies that draw from whatever theory of economics is favored by those in power.

In September 2008, the collapse of several important investment banks led to stock prices spiraling downward and fears that the American economic system was in peril. Congress reluctantly passed a "rescue" package of $700 billion in an attempt to quiet such fears, although many complained that the package essentially bailed out those on Wall Street who had caused the mess in the first place with their risky lending practices. After these dramatic events, few would soon again doubt the importance of economic policy to our nation, as well as to the world.

An Overview of the Policy-Making Process

★ Public policy

The set of laws, regulations, and rules that affect the whole of society.

Public policy refers to the set of laws, regulations, and rules that affect the whole of society. In the United States, the term public policy has come to be associated in particular with the response of public institutions—usually in the form of some principle, plan, or formal course of action—to events and conditions that occur both inside and outside the government.

Because the responsibilities and interests of private and public institutions often overlap, some battles that are waged primarily among private parties may still fall under the general subject of public policy—after all, government may seek to enact laws or regulations aimed at monitoring such disputes. Antitrust laws, for example, offer a public policy response to disputes that arise between competing private companies such as Microsoft and Netscape. Microsoft's dominance of the market for operating systems on personal computers afforded it the leverage and market power to demand that hardware manufacturers such as Dell and Gateway refuse to install other non-Microsoft products such as search engines; those demands in turn made it hard (some say impossible) for companies such as Netscape to compete. Government regulators feared that absent some form of competition, Microsoft would eventually be in a position to gouge consumers with artificially high prices on all its products. Thus the regulation of Microsoft and the agreements it entered into with manufacturers quickly became a matter of public policy in the 1990s, even though those agreements were technically between private entities.

Although the policy-making process tends to vary considerably from one subject area to another, most policies unfold in five separate stages:

★ The *recognition/definition stage*, in which objectives to be fulfilled and goals to be pursued through policy are first identified and defined according to how the problem fits within existing policy categories, and then prioritized;

★ The *formulation stage*, in which various alternative courses for this policy are considered, and a preferred course is selected;

★ The *adoption (or legitimation) stage*, in which the policy under consideration assumes the authority of law through ratification by Congress or through regulations issued by the relevant administrative agencies;

★ The *implementation stage*, in which a bureaucratic agency translates law into action though the adoption of administrative regulations and the dedication of agency resources to carry out the policy; and

★ The *evaluation stage*, in which the policy is assessed for its worth and effectiveness in meeting its original objectives and goals.

A large number of actors and institutions are involved in making policy in the United States. Bureaucrats in administrative agencies often play a key role at every stage of the policy-making process, helping to define the problem and identify the possible options, proposing alternatives and implementing the preferred course, and assisting in collecting information necessary to evaluate the policy.[1] In the Department of Commerce, for example, in addition to the Secretary of Commerce, the department employs at least six undersecretaries responsible for overseeing the formulation of numerous policy initiatives on behalf of the agency. Just one of those commerce officials, the Undersecretary for the National Oceanic and Atmospheric Administration, oversees a $4 billion bureaucracy that supervises the National Marine Fisheries Service, the National Ocean Service, and the National Weather Service, among other ocean-related agencies.

Congress and the president are most directly involved in the recognition, formulation, and adoption stages of policy making, when media attention is most intense; their influence over the other stages is limited by the practical need to delegate administrative details to agencies with the resources and expertise to handle such matters. The courts may play a role in ensuring that all proper procedures are followed in the formulation of policy and in interpreting rules, regulations, and policies that emerge from the policy-making process.[2]

Interest groups and "think tanks" (policy research institutes) tend to be most active in influencing program choices and decisions, where they have the opportunity to make significant gains on behalf of their members.[3] Think tanks are organizations that do intensive research and problem solving, either on behalf of other entities, or on their own (see Table 16.1, p. 486). Interest groups such as the Sierra Club, for example, lobby bureaucrats at the EPA and members of Congress on environmental committees

[1] Carl E. Van Horn, Donald Baumer, and William T. Gormley Jr., *Politics and Public Policy*, 3rd ed. (Washington, DC: CQ Press, 2001).
[2] Ibid., pp. 193–230.
[3] William T. Gormley Jr., "Interest Group Interventions in the Administrative Process" in Paul C. Herrnson, Ronald G. Shaiko, and Clyde Wilcox, eds., *The Interest Group Connection* (Chatham, NJ: Chatham House, 1998), pp. 213–223.

Table 16.1 Influential Policy Think Tanks

Institute	Date Established	Philosophy/Goals
American Enterprise Institute	1943	A conservative think tank dedicated to preserving "limited government, private enterprise . . . and a strong foreign policy and national defense."
The Brookings Institution	Roots trace back to 1916	To improve "the performance of American institutions and the quality of public policy" through the use of social science.
The Cato Institute	1977	Mostly libertarian; seeks to broaden the parameters of public policy debate to allow consideration of "the traditional American principles of limited government, individual liberty, free markets, and peace."
The Heritage Foundation	1973	Seeks "to formulate and promote conservative public policies based on the principles of free enterprise, limited government, individual freedom, traditional American values, and a strong national defense."
The Rand Corporation	1945	Seeks to provide policy analysis and solutions that address challenges facing the nation and the world, including education, poverty, crime, and the environment, as well as a range of national security issues.
The Progressive Policy Institute	1989	Affiliated with the Democratic Leadership Council; maintains as its mission the definition and promotion of a new progressive politics in America. Its work rests on three ideals: equal opportunity, mutual responsibility, and self-governing citizens and communities.

to ensure that the Clean Air Act is successfully updated to meet new challenges. The specialized committee structure of Congress encourages interest groups to focus their resources on those legislators and members of legislative staffs who have authority over relevant issue areas. Normally, a think tank staffed by researchers and policy analysts will produce an elaborate report detailing the implications of the problem it has studied; as with interest groups, it then seeks to publicize its findings, whether by holding a press conference, sponsoring a symposium or panel discussion, or some other means.

This chapter focuses on economic policy making, which encompasses all the legislative and rule-making initiatives that affect the management of wealth and resources within this country. For much of its history, the United States maintained one of the world's most entrepreneurially free economies, with minimal government regulation. The government's mostly hands-off approach to economic matters survived until the early part of the twentieth century, when the federal government began to insert itself more regularly in the economy. At first, government involvement was directed at antitrust matters and corporate abuses such as the employment of child labor; by the 1930s government involvement had begun to take a variety of new forms, as federal agencies actively oversaw the monetary system, supported struggling businesses, regulated the stock and bond markets, and otherwise reinforced the economic infrastructure as a whole. Indeed, immediately following the frightening events on Wall Street that occurred in September 2008, few from either political party questioned the wisdom of increasing government oversight of Wall Street. Today the government's role in managing the economy is significant—

often decided by voter perceptions of success or failure in this area. Overseeing the economy includes two distinct forms of policy making: fiscal policy making and monetary policy making.

Theory and Practice in Fiscal Policy

Fiscal policy is concerned with how to raise revenue through taxation and how to spend the revenue generated. Many economists believe that the nation's fiscal policy has direct implications for unemployment, that is, the percentage of the workforce that wants to work and is not currently employed, and **inflation,** or consistent increases in the prices of goods and services. The primary instrument by which the federal government manages fiscal policy is the *federal budget,* a comprehensive plan laying out what the government will spend for its various programs during the coming fiscal years and how it expects to raise the money to pay for them.

Fiscal policy can be thought of as lying on a spectrum. At one end of the spectrum is the policy of minimal government interference in the economy, in which the government exercises little or no budget-making power by authorizing only minimal spending, taxation, and regulation of private business practices. At the opposite end of the spectrum is fiscal policy that involves considerable government intervention in the economy, perhaps by taxing citizens or by offering subsidies to farmers in return for their agreement not to overproduce certain commodities.

A variety of economic theories explain the decision to craft fiscal policy at a given point along the fiscal policy spectrum. For example, the economic doctrine known as **laissez-faire** (a French phrase meaning literally "leave us alone") guided the fiscal policy that prevailed for much of the eighteenth and nineteenth centuries in the United States.[4] Laissez-faire favors less intervention in the economy, allowing businesses to conduct their affairs more or less free from governmental regulation. The theory came under attack toward the end of the 1800s, when increasing industrialization led to more frequent financial panics, bouts of severe unemployment, corrupt business practices, and the abuse of workers, especially in big cities. Government's involvement in the economy gradually increased, and in the 1930s widespread public support for President Franklin Roosevelt's New Deal programs, enacted to address the problems of the Great Depression, effectively spelled the end of laissez-faire theory as the guiding principle for the nation's fiscal policy.

As was discussed in the opening, FDR's New Deal policies were based on **Keynesian economic theory,** named for the British economist John Maynard Keynes. Keynesian theory argues that the government should increase spending when economic times are bad as a way of raising total demand. Total demand for goods and services, according to this theory, is the key determinant of whether the economy is performing well.[5] The economic recovery that occurred during World War II, when federal military spending increased significantly, is often used to support the validity of Keynesian theory. Administrations that attempted to draw on the theory quickly learned that although government spending may forestall or even end a **recession**—defined as an economic slowdown characterized by higher unemployment, reduced productivity, or some other negative economic indicators—it may also bring about other economic problems such as inflation and chronically high deficits.

Supply-side economics is an alternative to Keynesian economics, arguing that rather than increasing government spending, cutting taxes (and cutting the government spending such taxes help to fund) is the preferred way to increase economic productivity and spur the economy. According to supply-side theory, high taxes take money out of the economy that would otherwise be invested in goods and services; thus by decreasing taxes, money flows back into the economy, stimulating business, new jobs, and overall productivity. While campaigning for the presidency in 1980, Ronald Reagan seized on this theory to

★ **Fiscal policy**

Decisions by the federal government that relate to raising revenue through taxation and spending the revenue that is thereby generated.

★ **Inflation**

The overall general upward price movement of goods and services in an economy, normally measured by the Consumer Price Index (CPI).

★ **Laissez-faire economics**

Fiscal policy theory that favors minimal intervention in the nation's economy.

★ **Keynesian economic theory**

Fiscal policy theory that favors government taxation and spending during difficult economic times.

★ **Recession**

An economic slowdown characterized by high unemployment, reduced productivity, or other negative economic indicators.

★ **Supply-side economics**

Economic theory that favors cutting taxes as way of increasing economic productivity.

[4] See Adam Smith, *The Wealth of Nations*, reprinted in Adam Smith, *The Wealth of Nations* (New York: Modern Library, 1994).
[5] John Maynard Keynes's most famous work is *The General Theory of Employment, Interest, and Money* (New York: Harcourt Brace Jovanovich, 1936).

Chapter 16: American Economic Policy

propose that a program of tax cuts, spending cuts, and balancing the budget was the best means to get the economy out of recession. (As president, Reagan did secure passage of a large tax cut, but federal spending and deficits also multiplied during his eight years in office.)[6]

Assessing the Economy's Performance

Just as different economic theories guide the crafting of fiscal policy, different measures are used to assess whether the nation's fiscal policy has been a success. Listed below are several economic measures regarded as especially significant indicators of general economic performance:

★ Gross domestic product (GDP)

An estimate of the total money value of all the goods and services produced in the U.S. a one-year period.

★ **Gross domestic product (GDP)** is an estimate of the total money value of all the goods and services produced in the U.S. in a given one-year period. When GDP improves, workers are producing more in fewer hours, allowing employers in turn to increase wages without raising prices. By contrast, declining productivity signals higher labor costs and, ultimately, higher prices for consumers. Measured in constant dollars (that is, adjusting for inflation), the GDP enjoyed its highest one-year increase during the past half century in 1984, when it rose by 6.8 percent. The GDP has actually fallen in constant dollars in five separate years over that same fifty-year time span.

★ The *Consumer Price Index (CPI)* is an index of prices for goods and services regularly traded in the U.S. economy. A sustained rise over time in the CPI indicates that inflation is on the rise and consumers' buying power is on the decline. Although critics argue that the CPI overstates inflation by at least 1 percent per year, the government still heavily relies on the CPI in defining tax brackets and spending for certain entitlement programs, such as cost-of-living adjustments for Social Security recipients. In 1980, the CPI increase for urban consumers was 13.5 percent, the highest figure recorded in more than three decades. Since 1983, the CPI has not increased by more than 6 percent in any given year.

★ The *unemployment rate* measures the percentage of people unemployed and actively looking for work in the U.S. labor market. Although a major goal of the economic programs of most Western governments (including the United States) is to keep unemployment relatively low, full employment remains an elusive goal due to seasonal factors, voluntary job changes, and routine shifts in economic conditions (such as the rise in interest rates) that assist some businesses (construction companies and home loan financing companies) and de-emphasize others (apartment rental firms). In recent years, a rate of 5 percent has been considered a realistic minimum for unemployment in the United States. That rate is certainly better than the unemployment rate of nearly 10 percent recorded in 1982 and early 1983.

★ Budget deficit

The amount of money spent by the U.S. government beyond that which it collects in taxes and other revenue in a single year.

★ Budget surplus

The amount of money left over in a single year after the government has spent all its revenue for that year.

★ The **budget deficit** is the amount of money spent by the U.S. government over and above what it collects in taxes and other revenue in a single year. A **budget surplus,** on the other hand, is the amount of money left over after the government has spent all of its revenue. The federal government has posted annual budget surpluses just eleven times since 1931, although it did so four straight years from 1998 through 2001. Prior to 1998, the last surplus recorded was in 1969, the first year of Richard Nixon's presidency. Although budget deficits are often compelled by national crises that require the quick allotment of funds for

American Government: Historical, Popular, and Global Perspectives

---

[6] See David Stockman, *The Triumph of Politics: How the Reagan Revolution Failed* (New York: Harper & Row, 1986).

some specific purpose (such as responding to the September 11 terrorist attacks), critics argue that continued budget deficits beyond a short period of time can lead to politically unpopular remedies such as tax increases or spending cuts, or alternatively, to a burgeoning national debt that can slow economic growth in the long run.

Long lines at an unemployment office in St. Louis, Missouri, in 1975.

★ The **national debt** is the total sum of the outstanding debt obligations of the U.S. government, most often entered with individuals or organizations whenever they purchase interest-bearings U.S. savings bonds, U.S. treasury notes, and U.S. treasury bills. It represents the accumulated total of all government budget surpluses and deficits of past years as well.[7] In recent years the debt has reached into the trillions of dollars, requiring the government to pay in excess of $350 billion per year in interest costs alone. That means to meet interest obligations on the debt, the government must annually pay out the equivalent of about $1,000 for every man, woman, and child in the country.

★ The *Dow Jones Industrial Average* is perhaps the most widely used indicator of the overall condition of the stock market where publicly owned companies are actively traded each business day. "The Dow" is actually just a price-weighted average of thirty actively traded blue chip stocks (that is, from large companies), but its prominence on network newscasts each evening testifies to the important status it holds in the minds of consumers. Other stock market indexes include the Standard & Poor's 500 Index, which encompasses a broader range of large company stocks, and the NASDAQ, an index of high-tech company stocks.

★ *Housing starts* are a measure of the number of U.S. residential building construction projects begun during a specific period of time. Many experts believe that a decline in housing starts provides one of the first signs of an approaching economic downturn, and thus it is one of the first indicators consulted by those trying to assess the overall direction of the economy.

★ The *consumer confidence index* measures the public's evaluation of the economy by asking a representative sample of Americans how they feel about the current condition of the economy, their personal financial situation, and their prediction about the future of the economy.

★ *Balance of trade figures* (also called net exports) measure the sum of the money gained by a given economy by selling exports, minus the cost of buying imports. When a country exports more than it imports, that signifies that the country has a trade surplus, whereas the reverse situation denotes a trade deficit. The United States has posted an annual trade deficit dating back to the 1970s; this is perhaps a testament to the rising purchasing power American consumers enjoy around the world. Economists often debate whether such chronic trade deficits are a bad thing; regardless, because especially large trade deficits or surpluses may be a sign of some other economic problems, economists keep a watchful eye on these measures.

★ National debt

Total sum of the federal government's outstanding debt obligations.

---

7 John Steele Gordon, *Hamilton's Blessing: The Extraordinary Life and Times of Our National Debt* (New York: Penguin, 1998).

American Government . . . in Popular Perspective:
The Public and the Budget Deficit

Some economists liken government deficits to businesses or households that run deficits: by failing to match expenditures to revenues, the government is deemed to be acting irresponsibly. Others contend that government-run deficits can be a legitimate tool of fiscal policy if they are employed strategically, such as to stimulate the economy during a recession. Regardless, it is clear that deficits are a real concern for a majority of Americans as indicated by the results of two surveys conducted in 2005.

Associated Press/Ipsos-Public Affairs Poll (July 2005)

"How much do you worry about the size of the federal budget deficit? A lot, some, not much, not at all…"

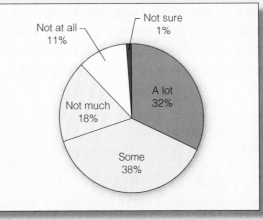

Source: Survey by Associated Press. Methodology: Conducted by Ipsos-Public Affairs, July 5–July 7, 2005.

Democracy Corps Poll (June 2005)

"I am going to read you a list of issues relating to the economy. For each issue I want you to tell me whether today you think it is a very serious problem, a serious problem, not too serious a problem, or not a problem at all in the current economy…. The federal deficit…"

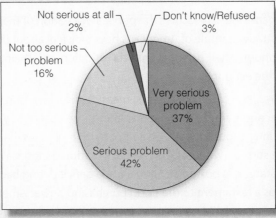

Source: Survey by Democracy Corps. Methodology: Conducted by Greenberg Quinlan Rosner Research, June 20–June 25, 2005.

In an effort to gauge the state of the economy as a whole, economists have attempted to combine these measures and others into some all-purpose economic indicator. For example, the misery index, measured by adding the inflation rate to the unemployment rate, is a rough indicator of how bad the economy is performing. Jimmy Carter capitalized on an exceedingly high misery index for 1975 to defeat incumbent President Gerald Ford, only to be victimized by an even higher misery index in 1979, which may well have cost Carter re-election in 1980.

Although most observers agree that presidents actually exert only a marginal impact on the economy, economic performance can still be a crucial factor in determining which party wins a presidential election.[8] The U.S. economy normally runs in cycles. The onset of a recession tends to deliver a "one-two punch" against the economy: first, federal revenues decline as profits decrease and fewer people work; then federal expenditures increase as people claim more and more *entitlements* (guaranteed government benefits such as food stamps and welfare) to get them through the jobless period. A recession is eventually followed by an economic recovery, marked by an upswing of positive economic indicators.

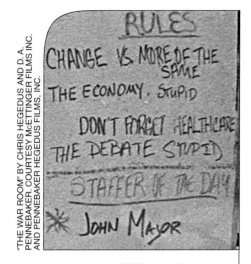

Bill Clinton's 1992 campaign emphasized a handful of major themes, as captured on this white board at campaign headquarters. The saying "it's the economy, stupid," reminded Clinton and top officials in his campaign that they needed to hammer away at the poor state of the nation's economy in 1992.

The Federal Budget-Making Process

Once considered to be little more than a document detailing sums of money to be spent for particular purposes, the federal budget today has become the primary instrument of federal fiscal policy. The Budget and Accounting Act of 1921 made the president formally responsible for initially formulating the national budget. Today, the president's budget establishes the position around which all subsequent budget battles will be fought. With passage of the Employment Act of 1946, Congress permanently committed the federal government to use the budgetary process to promote maximum employment, production, and purchasing power. Together, these two acts obligate the president to craft budgets strategically to strengthen the economy.

The budget process begins when federal agencies formulate their budget requests and pass them on to the Office of Management and Budget (OMB). A part of the Executive Office of the President, the OMB determines whether the agency's budget proposals are in accord with the president's program and then uses those proposals to prepare an overall budget for the coming fiscal year, setting guidelines for estimating revenue and allotting spending.[9]

After receiving the president's proposals, Congress offers its own budget resolution for the fiscal year, based on its own projections for revenue. The Appropriations committees of the House and the Senate are primarily responsible for such budget formulation. Each of the two committees plans overview hearings during which the OMB director and representatives of federal agencies discuss the president's budget priorities. Each of the Appropriations committees must eventually pass ten to twelve appropriations bills to keep the government running. House appropriations bills generally cover the topic areas listed below, with some variations from year to year:

1. Agriculture, rural development, and related agencies

2. Science, the Departments of State, Justice, and related agencies

3. Defense

4. Transportation, Treasury, Housing and Urban Development, the Judiciary, the District of Columbia

5. Energy and Water development

6. Foreign operations, export financing, and related programs

---

[8] For a more detailed discussion of this argument, see the work of Michael Lewis-Beck, including *Economics and Elections: The Major Western Democracies* (Ann Arbor: University of Michigan Press, 1990).

[9] Shelley Lynne Tomkin, *Inside OMB: Politics and Process in the President's Budget Office* (Armonk, NY: M. E. Sharpe, 1998).

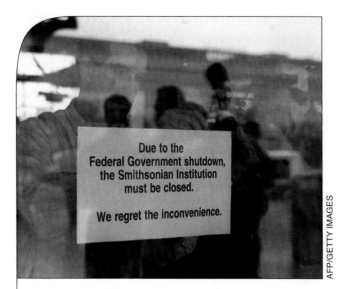

Due to the
Federal Government shutdown,
the Smithsonian Institution
must be closed.

We regret the inconvenience.

AFP/GETTY IMAGES

The Smithsonian Institution was among many government sites closed down during the 1995 government shutdown.

7. Homeland Security

8. Interior, Environment, and related agencies

9. Labor, Health and Human Services, and Education

10. Military Quality of Life and Veteran Affairs

All appropriations bills originate in the House; after the House Appropriations Committee has reported the bills to the full House, and after the full House has passed the each measure, the Senate Appropriations Committee takes its turn revising the House version. After Senate subcommittee work has been completed on the House bills, the Senate Appropriations Committee marks up its own versions of the bills and reports them to the Senate for floor action.

Congress created separate House and Senate Budget committees during the 1970s to oversee the budget process. The Budget and Impoundment Act of 1974 required Congress to set a maximum spending figure for the total budget and for each of several broad funding categories based on projections of future revenue. These figures are prepared by the Congressional Budget Office (CBO), which reports to Congress, and the OMB, which reports to the president. When the CBO and the OMB differ widely on estimates, as has happened frequently in recent years, Congress tends to side with its own agency. The House and Senate Budget committees may require cuts in spending to ensure that the overall budget targets can be reached. Eventually the House and Senate must reconcile their competing versions of the budget and secure additional votes from their members for approval of the final budget bill, which is then presented to the president for signature.

All these legislative obstacles must be navigated over a period of eight months, extending from the first Monday in February (when the president's budget proposal is delivered to Congress) through October 1, when the new fiscal year begins. If Congress and the president cannot agree on a final budget over this period of time, Congress may be forced to pass "continuing resolutions" to allow the government to keep running while final budget negotiations continue.[10] Occasionally, Congress and the president are at such loggerheads that a budget showdown is inevitable. In late 1995 the Republican Congress, led by House Speaker Newt Gingrich, insisted that President Bill Clinton sign a budget bill with spending cuts that Clinton's administration had strenuously opposed. When Congress refused to keep passing continuing resolutions, the resulting impasse led to two government shutdowns totaling twenty-seven days, during which all federal government institutions and buildings were forced to close.[11] Even after congressional leaders buckled under to the White House and reopened the government in January 1996, the fiscal year 1996 budget was still not fully enacted until April 24, 1996, almost six months late.

Even though the Senate and House Budget committees have brought more fiscal restraint to the budget process, some within and outside Congress attempted to introduce bolder budgetary reforms in response to the $200 billion deficits of the mid-1980s. The Gramm-Rudman-Hollings Act of 1985 set annual targets for reducing the deficit and required the General Accounting Office (GAO) to determine whether automatic spending cuts would take effect if Congress passed budgets that missed the established deficit target. In 1986, the Supreme Court struck down the act as unconstitutional because the GAO, accountable only to Congress, could not legally perform what were essentially "executive" acts.[12] The Budget Enforcement Act of 1990 set deficit targets that could be adjusted due to unforeseen economic changes; however, the act did not compensate for unexpected spending increases by requiring offsetting cuts elsewhere.

[10] See Allen Schick and Felix Lostracco, *The Federal Budget: Politics, Policy, Process* (Washington, DC: Brookings Institution Press, 2000).

[11] Elizabeth Drew, *Showdown: The Struggle Between the Gingrich Congress and the Clinton White House* (New York: Touchstone, 1997).

[12] *Bowsher v. Synar,* 478 U.S. 714 (1986).

Of course the central problem of the budget process—that it allows the federal government to spend more money than it takes in—remained in place even with such reforms. In recent years, Congress has debated passing a balanced budget amendment to the Constitution, which would require that annual federal spending be kept at or below revenue collected during the year. Proponents of the amendment argue that it would force free-spending lawmakers to become accountable: just as many taxpayers must live off what their income is (or even considerably less) the government should be expected to do likewise. Opponents of the amendment counter that the government might—in accordance with Keynesian principles—want to engage in deficit spending during times of recession as a method of economic stimulation. They also note that the federal government must be able to spend freely to defend the national security of the United States, even if that means running up large deficits. (Although recent versions of the amendment would allow Congress to waive the requirement in case of war or military conflict, critics argue that even more flexibility is necessary.) The Balanced Budget Amendment has been passed in one house but defeated in the other on five separate occasions since 1982. In 1995 and again in 1997, the amendment failed by a single vote in the U.S. Senate.

Taxation Policy

Taxation policies tend to fall into one of two general categories. **Redistributive tax policies** aim to provide a social safety net to meet the minimum physical needs of citizens. Such policies accomplish this end by following Robin Hood's principle of "taking from the rich and giving to the poor." For example, taxes that are channeled directly into public assistance programs are redistributive. **Distributive tax policies,** by comparison, theoretically promote the interests of all economic classes equally. Taxes that are directed toward the maintenance of national parks or the national highway system theoretically benefit all citizens.

All governments need revenue to pay the salaries of government workers and to fund its various activities. In July 1789, just four months after the creation of a new government, Congress passed its first revenue-raising bill: specifically, it levied **tariffs,** which are taxes on imported foreign goods. Up until the Civil War, tariffs provided approximately 90 percent of the federal government's revenue; yet as that war evolved into a long-lasting conflict, the Union needed far greater revenues than even high tariffs could provide. The exponential growth of the federal government after the Civil War exacerbated these demands further. Thus in the late nineteenth and early twentieth centuries, the federal government was forced to look elsewhere for major sources of funding. Eventually it started to draw more heavily on internal sources of revenue, including payroll taxes, corporate income taxes, and individual income taxes.

The Sixteenth Amendment to the U.S. Constitution authorizes Congress to tax an individual's increase in wealth, whether that wealth comes from wages, benefits, bonuses, or any other form of income. Today individual income taxes provide nearly half of all revenue that flows into the U.S. treasury. Although personal income taxes provide the single largest contribution to the nation's revenue, their fairness remains a subject of contentious debate. The federal government has traditionally imposed a **progressive tax** on incomes. With a progressive tax, the tax rate on an individual's income increases as the amount of income gets larger. Though President Reagan signed tax reform legislation in 1986 to cut top rates and close various loopholes, the personal income tax system still remained mostly progressive—today it goes up in several stages to a high of 35 percent for all wages earned over $319,101.

A **regressive tax** charges individuals the same amount, regardless of income. It thus exacts a larger percentage of income from the lower-wage earner than it does from the high-income earner. Most state sales taxes, for example, are regressive because they apply equally to every purchaser (for example, both a poor person and a wealthy person pay the same exact amount of sales tax for a gallon of gasoline) and thus in effect take a greater overall percentage of the income earned by the poor.

★ Redistributive tax policies

Taxation policies that aim to provide a social safety net to meet the minimum physical needs of citizens.

★ Distributive tax policies

Taxation policies that theoretically promote the interests of all classes equally.

★ Tariff

A tax on imported goods, charged at the time the goods are received in port.

★ Progressive tax

A tax whose effective rate on an individual's income increases as the person's income rises.

★ Regressive tax

A tax that charges individuals the same amount, regardless of income.

In his 2005 book, two-time presidential candidate Steve Forbes argued for a simplified flat tax form that would be the size of an index card.

GLEN DAVIS/FORBES

★Flat tax

A tax policy that draws money from all entities at the exact same rate as a proportion of their income.

Some people incorrectly confuse regressive taxes with **flat taxes.** Unlike regressive taxes, flat taxes tax all entities at the same rate *as a proportion of income.* Thus with a flat tax, a rich person may pay far more in total taxes than a poor person, although the two are still technically being taxed at the same rate of their overall income. In 1996 and 2000, presidential candidate Steve Forbes proposed that the federal government impose a flat tax of 15 percent on all income earned in the United States. Forbes argued that such a system would spread the tax burden more evenly, stop penalizing Americans for working harder to earn more, and dramatically simplify the current system.[13] Forbes's proposals have not fared well in the political arena; currently, neither of the two major parties is putting its weight behind a truly flat income tax for Americans.

Social Security taxes (a tax on personal income and on employers) contribute on average 35 percent to the federal government's overall revenues. Created in 1935, the Social Security system was intended to be self-supporting: payroll taxes would be taken directly out of each worker's paycheck and held until that employee's retirement many years later. In reality, however, the system has become "pay as you go," with current payroll taxes going directly to pay the benefits of current retirees.

During the past century Congress has also imposed corporate income taxes, which today comprise just less than 10 percent of the government's revenues. Other important revenue sources include federal taxes on gasoline and communications services, estates and large financial gifts, and customs duties. And if these revenue sources fall short of projected expenditures in the form of a deficit, the federal government must make up the difference by borrowing money in the form of issuing U.S. savings bonds, treasury bills, and the like.

Americans commonly complain about the high taxes they pay, and politicians do not like to be perceived as favoring tax increases; in 1984, Democratic presidential candidate Walter Mondale promised to raise taxes in response to skyrocketing

GLOBAL PERSPECTIVE

American Government . . . in Global Perspective:
A Brazilian Reflects on America's Fiscal Irresponsibility

Among the numerous Latin American states that have suffered turbulent financial times, Brazil has managed to strike a sharp contrast with its neighbors in recent years. After strategically micromanaging its economy out of the financial doldrums of the mid-1990s, the Brazilian government has cut inflation, increased privatization, and maintained a significant fiscal surplus for several years running. In early 2004, Brazilian journalist Boris Fausto of the liberal *Folha de Sao Paulo* expressed substantial alarm about America's suddenly increasing deficit:

. . . [E]xpenditures, added to tax cuts, within the framework of an economy in crisis, have resulted in the transformation of a fiscal surplus of $230 billion [. . .] into a deficit of $500 billion under the current administration . . . the principle of fiscal responsibility has been abandoned [by the U.S. government] in favor of security expenditures. . . . Since it is dubious to claim that expenditures of that nature stimulate the economy under the current circumstances, this is a good example of the predominance of ideology over pragmatism. . .

Source: World Press Review, January 2004, p. 40.

---

[13] Forbes's most recent proposal for a flat tax is discussed in Steve Forbes, *Flat Tax Revolution: Using a Postcard to Abolish the IRS* (Washington, DC: Regnery, 2005).

deficits, a promise that all but doomed his hopes of unseating President Ronald Reagan, the candidate more closely identified with lower taxes.

At the Republican National Convention in 1988, Vice President George H. W. Bush—having just been named his party's presidential nominee for the upcoming fall—sought to associate himself with the economic policies of the Reagan administration and its emphasis on tax cutting. In his speech accepting the nomination, Bush predicted that if elected president, the Democratic Congress would come to him, pushing him to raise taxes...

> *... and I'll say no, and they'll push, and I'll say no, and they'll push again, and I'll say to them: "READ MY LIPS: NO NEW TAXES."*

Bush's promise seemed politically astute at the time it was issued, and he coasted to victory that fall. But in 1990, with an economic recession firmly in place, Bush signed the Revenue Reconciliation Act, which aimed to reduce the federal deficit by $500 billion over the next five years. To accomplish that goal, the act called for $125 billion in new taxes, inviting charges that the president had flip-flopped on his 1988 pledge of "no new taxes." In the 1992 presidential campaign, Democratic candidate Bill Clinton attempted to capitalize on the flip-flop. Bush's defeat in the 1992 election was attributed in part to the lack of enthusiasm his candidacy had generated among conservatives, many of whom were still frustrated by the president's decision to sign that infamous tax bill in the first place. James Carville, chief political consultant to Clinton's 1992 presidential campaign, called it "the most famous broken promise in the history of American politics."

Still, despite all the complaints about high taxes, Americans' tax burden is quite low when compared with the tax burdens of other developed countries. Although U.S. citizens pay an income tax rate somewhere between 10 percent and 35 percent, citizens of Sweden pay twice that amount—between 33 percent and 60 percent of their income—to the Swedish government. Taxes paid by citizens in France, Germany, and Great Britain also tend to be higher (as a percentage of their income) than those paid by citizens of the United States. Of course such comparisons are not altogether fair—for example, Sweden, as part of its welfare system, provides all its citizens with an extensive tax-funded public child care system, dental care, and a ceiling on health care costs. England's tax-funded national health care service offers its citizens "free services" as well.

Then-Vice President George H. W. Bush, accepting the Republican Party's presidential nomination at its 1988 convention. Using a phrase he would later come to regret, Bush told the cheering crowd: "Read my lips . . . no new taxes."

Spending Policies—Dividing Up the Pie

Budget surpluses are a rarity in modern American politics because the federal government has demonstrated time and again its capacity to spend taxpayer money— government spending topped $2.6 trillion in fiscal year 2006 alone. Although the president is legally responsible for proposing budgets and has the power to veto spending decisions, Article I of the Constitution grants the Congress exclusive power to lay and collect duties "to pay the debts and provide for the common defense and general welfare of the United States." In reality, Congress allots funds from the U.S. treasury to federal departments and agencies and then gives them **budget authority,** which allows them to incur obligations to spend or lend that money. Budget authority for a fiscal year is essentially like the permission for an agency to enter a contract; it is not the same thing as how much the agency will spend in that fiscal year—that amount is called **outlays.**

Where does taxpayer money go? The truth about government spending might surprise you. Spending tends to fall into two general categories. **Mandatory spending** refers to spending not controlled by annual budget decisions—these funds are automatically obligated by virtue of previously enacted laws and may not be modified by annual budget decisions (although they can be modified by repeal or modification

★ **Budget authority**

The power federal departments and agencies maintain to incur obligations to spend or lend money.

★ **Outlays**

The power federal departments or agencies maintain to actually spend federal money in a given fiscal year.

★ **Mandatory spending**

Federal government spending that is not controlled by annual budget decisions, including entitlements such as Medicare and Social Security.

of the original legislation). Most mandatory spending occurs in the form of entitlements, government spending such as Social Security, Medicare (national health insurance for seniors), and veterans' benefits that must be paid to anyone meeting specific eligibility requirements. President Franklin Roosevelt's New Deal programs and President Lyndon Johnson's Great Society programs substantially expanded the number of entitlements, forcing future lawmakers to grapple with those entitlements when they considered reforms of their own. Since 1995, nearly two-thirds of all government spending has been mandatory, almost double the percentage of mandatory spending outlays of the early 1960s (see Figure 16.1, p. 498).

Discretionary spending encompasses all those spending categories that Congress does have the power to modify or eliminate in a given year. Budgeting is normally a give-and-take process between Congress and the president concerning the most appropriate levels of discretionary spending. Most federal spending on education, the environment, and national defense is based on discretionary spending outlays. When an administration's critics accuse the president of not being fiscally conservative enough with government spending, their criticisms usually focus on government spending as a whole; in fairness, however, only discretionary spending really lies within the president's immediate influence. In the eight years the Clinton administration was responsible for the federal budget (1994 through 2001), discretionary spending increased by an annual average of 3.4 percent; during the George W. Bush administration, discretionary spending has increased by an average of 10.5 percent annually.

Year in and year out, one particular mandatory spending category—Social Security spending—tops all the other categories. In fiscal year 2006, the federal government spent nearly $550 billion on the program, and Social Security expenditures of close to $600 billion are anticipated in the years to follow. Among the discretionary program outlays, national defense has traditionally constituted the largest part of the budget. In 1962, the federal government allotted $52.6 billion to defense, almost ten times the amount earmarked to any other discretionary program category. Four decades later, in 2006, over $500 billion was allotted to national defense. The growth in discretionary spending during the George W. Bush administration can be attributed in part to the administration's desire to increase spending on defense and homeland security in the wake of the terrorist attacks of September 11, 2001.

Theories and Practice in Monetary Policy

Monetary policy is the means by which the government controls the supply and price of money in the economy. Although this may seem like a nonpolitical, technical function, the exercise of monetary policy can have profound implications on unemployment rates and inflation, and thus is the focus of considerable political interest.

With few exceptions, the **Federal Reserve System,** which is headed by the **Federal Reserve Board** ("the Fed"), determines monetary policy in the United States. Since 1913, this independent agency has acted as the nation's central bank, supervising and regulating all of the nation's banks, and providing financial information to the public. In addition to the Federal Reserve Board, Congress established twelve nonprofit Federal Reserve Banks to serve as the operating arms of the central banking system. By law, all "member banks" in the United States (which includes all national banks and many state banks) must maintain fractional reserves—the portion of their deposits that must be kept on hand or at the Fed, as reserves to satisfy any demands for withdrawal. (Most fractional reserves are kept in accounts at the Federal Reserve Banks.) The Federal Reserve Banks in turn issue stock and pay dividends to member banks as partial compensation for the lack of interest they pay on member banks' required reserves. The Federal Reserve Board sets all rules and regulations for the Federal Reserve Banks.[14]

Perhaps the single most important responsibility of the Federal Reserve is to set the **discount rate** that all member banks and other depository institutions will be charged to borrow short-term funds. A high discount rate makes it more difficult for member banks to borrow money from the Federal Reserve Banks, but more profitable for banks

★ Discretionary spending

Forms of federal government spending that Congress can modify or eliminate in any given year, including spending on education, the environment, and national defense.

★ Monetary policy

Regulation of the money supply and interest rates by a central bank, such as the U.S. Federal Reserve Board, in order to control inflation and stabilize the currency.

★ Federal Reserve System

The central banking system of the United States, which controls the nation's money supply.

★ Federal Reserve Board

The Federal Reserve System's Board of Governors, which votes on monetary policy in the United States, supervises the nation's banks by setting rules for the twelve Federal Reserve Banks, and engages in open market operations.

★ Discount rate

The rate (expressed as a percentage) that all Federal Reserve member banks and other depository institutions will be charged by the Federal Reserve Banks to borrow short-term funds.

American Government: Historical, Popular, and Global Perspectives

---

[14] William Greider, *Secrets of the Temple: How the Federal Reserve Runs the Country* (New York: Simon & Schuster, 1989).

CHECKtheLIST

The Ten Countries with the Largest Defense Budgets

Even with the so-called peace dividend (the theoretical savings to military expenditures made possible when the Cold War with the Soviet Union ended in 1991), the United States managed to cut its defense budget the following year by only about $12 billion per year from the $303 billion it spent on the military in 1989. By 2005, the U.S. defense budget was greater than the world's next nine highest defense budgets combined! The ten countries with the largest defense budgets in 2005 were as follows. (All figures are in U.S. dollars, rounded off to the nearest billion.)

✔	**United States**	**$478 billion**
✔	**United Kingdom**	**$48 billion**
✔	**France**	**$46 billion**
✔	**Japan**	**$42 billion**
✔	**China**	**$41 billion**
✔	**Germany**	**$33 billion**
✔	**Italy**	**$27 billion**
✔	**Saudi Arabia**	**$25 billion**
✔	**Russia**	**$21 billion**
✔	**India**	**$20 billion**

Six of the countries listed above (Japan, the United Kingdom, Saudi Arabia, France, Germany, and Italy) can keep their defense budgets relatively low because they rely on the United States for indirect support of their own interests. This free rider problem offers a mixed blessing for the United States: it forces America to spend a disproportionate amount of money on the Western world's defense; but it also gives the nation some degree of leverage over these countries, because they are increasingly dependent on American goodwill.

Source: Stockholm International Peace Research Institute (www.sipri.org).

to lend money (because they'll secure a greater interest on their investment). The opposite is true when the Federal Reserve lowers the discount rate: banks are more apt to borrow money because it is cheaper, whereas lending money to others becomes less profitable. A second important function of the Federal Reserve is engaging in **open market operations,** by which it buys and sells government securities as a means of controlling the national money supply—buying bonds increases the amount of money in circulation, whereas selling has the opposite effect. Finally, the Federal Reserve sets the **reserve requirements** of member banks, determining the minimum liquid assets each bank must keep on hand to back customer loans. Any of these actions has the effect of either tightening or loosening the overall money supply.

In recent years, it has become common for investors to wait in eager anticipation of the Federal Reserve's announcement that it plans to adjust the interest rate up or down.[15] Although hardly an exact science, the Federal Reserve's setting of a new

★ Open market operations

The buying and selling of government securities by the Federal Reserve Board as a means of controlling the national money supply.

★ Reserve requirement

The minimum liquid assets each bank must keep on hand to back customer loans.

---

[15] This was especially true when Alan Greenspan headed the Federal Reserve. See Bob Woodward, *Greenspan's Fed and the American Boom* (New York: Simon & Schuster, 2001).

Figure 16.1 Where Do Federal Tax Dollars Come From and Where Do They Go?
Mandatory spending (required by law) represents such a large percentage of the budget (approximately two-thirds of all government spending) that lawmakers often complain that their hands are tied as they wrestle with ways to cut costs. Unlike most spending on our national defense, which Congress authorizes each year at its discretion, entitlements such as Social Security, Medicare, and the Food Stamp Program are examples of mandatory spending categories. The two pie charts shown here illustrate sources of federal revenues and the allocation of federal spending in Fiscal Year 2007.

Federal Revenues—FY 2007

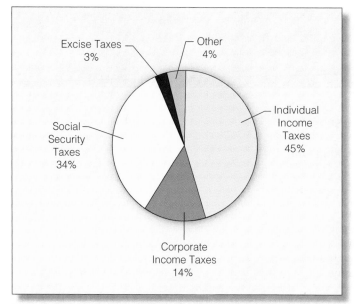

Source: Budget of the U.S. Government Fiscal Year 2009, Historical Tables, published by the Executive Office of the President.

Federal Spending—FY 2007

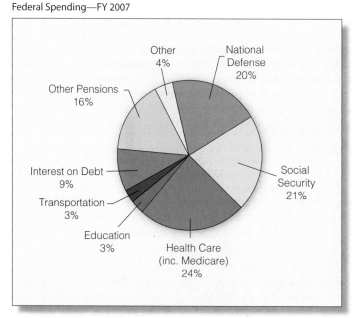

Source: Budget of the U.S. Government Fiscal Year 2009, Historical Tables, published by the Executive Office of the President.

discount rate can affect the economy in profoundly important ways. Why would the Federal Reserve choose to raise the discount rate? The primary goal of the Federal Reserve is to stabilize the economy and prevent dangerously wide fluctuations that can upset the economy. Although politicians may benefit in the short run from a quickly growing economy, the Federal Reserve may fear the eventual onset of high inflation. Under such circumstances, it may seek to tighten the money supply (the total amount of money available in the economy at a particular point in time) by increasing the discount rate. Such a move may be politically unpopular, because interest rates throughout the economy tend to rise along with the discount rate, making it harder for individuals to borrow money for houses and consumer goods. Investments by businesses may similarly be curtailed.

On the flip side, the Federal Reserve may choose to lower the discount rate as a way to stimulate investment and spur the economy forward. Lower interest rates allow individuals to borrow and invest more for consumer goods and real estate and businesses to borrow more money for capital investment. Some economists believe lower interest rates also keep unemployment at a minimum, because businesses are better able to maximize their production capacity.

When Congress enacted the Federal Reserve Act in 1913, it sought to ensure that the Federal Reserve could act independently of partisan political considerations, which often demand short-term fixes to the economy. Each of the Fed's seven members serves a term of fourteen years. Once appointed and confirmed, a board member may not be removed from office except through a cumbersome impeachment process for serious criminal violations. The president also determines (with the consent of the Senate) who will serve as Federal Reserve Chair for a period of four years, although in practice the Chair is often reappointed several times. Few officials in history have faced a more daunting challenge than Ben Bernanke, the Federal Reserve Chair appointed by President George W. Bush in January 2006. Bernanke replaced Alan Greenspan, the legendary chairman who presided over an unprecedented period of high economic growth and low inflation during his nineteen years at the helm of the Fed.

As was the case with the government's financial policy, its choice of monetary policy can significantly affect the overall direction of the nation's economy. Still, not all sectors will be affected evenly by these policies. A general rise in interest rates, for example, may deflate the housing market, though leaving other sectors relatively unaffected. Thus in discussing overall economic policy, it is useful to focus as well on a handful of more specific policy areas that shed light on how government intervention in public policy matters sometimes makes a difference. Though numerous sectors of the economy offer opportunities for analysis, this chapter focuses on three topics that continue to challenge federal and state officials to consider innovative policy solutions: agricultural policy, urban policy, and the politics of emergence relief policy.

Agriculture Policy

The United States was once primarily a nation of farmers, but by the 1880s, industry had replaced agriculture as the leading segment of the economy. By the early 1970s, only 4 percent of the civilian labor force could still be classified as farmers. Even so, agriculture continues to enjoy a disproportionate influence over the U.S. economy, and thus it continues to draw the attention of political officials at almost every level of government.

The federal government intervenes in agricultural policy today when it makes payments to farmers designed to encourage a change in production, called **subsidies,** or when it imposes price controls that set maximum or minimum prices for goods. The federal government may also impose tariffs, which raise the domestic price of imported goods by exacting a fee from importers who wish to sell their products in the United States. The Freedom to Farm Act of 1996 reduced farm subsidies and provided fixed payments to farmers, but overhauled the system of price supports and subsidies.

★ Subsidy

The amount paid by the government to entities such as farmers to encourage a change in the overall of amount production.

Growing dietary and health concerns, combined with the increased power of large supermarket and fast-food chains, have created a deepening crisis in the United States' agricultural sectors, which should prompt a new round of deliberations among policy experts about the future of U.S. agriculture policy.

Urban Policy

Despite the considerable growth of American suburbs during the latter half of the twentieth century, cities are where most Americans continue to work, shop, and enjoy a variety of cultural activities. In fact, the United States remains a predominantly urban nation in the sense that a clear majority of Americans today continue to live in metropolitan or urban areas.

Many government policies relating to cities have created a number of urban problems not experienced by those who live in rural areas or suburbs.[16] Beginning in the middle of the twentieth century government subsidies helped pay for road construction in general and the interstate highway system in particular. Some city planners hoped that highways leading directly into cities would help revitalize downtown districts by bringing in consumers from neighboring areas. Unfortunately, these access routes had the opposite effect, encouraging the population flight of wealthier citizens who could now more effectively commute from their homes in the suburbs to their jobs in the city.[17] Controversial urban renewal programs, in which local governments purchase private property for civic projects, were launched with the goal of cleaning up city centers increasingly marked by crime-infested slums, gangs, and other forms of urban blight. Yet urban renewal projects have just as often led to the creation of more highways, and mammoth-size housing projects that became new centers for crime, drug abuse, and other social problems. In 1961, social reformer Jane Jacobs published *The Death and Life of Great American Cities,* a comprehensive critique of contemporary large-scale urban renewal.[18] Within a decade, city groups across the nation had also awakened to the reality of urban renewal, and by the 1980s many major cities were actively resisting sweeping urban renewal programs.

In recent decades, urban policy has focused on the redevelopment (rather than the demolition) of existing neighborhoods and properties. In 1994, the Clinton administration designated nine so-called Empowerment Zones, including six urban areas (parts of Atlanta, Baltimore, Chicago, Detroit, New York City, and Philadelphia/Camden, NJ), which would be entitled to receive federal tax incentives and direct funding for physical improvements and social services. Yet none of these reforms have been able to address larger racial issues, and most metropolitan areas remain largely segregated by race. Efforts to reverse the flow of affluent people out of the cities, often referred to as gentrification projects, have enjoyed only modest successes to date.[19]

Emergency and Disaster Relief Policy

The U.S. Federal Emergency Management Agency (FEMA) has existed in one form or another for more than two centuries, providing relief after disasters that leave citizens homeless, penniless, or in need of significant medical care. Whenever the president of the United States declares a state of emergency in some affected geographical region, FEMA is able to exercise its power to coordinate federal relief efforts and offer assistance to individuals and governments to help them rebuild homes, businesses, and public facilities.[20]

Until quite recently, many Americans may have taken FEMA's role for granted; that changed as a result of the events following Hurricane Katrina's ravaging of the Gulf Coast in August 2005. The failure of President George W. Bush to pay an im-

[16] Charles C. Euchner and Stephen McGovern, *Urban Policy Reconsidered: Dialogues on the Problems and Prospects of American Cities* (New York: Routledge, 2003).
[17] Robert Fogelson, *Downtown: Its Rise and Fall, 1880–1950* (New Haven, CT: Yale University Press, 2001).
[18] See Jane Jacobs, *The Death and Life of Great American Cities* (New York: Vintage, 1963).
[19] For a discussion of the advantages and disadvantages of gentrification, see Rebecca Solnit, *Hollow City: Gentrification and the Eviction of Urban Culture* (New York: Verso, 2001).
[20] For more details on the financial aspects of disaster relief, see David Russell, *It's a Disaster: The Money and Politics That Follow Earthquakes, Hurricanes, and Other Catastrophic Losses* (Landsdowne, PA: Silver Lake Publishing, 1999).

American Government . . . in Historical Perspective:

Hurricane Relief that Calls for a "Hands-on" President

As a general matter, the president provides the general direction of economic policy, but leaves it to agency heads and bureaucracies to see that the policy is carried out effectively. Of course disaster relief is one exception to that rule—when nature strikes with harsh consequences, the nation wants to know that its president is on the scene, and not leaving FEMA workers and other subordinates to offer sympathy to the victims. Two presidents, both of whom hailed from Texas, learned that lesson the hard way.

On September 5, 1965, Hurricane Betsy, a Category 4 storm with winds in excess of 150 miles per hour, slammed into Louisiana. New Orleans was hit especially hard, as three-quarters of the city were left underwater. President Lyndon B. Johnson followed coverage of the storm from his office in Washington, DC. Preparing for two busy days ahead in the nation's capital, he was not inclined to visit the Gulf Coast. That all changed after Senator Russell Long (D-LA) and other lawmakers from the region urged the president to come immediately to New Orleans to survey the damage. Senator Long in particular felt that Johnson must reach out to citizens and give a human face to the federal government. Heeding the advice, Johnson hurried to New Orleans; his motorcade stopped repeatedly along the water-swept streets, allowing the president to personally reach out to the storm's victims. "I want them to know they're loved," LBJ said at the time. This was one instance in which the president's personal touch wasn't just nice—it was necessary.

On August 30, 2005, Hurricane Katrina, also a Category 4 storm with winds of up to 175 miles per hour, barreled into Louisiana and Southern Mississippi. The levees protecting New Orleans were once again breached, but this storm proved among the deadliest ever, as more than thirteen hundred fatalities and over $100 billion in damage were attributed to Katrina. At the time the storm hit, President Bush was vacationing at his ranch in Crawford, Texas. Returning to Washington, DC, in the days immediately following the hurricane, President Bush was captured by one photographer surveying the damage from Air Force One as it passed overhead on its way to the nation's capital. Many found the photograph troubling, as it seemed to present an image of a president "out of touch" with what was happening below. Eventually Bush did visit New Orleans, and he too reached out to the victims. Like LBJ, Bush had failed to see right away that entrusting subordinates to on-site activities is never enough in the context of natural disasters. At least in this context, policy administration requires a human face—that of the president of the United States.

mediate visit to the areas in southern Louisiana and Mississippi most affected by the hurricane led to a precipitous drop in his approval ratings. FEMA director Michael Brown also came under intense scrutiny following Hurricane Katrina; Brown was criticized both for FEMA's slow response to the disaster and for his own apparent disconnect with FEMA's on-site activities. (Brown resigned within weeks of the disaster.) The attention these events received in the media may help ensure that future administrations avoid the mistakes made in the wake of Hurricane Katrina. Three years later in September 2008 Hurricane Ike bore down on the Texas coast near Galveston, where it was destined to become the third costliest hurricane in history. This time, federal officials were conscious of the role that citizens have come to expect the federal government to play in attending to damaged areas and in providing emergency relief to the victims of disasters.

Perhaps the most controversial issue facing administrations responsible for disaster relief concerns whether or not they should attempt to rebuild homes and infrastructure in stricken areas that are just as likely to experience similar disasters in the future. Critics of FEMA claim that bureaucratic involvement at taxpayer

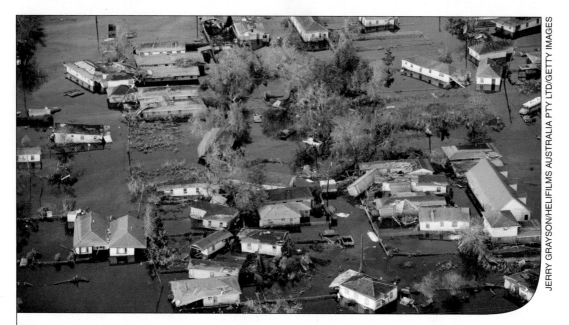

A New Orleans neighborhood destroyed by Hurricane Katrina.

expense increases the likelihood that sentimental value will affect the agency's decision making; they argue that if private companies were required to carry out the duties of FEMA, reconstruction would occur only in safer areas. This issue is likely to re-emerge in the years to come as officials determine the extent to which government subsidies should help to rebuild New Orleans, much of which remains susceptible to hurricane damage in the future. By the end of 2005, FEMA had already distributed the first $20 million installment of a $120 million community disaster loan to the city of New Orleans.

Now & Then: Making the Connection

Assuming no military operations or national security threats loom so large that they effectively dominate the national agenda, most modern presidents have seen their political fates rise and fall with the state of the economy. Herbert Hoover's presidency ended for all intents and purposes when the nation's economy fell into a great depression; Jimmy Carter's presidency coincided with a near record high misery index, and he too became a one-term president. The crisis on Wall Street in 2008 cast an especially large shadow on the presidential election contest waged that fall between John McCain and Barack Obama. It is no surprise, then, that those who win the presidency feel compelled to lay out a detailed economic plan early in their respective administrations; seeking to build support for their plans, presidents are eager to justify their economic proposals on the basis of sound economic theory.

Economic theories often help justify the plans presidents advocate for improving the nation's prosperity. In 1934, President Franklin Delano Roosevelt learned about John Maynard Keynes's "tax and spend" theories, and by 1938 FDR's economic policies clearly reflected Keynesian principles. In 2001, President George W. Bush was eager to put into practice the same supply-side (or "trickle down") economic theory that had helped Ronald Reagan win a second term in office, and Bush's administration steadfastly pushed for making tax cuts permanent even as the national deficit was exploding. History remembers FDR's tax-and-spend policies as kindly as it remembers President Reagan's application of supply-side economics. Although he secured a second term in office, the verdict is still out on whether Bush's decision to embrace trickle-down economics was a success. Of course it is easy to look back decades later at a president's economic policies and judge them as successes or failures. Presidents weighing fiscal policies that will affect millions in the short term do not have that luxury.

Politics InterActive!

When he was first approached in 1987 about the possibility of becoming Federal Reserve Board Chairman, Alan Greenspan did not want to take the job. As an economist working in New York, Greenspan preferred more mechanical types of economic analysis that drew on hard accounting principles. By contrast, Greenspan viewed the central task of the Federal Reserve—to make economic predictions—as a near impossible task. But he eventually accepted the position when President Reagan offered it to him, and Greenspan's emphasis on low interest rates during his nearly nineteen years in the position helped make him the most renowned Fed chairman in history. It even earned him a share of credit for an economic recovery that stretched throughout the 1990s with inflation rates and interest rates near record lows.

In fact, Greenspan became such a respected figure that even a simple appearance by him before Congress became a market-shifting event. For example, immediately after President Clinton in 1993 unveiled his economic plan aimed at deficit reduction, Greenspan told the Senate Banking Committee that Clinton's plan was both "serious" and "credible." Within a week of that endorsement, long-term interest rates began to fall, much to the delight of Clinton administration officials. Aware of his impact, Greenspan took great care to avoid offering sound bites that might be misinterpreted in the media. Indeed, he was often accused of using "constructive ambiguity" to promote incomprehensibility (and no doubt a degree of mystery) about his own opinions. Nevertheless, Greenspan was a cult figure in Washington, DC, and unlike past chairs of the Federal Reserve, he won't soon be forgotten.

On http://academic.cengage.com/ dautrich, find the Politics Interactive link for a detailed discussion of the challenges facing the current Federal Reserve Chairman, Ben Bernanke, including the Wall Street bailout of 2008. You will also find information that helps us to understand the modern Federal Reserve Board that Alan Greenspan shaped over two decades in historical, popular, and global perspectives.

THE FEDERAL RESERVE

Brokers on the NY Stock Exchange at work as they listen to former Federal Reserve Chairman Alan Greenspan testifying before Congress.

http://academic.cengage.com/dautrich

Chapter Summary

★ The policy-making process generally unfolds in five stages: a recognition/definition stage, a formulation stage, an adoption stage, an implementation stage, and an evaluation stage. Bureaucrats in administrative agencies, interest groups (including think tanks), Congress, and the president are all actively involved throughout the process.

★ Fiscal policy is concerned with the raising of revenue through taxation and the spending of whatever revenue has been generated. The federal budget, which lays out a comprehensive plan of government spending, is the primary means by which government carries out fiscal policy.

★ Laissez-faire capitalism, which favors minimal government interference in the economy, dominated the U.S. economy for much of the eighteenth and nineteenth centuries; however, beginning in the 1930s, the government began to apply the principles of Keynesian economic theory, which favors government spending during difficult economic times. During the past quarter century, some presidents have turned to supply-side economics, which favors cutting taxes as way of increasing economic productivity.

★ The most significant indicators of U.S. economic success or failure include the nation's gross domestic product, the consumer price index, the unemployment rate, the budget deficit, and the Dow Jones Industrial Stock Average.

★ Today's budget-making process is dominated by the president, who proposes an initial budget that will serve as the framework for all budget negotiations. Congress responds initially through its Appropriations committees and Budget committees, which in turn formulate budget proposals based on its own projections for future revenue. Occasionally Congress and the president struggle to find a compromise, and in some extreme cases the federal government has been forced to shut down until some compromise can be reached.

★ Taxation policies may be redistributive (benefiting the poor at the expense of the rich) or distributive (promoting the interests of all economic classes equally).

★ A large percentage of taxpayer funds go to mandatory spending (usually in the form of entitlements such as Medicare and Social Security) that is unaffected by annual budget decisions. Discretionary spending categories include defense, education, and the environment.

★ The Federal Reserve supervises the nation's monetary policy by setting the discount rate its Federal Reserve Banks may charge member banks to receive loans and by determining the minimum assets banks must keep in hand, called the reserve requirements. When the Federal Reserve lowers the discount rate, it may stimulate economic investment, but it risks setting off higher inflation rates.

★ The federal government continues to be concerned with changes in the nature of farming across the nation and with shifts in the population of American metropolitan areas; thus agricultural and urban policy making remain important areas of public policy making. The thorny politics of natural disaster relief has also provided a challenge to federal officials.

Key Terms

Budget authority (p. 495)

Budget deficit (p. 488)

Budget surplus (p. 488)

Discount rate (p. 496)

Discretionary spending (p. 496)

Distributive tax policies (p. 493)

Federal Reserve Board (p. 496)

Federal Reserve System (p. 496)

Fiscal policy (p. 487)

Flat tax (p. 494)

Gross domestic product (GDP)
   (p. 488)

Inflation (p. 487)

Keynesian economic theory
   (p. 487)

Laissez-faire economics (p. 487)

Mandatory spending (p. 495)

Monetary policy (p. 496)

National debt (p. 489)

Open market operations (p. 497)

Outlays (p. 495)

Progressive tax (p. 493)

Public policy (p. 484)

Recession (p. 487)

Redistributive tax policies (p. 493)

Regressive tax (p. 493)

Reserve requirement (p. 497)

Subsidy (p. 499)

Supply-side economics (p. 487)

Tariff (p. 493)

Resources

Important Books

Dye, Thomas. *Understanding Public Policy.* New York: Prentice Hall, 2001.

Forbes, Steve. *Flat Tax Revolution: Using a Postcard to Abolish the IRS.* New York: Regnery, 2005.

Greider, William. *Secrets of the Temple: How the Federal Reserve Runs the Country.* New York: Simon & Schuster, 1989.

Jacobs, Jane. *The Death and Life of American Cities.* New York: Vintage, 1992.

Kingdon, John. *Agendas, Alternatives and Public Policies,* 2nd ed. New York: Addison-Wesley Publishing, 1997.

Phillips, Kevin. *Bad Money: Reckless Finance, Failed Politics and the Global Crisis in American Capitalism.* New York: Viking Adult, 2008.

Stone, Deborah. *Policy Paradox: The Art of Political Decisionmaking,* rev. ed. New York: W. W. Norton, 2001.

Weisman, Steven R. *The Great Tax Wars: Lincoln to Wilson—The Fierce Battles over Money and Power That Transformed a Nation.* New York: Simon & Schuster, 2002.

Internet Sources

Websites for the various think tanks mentioned in this chapter: http://www.aei.org (The American Enterprise Institute), http://www.brookings.org (The Brookings Institution), http://www.cato.org (the Cato Institute), http://www.heritage.org (The Heritage Foundation), http://www.rand.org (The Rand Corporation), and http://www.ppionline.org (The Progressive Policy Institute)

http://www.epn.org (the site of the electronic policy network, a leading source of information on economic policy matters)

http://www.federalreserve.org (the official site of the Federal Reserve Board)

http://www.fema.gov (the official site of the Federal Emergency Management Agency; includes a history of the agency, its strategic plan, and information about active disasters and emergencies)

http://www.atr.org/index.html (official site for "Americans for Tax Reform," one of the most influential organizations in the country pushing for lower taxes)

17 American Social Policy

President Bush joins a senior citizen picking up her prescriptions under the new federal plan.

When Heartfelt Passions Confront Political Reality: Now & Then

The problem had been festering for far too long. To address it, the president demanded sweeping, vigorous policy reform to reconsider the issue and offer comprehensive solutions. Although leaders of both parties conceded the need for reform, the president's proposals soon met with considerable skepticism in Congress. As a result, the policy-making process quickly bogged down in legislative gridlock. In a time of relative prosperity for the country as a whole, increased momentum for the president's grander proposals seemed unlikely. In the end, a far more modest version of the president's proposals became the law of the land. It was a start, but not what the president had in mind. The limited change that ultimately occurred proved that to enact broader reforms, far more people would have to be convinced that such extensive change was necessary.

President Theodore Roosevelt, at Yosemite Park

NOW &

2030 | 2020 | 2010 | 2000 | 1990 |

2003

Now. . . By the 1990s, the glacial pace of lawmaking had exacerbated the national crisis over affordable health care for all Americans. Spiraling costs and widespread complaints about limited access to care had forced the issue to the forefront of the political agenda. The Medicare and Medicaid laws (the federal health insurance programs for seniors and the poor, respectively) passed in the 1960s no longer met the needs of these populations. Accordingly, in 1993 President Bill Clinton urged Congress to pass a sweeping health care reform plan that would have offered guarantees of universal health care to the indigent and controlled health care costs for all Americans. Yet even before the details of the plan were made public, insurance lobbies poured millions of dollars into a media and lobbying campaign that doomed the proposal in Congress.[1] Nearly a decade later, President George W. Bush managed to achieve a far more limited reform in heath care insurance when he signed into law the Medicare Prescription and Modernization Act of 2003. This new law was the first reform to Medicare in nearly three decades and set some limits on spiraling prescription drug costs for the elderly. Still, this more modest plan did nothing to alter the basic structure of the American health care system, which continued to oppose universally guaranteed health care coverage.

---

[1] Nicholas Laham, *A Lost Cause: Bill Clinton's Campaign for National Health Care Insurance* (Westport, CT: Praeger, 1996), pp. 208–209.

1950   1940   1930   1920   1910

Then. . .

President Theodore Roosevelt's romanticism about nature and the wilderness dated back to his days as an amateur rancher in the badlands of North Dakota during the late 1880s. As his political career progressed, he watched with frustration as conglomerate trusts abused the environment in the name of industrial progress. He believed that natural resources were like a family trust—they existed to be used, but they had to be used wisely. At the outset of his administration, Roosevelt announced that the conservation of forest and water resources would be considered a national issue of vital importance.[2] In the area of forest preservation, he enjoyed some early successes—by executive order he designated many federal tracts as game reserves, and he reserved more than 150 million acres in all as national forest reserves protected from unregulated strip mining. Yet to effectively conserve water resources, there was only so much the president could do without the help of Congress; unfortunately for Roosevelt, business interests had successfully prevailed on the legislative branch to go slow in protecting all aspects of the environment. Congress refused Roosevelt's entreaties to pass laws to protect the nation's water resources. In 1907, Congress even passed a law curtailing presidential authority to create additional forest reserves (Roosevelt quickly found a way around the law). Ultimately Roosevelt's administration saved the forests but did little else; it wasn't until 1948, during the Harry Truman administration, that the first water pollution control act was passed. Innovative new social policies often invite legislative foot dragging. Roosevelt's efforts to introduce conservation policies met with this sort of delay, as did Clinton's health care reform proposal almost a century later.

---

[2] Paul R. Cutright, *Theodore Roosevelt: The Making of a Conservationist* (Urbana: University of Illinois Press, 1985).

Grand policy-planning strategies are often unrealistic in a system where passing laws of any kind is so difficult. The separation of governmental powers, the involvement of interest groups at every stage of the process, and the intense media scrutiny all conspire to slow down policy-making mechanisms, if not grind them to a halt. Officials must often resort to incremental and haphazard breakthroughs. In the 1950s, Professor Charles E. Lindblom described the domestic policy-making process as the "science of muddling through."[3] Lindblom's view challenged the prevailing rational-comprehensive model of policy making, in which rational decision makers utilized scientific analysis and sound logic to develop public policy. Lindblom felt that this model was unrealistic because of the political and human factors involved in the process. By lending scholarly credence to the "science of muddling through," he forced a generation of scholars to consider the role that timing, opportunity, and even luck can play in the policy process. Of course not all scholars agree with Lindblom's theory. For example, political scientists Bryan Jones and Frank Baumgartner have argued that public policy can be explained by "punctuated equilibrium" in which long periods of stability are broken up by sudden and abrupt change.[4] Yet Lindblom's theory continues to serve as the baseline by which so many other theories are often measured.

Lindblom's theory of "muddling through" applies to all areas of public policy, but it may be especially applicable in the area of social policy, where passionate advocates can undermine an efficient and logical policy-making process. Neither President Theodore Roosevelt nor President Bill Clinton was satisfied with the speed of the policy process in dealing with their overriding concerns—conservation and health care, respectively. Even public consensus that significant reforms were necessary did not provide the sense of urgency in Congress that is normally required to forge grand change. But the policy-making process did allow for incremental or limited fixes, whether by executive order or more modest legislation, laying the groundwork for broader reforms in the years to follow. Presidents hemmed in by the confines of four-year terms rarely exhibit much patience in this regard. But "muddling through" with small incremental policy change remains a hallmark of the policy process, preventing ill-conceived, sweeping changes in the American political system. In the final analysis, "muddling through" occurs precisely because the American political system is set up to encourage this inexorably slow, incremental process.

The term **social policy** refers to the rules, regulations, and policy making pertaining to the quality of life, welfare, and relations of human beings in the United States. There are many different types of social policy, and in this chapter we review some of the major ones including crime policy, health care policy, social security, environmental policy, and some aspects of the relationship between religion and public policy. In each instance, we will consider the evolution of social policy within the overall framework of policy making discussed in the previous chapter.

Former New York City mayor Rudolph Giuliani, seen here in 2007, campaigning for the presidency on his record of reducing the city's crime rates during the mid 1990s. A fellow Republican, California governor Arnold Schwarzenegger, is seen in the background on the right.

MARIO ANZUONI/REUTERS/LANDOV

★ Social policy

Rules, regulations, and policy making pertaining to the quality of life, welfare, and relations of human beings in the United States.

The Nature and Practice of Crime Policy

Perhaps the most fundamental way in which modern societies manage relations among human beings residing within their jurisdictions is through the use of a comprehensive criminal justice system. Democratic systems must strike a careful balance between maintaining public order and protecting individual freedom—the rules and practices of the criminal justice system determine where and how that balance will be struck. For example, especially severe and strict forms of law enforcement could prove effective at

[3] Charles Lindblom, "The Science of Muddling Through," *Public Administration Review* 19 (Spring 1959), 79–88.
[4] Bryan Jones and Frank Baumgartner, "A Model of Choice for Public Policy," *Journal of Public Administration Research and Theory Online* 15 (2005), 325–351.

making citizens safe, but only at a very high cost in taxpayers' money and possibly some loss of individual freedom as well.

In 1968, social scientist Herbert Packer defined two different models of criminal justice policy making: the "crime control model" and the "due process model."[5] The **crime control model** views the controlling of criminal behavior as the most important function of criminal justice. Packer depicts the crime control model as a type of "assembly line justice" because it tries to move cases quickly and efficiently though the system. The process requires that police and prosecutor make crucial judgments about defendants' guilt early in the process; the crime control model thus relies extensively on negotiations between defense attorneys and state prosecutors early on, to avoid the uncertainty and high costs associated with a full-blown trial. In theory, the guilty will be routinely pressed to enter plea bargains, whereas the innocent should hope to see their indictments dismissed early in the process. Of course the quick nature of this process increases the likelihood that public officials and defense attorneys will not always make the best judgments.

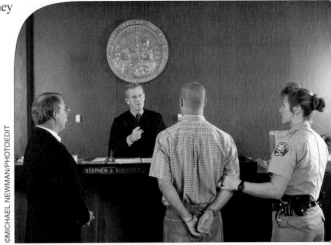

A defendant being arraigned in one of the nation's criminal courtrooms.

By contrast, in the **due process model** the principal goal is justice, which focuses just as much on acting to protect the innocent as it does on convicting the guilty. Stressing the adversarial process and the need for hearings, the model endeavors to guarantee that all criminal justice decisions will be based on reliable information at every stage of the process, with the government forced to meet far higher standards than the accused along the way. By placing a premium on protecting the rights of individuals, some guilty defendants may go free simply because the state has not met its high burden of proving guilt "beyond a reasonable doubt."[6]

The American system of criminal justice can be characterized as a tug-of-war between both these models, with no-name, relatively run-of-the-mill, usually poor defendants generally falling into the crime control "assembly line," whereas bigger-name, higher-profile, and wealthy defendants are far more likely to experience the due process model.

Critics of the criminal justice system charge that racial disparities have become the norm, with African Americans, Hispanic Americans, and other racial and ethnic minorities entering the system at numbers disproportionate to what they make up within the general population.[7] They point also to the controversy surrounding police use of racial profiling, in which African Americans in particular are often stopped and interrogated simply because they possess the same racial characteristics of others who have committed crimes. Defenders of the system contend that racial minorities commit a larger percentage of crimes, perhaps a product of their relative economic disadvantage in society as a whole. That defense does not take into account alarming statistical trends showing that race figures directly into sentencing decisions. For example, a 1990 study demonstrated that killers of whites in Georgia were 4.3 times more likely to be sentenced to death than killers of African Americans.[8] Because racism remains a problem in American society as whole, judicial sentencing and racial stereotyping may well be tainted by feelings of racism that lie below the surface.

★ Crime control model

Criminal justice policy-making model that views the controlling of criminal behavior as the system's most important function.

★ Due process model

Criminal justice policy-making model that views the attainment of justice—which includes protection of the innocent—as the principal goal of the system.

An African American man being arrested. Racial profiling targets stopping and interrogating members of racial minorities simply because their racial characteristics are similar to others who have committed crimes.

[5] Herbert Packer, *The Limits of the Criminal Sanction* (Stanford, CA: Stanford University Press, 1968).
[6] For a discussion of criminal justice in America more generally, see George Cole and Christopher Smith, *The American System of Criminal Justice* (Belmont, CA: Wadsworth, 2001).
[7] Larry J. Siegel and Joseph J. Senna, *Introduction to Criminal Justice* (Boston: Wasdworth, 2005), p. 412.
[8] David Baldus, George Woodworth, and Charles Pulaski, *Equal Justice and the Death Penalty: A Legal and Empirical Analysis* (Boston: Northeastern University Press, 1990).

For as long as crimes have been committed, politicians have sought to implement public policies that address the "crime problem"—so much the better for the re-election prospects of public officials who can more rightfully claim to be "law and order" politicians who "clean up the streets" for honest citizens. In recent years, even Congress has sought its share of credit for reducing crime, passing with overwhelming bipartisan support an act prohibiting possession of guns in school zones and a federal carjacking act, among other crime-fighting initiatives. Of course, politicians disagree vehemently on the best method for fighting crime; sometimes the innovative new methods of the moment can be relegated to the dustbin of law enforcement within a few decades.

During the mid- to late nineteenth century, law enforcement agencies increasingly believed that even evil wrongdoers had the power within themselves to resist the temptation to commit crimes, so long as they embraced discipline and hard work. Thus law enforcers devoted large portions of their budgets to discouraging "rowdy and undisciplined behavior," even though such minor offenses were not always committed by bad or evil people. City police officers in particular drastically increased the number of arrests they made for drunkenness and vagrancy on the theory that those smaller, less "harmful" crimes contributed to a general state of moral decline. No less notable a law enforce-

ment official than Theodore Roosevelt, New York City Police Commissioner in the mid-1890s, saw police work as "a fight to clean up vice to promote the advance of civilization and decency." This emphasis on public order maintenance receded somewhat after the turn of the century, especially in the 1920s, as police officers increasingly viewed themselves as "professional crime fighters" who needed to focus on more serious offenses such as murder, rape, and burglary. "Order maintenance," by contrast, was de-emphasized.

A vagrant is hauled off by city policemen as part of law enforcement's emphasis on public order maintenance.

From the 1940s through the 1970s, the theory of rehabilitation, which argued that convicted offenders could be restored to a constructive place in society by means of training, therapy, or other methods, played a dominant role in the treatment of criminal offenders across the nation. Most state criminal justice systems relied on indeterminate sentencing, featuring no fixed release date set by a judge, on the ground that prisoners who knew in advance when they would be released would have little motivation to participate in treatment or therapy programs while they were

Up through the 1980s, criminal justice policy making mostly occurred within state and local governments. In recent decades, however, Congress has acted to criminalize and/or increase sentences for a host of unlawful activities at the federal level.[9] Passage of the federal Gun-Free School Zones Act of 1990 that outlawed the possession of guns within a specified proximity of a school building, a 1996 federal carjacking statute, and federal crime bills that expand the death penalty to cover certain federal crimes, are all representative of this modern policy-making trend.[10] Congress has also been actively involved in the "war on drugs," passing numerous federal statutes outlawing the possession, use, and sale of certain illegal drugs.

Occasionally Congress has overstepped its constitutional bounds in passing crime laws—in 1995 the Supreme Court struck down the Gun-Free Schools Zones Act as an unconstitutional usurpation of each state's prerogative to criminalize acts that take place solely within its jurisdiction.[11] Still, given the public's favorable response to

[9] Lawrence M. Friedman, *Crime and Punishment in American History* (New York: Basic Books, 1993), pp. 264–265.
[10] Jeffrey Rosen, "Dual Sovereigns," *The New Republic* (July 28, 1997), 16–19.
[11] *United States v. Lopez*, 514 U.S. 549 (1995).

incarcerated. By the 1980s, this model was increasingly questioned by scholars who challenged whether there was any clear and provable link between poverty and low self-esteem on one hand and criminal activities on the other hand. Indeterminate sentences soon gave way to fixed and determined sentences that allowed wardens and other public officials to more effectively manage the criminal populations under their charge.

In the 1980s, a new version of an older theory gained momentum once again. In 1982, social scientists James Q. Wilson and George Kelling wrote an article titled "Broken Windows: The Police and Neighborhood Safety." In a modern spin on the public order theories advanced more than a century earlier, they argued that disorderly behavior left unregulated and unchecked signals to residents that they are and will continue to be unsafe. By contrast, quickly cleaning up vandalism, such as fixing broken windows right away, deters further petty crimes and antisocial behavior in the short run and deters major crimes in the long run. It also encourages law-abiding residents to stay put, rather than fleeing the neighborhood. Wilson and Kelling's "broken windows theory" attracted widespread national attention in the 1980s and again in the early 1990s when New York City Mayor Rudolph Giuliani spoke of "quality of life" and "zero tolerance" in his approach to cleaning up crime in New York City. Subway fare dodgers were

soon prosecuted to the full extent of the law, and New York City police also rid the streets of "squeegee men," who demanded payment for cleaning the windshields of drivers entering the city, even though the drivers did not ask for and often did not want the service provided. Sociologists today disagree over whether the broken windows theory could account for the overall drop in crime in New York City or in any of the other urban centers that focused efforts on addressing such petty offenses. The problem with verifying that link is that the zero tolerance effect on serious crime remains difficult, if not impossible, to disentangle from other crime-fighting initiatives that are taking place simultaneously.

Wilson and Kelling's "broken windows" theory argued that even minor disorderly conduct, if left unregulated, signals to law-abiding residents that they will never be safe.

such laws, it is tough to imagine Congress withdrawing from this area of policy making any time soon.

The Welfare State

The term **welfare state** refers to a social system in which the state assumes a considerable degree of responsibility for citizens in matters of health care, employment, education, and retirement income. In its ideal form, a welfare state is expected to do more than merely guarantee a minimum level of subsistence in these matters; thus welfare states do not simply ensure a "safety net" for their citizens. (Naturally, these welfare states require higher levels of taxation than do more strictly capitalist systems.) The actual amount of welfare provided varies widely from nation to nation. Nearly all modern welfare states sit somewhere on a spectrum between pure **capitalism** (an economic system in which all or most of the

★ Welfare state

Social system in which the state assumes a considerable degree of responsibility for citizens in matters of health care, employment, education, and retirement income.

★ Capitalism

Economic system in which all or most of the means of production are privately owned under competitive conditions.

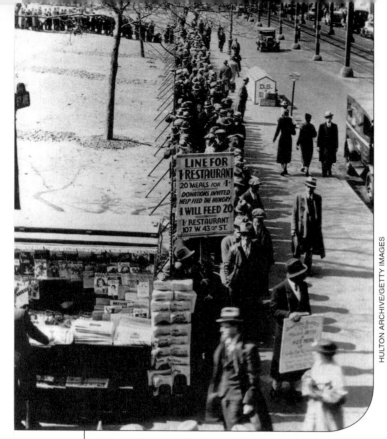

Long lines of people in New York City waited patiently for handouts during the Great Depression.

age, beneficiaries today are paid primarily from taxes drawn out of the paychecks of current workers. Additionally, because people are now living longer, more funds have been drawn from the trust fund than was originally anticipated. Some economists fear that the Social Security system will become even weaker in the years ahead, as a greater percentage of the disproportionately large baby boom generation (those born between 1946 and 1964) reaches retirement age during the first decade of the twenty-first century.[18]

Because they represent the largest single sustained growth of the population in the history of the United States, baby boomers have placed significant strains on schools and other public resources as they've proceeded through life. Today the oldest baby boomers have already celebrated their sixtieth birthday and soon will be drawing payments from Social Security. By the year 2030, when all baby boomers will be eligible for Social Security, the system may face solvency issues. In fact, a substantial percentage of baby boomers are not all that optimistic about their prospects of receiving Social Security: in a 2003 poll conducted for the American Association of Retired Persons (AARP), just 54 percent felt very or somewhat confident that Social Security would even be around when they retire.[19]

Social Security thus represents a conundrum for politicians: many recognize the need for large-scale reform of the system, but public opinion and interest groups that favor the current system have proven just as stubborn. The broad political support Social Security enjoys is based largely on the premise that the system is not simply another form of welfare; although lower-income contributors do receive some breaks, rich and poor employees alike pay into the system and receive its benefits. Running for president in 2000, George W. Bush proposed the partial "privatization" of Social Security, allowing younger workers to invest a portion of their Social Security taxes in personal retirement accounts linked to the stock market. Yet when the market did poorly in 2001 and 2002, President Bush de-emphasized his privatization proposal for the remainder of his first term.[20]

Because of the concern over the long-run solvency of the Social Security system, many future retirees have been forced to adjust their savings strategies to plan for a future without any guarantee of Social Security. Traditionally, government employees and people who work for larger companies or organizations have enjoyed conventional pension plans that guarantee a monthly benefit after retirement. Unfortunately, employees normally have no control over the investment of pension funds—many employees learn that their company's pension fund has been depleted by unwise investments only after the damage has been done. Additionally, most pension plans provide significant benefits only for employees who work at a particular organization for the long haul—perhaps for twenty-five or thirty years. In an increasingly mobile economy such as ours, fewer and fewer workers fit this description.

Through the use of tax incentives, the federal government has recently played a role in encouraging people to put aside extra savings for retirement. As a result, millions today directly invest a substantial portion of their savings in the stock market through the use of tax-favored retirement vehicles. Not only do such vehicles help provide an extra retirement cushion; they also have helped to ensure that a stream of investment capital continues to flow into publicly traded companies on the stock market, which in turn contribute to the well-being of the economy. These tax-favored investment plans include the following:

---

[18] See Paul Light, *Still Artful Work: The Continuing Politics of Social Security Reform* (New York: McGraw Hill, 1994).

[19] "Baby Boomers Envision Retirement II: Survey of Baby Boomers' Expectations for Retirement," survey conducted for AARP by RoperASW, October 9–23, 2003 (see http://www.research.aarp.org/).

[20] For more detailed criticism of Social Security privatization, see Henry Aaron and Robert Reischauer, *Countdown to Reform: The Great Social Security Debate* (New York: Century Foundation Press, 1999).

American Government: Historical, Popular, and Global Perspectives

employers. Still, approximately one in seven Americans under the age of sixty-five do not have any health insurance at all, and 78 percent of those who are uninsured are full-time workers or their dependents. Some of those individuals may have made conscious decisions not to pay for health insurance. Others simply cannot afford the mounting health insurance expenses—consider that the annual premium that a health insurer charged an employer for a health plan covering a family of four averaged $11,480 in 2006.[22] Still others are hindered by a lack of access to primary care: more than 20 million people in the United States live in rural areas or inner-city neighborhoods that have a shortage of physicians to meet their basic health care needs.[23] Rural residents are particularly disadvantaged: according to the U.S. Department of Health and Human Services, residents of rural areas maintain the highest death rates for unintentional injuries generally and for motor-vehicle injuries specifically, due in large part to the shortage of physicians in such areas.

President Bill Clinton holding up his proposed "universal health care card" in a 1993 address to Congress. Clinton's health care plan was soundly defeated.

Attempts during the past century to overhaul the system have all been turned back by the lobbying strength of physicians groups and other organized interests. In the 1920s, the American Medical Association (AMA) opposed compulsory heath insurance enrollment schemes for manual laborers. President Harry Truman's support for a bill to provide health insurance to all those paying Social Security taxes (and their families) also went nowhere. President Clinton in the early 1990s proposed a health insurance program that would have covered all Americans through large health insurance purchasing cooperatives; his plan ended up going down in political flames amid a well-organized lobbying campaign by the health insurance industry and others. Among the president's most determined critics was the Health Insurance Association of America (HIAA), a trade association representing nearly thirteen hundred health insurance companies across the country. The HIAA spent $17 million to defeat the plan—some of those funds were spent on one particularly damaging television commercial. In the now infamous TV spot, an older couple, "Harry and Louise," sat around their kitchen table lamenting the complexity of Clinton's plan and the menace of a new "billion-dollar bureaucracy." They expressed the fear that people would lose their choice of doctors and that insurance would become so expensive that their own employers would drop it. To disappointed advocates of universal care, Harry and Louise symbolized everything that went wrong with the great health care struggle of 1994: a powerful advertising campaign, financed by the insurance industry, that played on people's fears and helped derail the process. Because sweeping reform proposals have been repeatedly defeated, reformers have been forced to offer piecemeal responses to the heath care crisis: HMOs, limited prescription drug benefits, and the like.

Environmental Policy

Prior to the twentieth century, there was no environmental policy in the United States to speak of. The Progressive-era conservation movement only began at the turn of that century when President Theodore Roosevelt led the push to preserve national parks and wildlife refuges. In 1905, Roosevelt's administration founded the National Forest Service, an agency charged with protecting land from rapid development. More than fifty years later, Congress created the U.S. Fish and Wildlife Service as a means of protecting fish and wild animals.

Contemporary environmental policy was crafted piecemeal during the 1960s and early 1970s.[24] The National Environmental Policy Act of 1969 imposed restrictions on all federally funded projects that might cause damage to the environment; the 1960 Clean Water Act and the 1963 Clean Air Act spelled out specific requirements to be met by all businesses whose activities might cause pollution. The 1964 Federal Wilderness Act protects more than 650 million acres of federal land in forty-four states from logging, mining, oil and gas drilling, off-road vehicles, and further road building. Perhaps the single biggest governmental commitment to the environmental movement came with the creation of the **Environmental Protection Agency (EPA)** in 1970. The EPA coordinates all the above programs into a single

★ Environmental Protection Agency (EPA)

Federal agency that administers and enforces all of the nation's environmental programs and spells out the requirements of legislative initiatives to control the quality of the environment.

[22] Tony Pugh, "Health Insurance Premiums Continue to Soar," McClatchy Newspapers, September 27, 2006 (see http://www.commondreams.org/headlines06/0927-09.html).

[23] William Gesler and Thomas Ricketts, eds., *Heath Care in Rural North America: The Geography of Health Care Services in North America* (Newark, NJ: Rutgers University Press, 1992).

[24] For an especially readable introduction to environmental policy, see Daniel J. Fiorino, *Making Environmental Policy* (Berkeley: University of California Press, 1995).

J. DAVID AKE/AFP/GETTY IMAGES

American Government ... in Global Perspective:
The Grass Only *Looks* Greener for Canadian Health Care

More than a decade after President Bill Clinton's proposal for universal health care went down in flames, debates over the U.S. government's responsibility for providing more affordable health care rage on. In the meantime, some American citizens look longingly to the north for answers: from the vantage point of some, Canada's health care system—70 percent of which is funded by the government—seems eminently more sensible than our own. Certainly Canadians benefit from a system that keeps malpractice lawsuits (and the high costs associated with them) to a minimum and makes cheaper generic drugs available sooner without sacrificing the quality of doctors in the process. The Canadian government's willingness to buy drugs in bulk allows Canada to keep prices for many brand-name drugs much lower as well—not surprisingly, elderly Americans living near the border with Canada have tried to fulfill many of their prescription drug needs in that country, taking advantage of an international loophole.

Is the American system really so much worse than the Canadian system?

In her 2004 book titled, *Miracle Cure: How to Solve America's Health-Care Crisis and Why Canada Isn't the Answer*, Canadian-born scholar Sally C. Pipes provides a different perspective on the Canadian heath care system, noting that it is often beset with rationing, delays, and long waits, because numerous government hurdles prevent many new drugs from reaching the Canadian consumer quickly, if at all. According to Pipes, it has taken twice as long to get AIDS drugs approved in Canada as it did to get them approved in the United States. She thus offers one outsider's view of America's health care system that is much more positive:

The myth of the U.S. health care system is that it is a free-wheeling, cold-hearted, for-profit system ... it is true that for-profit insurance companies, medical supply corporations, hospitals and physician practices are notable actors in the U.S. health care environment. It is for that reason that the United States has the most dispersed and dynamic health care system in the world.

Source: Sally C. Pipes, *Miracle Cure: How to Solve America's Health-Care Crisis and Why Canada Isn't the Answer* (San Francisco: Pacific Research Institute, 2004), p. 1.

regime of law enforcement; it also issues regulations spelling out the requirements of vague legislative initiatives to control the quality of the environment.[25]

In recent decades, the EPA has been much more active in tightening pollution standards and regulating environmental risks more closely, including those that affect wildlife as well as humans. Still, the EPA was allotted merely $7.6 billion in fiscal year 2008, considerably less than that earmarked for competing programs such as transportation ($67 billion). EPA Administrator Christine Todd Whitman resigned from that position just two and a half years into George W. Bush's first term in office—her pro-environment instincts were reportedly frustrated by the White House, which backed away from a worldwide treaty to slow global warming and had supported an increase in off-coast oil drilling in Alaska. As long as future administrations must concern themselves with economic productivity and the cultivation of new energy sources, future EPA administrators are likely to find themselves torn between two masters: the environment and their own bosses.

A final word should be offered concerning the powerful environmental movement, which advocates the protection, management, and restoration of the natural environment worldwide. This movement has often found itself at odds with modern trends such as globalization, defined as the growing economic interdependence of countries worldwide. Some environmental activists see globalization as the promo-

[25] For a more critical look at the EPA during much of its existence, see Mark Landy et al., *The Environmental Protection Agency: Asking the Wrong Questions: From Nixon to Clinton* (New York: Oxford University Press, 1994).

The sharp spike in oil prices during the spring and summer months of 2008 led to significant increases in the cost of gasoline and home energy costs. Reducing America's dependence on foreign oil became a critical issue in the 2008 presidential race.

An August 2008 national survey, conducted by the Wall Street Journal/NBC

News Poll, presented Americans with a number of possible solutions to making the nation less dependent on foreign oil. This chart lists the percentage of respondents who said each solution would accomplish "a great deal" toward solving America's energy needs.

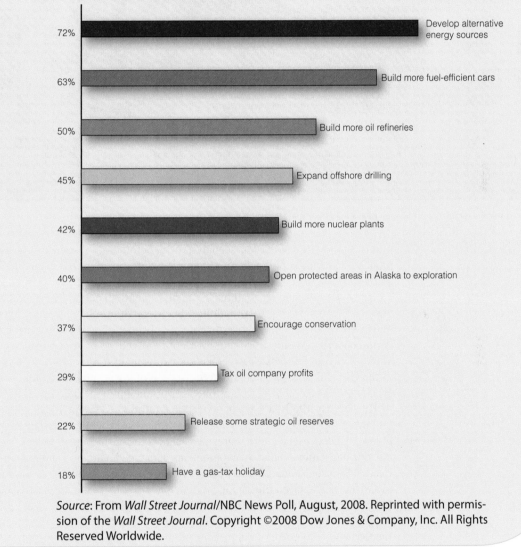

Percentage	Solution
72%	Develop alternative energy sources
63%	Build more fuel-efficient cars
50%	Build more oil refineries
45%	Expand offshore drilling
42%	Build more nuclear plants
40%	Open protected areas in Alaska to exploration
37%	Encourage conservation
29%	Tax oil company profits
22%	Release some strategic oil reserves
18%	Have a gas-tax holiday

Source: From *Wall Street Journal*/NBC News Poll, August, 2008. Reprinted with permission of the *Wall Street Journal*. Copyright ©2008 Dow Jones & Company, Inc. All Rights Reserved Worldwide.

tion of a corporatist agenda that does not take the interest of the environment into account. Environmentalists were thus well represented among the massive protests against the World Trade Organization when it convened in Seattle in 1999.

Education Policy

Education has traditionally been a state and local responsibility. The movement to create taxpayer-funded public schools, which began in the 1840s and gained

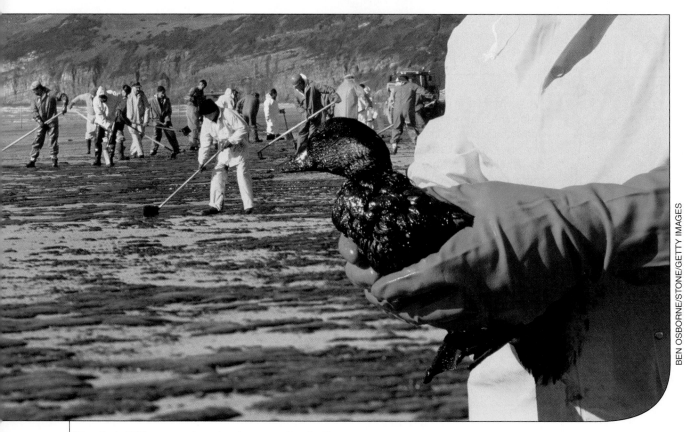

Oil-soaked wildlife recovered on a beach near a major oil spill.

momentum in the 1860s, was seen as a local, community responsibility. This approach to education policy helps explain the widespread variations in quality and administration of school programs across the nation: The public school systems created by many state legislatures in the mid-twentieth century were marked by harshly unequal per-pupil expenditures between white schools and segregated black schools. The federal government's involvement in education during this period occurred mainly as an outgrowth of its functions as supervisor of veterans' affairs. For example, the Servicemen's Readjustment Act of 1944, popularly known as the G.I. Bill of Rights, provided for college or vocational education for returning World War II veterans, as well as one year of unemployment compensation.

By the early 1960s, a wave of educational reform had swept Washington, DC. Following the Supreme Court's unanimous ruling in *Brown v. Board of Education* (1954) that declared racially segregated schools unconstitutional, federal legislators decided national educational problems demanded national solutions. President Lyndon Johnson's Great Society program included not only the Head Start program to assist disadvantaged preschool children, but also the Elementary and Secondary Education Act of 1965, which offered the first comprehensive federal aid program for public education in the United States. Since then, the federal government has funded nearly 7 percent of public education, amounting to approximately $30 billion annually. Higher education students have been helped indirectly by federal spending, and more directly by a federal student loan program that provides $10 billion in loans each year. If you received a student loan from a commercial bank, it may well be guaranteed by the federal government, which pays nearly $3 billion in defaulted student loans to banks each year.

The federal government's greater economic role in education has led to some sacrifice in local and state autonomy in education matters. Federal spending on local education is often accompanied by conditions that state administrators must follow. For example, amendments to the Elementary and Secondary Education Act in recent

Figure 17.1 The Thorny Politics of Drilling for Oil in Alaska

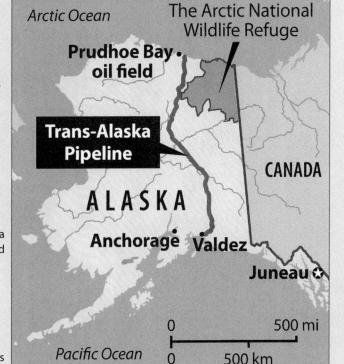

The United States has been accurately termed the "land of the automobile"—cars have pervaded much of American life since the 1920s, embodying our nation's consumer culture and the desire of so many Americans to hit the open road. Unfortunately, American demand for petroleum to run cars (as well as heat homes) had far exceeded domestic production by the early 1970s. By the 1990s, fully 50 percent of total U.S. consumption of oil came from foreign imports. Officials have grown especially concerned with America's increased dependence on oil from the politically unstable Middle East. Eager to keep oil prices low, officials in recent decades have increasingly turned their attention to Alaska and its vast potential as a supplier of crude oil to the United States and elsewhere.

Yet such oil drilling efforts in Alaska have recently run into a political quagmire. After years of legal wrangling and production problems, a trans-Alaska pipeline was finally completed in 1977, transporting oil more than eight hundred miles from Alaska's north slope to the port of Valdez on Prince William Sound. By 1982, fully 87 percent of the state's revenue came from the oil industry. At the same time, Congress in 1980 passed the Alaska National Interests Land Conservation Act, making it exceedingly difficult for oil producers to explore new areas for drilling in that region. A major offshore oil spill by the tanker *Exxon Valdez* in 1989 added to the controversy surrounding the impact oil production has had on the state's wildlife and natural resources. In 2001, newly elected President George W. Bush showed interest in renewing efforts to drill in Alaska's Arctic National Wildlife Refuge, but the U.S. Senate twice rejected such efforts during Bush's first term in office. Given Americans' continued devotion to the automobile, the search for alternative sources of oil in Alaska and elsewhere is not likely to diminish any time soon.

years have required public and private schools alike to offer an "individualized education program" for disabled students, a special accommodation necessary to keep disabled students mainstreamed with others. Such accommodations can prove quite costly to local schools, which may be required to hire high-priced specialists at their own expense. Concerns have also been raised about the content of curricula and the quality of teaching. The states have implemented various reforms to improve standards for the training of teachers and the testing of students. In 2002, President Bush signed the **No Child Left Behind Act,** which required mandatory testing of students to meet basic competencies.[26] This policy has been controversial, because it means schools with a high percentage of low-income or underprivileged children can be labeled as "failures" under the policy. Penalties for failing to meet standards include the forced hiring of tutors and other academic assistants, substantially straining the economic burdens on these schools.

Federal courts have been especially active in overseeing state educational matters since the 1960s. Fifteen years after *Brown v. Board of Education*, the Supreme Court was still enforcing desegregation decrees in recalcitrant school districts. Some integration efforts, such as the busing of children over long distances to guarantee diverse student bodies, met with opposition from African Americans and whites alike.

★ No Child Left Behind Act

Federal legislation passed in 2002 that requires mandatory testing of students to meet basic competencies.

[26] See Patrick J. McGuinn, *No Child Left Behind and the Transformation of Federal Education Policy, 1965–2005* (Lawrence: University Press of Kansas, 2006).

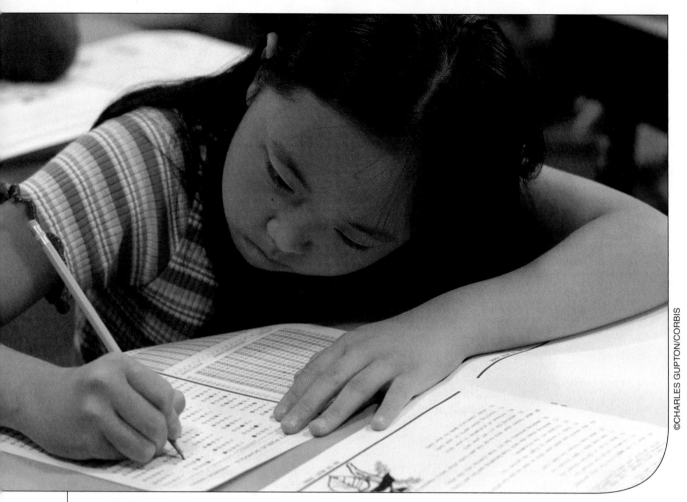

An elementary school student taking a standardized test as mandated by federal "No Child Left Behind" legislation.

Yet by 2007 even the Supreme Court had joined the opposition to race-conscious remedies in education, declaring that "the way to stop discrimination on the basis of race is to stop discriminating on the basis of race."[27] However, battles between local and federal authorities over the direction of education promise to continue well into the twenty-first century.

Religion and Public Policy

Religion has enjoyed a central and influential place in American history. In 1835, the European observer Alexis de Tocqueville wrote that "there is no country in the world where the Christian religion retains a greater influence over the souls of men than in America," and he was surely correct. Although the reach of religion into American politics in particular was quite evident in the late eighteenth and nineteenth centuries, religious leaders and movements usually acted outside the policy-making institutions of government. With few exceptions, religious groups were often quite cautious about tying their fates to specific political parties. Prior to the Civil War, some religious groups supported the abolitionist movement that opposed slavery and called for the immediate emancipation of all slaves; religious groups also played an influential role in helping to improve factory conditions for women and child laborers. At the beginning of the twentieth century, the influence of religion and religious groups was diffused somewhat by an increase in the number of new religions, new sects, and widely varying religious practices. Religious groups often disagreed among themselves about public policy, further diminishing

[27] *Parents Involved in Community Schools v. Seattle School District No. 1,* 127 S.Ct. 2738 (2007).

their influence. For example, traditional fundamentalist Christian groups opposed more modernist Christian groups over the direction of culture in general. Some defenders of traditional Christian practice and belief responded by withdrawing from public life altogether.

It wasn't until the 1970s that religion generally, and many fundamentalist religious groups in particular, re-emerged as a powerful force in American politics. Some of the Supreme Court's controversial rulings on religious matters during the 1960s, such as that forbidding public prayer in public schools, galvanized these groups to become increasingly involved in politics and the shaping of public policy. Richard Nixon's 1968 campaign for the presidency focused on wrestling southern voters away from their traditional allegiance to the Democratic Party. The preponderantly Republican affiliation of conservative and evangelical forms of Protestantism in the South proved crucial to Nixon's success in 1968 and 1972. The church unification movement, which joined together numerous large churches into even larger, more powerful entities, facilitated political organizational efforts. The Supreme Court's 1973 decision in *Roe v. Wade* that protected a woman's right to abortion drew even more religious groups into the political process. By 1980, the so-called religious right, a label that applies to a number of religious movements and groups that are especially conservative on such social issues, had started to exert its influence at the national level.[28] In his campaign for the presidency that year, Republican candidate Ronald Reagan positioned himself as a social conservative and promised to appoint judges who would reverse the Supreme Court's school prayer and abortion decisions. In both 1980 and 1984, conservative Christians became the foot soldiers of the Republican Party.

Former President George W. Bush, seen here celebrating the National Day of Prayer in 2007 with James Dobson (left, with his hands folded), the chairman of "Focus on the Family," an organization that defends the interests of Evangelical Christians in the United States. Bush, a self-described born-again Christian, actively courted social conservatives throughout his presidency.

---

[28] Ruth Murray Brown, *For a Christian America: A History of the Religious Right* (Amherst, NY: Prometheus Books, 2002).

The rise of Republican-oriented religious movements during the past quarter century such as Jerry Falwell's Moral Majority and Pat Robertson's Christian Coalition added new religious issues onto the national policy agenda. Republican administrations have routinely addressed those groups' policy priorities—in addition to advocating in favor of school prayer and opposing abortion rights, they've successfully pressed for legislation ensuring tougher immigration controls, pornography regulations, and opposition to gay rights. The Communications Decency Act, the Partial Birth Abortion Act, and the Defense of Marriage Act all emerged from a Republican-controlled Congress in which the religious right enjoyed significant influence.

The connection between religion and politics took a new turn in January 2001 when the George W. Bush administration established the White House Office of Faith-Based and Community-Based Initiatives, which encouraged religious organizations to compete for government welfare contracts and grants, without requiring a strict separation between their religious activities and social service programs. In defending the new initiative, President Bush argued that religious organizations would be more effective than the government in managing social programs. Under programs administered by the new office, religious groups receive federal money to help them run food and housing assistance programs, drug abuse prevention programs, and other social welfare services. Beyond concerns about the constitutional separation of church and state posed by this new program, critics also claimed that it did not offer clear enough protections against those same religious groups proselytizing as they provide the services and discriminating in their hiring policies.

Now & Then: Making the Connection

Social welfare policy in the United States has been a source of continued frustration for many. This nation's status as perhaps the richest nation in the world over the past century might imply a responsibility on the part of the government to spread around those riches so that each person is assured at least a minimum level of subsistence and welfare, as well as the right to enjoy such public goods as clean water and clean air. At the same time, the U.S. capitalist system tends to foster a "pull yourself up by your bootstraps" culture, which is at odds with any public policy efforts leading to the systematic provision of goods and services to needy people. U.S. culture has instead traditionally emphasized a reliance on churches and other nonprofit organizations to provide that level of security. In the modern era, the U.S. government has attempted to strike a balance between these two positions, to the satisfaction of few.

Prior to the New Deal, the government's role in providing social welfare was quite limited. Since the 1930s, and especially since the 1960s, the government's social welfare functions have increased substantially. Of course innovative social welfare policies do not emerge overnight. The controversy that surrounds governmental welfare schemes often invites as much resistance as it does cheerleading. Theodore Roosevelt's attempt to establish landmark environmental conservation policy met with resistance in Congress; similarly, President Bill Clinton's high hopes for universal health insurance in the early 1990s bogged down into legislative gridlock and produced little change of note in health care policy during his presidency. Both Roosevelt and Clinton did, however, set the stage for broader policy reform in later years: future administrations would preside over passage of clean air and water acts, as well as enactment of a prescription drugs bill that made limited fixes to America's system of health care insurance. Clearly Charles Lindblom's "science of muddling through" is a policy-making process for the patient only.

The Social Security Act of 1935 essentially introduced U.S. citizens to the welfare state. The primary purpose of the law was to provide adequate income to American retirees at a time when an economic depression was making it difficult for many seniors to make ends meet. Social Security today has become a central feature of American work life and retirement. Without this public retirement system, more than half of America's senior citizens would have been forced to live on incomes that place them below the poverty level. The retirement portion of today's Social Security system requires American workers and their employers to provide the revenue to keep the system afloat, while payments are made to retirees. Payment benefits are based on a formula that takes into account the amount of money a retiree contributed to the system and the age at which that individual retired. Because revenues currently outpace outlays, the system today is financially healthy. Most economists agree, however, that the financial security of the Social Security system will soon be threatened, because payments to Social Security recipients will start to outpace contributions to the system within the next decade. This problem will be caused by the large population of baby boomers who are now beginning to retire and are beginning to draw money from the system rather than contribute to it. Though a number of proposals have been offered to fix this impending problem, none so far have been adopted. Recently the administration of President George W. Bush proposed a number of measures to privatize the system. The nation's focus on international events, a poorly performing stock market (which would be used to accomplish privatized retirement savings account under the Bush plan), and strong opposition from the Democrats doomed these proposals.

On http://academic.cengage.com/dautrich, find the Politics Interactive link for details on the politics of Social Security. Consult as well the various links that provide historical, popular, and global perspectives on the Social Security system.

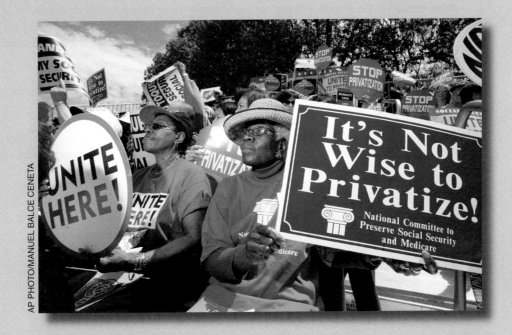

AP PHOTO/MANUEL BALCE CENETA

http://academic.cengage.com/dautrich

Chapter Summary

★ Social policy refers to the rules, regulations, and policy making pertaining to the quality of life, welfare, and relations of human beings in the United States. There are many different types of social policy, including crime policy, health care policy, social security policy, and environmental policy.

★ Democratic governments must strike a delicate balance between maintaining public order and protecting individual freedom. Especially severe and strict forms of law enforcement would make citizens safe, but with a very high cost to taxpayers and possibly some loss of individual freedom as well.

★ Though criminal justice policy making has been an area of law reserved primarily to state governments, the federal government has more recently become more proactive in legislating such areas as gun control, drug-trafficking, and carjacking.

★ The welfare state is a social system in which the state assumes a considerable degree of responsibility for citizens in matters of health care, employment, education, and retirement income. The actual amount of welfare provided varies widely from nation to nation. Most modern welfare states sit somewhere on a spectrum between pure capitalism and pure socialism.

★ The United States generally resisted any meaningful attempt to provide welfare benefits to all citizens until the 1930s. In response to the severe economic depression, President Franklin D. Roosevelt proposed—and Congress passed—a "New Deal" of programs that provided certain welfare services, such as Social Security.

★ President Lyndon Johnson's Great Society programs of the mid-1960s further advanced welfare programs in the United States, introducing such programs as Medicare and Medicaid.

★ Social Security is a retirement benefit program for members of the U.S. workforce. Though it has provided retirement income for millions of retirees since 1935, many economists predict that by about year 2030 the system will pay out significantly more than it brings in. A number of proposals to privatize Social Security have been suggested; however, to date the U.S. Congress has enacted no major policy changes, and the crisis on Wall Street in September 2008 put off all discussion of privatization for the time being.

★ The U.S. government encourages private retirement investing through tax-free investment vehicles such as IRAs, Keoghs, and 401(k) plans.

★ The U.S. health care system contrasts sharply with systems found in other Western democracies that feature universal health care. Criticisms of the U.S. system focus on limitations on access and excessively high costs.

★ Education has traditionally been a state and local responsibility. LBJ's Great Society of the 1960s included programs to assist disadvantaged preschool children and programs offering federal aid for public education and low-cost student loans for college.

★ Since the 1970s, religion has become a powerful influence in American politics. The rise of religious movements favoring the Republican party in particular has pushed issues such as abortion, school prayer, and gay rights onto the national policy-making agenda.

Key Terms

Capitalism (p. 513)

Crime control model (p. 511)

Due process model (p. 511)

Environmental Protection Agency
(EPA) (p. 519)

Health maintenance organization
(HMO) (p. 518)

Medicaid (p. 515)

Medicare (p. 515)

No Child Left Behind Act (p. 523)

Social policy (p. 510)

Socialism (p. 514)

Universal health care (p. 517)

Welfare state (p. 513)

Resources

Important Books

Beland, Daniel. *Social Security: History and Politics from the New Deal to the Privatization Debate.*
Lawrence: University Press of Kansas, 2005.

Blank, Rebecca. *It Takes a Nation: A New Agenda for Fighting Poverty.* Princeton, NJ: Princeton University Press, 1998.

Feldman, Noah. *Divided by God: America's Church-State Problem—and What We Should Do About It.*
New York: Farrar, Straus and Giroux, 2005.

Friedman, Thomas L. *Hot, Flat, and Crowded: Why We Need a Green Revolution—and How It Can Renew America.* New York: Farrar, Straus, and Giroux, 2008.

Gore, Albert, Jr. *An Inconvenient Truth: The Planetary Emergency of Global Warming and What We Can Do About It.* New York: Bloomsbury Books, 2006.

Patterson, James T. *America's Struggle Against Poverty.* Cambridge, MA: Harvard University
Press, 1994.

Skocpol, Theda. *Social Policy in the United States.* Princeton, NJ: Princeton University Press, 1995.

Internet Sources

http://www.epa.gov (the official website of the Environmental Protection Agency, which features information on environmental projects and programs, news and events, as well as rules and regulations)

http://www.ssa.org (Social Security online is the official website of the Social Security Administration, which includes information on services, benefits, research and data, Social Security laws, and other frequently asked questions about Social Security in the United States)

http://www.welfaretowork.org (the official website of the Welfare-to-Work Partnership, a nonpartisan group organized to help businesses hire people on public assistance)

http://www.medicare.gov (the official U.S. website on the Medicare program which features information about Medicare enrollment and the Medicare Prescription Dug Improvement and Modernization Act of 2003)

18 American Foreign Policy

President George W. Bush speaking to U.S.
Marines at Camp Pendleton in California

esident Woodrow Wilson (in top hat) marching
a Liberty Loan Parade during World War I

A Domestic Focus Yields to International Realities: Now & Then

During his campaign for the presidency, he repeatedly criticized previous administrations for engaging in foreign policy initiatives that overextended America's military abroad. Rather, he argued that the United States should avoid acting as the world's policeman. In fact, the candidate openly questioned the need to send troops to countries where U.S. immediate interests were not being threatened. His position squared well with public attitudes of the time: foreign policy barely registered on the public's conscience throughout the presidential campaign. Eventually he was elected president on the strength of his ambitious domestic agenda. Yet once elected, dramatic events quickly tipped the political scales in favor of increased U.S. involvement abroad. This chief executive who had campaigned against international forays by American forces now, as president, went before a joint session of Congress to demand that immediate military action be taken in another part of the world. More active participation in international conflicts, the president believed, would increase the U.S. government's leverage to dictate the future rules governing the international order. Ironically, the primary legacy this president would leave to the nation would not be any lasting successes achieved in the domestic sphere; rather, he would be best remembered for his actions as commander-in-chief of the U.S. armed forces and for his attempts to spread democracy as part of a new international order he helped to create.

2001

2020   2000   1980   1960   1940

Now. . . Although the son of a president who had led the nation into war in the early 1990s, President George W. Bush never imagined that his tenure in office would be dominated by military operations in Afghanistan, Iraq, and other countries as a result of his own administration's war on terrorism. Indeed, he viewed his father's failed bid for re-election in 1992 as a warning that Americans wanted their chief executives to emphasize issues at home—in particular, the state of the economy, health care, and domestic law enforcement issues. But the events of September 11, 2001, shifted the new president's priorities: reacting swiftly to the terrorist attacks on the World Trade Center and the Pentagon, Bush shifted his primary focus to foreign policy matters. Over the next year and a half, the Bush administration would (1) shepherd through Congress the USA Patriot Act, giving federal law enforcement officials countless new tools to fight the war on terrorism; (2) establish a new cabinet-level bureaucratic structure called the Department of Homeland Security, charged with coordinating the nation's defense against military threats; and (3) send U.S. troops into both Afghanistan and Iraq, toppling the governments of each of those nations in succession. Less than two years after criticizing those who had advocated an increased U.S. role as an international policeman, George W. Bush had proven his readiness to flex U.S. military power overseas.

American Government: Historical, Popular, and Global Perspectives

1917

1920   1900   1880   1860   1840

Then. . .

President Bush was not the first American chief executive to see his own carefully conceived domestic agenda swept away in the face of unanticipated foreign policy demands. Woodrow Wilson ran for president twice as the Democratic candidate most closely associated with progressive domestic reforms. Who would have imagined that he would one day become the president responsible for unprecedented military interventions overseas? To be sure, Wilson's first term in office focused on addressing the ill effects of the Industrial Revolution at home, even as World War I was being fought in Europe. Not even the German sinking in 1915 of the British liner *Lusitania*, with 128 Americans aboard, could shift Wilson from his isolationist position. The following year Wilson even campaigned successfully for re-election on the slogan: "He kept us out of the war." After Wilson's second inauguration, however, the war began to hit home once Germany resumed its policy of unrestricted submarine warfare in the Atlantic: German subs sank three American merchant ships in early 1917. This act led Wilson to condemn the German campaign before Congress, as he urged Americans to fight to make the world "safe for democracy." U.S. involvement in World War I eventually tipped the military balance in favor of the Allies; it also assured Wilson's status as a key player in shaping the treaty for peace following the war.[1]

---

[1] H. W. Brands, *Woodrow Wilson, 1913–1921* (New York: Times Books, 2003).

Both Bush and his predecessor of nearly a century ago faced similar dilemmas. Foreign policy always seems to sit on the back burner of American politics—at least until the nation is unexpectedly attacked. Then, even those leaders who were elected on a platform of noninterventionism lead the charge for military solutions. Franklin Delano Roosevelt's aggressive domestic agenda lost considerable steam by the end of his second term, as the United States increasingly turned its attention to the looming threat of World War II. Just as dramatically, the expansion of the Vietnam War brought an abrupt halt to Lyndon Johnson's domestic agenda beginning in the summer and early fall of 1965.[2]

Both Wilson and Bush alternated first as beneficiaries and then later as victims of this inexorable pull toward foreign policy priorities. Each man, by his words and actions, contributed heavily to the shape of U.S. foreign policy during his presidency, and the American people would eventually issue blame or credit to each of them according to the success of their policies in the world arena. Yet presidents do not act alone in making foreign policy. As we shall see, other actors within and outside of government also play a role in influencing America's foreign policy. The political activities of these other actors provide an enlightening window into the American political system as a whole.

The Constitutional Framework of American Foreign Policy

A nation's foreign policy comprises all of its activities directed at conducting relations with other countries, including military operations and diplomatic activities (such as the building up of trade practices and the making of treaties). In the 200-plus-year history of the United States, few have disputed the federal government's exclusive authority to manage the nation's foreign policy. Indeed, two of the three original cabinet departments created by Congress were the Department of State and the Department of War, a sign of just how important these two functions would be to the nation.

Article I of the Constitution gives Congress the exclusive power to declare war, raise armies, punish maritime crimes, and regulate foreign commerce. Under Article II, the president is empowered as commander-in-chief to conduct the course of war. The Founders' intent in separating the power to command from the power to fund the military was to check the war power from being abused. The Constitution also gives the president the authority to negotiate treaties and to appoint and receive ambassadors.

Perhaps the most basic elements of foreign policy during the eighteenth and nineteenth centuries were the treaties the United States entered into with foreign nations. Because the Senate alone was vested with the authority to ratify such treaties (by a two-thirds vote), many expected that this small legislative body (there were just twenty-six senators at the outset) would exert a strong influence over the nation's foreign policy.

Within the next two centuries, control over foreign affairs, including the power to make war, would shift from Congress to the White House. Fundamental changes in America's role in world affairs during the twentieth century spurred this transfer of power. America's ascendancy to superpower status in the early part of the twentieth century led to U.S. involvement in world affairs. The presidency was well-suited to respond to these new demands on America's attention; within the three branches of government, the single chief executive is best-positioned to respond to sudden changes in circumstances around the globe in a quick and forceful manner. Unlike Congress, the president can use the "bully pulpit" of the office to communicate policies and generate support for the administration's goals. Highly activist presidents, including Theodore Roosevelt, Woodrow Wilson, and Franklin Delano Roosevelt,

---

[2] Two of the best overviews of American foreign during the latter half of the twentieth century are Stephen Ambrose and Douglas Brinkley, *Rise to Globalism: American Foreign Policy Since 1938* (New York: Penguin, 1997); and Thomas Paterson, J. Garry Clifford, and Kenneth Hagan, *American Foreign Policy: A History* (New York: D. C. Heath, 1997).

American Government ... in Historical Perspective:
Presidential Dominance of the Warmaking Power

The Constitution vests Congress alone with the authority to declare war; the president's role as commander-in-chief is theoretically limited to making strategic decisions about how to wage war, and arguably, to repelling unexpected attacks from foreign powers. In reality, however, the president has come to dominate the declaration and exercise of war making power in everything but name.

In 1861, President Abraham Lincoln waged "war" for almost three months against the Confederate States without even calling Congress into session. From April 12 (the day the Southern rebels first fired on a federal military installation at Fort Sumter in South Carolina) through July 6, Lincoln proclaimed a blockade of the southern states, increased the size of the army, expended funds for military purposes without congressional approval, and suspended the writ of habeas corpus (which limited the holding of prisoners without a trial). Although Lincoln defended each of these measures as defensive in nature, critics of his administration complained that he exceeded his constitutional authority. In at least one respect the Supreme Court agreed: in 1866, it declared the suspension of habeas corpus unconstitutional.

In 1964, President Lyndon Johnson secured near unanimous consent from Congress for passage of the Gulf of Tonkin resolution, which authorized the White House to use armed military force to protect U.S. soldiers in South Vietnam and to deter further aggression from North Vietnam. Congressional leaders believed at the time that they were merely helping Johnson assume a stronger defensive posture in the wake of numerous North Vietnamese gunboat attacks on U.S. destroyers. But in subsequent years, Johnson interpreted the resolution to provide him with a virtual blank check for further military action in Vietnam. He eventually sent close to half a million troops to fight in what remained an undeclared war and ordered the offensive bombing of North Vietnamese strongholds, all on the basis of the Gulf of Tonkin resolution's slim grant of war making authority.

In 1983, President Ronald Reagan provided a vivid illustration of just how much war making discretion presidents actually have when he ordered the U.S. intervention in Grenada, a small Communist-held island off the coast of South America. The Marxist government in that country had recently begun constructing an airstrip that could eventually be used for staging Cuban and Soviet military flights. With unrest growing in Grenada, the Reagan administration also expressed concern for the safety of a thousand or so American citizens (mostly medical students) on the island. After the country's prime minister was assassinated, Reagan ordered an invasion of seventeen hundred marines with air support; the American forces quickly overran the island. The brief battle cost the lives of eighteen U.S. servicemen; meanwhile, Congress remained on the sidelines throughout the conflict.

capitalized on these assets by communicating frequently with world leaders and their own publics on pressing affairs around the world.

Although the Constitution appears to give Congress primary authority over foreign and military affairs, the large and often unwieldy Congress has proven no match for modern presidents on the world stage. Political scientist Aaron Wildavsky's **two presidencies theory** posits the existence of a more powerful presidency in foreign affairs and a more limited presidency in the domestic sphere. Of course the president's dominance over foreign affairs hasn't stopped Congress from at least trying to reassert its authority in this realm.

★ **Two presidencies theory**

Theory articulated by political scientist Aaron Wildavsky that posits the existence of a more powerful presidency in foreign affairs and a more limited presidency in the domestic sphere.

A napalm strike erupts in a fireball near U.S. soldiers in Vietnam in 1966.

★ War Powers Resolution

Largely ignored congressional policy that restricts the president's power to engage in war except (1) when Congress has declared war, (2) when Congress has specifically granted the president permission to use armed forces, or (3) when the nation is under attack. The resolution further requires the president to report to Congress whenever American forces are entered into hostilities.

In 1973, with public opinion shifting against military involvement around the globe, Congress passed the **War Powers Resolution,** overriding President Richard Nixon's veto in the process. The resolution theoretically restricted the president's power to engage in war to instances in which Congress had declared war or specifically granted the president permission to use armed forces, or to cases where the nation was under attack. The resolution required the president to report to Congress whenever American forces were entered into hostilities and attain congressional permission to engage those forces for more than sixty days. Every president since Nixon has either evaded or ignored the War Powers Resolution, arguing that it unconstitutionally infringes on the president's war powers. In fact, no court to date has ever ruled definitively on whether the president must comply with the law's provisions.

With some exceptions, the rise of the president to become the key actor in foreign affairs was a twentieth-century development. Initially, the Founders' hopes for an American foreign policy built on consensus among the political branches of government were for the most part realized. But this new decision-making apparatus faced severe tests in the decades following the American Revolution.

The Roots of American Foreign Policy

As a new nation with a limited military, the United States was at first heavily dependent on maintaining good foreign relations to avoid disadvantageous military engagements. Fortunately, the great distance that separated America from Western European superpowers provided a measure of protection from frequent threats and incursions. More than two centuries later, the nation's status as a military superpower affords it far more leverage in its relations with foreign powers. Still, with advances in communications and transportation effectively shrinking the size of the global community, the United States must expend considerable resources and energy to successfully navigate through an increasingly complex foreign policy landscape. American foreign policy has always stood front and center in the list of U.S. government priorities.

The Isolationist Tradition and the Monroe Doctrine

The successful transition of the former British colonies in America into an independent nation was the product of astute foreign policy initiatives by some high-profile figures. George Washington's Continental army struggled for victories throughout the war for American independence; American fortunes in the war were raised only after Benjamin Franklin helped convince France in 1778 to join the war on the side of the colonies. Indeed, many historians and analysts attribute the Americans' victory over Britain to this crucial Franco-American alliance, which provided the colonies with resources to threaten British ships off the waters near the Atlantic Coast. However, under the leadership of President George Washington, the newly formed United States of America set aside the alliance with France and declared formal neutrality when England and revolutionary France went to war in 1793. In his farewell address to the nation in 1796, Washington urged his fellow Americans to steer clear of permanent alliances of any kind.

During the nation's early years, the United States maintained a foreign policy marked by **isolationism,** defined as opposition to both (1) interventions in distant wars (that is, outside the Western hemisphere) and (2) involvement in permanent military alliances. The policy of isolationism dominated America's foreign affairs for nearly a century and a half, preserving America's freedom to refuse to act until the very last minute, and in most cases allowing it to forgo intervention altogether. Isolationism is distinguished from **pacifism,** a policy that refuses to sanction *any* military conflict and opposes all war making. Consistent with its general policy of isolationism, during the nineteenth century the United States fought wars in lands that bordered the nation or lay within U.S. boundaries in 1812 (against Britain), in 1846 (against Mexico), and in 1898 (against Spain in the Caribbean). Finally, the policy of military isolationism did not mean complete isolation from the world's culture or commerce, as Americans enthusiastically learned from other nations and welcomed visitors and products from abroad throughout this period.

America's brand of military isolationism never applied to the Western hemisphere. On December 2, 1823, President James Monroe declared the nation's commitment to a foreign policy that would eventually become known as the **Monroe Doctrine.** Specifically, Monroe proclaimed that both North and South America should not be considered "as subjects for future colonization by any European power," and that the United States would consider any efforts by Europeans to colonize these areas "as dangerous to our peace and safety." The implications of the Monroe Doctrine were profound: America would consider any new colonization efforts on its side of the Atlantic Ocean as tantamount to an act of war against the United States. This doctrine did not cause much controversy for most of the nineteenth century. Yet the degree to which European nations actually deferred to the United States because of the doctrine (as opposed to deferring because it was in their interests to do so) is difficult for historians to assess.

With the rise of European imperialism at the end of the nineteenth century, the United States eventually took action on its own to invoke the Monroe Doctrine. In 1895, the United States intervened in a dispute between Great Britain and Venezuela over the boundaries between Venezuela and British Guiana (present-day Guyana). In the early twentieth century, the United States prevented European nations from interfering in the affairs of debt-ridden Latin American countries by taking over the struggling economies of the Dominican Republic (1907) and Nicaragua (1911). Concerned about German influence over the Republic of Haiti, the United States even occupied that small country in 1915. The United States also actively encouraged the revolt of Latin American nations against Spain in the early part of the

★ **Isolationism**

Foreign policy doctrine that opposes (1) intervention in distant wars and (2) involvement in permanent military alliances.

★ **Pacifism**

Doctrine of foreign relations that refuses to sanction any military conflict and that opposes all war making.

★ **Monroe Doctrine**

U.S. foreign policy that proclaimed North and South America unavailable for future colonization by any European power and that declared any such colonization would be viewed as an act of war on the United States.

A cartoon satirizing President Theodore Roosevelt's approach to foreign policy: "Walk softly and carry a big stick."

★ Expansionism

Doctrine that favors a country expanding its own territory and influence.

★ Manifest destiny

U.S. policy of the mid-nineteenth century that advocated acquiring lands and occupying the entire American continent from one ocean to the other.

twentieth century, even though Spanish possession of these territories predated the Monroe Doctrine.

Expansionism and the Birth of a Superpower

U.S. opposition to further European colonization in the Western hemisphere helped the nation to establish itself as the pre-eminent power in the Americas. Meanwhile, the United States practiced a policy of expansionism on the North American continent. **Expansionism** is the doctrine of expanding the territory or economic influence of one's own country. The policy began as a systematic effort to pursue what many American officials viewed as the nation's defining ideology: its **manifest destiny** to acquire lands and occupy the entire continent from the Atlantic to the Pacific Ocean. America's purchase of the massive Louisiana Territory from the French in 1803 more than doubled the land size of the United States at the time. The federal government went on to annex Florida after conquering Spanish holdings there between 1817 and 1819. Resolution of border conflicts with Great Britain in the 1840s established the northeastern boundary of Maine and of the Oregon territory. The United States annexed the independent Republic of Texas in 1845, and following a successful war against Mexico in 1846–1848 gained all of present-day California, Nevada, and Utah and parts of present-day Arizona, New Mexico, Colorado, and Wyoming.

Adherence to isolationism in principle also did not preclude the United States from setting its imperial sights on territories in the Pacific Ocean and the Caribbean Sea. In the late 1890s, Congress annexed Hawaii around the same time that it fought the Spanish-American War to free Cuba from Spain. The United States gained possession of the Philippine Islands as a result of the Philippine-American War of 1898–1902. Although the United States mostly discontinued its quest for territorial acquisitions abroad after the turn of the century, it continued to play an active role in opposing the imperialist designs of other nations.

America's increasing willingness to intervene militarily in foreign affairs signaled a potential shift in the traditional balance of powers, as the United States increasingly found itself a major player on the world stage. Nevertheless, up until World War I the United States remained primarily separate from the rest of the world militarily. Even the outbreak of World War I in 1914 produced no immediate change in U.S. foreign policy; President Woodrow Wilson openly proclaimed U.S. neutrality in the dispute and between 1915 and 1917 continually attempted mediation among the warring parties. Only when those efforts to settle the war failed, and Germany began to relentlessly attack U.S. vessels in 1917, did America enter the war on the side of the Allies—Great Britain, France, Italy, and Russia.

By the end of World War I, the European Allies owed more than $11 billion to the United States, making America a creditor nation for the first time in its history. Other world powers looked to the United States for guidance and resources to help construct a new international order, and together with President Wilson, in 1919 they drafted the Treaty of Versailles, which established a system of reparations and called

MPI/GETTY IMAGES

for the creation of a League of Nations, which was intended to arbitrate international disputes and thereby avoid future wars. Yet preferences for a policy of isolationism still ran strong throughout America. After an overconfident Wilson engaged in a series of political missteps in selling the Treaty of Versailles to the public, the Republican-controlled U.S. Senate balked at the risk that the League of Nations might force the U.S. president to engage in military action; the Senate wanted Wilson to modify those aspects of the League covenant, but he refused. Facing an unyielding president on the issue, the Senate voted against U.S. membership in the League, which thereafter proved ineffective in maintaining peace and preventing aggression and was eventually dissolved in 1946. Thus American isolationism continued to prevail in the years between the two world wars.

As the second world war approached in the late 1930s and early 1940s, President Franklin Roosevelt made clear where the sympathies of the U.S. government lay, first by utilizing a lend-lease program with Britain that supplied that country with arms at little or no cost, and later, by increasing economic pressures on the Japanese in the Pacific.[3] The Japanese attack on Pearl Harbor on December 7, 1941, propelled the United States into the war against Germany, Japan, and Italy.

U.S. involvement in World War II proved critical to the final outcome: American manpower and resources were an important component in the success of the D-Day invasion of France and much of Western Europe in 1944. The United States detonated two atomic bombs over Japan in August 1945, forcing the Japanese to surrender. After the war, the European victors looked to the United States again to help keep international peace. This time they were not disappointed, as they had been when the U.S. Senate refused to support the League of Nations three decades earlier. In 1945, the United States joined the newly created **United Nations (UN),** an international organization formed to promote and maintain international security and peace.

After World War II, America's prevailing foreign policy changed from one marked by isolationism to one featuring **internationalism**—the United States now actively participated in a process that collectively secured the political independence and territorial boundaries of other countries by a system of economic and military sanctions against aggressor nations. In fact, America went even further than other nations in this regard. The **Marshall Plan** (formally the European Recovery Program) introduced by Secretary of State George Marshall in 1947 provided $13 billion in loans to Western European countries whose economies had been ravaged by World War II. Some countries used the money to combat inflation or retire state debts; others (defeated Germany, Austria, and Italy among them) used the assistance to buy food. Proponents of the plan deemed it a humanitarian policy intended to alleviate suffering, whereas critics argued that the aid had a more strategic purpose: to increase European dependence on the United States and discourage potential new alliances with the Soviet Union.[4]

Foreign Policy During the Cold War

Out of the wreckage of World War II emerged two global military and political superpowers, the United States and the Soviet Union, locked in a nearly half-century-long struggle called the **Cold War.**[5] This conflict over ideological differences (the promotion of democracy by the United States versus the promotion of communism by the Soviet Union) lasted from 1945 until the dissolution of the Soviet Union in 1991 and was carried on by a variety of methods including economic warfare, arms buildups, and tense diplomacy. Postwar leaders in the United States believed that the nation had fought in World War II to protect self-determination and open trade, and together with other Western European nations including Great Britain and France, it formed military, political, and at times, economic alliances. Formally created in 1949, the **North Atlantic Treaty Organization (NATO)** bound the United States to the military defense of Western Europe. Meanwhile the Soviet Union in the late 1940s

★ United Nations (UN)

International organization formed after World War II to promote and maintain international security and peace.

★ Internationalism

Doctrine that favors active participation of the nation in collective arrangements that secure the political independence and territorial boundaries of other countries.

★ Marshall Plan

The 1947 U.S. policy that provided loans and aid to Western European countries whose economies had been ravaged by World War II.

★ Cold War

The nearly half-century struggle over ideological differences between the United States and the Soviet Union. Waged through economic warfare, arms buildups, and tense diplomatic talks, the Cold War never broke out into a sustained military engagement between the two nations and ended with the dissolution of the Soviet Union in 1991.

★ North Atlantic Treaty Organization (NATO)

A military, political, and economic alliance of nations formally bound to protect self-determination and open trade in Western Europe.

[3] Robert Dallek, *Franklin Delano Roosevelt and American Foreign Policy, 1932–1945* (New York: Oxford University Press, 1995).
[4] A detailed (if uncritical) look at the events leading up to the Truman Doctrine and the Marshall Plan can be found in Joseph M. Jones, *The Fifteen Weeks* (New York: Harcourt, Brace, 1955).
[5] D. F. Flemming, *The Cold War and Its Origins: 1917–1960* (New York: Doubleday, 1961).

★ Warsaw Pact

Formal alliance of nations within the Soviet sphere during the Cold War.

★ Truman Doctrine

Doctrine articulated by President Harry Truman in the late 1940s by which money and resources were provided to support and sustain non-Communist governments in areas strategically vital to the United States.

★ Containment

U.S. foreign policy that sought to restrict Soviet power (and Communist influence) to its existing geographical sphere.

★ Domino theory

Theory that held that Communist takeovers of countries in Southeast Asia and elsewhere would be followed by subsequent Communist takeovers of nearby countries.

dominated its Eastern European neighbors, including Poland and Romania. In 1955, those nations and others within the Soviet sphere formed the **Warsaw Pact.** Germany, divided in two following World War II, was split between the two alliances, with West Germany as a model democratic nation in NATO, and East Germany serving as a western outpost for Soviet communism in the Warsaw Pact.

In 1947, President Harry Truman articulated the **Truman Doctrine,** which provided money and resources to sustaining non-Communist governments in areas strategically vital to the United States, such as the Mediterranean and the Middle East. American foreign policy during the Cold War generally adhered to a policy of **containment**—restricting Soviet power to its current geographical sphere and resisting any efforts to expand Communist influence. When the Soviets in 1949 blockaded the city of Berlin (a West German city located entirely within Soviet-controlled East German territory), the United States airlifted supplies to the city for nearly a year. Aerial reconnaissance allowed the Cold War adversaries to keep a more careful eye on each other beginning in the 1950s. It also led to the Cuban Missile Crisis in October 1962, when President John F. Kennedy's demands that the Soviet Union remove missiles from nearby Cuba led to a tense standoff with the Soviets and nearly ignited a nuclear war. U.S. military involvement in both the Korean and Vietnam Wars was spurred by U.S. government fears of a total Communist takeover of those two countries. Most U.S. presidents during the Cold War subscribed to some version of the **domino theory,** which posited that Communist takeovers of these Southeast Asian countries would be followed by takeovers of Taiwan, India, Iran, and possibly other nations as well.

The American military failure in the Vietnam War in particular led officials at every level of the American government to revisit some of the most fundamental premises of U.S. foreign policy, including the theory of containment.[6] The American phase of that war, extending from 1964 until 1973, proved longer lasting and more divisive than any other war involving the United States.[7] The conflict eventually left fifty-eight thousand Americans dead or missing and cost the U.S. government more than $167 billion. Despite all the bloodshed, none of the U.S. aims in the war—to repel North Vietnam aggression, help negotiate a lasting peace, and encourage South Vietnam as a self-sufficient republic—were accomplished. The final peace agreement allowed for extrication of U.S. forces and return of prisoners of war, but little else; and by 1975 South Vietnam had fallen to the Communists.[8] The decade-long Vietnam quagmire struck a blow against the domino theory. Future military interventions would require that administrations present some additional evidence of a direct threat to America's strategic interests abroad or at home.

During the 1970s, the United States and the Soviet Union engaged in a period of somewhat eased tensions, or limited détente. During this time they agreed on several strategic arms limitation treaties (SALT I and SALT II) that set restrictions on nuclear missiles.[9] But such détente proved

A distraught President Ronald Reagan and Soviet leader Mikhail Gorbachev leaving their unsuccessful arms limitations talks in Reykjavik, Iceland, in October 1986.

©CORBIS

American Government: Historical, Popular, and Global Perspectives

[6] David DiLeo, *George Ball, Vietnam and the Rethinking of Containment* (Chapel Hill: University of North Carolina Press, 1991).
[7] Stanley Karnow, *Vietnam: A History* (New York: Penguin, 1997).
[8] Frank Snepp, *Decent Interval: An Insider's Account on Saigon's Indecent End* (New York: Vintage Books, 1978).
[9] Robert Litwak, *Détente and the Nixon Doctrine* (Cambridge: Cambridge University Press, 1986).

short-lived, as confrontations in underdeveloped Third World nations continued to inject tensions into the Cold War landscape. President Ronald Reagan, denouncing the Soviet Union as an evil empire, outlined a new defense plan, the controversial **Strategic Defense Initiative (SDI),** an antimissile system based on the use of lasers and particle beams to shoot down Soviet nuclear missiles in outer space.[10]

East–West tensions eased with the ascension of reform-minded Mikhail Gorbachev to the leadership of the Soviet state in 1985. Gorbachev's reforms aimed at restructuring the faltering Soviet economy with greater competition and at liberalizing dissent by introducing press freedoms could not be reconciled with a continuation of the costly arms race with the United States. The Cold War formally came to a close in 1991, when Gorbachev resigned his position with the Soviet government amid extremely difficult economic times. In addition to the former Soviet-bloc countries, ten former Soviet republics, including Russia, declared their independence.[11] Following the end of the Cold War, U.S. leaders redirected their foreign policy thinking toward a new world order characterized by conflicts in the Third World, a war on terrorism, and threats of nuclear attack from both terrorists and rogue nations.

★ Strategic Defense Initiative (SDI)

A theoretical antimissile system based on the use of lasers and particle beams to shoot down Soviet nuclear missiles in outer space.

New World Order and New World Disorder

U.S. responsibilities around the world have not decreased much at all in the aftermath of the Cold War. In his January 1991 State of the Union speech, President George H. W. Bush spoke of the onset of a **new world order,** in which numerous nations would work together for the purpose of securing collective peace, security, freedom, and the rule of law.[12] Maintaining this new world order has been a challenge for American political leaders ever since.

Further complicating the foreign affairs landscape was the looming presence of China. Still a Communist nation, China is a crucial market for U.S. goods and products, given that it contains one-fifth of the world's population. In the 1990s, both Presidents George H. W. Bush and Bill Clinton emphasized the need for liberalization of global trade, and in 1993 Congress approved the North American Free Trade Agreement (NAFTA), which lifted trade barriers such as protective tariffs and investment restrictions between the United States and Canada and Mexico. With the U.S. economy increasingly intertwined with the global economy, economic relations with East Asia, Europe, and other countries in the Western hemisphere continue to be a central factor in American foreign policy. Of course economic concerns do not eliminate other interests—tragic human rights abuses in Somalia and Bosnia put pressure on the George H. W. Bush and Clinton administrations to intervene on humanitarian grounds in those countries. The balance both presidents struck in those instances, providing limited aid but no military assistance, prompted criticisms that they had failed to wield America's superpower status in the most appropriate fashion.[13]

★ New world order

President George H. W. Bush's description of the post–Cold War world, in which nations would work together for the purpose of securing collective peace, security, freedom, and the rule of law.

The U.S. Government Confronts the Middle East

Although the Cold War has ended, among the current generation of policy makers the specter of the Vietnam War continues to cast a large shadow on foreign policy deliberations. Discussions of American military intervention since the early 1970s have occurred with the lessons of the Vietnam War looming ominously in the background. Some hawkish conservatives even complain of what they call a "Vietnam syndrome," in which the problems of Vietnam produce an undesirable pacifism on the part of American leaders. Politicians live in fear of supporting yet another war in which public support is flimsy, the military objectives are unclear, and an exit strategy remains ill defined. American interventions in the Balkans and Somalia in the 1990s

---

[10] John Newhouse, "The Missile Defense Debate," *Foreign Affairs 80*, no. 4 (July/August 2001).

[11] John Lewis Gaddis, *The Cold War: A New History* (New York: Penguin, 2005).

[12] One of the key architects of this new understanding was Bush's secretary of state, James A. Baker III. See James A. Baker III, *The Politics of Diplomacy* (New York: Putnam, 1995).

[13] Many of these criticisms are discussed in Samantha Power's award-winning book, *A Problem from Hell: America and the Age of Genocide* (New York: Harper Perennial, 2003).

were limited by fears that increased U.S. involvement in those countries would escalate into another Vietnam. During the first Persian Gulf War of 1991, Joint Chiefs of Staff Chairman Colin Powell urged the nation to avoid Vietnam-like entanglements in which fear of escalation placed the military in an essentially unwinnable conflict.

President George W. Bush's administration has faced inevitable comparisons between the Vietnam War and U.S. intervention of Iraq in 2003. When the military failed to unearth "weapons of mass destruction" cited as partial justification of the war, critics of the Iraqi intervention argued that U.S. interests in the region were just as unclear as they had been in Southeast Asia during the 1960s. Furthermore, the U.S. military's failure to contain rebel insurgents even after taking control of Baghdad invited comparisons to guerrilla war in North Vietnam. In response, President Bush proclaimed that the Iraqi invasion had both removed a brutal dictator, Saddam Hussein, from power and restored a democratic government, in the form of duly held elections, to the previously oppressed nation. Up through late 2008, Bush continued to claim that his administration was committed to having the American military stay in Iraq until democracy and stability were established, a clear attempt to distinguish this event from the

A U.S. soldier guarding the scene of a car bomb explosion in Baghdad.

AP PHOTO/HUSSEIN MALLA

nation's tenuous hold of the South Vietnamese city of Saigon, which the United States abandoned in 1975.

Militarily, the greatest threats to U.S. security during the first decade of the twenty-first century appear to be in two areas of the world: the Middle East and North Korea. More of the U.S. government's attention in recent decades has been focused on the former locus of conflict. Since it first recognized the newly created independent nation of Israel in 1948, the United States has been committed in its support for that country as a political haven for Jews. Meanwhile, Israel has emerged as a modernized democratic presence in a region of the world dominated by Arab countries largely hostile to Western economic power and its cultural domination. U.S. support for Israel has assured the United States of a friendly ally in the Middle East, yet it has also at times run counter to fundamental principles of self-determination as U.S. officials have been forced to confront another dilemma—what to do with the tens of thousands of Palestinian refugees uprooted from their homes in the years following Israel's occupation of former Palestinian territory.

President Jimmy Carter's successful mediation of disputes between Israel and Egypt in 1978 demonstrated that the United States can play a role in resolving conflicts, but long-term peace between Israel and its neighbors has remained elusive despite such efforts. The George H. W. Bush administration encouraged negotiations between Palestinian Liberation Organization head Yasir Arafat and the Israeli government—the resulting Oslo accords of 1993 called for the exchange of Israeli territory and ultimate Palestinian self-determination for the guarantee of peace. Unfortunately, the accords left unclear the precise boundaries and the specific characteristics of Palestinian rule. Right-wing Israeli extremists murdered Israeli Prime Minister Yitzhak Rabin two years later, and both sides hardened against the accords. The Clinton administration attempted to renew negotiations between the two sides in the late 1990s, but the impasse continues today, with Palestinian suicide bombers and Israeli government bombings becoming a routine feature of Israeli and Palestinian daily life in the early part of the twenty-first century.

Distrust of the United States by many Middle East countries has intensified in the wake of recent administrations' overwhelming support for Israel, and the continued presence of the U.S. military in the Middle East, facilitated by the granting of military bases to the United States in Saudi Arabia and Kuwait. Activities by revolutionary forces have occasionally fomented in the region, threatening U.S. interests directly and indirectly. In 1979, the new fundamentalist Iranian regime under Ayatollah Khomeni seized the United States Embassy and held U.S. hostages for more than a year. In late 1990, Iraq President Saddam Hussein invaded Kuwait, threatening U.S. economic interests in the region and spurring the first Bush administration to militarily expel Hussein's army from Kuwait in early 1991.

Navigating the New World Order After the September 11 Attacks

The events of September 11, 2001, refocused the U.S. government's foreign policy energies toward a global war on terrorism. After a short-lived war in Afghanistan that purportedly expelled the Al Qaeda terrorist network from that country, the George W. Bush administration turned its attention back to Saddam Hussein's government in Iraq, which it accused of supporting terrorism abroad and concealing weapons of mass destruction. After less than six weeks of fighting, American military forces liberated the country of Hussein's dictatorial government during the spring of 2003. Yet the aftermath of the Iraq war has proved highly problematic, with insurgent forces in and around the nation's cities posing an ever-present threat to the more than 150,000 American forces who remained there as part of the occupation.[14] By early 2007, over 3,000 Americans had died in Iraq, and Congress began putting pressure on the Bush administration to lay out a timetable and plan for eventual American withdrawal. Rejecting those entreaties, in early 2007 President Bush increased by over 20,000 the number of troops deployed to Iraq in what came to be known as the "Iraq war troop surge of 2007." (Administration officials attributed a general drop in violence during 2007–08 to this increased military presence.)

© SEAN ADAIR/REUTERS/CORBIS

Meanwhile, threats of nuclear and biological terrorism remain ever present in the Middle East where terrorists continue to operate underground. In the past decade, North Korea has also emerged as a potential nuclear threat. Critics charge that the end of the Cold War has in fact ushered in a "new world disorder," featuring ever-shifting alliances and grave terrorist threats from entities not formally associated with any specific nation.

Within this constantly shifting international terrain, America continues to search for its role and identity in the twenty-first-century world. In *Colossus: The Rise and Fall of the American Empire,* British-born Harvard Professor Niall Ferguson argues that like the great British empire of old, the United States needs to embrace its imperial character and commit to more securely establishing the types of democratic institutions around the world that foster long-term prosperity.[15] In another influential book, *Soft Power: The Means to Success in World Politics,* Joseph Nye argues that rather than relying on unilateralism and military power, the United States should endeavor to win the voluntary cooperation of foreign governments.[16] Is the United States an empire? Does it want to be? In light of the difficulties U.S. military forces have faced in postwar Iraq, many of these questions will continue to be debated in the years ahead.

[14] Perhaps the best book written to date about the problems in the military's 2003 intervention in Iraq is Michael Gordon and Bernard Trainor's *Cobra II: The Inside Story of the Invasion and Occupation of Iraq* (New York: Pantheon, 2006).
[15] Niall Ferguson, *Colossus: The Rise and Fall of the American Empire* (New York: Penguin Books, 2005).
[16] Joseph Nye, *Soft Power: The Means to Success in World Politics* (New York: PublicAffairs, 2005).

The Structure of American Foreign Policy Making

The Constitution designates specific roles for the president and the Senate in making U.S. foreign policy. Yet over the course of two centuries, the president of the United States and the executive branch that reports to the president have assumed an increasingly significant role in the process, rendering Congress, interest groups, and citizens themselves less significant in foreign policy making.

Challenged for his lack of foreign policy experience, Democratic presidential candidate Barack Obama traveled to the Middle East and Europe in the summer of 2008 to meet with a number of foreign leaders. The candidate is seen here meeting with Israeli president Shimon Peres in Jerusalem.

★ Department of State

Executive branch agency that is primarily responsible for most foreign policy programs within the executive branch, including diplomatic missions, foreign aid, and contributions to international organizations.

★ International organization

Entity of international scope or character, usually established by treaty, such as the World Bank or the International Monetary Fund.

The Role of the Executive Branch

Many actors and institutions attempt either formally or informally to influence American foreign policy. The president of the United States sits squarely at the center of foreign policy making—within the federal government, the president often dictates its terms with little interference from the other branches.[17] On the positive side, presidential dominance of foreign policy allows the U.S. government to act immediately and decisively in response to developments abroad. The quick responses to the bombing of Pearl Harbor, the threat of nuclear missiles in Cuba, and the 9/11 terrorist attacks might not have been possible had the principal decision makers been a legislative body or council. At the same time, more controversial foreign policy forays such as America's involvement in the Vietnam War, the trading of arms for hostages with Iran in the 1980s, and military intervention in Iraq without proof of weapons of mass destruction might well have been avoided had so much power not been vested in one individual. Although the president is at the center of foreign policy making, other executive branch departments and agencies help formulate and implement foreign policy.

The **Department of State,** headed by the secretary of state, maintains primary responsibility for many foreign policy programs. State Department programs include diplomatic missions to other countries, foreign aid to developing nations, and contributions to **international organizations** (official entities of international scope or character, usually established by treaty, such as the World Bank and the International Monetary Fund). During the latter half of the twentieth century, the secretary of state emerged as a principal spokesperson for the U.S. government on all foreign policy matters.

Few individuals have enjoyed a higher profile at the state department in recent decades than Colin Powell, secretary of state during George W. Bush's first term in office. In 1989, President George H. W. Bush appointed Powell as chairman of the Joint Chiefs of Staff, the highest position in the American military. In that capacity, Powell first articulated the framework for intervention in that war, later termed the "Powell Doctrine": military action should be used as a last resort and then only with clear popular support, overwhelming force, and a clear exit strategy.

The 1991 Persian Gulf War met Powell's criteria, although America's quick exit left Saddam Hussein still in power. As secretary of state a decade later, Powell engaged in a form of shuttle diplomacy over the George W. Bush administration's threat to engage in a second Iraq war—he tried in vain to line up many of America's European allies in a coalition during late 2002 and early 2003.[18] Yet unlike in 1991, the Powell Doctrine did not appear to guide the war effort; the United States went to war despite divisions

[17] Louis Fisher, "Without Restraint: Presidential Military Initiatives from Korea to Bosnia," in Eugene Wittkopf and James McCormick, eds., *Domestic Sources of American Foreign Policy*, 3rd ed. (Lanham, MD: Rowman and Littlefield, 1999), pp. 141–155.

[18] Powell's shuttle diplomacy was described in great detail in Bob Woodward, *Plan of Attack* (New York: Simon & Schuster, 2004).

American Government: Historical, Popular, and Global Perspectives

among its allies, and to a lesser extent within the public as well. The exit strategy after the war was also subject to constant revision. Although Powell remained a key figure in the administration for the remainder of George W. Bush's first term, his star seemed to lose its luster as the administration's hawks continued to dominate the administration's foreign policy. Powell stepped down as secretary of state at the end of Bush's first term in office and was replaced by Condoleezza Rice.

Military power is an important factor in U.S. foreign relations. **The Department of Defense** plays a critical role in helping formulate and implement U.S. foreign policy by managing the nation's military. The secretary of defense is the principal civilian adviser to the president on military matters. On the military side, the president is advised by the **Joint Chiefs of Staff (JCS),** which consists of the chief officers of the four branches of the armed forces (army, navy, air force, and marines) as well as the JCS chair and vice chair. The JCS delivers the president's orders to the military commands involved in a particular operation. During the 2003 war in Iraq, Secretary of Defense Donald Rumsfeld emerged as the principal spokesman for the administration, holding frequent press conferences to report on the operation's progress and reaffirm the administration's objectives. Three years later, several retired army officers complained that when the decision was made to go to war in Iraq, Rumsfeld bypassed the advice of the Joint Chiefs of Staff. Rumsfeld resigned in November 2006, at which point he was already the second-longest-serving defense secretary in American history (only Robert McNamara, who served during the 1960s for the Kennedy and Johnson administrations, served longer).

In 1947, the National Security Act established the **National Security Council (NSC)** as an advisory body to the president, coordinating information about foreign, military, and economic policies that affect national security. By law the NSC must include the president, vice president, and the secretaries of state and defense. But recent presidents have also appointed a national security adviser to supervise the council and monitor the implementation of national security decisions made by the president. Dating back to the 1960s, the national security adviser has served as both a key adviser and policy maker for most modern presidents.[19]

With three executive branch officials (the secretary of defense, the secretary of state, and the national security adviser) in a position to advise the president on foreign policy, some conflicts are inevitable. During George W. Bush's first term as president, National Security Advisor Condoleezza Rice, Secretary of State Colin Powell, and Secretary of Defense Donald Rumsfeld all served as critical advisers in helping the president formulate national security policy in the wake of the 9/11 terrorist attacks. The war in Afghanistan that followed generated widespread support throughout the country, and among these officials as well. But when the Bush administration turned its attention to a possible war in Iraq, sharp divisions among the three officials emerged. Although such terms may be oversimplified, the administration's **hawks**—who called for aggressive military action wherever hostile forces might be found—were led by Rumsfeld, Rice, and Vice President Dick Cheney. On the other side of this divide were the **realists,** led by Powell, who counseled diplomacy as the primary means of protecting U.S. interests abroad. Powell was particularly concerned that a military attack on Iraq might reduce support for democratic reforms in Saudi Arabia and strain relationships with important Western European allies such as France and Germany. Ultimately the hawks won the day, because the Bush administration waged the 2003 war in Iraq without support from the United Nations and many of its allies. Powell remained in his position until after the 2004 presidential election.

Although not directly responsible for formulating the administration's overall foreign policy direction, other agencies and executive branch officials also influence aspects of foreign policy. In the aftermath of the 9/11 terrorist attacks, the Bush administration sought to create a unified security structure to coordinate the protection of U.S. citizens against terrorist threats within the nation's own borders. Accordingly, Congress in 2002 established the **Department of Homeland Security (DHS).**

★ **Department of Defense**

Executive branch agency that is responsible for managing the nation's military and advising the president on all military matters.

★ **Joint Chiefs of Staff (JCS)**

Group of chief officers of the four branches of the armed forces as well as a JCS chair and vice chair, which advises the president on military matters and delivers the president's orders to the military.

★ **National Security Council (NSC)**

Advisory body to the president charged with coordinating information about foreign, military, and economic policies that affect national security.

★ **Hawks**

Members of the president's administration who call for aggressive military actions wherever hostile forces may be found.

★ **Realists**

Members of the president's administration who advocate diplomacy as the primary means of protecting U.S. interests abroad.

★ **Department of Homeland Security (DHS)**

Executive branch agency established in 2002 to coordinate government entities in protecting U.S. citizens against terrorism within the nation's borders.

[19] Geoffrey Kemp, "Presidential Management of the Executive Bureaucracy," in Robert J. Art and Seyom Brown, eds., *United States Foreign Policy: The Search for a New Role* (Upper Saddle River, NJ: Prentice Hall, 1993).

President Bush standing by as his new Director of National Intelligence, Michael McConnell, is sworn into office in February 2007.

★ **Central Intelligence Agency (CIA)**

Federal agency charged with evaluating and disseminating intelligence information, performing public relations functions that affect international perceptions of the United States, and engaging in overt and covert operations at the direction of the president.

Various governmental divisions responsible for U.S. security have been brought under DHS control, including border and transportation security, infrastructure protection, the U.S. Coast Guard, the U.S. Secret Service, the Federal Emergency Management Agency (FEMA), and the Bureau of Citizenship and Immigration Services. The DHS secretary is responsible for overseeing the efforts of more than 180,000 government employees in the department's efforts to strengthen U.S. borders, provide for intelligence analysis and infrastructure protection, and improve the use of science and technology to combat terrorist threats. The DHS is also responsible for formulating a comprehensive response and recovery capability in the event of an unexpected threat.

The National Security Act of 1947 created the **Central Intelligence Agency (CIA)** to correlate, evaluate, and disseminate intelligence information from throughout the world that affects national security. Unlike the NSC, the CIA is also responsible for disseminating propaganda or performing public relations functions on behalf of the U.S. government, and for engaging in overt or covert activities at the direction of the president.

Since the fall of the Soviet Union in 1991, the CIA has struggled to define its role in the post–Cold War era, particularly with regard to the Middle East and the recent war on terrorism. The first CIA director during the George W. Bush administration, George Tenet, came under heated criticism both for the failure of his agency to coordinate information about the Al Qaeda terrorist network in advance of the 9/11 attacks and for mistakenly allowing President Bush to make false claims about Iraq's nuclear capabilities during a State of the Union address.

With the continued need for information about activities in the Middle East, the Balkans, and North Korea, the CIA still plays a critical role in helping American leaders craft foreign policy.[20] Congress has increasingly pressed the agency to improve its operations and justify its specific operations. A House-Senate Intelligence Committee investigating the 9/11 attacks complained that the traditional post of Director of Central Intelligence was outdated and poorly suited to coordinate intelligence coming from so many different parts of government; accordingly, it recommended the establishment of a new cabinet-level post on intelligence matters. In 2004, the Bush administration created the new position of Director of National Intelligence (DNI), charged with leading the intelligence community across all government agencies.

[20] See Bruce Berkowitz, "Information Age Intelligence," *Foreign Policy* 103 (Summer 1996), 35–50.

American Government . . . in Popular Perspective:
Changing Fortunes in Iraq?

When American troops invaded Iraq on March 20, 2003, President Bush could count on a solid foundation of support from the American people for his decision to go to war. At that time, more than seven in ten Americans approved of the way the president was handling the situation in Iraq, and nearly the same number believed it was worth invading Iraq, given Bush's arguments that Iraq represented a potential threat with its weapons of mass destruction.

On April 9, 2003, Baghdad fell to American forces, and three weeks later,

the United States declared an end to its major combat operations in the country. Yet two and a half years later, with no weapons of mass destruction ever found and the American death toll in Iraq topping two thousand, Americans began turning against the war in increasing numbers. To gauge these shifting fortunes, consider these results of Gallup/ CNN surveys conducted between 2003 and 2008 that asked Americans whether the decision to go into Iraq in the first place was a mistake.

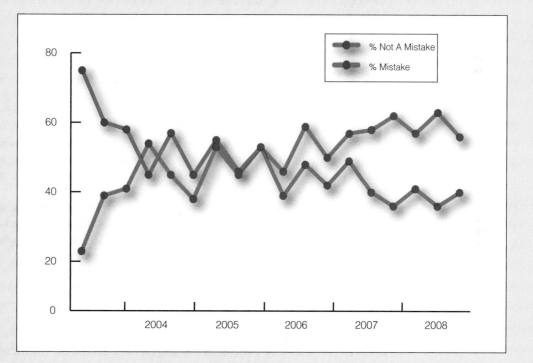

Source: CNN/USA Today/Gallup Poll. Adults nationwide.

Other Foreign Policy Actors and Interests

Although generally more oriented toward domestic affairs, Congress possesses various constitutional powers that give it some stake in crafting U.S. foreign policy. Though presidents have committed troops to battle more than a hundred times in our nation's history without a formal declaration of war from Congress—including most notably in Korea and Vietnam—modern chief executives have learned that there may be some political benefits to asking for a congressional resolution to support military action. Congressional approval of such actions can help rally public support and possibly provide some political cover should those military operations fail. In October 2002, for example, Congress passed a resolution backing the use of military force in Iraq. In the months that followed the invasion when guerrilla warfare continued to threaten American soldiers, many Democratic senators who voted for the resolution were hard-pressed to criticize the president's decision to invade.

Legislators on the Foreign Relations committees of the Senate and the House may take the lead in initiating investigations into a broad range of foreign policy initiatives undertaken by the executive branch.[21] The secretary of state reports regularly to both committees, which oversee relations with foreign nations, executive agreements in foreign affairs, international organizations, and foreign interventions. The secretary of defense reports regularly to the House and Senate Armed Services committees, which are responsible for overseeing defense and national security issues. The diffusion of power among so many separate committees and individual legislators tends to hamstring congressional efforts to encourage the executive branch to consult with the committees before taking some action. Further, the possibility that members of congressional committees might leak information provides the White House with the incentive to conceal information by claiming executive privilege. The Senate's constitutionally vested power to ratify all treaties may also thwart a president eager to move forward. For example, in the case of the Senate's ratification of two Panama Canal treaties in the late 1970s, senators offered no less than 145 amendments to the treaties, which returned the Panama Canal from U.S. control back to Panama.

Groups of legislators frequently tour other nations to learn firsthand the nature of particular foreign policy problems. In rare cases, individual legislators may choose to act on their own to influence foreign policy, sometimes causing headaches for White House officials determined to present a unified front to foreign nations. For example, during the 1980s, Representative Charlie Wilson (D-TX), a maverick congressman from East Texas, worked behind the scenes to help the Central Intelligence Agency arm and sustain a rebel Afghanistan group, the Mujahidin, in its revolt against military occupation by the Soviet Union.[22] More recently, in November 2005, Congressman John Murtha (D-PA), a former Marine and noted war hawk, spoke out forcefully against the Iraq war. After attempts to paint Murtha as an extremist failed, Bush administration officials, including Vice President Dick Cheney, scrambled to respond to Murtha's comments with specific plans for the occupation.

Certainly some private citizens may be in a position to pursue similar initiatives on their own; before making his first presidential bid in 1992, millionaire Ross Perot helped rescue two employees of his corporation from an Iranian prison.[23] Yet most Americans seeking to influence foreign policy organize themselves into special-interest or "pressure" groups for the purpose of doing so. The power that the so-called pro-Israel lobby wields in Congress is well-known: the American-Israel Public Affairs Committee (AIPAC) has influenced important appropriation decisions on Capitol Hill during the past thirty years, helping to ensure the continuation of American aid to Israel. AIPAC's tactics have included letter-writing campaigns and active involvement in election campaigns to assist members of Congress whom it believes are sympathetic to Israel.

Private-sector interest groups have been especially active with regard to most aspects of general trade policy. Textile manufacturers' lobbies have fought to limit imports of foreign garments, whereas farmers' lobbies have pressured the government to pass tariffs on agricultural products imported from other countries. U.S. business interests seeking to export high-tech goods, such as computer and software firms and aerospace manufacturers, have opposed all efforts to impose trade restrictions and sanctions on large potential markets such as China. Is it appropriate for such interest groups to attempt to influence foreign affairs? Critics contend that the lobbying activities of these pressure groups may inadvertently undermine

---

[21] Jeremy D. Rosner, *The New Tug-of-War: Congress, the Executive Branch and National Security* (Washington, DC: Carnegie Endowment for International Peace, 1995).
[22] George Crile, *Charlie Wilson's War* (New York: Grove Press, 2004).
[23] Perot's daring rescue effort is described in dramatic fashion in Ken Follett, *On Wings of Eagles* (New York: William Morrow, 1983).

American foreign policy or even threaten American national security interests. Despite these concerns, interest groups continue to play an active and aggressive role in the process.

The term **military-industrial complex** refers to the vast network of defense industries in America, such as manufacturers of weapons, missiles, aircraft, submarines, and so forth, and their bureaucratic allies. The complex as a whole maintains a keen interest in foreign policy making that is concerned with defense and national security. These industries expanded during the Cold War as U.S. defense budgets rose to as much as 40 percent of annual federal spending. In the late 1990s, defense spending amounted to just 15 percent of the budget, generating ever more feverish efforts by members of the military-industrial complex to either increase that allotment or shift the focus of defense spending to weapons and resources that meet their own areas of expertise.

★ Military-industrial complex

The vast network of defense industries in America (including manufacturers of weapons, missiles, aircraft, and so forth) and their allies in the federal bureaucracy.

American Foreign Policy and Public Opinion

Public opinion on foreign policy issues is a central concern for key actors in the U.S. foreign policy-making arena, including the president, in part because those actors won't keep their jobs for long if they ignore popular sentiments. When the public punishes officials at the polls for their ill-advised foreign policy decisions, observers are quick to criticize those officials for ignoring the will of the people.[24] Certainly when President George W. Bush ordered a "surge" of twenty thousand more U.S. forces in Iraq in early 2007, he was not responding to public opinion as much as he was hoping to shift it in a pro-war direction. However, many political defeats occur because officials have misinterpreted public attitudes, rather than ignoring them outright. Even Lyndon Johnson, whose Vietnam policy proved so unpopular that he was forced to drop of out of the presidential election race in 1968, was known to have carried in his pajama pockets the results of public opinion polls about foreign policy.

Part of the challenge facing U.S. officials is that public attitudes toward foreign affairs often defy easy analysis and interpretation. Modern presidents have managed to generate considerable public support for foreign policy objectives that protect American jobs, control illegal immigration, or counter the illegal drug trade. Foreign policy initiatives that promote human rights or advance democracy abroad have been far less likely to garner support. The 1991 Persian Gulf War generated public support from the outset because an adversary had engaged in aggressive military action against a U.S. ally. By contrast, the Clinton administration fought an uphill battle against public opinion in its Operation Restore Hope to counter widespread famine in Somalia and in its limited military interventions in Bosnia.

Political scientist John Mueller offered the following four propositions to describe American public opinion concerning foreign policy:

1. Americans will tolerate a substantial loss of American lives only if the enemy is seen to be truly powerful and set on jeopardizing vital American interests;

2. The advantage to a president of a success in minor foreign policy ventures is marginal; the disadvantage to a president of a failure in such a venture is more than marginal;

3. If they are not being killed, American troops can remain in peacekeeping or other ventures virtually indefinitely with little public criticism; and

4. Although few concerns can turn the public's attention to foreign affairs, nuclear weapons retain the capacity to arrest the public's attention, and the same may hold for biological and chemical weapons.[25]

The events of September 11, 2001, turned the attention of Americans to foreign policy like few other events of the past thirty years. The George W. Bush administration has

---

[24] See William B. Quandt, "The Electoral Cycle and the Conduct of American Foreign Policy," *Political Science Quarterly* 101 (1986), 825–837.
[25] John Mueller, "Public Opinion and Foreign Policy: The People's Common Sense," in Eugene Wittkopf and James McCormick, eds., *Domestic Sources of American Foreign Policy*, 3rd ed. (Lanham, MD: Rowman and Littlefield, 1999), pp. 51–60.

sought to characterize its foreign policy initiatives in Afghanistan, Iraq, and elsewhere in terms designed to be acceptable to public opinion. The war on terrorism is framed in terms of a worldwide threat of seismic proportions. Officials may have delayed the 2003 war to lay the groundwork for clear-cut and unambiguous military success. Even after the formal military engagement of that war was concluded, President Bush continued to couch the threat in terms of intelligence received that Iraq possessed nuclear capabilities. As with presidents before him, Bush is continually attentive to the dynamics of American public opinion.

The thorny politics of foreign occupation that occurs following most military battles—when the victors must (at least temporarily) control the area that has been seized by military force—can weigh especially heavily in the court of public opinion. Public support for the war tends to tail off once the opposing armies have been defeated. If the occupation fails, the defeated or other hostile entities may seize the opportunity to reverse the war's outcome. America's military history features numerous successful military occupations, such as that over West Germany and Japan in the aftermath of World War II. By contrast, the George W. Bush administration has invested more than $1 billion per day in the occupation of Iraq; yet far more American troops were killed during the occupation than during the brief six-week military conflict.

Foreign Policy Dilemmas for the Twenty-first Century

JENS MEYER/AP PHOTO

During his campaign for the presidency in 2008, Barack Obama visited Germany, where he was warmly received by thousands of Europeans.

Some foreign policy dilemmas of the twenty-first century, such as the problematic occupation of Iraq by U.S. forces after the 2003 Iraq war, represent new versions of age-old challenges that the U.S. government has faced on an intermittent basis since the nation's founding. Others represent unforeseen obstacles produced by circumstances unique to the modern, post–Cold War world. Regardless, American officials must always be on the lookout for foreign policy challenges that arise with little or no warning and that can overshadow all other aspects of the federal government's agenda if they are not kept under control. Officials must also be prepared to justify their actions according to some theory or well-articulated rationale, lest they be accused of conducting foreign policy "on the fly" with little real reason for endangering American resources, and in some instances, for putting American troops in harm's way.

The "Pre-emption Doctrine"—Is It Justifiable?

Only a year after the collapse of the Soviet Union in 1991, the first hint of a dramatic transformation in America's foreign policy could be seen. In 1992, several Pentagon planners working in the George H. W. Bush administration drafted a policy statement asserting that the American government should assume a far more activist role in foreign affairs, especially in the Middle East. Their statement specifically reserved the right of the U.S. military to use advance strikes to stop rogue states from developing weapons of mass destruction. Later termed the **pre-emption doctrine,** this statement sparked considerable controversy after it was leaked to the *New York Times*. In 1997 one of its original authors, Paul Wolfowitz, joined Donald Rumsfeld and other conservative foreign policy advocates to warn President Bill Clinton that America's containment of

★ Pre-emption doctrine

Doctrine of war making that reserves the right of the U.S. military to use advance strikes to stop rogue states from developing weapons of mass destruction.

Iraq had failed. They urged the government to shift its focus to the outright removal of Iraqi leader Saddam Hussein, who had remained in power even through the American military's conquering of his country during the Persian Gulf War of 1991.

With George W. Bush's election as president in 2000 and the more intense focus on international terrorism that followed the September 11, 2001, attacks, the emphasis on pre-emption became ingrained in U.S. policy. Rumsfeld, who had become secretary of defense, joined others in pressing the administration to exercise its military power, unilaterally if necessary, to confront hostile states bent on acquiring weapons of mass destruction. Bush named Wolfowitz as deputy secretary of defense, a platform from which he more forcefully stressed the merits of a strategic pre-emption doctrine.

Even advocates of this doctrine do not dispute that pre-emption carries with it some significant risks. The fundamental paradox of pre-emption is that it can be effectively applied only to a country that lacks the capacity to retaliate. Though Iraq suffered from pre-emptive American attacks in the spring of 2003, North Korea and Iran—two nations similarly charged with posing international threats—are less likely to be targets of a U.S. pre-emptive attack because neither is viewed as so weak or vulnerable as was Saddam Hussein's regime. Critics of pre-emption doctrine also charge that although this policy may be justified in the rare instance when a rival power's attacks are imminent, it cannot be justified to prevent attacks in the distant and more ambiguous future.

Cultivating Relations with the New Russian Federation

Although many now view America as the world's lone remaining superpower, the fall of the Soviet Union did not by any means eliminate all threats to the United States from that part of the globe. The Russian Federation now headed by Dmitry Medvedev (elected in March 2008 to succeed Vladimir Putin, who then became prime minister of the Russian Federation) controls a land mass of more than 6 million square miles, nearly twice the size of both China and the United States. It also maintains one of the world's most powerful military threats, because most of the nuclear capabilities of the former Soviet Union were passed on to Russia. Though U.S. foreign policy must address each of the twelve independent nations of the former Soviet Union on their own merits, the Russian Federation continues to capture the bulk of attention from American foreign policy makers.

Russian Federation President Vladimir Putin and President Bush at a joint White House news conference in September 2005.

Concerns around the world have been raised about Russia's occasional use of military force: for example, it subdued the smaller Republic of Chechnya, the site of bloody Chechen-Russian War of 1994–1996. More recently in August 2008, Russia temporarily occupied the nearby country of Georgia by force after months of skirmishes and increasing tensions between the two nations. Both American and Russian officials have strong incentives to cultivate friendly relations with each other. Russia's efforts to establish itself as a member of the club of democratic nations in good standing require it to demonstrate to the world that it can conduct responsible foreign policy with the United States. Meanwhile, the United States needs Russian cooperation to allow the stationing of U.S. forces in distant sites, such as the central Asian republic of Tajikistan, in order to combat terrorist threats in that part of the globe. The United States may also seek to revive negotiations with Russia on arms limitations. Finally, a strong relationship with Russia assists the United States in encouraging some of its allies, particularly France and Germany, to go along with

Who Gives the Most Foreign Aid?

Although the U.S. foreign-aid budget as a percentage of gross national income (GNI) is exceedingly small (0.16 percent), the United States is the world's top donor of economic aid. In 2004, these five nations provided the most overall economic assistance to other countries:

✔	1.	**United States**	$19 billion
✔	2.	**Japan**	$8.86 billion
✔	3.	**France**	$8.48 billion
✔	4.	**United Kingdom**	$7.84 billion
✔	5.	**Germany**	$7.5 billion

Source: Larry Nowels, "Foreign Aid: Understanding Data Used to Compare Donors," Organization for Economic Cooperation and Development. *CRS Report for Congress*, Order Code RS 22032. Updated May 23, 2005, p. 5.

American operations. Russia's refusal to support the 2003 war in Iraq may have helped embolden those two Western European countries to withhold support for the American-led war.

Foreign Aid—What Role Does It Play in the New International Order?

The American government's legacy of providing monetary aid to struggling nations and allies was first established on a monumental scale with the Marshall Plan to help Western European nations recover after World War II. Although humanitarian concerns continue to influence such aid, U.S. economic and national security interests also affect foreign aid decisions. Expanded foreign markets would purchase domestic products and agricultural goods, boosting the U.S. economy. New states would also be more likely to join the expanding capitalist world economy if U.S. aid contributed to their recovery and encouraged them to reject anticapitalist economic systems.

Because the dissolution of the Soviet Union has weakened some of the strategic rationale for foreign aid, there have been substantial reductions in such aid during the past decade. Critics of foreign aid also charge that much of the money provided by America goes to elites in the recipient nations, rather than to those who need help. Defenders of aid respond that even when elites control a sizeable portion of the aid, the recipient nation is able to expand its national output, which leads to higher living standards for all. But this "trickle down" theory of foreign aid has been cast aside in recent years by experts such as economist Peter Boone of the London School of Economics. After assessing the experience of nearly one hundred nations, Boone concluded that because foreign transfers only tend to increase government consumption (which has no positive effect on growth), foreign aid has had little or no impact on the recipient country's overall investment levels.[26]

[26] Peter Boone, "The Impact of Foreign Aid on Savings and Growth," *Center for Economic Performance Working Paper No. 1265*, London, October 1994, pp. 25–26.

The United States continues to be a leading contributor to such international aid institutions as the World Bank, which since 1945 has extended credit to nations for building and economic development. America also contributes substantially to the International Monetary Fund, which helps to maintain the value of foreign currencies during times of crisis. But the heyday of foreign aid—when it served as a critical instrument of U.S. foreign relations—appears to be a thing of the past.

Does the United Nations Still Serve an Important Function?

The United Nations (UN), founded at the conclusion of World War II, is structured around five separate governing bodies: (1) the General Assembly, which is made up of all member states (at present there are 192 member states); (2) the Economic and Social Council, which is made up of 54 members chosen by the General Assembly and serves primarily an advisory body to the General Assembly on matters of international economic and social cooperation; (3) the Secretariat, which supports the other UN bodies and carries out tasks as directed by the other bodies; (4) the International Court of Justice, the UN's judicial organ that has jurisdiction to try certain international war criminals and settles disputes submitted to it by duly authorized international entities; and (5) the Security Council, which maintains peace and security among nations by issuing resolutions that (at least in theory) are binding on UN members. The separation of the Security Council from the larger General Assembly is significant. As currently constituted, the Security Council consists of five permanent members (China, France, the Russian

American Government ... in Global Perspective:
One Iranian's Perspective on American Foreign Policy

During the late 1970s, the American media delivered a disconcerting picture of revolutionary Iran to Americans. In 1979, Iranian student revolutionaries, acting with the blessings of the new government led by the Ayatollah Khomeini, seized American hostages from the U.S. embassy. Images of President Jimmy Carter were burned in effigy in the public square of Tehran. Although Khomeini is no longer in power, Iran remains an isolated country dominated by extremist Islamic factions. Does Iran even desire a normalization of relations with the United States? Under certain circumstances, yes, states Mahmood Sariolghalam, editor of the journal *Discourse: An Iranian Quarterly*, and a professor at one of Iran's top universities:

In less than a decade, new and young faces will lead the Middle East. The new leaders have no choice but to lead their countries to greater economic and political liberalization. . . . The crucial element in this historic shift is political and methodical proximity to a West, and especially the United States, that appreciates procedural and cultural nuances. The United States deserves to provide thought and leadership to the world but it need not advertise its desire to be hegemonic. U.S. bluntness about being the only leader in the world may not be psychologically wise. . . . Washington needs to employ much greater subtlety in its multifaceted projection of power, especially at a time when new leaders exposed to mass politics are about to emerge.

Source: Mahmood Sariolghalam, "Justice for All," in Alexander Lennon, *What Does the World Want from America?* (Cambridge, MA: MIT Press, 2002), p. 73.

Federation, the United States, and Great Britain) and ten nonpermanent rotating members. Each of the five permanent members maintains the absolute right to veto decisions of the all-important council, the only UN body with the power to authorize economic sanctions or military force. However, the General Assembly retains the exclusive power to enforce Security Council decisions.

The United States dominated the UN on all security issues during its first forty years, but as U.S. influence over the body has declined, calls have increased within Congress to reduce American aid to the organization and to ignore its dictates whenever American security interests were at issue. Most recently in 2003, America went to war in Iraq even though the UN Security Council was unwilling to offer advance authorization for any such military action. Yet immediately after the war with Iraq had concluded, the United Nations began relief and reconstruction activities in the war-torn nation, and began pushing for a resolution that would broaden international control over the region. Thus in the twenty-first century, the United Nations seems destined to play at least a limited role in international affairs, asserting its authority most strongly during peacekeeping and relief missions that follow military action.

Now & Then: Making the Connection

As much as individual presidents like to think that they control the agendas of their presidencies, unforeseen crises have a way of scuttling such carefully laid plans and bringing new priorities to the table. Both Woodrow Wilson and George W. Bush may have anticipated that given the American public's recent hesitancy to overextend its military commitments abroad, their terms in the White House would be spent mainly attending to domestic concerns. Woodrow Wilson managed to do just that during his first term, but nearly his entire second term was occupied with the management of World War I and its aftermath. George W. Bush had not even served a full year as president when the tragic events of September 11, 2001, launched his administration into the war on terrorism; domestic issues temporarily fell off the public's radar screen during these periods.

The president in particular enjoys considerable discretion in pursuing a foreign policy agenda; Congress and other governmental actors play only a subordinate role in such affairs. Actors outside of government also have only limited influence to affect foreign policy decisions. Not surprisingly, many presidents, including most recently, Presidents Clinton and Nixon, found foreign policy to be a welcome diversion from the scandals that were rocking their respective presidencies. At the same time, many foreign policy issues—relations with Russia, the Arab–Israeli conflict, the military occupation in Iraq, to name just a few—are among the most complicated and difficult issues a president faces. As a result, though some presidents enjoy short-term successes in foreign affairs, few are able to offer long-term solutions, and many only tend to exacerbate the problems faced by their predecessors.

EMMANUEL DUNAND/AFP/GETTY IMAGES

Mahmoud Ahmedinejad, president of Iran.

Since the overthrow of the Iraqi government by U.S. military forces in the spring of 2003, the American military has added the occupation of that country to its already sizeable list of responsibilities in Europe, the Pacific, and elsewhere. To meet these growing military demands, in February 2007 Secretary of Defense Robert Gates proposed that the United States increase the overall size of its military by approximately 92,000 troops over the following five years. That would bring the total active-duty force of the United States to approximately 1,479,000 soldiers and personnel.

Gates has publicly expressed concern not just about Iraq, but about other threats as well. Specifically, the already stretched capacity of the U.S. military leaves it in little position to even rattle its sabers to gain leverage against upstarts such as Iran, which fired unarmed missiles on November 2, 2006, as part of a series of military war games. Since 1992 Iran has produced its own tanks, armored personnel carriers, guided missiles, submarines, and even one fighter plane. Meanwhile, Iran's current president, Mahmoud Ahmadinejad (pictured above), has so far refused the demands of the United Nations Security Council to stop Iran's nuclear program, claiming that Iran's nuclear enrichment program is for peaceful purposes only.

As one of the three members of President George W. Bush's declared "axis of evil" (along with Iraq and North Korea), Iran's warlike gestures may ultimately force the U.S. government to once again exercise its military power in the Middle East. Yet even if Secretary Gates's requests are met, is America really in a position to offer a real challenge to Iran at the same time as it is maintaining an occupying force in Iraq? Furthermore, should it be prepared to do so?

On http://academic.cengage.com/dautrich, find the Politics InterActive link for the latest details on the military threat from Iran, and a discussion of how the current administration is reacting to these threats. Consult as well the various links that provide historical, popular, and global perspectives on the Iran–U.S. relationship.

http://academic.cengage.com/dautrich

Chapter Summary

★ The federal government maintains exclusive authority over foreign policy in the United States. The president is the commander-in-chief and has the power to negotiate treaties and appoint and receive ambassadors; Congress has the power to declare war, raise armies, and regulate foreign commerce, among its other functions.

★ Over two centuries, the practical power to make war has shifted from Congress to the president, who as commander-in-chief, is far better suited to respond to sudden changes in circumstances around the world. Thus the president has become even more powerful in foreign affairs than in domestic affairs.

★ The United States adhered to a policy of isolationism from the time of its founding until the late nineteenth century, generally forgoing intervention in foreign wars during that period. However, in the mid-nineteenth century the U.S. government practiced aggressive expansionism in North America; near the end of the century it also annexed Hawaii and gained possession of the Philippine Islands.

★ With its entry into World War I and World War II, the United States rose to the status of world superpower, with many smaller nations looking to the U.S. government to preserve international peace. America's foreign policy eventually shifted to an emphasis on internationalism, by which it participated in a system of collective security.

★ The Cold War, pitting the United States against the Soviet Union from 1945 until 1991, was waged through economic warfare, arms buildups, and moments of tense diplomacy that fell short of direct military engagements between the two superpowers. The demise of Soviet-run regimes in Russia and elsewhere beginning in the late 1980s failed to decrease U.S. involvement around the world.

★ The Middle East remains a source of great concern for U.S. foreign policy in the twenty-first century. After the 9/11 attacks, the federal government launched an aggressive war on terrorism. The U.S. military overthrew the governments of Afghanistan and Iraq in 2001 and 2003, respectively, as part of the war on terrorism. However, occupation of Iraq by U.S. forces after the Iraqi war has been a continuing source of debate among political officials in the United States.

★ In formulating foreign policy, the president is assisted by the secretary of state, the secretary of defense, the Joint Chiefs of Staff, the national security adviser, and the Director of National Intelligence.

★ The Department of Homeland Security, created by an act of Congress in 2002, is responsible for border and transportation security, intelligence analysis, infrastructure protection, and all other government divisions that play a role in protecting against terrorist threats in the United States.

★ Congress oversees foreign policy through its Foreign Relations committees, which receive regular reports from the secretary of state and the secretary of defense. Groups of legislators frequently travel overseas to learn firsthand about foreign policy problems.

★ Public opinion concerning American foreign policy often defies easy interpretation. Many presidents have been punished at the polls for ill-advised foreign policy decisions, whereas others have essentially rescued their presidencies by engaging in successful foreign policy initiatives.

★ Foreign policy dilemmas facing American officials in the twenty-first century include questions about when (if at all) a pre-emptive military attack is justified, what role (if any) the United States should play in supporting the United Nations, and whether the United States should increase or decrease foreign aid in general.

Key Terms

Central Intelligence Agency (CIA) (p. 546)

Cold War (p. 539)

Containment (p. 540)

Department of Defense (p. 545)

Department of Homeland Security (DHS) (p. 545)

Department of State (p. 544)

Domino theory (p. 540)

Expansionism (p. 538)

Hawks (p. 545)

International organization (p. 544)

Internationalism (p. 539)

Isolationism (p. 537)

Joint Chiefs of Staff (JCS) (p. 545)

Manifest destiny (p. 538)

Marshall Plan (p. 539)

Military-industrial complex (p. 549)

Monroe Doctrine (p. 537)

National Security Council (NSC) (p. 545)

New world order (p. 541)

North Atlantic Treaty Organization (NATO) (p. 539)

Pacifism (p. 537)

Pre-emption doctrine (p. 550)

Realists (p. 545)

Strategic Defense Initiative (SDI) (p. 541)

Truman Doctrine (p. 540)

Two presidencies theory (p. 535)

United Nations (UN) (p. 539)

War Powers Resolution (p. 536)

Warsaw Pact (p. 540)

Resources

Important Books

Ambrose, Stephen, and Douglas Brinkley. *Rise to Globalism: American Foreign Policy Since 1938.* New York: Penguin, 1997.

Ferguson, Niall. *Colossus: The Price of America's Empire.* New York: Penguin, 2004.

Kissinger, Henry. *Crisis: The Anatomy of Two Major Foreign Policy Crises.* New York: Simon & Schuster, 2003.

Mead, Walter Russell. *Special Providence: American Foreign Policy and How It Changed the World.* New York: Routledge, 2002.

Nye, Joseph, Jr. *The Paradox of American Power: Why the World's Only Superpower Can't Go It Alone.* New York: Oxford University Press, 2002.

Wittkopf, Eugene R., and James M. McCormick. *The Domestic Sources of Foreign Policy*, 3rd ed. Lanham, MD: Rowman and Littlefield, 1999.

Woodward, Bob. *The War Within: A Secret White House History, 2006–2008.* New York: Simon & Schuster, 2008.

Internet Sources

http://www.defenselink.mil (the official website of the Department of Defense; contains information on all branches of the military, speeches and press resources, reports from the secretary of defense, and so on)

http://www.state.gov (the official website of the U.S. Department of State, featuring reports on world affairs, information about traveling and living abroad, and so forth)

http://www.un.org/english (the official home page of the United Nations; includes daily briefings and information about breaking developments in world affairs, documents and maps, conferences and publications, and a link to a live UN web cast)

http://www.peacecorps.gov (the Peace Corps home page; includes sections on how to volunteer, information about other countries, Peace Corps news, and links to other agencies)

APPENDIX

The Declaration of Independence

In Congress, July 4, 1776.
A DECLARATION
By the Representatives of the United States of America,
In General Congress Assembled.

When in the Course of human Events, it becomes necessary for one People to dissolve the Political Bands which have connected them with another, and to assume among the Powers of the Earth, the separate and equal Station to which the Laws of Nature and of Nature's God entitle them, a decent Respect to the Opinions of Mankind requires that they should declare the causes which impel them to the Separation.

We hold these Truths to be self-evident, that all Men are created equal, that they are endowed by their Creator with certain unalienable Rights, that among these are Life, Liberty, and the Pursuit of Happiness—That to secure these Rights, Governments are instituted among Men, deriving their just Powers from the Consent of the Governed, that whenever any Form of Government becomes destructive of these Ends, it is the Right of the People to alter or abolish it, and to institute new Government, laying its Foundation on such Principles, and organizing its Powers in such Form, as to them shall seem most likely to effect their Safety and Happiness. Prudence, indeed, will dictate that Governments long established should not be changed for light and transient Causes; and accordingly all Experience hath shewn, that Mankind are more disposed to suffer, while Evils are sufferable, than to right themselves by abolishing the Forms to which they are accustomed. But when a long Train of Abuses and Usurpations, pursuing invariably the same Object, evinces a Design to reduce them under absolute Despotism, it is their Right, it is their Duty, to throw off such Government, and to provide new Guards for their future Security. Such has been the patient Sufferance of these Colonies; and such is now the Necessity which constrains them to alter their former Systems of Government. The History of the present kind of Great Britain is a History of repeated Injuries and Usurpations, all having in direct Object the Establishment of an absolute Tyranny over these States. To prove this, let Facts be submitted to a candid World.

He has refused his Assent to Laws, the most wholesome and necessary for public good.

He has forbidden his Governors to pass Laws of immediate and pressing importance, unless suspended in their Operation till his Assent should be obtained; and when so suspended, he has utterly neglected to attend to them.

He has refused to pass other Laws for the Accommodation of large Districts of People, unless those People would relinquish the Right of Representation in the Legislature, a Right inestimable to them, and formidable to Tyrants only.

He has called together Legislative Bodies at Places unusual, uncomfortable, and distant from the Depository of their public records, for the sole Purpose of fatiguing them into Compliance with his Measures.

He has dissolved Representative Houses repeatedly, for opposing with many Firmness his Invasions on the Rights of the People.

He has refused for a long Time, after such Dissolutions, to cause others to be elected; whereby the Legislative Powers, incapable of Annihilation, have returned to the People at large for their exercise; the State remaining in the mean time exposed to all the Dangers of Invasion from without, and Convulsions within.

He has endeavoured to prevent the Population of these States; for that Purpose obstructing the Laws for Naturalization of Foreigners; refusing to pass others to encourage their Migrations hither, and raising the Conditions of new Appropriations of Lands.

He has obstructed the Administration of Justice, by refusing his Assent to Laws for establishing Judiciary Powers.

He has made Judges dependent on his Will alone, for the Tenure of their Offices, and the Amount and Payment of their Salaries.

He has erected a Multitude of new Offices, and sent hither Swarms of Officers to harass our People, and eat out their Substance.

He has kept among us, in Times of Peaces, Standing Armies, without the consent of our Legislatures.

He has affected to render the Military independent of and superior to the Civil Power.

He has combined with others to subject us to a Jurisdiction foreign to our Constitution, and unacknowledged by our Laws; giving his Assent to their Acts of pretended Legislation:

For quartering large Bodies of Armed Troops among us:

For protecting them, by a mock Trial, from Punishment for any Murders which they should commit on the Inhabitants of these States:

For cutting off our Trade with all Parts of the World:

For imposing Taxes on us without our Consent: For depriving us, in many Cases, of the Benefits of Trial by Jury:

For transporting us beyond Seas to be tried for pretended Offences:

For abolishing the free System of English Laws in a neighbouring Province, establishing therein an arbitrary Government, and enlarging its Boundaries, so as to render it at once an Example and fit Instrument for introducing the same absolute Rule into these Colonies:

For taking away our Charters, abolishing our most valuable Laws, and altering fundamentally the Forms of our Governments:

For suspending our own Legislatures, and declaring themselves invested with Power to legislate for us in all Cases whatsoever.

He has abdicated Government here, by declaring us out of his Protection and waging War against us.

He has plundered our Seas, ravaged our Coasts, burnt our Towns, and destroyed the Lives of our People.

He is, at this Time, transporting large Armies of foreign Mercenaries to compleat the Works of Death, Desolation, and Tyranny, already begun with circumstances of Cruelty and Perfidy, scarcely parelleled in the most barbarous Ages, and totally unworthy the Head of a civilized Nation.

He has constrained our fellow Citizens taken Captive on the high Seas to bear Arms against their Country, to become the Executioners of their Friends and Brethren, or to fall themselves by their Hands.

He has excited domestic Insurrections amongst us, and has endeavoured to bring on the Inhabitants of our Frontiers, the merciless Indian Savages, whose known Rule of Warfare, is an undistinguished Destruction, of all Ages, Sexes and Conditions.

In every stage of these Oppressions we have Petitioned for Redress in the must humble Terms: Our repeated Petitions have been answered only by repeated Injury. A Prince, whose Character is thus marked by every act which may define a Tyrant, is unfit to be the Ruler of a free People.

Nor have we been wanting in Attentions to our British Brethren. We have warned them from Time to Time of Attempts by their Legislature to extend an unwarrantable Jurisdiction over us. We have reminded them of the Circumstances of our Emigration and Settlement here. We have appealed to their native Justice and Magnanimity, and we have conjured them by the Ties of our common Kindred to disavow these Usurpations, which, would inevitably interrupt our Connections and Correspondence. They too have been deaf to the Voice of Justice and of Consanguinity. We must, therefore, acquiesce in the Necessity, which denounces our Separation, and hold them, as we hold the rest of Mankind, Enemies in War, in Peace, Friends.

We, therefore, the Representatives of the UNITED STATES OF AMERICA, in GENERAL CONGRESS, Assembled, appealing to the Supreme Judge of the World for the Rectitude of our Intentions, do, in the Name, and by Authority of the good People of these Colonies, solemnly Publish and Declare, That these United Colonies are, and of Right ought to be, FREE AND INDEPENDENT STATES; that they are absolved from all Allegiance to the British Crown, and that all political Connection between them and the State of Great-Britain, is and ought to be totally dissolved; and that as FREE AND INDEPENDENT STATES, they have full Power to levy War, conclude Peace, contract Alliances, establish Commerce, and to do all other Acts and Things which INDEPENDENT STATES may of right do. And for the support of this Declaration, with a firm Reliance on the Protection of divine Providence, we mutually pledge to each other our Lives, our Fortunes, and our sacred Honor.

John Hancock

Georgia:
  Button Gwinnett
  Lyman Hall
  George Walton

North Carolina:
  William Hooper
  Joseph Hewes
  John Penn

South Carolina:
  Edward Rutledge
  Thomas Heyward, Jr.
  Thomas Lynch, Jr.
  Arthur Middleton

Maryland:
  Samuel Chase
  William Paca
  Thomas Stone
  Charles Carroll of Carrollton

Virginia:
  George Wythe
  Richard Henry Lee
  Thomas Jefferson
  Benjamin Harrison
  Thomas Nelson, Jr.
  Francis Lightfoot Lee
  Carter Braxton

Pennsylvania:
  Robert Morris
  Benjamin Rush
  Benjamin Franklin
  John Morton
  George Clymer
  James Smith
  George Taylor
  James Wilson
  George Ross

Delaware:
  Caesar Rodney
  George Read
  Thomas McKean

New York:
  William Floyd
  Philip Livingston
  Francis Lewis
  Lewis Morris

New Jersey:
  Richard Stockton
  John Witherspoon
  Francis Hopkinson
  John Hart
  Abraham Clark

New Hampshire:
  Josiah Bartlett
  William Whipple

Massachusetts:
  Samuel Adams
  John Adams
  Robert Treat Paine
  Elbridge Gerry

Rhode Island:
  Stephen Hopkins
  William Ellery

Connecticut:
  Roger Sherman
  Samuel Huntington
  Oliver Wolcott

New Hampshire:
  Matthew Thornton

Federalist No. 10

November 23, 1787
TO THE PEOPLE OF THE STATE OF NEW YORK

Among the numerous advantages promised by a well-constructed Union, none deserves to be more accurately developed than its tendency to break and control the violence of faction. The friend of popular governments never finds himself so much alarmed for their character and fate, as when he contemplates their propensity to this dangerous vice. He will not fail, therefore, to set a due value on any plan which, without violating the principles to which he is attached, provides a proper cure for it. The instability, injustice, and confusion introduced into the public councils, have, in truth, been the mortal diseases under which popular governments have everywhere perished; as they continue to be the favorite and fruitful topics from which the adversaries to liberty derive their most specious declamations. The valuable improvements made by the American constitutions on the popular models, both ancient and modern, cannot certainly be too much admired; but it would be an unwarrantable partiality, to contend that they have as effectually obviated the danger on this side, as was wished and expected. Complaints are everywhere heard from our most considerate and virtuous citizens, equally the friends of public and private faith, and of public and personal liberty, that our governments are too unstable, that the public good is disregarded in the conflicts of rival parties, and that measures are too often decided, not according to the rules of justice and the rights of the minor party, but by the superior force on an interested and overbearing majority. However anxiously we may wish that these complaints had no foundation, the evidence of known facts will not permit us to deny that they are in some degree true. It will be found, indeed, on a candid review of our situation, that some of the distresses under which we labor have been erroneously charged on the operation of our governments; but it will be found, at the same time, that other causes will not alone account for many of our heaviest misfortunes; and, particularly, for that prevailing and increasing distrust of public engagements, and alarm for private rights, which are echoed from one end of the continent to the other. These must be chiefly, if not wholly, effects of the unsteadiness and injustice with which a factious spirit has tainted our public administrations.

By a faction, I understand a number of citizens, whether amounting to a majority or a minority of the whole, who are united and actuated by some common impulse of passion, or of interest, adversed to the rights of other citizens, or to the permanent and aggregate interests of the community.

There are two methods of curing the mischeifs of faction: the one, by removing its causes; the other, by controlling its effects.

There are again two methods of removing the causes of faction: the one, by destroying the liberty which is essential to its existence; the other, by giving to every citizen the same opinions, the same passions, and the same interests.

It could never be more truly said than of the first remedy, that it was worse than the disease. Liberty is to faction what air is to fire, an aliment without which it instantly expires. But it could not be less folly to abolish liberty, which is essential to political life, because it nourishes faction, than it would be to wish the annihilation of air, which is essential to animal life, because it imparts to fire its destructive tendency.

The second expedient is as impracticable as the first would be unwise. As long as the reason of man continues fallible, and he is at liberty to exercise it, different opinions will be formed. As long as the connection subsists between his reason and his self-love, his opinions and his passions will have a reciprocal influence on each other; and the former will be objects to which the latter will attach themselves. The diversity in the faculties of men, from which the rights of property originate, is not less an insuperable obstacle to a uniformity of interests. The protection of these faculties is the first object of government. From the protection of different and unequal faculties of acquiring property, the possession of different degrees and kinds of property immediately results; and from the influence of these on the sentiments and views of the respective proprietors, ensues a division of the society into different interests and parties.

The latent causes of faction are thus sown in the nature of man; and we see them everywhere brought into different degrees of activity, according to the different circumstances of civil society.

A zeal for different opinions concerning religion, concerning government, and many other points, as well of speculation as of practice; an attachment to different leaders ambitiously contending for pre-eminence and power; or to persons of other descriptions whose fortunes have been interesting to the human passions, have, in turn, divided mankind into parties, inflamed them with mutual animosity, and rendered them much more disposed to vex and oppress each other than to co-operate for their common good. So string is this propensity of mankind to fall into mutual animosities, that where no substantial occasion presents itself, the most frivolous and fanciful distinctions have been sufficient to kindle their unfriendly passions and excite their most violent conflicts. But the most common and durable source of factions has been the various and unequal distribution of property. Those who hold and those who are without property have ever formed distinct interests in society. Those who are creditors, and those who are debtors, fall under a like discrimination. A landed interest, a manufacturing interest, a mercantile interest, a moneyed interest, with many lesser interests, grow up of necessity in civilized nations, and divide them into different classes, actuated by different sentiments and views. The regulation of these various and interfering interests forms the principal task of modern legislation, and involves the spirit of party and faction in the necessary and ordinary operations of the government.

No man is allowed to be a judge in his own case, because his interest would certainly bias his judg-ment, and, not improbably, corrupt his integrity. With equal, nay with greater reason, a body of men are unfit to be both judges and parties at the same time; yet what are many of the most important acts of legislation, but so many judicial determinations, not indeed concerning the rights of single persons, but concerning the rights of large bodies of citizens? And what are the different classes of legislators but advocates and parties to the causes which they determine? Is a law proposed concerning private debts? It is a question to which the creditors are parties on one side and the debtors on the other. Justice ought to hold the balance between them. Yet the parties are, and must be, themselves the judges; and the most numerous party, or, in other words, the most powerful action must be expected to prevail. Shall domestic manufactures be encouraged, and in what degree, by restrictions on foreign manufactures? are questions which would be differently decided by the landed and the manufacturing classes, and probably by neither with a sole regard to justice and the public good. The apportionment of taxes on the various descriptions of property is an act which seems to require the most exact impartiality; yet there is, perhaps, no legislative act in which greater opportunity and temptation are given to a predominant party to trample on the rules of justice. Every shilling with which they overburden the inferior number, is a shilling saved to their own pockets.

It is in vain to say that enlightened statesmen will be able to adjust these clashing interests, and render them all subservient to the public good. Enlightened statesmen will not always be at the helm. Nor, in many cases, can such an adjustment be made at all without taking into view indirect and remote considerations, which will rarely prevail over the immediate interest which one party may find in disre-garding the rights of another or the good of the whole.

The inference to which we are brought is, that the *causes* of faction cannot be removed, and that relief is only to be sought in the means of controlling its *effects*.

If a faction consists of less than a majority, relief is supplied by the republican principle, which enables the majority to defeat its sinister views by regular vote. It may clog the administration, it may convulse the society; but it will be unable to execute and mask its violence under the forms of the Constitution. When a majority is included in a faction, the form of popular government, on the other hand, enables it to sacrifice to its ruling passion or interest both the public good and the rights of other citizens. to secure the public good and private rights against the danger of such a faction, and at the same time to preserve the spirit and form of popular government, is then the great object to which our inquiries are directed. Let me add that it is the great desideratum by which this form of government can be rescued from the opprobrium under which it has so long labored, and be recommended to the esteem and adoption of mankind.

By what means is this object attainable? Evidently by one of two only. Either the existence of the same passion or interest in a majority at the same time must be prevented, or the majority, having such coexistent passion or interest, must be rendered, by their number and local situation, unable to concert and carry into effect schemes of oppression. If the impulse and the opportunity be suffered to coincide, we well know that neither moral nor religious motives can be relied on as an adequate control. They are not found to be such on the injustice and violence of individuals, and lose their efficacy in proportion to the number combined together, that is, in proportion as their efficacy becomes needful.

From this view of the subject it may be concluded that a pure democracy, by which I mean a society consisting of a small number of citizens, who assemble and administer the government in person, can admit of no cure for the mischiefs of faction. A common passion or interest will, in almost every case, be felt by a majority of the whole; a communication and concert result from the form of government itself; and there is nothing to check the inducements to sacrifice the weaker party or an obnoxious individual. Hence it is that such democracies have ever been spectacles of turbulence and contention; have ever been found incompatible with personal security or the rights of property; and have in general been as short in their lives as they have been violent in their deaths. Theoretic politicians, who have patronized this species of government, have erroneously supposed that by reducing mankind to a perfect equality in their political rights, they would, at the same time, be perfectly equalized and assimilated in their possessions, their opinions, and their passions.

A republic, by which I mean a government in which the scheme of representation takes place, opens a different prospect, and promises the cure for which we are seeking. Let us examine the points in which it varies from pure democracy, and we shall comprehend both the nature of the cure and the efficacy which it must derive from the Union.

The two great points of difference between a democracy and a republic are: first, the delegation of the government, in the latter, to a small number of citizens elected by the rest; secondly, the greater number of citizens, and greater sphere of country, over which the latter may be extended.

The effect of the first difference is, on the one hand, to refine and enlarge the public views, by passing them through the medium of a chosen body of citizens, whose wisdom may best discern the true interest of their country, and whose patriotism and love of justice will be least likely to sacrifice it to temporary or partial considerations. Under such a regulation, it may well happen that the public voice, pronounced by the representatives of the people, will be more consonant to the public good than it pronounced by the people themselves, convened for the purpose. On the other hand, the effect may be inverted. Men of factious tempers, of local prejudices, or of sinister designs, may, by intrigue, by corruption, or by other means, first obtain the suffrages, and then betray the interests, of the people. The question resulting is, whether small or extensive republics are more favorable to the election of proper guardians of the public weal; and it is clearly decided in favor of the latter by two obvious considerations:

In the first place, it is to be remarked that, however small the republic may be, the representatives must be raised to a certain number, in order to guard against the cabals of a few; and that, however large it may be, they must be limited to a certain number, in order to guard against the confusion of a multitude. Hence, the number of representatives in the two cases not being in proportion to that of the two constituents, and being proportionally greater in the small republic, it follows that, if the proportion of fit characters be not less in the large than in the small republic, the former will present a greater option, and consequently a greater probability of a fit choice.

In the next place, as each representative will be chosen by a greater number of citizens in the large than in the small republic, it will be more difficult for unworthy candidates to practice with success the vicious arts by which elections are too often carried; and the suffrages of the people being more free, will be more likely to centre in men who possess the most attractive merit and the most diffusive and established characters.

It must be confessed that in this, as in most other cases, there is a mean, on both sides of which inconveniences will be found to lie. By enlarging too much the number of electors, you render the representatives too little acquainted with all their local circumstances and lesser interests; as by reducing it too much, you render him unduly attached to these, and too little fit to comprehend and pursue great and national objects. The federal Constitution forms a happy combination in this respect; the great and aggregate interests being referred to the national, the local and particular to the State legislatures.

The other point of difference is, the greater number of citizens and extent of territory which may be brought within the compass of republican than of democratic government; and it is this circumstance principally which renders factious combinations less to be dreaded in the former than in the latter. The smaller the society, the fewer probably will be the distinct parties and interests composing it; the fewer the distinct parties and interests, the more frequently will a majority be found of the same party; and the smaller the number of individuals composing a majority, and the smaller the compass within which they are placed, the more easily will they concert and execute their plans of oppression. Extend the sphere, and you take in a greater variety of parties and interests; you make it less probable that a majority of the whole will have a common motive to invade the rights of other citizens; or if such a common motive exists, it will be more difficult for all who feel it to discover their own strength, and to act in unison with each other. Besides other impediments, it may be remarked that, where there is a consciousness of unjust or dishonorable purposes, communication is always checked by distrust in proportion to the number whose concurrence is necessary.

Hence, it clearly appears, that the same advantage which a republic has over a democracy, in controlling the effects of faction, is enjoyed by a large over a small republic,—-and is enjoyed by the Union over the States composing it. Does the advantage consist in the substitution of representatives whose enlightened views and virtuous sentiments render them superior to local prejudices and schemes of injustice? It will not be denied that the representation of the Union will be most likely to possess these requisite endowments. Does it consist in the greater security afforded by a greater variety of parties, against the event of any one party being able to outnumber and oppress the rest? In an equal degree does the increased variety of parties comprised within the Union, increase this security. Does it, in fine, consist in the greater obstacles opposed to the concert and accomplishment of the secret wishes of an unjust and interested majority? Here, again, the extent of the Union gives it the most palpable advantage.

The influence of factious leaders may kindle a flame within their particular States, but will be unable to spread a general conflagration through the other States. A religious sect may degenerate into a political faction in a part of the Confederacy; but the variety of sects dispersed over the entire face of it must secure the national councils against any danger from that source. A rage for paper money, for an abolition of debts, for an equal division of property, or for any other improper or wicked project, will be less apt to pervade the whole body of the Union than a particular member of it; in the same proportion as such a malady is more likely to taint a particular county or district, than an entire State.

In the extent and proper structure of the Union, therefore, we behold a republican remedy for the diseases most incident to republican government. And according to the degree of pleasure and pride we feel in being republicans, ought to be our zeal in cherishing the spirit and supporting the character of Federalists.

PUBLIUS

Federalist No. 51

February 8, 1788

TO THE PEOPLE OF THE STATE OF NEW YORK

To what expedient, then, shall we finally resort, for maintaining in practice the necessary partition of power among the several departments, as laid down in the Constitution? The only answer that can be given is, that as all these exterior provisions are found to be inadequate, the defect must be supplied, by so contriving the interior structure of the government as that its several constituent parts may, by their mutual relations, be the means of keeping each other in their proper places. Without presuming to undertake a full development of the important idea, I will hazard a few general observations, which may perhaps place it in a clearer light, and enable us to form a more correct judgment of the principles and structure of the government planned by the convention.

In order to lay a due foundation for that separate and distinct exercise of the different powers of government, which to a certain extent is admitted on all hands to be essential to the preservation of liberty, it is evident that each department should have a will of its own; and consequently should be so constituted that the members of each should have as little agency as possible in the appointment of the members of the others. Were this principle rigorously adhered to, it would require that all the appointments for the supreme executive, legislative, and judiciary magistracies should be drawn from the same fountain of authority, the people, through channels having no communication whatever with one another. Perhaps such a plan of constructing the several departments would be less difficult in practice than it may in contemplation appear. Some difficulties, however, and some additional expense would attend the execution of it. Some deviations, therefore, from the principle must be admitted. In the constitution of the judiciary department in particular, it might be inexpedient to insist rigorously on the principle: first, because peculiar qualifications being essential in the members, the primary consideration ought to be to select that mode of choice which best secures these qualifications; secondly, because the permanent tenure by which the appointments are held in that department, must soon destroy all sense of dependence on the authority conferring them.

It is equally evident, that the members of each department should be as little dependent as possible on those of the others, for the emoluments annexed to their offices. Were the executive magistrate, or the judges, not independent of the legislature in this particular, their independence in every other would be merely nominal.

But the great security against a gradual concentration of the several powers in the same department, consists in giving to those who administer each department the necessary constitutional means and personal motives to resist encroachments of the others. The provision for defense must in this, as in all other cases, be made commensurate to the danger of attack. Ambition must be made to counteract ambition. The interest of the man must be connected with the constitutional rights of the place. It may be a reflection on human nature, that such devices should be necessary to control the abuses of government. But what is government itself, but the greatest of all reflections on human nature? If men were angels, no government would be necessary. If angels were to govern men, neither external nor internal controls on government would be necessary. In framing a government which is to be administered by men over men, the great difficulty lies in this: you must first enable the government to control the governed; and in the next place oblige it to control itself. A dependence on the people is, no doubt, the primary control on the government; but experience has taught mankind the necessity of auxiliary precautions.

This policy of supplying, by opposite and rival interests, the defect of better motives, might be traced through the whole system of human affairs, private as well as public. We see it particularly displayed in all the subordinate distributions of power, where the constant aim is to divide and arrange the several offices in such a manner as that each may be a check on the other—-that the private interest of every individual may be a sentinel over the public rights. These inventions of prudence cannot be less requisite in the distribution of the supreme powers of the State.

But it is not possible to give to each department an equal power of self-defense. In republican government, the legislative authority necessarily predominates. The remedy for this inconveniency is to divide the legislature into different branches; and to render them, by different modes of election and different principles of action, as little connected with each other as the nature of their common functions and their common dependence on the society will admit. It may even be necessary to guard against dangerous encroachments by still further precautions. As the weight of the legislative authority requires that it should be thus divided, the weakness of the executive may require, on the other hand, that it should be fortified. An absolute negative on the legislature appears, at first view, to be the natural defense with which the executive magistrate should be armed. But perhaps it would be neither altogether safe nor alone sufficient. On ordinary occasions it might not be exerted with the requisite firmness, and on extraordinary occasions it might be perfidiously abused. May not this defect of an absolute negative be supplied by some qualified connection between this weaker department and the weaker branch of the stronger department, by which the latter may be led to support the constitutional rights of the former, without being too much detached from the rights of its own department?

If the principles on which these observations are founded be just, as I persuade myself they are, and they be applied as a criterion to the several State constitutions, and to the federal Constitution it will be found that if the latter does not perfectly correspond with them, the former are infinitely less able to bear such a test.

There are, moreover, two considerations particularly applicable to the federal system of America, which place that system in a very interesting point of view.

First. In a single republic, all the power surrendered by the people is submitted to the administration of a single government; and the usurpations are guarded against by a division of the government into distinct and separate departments. In the compound republic of America, the power surrendered by the people is first divided between two distinct governments, and then the portion allotted to each subdivided among distinct and separate departments. Hence a double security arises to the rights of the people. The different governments will control each other, at the same time that each will be controlled by itself.

Second. It is of great importance in a republic not only to guard the society against the oppression of its rulers, but to guard one part of the society against the injustice of the other part. Different interests necessarily exist in different classes of citizens. If a majority be united by a common interest, the rights of the minority will be insecure. There are but two methods of providing against this evil: the one by creating a will in the community independent of the majority that is, of the society itself; the other, by comprehending in the society so many separate descriptions of citizens as will render an unjust combination of a majority of the whole very improbable, if not impracticable. The first method prevails in all governments possessing an hereditary or self-appointed authority. This, at best, is but a precarious security; because a power independent of society may as well espouse the unjust views of the major as the rightful interests of the minor party, and may possibly be turned against both parties. The second method will be exemplified in the federal republic of the United States. Whilst all authority in it will be derived from and dependent on the society, the society itself will be broken into so many parts, interests, and classes of citizens, that the rights of individuals, or of the minority, will be in little danger from interested combinations of the majority. In a free government the security for civil rights must be the same as that for religious rights. It consists in the one case in the multiplicity of interests, and in the other in the multiplicity of sects. The degree of security in both cases will depend on the number of interests and sects; and this may be presumed to depend on the extent of country and number of people comprehended under the same government. This view of the subject must particularly recommend a proper federal system to all the sincere and considerate friends of republican government, since it shows that in exact proportion as the territory of the Union may be formed into more circumscribed Confederacies, or States oppressive combinations of a majority will be facilitated: the best security, under republican forms, for the rights of every class of citizens, will be diminished; and consequently the stability and independence of some member of the government, the only other security, must be proportionately increased. Justice is the end of government. It is the end of civil society. It ever has been and ever will be pursued until it be obtained, or until liberty be lost in the pursuit. In a society under the forms of which the stronger faction can readily unite and oppress the weaker, anarchy may as truly be said to reign as in a state of nature, where the weaker individual is not secured against the violence of the stronger; and as, in the latter state, even the stronger individuals are prompted, by the uncertainty of their condition, to submit to a government which may protect the wear as well as the more powerful. It can be little doubted that if the State of Rhode Island was separated from the Confederacy and left to itself, the insecurity of rights under the popular form of government within such narrow limits would be displayed by such reiterated oppressions of factious majorities that some power altogether independent of the people would soon be called for by the voice of the very factions whose misrule had proved the necessity of it. In the extended republic of the United States, and among the great variety of interests, parties, and sects which it embraces, a coalition of a majority of the whole society could seldom take place on any other principles than those of justice and the general good; whilst there being thus less danger to a minor from the will of a major party, there must be less pretext, also, to provide for the security of the former, by introducing into the government a will not dependent on the latter, or, in other words, a will independent of the society itself. It is no less certain than it is important, notwithstanding the contrary opinions which have been entertained, that the larger the society, provided it lie within a practical sphere, the more duly capable it will be of self-government. And happily for the *republican cause*, the practicable sphere may be carried to a very great extent, by a judicious modification of mixture of the *federal principle*.

PUBLIUS

Presidents of the United States

Name of President	Dates of Service	Political Party Affiliation	Vice President(s)	Major Party Candidate(s) Defeated in General Election
George Washington	1789–97		Adams	
John Adams	1797–1801	Federalist	Jefferson	Jefferson
Thomas Jefferson	1801–09	Democratic-Republican	Burr/Clinton	Adams, Pinckney
James Madison	1809–17	Democratic-Republican	Clinton/Gerry	Pinckney, D. Clinton
James Monroe	1817–25	Democratic-Republican	Tompkins	King
John Quincy Adams	1825–29	Democratic-Republican/Democratic	Calhoun	Jackson
Andrew Jackson	1829–37	Democratic	Van Buren	J. Q.Adams, Clay
Martin Van Buren	1837–41	Democratic	Johnson	Harrison
William Harrison	1841	Whig	Tyler	Van Buren
John Tyler	1841–45	Whig	vacant	
James Polk	1845–49	Democratic	Dallas	Clay
Zachary Taylor	1849–50	Whig	Fillmore	Cass
Millard Fillmore	1850–53	Whig	vacant	
Franklin Pierce	1853–57	Democratic	King/vacant	Scott
James Buchanan	1857–61	Democratic	Breckinridge	Fremont
Abraham Lincoln	1861–65	Republican	Hamlin/Johnson	Breckinridge, Douglas, McClellan
Andrew Johnson	1865–69	Democratic	vacant	
Ulysses S. Grant	1869–77	Republican	Colfax/Wilson/vacant	Seymour, Greeley
Rutherford B. Hayes	1877–81	Republican	Wheeler	Tilden
James Garfield	1881	Republican	Arthur	Hancock
Chester Arthur	1881–85	Republican	vacant	
Grover Cleveland	1885–89	Democratic	Hendricks/vacant	Blaine

Name of President	Dates of Service	Political Party Affiliation	Vice President(s)	Major Party Candidate(s) Defeated in General Election
Benjamin Harrison	1889–93	Republican	Morton	Cleveland
Grover Cleveland	1893–97	Democratic	Stevenson	Harrison
William McKinley	1897–1901	Republican	Hobart	Bryan
Theodore Roosevelt	1901–09	Republican	vacant/Fairbanks	Parker
William Taft	1909–13	Republican	Sherman/vacant	Bryan
Woodrow Wilson	1913–21	Democratic	Marshall	T. Roosevelt, Taft, Hughes
Warren G. Harding	1921–23	Republican	Coolidge	Cox
Calvin Coolidge	1923–29	Republican	vacant/Dawes	Davis
Herbert Hoover	1929–33	Republican	Curtis	Smith
Franklin D. Roosevelt	1933–45	Democratic	Garner/Wallace/ Truman	Hoover, Landon, Wilkie, Dewey
Harry Truman	1945–53	Democratic	vacant/Barkley	Dewey
Dwight Eisenhower	1953–61	Republican	Nixon	Stevenson
John F. Kennedy	1961–63	Democratic	Johnson	Nixon
Lyndon Johnson	1963–69	Democratic	vacant/Humphrey	Goldwater
Richard Nixon	1969–74	Republican	Agnew/vacant/Ford	Humphrey, McGovern
Gerald Ford	1974–77	Republican	vacant/Rockefeller	
Jimmy Carter	1977–81	Democratic	Mondale	Ford
Ronald Reagan	1981–89	Republican	G. H.W. Bush	Carter, Mondale
George H.W. Bush	1989–93	Republican	Quayle	Dukakis
William Clinton	1993–2001	Democratic	Gore	G. H. W. Bush, Dole
George W. Bush	2001–2009	Republican	Cheney	Gore, Kerry
Barack Obama	2009–present	Democratic	Biden	McCain

Glossary

A

Administrative discretion the freedom of agencies to decide how to implement a vague or ambiguous law passed by Congress.

Administrative law a law that relates to the authority of administrative agencies and the rules promulgated by those agencies.

Affirmative action programs, laws, or practices designed to remedy discriminatory hiring practices, government contracting, and school admissions.

Agenda setting theory the theory that holds that although the effects of television exposure may be minimal or difficult to gauge, the media are quite influential in telling the public what to think about.

Agents of political socialization factors that have a significant impact on an individual's socialization to politics.

Amendments modifications or additions to the U.S. Constitution passed in accordance with the amendment procedures laid out in Article V.

Amicus curiae briefs written documents filed by outside parties in the case with an interest in the outcome of the litigation expressing their own views on how the Court should decide a particular case.

Anarchy a situation in a society where there is no government and that is characterized by lawlessness and discord in the political system.

Anti-Federalists those who opposed ratification of the proposed Constitution of the United States.

Appellate jurisdiction the authority of a court to review decisions handed down by another court.

Articles of Confederation the document creating a "league of friendship" governing the thirteen states during and immediately after the war for independence; hampered by the limited power they vest in the legislature to collect revenue or regulate commerce, the Articles eventually proved unworkable for the new nation.

Authoritarianism a form of government in which one political party, group, or person maintains such complete control over the nation that it may refuse to recognize and, if it chooses to, suppress all other political parties and interests.

Authority the ability of public institutions and the officials within them to make laws, independent of the power to execute them.

B

Bail an amount of money determined by a judge that the accused must pay to a court as security against a defendant's freedom before trial.

Battleground states states identified as offering either major-party candidate a reasonable chance for victory in the Electoral College.

Bicameral legislature a legislature composed of two separate chambers.

Bill a proposed law presented for consideration to a legislative body.

Bill of attainder an act of a legislature declaring a person (or group) guilty of some crime, and then punishing them without a trial. The Constitution denies Congress the ability to issue a bill of attainder.

Bill of Rights the first eight amendments to the U.S. Constitution, which protect various rights of the people against the new federal government.

Bipartisan Campaign Reform Act (BCRA) of 2002 also called the McCain-Feingold Act, the federal legislation that (1) restricted soft money spent by political parties, (2) regulated expenditures on ads that refer to specific candidates immediately before an election, and (3) increased limits on hard money donated directly to candidates and their campaigns.

Block grants grants from the federal government to the states that may be used at the discretion of states to pursue more generalized aims.

Blogs derived from the term *weblogs,* these are Internet sites that include a combination of editorial page, personal web page, and online diary of personal observations in real time about news events and issues.

Briefs written documents filed by parties in an appealed case arguing why constitutional or statutory law weighs in favor of their respective positions.

***Brown v. Board of Education* (1954)** the 1954 U.S. Supreme Court decision that declared school segregation to be unconstitutional.

***Buckley v. Valeo* (1976)** the 1976 Supreme Court opinion that held that spending money to influence elections is protected First Amendment speech, and that prohibited limitations on independent expenditures or personal money spent by candidates on their own campaigns.

Budget authority the power federal departments and agencies maintain to incur obligations to spend or lend money.

Budget deficit the amount of money spent by the U.S. government beyond that which it collects in taxes and other revenue in a single year.

Budget surplus the amount of money left over in a single year after the government has spent all its revenue for that year.

Bureaucracy an organization set up in a logical and rational manner for the purpose of accomplishing specific functions.

Bureaucratic adjudicating determining the rights and duties of particular parties within the scope of an agency's rules or regulations.

C

Cabinet the collection of the principal officers in each of the executive departments of the federal government who serve as key advisers to the president.

Cabinet departments those federal agencies that qualify as the major administrative organizations of the executive branch.

Capitalism economic system in which all or most of the means of production are privately owned under competitive conditions.

Casework the direct assistance that a member of Congress provides to a constituent, community group, or a local or state official.

Caucus a method of choosing party nominees in which party members attend local meetings at which they choose delegates committed to a particular candidate.

Central Intelligence Agency (CIA) federal agency charged with evaluating and disseminating intelligence information, performing public relations functions that affect international perceptions of the United States, and engaging in overt and covert operations at the direction of the president.

Charter a state law that grants a local government the authority to provide public services, enact and enforce regulations, and raise revenue to support its operations.

Checks and balances a system of limits imposed by the Constitution that gives each branch of government the limited right to change or cancel the acts of other branches.

City the type of local government that has been chartered by a state to serve the needs of a more urbanized or densely populated area.

Civil law there are actually two meanings to this term: (1) Legislative codes, laws, or sets of rules enacted by duly authorized lawmaking bodies such as Congress, state and local legislatures, or any executive authority entrusted with the power to make laws; (2) the body of non-criminal laws of a nation or state that deal with the rights of private citizens.

Civil liberties those specific individual rights that cannot be denied to citizens by government that are guaranteed by the Constitution. Most of these rights are in the first eight amendments to the Constitution, known as the Bill of Rights.

Civil rights those positive rights, whether political, social, or economic, conferred by the government on individuals or groups.

Civil Rights Act of 1964 the federal law that banned racial discrimination in all public accommodations, including those that were privately owned; prohibited discrimination by employers and created the Equal Employment Opportunity Commission to investigate complaints of discrimination; and denied public funds to schools that continued to discriminate on the basis of race.

Civil Rights Act of 1968 the federal law that banned race discrimination in housing and made interference with a citizen's civil rights a federal crime.

Civil service the system whereby workers in the federal bureaucracy are supposed to be immune from partisan political maneuvering.

Civil Service Reform Act of 1978 the federal act that replaced the Civil Service Commission (the agency that oversaw federal hiring and firing practices) with the Office of Personnel Management

(OPM) and the Merit Systems Protection Board (MSPB).

Civil War Amendments the Thirteenth Amendment (ratified in 1865) banished slavery from all states and U.S. territories. The Fourteenth Amendment (ratified in 1868) granted full U.S. and state citizenship to all people born or naturalized in the United States and guaranteed to each person "the equal protection of the laws." The Fifteenth Amendment (1870) forbade the denial or abridgement of the right to vote by any government on account of race.

Class action lawsuit a lawsuit filed by a large group of persons with clearly defined common interests.

Closed primary an election that requires voters to declare their party affiliation ahead of time.

Closed rule a rule of procedure adopted by the House Rules Committee that severely limits the ability of members of Congress to amend the bill.

Closed shop the law that requires employees to become members of the union as a condition of employment in unionized workplaces.

Cloture a Senate debate procedure that permits that body to end debate and force a vote on a bill by a vote of sixty senators.

Coattail effect the potential benefit that successful presidential candidates offer to congressional candidates of the same political party during presidential election years.

Cold War the nearly half-century struggle over ideological differences between the United States and the Soviet Union. Waged through economic warfare, arms buildups, and tense diplomatic talks, the Cold War never broke out into a sustained military engagement between the two nations and ended with the dissolution of the Soviet Union in 1991.

Commission form the form of local government that features an elected group of commissioners with each commissioner having administrative authority over a specific aspect of government.

Common law judge-made law handed down through judicial opinions, which over time establish precedents.

Complaint a document written by the plaintiff arguing why the court is empowered to hear the case and explaining why he or she is entitled to some form of relief under the current law.

Concurrent powers those powers shared by the federal and state governments under the Constitution.

Concurring opinion the opinion of one or more justices that agrees with the end result reached by the majority but disagrees with the reasons offered for the decision.

Confederation a system of government (or "league") in which two or more independent states unite to achieve certain specified common aims.

Conference committee a joint committee of Congress appointed by the House of Representatives and the Senate to resolve differences on a particular bill.

Congressional agencies government bodies formed by and relied on by Congress to support members of Congress in performing their functions.

Congressional district a geographic region (either a state itself or a region located entirely within one state) whose residents select one member to represent it in the House of Representatives.

Congressional oversight Congress's exercise of its authority to monitor the activities of agencies and administrators.

Congressional personal staff a group of workers who assist an individual member of Congress in performing his or her responsibilities.

Conservative ideology a political orientation that generally favors government activism in defense of more traditional values on social issues, but that also favors government restraint in economic redistribution.

Constitutional Convention meeting of delegates from twelve states in Philadelphia during the summer of 1787, at which was drafted an entirely new system of government to govern the United States.

Containment U.S. foreign policy that sought to restrict Soviet power (and Communist influence) to its existing geographical sphere.

Continuity (in public opinion) a tendency for political preferences to remain generally stable over time.

Cooperative federalism the doctrine of federalism that affords Congress nearly unlimited authority to exercise its powers through means that often coerce states into administering and/or enforcing federal policies.

Council-manager form the form of local government structure that places management of the city or town in the hands of a nonelected professional appointed by the council.

County a form of local government that varies in importance and scope of activity across the states, and that usually coexists with city or town governments.

Crime control model criminal justice model that views the controlling of criminal behavior as the system's most important function.

Critical election an election that produces sharp changes in patterns of party loyalty among voters.

Cultivation theory the theory of media effects that suggests that heavy television exposure helps develop an individual's overall view of the world.

D

Dealignment a decline in voter attachment to parties and in clarity of party coalitions.

Declaration of Independence formal document listing colonists' grievances and articulating the colonists' intention to seek independence; formally adopted by the Second Continental Congress on July 4, 1776.

Defendant the target of a plaintiff's complaint explaining why he or she is entitled to some form of relief under the current law.

Delegation of congressional power Congress's transferring of its lawmaking authority to the executive branch of government.

Democracy form of government in which the people, either directly or through elected representatives, hold power and authority. The word *democracy* is derived from the Greek *demos kratos,* meaning "rule by the people."

Department of Defense executive branch agency that is responsible for managing the nation's military and advising the president on all military matters.

Department of Homeland Security (DHS) executive branch agency established in 2002 to coordinate government entities in protecting U.S. citizens against terrorism within the nation's borders.

Department of State executive branch agency that is primarily responsible for most foreign policy programs within the executive branch, including diplomatic missions, foreign aid, and contributions to international organizations.

Deregulation the elimination of government oversight and government regulation of certain activities.

Devolution the transfer of power and responsibilities for certain regulatory programs from the federal government back to the states.

Digital divide the term indicating the large differences in usage of the Internet between younger and older people, lower- and middle/upper-class people, lesser and better educated, and minority groups and nonminority groups.

Dillon's Rule the Iowa court ruling that gives state government clear authority over local governments to issue directives ordering localities to do what the state wishes.

Direct democracy a system of government in which all citizens participate in making policy, rules, and governing decisions.

Direct primary election an open election, rather than an election by party leaders, to choose candidates for the general election.

Direction (of public opinion) a tendency toward a particular preference, usually (though not always) characterized as either positive or negative.

Discount rate the rate (expressed as a percentage) that all Federal Reserve member banks and other depository institutions will be charged by the Federal Reserve Banks to borrow short-term funds.

Discovery a stage of pretrial litigation in which the plaintiff and defendant have the right to learn what information the other side has about the case by requesting documents or materials, access to property, and/or examinations, or by offering answers to questions about the litigation either in written form, or verbally at a deposition.

Discretionary spending forms of federal government spending that Congress can modify or eliminate in any given year, including spending on education, the environment, and national defense.

Dissenting opinion the opinion of one or more justices who disagree with the result reached by the majority.

Distributive tax policies taxation policies that theoretically promote the interests of all classes equally.

Divided government split party control of Congress and the presidency.

Domino theory theory that held that Communist takeovers of countries in Southeast Asia and elsewhere would be followed by subsequent Communist takeovers of nearby countries as well.

Double jeopardy the constitutional protection that those accused of a crime cannot be tried twice for the same crime.

Dual federalism the doctrine of federalism that holds that state authority acts as a limit on congressional power under the Constitution.

Due process model criminal justice model that views the attainment of justice—which includes protection of the innocent—as equally important goals of the system.

E

Economic equality may be defined either as providing all groups the equality of opportunity for economic success, or as the equality of results. In the United States, the latter has been the more common understanding of economic opportunity.

Economic interest group an organized group that exists to promote economic conditions favorable to and economic opportunities for its members.

Economic protest party a party that emerges in times of economic recession to express discontent with the ruling party.

Electoral College the constitutional mechanism by which presidents are chosen. Each state is allocated Electoral College votes based on the sum of that state's U.S. senators and House members.

Electors individuals appointed to represent a state's presidential vote in the Electoral College; in practice, voters in presidential elections vote for a slate of electors committed to a particular candidate, rather than voting directly for the candidate.

Enumerated powers express powers explicitly granted by the Constitution such as the taxing power specifically granted to Congress.

Environmental Protection Agency (EPA) federal agency that administers and enforces all of the nation's environmental programs and spells out the requirements of legislative initiatives to control the quality of the environment.

Equal time rule the FCC mandate that radio and TV stations sell equal amounts of airtime to all political candidates who want to broadcast advertisements.

Establishment clause the clause in the First Amendment that prohibits government from enacting any law "respecting an establishment of religion." Separationist interpretations of this clause affirm that government should not support any religious activity. Accommodationists say that support for a religion is legal provided that all religions are equally supported.

Ex post facto laws a law that punishes someone for doing something in the past, at a time when the act was not illegal. The Constitution denies government the ability to write laws ex post facto.

Exclusionary rule the legal rule requiring that all evidence illegally obtained by police in violation of the Bill of Rights must be "excluded" from admission in a court of law, where it might have assisted in convicting those accused of committing crimes.

Executive agreement a pact reached between the president and a foreign government that does not require the consent of Congress.

Executive Office of the President the staffers who help the president of the United States manage the rest of the federal bureaucracy.

Executive orders rules or regulations issued by the chief executive that have the force of law and do not require the consent of Congress.

Expansionism doctrine that favors a country expanding its own territory and influence.

Extradition the clause in Article IV of the U.S. Constitution that requires a state to surrender a fugitive accused of committing a crime in another state back to the state where the crime was committed for legal prosecution.

F

Factional party a party that has split off from one of the major parties.

Federal Election Campaign Act (FECA) the federal legislation passed in 1971 that established disclosure requirements and restricted individual campaign contributions.

Federal Election Commission the agency created in 1974 to enforce federal election laws.

Federal Register the journal that publishes draft regulations that implement a federal program.

Federal Reserve Board the Federal Reserve System's Board of Governors, which votes on monetary policy in the United States, supervises the nation's banks by setting rules for the twelve Federal Reserve Banks, and engages in open market operations.

Federal Reserve System the central banking system of the United States, which controls the nation's money supply.

Federalism the doctrine underlying a system of government in which power is divided between a central government and constituent political subunits.

Federalist Papers a series of articles authored by Alexander Hamilton, James Madison, and John Jay, which argued in favor of ratifying the proposed Constitution of the United States; the Federalist Papers outlined the philosophy and motivation of the document.

Federalists those who supported ratification of the proposed Constitution of the United States between 1787 and 1789.

Fifteenth Amendment the amendment to the Constitution that guaranteed the franchise regardless of race, color, or any previous condition of servitude.

Filibuster the action by a single senator or a minority of senators to block a bill from passage by refusing to end discussion.

Fiscal policy decisions by the federal government that relate to raising revenue through taxation and spending the revenue that is thereby generated.

Flat tax a tax policy that draws money from all entities at the exact same rate as a proportion of their income.

Franchise (or suffrage) the right to vote.

Franking privilege the traditional right of members of Congress to mail materials to their constituents without paying postage.

Free exercise clause the religious freedom clause in the First Amendment that denies government the ability to prohibit the free exercise of religion. Debate over the clause has largely focused on whether government laws can force adherents of a certain religion to engage in activities that are prohibited by their religious beliefs or prevent them from performing acts that are compelled by their religious beliefs.

Free rider an individual who does not join or contribute to an interest group that is representing his or her interests

Frontloading the recent trend of states moving their primaries and caucuses earlier in the year to attract greater attention from the candidates and the media.

Full faith and credit clause the clause in Article IV, Section 1 of the Constitution that forces states to abide by the official acts and proceedings of all other states.

G

Gerrymandering the drawing of House district boundaries to the benefit of one political party over another. The term is named for Elbridge Gerry, a Massachusetts delegate to the Constitutional Convention, who (as governor) redrew districts in this fashion to favor the Democratic-Republicans.

Gibbons v. Ogden (1824) the Supreme Court case that held that a federal license to operate steamboats overrides a state-granted monopoly of New York water rights under the Constitution.

Good faith exception an exception to the exclusionary rule that states that if a search warrant is invalid through no fault of the police, evidence obtained under that warrant may still be admitted into court.

Government the collection of public institutions in a nation that establish and enforce the rules by which the members of that nation must live.

Government corporations units in the federal bureaucracy set up to run like private companies that depend on revenue from citizens to provide their services.

Grand jury a jury that meets to decide whether evidence is sufficient to justify a prosecutor's request that a case go to trial. Grand juries do not decide on a defendant's guilt or innocence.

Grants-in-aid grants from the federal government to states that allow state governments to pursue specific federal policies such as highway construction.

Grassroots lobbying communications by interest groups with government officials through the mobilization of public opinion to exert influence on government action.

Great Compromise a proposal also known as the "Connecticut

Compromise" which provided for a bicameral legislature featuring an upper house based on equal representation among the states and a lower house whose membership was based on each state's population; approved by a 5–4 vote of the state delegations.

Great Society a set of aggressive federal domestic policies, proposed by President Lyndon Johnson and passed by Congress in the 1960s, that further enhanced the role of the presidency.

Gross domestic product (GDP) an estimate of the total money value of all the goods and services produced in the U.S. in a given one-year period.

H

Hard money donations made directly to political candidates and their campaigns that must be declared with the name of the donor (which then becomes public knowledge).

Hatch Act of 1939 the 1939 law that insulated the civil service from partisan politics by prohibiting employee dismissals for partisan reasons and by prohibiting federal workers from participating in political campaigns.

Hawks members of the president's administration who call for aggressive military actions wherever hostile forces may be found.

Health maintenance organization (HMO) prepaid group medical practice arrangements that attempt to limit health care costs through the establishment of flat monthly rates.

I

Ideological party a party that promotes broad ideas about the purpose and role of government.

Impeachment the first step in a two-step process outlined in Article II, Section 4 of the U.S. Constitution to remove a president or other high official from office. The House of Representatives, by majority vote, may impeach if the official has committed "treason, bribery, or other high crimes or misdemeanors." The second step requires a conviction in the Senate by a two-thirds vote.

Incorporation the process by which the U.S. Supreme Court used the due process clause of the Fourteenth Amendment to make applicable to the states most of the individual rights guaranteed by the Bill of Rights. Incorporation provided that state and local governments, as well as the federal government, could not deny these rights to citizens.

Incumbent race a general election race pitting a person currently holding the office against a challenger.

Independent agency a department that focuses on a narrower set of issues than do higher-status Cabinet departments.

Independent campaign expenditures political donations that PACs or individuals spend to support campaigns, but do not directly contribute to the campaigns.

Indiana ballot the voting ballot format in which the name of the political party appears at the top of the column and candidates for the various offices appear below the party label, thus cuing the voters to partisan-based voting.

Indictment a decision by a grand jury authorizing the government to proceed to trial against the defendant.

Individualism the value that individuals are primarily responsible for their own lot in life and that promotes and rewards individual initiative and responsibility. This value underlies America's reliance on a capitalist economy and the free-market system.

Inflation the overall general upward price movement of goods and services in an economy, normally measured by the Consumer Price Index (CPI).

Initiative a question that goes directly before the voters for approval or rejection without having first to be proposed by the state legislature.

Intensity (of public opinion) the degree of strength or commitment the public feels about the opinion it holds.

Interest group an organization of people with shared goals that tries to influence public policy through a variety of activities.

Intergovernmental lobby any interest group that represents the collective interests of states, cities, and other governments.

International organization entity of international scope or character, usually established by treaty, such as the World Bank or the International Monetary Fund.

Internationalism doctrine that favors active participation of the nation in collective arrangements that secure the political independence and territorial boundaries of other countries.

Invisible primary the competition among candidates seeking the party nomination for front-runner status prior to the primaries and caucuses.

Iron triangle a three-sided network of policy making that includes congressional committees (and subcommittees) in a specific policy area, executive agencies with authority over that area, and private interest groups focused on influencing that area.

Isolationism foreign policy doctrine that opposes (1) intervention in distant wars and (2) involvement in permanent military alliances.

Issue and ideological group an organized group that focuses on specific issues and ideological perspectives.

Issue network the broad array of actors (beyond just the iron triangle) that try to collectively influence a policy area in which they maintain a vested interest.

Issue party a party that tends to form on the basis of a single issue.

J

Jim Crow laws laws used by some southern states that required segregation of blacks and whites in public schools, railroads, buses, restaurants, hotels, theaters, and other public facilities. The laws excluded blacks from militias and denied them certain education and welfare services.

Joint Chiefs of Staff (JCS) group of chief officers of the four branches of the armed forces as well as a JCS chair and vice chair that advises the president on military matters and delivers the president's orders to the military.

Joint committee a committee comprised of members of both the House and the Senate that is investigative in nature.

Judicial review the power of courts to declare acts of the other branches of government to be unconstitutional and thus invalid.

K

Katz **test** the legal standard that requires the government to attain a warrant demonstrating "probable cause" for any "search" that violates a person's actual and reasonable expectation of privacy.

Keynesian economic theory fiscal policy theory that favors government taxation and spending during difficult economic times**.**

L

Laissez-faire economics fiscal policy theory that favors minimal intervention in the nation's economy.

Layer cake federalism description of federalism as maintaining that the authority of state and federal governments exists in distinct and separate spheres.

Legitimacy the extent to which the people afford the government the authority and right to exercise power.

Lemon **test** the legal test that determines if a government statute aiding public or private schools is an unconstitutional violation of the establishment clause. The statute is unconstitutional if: the statute has no secular purpose; its principal or primary effect advances or inhibits religion; or it fosters "an excessive government entanglement with religion."

Libel printing or disseminating false statements that harm someone.

Liberal ideology a political orientation that favors a more assertive role in the redistribution of economic resources, but emphasizes individual freedom on a range of social issues.

Limited government the value that promotes the idea that government power should be as restricted as possible.

Literacy test the requirement that individuals prove that they can read and write before being allowed to vote.

Litigation any judicial contest, including all the events that lead up to a possible court event.

Lobbying the means by which interest groups attempt to influence government officials to make decisions favorable to their goals.

Logrolling the trading of influence or votes among legislators to achieve passage of projects that are of interest to one another.

Loose construction Constitutional interpretation that gives constitutional provisions broad and open-ended meanings.

M

Majoritarianism the principle that the choice that is supported by the most voters is the choice that prevails.

Majority caucus the members of the party that has the majority of seats in a particular chamber.

Majority leader in the Senate, the controlling party's main spokesperson who leads his or her party in proposing new laws and crafting the party's platform. The Senate majority leader also enjoys the power to make committee assignments. In the House, the majority leader is the controlling party's second in command, who helps the Speaker to oversee the development of the party platform.

Majority opinion the opinion of a majority of members of the U.S. Supreme Court, which carries the force of law.

Majority rule the notion that the will of the majority should guide decisions made by American government.

Mandatory spending federal government spending that is not controlled by annual budget decisions, including entitlements such as Medicare and Social Security.

Manifest destiny U.S. policy of the mid-nineteenth century that advocated acquiring lands and occupying the entire American continent from one ocean to the other.

Marble cake federalism description of federalism as intertwining state and federal authority in an inseparable mixture.

Marginal seat congressional districts that tend to have relatively similar numbers of Democratic and Republican voters.

Marshall Plan the 1947 U.S. policy that provided loans to West European countries whose economies had been ravaged by World War II.

Martin v. Hunter's Lessee **(1819)** the Supreme Court case that established that state governments and state courts must abide by the U.S. Supreme Court's interpretation of the federal constitution.

Massachusetts ballot the voting ballot format that organizes the slate of candidates on the basis of the office they are seeking and simply supplies a label indicating the candidate's party affiliation.

Material benefits (of group membership) the specific, tangible benefits individuals receive from interest group membership, such as economic concessions, discounts on products, etc.

Mayor-council form the form of local government that is modeled on the executive and legislative branches of the federal government and the fifty state governments.

McCulloch v. Maryland (1819) the Supreme Court case that established that Congress enjoys broad and extensive authority to make all laws that are "necessary and proper" to carry out its constitutionially delegated powers.

Medicaid federal program that provides limited health care services to the poor.

Medicare federal program that provides health insurance for the elderly.

Merit system a system of appointing and promoting civil service personnel based on merit rather than political affiliation or loyalty.

Midterm congressional elections congressional elections held midway between successive presidential elections.

Military-industrial complex the vast network of defense industries in America (including manufacturers of weapons, missiles, aircraft, and so on) and their allies in the federal bureaucracy.

Minimal effects theory the theory that deep-seated, long-term factors, such as party identification, had much greater influence on vote decisions than did news media coverage.

Minority caucus the members of the party that has a minority of seats in a particular chamber.

Minority leader the leader of the minority party in each chamber.

Miranda warning the U.S. Supreme Court's requirement that when an individual is arrested he or she must be read a statement that indicates the person's right to remain silent and the right to an attorney.

Monarchy a form of government in which one person, who is usually a member of a royal family or a royal designate, exercises supreme authority.

Monetary policy regulation of the money supply and interest rates by a central bank, such as the U.S. Federal Reserve Board, in order to control inflation and stabilize the currency.

Monroe Doctrine U.S. foreign policy that proclaimed North and South America unavailable for future colonization by any European power and that declared that any such colonization would be viewed as an act of war on the United States.

Motor Voter law the federal law that mandates that when an individual applies for or renews a state driver's license, the state must also provide that individual with voter registration materials.

Multiparty system a political system in which many different parties are organized on the basis of political ideologies, economic interests, positions on a single issue or set of issues, religion, or geography.

N

National committee the committee that oversees the conduct of a party's presidential campaign and develops strategy for congressional elections.

National committee chair the head of the national committee for one of the two major parties.

National debt total sum of the federal government's outstanding debt obligations.

National party convention a large meeting that draws together party delegates from across the nation to choose (or formally affirm the selection of) the party's presidential and vice presidential candidates.

National party organization the institution through which political parties exist at the national, state, and local levels, primarily focused on articulating policy positions, raising money, organizing volunteers, and providing services to candidates.

National Security Council (NSC) advisory body to the president charged with coordinating information about foreign, military, and economic policies that affect national security.

National supremacy doctrine Chief Justice John Marshall's interpretation of federalism as holding that states have extremely limited sovereign authority, whereas Congress is supreme within its own sphere of constitutional authority.

Natural law according to John Locke, the most fundamental type of law, which supersedes any law that is made by government. Citizens are born with certain natural rights (including life, liberty, and property) that derive from this law that government cannot take away.

Necessary and proper clause the clause in Article I, Section 8 of the Constitution that affords Congress the power to make laws that serve as a means to achieving its expressly delegated powers.

New Deal an aggressive set of federal domestic policies proposed by President Franklin Roosevelt in the 1930s and passed by Congress as a response to the Great Depression, which ultimately transformed the presidency into an institution marked by permanent bureaucracies and well-established repositories of power.

New Jersey Plan a proposal known also as the "small states plan" that would have retained the Articles of Confederation principle of a legislature where states enjoyed equal representation.

New media media outlets that rely on relatively newer technologies for communicating, such as the Internet, DVDs, fax machines, cell phones, satellites, cable TV, and broadband.

New world order President George H. W. Bush's description of the post–Cold War world, in which nations would be forced to work together for the purpose of securing collective peace, security, freedom, and the rule of law.

Nineteenth Amendment the constitutional amendment that guarantees women voting rights.

No Child Left Behind Act federal legislation passed in 2002 that requires mandatory testing of students to meet basic competencies.

Nomination campaign the political season in which the two major parties hold primaries and caucuses in all the states to choose party delegates committed to specific candidates.

Noneconomic interest group an organized group that advocates for reasons other than their membership's commercial and financial interests.

Normal vote the percentage of voters that can be expected with reasonable certainty to cast a ballot for each of the two major political parties.

North Atlantic Treaty Organization (NATO) a military, political, and economic alliance of nations formally bound to protect self-determination and open trade in Western Europe.

O

Objectivity the journalistic standard that news reporting of events must be factual, accurate, fair, and equitable.

Oligarchy a form of government in which a small exclusive class, which may or may not attempt to rule on behalf of the people as a whole, holds supreme power.

Open market operations the buying and selling of government securities by the Federal Reserve Board as a means of controlling the national money supply.

Open primary an election that allows voters to choose on the day of the primary election the party in which they want to vote.

Open rule a rule of procedure adopted by the House Rules Committee that permits amendments to a bill.

Open seat election general election race in which neither candidate is the incumbent.

Open shop the law that allows employees the option of joining or not joining the certified union at a unionized workplace

Original jurisdiction the authority of a court to be the initial court in which a legal decision is rendered.

Outlays the power federal departments or agencies maintain to actually spend federal money in a given fiscal year.

Overriding a veto the power of the Congress to enact legislation despite a president's veto of that legislation; requires a two-thirds vote of both houses of Congress.

P

Pacifism doctrine of foreign relations that refuses to sanction any military conflict and that opposes all war making.

Pardon the president's constitutional authority to relieve an individual of both the punishment and the guilt of violating the law.

Partisan press era a period, from the late 1700s to the mid-1800s, when newspapers typically supported a particular political party.

Party identification the psychological attachment that an individual has to a particular party.

Party platform a document outlining the party's position on important policy issues.

Patronage the practice of appointing people to government positions.

Pendleton Civil Service Reform Act the 1883 law that created a merit system for hiring many federal workers, protected them from being fired for partisan reasons, and set up a Civil Service Commission to oversee the hiring and firing process.

Plaintiff the party that chooses to initiate formal legal proceedings in a civil case.

Plea bargain a pretrial negotiated resolution in a criminal case in which the defendants seek to reduce their jail sentences by pleading guilty and in return prosecutors are willing to trade down the severity of the punishment.

***Plessy v. Ferguson* (1896)** the 1896 Supreme Court case that upheld a Louisiana segregation law on the theory that as long as the accommodations between the racially segregated facilities were equal, the equal protection clause was not violated. The Court's ruling effectively established the constitutionality of racial segregation and the notion of "separate but equal."

Pluralism the theory that public policy largely results from a variety of interest groups competing with one another to promote laws that benefit members of their respective groups.

Pocket veto the indirect veto of a bill received by the president within ten days of the adjournment of Congress, effected by the president's retaining the bill unsigned until Congress adjourns.

Policy implementation the process of carrying out laws, and the specific programs or services outlines in those laws.

Political action committee (PAC) the political arm of an interest group that promotes candidates in election campaigns primarily through financial campaigns.

Political culture the values and beliefs about government, its purpose, and its operations and institutions that are widely held among citizens in a society; it defines the essence of how a society thinks politically and is transmitted from one generation to the next.

Political equality a condition in which members of different groups possess substantially the same rights to participate actively in the political system. In the United States, these rights include voting, running for office, petitioning the government for redress of grievances, free speech, free press, and the access to an education.

Political ideology a philosophical guide that people use to help translate their values and beliefs into political preferences.

Political orientations the translation of values and beliefs into a systematic way of assessing the political environment.

Political party an organization that seeks to win elections for the purpose of influencing the outputs of government.

Political preferences the attitudes people maintain regarding the performance of political leaders and institutions, their candidate preferences in elections, and specific policy issues.

Political socialization the process by which an individual acquires values, beliefs, and opinions about politics.

Politics the way in which the institutions of government are organized to make laws, rules, and policies, and how those institutions are influenced.

Poll tax the requirement that individuals pay a fee before being allowed to vote.

Popular sovereignty the idea that the ultimate source of power in the nation is held by the people.

Pork-barrel legislation a government project or appropriation that yields jobs or other benefits to a specific locale and patronage opportunities to its political representative.

Power the ability to get individuals to do something that they may not otherwise do, such as pay taxes, stop for red lights, or submit to a search before boarding an airplane.

Power of appointment the president's constitutional power to hire and fire those charged with administrative authority to help execute federal laws, including ambassadors, federal judges including those on the Supreme Court, and all other federal officers under the president's charge. Most of these appointments require the consent of the Senate.

Power of incumbency the phenomenon by which incumbent members of Congress running for re-election are returned to office at an extremely high rate.

Preemption the constitutional doctrine that holds that when Congress acts affirmatively in the exercise of its own granted power, federal laws supersede all state laws on the matter.

Pre-emption doctrine doctrine of war making that reserves the right of the U.S military to use advance strikes to stop rogue states from developing weapons of mass destruction.

Prenomination campaign the political season in which candidates for president begin to explore the possibility of running by attempting to raise money and garner support.

President pro tempore in the absence of the vice president, the senator who presides over the Senate session. By tradition, this is usually the senator from the majority caucus who has served the longest number of consecutive years in the Senate.

Presidential primary a statewide election to select delegates who will represent a state at the party's national convention.

Primacy tendency the theory that impressions acquired while an individual is younger are likely to be more influential and long-lasting.

Prior restraint the government's requirement that a story be approved by government before it can be published.

Privatization the process of replacing government-provided services with services provided by the private sector.

Progressive tax a tax whose effective rate on an individual's income increases as the person's income rises.

Proportional representation a system of electing a national legislature in which the percentage of the vote that a party receives is reflected in the number of seats that the party occupies.

Protectionism economic policy of imposing quotas or tariffs on imports to protect domestic industries from foreign competition.

Pseudo-poll phone calls from political campaigns or PACs that present themselves as pollsters for the purpose of planting messages with voters rather than measuring public opinion.

Public interest group an organized group that promotes the broad, collective good of citizens and consumers.

Public opinion the summation of individual opinions on any particular issue or topic.

Public opinion poll a method of measuring the opinions of a large group of people by asking questions to a subset of the larger group and then generalizing the findings to that larger group.

Public policy the set of laws, regulations, and rules that affect the whole of society.

Purposive benefits (of group membership) rewards that do not directly benefit the individual member, but benefit society as a whole.

R

Racial profiling the law enforcement practice of taking race into account when identifying possible suspects of crimes.

Random-digit dialing (RDD) a probability technique for scientific telephone polling that randomly assigns the last four digits to known information about telephone area codes and exchanges.

Realigning election an election in which voter preferences shift as part of a lasting reconfiguration.

Realists members of the president's administration who advocate diplomacy as the primary means of protecting U.S. interests abroad.

Reapportionment the allocation of a fixed number of House seats to the states.

Recall a ballot measure allowing voters to remove duly elected officials from office prior to the end of their term.

Recession an economic slowdown characterized by high unemployment, reduced productivity, or other negative economic indicators.

Redistributive tax policies taxation policies that aim to provide a social safety net to meet the minimum physical needs of citizens.

Redistricting the act of redrawing congressional boundaries to achieve equal representation in each of the congressional districts.

Referendum a question that appears on the ballot that asks voters to approve or reject a policy action either recommended by the state legislature or already approved by the state legislature.

Regressive tax a tax that charges individuals the same amount, regardless of income.

Regulations rules or other directives issued by government agencies.

Regulatory agency a government body responsible for the control and supervision of a specified activity or area of public interest.

Reporting legislation the exclusive power of standing committees to forward legisla-

tion to the full House or Senate. Neither chamber can vote on a bill unless the committee votes to approve it first.

Representative democracy a form of government designed by the U.S. Constitution whereby free, open, and regular elections are held to allow voters to choose those who govern on their behalf; it is also referred to as *indirect democracy* or a *republican* form of government.

Reprieve the president's constitutional authority to reduce the severity of a punishment without removing the guilt for those who have violated the law.

Reserve requirement the minimum liquid assets each bank must keep on hand to back customer loans.

Reserved powers those powers expressly retained by the state governments under the Constitution.

Retrospective voting an explanation of vote choice that asserts that voters' evaluations of a candidate's past performance in office provides an important cue for vote decisions.

Rules Committee a committee in the House of Representatives that determines the rules by which other bills will come to the floor, be debated, and so on.

S

Safe seat a congressional seat from a district that includes a high percentage of voters from one of the major parties.

Sampling error the amount of error in a poll that results from interviewing a sample of people rather than the whole population under study; the larger the sample, the less sampling error.

Scientific sample a randomly selected subgroup drawn from a population using probability theory.

Sedition the crime of advocating the overthrow of the existing system of government.

Select committee a committee established by a resolution in either the House or the Senate for a specific purpose and, usually, for a limited time.

Senior Executive Service (SES) since the late 1970s, a defined group of approximately seventy-five hundred career professionals in the federal bureaucracy who provide continuity in the operations of the bureaucracy from one presidential administration to the next.

Separation of powers the principle that each branch of government enjoys separate and independent powers and areas of responsibility.

Shays's Rebellion armed uprising by debt-ridden Massachusetts farmers frustrated with the state government.

SLAPS test a standard that courts established to determine if material is obscene based in part on whether the material has serious literary, artistic, political, or scientific value. If it does, then the material is not obscene.

Social capital the "social connectedness" of a community, or the extent to which individuals are socially integrated into their community.

Social contract from the philosophy of Jean-Jacques Rousseau, an agreement people make with one another to form a government and abide by its rules and laws, and in return, the government promises to protect the people's rights and welfare and promote their best interests.

Social equality equality, and fair treatment of all groups within the various institutions in society, both public and private, that serve the public at large, including in stores, theaters, restaurants, hotels, and public transportation facilities among many other operations open to the public.

Social learning theory the theory that argues that viewers imitate what they view on television through observational learning.

Social movement a large informal grouping of individuals and/or organizations focused on specific political or social issues.

Social policy rules, regulations, and policy making pertaining to the quality of life, welfare, and relations of human beings in the United States.

Socialism economic system in which all or most of the means of production are owned by the community as a whole.

Soft money money not donated directly to a candidate's campaign, but rather to a political advocacy group or a political party for "party building" activities.

Solicitor general the lawyer representing the U.S. government before the U.S. Supreme Court.

Solidary benefits (of group membership) satisfaction that individuals receive from interacting with like-minded individuals for a cause.

Sovereignty the supreme political power of a government to regulate its affairs without outside interference.

Speaker of the House the leader of the House of Representatives, responsible for assigning new bills to committees, recognizing members to speak in the House chamber, and assigning chairs of committees.

Spoils system the postelection practice of rewarding loyal supporters of the winning candidates and party with appointive public offices.

Standing the requirement that a party must be uniquely or singularly affected by a controversy in order to be eligible to file a lawsuit.

Standing committee a permanent committee that exists in both the House and Senate; most standing committees focus on a particular substantive area of public policy, such as transportation, labor, foreign affairs, and the federal budget.

State constitution the fundamental law governing the structure and activities of state and local government.

State of the Union address an annual speech that the president delivers to Congress laying out the status of the nation and offering suggestions for new legislation.

Strategic Defense Initiative (SDI) a theoretical antimissile system based on the use of lasers and particle beams to shoot down Soviet nuclear missiles in outer space.

Straw poll an unscientific poll that gathers the opinions of people who are conveniently available in a gathering place.

Strict construction constitutional interpretation that limits the government to only those powers explicitly stated in the Constitution.

Strict scrutiny a legal standard set in *Brown v. Board of Education* for cases related to racial discrimination that tends to invalidate almost all state laws that segregate racial groups.

Subsidy the amount paid by the government to entities such as farmers to encourage a change in the overall amount production.

Supply-side economics economic theory that favors cutting taxes as way of increasing economic productivity.

Supremacy clause the provision in Article VI, Paragraph 2 of the Constitution that provides that the Constitution and federal laws override any conflicting provisions in state constitutions or state laws.

Symbolic speech nonspoken forms of speech that might be protected by the First Amendment, such as flag burning, wearing armbands at school to protest a war, or camping out in public parks to protest the plight of the homeless.

T

Talk radio a specialized form of radio programming in which one or more hosts provide commentary and often invite listeners to call in to the show and offer their own opinions.

Tariff a tax on imported goods, charged at the time they are received in port.

Theocracy a form of government in which a particular religion or faith plays a dominant role in the government.

Thirteenth Amendment the amendment to the Constitution that abolished slavery.

Three-fifths Compromise a compromise proposal in which five slaves would be counted as the equivalent of three free people for purposes of taxes and representation.

Title IX the section of the Federal Educational Amendments Law of 1972 that prohibits the exclusion of women from an educational program or activity receiving financial assistance from the federal government. Courts have interpreted those provisions to force colleges and universities to provide as many athletic teams for women as they do for men.

Town meeting the form of local government found exclusively in some small towns in the New England states where all citizens are invited to vote on policy issues and management matters.

Townships the name for the type of local government that typically serves rural areas or geographic outgrowths of cities.

Trade association a business association that focuses on one particular industry, with membership drawn exclusively from that industry.

Truman Doctrine doctrine articulated by President Harry Truman in the late 1940s by which money and resources were provided to support and sustain non-Communist governments in areas strategically vital to the United States.

Twenty-fourth Amendment a 1964 constitutional amendment that banned poll taxes in federal elections.

Twenty-second Amendment passed in 1951, this constitutional amendment restricts any one person from being elected to the presidency "more than twice," or from acting as president for longer than two and a half terms.

Twenty-sixth Amendment the constitutional amendment that lowered the voting age to eighteen in all local, state, and federal elections.

Twenty-third Amendment the constitutional amendment providing electoral votes to the District of Columbia, thus giving District residents the right to vote in presidential elections.

Two-party system a party system dominated by two major parties that win the vast majority of elections.

Two presidencies theory theory articulated by political scientist Aaron Wildavsky that posits the existence of a more powerful presidency in foreign affairs and a more limited presidency in the domestic sphere.

U

Unfunded mandate a directive from the federal government to the states requiring that they perform certain functions, with no accompanying funds to support those functions.

Union shop the law that requires that employees in unionized workplaces either join the union or pay the equivalent of union dues to it after a set period of time.

Unit rule the system in forty-eight states by which the candidate who wins the most votes among the popular votes cast for presi-

dent in a state receives all the electoral votes from that state; also known as the "winner-take-all" system.

Unitary system of government a system of government in which the constituent states are strictly subordinated to the goals of the central government as a whole.

United Nations (UN) international organization formed after World War II to promote and maintain international security and peace.

Universal health care national health care system in which full access to health care is provided to citizens at government expense.

Universal suffrage the idea that all citizens in a nation have the right to vote.

Unscientific poll a poll in which the sample of people interviewed is not representative of any group beyond those who register their opinion.

V

Values and beliefs the broad principles underlying the American political culture that citizens support and adhere to.

Veto the constitutional procedure by which the president refuses to approve a bill or joint resolution, and thus prevents its enactment into law.

Virginia Plan a proposal known also as the "large states plan" that empowered three separate branches of government, including a legislature with membership proportional to population.

Voter turnout the number of people who turn out to vote as a percentage of all those eligible to vote.

Voting the political mechanism that ensures that the will of the majority will rule.

Voting Rights Act of 1965 the federal law that invalidated literacy tests and property requirements and required select states and cities to apply for permission to the Justice Department to change their voting laws. As a consequence, millions of African Americans were effectively re-enfranchised in the South.

W

War Powers Resolution largely ignored congressional policy that restricts the president's power to engage in war except (1) when Congress has declared war, (2) when Congress has specifically granted the president permission to use armed forces, or (3) when the nation is under attack. The resolution further requires the president to report to Congress whenever American forces are entered into hostilities.

Warrant a document issued by a judge or magistrate that allows law enforcement to search or seize items at a home, business, or anywhere else that might be specified.

Warsaw Pact formal alliance of nations within the Soviet sphere during the Cold War.

Welfare state social system in which the state assumes a considerable degree of responsibility for citizens in matters of health care, employment, education, and retirement income.

Whips (majority and minority) member of Congress elected by his or her party to count potential votes and promote party unity in voting.

White House Chief of Staff the manager of the White House staff, which serves the president's organizational needs, including speech-writing, advance work for presidential appearances, scheduling, congressional relations, public relations, and communications.

White House Office of Legislative Affairs a presidential office that serves as a liaison between the president and Congress. This office helps the president develop the strategy used to promote passage of the president's legislative agenda.

White House Press Secretary the person on the White House staff who plays an especially important role in briefing the press, organizing news conferences, and even briefing the president on questions that may be asked.

Writ of certiorari the formal term for an order by which the Supreme Court acts in its discretion to hear a case on appeal.

Credits

Chapter 1. 4: Source: www.cnn.com/specials/cold.war/experience/the .bomb. 7: Source: Statistical Abstract of the United States, 2002. 13: Source: Daniel J. Elazar, 'American Federalism: A View from the States' (New York: Thomas Y. Crowell, 1966). 19: From 'Vital Statistics on American Politics,' Howard W. Stanley and Richard G. Niemi (CQ Press, 2006). Copyright © 2006 CQ Press, a division of Sage Publications. 8–9: Pew Global Attitudes Project, 2002, 2005.

Chapter 2. 33: Used by permission of James Allison. 40: From the website of the 'GIS for History Project' at the University of Illinois at Chicago-http://www.gisforhistory.org. 41: Source: "Mexico: Oil Depletion and Illegal U.S. Immigration," at worldpress.org (website of World Press Review), April 25, 2006 50: Based on Paul Murphy, 'Background of the Bill of Rights' (New York: Taylor & Francis, 1990). 53: Methodology: Conducted by ABC News, June 11–June 15, 2003. Courtesy of ABC NEWS.

Chapter 3. 66: Source: Pew Research Center for the People and the Press, 2008. 74: Source: Massachusetts Budget and Policy Center (www.massbudget.org). 74: Source: Office of Management and Government. 74: Source: State of California Legislative Analyst's Office (www.lao.ca.gov). 78: Source: http://www.latinamericanpost.com/index.php?mod=seccion&secc=82&conn=2589.

Chapter 4. 102: Source: David R. Hoffman, "Great Lies of the American Free Press," 'Pravda,' May 23, 2005, republished in Worldpress. org. 108: Source: David Yalof, Kenneth Dautrich, and Mark Hugo Lopez, "The Future of the First Amendment" (Lanham, MD: Rowman & Littlefield, 2008). 116: Source: Bernard Schwartz, "A Book of Legal Lists" (New York: Oxford University Press, 1997).

Chapter 5. 136: From Bernard Grofman, Lisa Handley and Richard G. Niemi, "Minority Representation and the Quest for Voting Equality" (New York: Cambridge University Press, 1992). Reprinted with the permission of Cambridge University Press. 145: From Nicholas Spuelda and Mary McIntosh, "Global Gender Gaps" (Released May 13, 2004), Pew Global Attitudes Project (see http://pewglobal.org/commentary/display.php?AnalysisID=90).

Chapter 6. 164: © 2007 The Gallup Organization. 174: From "Political Dynasties" by Ernesto Dal Bo (University of California, Berkeley), Pedro Dal Bo (Brown), and Jason Snyder (Northwestern) in 'The Atlantic Monthly,' June 2007, p. 32. 182: From The Pew Research Center for the People and the Press, 'Pew Global Attitudes Project: Nine Nation Survey' (March 2004), Q. 11, p. 32 (http//people-press.org/reports/questionnaires/206.pdf).

Chapter 7. 200: Source: John Harbeson, "Harbeson's Dreams and the African Agenda," 'Daily Nation," August 16, 2008 (http://www.nation.co.ke/News/world/-/1068/457288/-/rx0emi/-/index.html; accessed on August 19, 2008). 202: Sources: Schlesinger Jr. Poll, 1996; Intercollegiate Studies Institute Poll, 1998. 204: From The Pew Research Center for the People and The Press, 'Pew Global Attitudes Project: Nine Nation Survey' (March 2008). 211: Source: Office of the Clerk of the House.

Chapter 8. 229: From National survey of American adults conducted by Pew Center for People and the Press, October 2005. N=1,500 adults nationwide. 230: Source: www.firstgov.gov. 233: Source: Taxpayers for Common Sense website: www.taxpayer.net. 236: Source: Beppe Severgnini, 'Ciao, America! An Italian Discovers the U.S.' (New York: Broadway Press, reprint edition 2003), pp. 13–14.

Chapter 9. 273: From ABC News/Washington Post Polls, September 1987. Courtesy of ABC NEWS.: 279: Source: 'London Times.' May 28, 2007.

Chapter 10. 299: From Pew Research Center, 'Trends 2005' (Washington, DC: Pew Research Center, 2005), p. 25. 301: American National Election Studies (www.electionstudies.org). 302: ABC News/Money Magazine Polls. Courtesy of ABC NEWS. 303 bottom: Source: The

Gallup Organization. © 2003–2004 The Gallup Organization. 303 top left: Source: The Gallup Organization. © 2001 The Gallup Organization. 303 top right: American National Election Studies (www.electionstudies .org). 304: Source: Kaiser Foundation, 2001. 307: Source: "Don't Panic" by Andisheh Nouraee (7/5/06) on website http://atlanta.creativeloafing .com/gyrobase/Content?oid=oid 318: Source: A list articulated by members of the National Council on Public Polls.

Chapter 11. 330: Source: 'Democracy in America' (1835). 334 bottom: From The Pew Research Center for the People and the Press survey conducted by Princeton Survey Research Associates International, Feb. 1–5, 2006. N=757 adults nationwide. MoE+4 (Form 1). 334 top left: From The Pew Research Center for the People and the Press survey conducted by Princeton Survey Research Associates International, April 7–16, 2006. N=1,501 adults nationwide. MoE+3 (for all adults). 334 top right: From The Pew Research Center for the People and the Press survey conducted by Princeton Survey Research Associates International, Feb. 1–5, 2006. N=1,502 adults nationwide. MoE+3 (for all adults). 342: www.opensecrets.org, the website of The Center for Responsive Politics, June 2007. 344: Reprinted with permission from Almanac of American Politics, 2006. Copyright 2008 by National Journal Group, Inc. All rights reserved. 348: From The Center for Responsive Politics, June 2007.

Chapter 12. 370: Based on a 2005 survey conducted at the University of Connecticut. 376–77: Based on national surveys of American adults, conducted at the University of Connecticut in October 2003 and April 2005. 378: From Eric Margolis, "Bush's tame U.S. media may yet have teeth," 'Toronto Sun,' September 21, 2003.

Chapter 13. 393: From Pew Global Attitudes Survey, 2004. 399 bottom left: CBS News Poll, April 2005. Copyright © 2005 CBS Broadcasting, Inc. All Rights Reserved. Used courtesy of CBS News. 399 bottom right: Los Angeles Times poll, December 2003. 399 top left: Based on May 2005 survey by the Boston Globe. 399 top right: Pew Center poll, March, 2005. 400: 402 bottom: Source: Congressional Quarterly Weekly. 402 top: Source: Congressional Quarterly Weekly. 405: Source: 2004 American National Election Study, University of Michigan.

Chapter 14. 422: Source: http:// www.GenerationVote.com. 426: From a Pew Research Center for the People and The Press poll, 2006. 427: From a Pew Research Center for the People and The Press poll, 2006. 432: Source: International Institute for Democracy and International Assistance. 434: Source: American National Election Studies, 1952–2004. 437: Source: The Gallup Organization. © 1936–2008 The Gallup Organization.

Chapter 15. 451: Source: Mora Malram, 'Egypt Daily News,' 10/7/08. 468: Source: The Gallup Organization. © 2004 The Gallup Organization. 471: From Harold W. Stanley and Richard G. Niemi, "Vital Statistics on American Politics 2004–2005," p. 103 (Washington, DC: CQ Press, 2006). Copyright © 2006 CQ Press, a division of Sage Publications. 476: From Harold W. Stanley and Richard G. Niemi, "Vital Statistics on American Politics, 2005–2006," pp. 48–49. (Washington, DC: CQ Press, 2006). Copyright © 2006 CQ Press, a division of Sage Publications.

Chapter 16. 490 bottom: Source: Survey by Democracy Corps. Methodology: Conducted by Greenberg Quinlan Rosner Research, June 20–June 25, 2005. 490 top: Source: Survey by Associated Press. Methodology: Conducted by Ipsos-Public Affairs, July 5–July 7, 2005. 494: Source: World Press Review, January 2004, p. 40. 497: Source: Stockholm International Peace Research Institute (www.sipri.org). 498: Source: Budget of the U.S. Government, Historical Tables, published by the Executive Office of the President. 498: Source: Budget of the U.S. Government, Historical Tables, published by the Executive Office of the President.

Chapter 17. 518: From the Organization for Economic Co-operation and Development, 'OECD Health Data 2006,' from the OECD Internet subscription database, updated October 10, 2006. Copyright © OECD 2006. Any other reproduction of OECD material in another work is subject to written permission from the OECD. 520: Source: Sally C. Pipes, "Miracle Cure: How to Solve America's Health-Care Crisis and Why Canada Isn't the Answer" (San Francisco: Pacific Research Institute, 2004), p. 1. 521: From Wall Street Journal/NBC News Poll, August, 2008. Reprinted with permission of the Wall Street Journal, Copyright © 2008 Dow Jones & Company, Inc. All Rights Reserved Worldwide.

Chapter 18. 547: Sources: CNN/USA Today/Gallup Polls. Adults nationwide. 552: Source: Larry Nowels, "Foreign Aid: Understanding Data Used to Compare Donors," Organization for Economic Co-operation and Development. 'CRS Report for Congress,' Order Code RS 22032, updated May 23, 2005, p. 5. 553: Source: Mahmood Sariolghalam, 'Justice for All' in Alexander Lennon, "What Does the World Want from America?" (Cambridge, MA: MIT Press, 2002), p. 73.

End Sheet Back Cover. Courtesy of Michael Gastner, Cosma Shalizi, and Mark Newman, University of Michigan. Courtesy of Michael Gastner, Cosma Shalizi, and Mark Newman, University of Michigan. Used by permission of Robert Vanderbei.

Index

Note: Terms in boldface type are key terms defined in the glossary. Page numbers in italics refer to tables, figures, and boxed features.

at Republican National
Convention, 460
Romney, Mitt, *vs., 457*
tax cuts and, 482
McCain-Feingold Act, 473
McCarthy, Eugene, 460
McCarthy, Joseph, 102, *285,* 361, 366
McCluhan, Marshall, 367
McConnell, Michael, *546*
McConnell, Mitch, *168, 169, 344*
McConnell v. F.E.C., 473
McCorvey, Norma, 115
McCulloch, James W., 70
McCulloch v. Maryland (1819), 54,
70, 72, 270. *See also* Second
National Bank
McCullough, David, 34
McGovern, George, 460, 462
McKinley, William, 199, 200, 396
assassination of, 200
foreign policy and, *395*
McLaurin v. Okla. State Regent, 132
McNamara, Robert, 545
McVeigh, Timothy, 264, *360*
Media, 354–381
criticisms of, 376–379
"digital," 372–373
effects of, 374–376
electronic, 364–366, 370–373
"embedded" reporters in, *378*
as "fourth estate," 362
functions of, 359, 360–363
government regulation of,
358–359
as "government watchdog,"
362–363
historical development of, 363–369
lapses in journalistic ethics in, *360*
liberal *vs.* conservative, 361
local party organizations and, 411
new, 371
news sources used most in, 370, *370*
objectivity in, 3861
ownership of, 373–374, 379
partisan press era and, 363
policy making and, 485, 510
political cartoons and, *364–365*
political parties and, 411
political talk shows in, 361, 365–366
(*See also* **Talk radio**)
in politics, 355, 358–363
popular perspective on bias in,
376–377
presidential debates and, 366–368
presidential elections and, 440–441
presidential press conferences in,
368–369
presidents and, 218–219
print, 369–370
protestors and, 441
public debate and, 361–362
public opinion
expression of, and, 298
influence on, 310

television networks' ownership,
373, *374*
"yellow journalism" in, 20, 357
Medicaid, 203, 515
Medical research
Department of Health and Human
Services and, *241*
federal bureaucracy and, 231
Medicare, 203, 515, 518
mandatory spending for, 496, *498*
prescription drugs and, 508,
518, 526
reform of, 508
Medicare Prescription and
Modernization Act, 508
Medvedev, Dmitry, 551
Meet the Press, 362
"Melting pot," 13
Menendez, Bob, *160*
Merit plan (for selecting judges), 274
Merit system (in **civil service**), 250
Merit Systems Protection Board
(MSPB), 230, 250
Mexican-American War, 198
Mexican Americans, 148
Mexican immigrants, 148
Mexico
NAFTA and, 541
war with, 537, 538
Wilson, Woodrow, and, 206
Meyer, Philip, 361
Miami Herald, 370
Microsoft, 20, 207, 485
Middle East, 541–543
Central Intelligence Agency
and, 546
Department of Energy and oil
from, *241*
Midterm congressional elections, 474
Miers, Harriet, 183–184, 207, *275, 276*
Military draft, 193
Military-industrial complex, 549
Military personnel
Department of Defense and, *240*
Department of Veterans Affairs
and, *241*
Military power, 545–546
Miller v. California, 104, 106
Million Man March, *126,* 136–137
Mills, C. Wright, 331
Minimal effects theory, 375
Minimum scrutiny, 143
Minimum wage, 77, *241*
Minorities
criminal justice system and, 511
media and, 310
two-party system and, 404
Minority caucus, 166, 171
Minority leader, 169, 171
Minority-owned businesses, Department
of Commerce and, *240*
Minority rights, 12
affirmative action and, 15
values and beliefs about, 300

Miracle Cure, 520
Miranda v. Arizona, 113, 284
Miranda warnings, 113–114
Missouri Ex. Rel. Gaines v. Canada, 132
Missouri Plan, 274
Mitchell, George, 218
Monarchy, 6
Mondale, Walter, 214, 474
"image score" of, 440
in presidential debate, 465
taxes and, 494–495
Monetary policy, 496–499, *498*
Money
contributed to political parties, *421*
Department of Treasury and
printing, *240*
hard *vs.* soft, 472, 473
politics and, 16, 20 (See also
Campaign funding)
public opinion and, 298
Monroe, James, 197, *453. See also*
Monroe Doctrine
Monroe Doctrine, 198, 201, 537
Montesquieu, Baron de, 42, 206, 296
Moore, Roy, 272
Moral Majority, 526
Moralistic subculture, *13*
Morgan, J. Pierpont, 20
Mormons, 95, 96–97
Morning Edition, 373
Morris, Gouverneur, 33
Morton, Marcus, *422*
MOSAIC, 372
Motor Voter law, 425
Moynihan, Patrick, *46*
MSPB. *See* Merit Systems Protection
Board (MSPB)
"Muckrakers," 362, 379
Mueller, John, 549
Mujahidin, 548
Muller v. Oregon, 141
Multiparty system, 403–404
"Multiplicity of interests," 45
Municipal government(s), number
of, *7*
Murphy, Patrick, *175*
Murrow, Edward R., 365
Murtha, John, 548
Muslim Americans, 147, 153
Muslim countries, *307*
Muslims, *307*
gender equality and, *145*
two-party elections and, *393*
Myers v. United States, 208

N

NAACP. *See* National Association for
the Advancement of Colored
People (NAACP)
Nader, Ralph, 332, 343, 386, *386,*
388, 412
Green Party of, 406, *407*
journalists' votes for, *377*
Nader's Raiders, 343

Electoral College Maps

Electoral College results, 1996–2008

2008

Electoral votes*
- Obama (D) 365
- McCain (R) 173

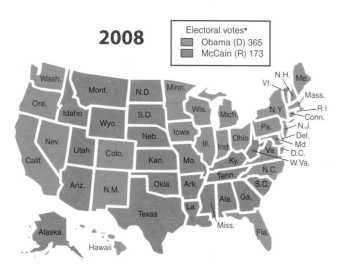

*At the time this book went to press, Missouri appeared to be leaning to John McCain, with the final results not yet certified.

2004

Electoral votes*
- Kerry (D) 251
- Bush (R) 286

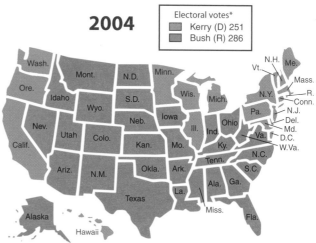

* A Minnesota elector pledged to Kerry cast a ballot for John Ewards [sic].

2000

Electoral votes*
- Gore (D) 266
- Bush (R) 271†

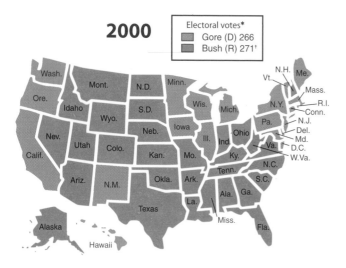

*A District of Columbia elector pledged to Gore cast no ballot as a protest against the District of Columbia's lack of representation in the U.S. Congress

†The state of Florida certified Bush the winner on November 26, a result that Gore contested in court.

1996

Electoral votes
- Clinton (D) 379
- Dole (R) 159

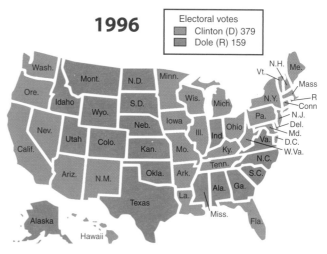